MEDICINE AND HEALTH CARE INTO THE TWENTY-FIRST CENTURY

The Pennsylvania Academy of ... lications

Books and Jo... al

Editor: Shyamal K. Majumdar
Professor and Head of Biology, Lafayette College
Easton, Pennsylvania 18042

1. *Energy, Environment, and the Economy,* 1981. ISBN: 0-9606670-0-8. Editor: S.K. Majumdar.
2. *Pennsylvania Coal: Resources, Technology and Utilization,* 1983. ISBN: 0-9606670-1-6. Editors: S.K. Majumdar and E.W. Miller.
3. *Hazardous and Toxic Wastes: Technology, Management and Health Effects,* 1984. ISBN: 0-9606670-2-4. Editors: S.K. Majumdar and E. W. Miller.
4. *Solid and Liquid Wastes: Management, Methods and Socioeconomic Considerations,* 1984. ISBN: 0-9606670-3-2. Editors: S.K. Majumdar and E.W. Miller.
5. *Management of Radioactive Materials and Wastes: Issues and Progress,* 1985. ISBN: 0-9606670-4-0. Editors: S.K. Majumdar and E.W. Miller.
6. *Endangered and Threatened Species Programs in Pennsylvania and Other States: Causes, Issues and Management,* 1986. ISBN: 0-9606670-5-9. Editors: S.K. Majumdar, F.J. Brenner, and A.F. Rhoads.
7. *Environmental Consequences of Energy Production: Problems and Prospects,* 1987. ISBN: 0-9606670-6-7. Editors: S.K. Majumdar, F.J. Brenner and E.W. Miller.
8. *Contaminant Problems and Management of Living Chesapeake Bay Resources,* 1987. ISBN: 0-9606670-7-5. Editors: S.K. Majumdar, L.W. Hall, Jr. and H.M. Austin.
9. *Ecology and Restoration of The Delaware River Basin,* 1988. ISBN: 0-9606670-8-3. Editors: S.K. Majumdar, E.W. Miller and L.E. Sage.
10. *Management of Hazardous Materials and Wastes: Treatment, Minimization and Environmental Impacts,* 1989. ISBN: 0-9606670-9-1. Editors: S.K. Majumdar, E.W. Miller and R.F. Schmalz.
11. *Wetlands Ecology and Conservation: Emphasis in Pennsylvania,* 1989. ISBN: 0-945809-01-8. Editors: S.K. Majumdar, R.P. Brooks, F.J. Brenner and R.W. Tiner, Jr.
12. *Water Resources in Pennsylvania: Availability, Quality and Management,* 1990. ISBN: 0-945809-02-6. Editors: S.K. Majumdar, E.W. Miller and R.R. Parizek.
13. *Environmental Radon: Occurrence, Control and Health Hazards*, 1990. ISBN: 0-945809-03-4. Editors: S.K. Majumdar, R.F. Schmalz and E.W. Miller.
14. *Science Education in the United States: Issues, Crises, and Priorities,* 1991. ISBN: 0945809-04-2. Editors: S.K. Majumdar, L.M. Rosenfeld, P.A. Rubba, E.W. Miller and R.F. Schmalz.
15. *Air Pollution: Environmental Issues and Health Effects,* 1991; ISBN: 0-945809-05-0. Editors: S.K. Majumdar, E.W. Miller, and J.J. Cahir.
16. *Natural and Technological Disasters: Causes, Effects and Preventive Measures*, 1992; ISBN: O-945809-06-9. Editors: S.K. Majumdar, G.S. Forbes, E.W. Miller, and R.F. Schmalz.
17. *Global Climate Change: Implications, Challenges and Mitigation Measures*, 1992; ISBN: 0-945809-07-7. Editors: S.K. Majumdar, L.S. Kalkstein, B. Yarnal, E.W. Miller, and L.M. Rosenfeld.
18. *Conservation and Resource Management,* 1993; ISBN: 0-945809-08-5. Editors: S.K. Majumdar, E.W. Miller, D.E. Baker, E.K. Brown, J.R. Pratt, and R.F. Schmalz.
19. *Biological Diversity: Problems and Challenges,* 1994; ISBN: 0945809-09-3. Editors: S.K. Majumdar, F.J. Brenner, J.E. Lovich, J.F. Schalles, and E.W. Miller.
20. *The Oceans: Physical-Chemical Dynamics and Human Impact,* 1994; ISBN: 0945809-10-7. Editors: S.K. Majumdar, E.W. Miller, G.S. Forbes, R.F. Schmalz, and A.A. Panah.
21. *Medicine and Health Care Into the 21st Century,* 1995; ISBN: 0945809-11-5. Editors: S.K. Majumdar, L.M. Rosenfeld, D.B. Nash, and A.M. Audet.

MEDICINE AND HEALTH CARE INTO THE TWENTY-FIRST CENTURY

EDITED BY

S.K. MAJUMDAR, Ph.D.
Marshall R. Metzgar
Professor and Head of Biology
Department of Biology
Lafayette College
Easton, PA 18042

L.M. ROSENFELD, Ph.D.
Assistant Professor of Physiology,
Jefferson Medical College, and
Assistant Dean, College of Graduate Studies,
Thomas Jefferson University
Philadelphia, PA 19107

D.B. NASH, M.D., M.B.A., F.A.C.P.
Director of the Office of Health Policy and Clinical Outcomes
Thomas Jefferson University, and
Associate Professor of Medicine
Jefferson Medical College
Philadelphia, PA 19107

A.M. AUDET, M.D.
Assistant Medical Director for Quality Improvement
Massachusetts Peer Review Organization, Inc.
Waltham, MA 02154

Founded on April 18, 1924

A Publication of
The Pennsylvania Academy of Science

Library of Congress Cataloging in Publication Data

Bibliography
Index
Majumdar, Shyamal K. 1938-, ed.

Library of Congress Catalog Card No.: 95-67144

ISBN-0-945809-11-5

A Publication of
The Pennsylvania Academy of Science, Easton, PA 18042

Printed in the United States of America by

Typehouse of Easton
Easton, PA 18042

PREFACE

History has taught that change is ever with us . . . for the individual, institution and society. As we approach the dawn of the twenty-first century, the pace of change escalates. Nowhere have we seen the potential and reality of change as significantly as in medicine and health care. The years 1993 and 1994 will be described, in various quarters, as ones of re-examination, re-evaluation, revision and revolution! There is much fear, uncertainty and turmoil. This volume does not presume to solve the problem or give all of the answers. It attempts to utilize the knowlege, experience and views of some of the best medical thinkers, educators, practitioners, administrators, nursing and allied health professionals, as well as key policy-makers at the local, state, national and international level to present a balanced analysis of a most timely and vital core issue and interject light into darkness.

Societal and economic forces have conspired to demand a thorough re-examination of health care structure, delivery and financing in the United States and to differing degrees, throughout the world. Change is being demanded and is occurring! Often, however, these changes are reactive, based on fear and uncertainty, rather than proactive, based on logic, foresight and knowledge.

The book is organized into six major sections, preceded by introductory statements by Robert P. Casey, Governor of the Commonwealth of Pennsylvania (1987 - 1995) and Carroll A. Campbell, Governor of South Carolina (1987 - 1995) and Chairman of the National Governor's Association (NGA) (1993 - 1994). NGA has been active nationally in striving for viable, locally-relevant, bipartisan solutions to real problems.

Part I presents the views of three important voices in the health care debate: Senator Harris Wofford of Pennsylvania (1991 - 1995), who perhaps more than anyone else, brought health care to the center of political debate; U.S. Representative Jim Cooper of Tennessee (1987 - 1995), a strong proponent of managed care; and William A. Glaser, an important commentator on international health issues.

Part II presents insightful views on health care by key leaders in academic health care, the National Governor's Association, the American and Pennsylvania Hospital Associations and the World Health Organization.

Part III explores emerging methods to influence and improve the practice of Medicine. Included are the role of government in setting standards of care with practice guidelines, as well as technology assessment, quality management, decision analysis and the patient's role in decision making (evolving from passive to a much more active position). Also developed in this section are the information explosion causing an increased demand for health care with enhancement of technology and the politics of generating a balanced physician supply.

Medical education and physician supply are investigated on many fronts in Part IV: undergraduate preparation for medicine; development of an adequate supply of physician generalists and of the emerging vital new class of physician managers; the important role of graduate education and of biomedical research; the rapidly evolving roles and duties of nurses, and the broad spectrum of allied health professionals. The importance of balancing the physical, psychic and social sides of health and disease is underscored.

The social context of medicine and health care is stressed in Part V in the context of whether health care is a right and whether medicine is a humanity as well as a science. Other issues explored include resource allocation; the increasing significance of violence as a public health epidemiological concern; preservation of medical professionalism in the face of health care reform; importance of preservation of physician wellness in an era of rapid change; increasing significance of the aged in health care system evaluation; the patient-physician relationship; the relationship-interrelationship of religion and medicine.

The forces which demand health care re-examination and change are certainly not unique to the United States. Part VI covers an excellent comparative overview of health care systems around the globe and ten (10) specific national health care systems: Argentina, Bermuda, Britain, Canada, China, Finland, Hungary, Israel, Nigeria, and South Africa. We can each learn from the experiences of others.

The editors trust that this book will be a valuable asset to a wide audience; not only to clinicians and educators but to all individuals who are concerned about the true state of medicine and health care in the United States and around the world. We include a cross-section of the best current thought and analysis on how these systems will evolve into the twenty-first century. We express our deep appreciation to the contributing chapter authors for their dedication to this project, the quality of their work and for excellent cooperation as the volume developed. Special gratitude is extended to Lafayette College, Jefferson Medical College/Thomas Jefferson University, American College of Physicians, and Massachusetts Peer Review Organization for providing facilities and support for the editors. Lastly, the editors extend heartfelt thanks to their spouses and families for their encouragement and help during the preparation of this book.

The Editors
January, 1995

Medicine and Health Care Into the Twenty-First Century

Table of Contents

Part Three: State of the Art Methods to Influence and Improve the Practice of Medicine

Part Four: Medical Education and Physician Supply

Part Five: Medicine and Health: The Social Context

Part Six: Comparative Health Care Systems

FOREWORD

Leonard M. Rosenfeld, Ph.D.
President (1992 - 1994)
Pennsylvania Academy of Science

This month marks the 70th anniversary of the founding of the Pennsylvania Academy of Science in Harrisburg, PA on April 18, 1924. The Academy serves the citizenry, professions and government of the Commonwealth of Pennsylvania, represents all of the sciences and draws membership from academia, government and the corporate sector. There is a 70-year tradition of the Academy working to enhance science education, research capability and competitiveness within the Commonwealth.

In 1980, the Academy initiated publication of a series of monographs, initially dealing with local scientific issues and evolving to scientific issues of a regional, national and eventually, global nature. **Medicine and Health Care into the Twenty-First Century** represents the twentieth volume in this series and addresses one of the most vital public policy issues of our day. Personally, it has been a joy working on this project as a co-editor. We are fortunate to have had co-editors of the caliber of Shyamal K. Majumdar (Lafayette College), David B. Nash (Jefferson Medical College) and Anne Marie Audet (American College of Physicians and now the Massachusetts Peer Review Organization).

As in all issues, the Academy approaches health care with a responsibility to present issues broadly, as viewed by exceptionally knowledgeable practitioners and policy-makers in the field. Our author corps represents the finest current thought in medical education and research, clinical practice and management of health care delivery systems and of important policy-makers in domestic and international health care.

Much public turmoil accompanies examination of the current health care system. Potential change generates fear and uncertainty if not accompanied by fact and reason. I take great pride in the responsible and principled manner in which my colleagues and the Pennsylvania Academy of Science have approached this issue. This volume, then, is a fitting capstone to 70 years of service by the Academy. In this spirit, we proudly present it for your review.

Leonard M. Rosenfeld, Ph.D.
President (1992 - 1994)
Pennsylvania Academy of Science
Jefferson Medical College
Philadelphia, PA
April, 1994

There is a revolution on the financing side of health care as well. Increasingly, employers are selecting managed care insurers for their employees and are promoting wellness programs. Even state government is actively moving Medicaid recipients into managed care. The shifting of costs within the health care financing system have become more evident, costly, and controversial. A growing number of large employers have become self-insured, partly to insulate themselves from these cost-shifts.

Other employers have actually encouraged cost-shifting by rewarding workers who elect coverage under their spouse's plan. Consumer choice is being eroded by employers who cover their employees through a single, restricted-provider health care network.

With these marketplace changes, it is fair to ask what the appropriate role for government should be. I believe the answer is clear. Government should help manage these changes to assure that everyone has access to health care and the ability to pay for it. Government should protect consumers by licensing providers and insurers and ensuring that complaints are resolved. Government should protect consumers' freedom to choose a health plan, their doctor, and their hospital. Government should ensure that consumers have the information they need to make informed decisions in a competitive marketplace.

These functions, and probably others, are appropriate roles for the state and federal government. To address these objectives in Pennsylvania, I have proposed comprehensive health reform legislation.

The "Pennsylvania Health Security Act" responds to all those challenges. By providing health insurance coverage to all, we will not only be fulfilling a basic human right—we will be able to contain health care costs.

The plan will guarantee health insurance coverage for all Pennsylvanians through a guaranteed benefits package, financed by both employers and workers. Payments by small businesses and low-income Pennsylvanians would be subsidized, and small business payments would be capped at seven percent of payroll. Benefits offered would include immunizations, mammography screening, drug and alcohol treatment, and a comprehensive range of child and maternal health services. No individual would be denied coverage, regardless of their age, race, sex, employment status or health history.

The plan will control costs and improve the quality of care by fostering competition among health care providers throughout the state. Under the plan, physicians in eight health service regions will compete for patients, based on the quality and cost-effectiveness of their care. The plan emphasizes preventive care and forges broader linkages between public health, health education, and direct medical services.

Finally, our plan encourages individual responsibility for health, by having every individual bear a portion of their health care costs, and by empowering individuals, not their employers, to make decisions who their insurer, doctor and hospital will be.

The "Pennsylvania Health Security Act" demonstrates that Pennsylvania is a step ahead of the rest of the nation and that we are doing much more than talking about health care reform.

Our ultimate goal is to design and establish an adequate health care system that will serve everyone, assuring them of the basic health care they need to live full and rewarding lives.

The "Pennsylvania Health Security Act" reflects our commitment to the future. It sets the stage for the future, safeguarding the health of our Commonwealth as we approach the 21st century.

Robert P. Casey
Governor (1987 - 1995)
Commonwealth of Pennsylvania
May, 1994

NATIONAL
GOVERNORS'
ASSOCIATION

MESSAGE

Carroll A. Campbell, Jr.
Governor of South Carolina (1987 - 1995)

It is nearly impossible to over-estimate the difficulty of arriving at a national health care reform strategy that will meet the needs of the 55 states, commonwealths, and territories. Yet, if reform is not sufficiently flexible to allow states to tailor health care to meet the diverse needs of their people, it will surely fail.

That has been the challenge for the National Governors' Association (NGA) as we have participated in the debate.

A bipartisan group of Governors and staff has spent an enormous amount of time working with the administration, beginning during the transition and continuing as Mrs. Clinton's health care task force developed their proposal. While we had some impact on the structure and details of the Clinton plan, it was clear early on that there would be serious philosophical differences about the basic priniciples, namely employer mandates, global budgets requiring price controls, and mandatory government-run health alliances.

Yet, in spite of our differences, we realized that there was a great deal of common ground between us about strategies to address the nation's health care problems. There also was a strong belief that these reforms had to be undertaken this year.

My goal, as a governor and as chairman of the National Governors' Association, is to break down the health care problem into components that can be addressed and solved. Thoughtful officials must coalesce around alternatives that recognize the areas and the people that are truly in crisis.

At the National Governors' Association 1994 mid-winter meeting, an important step was taken toward a bipartisan framework for reform. While there is not total unanimity among the governors, we are convinced that we can contribute most to the national debate by adopting policy that reflects our consensus position. That NGA policy includes several important provisions:

- Insurance reform to insure portability of coverage;
- A core benefits package that will be offered, but not necessarily paid for, by employers;
- A cap on tax deductibility that is the same for everybody;
- Subsidies for low-income individuals who cannot afford insurance;
- Flexibility to move the current Medicaid population to managed care settings;
- Malpractice reform and antitrust relief;
- State-based health care purchasing cooperatives;
- Federally organized outcome and quality standards and administrative simplifications; and
- The ability for states to get ERISA waivers.

These are reforms that Congress could enact quickly and that could improve our health care system.

These reforms are not insignificant and, indeed, should the nation agree that they are reforms we should pursue, they will not be easy to flesh out. Yet a political consensus is building around these kinds of changes. This consensus could bring us a bipartisan coalition that believes these are the first steps that must be taken.

Some would say these steps, by themselves, are adequate; I believe that's a real possibility. Others would say these are first steps. But the point is, these things are both positive and possible. Why should we wait?

As chairman of the National Governor's Association, I understand the political sensitivities that prevent public officials of good will from moving ahead in an environment where the administration and others have staked out clear policy positions. Yet the opportunity before us—spurred in large part by the high stakes attached to health care by the Clinton administration—is so great that it would be tragic to waste it.

Let's not polarize so that meaningful health reform becomes undoable this year. My hope is to get beyond the rhetoric and to get down to the realities of health care reform—what is possible, what is not; what can move us forward, what stalls any reform at all—and enact the best health care reform we can in 1994. I believe the nation's governors, with the policy positions we have enacted in the last year, can be catalysts to help arrive at that result.

I commend the Pennsylvania Academy of Science for undertaking this ambitious project, which will contribute to the congressional debate on health care, and to the ultimate goals of improving the nation's health care system.

Carroll A. Campbell, Jr.
Chairman, National Governors' Association (1993 - 1994)
March, 1994

Medicine and Health Care Into the Twenty-First Century. Edited by S.K. Majumdar, L.M. Rosenfeld, D.B. Nash and A.M. Audet. © 1995, The Pennsylvania Academy of Science.

Chapter One

THE RECENT POLITICS OF HEALTH CARE REFORM

SENATOR HARRIS WOFFORD
United States Senate

Senator Harris Wofford
(Pennsylvania, 1991-1995)

THE STAGE IS SET

The 1991 Senate election in Pennsylvania made health care a national priority and sent me to Washington with a mandate to work for legislative action. The road has not been easy, but I've been in long battles before.

In 1941, the fate of Britain, western civilization, and the world hung in balance. People worried that America would not do enough to enable Britain to withstand the expected Nazi onslaught. Winston Churchill said, "I have confidence that the American people, in their good common sense, will, in the end, do the right thing . . . *after* they have tried every other alternative."

THE TERMS OF DEBATE

Those who have followed the health care issue over the past three years know that there has been a spirited debate among those advocating various approaches to health reform. Some on the Democratic side of the aisle favored the so-called "single payer" approach, a publicly-financed insurance system similar to the current Canadian approach. Others supported an approach that came to be known as "pay or play," a mandate on employers to provide insurance to their employees or to pay into a public pool that would provide such coverage.

More recently, the debate has centered on an approach called "managed competition," an idea which comes from many in business and the health care industry itself. In various forms, managed competition has many supporters among both Democrats and Republicans in Congress, myself included. Indeed, in 1992 I joined with Princeton professor Paul Starr, with whom I had been consulting since the summer of 1991, in pressing Democrats—including then-candidate Bill Clinton—to marry the market-based structure of consumer purchasing cooperatives with a system of guaranteed, universal coverage.

California's Insurance Commissioner, John Garamendi, had made real progress in this direction. I invited Garamendi to present his ideas to a group of Democratic Senators keenly interested in moving the health care debate forward. He, too, helped convince Bill Clinton to present a health care proposal in his general election campaign which relied on a restructured, more competitive, private health care marketplace. Senator Jay Rockefeller and I joined Clinton at the Merck company in New Brunswick, New Jersey when he made that proposal in September, 1992.

Over two years ago, I joined with Senator Tom Daschle (D-S.D.) to introduce a bill called the American Health Security Plan. We sought to put the old labels behind us and craft a sensible plan that incorporated the best thinking of everyone invoM in the health care debate.

The key elements of the Daschle-Wofford bill were to create a comprehensive, standard package of health benefits available to everyone throughout their lives, regardless of where they live or work and to offer health insurance through a decentralized system of regional health purchasing cooperatives.

This approach permitted choice of doctor and greatly simplified the existing maze of paperwork and bureaucracy through an electronic billing system. Instead of hundreds of different forms from private insurers and government, there would be a single claims form. Every person would have a "health security card" that would provide access to care.

Most important, in developing this plan with Senator Daschle I committed myself to working towards legislation to address a simple yet crucial set of goals. These include:

- Guaranteeing that every American has private health insurance that is there when it is needed.
- Controlling the inflation of health care costs.
- Improving the quality of health care and giving priority to preventive and primary care.
- Increasing each individual's ability to choose his own or her own doctor and health care plan.
- Ending discriminatory and unfair insurance industry practices, such as exclusions for pre-existing conditions and different rates for different people based solely on personal characteristics.
- Protecting and expanding the health care of older Americans by offering prescription drug coverage and taking a strong step forward in providing long-term care.

Though the Daschle-Wofford bill was not adopted, I expect that many of its ideas and innovations will be evident in the final health reform legislation.

WHERE ARE WE TODAY

The Health Security Act proposed by the President and Hillary Clinton in the autumn of 1993 was an impressive piece of work that offers a useful guide to how health reform might be implemented. However, it was only a step in the process, not the end of the process.

It was certainly a large and complicated bill; it's length alone has invited substantial criticism. It is worth noting that the bill is not as complicated as other legislation Congress has recently considered. For instance, the NAFTA treaty consisted of five volumes, each of which was as big as the Health Security Act. Citizens and Members of Congress nonetheless grasped the important choices presented by that complex agreement. A certain level of detail is to be expected; but it cannot be used as an excuse for doing nothing. In fact, trying to explain the maze of the current health care system would be far more complicated than any reform plan on the table.

Nonetheless, the Clinton bill as originally drafted was too long and complicated. Health reform legislation can be much shorter, simpler, less bureaucratic, and easier to understand. I have always been impressed by the fact that the 1933 Civilian Conservation Corps Act which put hundreds of thousands of young unemployed men to work during the Depression was only one-and-one-half pages long. The bill empowered the President to create a Civilian Conservation Corps, the army to provide the camps and the discipline, the Labor Department to find youth to do the work and the Interior Department to find the hardest conservation jobs in the country, as well as authorizing the necessary funds. Within six months, 300,000 young men were in 1,500 CCC camps and George Marshall, a young colonel who organized many of those camps, first came to the nation's attention.

I wish a health reform bill could be that simple and straightforward. Of course, it cannot. However, dramatic improvements are both possible and necessary.

Over the past several months, I have worked to streamline health reform legislation without sacrificing the key principles of reform that I outlined above. In discussing this streamlining process, I would divide the bill into three categories—those sections that should be rewritten, those sections that can be removed, and those sections that are open to negotiation.

Others committed to health reform joined me in seeking areas of agreement and consensus. After blocking comprehensive reform, however, it soon became clear that the opponents of reform would block even a practical first step toward making health insurance more secure. It's a sad fact that the debate about one of the most serious issues facing our country was dominated by partisanship, special interest lobbying, and ultimately by obstructionist tactics.

But I have been in long battles before, and I will continue to fight for greater health security for all Americans. The health reform issue will not go away. We will be brought back to this issue next year by the clear and harsh facts: continuing discriminatory and unfair insurance practices; more Americans losing coverage; rising health care costs. And when we return to health reform next year, I'll continue to apply my own prime test for reform: that it should enable all Americans to have the kind of guaranteed health care benefits and choice of doctor and health plans that members of Congress and millions of federal employees now get through the Federal Employees Health Benefits Program (FEHBP).

FEHBP is like the health insurance system many Americans are already familiar with. The employer and employees each contribute to the premiums, with the employer paying an average of 72 percent. But unlike an increasing number of employer-provided coverage, all employees can choose for themselves from a menu of private health plans, from the full Blue Cross/Blue Shield choose-your-own-doctor plan to a potentially lower-cost HMO.

Members of Congress have the ability to change plans once a year, and protections against unfair insurance practices such as pre-existing condition exclusions and price discrimination based on personal characteristics. That is exactly the type of health security that the American people want, and yet fewer and fewer of them can afford.

A second test for successful health reform is that it must not increase the federal deficit. Instead, our efforts should make sure health reform *decreases* the deficit.

Third, our bill must redesign the so-called "alliances" in the President's plan to make them voluntary consumer purchasing co-operatives, an approach I've long been advocating. We must eliminate the potential for added bureaucracy and government control that concerned me and many others in our hearings over the past six months.

Fourth, any final bill should include new protections for older citizens that I've been urging over the past year:

- A new self-financed, voluntary insurance system for nursing home care. This will be of tremendous help to millions of older citizens and their families who under today's absurd system are forced to spend-away their life savings—and often their dignity—in order to qualify for nursing home assistance under Medicaid.
- A Retiree Health Benefits Protection provision which would give early retirees greater legal safeguards against employers who try to drop their promised health benefits. Unisys retirees in the Philadelphia area, Allegheny-International retirees in the Pittsburgh area and many others across our country who have been hurt by cutbacks in their promised benefits understand all too well why this is so crucial.

COMING TO CLOSURE

There have been many bumps in the long road to health care reform. There will be many more before we reach our destination. Finding a clear, smooth path toward universal coverage will take both probing debate and practical compromise. To that end, I thank the Pennsylvania Academy of Science and the contributing authors for preparing this book, which examines possible solutions to the very difficult issues Congress is currently grappling with.

My own political background includes deep involvement with the civil rights movement. From our 1950 experience in India, my wife Clare and I wrote a book advocating that this country adopt Ghandian tactics of nonviolent civil disobedience as part of its civil rights strategy (4). This led to an early association with Martin Luther King, Jr. In 1960, I was also asked to organize and coordinate the Civil Rights Section of John F. Kennedy's presidential campaign. I witnessed first hand how deep divisions among Americans over the civil rights of Black Americans threatened to tear this country apart.

Looking back now, Americans wonder how this country could have tolerated a situation in which one-third of its people could not vote, could not ride in the front of public buses, and could not sit at lunch counters.

It will not be very long before we look back on the health care debate of our time and wonder how we could have tolerated a health care system that stripped Americans of their health insurance when they lost a job. How could we have permitted a health care system in which someone could not leave welfare to take a job because the job did not provide health coverage comparable to what he or she received on Medicaid? How could we have had a health care system in which those with pre-existing conditions had to fear losing or being denied coverage for the very condition that made insurance necessary? How could we have had such good health care but a health insurance system that was so unfair?

Passing health care reform is one of the most important challenges America has faced since the debate over the creation of Social Security in August 1935. We know it won't be easy. But history won't forgive us if we fail to seize this opportunity to find the highest common ground, instead of the lowest common denominator. It will be a test of our good will, of our ability to act in the interest of the common good. We have a long road still to go, but I am confident that in the end after we have looked at all the alternatives, we will, in Churchill's words, "do the right thing," and turn the right to affordable [*private*] health insurance into a reality for all Americans.

LITERATURE CITED

1. Truman, Harry S. 1956. *Memoirs by Harry S. Truman: Volume 2 - Years of Trial and Hope.* Doubleday & Company, Inc.: New York, pp. 17-24.
2. U.S. Library of Congress. Congressional Research Memorandum. *President Nixon's Comprehensive Health Insurance Act of 1974.* May 19, 1994.
3. Minority Leader Robert Dole in a speech before the American Hospital Association, January 31, 1994.
4. Wofford, Harris and Clare. 1951. *India Afire.* The John Day Company: New York.

Medicine and Health Care Into the Twenty-First Century. Edited by S.K. Majumdar, L.M. Rosenfeld, D.B. Nash and A.M. Audet.

Chapter Two

A MANAGED COMPETITION PRIMER

REPRESENTATIVE JIM COOPER

Congress of the United States
House of Representatives
125 Cannon Building
Washington, DC 20515

Rep. Jim Cooper
(Tennessee, 1987-1995)

Until last year, few people had ever heard of managed competition in health care reform. Today the term is used by so many, it has nearly lost its meaning. Many people have forgotten that certain elements are essential in order for managed competition to work.

Managed competition was conceived by the Jackson Hole Group, a collection of academics and industry leaders who have met regularly over the past two decades in Jackson Hole, Wyoming. My colleagues in the Conservative Democratic Forum (CDF) and I introduced a pure managed competition bill using the Jackson Hole model last Congress. The Democratic Leadership Council (DLC) and the Progressive Policy Institute (PPI) also embraced this approach in their book *Mandate for Change.*

Managed competition has proven to be politically attractive because it represents a compromise between complete government takeover and laissez-faire in health care. However, the balance managed competition strikes between regulation and competition is not arbitrary. One cannot simply adjust it for political expediency without ruining the mechanism which makes it work.

Managed competition requires just enough government intervention to establish ground rules for health plans competing in the system, to enhance the power of consumer choice in the market, and to guarantee access to coverage for all Americans.

What are the key elements of managed competition and where does it draw the line between government responsibilities and the role of the market? Here is a guide:

Insurance Market Reforms: There is competition in today's market, but it is destructive competition among insurance companies trying to avoid sick customers. The new Accountable Health Plans (AHPs) will be required to offer coverage to everyone. They will not be able to deny coverage or charge more for a pre-existing medical condition. Coverage will be portable.

Insurers have also competed negatively by crafting hundreds of different benefits packages. There must be a standardized benefits package which all health plans offer so that consumers can make "apple-to-apple" comparisons. All benefits would be fully and freely available as long as it did not duplicate standard coverage.

Standardization must apply to copays and deductibles as well (only allowing higher cost-sharing for health plans with an out-of-network option). Some have suggested different benefits packages for different types of health plans (e.g. HMOs, PPOs and fee-for-service). This would create opportunities for adverse selection and could subvert effective competition.

As price competition intensifies, health plans and their providers must be held accountable for the quality of the care they deliver. Consumers should have comparative quality information on all health plans. This information should not be limited to process measures (e.g. immunization or mammography rates), it must include analysis of clinical and functional outcomes. Providers must be constantly challenged to improve their care of patients.

Because AHPs will be held accountable for price and quality, they must have the ability to establish networks and to exclude inefficient or poor-quality providers. AHPs also must be free to reimburse their providers any way they choose.

Purchasing Groups: Pooling the buying power of individuals and small businesses will give them market advantages only the largest employers enjoy today: large risk pool; choice of multiple health plans; lower administrative costs; market power; and group rates.

In order for managed competition to be effective, health plan purchasing groups must be neutral farmers' markets, not regulators. They must offer all qualifying health plans in the area, allowing consumer choice to determine which health plans succeed and which fail. Purchasing groups should not have the power to limit enrollment in plans, regulate premiums, or set provider fees. Finally, purchasing groups must not bear risk or have a financial stake in any health plan. Managed competition purchasing groups are designed to enhance consumer choice, not limit it.

Since large employers already have the benefits of group purchasing, they don't need much government help. Through direct contracting with AHPs or through self-insuring, large-employer purchasing will provide an important counterbalance to the HPPC in the marketplace. Of course, large-employer plans must meet the same access and quality standards as any other AHP.

Tax Reform and Employer Contributions: In order for managed competition to slow increases in health care spending, buyers must bear the cost of choosing wasteful or excessive health plans. Subsidizing the cost of expensive health plans, as employers and federal tax policy do today, is anti-competitive. It actually discourages health plans from reducing their prices.

Employers must not be allowed to vary their contribution to employees' health benefits according to the health plan an employee has chosen. They must be required to "define" a specific dollar amount for their contribution, so their employees don't receive a greater contribution if they pick a higher-priced plan. Employers could still define their contribution to be the price of the most expensive plan, but employees must be able to choose a less expensive plan and receive a rebate for the difference.

Federal tax policy shields employers from the full cost of choosing relatively expensive health plans because it allows employers unlimited deductibility of the cost of health benefits provided to employees. Limiting employer deductibility to spending on the standardized benefits package, as some have proposed, is not sufficient because it does not influence the purchaser's decision among health plans offering those benefits. Deductibility must be limited to the price of the most cost-effective plan meeting federal quality standards.

Artificial Price Constraints: Government-imposed limits on what health plans or providers may charge are fundamentally incompatible with managed competition. If after several years, fully implemented managed competition fails to sufficiently constrain health care cost increases, then government regulation may be necessary. But trying to combine managed competition with global budgets or price regulation from the outset will prevent managed competition from working.

The failures of price controls to contain spending in health care and other segments of the economy are legion. History has shown us time and again that we lack the necessary data to set them fairly and the tools to enforce them. We must change the underlying incentives in the system before we can make real headway on cost containment. Managed competition tries to do that by giving health plans and providers the financial incentive to provide only high-quality cost-effective care.

treatment of disease, and transformed its own population. Among developed countries, infant mortality has diminished, life expectancy has increased, infectious diseases (such as smallpox and diphtheria) have been prevented or cured, and profiles of morbidity and mortality are now associated primarily with aging and affluence.

Originating in Europe and North America during the eighteenth and nineteenth centuries, scientific medicine's understanding of health and therapeutic methods spread throughout the world. Medical school curricula, textbooks, journals, diagnostic and treatment techniques, technology, and pharmaceutical drugs have spread everywhere and have become remarkably alike. A new class of doctors, nurses, hospital managers, and health educators throughout the Third World study scientific medicine in their own medical schools, gain specialized skills in postgraduate residencies in Europe and North America, and receive constant updates at home in workshops taught by Western experts visiting under the auspices of international technical assistance programs. These programs are conducted by several agencies in the United Nations system (such as the World Health Organization and the United Nations Children's Fund) and by national technical assistance programs. Among their achievements have been mass vaccinations, improved maternal and child care, and public health reforms (1).

In all countries, these medical innovations produce a sequence in the population structure, economy, and environment. At first, infant mortality greatly diminishes. People gain healthier food, water, and housing. Fewer people succumb to disease and injuries. The population and labor force increase greatly. Eventually women (and mothers) become emancipated, and the fertility rate diminishes. After a long time, the population stabilizes in size and ages in composition (2).

In Europe and North America, medical care is so successful that everyone wants it. The mirage of perfect health and long life is fed by the claims of clinicians, equipment manufacturers, and pharmaceutical companies. Each individual seeks maximum and immediate care. Every affluent country develops institutions to provide access to all citizens, create and update the best services in all regions, and also to allocate appropriate shares of society's resources. The health sector's demand for money rises rapidly, as the population's utilization increases and as new techniques are invented.

At first in Europe, access and financing were accomplished by voluntary mutual aid associations, uniting many families in certain occupations and religious communities. All members paid into a pool and received benefits when needed. The funds paid disability benefits, pensions after retirement, and the services of doctors, midwives, and hospitals. Churches and local governments offered benefits to the urban poor who did not belong to mutual aid associations (3, 6). Eventually every government in Europe expanded and strengthened these separate private efforts by enacting social security programs, including old age pensions, work accident services, disability benefits for workers, and national health insurance for workers and their families. The political impetus came from the trade unions, the political parties of the Left, and the ordinary population. The inspiring ideology was "social solidarity", whereby everyone paid into the several accounts, and the funds covered persons when needed. The financing system used earmarked percentage-of-wages payroll taxes and was redistributive, so that upper-income people tended to pay in more than the value of their health and other benefits, while the poor and less healthy drew out more than they paid in (5).

These methods evolved in an orderly fashion over many years throughout Europe. France, Germany, Belgium, Holland, and Austria still have their national health insurance systems, now covering their entire populations, paying the still independent doctors and hospitals, and controlling costs every year (6). A few countries—particularly Britain and Sweden—substituted national health services, wherein the government owns the hopsitals, employs or contracts with the doctors, and pays everything through the central government budgets, but their arrangements are unusual (7). Canada was unable to develop the building blocks of nonprofit mutual aid associations across the country and now covers its population through governmental general-revenue payments to independent self-employed doctors and hospitals, but no other country has a method like this (8).

The developed countries cemented their national health insurance and national health services after World War II, but the Third World experienced faster and upsetting changes. Immunizations, public health measures, and Western medical methods rapidly reduced infant mortality and adult morbidity. The populations exploded in size, spread across the landscape, and greatly exceeded the employment capabilities of the economies. Environments in both cities and countryside deteriorated, forests and wildlife were destroyed, and the global atmosphere worsened. Angry unemployed young men became urban misfits and joined revolutions against their own governments and against the West. Class antagonisms grew between the angry poor and the elites who ran Western-style organizations, enjoyed a Westernized lifestyle, and benefitted from Westernized health services. The Western countries that had transformed these societies by their teachings, medical experts, and technical assistance now became targets of a backlash (9, 10).

The developed countries based their health care coverage, service delivery, and financing methods on an ideology of social solidarity, on redistributive financing, and on a capacity to organize and operate nationwide institutions. Among the affluent countries the United States has been the only significant exception. During the first half of the twentieth century, American policy thinkers participated in the world-wide debate that finally produced "welfare states" in Europe. The Americans enacted social security and numerous economic reforms (such as government-protected labor relations) but postponed—temporarily, they thought—national health insurance (11). Instead, labor unions forced business firms to grant health care and other fringe benefits, organized and financed by employers' group contracts with private insurance companies (12). Many business firms have always refused to cover health costs, and their many workers and family members must buy expensive individual policies or must go without coverage. In order to cut labor costs, employers are free to reduce benefits, increase the beneficiaries' point-of-service cost sharing, or drop coverage completely. Many large employers now manage their own health care claims and finances. The result is a complete lack of standardization, frequent changes within each employed group, much uncertainty by everyone, many disputes, many uninsured persons, and many uncollectible provider claims. Instead of practicing social solidarity and redistributive finance, each employer is self-centered, tries to pay the least money for its own employees, and contributes nothing for others. America's dominant ideology has been the pursuit of individual self-interest in a competitive free market. No other developed country tries to cover its population by employer-group contracts, private insurance, and free markets. No other country experiences the results (6).

In other developed countries, cost containment requires constant vigilance. Payroll taxes and government subsidies must be limited, so that industrial prices and employment are not jeopardized, so that society can continue to pay for other important purposes. Since these countries have organized national systems, each system can be used to monitor utilization and spending, can be used to set priorities and curb increases in spending. In democratic developed countries, government never dictates unilaterally. Rather, elaborate machinery of decision-making—involving health providers, varied interest groups, consumers, health insurance carriers, taxpayers, and government agencies—set targets for annual increases in total spending, negotiate the payment of doctors, regulate utilization and payment of hospitals, allocate expensive equipment to the most appropriate sites, promote efficiency, and settle conflicts of interest (13, 14).

Because the United States has no system, it cannot contain costs. Doctors, hospitals, equipment companies, drug companies, and other providers have great discretion in deciding the volume and complexity of care given to patients. Insurance carriers, employers, and even the few government financing programs have no organized collective methods of evaluating providers' claims but have paid them. American philosophy is to let every carrier, employer, and patient pursue its own self-interest, and perhaps efficiency and economy will ultimately result, if only the free competitive market can be made to work. Recently, each employer and each carrier has attempted to impose methods of "managed care" on patients, doctors, hospitals, and other providers, but the system as a whole is unmanaged, the administration of so many diverse "managed care" arrangements adds new costs, and providers are still left to shift higher charges to patient encounters outside of managed care (15, 16). As a result, this latest attempt to "make the market work" has not brought American costs down to the levels of other developed countries. Small business firms have become more reluctant than ever to incur the burden of health coverage of their workers.

America's high spending and unorganized system have produced some benefits. Drug and equipment manufacturers can sell their products throughout the country at high prices, and the United States has become the center for the development and testing of new methods. Hospitals are constantly modernized. Private and public money supports new clinical research in technically advanced centers in every city, making the United States the world's leader in research. Physicians, hospital directors, many other providers, and management consultants earn very high incomes. Medical equipment is an important export (17, 18).

America's elaborate clinical styles have great influence abroad. American journals and treaties are avidly read in Europe and the Third World. Clinicians from abroad attend American conferences. Until European teaching hospitals modernized during the 1960's and 1970's, many young specialists took post-graduate education in American medical centers before returning home to lead education and practice there. Now many Americans conduct technical assistance workshops throughout the Third World, to demonstrate the newest clinical methods.

But American clinical styles mislead the Third World in many ways. Medical practice is defined as high-tech specialized care, when many needs of the population—even in the United States—lie in primary care and preventive medicine. The glamour and income of high-tech specialization attracts young Third World doctors; instead of working in the urban ghettoes and rural areas of their countries, they search for specialized niches in their affluent city neighborhoods or emigrate to the United States. The poor in cities and countryside receive few of these services and still rely on traditional local practitioners. The poor resent the concentration of health investments and services among the urban upper and middle classes; the unequal delivery of health care becomes one of the grievances in the Third World against their own governments and against the West.

By the 1990's, American domestic public policy had to face tradeoffs. The country's diffuse and uncontrolled health care system used a rapidly mounting share of the national income, while also producing advanced techniques, improving the life expectancy and comfort of many people, and conferring high incomes on providers. But access and quality of care varied widely. Many high-tech diagnostic and therapeutic interventions in surgery and many other fields were clinically useless, damaging to some patients, and financially wasteful (19, 20). Disputes and uncertainties were constant. The question is whether a more comprehensive system can preserve the strengths of American health care while controlling costs, expanding access, improving primary care, reducing disputes, and simplifying administration. Once eager for foreign lessons in clinical, educational, and organizational methods, American policymakers by the 1990's had become too accustomed to their clinical pre-eminence in the world and too blinded by ideology, so that they now assume they have nothing to learn from abroad on any subject. Instead, they are again searching for peculiarly American methods to "make the market work". Doubtless they will be disappointed, since current problems result from American's dedication to an unorganized market and to an ideology encouraging everyone to pursue his self-centered economic interest. Other developed countries with national health insurance demonstrate that the desiderata of cost containment, universal access, up-to-date clinical techniques, generous benefits, provider autonomy, and maximum patient choice can be accomplished in organized systems inspired by social solidarity (21).

REFERENCES

1. Basch, Paul F. 1990. *International Health.* New York: Oxford University Press, Second edition.
2. *International Encyclopedia of Population.* 1982. New York: The Free Press, pp. 146-147, 519-525, etc. passim.

3. Bennet, Jean. 1975. *La Mutualité Francaise à travers sept siècles d'histoire.* Paris: Coopèrative d'information et d'Edition Mutualiste.
4. Van der Linden and Jan Lucassen (editors). 1994. *The Comparative History of Mutual Benefit Societies.* Bern: Peter Lang.
5. Köhler, Peter A. and Hans F. Zacher (editors). 1982. *The Evolution of Social* Insurance 1881-1981. London: Frances Pinter.
6. Glaser, William A. 1991. *Health Insurance in Practice.* San Francisco: Jossey Bass, Inc.
7. Sidel, Victor W. and Ruth Sidel. 1983. *A Healthy State.* New York: Pantheon Books, Second edition.
8. Crichton, Anne and David Hsu. 1990. *Canada's Health Care System.* Ottawa: Canadian Hospital Association Press.
9. Gupte, Pranay. 1990. *The Silent Crisis.* New Delhi: Vikas Publishing House.
10. Nelson, Joan M. 1992. "Poverty, Equity, and the Politics of Adjustment", in Stephen Haggard and Robert R. Kaufman (editors), *The Politics of Economic Adjustment.* Princeton: Princeton University Press, pp. 221-269.
11. Derthick, Martha. 1979. *Policymaking for Social Security.* Washington: The Brookings Institution.
12. Munts, Raymond. 1967. *Bargaining for Health: Labor Unions, Health Insurance, and Medical Care.* Madison: University of Wisconsin Press.
13. Glaser, William A. 1993. "How Expenditure Caps and Expenditure Targets Really Work", *The Milbank Quarterly,* Volume 71, Number 1 (1993), pp. 97-128.
14. Glaser, William A. 1987. *Paying the Hospital.* San Francisco: Jossey-Bass.
15. Kongstvedt, Peter R. 1993. *The Managed Care Handbook.* Gaithersburg, Md.: Aspen Publishers, Second edition.
16. Boland, Peter (editor). 1993. *Making Managed Healthcare Work.* Gaithersburg, Md.: Aspen Publishers.
17. Moreau, Jean-Georges and Patrice Bimont. 1980. "L'industrie du matériel biomédical," *Revue française des affaires sociales,* Volume 34, Number 4 (October-December 1980), pp. 191-204.
18. *Federal Policies and the Medical Device Industry.* 1984. Washington: Office of Technology Assessment, U.S. Congress, Ch. 1.
19. Eisenberg, John M. 1986. *Doctors' Decisions and the Cost of Medical Care.* Ann Arbor, Mich.: Health Administration Press.
20. Bunker, John P., Benjamin A. Barnes and Frederick Mosteller (editors). 1977. *Costs, Risks and Benefits of Surgery.* New York: Oxford University Press.
21. Glaser, William. A. 1993. "Universal Health Insurance that Really Works: Foreign Lessons for the United States", *Journal of Health Politics, Policy and Law,* Volume 18, Number 3 (Fall 1993), pp. 695-722.

Medicine and Health Care Into the Twenty-First Century. Edited by S.K. Majumdar, L.M. Rosenfeld, D.B. Nash and A.M. Audet.

Chapter Four

VISION OF HEALTH CARE TODAY AND THE ROLE OF MEDICAL INSTITUTIONS

PAUL C. BRUCKER, M.D.
President
Thomas Jefferson University
1025 Walnut St.
641 Scott Building
Philadelphia, PA 19107-5587

INTRODUCTION

The United States health care system continues to be the subject of intense concern and debate. In the search for alternatives, payors (the government, labor, business and insurers), health professionals, and patients compare and contrast our system with those of other countries.

Such comparisons, however, are difficult. The complexity of problems faced by the U.S. health care system is increased by wide regional variations and exacerbated as some state legislatures move ahead with localized health care reforms while others wait impatiently for federally mandated change.

Proposed reforms focus on three aspects of the U.S. health care system: the rising cost of care, the lack of access to the system for many U.S. citizens, and the need to maintain or increase quality while correcting other deficiencies in the system. Of the "system deficits", the cost of care attracts the most attention since its growth is most easily measured and directly related to the expanding federal deficit.

Payment of health benefits represented 107.9% of after-tax profits of American corporations in 1990 (12). Payments for health benefits currently are not subject to personal income or social security taxes. If they were, it is estimated that federal revenues would increase by $56 billion (13).

Many competitive insurance plans use a system of experience, rather than community, rating. Since 4% of insured individuals generate 50% of claim expenses and 20% of enrollees generate 80% of claims, it is easy to understand why "community" rating insurers with open enrollment irrespective of health status are more expensive than "experience" rated ones (14).

Private insurance design is shifting from traditional indemnity insurance to managed care plans which monitor utilization of hospitalization, physician consultants, and the use of expensive diagnostic technologies more closely, often through the use of primary physician "gatekeepers". There are financial incentives for patients to use the approved providers who are increasingly required to bear some level of financial risk. Although managed care plans tend to insure a relatively healthier, younger, employed population, they do demonstrate an ability to control costs more effectively than indemnity insurance models. In 1992, the difference in costs was approximately 15.3% (15).

The other key insurers include Medicare, which pays for only 90% of the cost of care for the elderly, and Medicaid, which pays for only 80% of the cost of indigent hospital care. These separate programs add to the confusion of the system and also to the tension between providers and private payors regarding who should absorb the expense of public payor underpayment (16).

Enacted in 1965, Medicare consists of two parts: a compulsory Part A that pays primarily for hospital services and Part B that pays for physician services, outpatient hospital care, and independent laboratory services. Thirty-five million people are insured under Medicare. A 1.45% payroll tax, imposed equally on employers and employees, funds Part A. The current average value of a beneficiary's Medicare hospital benefit exceeds a subscriber's contribution by five to one. A voluntary, monthly premium funds Part B. The sum of Part B premiums fund only 25% of program costs (17). General revenues pay for the remainder. In recent years, there have been increasing controls on both hospitals and physicians in an attempt to control the cost and volume of Medicare services (18). When there was an attempt to shift some of the costs to the more affluent elderly (The Catastrophic Insurance

---

(12) Iglehart, John K. June 18, 1992. The American Health Care System. *Health Policy Report.* 25:1715-1720.

(13) DeLew, Nancy, George Greenberg, and Kraig Kinchen. Fall 1992. A Layman's Guide to the U.S. Health Care System. *Health Care Financing Review.* 14:151-169.

(14) Iglehart, John K. June 18, 1992. American Health Care System. *Health Policy Report.* 25:1715-1720.

(15) Mr. John Klemm, Health Care Financing Administration.

(16) DeLew, Nancy, George Greenberg, and Kraig Kitchen. Fall 1992. A Layman's Guide to the U.S. Health Care System. *Health Care Financing Review,* 14:151-159.

(17) Mr. Dan Waldo, Health Care Financing Administration.

(18) DeLew, Nancy, George Greenberg, and Kraig Kinchen. Fall 1992. A Layman's Guide to the U.S. Health Care System. *Health Care Financing Review.* 14:151-169.

Act of 1988), there was such a furor that the Act was repealed less than a year after it was first passed (19).

The growth in Medicaid expense, shared by the states and the federal government, is a key factor in the current "crisis". Rapid growth in Medicaid funding is due to federally mandated expansions in coverage, expanded eligibility requirements for the poor, the recession with the increased number of unemployed, and the increased payment for services. The total spent by federal ($55.5 billion) and state governments in 1991, was $92.5 billion (20).

Excess Capacity

The United States has a surplus of acute care hospital beds and physicians. Approximately 68.8% (1,201,529) of acute hospital beds were filled on any given day in 1992 (21). The estimated cost of an empty bed is approximately $16,000 per year, and the total cost for unused or vacant beds is somewhere in the neighborhood of $3.1 billion per year (22). The reasons for this excess capacity include overbuilding of acute hospitals (often subsidized by tax-free municipal bonds), a drastic shortening in the length of hospital stay, and a recent emphasis on ambulatory care and same day surgery.

It is estimated that the United States has an adequate to almost excessive number of physicians. This is the result of the large increase in medical schools and medical school class size since the 1950's, and also the large number of international medical school graduates subsequently practicing in the United States (23).

Medical Technology

Many economists believe that new medical technologies are the principal factor for the average annual 10.6% rate of increase in health care costs over the past 3 decades (24). For those with access to the U.S. health care system, the best and most sophisticated technologies are readily available. Although technological innovation certainly adds to the cost of care, new technologies also save or improve the quality of life and in some cases actually decrease costs. In 1990, the diagnosis of a brain tumor with MRI (magnetic resonance imaging) not only replaces a 1950 hospital admission, but also a spinal tap, contrast or dye-requiring x-rays, and air insufflation tests. Hip replacement has allowed many a disabled individual to return to productive work. Some would argue that the business of developing and using medical technologies is good for the nation's overall economy. It is estimated that

(19) Source Book of Insurance Data By The Health Insurance Association of America. 1992. Appendix.
(20) Letsch, Suzanne W. Spring 1993. Data Watch: National Health Care Spending in 1991. *Health Affairs*. 94-110.
(21) American Hospital Association 1992 & 1993 Statistics.
(22) Medical Benefits, June 15, 1990, Volume 7, #11, pg. 2.
(23) COGME: Conclusions From Aggregate Supply Projections: Implications for MD's. - October 1992.
(24) Anderson, Christopher. July 23, 1993. Research and Health Care Costs. *Science*. 261:416-418.

that biotechnology sales will be $50 billion by the year 2000 (25). The dilemma, however, is that technology assessment methodologies are less sophisticated than the technologies themselves. New technologies often do not replace older ones and we have not yet developed sound methodologies for demonstrating efficacy.

Care of the Elderly

Although 13% of the U.S. population is 65 years of age or older, this population segment accounts for 40% of U.S. health care spending (26). The percentage of the elderly will increase to 15% in 2010 and 22% in 2030, placing additional strain on the health care system (27). Not only is the number of elderly increasing, but the percentage of the very old (above 85 years) continues to increase. Hospital care costs for this group is twice as much per capita as for those from 65-69 years of age. Interestingly, dying at older ages typically costs fewer dollars than dying from age 65-69, for fewer extensive courses of treatment are initiated. Similarly, there is evidence that individuals with advanced directives consume considerably less resources in the last two years of life than those without them (28). Yet it is estimated that in 1987, only 9% of the population have such instruments in place (29). The health care system does not address the special needs of the elderly and these "design failures" add significantly to health care costs. When sufficient family support is not available, inadequate provision for non acute and custodial care drives older adults to more expensive acute care settings.

Liability Issues

Providers of health care are subject to the negligence "rule of liability", with "negligence" defined as a departure from the customary standard of care. Patients who suffer a poor outcome caused by negligence are entitled to compensation for monetary and non-monetary losses. From 1975 to 1984, malpractice claims per physician rose at an average rate of 10% per year; and between 1982 and 1986 claim frequency per 100 physicians rose from 13.5% to 17.2% per year. Claim severity increased at roughly twice the rate of the Consumer Price Index from 1975 to 1984, and not surprisingly the costs of malpractice insurance have increased dramatically (30). An AMA survey in 1987, indicated malpractice premiums and damage payments comprised $5.7 billion of the $102.7 billion spent on physician

(25) Health Industry Manufacturers Association - 1990 Data.
(26) Mr. Dan Waldo, Health Care Financing Administration (Unpublished data).
(27) U.S. Census Bureau - projections based on the 1990 Census.
(28) Tempkin, Helen A. 1992. The Use & Cost of Health Services Prior to Death: A Comparison of the Medicare-only and the Medicare-Medicaid Elderly Populations. *The Milbank Quarterly*. Vol. 70, Number 4:679-701.
(29) Emanuel, Linda L., et al. March 28, 1991. Advance Directives for Medical Care - A Case for Greater Use. *New England Journal of Medicine*. Vol. 334, Number 13:889-895.
(30) Danzon, Patricia M., Mark V. Pauly, and Raynard S. Kington. The Effects of Malpractice Litigation on Physicians' Fees and Incomes. *AEA Papers and Proceedings*. May 1990. Volume 80, No. 2. pgs. 122-127.

services. The respondents claimed that defensive medicine cost an additional $19.3 billion (31). The average award to plaintiffs in jury trials went from approximately $405,000 in 1980, to $1,415,804 in 1989. Plaintiff attorneys usually receive one third of an award while defense attorneys, billing on an hourly basis, usually receive about the same as the plaintiff's attorney (32).

There are certainly patients who deserve compensation for injury resulting from negligence. Unfortunately, outcomes' analysis, even based solely on mortality issues, is not sufficiently developed to be a reliable and valid indicator of the quality of care. Outcomes' analysis must also pay attention to input variables such as comorbid conditions, social situations and the severity of problems.

ACCESS TO HEALTH CARE

Access to health care is limited by various factors. The most frequently cited statistic regarding access to care measures the number of Americans who are underinsured or have no insurance at all. The number most frequently cited is 37 million, or 14.5% of the population (33). This number is deceptive since it does not include individuals who are uninsured because they are "between jobs" or those who, for fear of losing insurance, remain in undesirable work situations. It ignores young adults who feel that they are "immortal" and do not need health insurance. It also excludes those with health care insurance that does not adequately cover outpatient, preventive, and long term care. It is the uninsured and the underinsured who provide the basis for the many anecdotes about the inadequacy of the United States health care system. Their stories, and the realistic anxiety of many who face the possible loss of their health insurance, contribute to the attractiveness of universal access-coverage.

The shortage and uneven distribution of primary physicians makes it difficult for individuals to enter the health care system. It results in care lacking continuity since patients often must rely on urgicenters and emergency rooms which are not designed or equipped for comprehensive care. In many rural areas, the closure of small hospitals forces patients to travel great distances for required care. Similarly, there is a shortage of affordable skilled and long-term facilities in most of the United States.

HEALTH CARE REFORM

As this chapter was being written, the Clinton administration submitted its health care reform proposal to the Congress. There, it will be considered by at least forty committees and subcommittees. Few can dispute the principles promoted by the

(31) Hospitals. August 5, 1990.
(32) Hudson T. *Hospitals.* May 20, 1990. Tort Reform Legislation: Can it help hospitals?

President, particularly those relating to universal coverage, prevention, and cost-constraint. There will undoubtedly be considerable debate as to how, at what rate and when these might be achieved. The principal discussions will revolve about the economic impact of health care reform on the economy and how it should be financed, the advantages and disadvantages of managed competition, and the role that the government should play in managing health care delivery. In the meantime, the health care industry is undergoing extensive change in anticipation of a new federal mandate to change. The populace is not debating whether there should be change, but are certainly concerned about what the change might be and how it might affect them.

As the year 2000 approaches, our nation must face the following dilemma: A larger number of individuals will need and/or want to seek more health care services, including technological innovations, available at little or no increase in total cost. Whether government or market forces drive change, our health care system will be significantly restructured. Without a global budget and a comprehensive approach to reform, change will be incremental and fragmented.

Structural Reform: Reimbursement

In the past decade, payors have attempted to modify provider and patient behavior through changes in the reimbursement structure: The federal government has revised Medicare reimbursement methodologies, paying hospitals prospectively set rates to control utilization, and paying physicians on the basis of relative value scales in a less than successful attempt to control costs as well as reward "cognitive" vs. procedure oriented specialties. To place cost and utilization controls on both patients and providers, Medicare has recently funded several pilot managed care programs; only 2 million of the 34 million eligible are currently enrolled.

Private insurers have established managed care products, with primary care physicians acting as gatekeepers, restricted provider networks often at financial risk for the inefficient delivery of services, and tight utilization controls. In 1992, 42 million people were enrolled in managed care programs (34). Critics of managed care claim that these plans achieve impressive utilization statistics by enrolling primarily healthy, younger patients and take exorbitant profits from the already limited health dollar. However, the managed care industry is maturing, with smaller players consolidating into large regional and national companies with powerful information and management systems. They are capable of utilizing clinical, financial, and demographic information to not only manage resources but also to track efficacy, continuity and comprehensiveness of care, and patient satisfaction. These developing, reliable management and information systems will provide the foundation for true health care reform.

Jumbo managed care companies are most definitely leading the health care industry away from a system in which dollars drive expansion more or less for the

---

(34) Group Health Association of America, Research & Analysis Department - HMO Industry Profile Report - 1993.

sake of expansion. It is unclear, however, if and when current trends will result in a seamless, integrated system which provides capabilities and incentives for care which is appropriate, demonstrably effective and rendered on a timely basis in the least costly setting.

Thus the debate over "managed competition". Charles Weller describes the traditional system of fee-for-service, solo practice, free choice of provider, and payment by a remote third party a "guilt free choice" system, allowing the patient to choose his or her doctor and thus eliminating the insurer's bargaining power. Physicians' control their income by the amount of service provided.

Alain C. Enthoven, the architect of managed competition, defines managed competition as "*value-for-money*" competition, "*a purchasing strategy to obtain maximum value for consumers and employers, using rules for competition derived from microeconomic principles.*" A sponsor (either an employer, a governmental entity, or a purchasing cooperative), acting on behalf of a large group of subscribers manages the enrollment process, organizes a provider network based on quality standards and price. Some of the features of managed competition include:

1. the sponsor's contribution to the premiums must not exceed the cost of the lowest-priced plan, and therefore can always take business away from a higher priced plan;
2. the sponsor sets its contribution after the health plans have submitted their quotes;
3. a standardization of coverage contract exists which should deter product differentiation, facilitate price comparisons, and counter market segmentation;
4. reliable, quality information;
5. a market structured to offer annual choice of plan at the individual subscriber level.

Enthoven claims that managed competition "*is compatible with strong American cultural preferences, as articulated by Alexis de Tocqueville, for limited government, voluntary action, decentralized decision making, individual choice, multiple competing approaches, pluralism, and personal and local responsibility*" (35).

As our nation debates which model will best reward quality, curtail costs and provide access, the "managed competition" and "guilt free choice" systems will be compared and contrasted frequently.

Structural Reform: The Workforce

Despite their increasing dissatisfaction with the present system, physicians fear the proposed changes even more. They complain about loss of clinical autonomy to the government and insurers, an increased hassle over financial matters including the erosion of the fee-for-service system, the threat of malpractice and the necessity to practice defensive medicine. Some resent the basic principles of HMO's which

(35) Endoven, Alain, C. Supplement 1993. The History and Principles of Managed Competition. *Health Affairs.* 24-48.

urban areas where the percentage of poor and elderly patients is greater. Funded by research, patient services, government funds, and tuition charges, the academic health centers have seen their patient revenue base diminish with more price competition and greater geographic extension of tertiary care. University hospitals simply can not complete financially in an urban setting with the many excellent suburban hospitals located in more affluent settings. This reduction in the available funds that have traditionally subsidized educational efforts, is accompanied by the reluctance of the majority of managed care insurers to provide such funding. Increased emphasis on primary care and the ambulatory setting will require even more labor intense efforts to train such health professionals.

Medical Malpractice Liability Reform

Many suggestions have been offered to improve access to fair compensation for negligence and, at the same time, reduce the costs of medical malpractice liability premiums and defensive medicine.

Proposals abound requiring medical liability questions to be initially resolved by a dispute resolution process before being eligible to enter the court system.

There are suggested caps on non-economic damages, and there is a plan to have court awarded punitive damages paid to the State to further reduce medical malpractice premiums. Punitive damages against a medical product producer would not be awarded if the product was approved in a creditable way by the FDA or other regulatory board. Caps have been suggested for attorneys' contingency fees along with a uniform statute of limitations for plaintiffs of all ages. In order to discourage frivolous, expensive court actions, some propose having the plaintiff pays the defendant's legal fees if the plaintiff loses the case.

CONCLUSION

The role of the government in reform is controversial. Many believe the government should play a larger role in health care administration and oversight, while others would prefer a government that facilitates and monitors, rather than micro manages. The timing is right for debate about necessary change that is acceptable and affordable. As outlined in this chapter, the complex components of our health care system will make the rapid overhaul or abrupt change difficult.

REFERENCES

American Hospital Association 1992 & 1993 Statistics.

Anderson, Christopher. *Science.* Research and Health Care Costs. July 23, 1993. 261:416-418.

COGME: Conclusions From Aggregate Supply Projections: Implications for MD's. - October 1992.

Council on Graduate Medical Education Third Report - Improving Access to Health Care Through Physician Workforce Reform: Directions for the 21st Century. October 1992. U.S. Department of Health & Human Services.
Danzon, Patricia M., Mark V. Pauly and Raynard S. Kington. *AEA Papers and Proceedings.* May 1990. The Effects of Malpractice Litigation on Physicians' Fees and Incomes. Volume 80, No. 2. pgs. 122-127.
DeLew, Nancy, George Greenberg and Kraig Kinchen. *Health Care Financing Review.* Fall 1992. A Layman's Guide to the U.S. Health Care System. 14:151-169.
Emanuel, Linda L., et al. *New England Journal of Medicine.* March 28, 1991. Advance Directives for Medical Care - A Case for Greater Use. Vol. 324, Number 13:889-895.
Ezekiel J. Emanuel. Single Payer System. Wall Street Journal. February 16, 1993.
Enthoven, Alain, C. *Health Affairs.* Supplement 1993. The History and Principles of Managed Competition. 24-48.
Fuchs, Victor R. *Milbank Quarterly.* Spring 1984. Though Much Is Taken: Reflections on Aging, Health and Medical Care. 62:143-166.
Gaul, Gilbert. August 5, 1993. Study Links Paperwork to 25% of Hospital Costs. The Philadelphia Inquirer.
Group Health Association of America, Research & Analysis Department - HMO Industry Profile Report - 1993.
Health Industry Manufacturers Association - 1990 Data.
Highlights at the Eighth International Conference on AIDS by American Hospitals Association in September 1992.
Hospitals. August 5, 1990.
Hudson, T. *Hospitals.* May 20, 1990. Tort Reform Legislation: Can it help hospitals?
Iglehart, John K. *Health Policy Report.* The American Health Care System. June 18, 1992. 25:1715-1720.
Klemm, John. Health Care Financing Administration.
Letsch, Suzanne W. *Health Affairs.* Spring 1993. Data Watch: National Health Care Spending in 1991. 94-110.
Medical Benefits, Volume 7, Number 11. June 15, 1990. pg. 2.
Medical Benefits, Volume 10, Number 6. March 30, 1993, pg. 1-2.
Schwartz, M.D., Leroy L. and Mark W. Stanton. *The Internist.* July-August 1992. Social Problems That Escalate America's Health Care Costs. 15-17.
Source Book of Insurance Data by the Health Insurance Association of America, 1992, pg. 58.
Temkin, Helen A. *The Milbank Quarterly.* 1992. The Use & Cost of Health Services Prior to Death: A Comparison of the Medicare-only and the Medicare-Medicaid Elderly Populations. Vol. 70, Number 4:679-701.
U.S. Census Bureau - projections based on the 1990 Census. Waldo, Dan. Health Care Financing Administration.
Wennberg, John E., Goodman, David C., Nease, Robert F. and Robert B. Keller. *Health Affairs.* Summer 1993. Finding Equilibrium in U.S. Physician Supply. pgs. 89-103.

Medicine and Health Care Into the Twenty-First Century. Edited by S.K. Majumdar, L.M. Rosenfeld, D.B. Nash and A.M. Audet. © 1995, The Pennsylvania Academy of Science.

Chapter Five

NATIONAL HEALTH CARE REFORM AND THE CLINTON HEALTH SECURITY ACT: A View From The States

RAYMOND C. SCHEPPACH, Ph.D. and
L. CARL VOLPE, Ph.D.[1]
National Governors' Association
Suite 267
444 N. Capitol Street
Washington, DC 20001

INTRODUCTION

On September 22, 1993, President Bill Clinton formally announced his long-awaited plan for health care reform. After some revisions, it was formally introduced in November in Congress as the Health Security Act. With the introduction of the President's bill and a number of alternative health reform proposals, the national debate on health care reform had begun in earnest. To fully understand the states' perspective on health care reform and the President's plan, it is important to look at the impact of the health care crisis on state government and examine the strategies they used to address their growing health care problems during the late 1980s and early 1990s.

---

[1]Raymond C. Scheppach, Ph.D., is the Executive Director of the National Governors' Association and L. Carl Volpe, Ph.D., is Deputy Director of the Human Resources Group for Health Policy and Legislation. The views expressed in this chapter are drawn, in large part, from formal positions taken by the nation's governors through the National Governors' Association. However, the authors bear sole responsibility for its content. (Note 1.)

THE FISCAL PRESSURES OF MEDICAID

When Governors and state legislators think of health care, they first think of Medicaid—the federal/state health care safety net for some of America's neediest people. (Note 2.) On average, for the last five years, states and the federal government have seen Medicaid grow in excess of 20 percent annually. Not only has Medicaid grown in absolute terms, but also it is increasing as a percentage of total state spending. In 1988, Medicaid represented 12 percent of spending; in 1992, it was up to 17 percent. In addition, twelve states had Medicaid spending above 20 percent, with Rhode Island at 27 percent and New Hampshire at 34 percent of total spending.

Overall, state spending on Medicaid is now greater than that for higher education, and it is beginning to approach the 21 percent spent on elementary and secondary education. (Note 3.) The growth in Medicaid spending, particularly during 1991 and 1992, was a major contributing factor to states increasing taxes by $25.3 billion over this two-year period. (Note 4.) This huge growth in Medicaid raised havoc with state spending priorities as spending for education, economic development, and other programs was cut and taxes were increased to fund this new "Pac man" of state government.

States have long argued that unfunded federal mandates have been the primary cause of the astronomical increases in Medicaid spending. Although a contributing factor, growth in Medicaid spending results from a complex combination of these unfunded federal eligibility and service mandates, with increases in enrollment in existing federal programs and increases in utilization patterns of Medicaid beneficiaries, especially among persons with disabilities. (Note 5.)

SHORT-TERM RELIEF FROM EXPLOSIVE MEDICAID COSTS

In the short run, there was little that states could do to control Medicaid costs or to generate additional revenues. Nevertheless, they made incremental changes in a number of areas to reduce their fiscal exposure.

Reducing and Eliminating Services

The most obvious approach to limiting a state's financial exposure was by eliminating or reducing eligibility and service entitlements. Although it may be simple to propose, Medicaid program cuts are very difficult to make. Reducing or eliminating services to Medicaid beneficiaries—the neediest of the needy—is an extremely difficult public policy choice and often is not politically popular. Denying Medicaid coverage to those currently in the program is even more difficult. In some states, however, the budget crisis has been so significant that state officials have cut the program despite the political risks. A less dramatic, but effective, approach to reducing Medicaid has been to reduce the amount of service that a beneficiary can receive. For example, states have limited the number of physician visits per year, rather than allowing unlimited visits.

Maximizing the Medicaid Match

As budgets tightened, states realized that a variety of Medicaid reimbursable services were being provided to Medicaid beneficiaries through state, county, and local government entities, but the federal matching funds were not claimed through the Medicaid program. Many states now have initiatives to ensure that every individual who receives services paid for with state funds and who could be enrolled in Medicaid is encouraged to do so. Moreover, states have tried to ensure that every state or local service dollar that could be matched with medicaid funds is claimed. It is hard to estimate the financial impact of this strategy, but it is reasonable to say that maximizing Medicaid dollars continues to be an important strategy for states.

Raising Revenues Through Provider Taxes and Voluntary Contributions

The most controversial step taken by states to address increasing health costs was the proliferation of provider tax and voluntary contribution programs. Unwilling or unable to raise state revenues through broad-based taxes, governors and legislators developed tax programs that often were supported by health care providers. Through these programs, states raised revenues or donations from providers—most of whom where Medicaid providers—and used the revenues to expand service or eligibility categories. These funds also were used to raise reimbursement rates to keep pace with increasing health care costs. In 1991, Congress enacted legislation that limited the way states could raise revenues through provider tax and voluntary contribution programs. Despite the limitations, provider taxes remain a viable option for states.

Providing Services Through Waivers

In recent years, governors have turned to health networks and managed systems of care to control costs. Within Medicaid, use of these delivery systems usually requires a federal waiver. More than 12 percent of all Medicaid beneficiaries receive care through managed care systems, and Medicaid managed care operates in more than thirty-six states. A recent General Accounting Office study reports that access to care for Medicaid beneficiaries is slightly better under managed care than traditional fee-for-service care, but cost savings were reported as inconclusive. (Note 6.) Despite this study, states report that Medicaid managed care is extremely cost efficient and is becoming more so as experience is gained in managed care systems.

States also have sought to control Medicaid and other health costs through waiver authority provided under Section 1115 of the Social Security Act. Although this waiver authority gives states much more latitude to change their health care systems, waivers are granted for a limited period of time—typically three to five years. Moreover, the conditions of acceptance are rather stringent. States must demonstrate that the waiver is for a true test of a health care innovation. The Oregon Health Plan waiver, the Hawaii Health QUEST waiver, and Tennessee's TennCare waiver were approved under this authority and are integral to each state's reform efforts. With the approval of the Hawaii and Tennessee waivers, states are looking seriously at the short-term use of this waiver authority to accomplish cost-efficient restructuring of their Medicaid programs while the debate on national health care reform continues.

For example, South Carolina will be applying for a federal Medicaid waiver in early 1994 that would extend coverage to many South Carolinians up to 100 percent of poverty. Using principles of managed competition, South Carolina and the federal government would achieve cost neutrality over the life of the project while expanding coverage and beginning to build a health care infrastructure that emphasizes personal responsibility, choice, prevention, and primary care.

STATE-INITIATED HEALTH CARE REFORM

States were moving to limit their financial risk from Medicaid, while simultaneously moving forward on broader health care reforms. Although the state of Hawaii has had universal health care since the mid-1970s, it was not until 1989, when Oregon began to enact a number of bills designed to make health insurance more affordable and accessible to all Oregonians, that a new round of state activity began. The Oregon bills focused mainly on increased Medicaid eligibility, cost-control measures, and the establishment of a high-risk pool for the uninsured. However, most of the publicity focused on the component that established a priority list of services and procedures that would be available for Medicaid beneficiaries. This provoked a national debate on "rationing" and, while controversial, it served to heighten the awareness of health care issues among average Americans.

The push by Oregon in 1989 and the continued shortcomings of the existing health care system led to a flurry of state activity in 1992 and 1993. By this time, reform was driven not only by the pressures of the Medicaid problem, but by the concerns and fears about health care security that were raised to governors as they traveled through their individual states. During this period, the problem of cost and the lack of available health insurance to small businesses were key concerns. Governors also heard from large corporations that feared their competitive position in the world marketplace was being eroded by spiraling health care costs and from average workers who had grown increasingly worried about losing health care benefits. Finally, they heard stories of the devastation to working families and the elderly from catastrophic or long-term illnesses. Governors were hearing these problems with increasing regularity throughout the states. Yet, federal action was still not forthcoming.

Early in 1993, Florida Governor Lawton Chiles signed into law the Florida Health Care Reform Act, which was designed to ensure access to basic health care for all Floridians by December 31, 1994. Minnesota followed shortly by passing a major package in 1993 aimed at slowing the rate of growth in costs by 10 percent for each of the next five years. There also were incentives to join integrated service networks in Minnesota as the state followed a managed competition model. On April 23, 1993, the state of Washington enacted a major health care reform package that requires all residents to have universal access to a uniform benefit package by 1995. Vermont also is on the frontier of health care reform by redesigning health care delivery.

Although most of these states enacted comprehensive state reform that would be phased in over time, none could fully implement their state legislation without changes in federal legislation—specifically, Medicaid and, to a much greater extent, the Employee Retirement Income Security Act (ERISA). (Note 7.) If states had been allowed to move forward as they adopted reforms, there would today be more data on which to base a federal system. As with most public policy, state innovation and experience often provide a clear path for federal action.

THE GOVERNORS' HEALTH CARE REFORM POLICY

As health care reform has been a major priority for a growing number of individual governors, collectively they have made it a priority of their national organization, the National Governors' Association (NGA). (Note 8.) Through NGA, the nation's governors have pursued health care reform policy on two tracks. The first calls for the enactment of a comprehensive federal framework with state flexibility; the second calls for immediate enactment of those federal legislative changes that are necessary to enable states to effectively reorganize the health care delivery system, increase access, and restrain costs. Taken together, these two complementary tracks form a cohesive and comprehensive state perspective that must be considered by Congress and the administration as they approach health reform.

In February 1993, the governors adopted a comprehensive policy on national health care reform that calls for universal access to affordable quality health care. The policy supports a national health care system that recognizes the importance of a federal framework for health care reform, but at the same time recognizes the essential roles and responsibilities of states. The governors support a framework inclusive of managed competition that guarantees universal access to coverage. It includes a core national benefits package that is tax deductible and emphasizes primary and preventive care, and allows portability of coverage; insurance reforms that address guaranteed renewability, portability, and availability; tort reform; antitrust changes; administrative simplifications; and the development of national health outcome measures so that Americans can assess the quality of their health care. The policy also calls for purchasing cooperatives at the state level. Although the governor's policy addresses purchasing cooperatives, it does not specify whether they should be mandatory or voluntary. There are differences of opinion among the governors on this issue.

The governors believe that strong cost control systems are integral to any health care reform system adopted for the nation, but that effective cost control can be achieved only in conjunction with universal access. As a group, the governors do not endorse enforceable budgets, preferring budget targets instead. The governors argue that setting enforceable budgets for one-seventh of the American economy requires a stable and objective national data system that does not now exist. Finally, the governors call for major reform of the Medicaid program so that all current Medicaid recipients can receive their acute care coverage in a mangaged care setting.

A Call for Action on National Reform

At their Winter Meeting in Washington in January 1994, Governors once again had an opportunity to meet and discuss the status of health care reform. They realized that despite differences on employer mandates, global budgets and mandatory alliances, there was a great deal of common ground about strategies to address many of the nation's health care problems. Also, they agreed that those strategies must be addressed this year. Governors became convinced that they would contribute most to the national debate by adopting a policy that reflected their consensus position. Therefore, they adopted a policy statement that calls upon President Clinton and Congress to pass health care legislation in 1994 that includes, at a minimum, the following:

- insurance reform;
- state-organized purchasing cooperatives;
- core benefits and access;
- limited tax deductibility of health care premiums;
- low income subsidies:
- changes to the current Medicaid system;
- medical malpractice and liability reform;
- relief from anti-trust statutes;
- relief from the Employee Retirement Income Security Act
- federally organized outcome and quality standards; and
- administrative simplifications.

They believe that these provisions should be included in any reform strategy. And as Governors, they did not vary in their support of these changes. In announcing their new policy, they urged Congress and the President to act as quickly as possible.

Immediate State Relief

Although the governors have pledged to continue working with President Clinton and Congress to enact comprehensive reform, they also believe that a number of reforms should be pursued now. Those reforms include allowing states to implement Medicaid managed care programs through state plan amendments (as opposed to waivers) and the establishment of a waiver process for ERISA so that states have the opportunity to implement broad-based financing mechanisms for state reform and to include self-insured plans in state-based reform programs. Managed care for the acute care portion of Medicaid will help recipients get appropriate prevention-oriented care. This will increase the quality of care in the Medicaid program, help to control costs, and provide a medical home for beneficiaries who historically have had trouble finding reliable care.

THE APPROPRIATE STATE ROLE IN HEALTH CARE REFORM

Through NGA, the governors have made it clear that they do not want to have fifty different state health care programs. The governors want health care benefits to be portable from state to state and for benefits to be tax deductible for all citizens equally. In addition, they are extremely sensitive to the concerns of large multistate employers who do not want to deal with statutes and regulations that differ from state to state. Furthermore, the governors understand the need for a system that is organized by the federal government and creates some uniform rules across state lines to ensure portability. It is for these reasons that through NGA, the governors support a strong federal framework that includes the following principles.

- The enactment of federal legislation to limit medical underwriting and minimize the variation in rates that different individuals and groups are charged. However, states should continue to enforce insurance regulations.
- The creation of core benefits package that all insurance companies and accountable health plans must offer.
- The setting of federal malpractice guidelines for states.
- The enactment of changes in federal antitrust legislation.
- The creation of medical outcome and quality information standards.
- The creation and enforcement of procedures for administrative streamlining.

Not only are these elements of a strong federal framework, but they also preempt state authority in a number of important areas. Nevertheless, they are necessary to develop an efficient delivery system for health care. State flexibility is the other major component necessary to develop an efficient system. States need to have the flexibility to administer, on a day-to-day basis, any system that is eventually enacted within this federal framework. This means flexibility in designing, regulating, and overseeing the regional alliances and accountable health plans. It also means flexibility in administering Medicaid and Medicare programs that are not fully integrated into the alliances.

It must be noted, however, that although there is significant agreement among the governors on the role of states in national health reform, they do not agree on all issues. For example, they disagree on the cost and financing of the new system. They also have different perspectives on the potential mandatory nature of the alliances.

THE GOVERNORS' REACTIONS TO THE PRESIDENT'S HEALTH SECURITY ACT

Like most Americans, the governors gave high marks to President Clinton for putting health care reform at the top of the national agenda. The governors also are grateful to the President for proposing a state-based system. There are a number of federal-state issues in the Clinton health care plan that the governors' policy supports, as well as some issues that are not supported by existing policy.

Alliances and Accountable Health Plans

The governors support the states' discretion on the number and regional boundaries of alliances. This will enable an individual state to take into account how its provider community and local governments are organized in determining regional boundaries. The governors support such latitude, but still have some questions about one aspect of this provision. The Health Security Act does not permit metropolitan statistical areas (MSAs) to be divided into different alliances. As it is understood, the policy was designed to preclude discriminatory practices in drawing alliance boundaries. The governors support the antidiscriminatory language in the act and, if necessary, would support stronger language to give states the broader flexibility at issue. However, at the very least, there should be a waiver provision to allow for the division of metropolitan statistical areas. It may be important in some states to draw boundaries that include rural areas with a part of the MSA. In addition, in some areas, it may be important to accommodate alliances that cross state boundaries. This may increase the quality of care that is available in rural areas. Finally, the governors support having the flexibility to select which legal entity will govern the alliance (i.e., a state agency, a quasi-governmental agency, or a private nonprofit organization).

Although few states are likely to pursue the single-payer system, the governors support having the flexibility to use this option as described in the act, with one modification. The act would require the single-payer system to be operated by the state or a designated agency of the state. The governors prefer to be able to contract out all or part of a state's operation to the private sector and would like the legislative language to specifically allow for this option. The governors also support additional flexibility to pursue alternate reform, as long as goals of access, quality, and cost containment can be met.

The governors support the authority vested in states to certify accountable health plans (AHPs), as well as to oversee the audits and guarantee funds. States already have considerable experience in this area because of their traditional role as regulators of insurance. It is critical that states have authority over both the alliances and the AHPs to ensure a cost-effective system.

Although the text of the act gives states flexibility in the establishment and administration of health alliances and AHPs, it confuses lines of authority between the federal and state governments by giving both the federal government and states some direct oversight and regulatory control over these entities. This could dilute accountability and may hurt the administrative efficiency of the system. Although the federal government has a legitimate interest in the efficient and effective operation of alliances and AHPs, the interest is best expressed through direct oversight by state governments, which can then regulate an oversee alliances and plans. The governors suggest that the federal government provide appropriate general guidelines rather than direct oversight.

Although the governors may have differing opinions on the need for setting fee-for-service rates, they appreciate having the ability to set rates for the entire state or to vest this authority in regional alliances, as appropriate.

There is some concern about the responsibility of states to ensure adequate access to a choice of health plans, as described in the act. The language calls not only for choice, but also for access to plans at or below the weighted average premium "to the maximum extent practicable." The availability of plans will, to some extent, be determined by the premium budget assigned to the alliance and the number of AHPs that choose to bid within that budget cap. Because states will have no control over the budget that will be set nationally, states may not have the tools to ensure choice. Moreover, the act stipulates a right to enforce state responsibilities through 42 U.S.C. §1983; giving individuals the right to sue states is a serious issue that will be vigorously opposed by the governors.

Finally, it appears that states are ultimately responsible for ensuring that individuals have access to health care. The governors are concerned that this provision will evolve into a situation where states will have financial responsibility when there are solvency problems for AHPs or if the federal government's contribution reaches the enacted cap. The governors also have some concerns that costs will be shifted to states or that benefits will be increased without additional federal funds.

Premium Caps

The governors are committed to meaningful cost containment that will bring the rate of growth in health care spending in line with the rate of growth in the national economy. The governors' policy supports budget targets in the early years of national reform, rather than immediate enforceable premium (budget) caps as detailed in the Health Security Act. Although the cap is determined and enforced by the federal government, the impact on states may be direct. If the federal government fails to set reasonable limits in the first several years, states may be left with the responsibility for correcting the damage done to providers, networks, and the availability of health care. The governors urge caution in setting premium caps in the early years of health reform. However, although urging caution, the governors do support the provision in the act that gives financial incentives to states to try to keep alliance spending under the budget. Without this incentive, each alliance could negotiate premiums equal to the premium cap set by the National Health Board.

Transition to the New System

States may begin implementing the new system as early as January 1, 1996, with all states participating within two years of this date. Although this deadline is somewhat ambitious, the governors believe that it can be met with the additional planning and start-up funds authorized in the proposed legislation. In fact, some states would prefer to begin operating a national system before the 1996 start date and will be seeking authority to do so.

Currently, about twelve states are establishing mandatory or voluntary alliances, and others will be considering such legislation next year. In addition, states have undertaken insurance reforms, budgeting, integration of public and private programs, and other initiatives consistent with the President's proposal. These states will serve as laboratories for the President's approach, and other states will be able to benefit from their experiences. Essentially, the two-year window will enable states such as Florida, Hawaii, Minnesota, Oregon, Vermont, and Washington to implement early, as many of them have already enacted major health care reform initiatives. Similarly, this start date will give other states more time to implement.

It is important to have planning and start-up funds in the proposed legislation. States will have strong incentives to implement early if they receive low-income and small business subsidies when they implement the new system.

Medicaid

Although there were significant staff and gubernatorial discussions with the President's health care task force, the Medicaid proposal outlined in the Health Security Act could have gone farther to streamline the system.

Acute Care. The governors have the most concerns with the acute care portion of the President's program. The governors believe strongly that the acute care portion of Medicaid should be incorporated into alliances and should cease to exist as a separate program. Unfortunately, given other interest groups, this may be difficult to accomplish. Individuals who are eligible for the Aid to Families with Dependent Children (AFDC) and the Supplemental Security Income (SSI) programs are part of Medicaid. As Medicaid beneficiaries, they receive their guaranteed national health benefits through an alliance. However, they may remain eligible for other Medicaid benefits than are currently either mandated or optional to states.

Those who currently recieve Medicaid through the noncash categorial programs, such as children and pregnant women with income up to 133 percent of poverty, will be eligible for the new low-income subsidy program and would not remain on the Medicaid rolls. However, children in these categories, as well as AFDC and SSI children, will be eligible for a set of acute care ancillary services that will augment the guaranteed national benefits package. This new program is federally funded. States continue to be responsible for low-income individuals who are eligible for both Medicaid and Medicare.

Such a structure is problematic. First, it requires states to maintain the complex eligibility and reimbursement systems that are the hallmark of Medicaid. Second, it continues to hold states accountable for Medicaid health care costs when the nation is trying to consolidate and streamline its health care programs. Third, the approach assumes that certain low-income individuals are worthier of ancillary health care benefits than other low-income individuals.

Low-income people have special problems in securing quality and affordable health care. The governors recognize that some of those circumstances will remain despite any national health reform approach. The nation has an unusual opportunity to restructure this system. The governors are well-positioned to play a major role in creating that system.

Institutional Long-Term Care. The Health Security Act establishes new national eligibility standards for the Medicaid institutional care program. Although these changes constitute a new unfunded federal mandate on states, there are no radical policy changes to the existing program.

New Community-Based Long-Term Care Program

The act creates a new community-based long-term care program for people with significant functional impairments. The governors support community-based alternatives to institutional care, and the act has several provisions, including this one, that are consistent with that position. The governors support the fact that states are given substantial flexibility, that community-based long-term care is a state entitlement program as opposed to an individual entitlement, and that this is an optional program. The major concern is that federal financial participation, though significant, is capped, while state financial exposure is not.

POTENTIAL ECONOMIC EFFECTS OF HEALTH CARE REFORM

As stewards of their states, the governors also are looking at health care reform from a broader economic perspective. In evaluating the potential economic impacts of the President's plan or other health care reform proposals, it is critical to differentiate between long- and short-term impacts.

Long-Term Impacts

Any proposal that significantly reduces the rate of increase in health care costs will have a major positive long-term economic impact because health care costs are virtually bankrupting all three levels of government and may be creating a drag on the country's competitiveness.

Dramatically lowering the rate of increase of health care costs will enable governments at all levels to change priorities, reduce taxes, and provide more funding for both human and physical capital. This means more funding for education and training, as well as roads, bridges, ports, and other types of infrastructure. Over time, such increases in public investment should help increase productivity, create jobs, and increase real income.

Not only will decreasing the rate of growth in health care costs help all levels of government, it should have a similar impact on the private sector. It is likely that cost reduction will help in three ways. First, firms will have higher profits that could be used for new capital investment, which would help increase productivity and real income. Second, goods produced by U.S. firms would have a lower cost. This should benefit U.S. consumers and make U.S. goods comparatively cheaper in the international market, which should further stimulate the growth in the U.S. economy. Finally, over time, wages would increase.

Short-Term Impacts

Although the long-term impact is positive, there is considerable uncertainty about the potential short-term impacts. The potential adjustments could take the following forms.

National Impacts. The health care industry has created one out of every six jobs in the United States over the last ten years. As the growth in health care spending slows, so will the industry's ability to create new jobs. In addition to this slowing of the rate of job creation, there will be some other negative economic impacts. First, there may be some negative impact on the insurance industry because of a reduction in the fee-for-service business. Second, because of the mandate to pay health care benefits, there may be a negative impact on some small businesses that do not now provide health coverage. On the other hand, there will be some positive economic impacts because approximately 37 million people who do not currently have health insurance will become insured. Also, there will be some positive impact from capping the cost of health care for many firms and governments. However, the net impact on employment and income is difficult to determine at this time.

Impacts Within a State. Currently, in many states, hospital occupancy is down and competition may force closure of some hospitals, probably in suburban and possibly in rural areas. This also may require new investments in clinics and other facilities in urban and, possibly, rural areas. Although such an adjustment may be necessary, it could cause some dislocation during the transition period in a number of states.

Impacts Across States. The President's plan, as introduced, as well as alternative reform bills, has the potential for distributional impacts across states. Although it is very difficult to quantify the various impacts, the following points are important.

- States with the largest number of uninsured residents, primarily the unemployed, will benefit after the employer mandate is implemented because they will be subsidized by the federal government.
- States with a high percentage of their population over age 65 and receiving Medicare, as well as those over age 50 who are pensioners, will benefit because these individuals will have federally paid drug benefits and subsidies.
- States with expensive health care costs relative to wages will benefit because the 7.9 percent caps will provide a federal subsidy to firms over the cap.
- States with a disproportionate share of small businesses that do not currently provide health insurance will lose. However, the impact is difficult to determine because it depends on the average wage as well as the average number of employees in those small firms.

The collective impact is difficult to quantify. However, it may depend substantially on the following:

- The underlying strength of the economy when health care reform is implemented. If economic growth is robust, then any potential short-term adjustments would be minimal. On the other hand, if the economy is fragile, the adjustment may be more difficult.
- The length of the transition period. In general, the longer the phase-in period, the more limited the short-term economic adjustment. However, the sooner the growth rate of health care costs is restrained, the more positive the impact.

ENDNOTES

1. Sections of this paper were previously published in an article by the authors that appeared in the *Journal of American Health Policy* (Vol. 3, No. 6, November/December 1993, pp. 25-31) and were included in testimony given by Governor Carroll A. Campbell Jr. and Governor Howard Dean on December 15, 1993, before the Ways and Means Committee, U.S. House of Representatives and on February 3, 1994 before the Committee on Finance, U.S. Senate.
2. The Medicaid program, established by Congress in 1965, provides health care to certain low income individuals who have both acute care and long term care needs. The program policy parameters are established federally; it is administered with some options for flexibility by states; and it is financed jointly with state and federal funds.
3. National Association of State Budget Officers, *1992 State Expenditure Report.* (Washington, DC: National Governors' Association, April 1993).
4. National Governors' Association and the National Association of State Budget Officers, *The Fiscal Survey of States.* (Washington, DC: National Governors' Association and the National Association of State Budget Officers, April 1993).
5. Feder, J., D.G. Rowland, J. Holahan, A. Salganicoff, and D. Heslam, *The Medicaid Cost Explosion: Causes and Consequences.* (The Kaiser Commission on the Future of Medicaid, February 1993).
6. General Accounting Office, *Medicaid: States Turn to Managed Care to Improve Access and Control Costs.* (Washington, DC: GAO/HRD-93-46, March 1993).
7. ERISA establishes a class of health insurance plans that are exempt from any form of state regulation. Any state choosing to establish a state-based comprehensive health care system would be precluded from including any of these plans in their design. As a result, states cannot establish basic benefits packages for all health plans, nor can they develop systems that might regulate payment rates. They are also precluded from mandating simplified administrative systems such as uniform claims systems or data reporting systems. Currently, about 40 percent of all care is provided through ERISA health plans.
8. The members of the National Governors' Association include the governors of the fifty states, the commonwealths of the Northern Mariana Islands and Puerto Rico, and the territories of American Samoa, Guam, and the Virgin Islands. Through NGA, the governors work together to deal collectively with issues of public policy and governance. The associations ongoing mission is to support the work of the governors by providing a bipartisan forum, to help shape and implement national policy, and to solve state problems.

Medicine and Health Care Into the Twenty-First Century. Edited by S.K. Majumdar, L.M. Rosenfeld, D.B. Nash and A.M. Audet.

Chapter Six

HOSPITALS AND THE EVOLVING UNITED STATES HEALTH CARE SYSTEM

JOANNE M. COOLEN, M.P.H., M.B.A.
Senior Vice President for Strategic Planning and Policy Development
The Hospital Association of Pennsylvania
P.O. Box 8600
Harrisburg, PA 17105

INTRODUCTION

The United States health care system stands on the precipice of the most dramatic change in its evolutionary history. Health care providers as they appear today will be remembered nostalgically as "dinosaurs" when we look back at the end of this decade. The alignment of political forces among consumers, providers, purchasers, insurers, and public policy makers seeking change is unprecedented. It is around the questions of what to change and how to change it that a clear consensus has yet to emerge.

This chapter will offer a brief recapitulation of the evolution of the United States health care system, covering the development highlights witnessed over the course of the 20th century. This will set the stage for an evaluation of its current status and an assessment of the prospects for change, with a special emphasis on the role of hospitals as a distinct class of health care providers.

As with all enterprises functioning within the national economy, the United States health care system is organized and operated as a function of both what is happening in the marketplace and, more importantly in the case of health care, what is happening in the public policy arena. Both of these have affected the course of evolution of the health care system, sometimes in compatible ways, sometimes in contradictory ways.

HISTORICAL OVERVIEW

Historically, the emphasis in United States health care policy has focused on one of three broad areas: quality of care, access to care, or cost of care. At various times, a different one of these three areas has dominated public policy agendas at the local, state, and national levels.

1900 - 1929: Quality

From the turn of the century until the Great Depression, most of the nation's attention was focused on the quality of health care. Concern about substandard hospitals and poorly-trained health care practitioners led to significant changes that influenced the entire course of the development and operation of the health care delivery system.

This period saw the formation of tighter standards for medical schools. Many schools closed. Medical education began to move into the hospital under the premise that supervised, hands-on clinical experience was an essential component of a clinician's education. States passed laws to create professional licensure systems. Tremendous strides also were made in public health with the development of penicillin and dramatic reductions in infectious diseases, such as typhoid, tuberculosis, and smallpox.

1929 - 1970: Access

During the Depression, important steps were taken to increase access to health care services in the United States. President Franklin D. Roosevelt initially hoped to include universal health coverage with Social Security as part of his New Deal. Although he withdrew support from health coverage when it became apparent that it would not pass, this proposal signaled the onset of an era of attempts by both the public and private sectors to expand services and access to them as broadly as possible throughout the nation. Cooperative insurance plans, now known as the Blue Cross and Blue Shield plans, were created beginning in 1932 to spread the risk of financing health care services and to remove financial access barriers associated with catastrophic illness.

Following World War II, a strong union movement took advantage of the postwar economic boom to press for increases in fringe benefits for workers. Private sector health care benefits typically came to include first-dollar, all-inclusive coverage for workers and their families. This movement established employment-based health care coverage as a fundamental and likely permanent feature of the United States health care system. In addition, the Hospital Survey and Construction Act (Hill-Burton program) was enacted by Congress in 1946 to assist states in constructing more hospitals. During this period, great emphasis also was placed on expanding the supply of health care professionals.

In 1965, in a political action that drastically altered both health care accessibility and financing in the United States, government became the largest single purchaser of health care services when the Medicare and Medicaid programs were instituted as part of President Lyndon B. Johnson's "Great Society" initiative. In committing government to pay for health care services for both the elderly and the poor, the United States took a major step forward in the effort to ensure universal access.

In the years since the inception of these programs, millions of the nation's elderly, disabled, and poor citizens have gained access to hospital care with greatly reduced concern for the personal financial consequences of illness or injury. In addition, revenues generated from these programs provided hospitals with the means to substantially enhance the comprehensiveness and sophistication of the services they offered. This is evidenced in Tables 1 and 2.

Once these programs were in place, Congress began to routinely approve expansions in both eligibility and benefits to keep pace with the private sector. The goal in both the public and private sectors was to provide more health care services to more people, with little attention paid to the long-term national cost implications of these commitments.

1970 - 1985: Cost

As the cost of providing expanded health care services to an ever-growing number of people continued to escalate, at a rate greater than general inflation, the attention of public policy makers shifted from access to cost. Beginning in the 1970s, a variety of piecemeal attempts were made to control health care costs. For example, professional standards review organizations (PSROs) and health systems agencies (HSAs) were created to review and control health care utilization and hospital capital expenditures, respectively. The turn of this decade also saw the imposition of an unsuccessful, short-term wage and price freeze by President Richard Nixon's administration.

As the 1980s opened, a recognition began to emerge that both retrospective, cost-based hospital reimbursement and fee-for-service physician payment had encouraged over-expansion and unquestionably had contributed to higher than anticipated Medicare and Medicaid program costs. In the public sector, this concern about Medicare and Medicaid cost escalation led to significant changes in hospital

TABLE 1

Community Hospital Characteristics: Selected Years 1946-1984

CHARACTERISTIC	1946	1950	1955	1960	1965	1970	1975	1980	1984
Community Hospitals	4,444	5,031	5,237	5,407	5,736	5,859	5,857	5,830	5,759
Beds (Thousands)	473	505	568	639	741	848	942	988	1,017
Admissions (Thousands)	13,655	16,663	19,100	22,970	26,463	29,252	33,435	36,143	35,155
Occupancy (Percent)	72.1	73.7	71.5	74.7	76.0	78.0	75.0	75.6	69.0
Outpatient Visits (Thousands)	Not Available				92,631	133,545	190,672	202,310	211,961
Average Length of Stay (Days)	9.1	8.1	7.8	7.6	7.8	8.2	7.7	7.3	

Source: Hospital Statistics, 1992-1993 edition, American Hospital Association.

payment mechanisms. These programs shifted almost overnight from retrospective payment systems based on cost plus administrative overhead, to prospective payment systems based on predetermined, diagnosis-related fees, generally set to meet the level of available funds. As can be seen in Table 3, this resulted in significant reductions in inpatient hospital utilization and in hospital operating margins, as well as a substantial increase in outpatient service utilization.

This period also saw the emergence of the private sector's concern with escalating health care costs. Businesses began to introduce employee cost-sharing, utilization controls, and wellness and managed care programs into their health benefit packages. In addition, private purchasers began to participate actively in efforts to shape public policies to curb health care inflation.

The health care sector's response to these initiatives was to enter an era of marketplace competition. The premise was that if the health care system were to operate according to competitive private business policies and practices, then efficiencies would be achieved and price inflation would be controlled without sacrificing quality and access.

1985 - Present

By the late 1980s it was clear that the competitive market strategy had failed to achieve an appropriate balance among the competing objectives of reasonable cost, high quality, and universal access. The private sector in the last decade has expressed

TABLE 2

Changing Patterns of Hospital Services: Selected Years 1948-1984
Percent of Community Hospitals with Selected Facilities and Services

Hospitals Reporting (Percent)	1948	1963	1973	1984
Pharmacy	41.3	52.8	87.5	96.4
Hospital Auxiliary	30.2	66.4	72.3	85.5
Physical Therapy Department	33.9	46.4	71.0	90.6
Blood Bank	30.5	56.9	64.8	73.6
Social Work Department	14.6	15.3	46.3	80.5
Dental Services	18.0	30.0	31.0	49.5
Occupational Therapy Department	8.2	9.7	17.8	40.1
Respiratory Therapy Services	—	—	70.7	93.7
Emergency Department	—	—	87.1	95.0
Outpatient Department	—	—	26.3	49.4
Open-Heart Surgery Facilities	—	—	8.5	11.8
Ambulatory Surgical Services	—	—	—	90.7
Ultrasound	—	—	—	82.4
Cardiac Catheterization	—	—	—	17.7
Hospice	—	—	—	10.8
Home Care Department	—	—	—	21.9
CT Scanners	—	—	—	47.9
Organ Transplant	—	—	—	4.6
Alcohol/Chemical Dependency Outpatient	—	—	—	14.4

Source: Hospital Statistics, 1992-1993 edition, American Hospital Association.

TABLE 3

Community Hospitals: Before and After PPS Implementation

CHARACTERISTICS	1975	1980	1981	1982	1983	1984	1985	1986	1987	1988	1989	1990	1991
Community Hospitals	5,857	5,830	5,813	5,801	5,783	5,759	5,732	5,678	5,611	5,533	5,455	5,384	5,342
Beds (Thousands)	942	988	1,003	1,012	1,018	1,017	1,001	978	958	947	933	927	924
Admissions (Thousands)	33,435	36,143	36,438	36,379	36,152	35,155	33,449	32,379	31,601	31,453	31,116	31,181	31,064
Occupancy (Percent)	75.0	75.6	76.0	75.3	73.5	69.0	64.8	64.3	64.9	65.5	66.2	66.8	66.1
Outpatient Visits (Thousands)	190,672	202,310	202,768	248,124	210,044	211,961	218,716	231,912	245,524	269,129	285,712	301,329	322,048
Average Length of Stay (Days)	7.7	7.6	7.6	7.6	7.6	7.3	7.1	7.1	7.2	7.2	7.2	7.2	7.2
PPS Operating Margins	—— PPS START IN OCTOBER 1983 ——					14.5	14.4	9.8	6.9	3.6	1	-1.5	-3.4
Total Hospital Margins	2.7	3.6	3.6	4.2	4.2	5.1	6	5.3	4.2	3.3	3.4	3.8	4.3

Sources: Hospital Statistics, 1992-1993 edition, American Hospital Association.
"Medicare and the American Health System: Report to the Congress," June 1993, Prospective Payment Assessment Commission, Washington, D.C.

growing concern about all three aspects of health care, with no overriding emphasis on any one aspect. While different private sector interests focused on a different aspect (i.e., employers on cost, labor on quality and individuals on access), the problem has now reached the point that all interests are voicing great dissatisfaction with the current health care system and demanding that the 1990s be the decade of comprehensive health care reform.

CURRENT STATE OF THE ART

Access

As the historical overview shows, there have been inadequate linkages over time between decisions on what care is to be provided, to whom and the level of national resources to be devoted to pay for that care. This has produced a health care system that is over-promised and under-funded, with serious continuing barriers to access, both geographic and financial. As can be seen in Table 4, growth of the health care system and the range and sophistication of services it offers has been substantial. At the same time, however, the problem of access to health care has become a national embarrassment for the United States. More than 37 million of its citizens are not insured for health care by either private or public programs, and there are almost another 25 million with health care coverage considered inadequate to meet their needs.

Private health care coverage in the United States continues to favor more expensive inpatient hospital care, with coverage for preventive, out-of-hospital, and specialty services generally absent or severely limited. This creates a different, but nonetheless important, kind of access problem. The dramatic shift to use of outpatient services in lieu of more expensive inpatient care has been supported by the combined effects of changing public payment systems and advancements in medical technology and practices.

Finally, health care resources are maldistributed across the various geographic areas of the country, with rural and inner-city areas experiencing a problem most acutely. The nation also currently has a glut of physician specialists, but a severe shortage of primary care practitioners.

A related access problem is produced as a by-product of the fragmented nature of the United States health care system. This fragmentation is so severe as to make the term "system" a misnomer. Individuals must muddle their way from one component of the system to another, as well as from the health care system to the social welfare system and back, all the time facing different, complex payment and coverage rules and limited information on the cost and quality of the providers they deal with. In addition, the referral process by which individuals are moved through the system is fraught with difficulties. The fact that patients' histories and diagnostic test results do not necessarily follow them gives testament to the problem.

Affordability

Health care in the United States is becoming increasingly unaffordable, in terms of both individual service prices and insurance premiums and aggregate societal expenditures. Government at all levels is faced with the dilemma of growing budget deficits and increasing programmatic/service obligations. Governments' response to this as it relates to the health care sector has been to reduce the level of resources devoted to funding these obligations and/or to seek tax revenue from health care providers who, to date, had been classified as non-taxable. These tactics simply shift responsibility for paying for these obligations to the private sector through indirect taxation, thereby exacerbating the affordability problem for businesses and individuals.

TABLE 4

Dynamics of Hospital Services: Changing Patterns from 1980-1987

	1980	1983	1987	Annual Rate of Change Pre-PPS 80-83 (Percent)	Annual Rate of Change Post-PPS 83-87 (Percent)
Hospitals Reporting (Percent)					
CT Scanner	22.4	39.7	61.4	21.0	12.0
Cardiac Catheterization Labs	16.2	17.0	22.0	2.0	7.0
Intensive Care Units	78.6	82.1	82.6	1.5	0.2
Burn Care Units	2.3	2.4	2.4	1.4	0.0
Cancer Programs	12.3	16.5	19.6	10.3	4.4
Neonatal Intensive Care	7.0	9.2	11.6	10.0	6.0
Open-Heart Surgery Capability	10.4	11.1	13.9	2.0	6.0
Alcohol/Chemical Dependency Beds	5.4	8.2	15.2	15.0	17.0
Psychiatric Outpatient Services	19.1	13.5	16.2	(11.0)	5.0
Rehabilitation Care Beds	4.3	5.7	10.5	10.0	17.0
Emergency Departments	95.7	96.6	97.2	0.5	0.2
Outpatient Departments	41.4	44.4	69.2	4.0	12.0
Home Care Programs	11.6	15.0	35.7	9.0	24.0
Separate Nursing Home LTC Units	11.6	13.9	17.9	6.0	7.0
Skilled Nursing Home Beds	10.4	11.5	16.8	3.0	10.0
Types of Hospitals					
General Medical/Surgical	6,121	6,049	5,853	(0.4)	(0.8)
Psychiatric	472	497	587	1.7	4.2
TB and Other Respiratory Diseases	11	8	5	(10.1)	(11.1)
Obstetrics & Gynecology	14	18	16	8.7	(2.9)
Eye, Ear, Nose, Throat	19	18	13	(1.8)	(7.8)
Rehabilitation	64	69	96	2.5	8.6
Orthopedic	9	9	9	0.0	0.0
Chronic Diseases	54	45	42	(5.9)	(1.7)
Other Specialty	100	93	79	(2.4)	(4.0)
Children's Hospitals	136	124	154	(3.0)	5.6

Source: Dynamics of Hospital Service, Technical Report 3-90-04/March 1990, Kirsten Iversen, Prospective Payment Assessment Commission, Washington, D.C.

The federal government embraced the concept of managed care as early as 1970, articulating a goal of making Health Maintenance Organizations (HMOs) available to 90 percent of the nation by 1980. While only approximately 15 percent of the population is currently enrolled in an HMO (see Table 5), a substantially greater percentage is part of other forms of managed care delivery systems. These delivery systems are characterized by three key operating principles: active management of the care of patients by a gatekeeper primary care practitioner; use of a select group of providers; and the assumption of some level of financial risk by the participating providers.

In the private sector, employers are testing a variety of different health care insurance and service financing and purchasing techniques to better control their expenditures and to enhance their competitiveness in the national and international marketplaces. These include: direct contracting with selected providers; group purchasing of such things as laboratory services; self-insurance; and managed care arrangements. Public purchasers are moving in the same direction, albeit at a slower pace.

In assessing the prospects for reform and the potential for balancing the objectives of universal access and affordability, many express concern about the necessity of instituting mechanisms for rationing so that access can be expanded without bankrupting the system. The issue really is not one of imposing rationing for the first time, but rather one of moving from the *de facto* rationing of health care services. Often the most difficult of these decisions are made at the bedside between caregivers and patients and their families.

Health Status

As can be seen in Table 6, the United States compares unfavorably to other industrialized nations in terms of its relatively poor performance on a variety of health status indicators, particularly given its relatively higher per capita investment in the health care sector of the economy.

This finding is not surprising if one considers that it has never been a clear national objective to establish and operate a health care "system." Disparate, fragmented public and private coverage, purchasing and payment policies and

TABLE 5

National HMO Enrollment Growth: 1980-1992

YEAR	HMO ENROLLMENT (Millions)	ANNUAL GROWTH (Percent)	HMO PERCENT OF NATIONAL POPULATION
1980	9.1	—	4.0
1982	10.8	18.7	4.7
1984	15.1	39.8	6.4
1986	23.7	57.0	9.9
1988	31.4	32.5	12.8
1990	33.6	7.0	13.5
1992	37.2	10.7	14.6

Source: Reprinted with permission of the publisher: InterStudy, Excelsior, MN.

TABLE 6

Comparison: U.S. Versus Other Countries
Selected Measures of Health Status and Total Health Expenditures

Country	Total Health Expenditure As Percent of GDP (1991)	Compound Annual Growth Rate (1985-1991)	Per Capita Health Spending (U.S. Dollars 1991)	Infant Mortality (Death per 1000 Live Births)	Life Expectancy at Birth (Males/Years)	Life Expectancy at Birth (Females/Years)
Canada	10.0	2.7	1,915	6.8	73.8	80.4
France	9.1	1.1	1,650	7.2	72.7	80.9
Germany	8.5	-0.4	1,659	7.1	72.6	79.0
Japan	6.8	0.8	1,307	4.6	75.9	81.9
Sweden	8.6	-0.4	1,443	6.0	74.8	80.4
Switzerland	7.6	0.6	1,713	6.8	74.0	80.9
United Kingdom	6.6	1.6	1,043	7.9	73.0	78.5
United States	13.2	3.9	2,868	9.1	72.0	78.8

Source: "Health Spending, Delivery, and Outcomes in OECD Countries," George J. Schieber, Jean-Pierre Poullier, Leslie M. Greenwald, Health Affairs, Summer 1993. This chart is reprinted with the publisher's permission: Health Affairs, 7500 Old Georgetown Road, Suite 600, Bethesda, MD 10814, (301) 656-7401.

practices driven by independent, often competing, individual interests have been characteristic of the forces driving the evolution of the health care delivery system. Absent has been any explicit national objective governing these policies and practices to coordinate health and social programs to achieve real improvements in the health of populations at an affordable cost. The United States health care system was never designed, operated, or financed to explicitly achieve such an objective. Rather, the emphasis has been on ensuring the highest quality and lowest cost of individual medical treatments.

Achieving optimal health status for populations at an affordable cost has only recently appeared on the national public policy agenda. Should this objective come to dominate the health care reform debate, the prospects for the development of a comprehensive, integrated, coordinated national health care policy are good. This, in turn, will drive the emergence of a more coordinated, integrated health care delivery system designed and financed to produce a healthier population.

Little recognition has been given to social and economic factors as the underlying causes of many health care problems in coverage, financing, payment, and purchasing policies and practices. While the United States has been an international leader in medical technology development, methods for evaluating efficacy and executing appropriate diffusion of this technology have been weak from the standpoint of achieving optimal improvements in the health status of populations. Medical practice patterns across the nation vary considerably, evidencing a related major weakness. In addition, while the notion of individual responsibility for lifelong health status has become a more prominent feature of American thinking, dedicated, coordinated educational and informational support systems continue to be lacking. The cultural diversity of American society makes effective execution of these types of support systems one of the nation's greatest challenges.

PROSPECTS FOR CHANGE

Public Policy - Health Care Marketplace Interface

The United States health care market is undergoing a period of rapid change as a consequence of two principal forces: the prospect of public policy driven health care reform and changes in the purchasing practices of major purchasers, specifically large employers and government. It is the latter category that is forging the most fundamental and likely permanent changes.

Many other countries that have imposed aggregate health care expenditure controls, such as the Netherlands, Germany and Japan, currently are experiencing increased pressure on their caps. Thus, they are seeking methods to change their payment and delivery systems to create incentives for greater efficiency in the production of health care services. Many of the major American health care reform thinkers and proposals today posit that a restructuring of the health care delivery system into integrated networks is essential to ensuring appropriate incentives both for efficiency and assumption of accountability for the health status of populations.

These networks are generally referred to as accountable health plans (AHPs).

An accountable health plan in its generic form is essentially a network of hospitals, physicians and other providers delivering insurance and health care as a single product, in competition with other AHPs. Individuals would select from among competing AHPs based upon the degree to which each is able to meet their health needs at a cost they consider affordable. The concept of AHPs goes beyond managed care systems as we know them today, involving a greater degree of integration and accountability for the health status of served populations.

Models of Integration

The merger of the insurance/administrative and health care systems can be accomplished in a variety of ways. The critical differences among the models is in the nature of the relationships among the participating parties. For purposes of illustration, a distinction will be made between contractual relationships and partnerships. Contractual relationships, which have dominated the health care delivery system throughout its history, involve time-limited, narrowly and precisely defined alliances between parties. They represent a coming together of competing economic interests, with the contract specifying conditions of mutal interest which have been delineated through a process of negotiation and compromise. Such relationships are fragile and not necessarily stable over time, as the interests of the parties change, often in diverse ways. Such relationships are transitory and involve a temporary commitment of the parties to work together on behalf of a particular mutual interest.

Because the health care system is rapidly evolving as this is written, such health plans are still being developed in a variety of formats. One good example of what is proposed is Minnesota's move to integrated service networks (ISN). The Minnesota Department of Health says tht ISNs are viewed differently from existing health plans based on the concepts of accountability and flexibility. ISNs will be held accountable for the cost, quality, and access of the care that they provide. Regulation will be flexible so that ISNs with a variety of structure can enter the market.

Partnerships, such as that achieved through a merger, involve a much more stable alignment of economic interests between parties. What is in the best interest of one partner is de facto in the best interest of the other partner(s). The degree to which the insurance/administrative and medical delivery systems are merged into a single operating entity within an AHP in large measure determines its stability potential over time.

An AHP in which these systems are integrated into a single entity theoretically has the most solid basis on which to compete and to assume explicit accountability for the health status of served populations. This form of AHP competes on a single front, whereas AHPs built partially or totally upon contractual relationships face competing interests on multiple fronts. The fully-integrated AHP is able to reinvest the time and resources previously devoted to economic competition among insurers, physicians and hospitals partly into competing with other AHPs and partly into improving the long-term status of their covered lives.

Exhibit 1 shows a simple schematic of the potential future evolution of the United States health care financing and delivery system. Traditional partnerships typically have been formed between like partners, with freestanding hospitals merging into multi-hospital systems, solo-practice physicians forming multi-specialty group practices, and insurers partnering with other insurers, such as Blue Cross plans merging with Blue Shield plans. A myriad of contractual relationships then have been maintained with all other parties to support the core partnerships.

It can be anticipated that the shift from these traditional alliances to partially and/or fully integrated AHPs will be chaotic, not only for those involved in health care financing and delivery, but also for the citizens who must continue to rely on a rapidly changing system for care. It also can be expected that if the promise of AHPs and health care reform is fully realized, businesses will no longer be compelled by cost pressures to self-insure and devote resources to establishing and maintaining a host of separate contractual relationships with hospitals, physicians and insurer/administrators.

CONCLUSION

The most salient characteristics of the American culture are its diversity and its emphasis on the rights and interests of the individual. Health care in America is

EXHIBIT 1

PROSPECTS FOR FUTURE EVOLUTION OF U.S. HEALTH CARE FINANCING AND DELIVERY SYSTEM

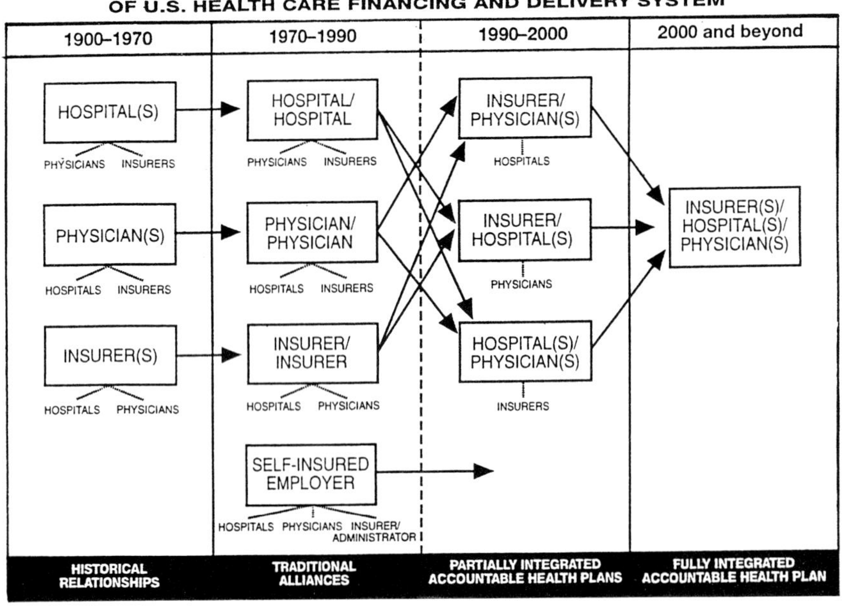

considered and delivered as a local product because of the diversity of needs and cultures existing across the variety of local communities. Increasingly, the economic diversity among American communities is having a negative effect on the nation's ability to realize the principle of equity in the availability, accessibility and financing of health care. A key challenge in any national health care reform effort will be the balancing of diverse individual interests with broader common interests. Specifically, broad societal interests will need to be balanced against a wide range of diverse individual interests.

This will need to occur concurrent with efforts to successfully balance aggregate expenditure controls with the efficient provision of health care services. AHPs afford the best opportunity for achieving a successful balance.

It is inevitable that these balancing efforts will be ongoing, with continual adjustments required over time. A recognition of the dynamic nature of the solutions to the United States' health care crisis is essential, if expectations are to be kept realistic and the future is not to be overpromised.

Medicine and Health Care Into the Twenty-First Century. Edited by S.K. Majumdar, L.M. Rosenfeld, D.B. Nash and A.M. Audet. © 1995, The Pennsylvania Academy of Science.

Chapter Seven

QUALITY IN A LARGER CONTEXT: Serving the People in our Communities

DEBORAH BOHR, M.P.H.[1] and **CHRISTINE IZUI**[2]
[1]Vice President
[2]Director, Quality of Case Studies
American Hospital Association
Hospital Research and Educational Trust
840 N. Lake Shore Drive
Chicago, IL 60611

INTRODUCTION

"We must serve the people of our communities in a way we haven't served them before," said Dick Davidson after becoming president of the American Hospital Association in 1991. Since then he has led the Association and its members to embrace a vision of health care reform with the ambitious aim of simultaneously expanding access and restraining costs without sacrificing quality.

With the welcome return to principles enunciated decades ago, the goal of improving an entire community's health now occupies center stage in the quality and health delivery debate. This chapter focuses on the important role that national organizations such as the AHA can play in promoting policies that improve the quality of care in the United States. The authors hope to illustrate how the critical concepts of *accountability* and *equity* clarify our understanding of the nature of quality, as well as provide a road map for constructive delivery reform. Helping health care providers to understand their communities' needs, and to apply principles of quality improvement to meet those needs, is uppermost on the AHA's agenda.

THE LESSONS OF HINDSIGHT

When many of today's hospitals were being formed years ago two things were true that are no longer so. First, to most people the hospital represented the centerpiece of the medical delivery system. Second, the hospitals were generally formed when community leaders came together to decide whether a hospital was needed and, if so, what resources would be required and how they would be used. At the same time, different community groups focused their attention on the development of other health services, such as nursing homes and visiting nurses associations.

As a result, the nation's health care institutions were built on certain assumptions which have had lasting consequences. On the one hand, the hospital's historic mission was to serve the needs of the surrounding community. On the other hand, various aspects of the delivery system were segregated from one another because they seemed to offer different services. The fact that they often served the same people, duplicated many aspects of organizational overhead, and neglected to coordinate what they were doing was lost in the individual institutions expanding their scope of services to a market niche. It wasn't long before health care institutions were competing among themselves for volunteers, clients, recognition, and funding (1).

Thus the hospital, by virtue of its acute care mission and concentration of resources, came to be viewed by many as the center of the community's "health care system," when in fact no true "system" ever developed at all. Individual entities provided their services separately, duplicated fundamental capabilities, spurred the development of separate payment, regulatory, and accreditation systems, and developed distinct organizational personalities and cadres of local supporters. The ability of health care providers to work together and build a system has become more difficult with each passing year (2).

The more recent experiences of the 1980s have shown us that health care competition focused solely on cost reduction can lead to duplication of services and excess capacity. Many factors have contributed to these negative outcomes, including: extensive insurance coverage that reduces the consumer's sensitivity to medical care prices, the ability of providers to shift uncovered costs across payers, and consumer vulnerability due to the high costs of making informed decisions. Managed competition may be able to resolve some of these deficiencies but as a lone approach to health care reform it lacks sufficient focus on local community health needs, especially among traditionally disadvantaged populations.

Today, with the benefit of hindsight, we can see that a significant part of the high price our nation pays for health care stems from these historic decisions. Having multiple, overlapping and redundant provider organizations, most now believe, does not foster cost-reducing competition. A growing body of research shows that in most communities more health care is consumed and health care costs are higher because of the presence of multiple uncoordinated, competing, and duplicate provider organizations. This is not to blame those who made these decisions. It merely points up the long-term costs of unplanned, institution-specific choices versus more global, community-focused strategies that would most likely have helped avoid the more difficult decisions that now must be made (3). In addition, competition among

---

(1) *Trustees and the Integration of Community Health,* HRET, 1993.

(2) *Ibid.*

(3) *Ibid.*

segmented health care providers has failed to focus on quality.

In recent years, proposals for redesigning our health care structure have focused largely on changing the regulatory and payment mechanisms that apply to each of the system's various parts. However, serious attention is now being directed once again to the community level. What if health care providers were brought together, or integrated, in some way with one another? What if communities were given the wherewithal to allocate fixed amounts of money in whatever way they saw fit, within agreed upon limits? What might happen if, in the light of long-term economic outlooks, new incentives were provided to encourage a fresh assessment of the consequences of those earlier crucial, and expensive, decisions (4)? The American Hospital Association and a growing number of other national organizations, believe that under this scenario, the components of health care would come together in more efficient, rational, and equitable structures.

A NEW LOOK AT OLD PRINCIPLES

The mission of the American Hospital Association is to promote high-quality health care and health services for all people through leadership in the development of public policy, leadership in the representation and advocacy of hospital and health care organizations' interests, and leadership in the provision of services to assist hospitals and health care organizations in meeting the health care needs of their communities. The mission of the AHA's research and educational affiliate has parallel concerns: The Hospital Research and Educational Trust exists to assist health care organizations and the communities they serve to improve the efficiency, quality, and accessibility of health care services. The Trust does this by conducting applied research, demonstration projects, and interpretive studies, and by disseminating the results through education, publications, and other media.

The American Hospital Association's vision for health care reform calls for a restructured health care delivery and financing system centered around community-based collaborative networks that it is calling Community Care Networks℠* in which the services of hospitals, physicians, other health providers, and social agencies would be available in a coordinated fashion for a fixed annual payment. Networks would be accountable to both patients and the larger community, measuring their success, for example, by community health status, consumer satisfaction, patient well-being, and their use of the financial resources allocated to them.

Restructuring of health care delivery is designed to accomplish several objectives:

1) return patients and communities to the center of health care delivery,
2) ensure access to all, including mainstreaming economically disadvantaged populations into health care delivery by maintaining focus on the entire community, and not just those who are well-insured,

---

(4) *Ibid.*

* CCN, Inc. and San Diego Community Healthcare Alliance use the name "Community Care Network" as their service mark (℠)and reserve all rights.

3) emphasize the prevention and minimizing of illness and disability,
4) make the system more user-friendly to all those who come in contact with it,
5) continually improve continuity and quality of health services, and
6) realign the incentives that affect decisions about the allocation and use of health resources so health is maximized while costs are constrained.

The AHA's reform vision is an important, indeed essential, component of the principle reform strategies being considered for the nation's health care system. Simply put, the AHA's goal is quality health care that meets the needs of the community, uses health care dollars wisely, and promotes integration and coordination of care. Community-level collaboration represents a viable mechanism for altering the prevailing pattern of inefficient competition by focusing on expanding access to care for all individuals in a community and reducing costs without sacrificing quality. Community networks also provide the vehicle for empowering residents of a community to participate in health care decision-making at the macro level so that local needs are addressed and rational resource allocation decisions can be made.

Ensuring access to basic health benefits and empowering the community are important concepts that address another aspect of quality—social equity. This is because the network model requires all stakeholders—purchasers, consumers, and providers—to consider health in its broadest terms, that is, the well-being of the community. The community's well-being can be enhanced when the health sector operates as part of a broader, multi-sector program of community involvement. To achieve this goal, the health care and social service sectors, which have operated independently for several decades, would coordinate their services to a much greater degree, offering community members a true "system" of care. This represents a renewed emphasis on the historical roots of hospitals, which were originally chartered to serve the entire community and were considered a public service. After a long and unfortunate absence from the health care debate, social equity has been re-introduced as a core concept of the AHA's health care reform vision (5).

Everyone knows that there is now great debate about what is wrong with the way health care is delivered. To date, however, discussions have tended to focus only on the medical treatment system, especially on calls for better research into which medical practices work for which patients and in which circumstances. Such research remains in its infancy and, while an important part of the quality improvement agenda, it is unlikely ever to tell us all we need to know. There are simply too many inputs to health that are obscured by our nearly exclusive reliance on the medical treatment model.

Two decades ago, Henrik Blum cautioned us about the inadequacy of the medical viewpoint: "verification of the validity or quality of medical innovation and intervention has not been made in terms of the influence on recipients of care, or on society, but rather on the technological accomplishment itself" (6). He asks us instead to measure health and the well-being of communities through the aggregated

---

(5) *In Sickness and in Health*, Seay and Vladeck, page 203.
(6) Henrik L. Blum, *Planning for Health* (New York, 1974), p. 78.

status of individuals (measurements of levels of various conditions, knowledge, behavior, accessibility to care, outcomes of care, aspiration levels relevant to satisfaction with prevailing services, etc. Health and well-being, Blum reminds us, are closely intertwined with and heavily dependent upon factors such as financial resources, health manpower, socioeconomic status, health services, education, and housing (7).

CONVERTING HEALTH INTO MEANINGFUL MEASURES

The AHA's reform agenda seeks to meet Blum's challenge by returning the principles enunciated decades ago. Thus the four key pillars of the AHA's vision are: focus on community health, provision of a seamless continuum of services, management within fixed resources, and public accountability.

Community Health Focus

The community is responsible for determining health priorities and working with health care providers to meet these priorities. In essence, networks of care are charged with the well-being of the community. Collaboration is therefore essential. Under this model, providers work with community leaders, local business leaders, health care purchasers, and consumers to shape the delivery system. The networks depend heavily on the development and dissemination of valid and reliable data with which they can measure and track improvement of health status. Collaboration and coordination remain constant themes for ensuring that the voice of all segments of society are heard. Data must fuel discussion on how well we are doing and how we can do it better.

Seamless Continuum of Care

In a model that manages and coordinates care, patients will not be expected to navigate the system on their own. Truly coordinated health care requires a single and consistent point of entry or access. The information necessary to offer coordinated care will require a unified information system that combines clinical and administrative data shared across settings. A health care system that meets the preferences and convenience of patients will be the hallmark of successful care networks. In addition to much better coordination among providers, substantial coordination between health care providers and other organizations will enable people to better utilize health services. For example, when people appear in a medical setting with health problems, related to nutrition, drug use, family violence, or housing, the health provider should be able to bring to bear the appropriate human services. Joint planning and decision-making across organizations will characterize the governance and management of new health delivery systems.

(7) *Ibid.*, pp. 181, 190.

Managing Within Fixed Resources

Any discussion related to the provision or improvement of health services must take resources into account as well. The AHA explicitly recognizes this as one of its four key factors for successful health services delivery reform: health providers must remain aware of the finite nature of resources and the need to allocate and manage them efficiently and fairly. Successful reform will therefore require the management of individual and community expectations, and the involvement of both in education and decision-making processes. Reorganizing and reallocating resources according to *expressed* community need, as opposed to individual need, will be the guiding principle. Incentives must shift to rewarding innovation, cost-effectiveness, prevention, and continuity.

Public Accountability

The ultimate judges of whether the new system is a success or failure are the local consumers of health care. New measures and information based on the needs and preferences of patients, their families, and the community will be necessary if the health care system is to respond to the consumers' judgements. New governance and leadership systems will support regular and structured dialogue and information exchange. The goal is to make the health care delivery system accountable to the community in much the same way that a corporation is accountable to its stockholders.

Clearly hospitals, health networks, and other providers, must view quality in a larger context than they have in recent years, looking beyond the walls of their institution. Relying on a broader definition of health, reconceptualizing the health care system, and reviewing accountability—the demonstration of quality and value—as an essential component of their mission, organizations can take responsibility for the quality of care provided and demonstrate commitment to meeting community need and seeking improvement (8).

LOOKING AT QUALITY IN A LARGER CONTEXT

Do principles of accountability and the equitable distribution of scarce resources complicate an already complex picture? How does redefining health care providers as "stewards" of their community's health—one of the original goals of the voluntary hospital—advance the state of quality measurement and improvement? The short answer is that these new principles and definitions help establish priorities for action. More precisely, the way we define *quality* has expanded to include issues of access and equity. In a landmark article reviewing twenty years of research on the quality of medical care, Avedis Donabedian defined the challenge we still face:

---

(8) David Lansky, Ph.D., "The New Responsibility: Measuring and Reporting on Quality," *The Joint Commission Journal on Quality Improvement,* Vol. 19, Number 12, December 1993.

"First and at a fundamental level, we need to look at the nature of quality itself, so that conceptions we have of it are socially more relevant and scientifically more valid. This requires that all presumed relationships between process and outcome be rigorously tested while our technical concerns are supplemented by attention to the interpersonal, social, even moral dimensions of quality" (9).

Philip Caper clarifies the issue by contrasting the prevailing definition of quality—with its focus on the individual—with a definition applied to populations: "For individuals, high-quality medical care is care that is effective and appropriate and results in patient satisfaction. For populations, high-quality medical care is care that is effective, appropriate and accessible and results in the delivery of optimal services for the greatest number of people within available resources" (10).

The common thread running through AHA's vision and the challenges posed by Blum, Donabedian and Caper, is the call for a definition of quality that encompasses both accountability and social equity. Should providers build on existing efforts, seek new ones, or use both? The answer is both. Quality must pass tests that go beyond medical efficacy and cost efficiency, although these characteristics remain central. One of the roles that the AHA and other national organizations must play, therefore, is to be an advocate for this expanded view of quality.

MULTIPLE LEVELS OF ACCOUNTABILITY

As health care providers become accountable for community health status, the structures, processes, and outcomes of care have changed. Consider, for example, structural measures of equipment. Under the current system, an adequate performance measure would gague the availability of equipment in a given institution. Under the reform vision, the unit of analysis shifts, and the questions become: Is there enough, or perhaps too much, equipment in the larger community, and are all who need it gaining access to it? New types of mesurement will be needed to balance the information needs of individual institutions and the overall system.

In the case of process measures, appropriateness of care extends beyond case by case management to considerations for entire populations. Education of both patients and the community, and their roles as active participants in decision-making, will become even more critical.

Outcomes will also have an expanded focus, both in terms of the health status of the individual and the health status of the community. Outcomes now include health priorities of the community such as the prevention of heart disease and teen pregnancy.

It is clear, then, that public accountability will challenge the scope of many of our quality improvement efforts. Traditionally, quality has been left to professionals

---

(9) Avedis Donabedian, "Twenty Years of Research on the Quality of Medical Care, 1964-1984," *Evaluations and the Health Professions,* Sage Publications, Inc., pp. 243-265.

(10) Caper, Philip, "Population-Based Measures of the Quality of Medical Care," *Health Care Quality Management for the 21st Century, Amercian College of Medical Quality,* 1991.

who have focused on performance in a single institution. Peer review, monitoring and evaluation activities, and quality studies have been kept exclusively within the purview of hospital and medical staff and other health care practitioners. The public is now challenging providers, who are beginning to respond, to demands for public performance information which cut across settings.

The following display illustrates how Donabedian's classic categorization of structure process and outcome can be translated from the current environment to a reformed delivery model:

CURRENT	**REFORM**
Structure	*In addition:*
• avaliability of equipment for specific treatment at an individual institution	• availability of equipment within a community to address health priorities (adequate access? unnecessary duplication?)
Process	
• treatment episode	• prevention, health promotion activities; outpatient, pre- and post-hospitalization care processes, including patient and family education and joint decision-making
Outcome	
• length of stay, short-term effects of treatment, costs of episode, complications	• chronic illness and disability measures, individual long-term functional and health status, population-based measures of health, overall financial performance related to maintaining health of populations, other population-based measures

AN AGENDA FOR QUALITY AND ACCOUNTABILITY

AHA's reform vision provides the context for a Quality and Acountability Agenda which calls on hospitals and networks to be publicly accountable to the community, and responsible for improving the health status of the community. The implication is that providers will have to measure their impact on community health, as well as document improvement of their results. National organizations should work toward promoting a common view of quality, including meaningful quality measures and models.

Given its research, demonstration, education, and dissemination activities, the Hospital Research and Educational Trust is positioned to play three major roles in promoting effective, efficient, and high-quality care. First, HRET can take the lead in identifying measures useful for both quality improvement and the demonstration of quality and value to patients, community members, health care practitioners, purchasers, and regulators. It is imperative, therefore, that HRET actively promote research and policies that lead to the development of common, compatible, and parsimonious data bases, and also to promote measures of quality and health status that capture the continuum of care. Second, HRET can test or monitor:

1) quality improvement tools, methods, and models;
2) case studies and other sources of best clinical and administrative practices;
3) innovative organizational and management approaches that promote effective, efficient, and high-quality care.

Third, HRET can serve as a resource, that is, as a central location for pooling or sharing information and analysis to promote more rapid information transfer in areas such as: benchmarking best practices, disseminating innovation, and coordinating efforts between multiple organizations.

A series of assumptions underlies these roles:

1) The measures and models for demonstrating accountability should grow out of tools developed to support internal management and quality improvement, whenever possible.
2) To meet the goals of continuous improvement and public accountability, hospitals and networks need valid and reliable measures of performance.
3) National organizations should provide leadership to promote a focus on the health status of populations served. (*This contrasts with a previous assumption of being accountable only for the quality and value of the services provided to patients within the system.*)
4) Quality measures and models should be determined by health priorities of the community and opportunities for clinical and administrative preformance improvement.
5) Performance measures should encompass more than technical quality. For example, issues of appropriateness (right service, right time, right place), access, cost, and both individual and community satisfaction must be evaluated in a way that is meaningful to patients, their families, and the community. In addition, measurement must address the entire spectrum of care.
6) Consumers are demanding a true system of health care that meets their needs, and quality can no longer be defined solely by health care professionals.

PRIORITIES FOR ACTION

In order to establish priorities for action, determining health priorities for the community is an essential first step before key measures of accountability are determined. These need to supplement the traditionally inwardly focused, technical quality measures. These performance indicators, in turn, become the basis for identifying key models of best practice for using this performance information to evaluate, communicate, and improve performance, and therefore, improve health.

Health Priorities / Opportunities for Improvement

↓

Key Measures of Accountability
(technical quality, community benefit, financial performance, access, satisfaction, individual and population health status, continuous improvement goals)

↓

Key Models for Using Measures to Evaluate, Communicate and Improve Performance

THE ROLE OF NATIONAL ORGANIZATIONS

Advocate, Evaluator, and Resource: These are the three key roles the American Hospital Association and its Hospital Research and Educational Trust should serve for its members and the field at large in their efforts to improve the quality of healthcare. As an *advocate* AHA should provide leadership in stimulating advancement in quality measurement and improvement; build consensus on quality measures, promote the use of appropriate and fair measures of quality, and stimulate the measurement of care across settings. As *evaluators,* AHA and HRET should play a role in testing tools, methods and models; encourage and highlight innovations and trends in quality improvement; determine which research findings are helpful; examine existing demonstration projects and initiatives. Lastly, AHA and HRET should serve as a *resource* to health care providers by: providing information on evolving science and research, encouraging comparisons with peers, pooling information on innovations, stimulating advancement in quality improvement models and methods.

PROMISING STEPS

Consider what is already being done. New understandings of the provider's role in promoting health and new ways of thinking about delivering prevention and care services are beginning to change the face of health care. There are hopeful models of collaboration among health care providers. In one example, a physicians' group practice, a hospital, and a community mental health center joined together to provide complete mental health services to rural areas around Petoskey, Michigan. In Franklin, New Hampshire, a hospital is collaborating with social service agencies, civic groups, and churches to create a community wellness center. The city of Nashville, Tennessee, is developing a comprehensive health care partnership hosted by the Chamber of Commerce. Participating are the Tennessee Hospital Association, local hospitals, the Metropolitan Health Department, the Nashville Academy of Medicine, the Tennessee Nurses Association, the Tennessee Primary Care Association, local insurers, local government, and neighborhood and local philanthropies.

Funded by grants from the Robert Wood Johnson Foundation and the United Hospital Fund, the Hospital Research and Educational Trust of the American Hospital Association has a demonstration project in five communities across the country called, "Community Health Intervention Partnerships." This project is examining the development of *equitable* relationships between community-based organizations and hospitals to assess a community's needs and resources, and develop a plan for reducing the top two or three health problems identified by the community. This partnership has very broad representation among diverse groups, such as health professionals, churches, schools, social service agencies, and other groups that work with the community. The goal is to create multiple opportunities for better meeting and coordinating the health needs of the community (11).

---

(11) Richard Bogue, "CHIPs Partnerships In Vanguard of New Community Networks," in *HRET/Seedco: Partnerships for Community Health* (1993).

CLOSING

Each of these projects helps restore the community to its rightful place at the center of the quality debate. Collectively, they hold out the promise of an integrated network of health care delivery that can at long last be called a "system". As Donald Bewick has pointed out: "It is the flow among organizations that now matters more than anything else in the production of community health, and only leaders can redraw the boundaries of the system" (12). Guiding hospitals and other health care providers in a time of great change, challenge and opportunity will require extraordinary skill and courage by leaders in all variety of health care settings. By redrawing our collective picture of health, we can indeed serve our communities in a way we haven't before.

FURTHER READING

Books

Blum, Henrik L., MD. 1974. *Planning for Health, Development and Application of Social Change Theory,* Human Sciences Press, Inc., New York.

Donabedian, Avedis, M.D. 1993. Twenty Years of Research on the Quality of Medical Care, 1964-1984. In: Stephen J. Williams, Sc.D, ed., *Contemporary Issues in Health Services,* Delmar Publishers, Albany, NY.

Lohr, Kathleen N., ed., and Institute of Medicine. 1990. *Medicare, A Strategy for Quality Assurance* (Vol. I), National Academy of Sciences.

Seay, David, J.D. and Bruce Vladek, PhD, eds. 1988. *In Sickness and in Health, The Mission of Voluntary Health Care Institutions,* McGraw-Hill, New York.

VHA, Inc. 1993. *Community Health Assessment: A Process for Positive Change,* Irving, Texas.

Journals / Reports / Articles

American Hospital Association. 1993. *Transforming Health Care Delivery – Toward Community Care Networks,* published by AHA.

Bogue, Richard J., PhD. 1993. CHIPs partnerships in the Vanguard of New Community Networks. Article published in *Partnerships For Community Health* magazine, published by HRET/Seedco.

HRET. 1992. *Bridging the Gap Between Theory and Practice: Exploring Clinical Practice Guidelines,* published by Hospital Research and Educational Trust, Chicago.

HRET. 1992. *Bridging the Gap Between Theory and Practice: Exploring Continuous Quality Improvement,* published by Hospital Research and Educational Trust, Chicago.

Lanksy, David J., PhD. 1993. The New Responsibility: Measuring and Reporting on Quality. Article published in the *Journal on Quality Improvement,* Vol. 19, No. 12.

(12) VHA, Inc., *Community Assessment: A Process for Positive Change,* 1993, Irving, Texas.

Medicine and Health Care Into the Twenty-First Century. Edited by S.K. Majumdar, L.M. Rosenfeld, D.B. Nash and A.M. Audet. © 1995, The Pennsylvania Academy of Science.

Chapter Eight

BEYOND 2000: Direction of World Health in the 21st Century

DAVID M. MACFADYEN, MSC., FRCP, EDIN.
Director, Programme Management
World Health Organization
Regional Office for Europe
8 Scherfigsvej
Copenhagen 2100, Denmark

UNDERSTANDING OUR OWN HUMANITY

The anthropologist, Jane Goodall observed at Gombe Stream in Kenya (van Lawick-Goodall, J., 1971) that disabled chimpanzees experiencing difficulty in collecting food, received no help from their fellows, who were indifferent to the plight of the sick and disabled. A clue as to the humanity of *Homo sapiens* is provided by Goodall's own reaction to an epidemic of paralytic poliomyelitis that ravaged the wild chimpanzees under her observation. The human, unlike the chimpanzee, was moved by the suffering of her fellow beings and administered polio vaccine to the primates.

ALTRUISM

Sixty-five-thousand years ago, in Shanidar, northern Iraq, two human beings, one disabled and one injured, appear to have survived through being cared for by their stone-age companions (Royal College of Physicians of Edinburgh, 1989).

Here is a reflection by two distinguished archaeologists on one of these human ancestors:

> "The subject . . . was a man, an arthritic one-armed cripple . . . Careful study of the skeletal remains has shown that the right arm and shoulder had never fully developed and that the arm had indeed been amputated below the elbow. . . . The fact that an individual so disabled from infancy should have been able to attain what must be regarded as old age argues for a degree of concern for the individual far transcending anything shown in animal societies. . . . The concern manifested for the cripple of Shanidar shows that love and compassion were especially necessary for human society. It was this solidarity, based on ethical considerations, that made possible the future achievements of man" (Clark G. & Piggott S., 1965).

Such altruism, by one human towards another, is captured in the famous seventeenth century meditation (Meditations XVII), of John Donne that:

> any man's death diminishes me
> for I am involved in mankind;
> and therefore never send to know for whom the bell tolls,
> it tolls for thee.

Conduct for the good of others, selflessness as distinct from selfishness, we now know by the word "altruism," coined in the nineteenth century by Auguste Comte, the father of sociology.

ACHIEVEMENTS OF THE PRESENT CENTURY

Scientists, historians and philosophers have failed, so far, to reach consensus on a descriptor that captures the achievements of the present century. Will the twentieth century come to be known as the century of altruism? The powerful idea that we are human because we show compassion for our fellow beings was put forward half a century ago by the physiologist Sir Charles Sherrington. A few words summarize his perception of our humanity: "altruism - extending to the family and beyond, to the tribe and beyond, knitting social ties of planetwide comradeship and good will. Love of life extends beyond self."

UNIVERSALITY OF ASPIRATIONS FOR HUMAN DEVELOPMENT

Aspirations to improve the economic, social and health conditions of the human species have been the dominant motivation for national and international endeavours during the second half of the twentieth century.

National and international visions for the year 2000 reflect this and illustrate the giant step taken by the human species in the latter half of this century. None of the year 2000 scenarios envisions our future advance in purely technological terms.

All include ennobling objectives which aspire to improvement in the physical, mental, social and spiritual domains.

THE PURSUIT OF WELL-BEING

In the immediate aftermath of World War II, global concern was to reduce human suffering. The century will draw to a close with humankind enjoying considerable progress in health—although, in the final decade, it is difficult to see this as a pandemic of HIV infection spreads to involve some 30-40 million of the world population by the year 2000. Since the infection was recognized just over a decade ago, there have been 2.5 million cases of AIDS, the great majority in sub-Saharan Africa. That survival quality of the human species—altruism to the total stranger—is being manifested in reciprocal aid between generations in Africa, as surviving elders care for AIDS orphans, the estimated number of whom is expected to reach 1 million in Uganda alone by the turn of the century. However, many countries *have* shaken free from the legacy of shortened life expectancy. Ninety-one countries with some 3600 million inhabitants attained a life expectancy at birth, in 1990, in excess of 60 years, compared to 74 countries a decade earlier (World Health Organization, 1993) - although this level was achieved by only two of the 37 least developed countries for which 1990 data were available.

HUMANITARIAN ASSISTANCE: A Permanent Phenomenon?

In addition to AIDS, there is justifiable concern at the high level of infant mortality. While many countries report increasing infant and child survival (World Health Organization, 1993, p. 341, Fig. 5), as many people are starving now in Africa as at any time in the past. The mortality rate of children between one and five years, which is perhaps the best indicator of nutrition, is 10 to 40 times higher in parts of Africa, Asia and Latin America, than it is in the U.S. Nevertheless, the population continues to increase in countries least able to increase food production, with the result that humanitarian assistance can no longer be considered a transitional phenomenon; food suppliers will always be the industrial west, and the recipients the 29 least developed countries.

THE MARVEL OF HUMAN PROGRESS

The all-absorbing concerns of poor countries in the 21st century will continue to be focused on improving child survival and on controlling poverty-related diseases. Nevertheless, the vision of global social transformation from unhealthy to healthy society is beginning to take effect. This is a marvel; a marvel that altruism towards the entire human species has become entrenched in the policies of all nations of the world; a marvel that we have agreed measures of progress; and a marvel that we have international structures to lead this transformation.

Governments committed to the World Health Organization's year 2000 goals, for a healthy society, have not been limited to the third world. The US Government is also committed to these collective health policies.

YEAR 2000 OBJECTIVES

In the decade of the 1980s, we were asked to look beyond the "medical model" toward public policies directed towards maintaining health and quality of life. Targets for the year 2000 were set for the US (United States Public Health Service, 1989), Europe (World Health Organization, 1991) and for individual European nations, such as England (Department of Health, 1992). This proliferation of Year 2000 health objectives is part of an historic shift in health policy which can be traced to Marc Lalonde, a former Canadian health minister. In 1974, in A New Perspective on the Health of Canadians, he concluded that, while health research and medical treatment are of great importance, public policy needs also to focus on individual, environmental and social determinants of well-being.

The US vision for the year 2000 is in line with a one nation/one world ethos. It is also practical and promotes, for example:

- Health system improvements (through primary care services);
- Healthy lifestyle (by promoting vitality and independence for older people);
- Environmental health (by reducing exposure to health-damaging toxins);

and

- Preventive services (by reducing vaccine-preventable diseases in children).

The Year 2000 objectives also extend health targets to improving quality of life.

TRACKING THE PROGRESS OF YEAR 2000 OBJECTIVES

Health for All, the aspirational policy of the World Health Organization, was also set around 1980 and was focused on the horizon of the year 2000. Adoption of that policy by the Organization's Member States in the European Region followed an analysis of health projections. Projections of European health trends therefore provided a scientific foundation for defining 38 specific targets as a strategy for attaining Health for All for the 850 million people in the WHO Region of Europe. For example, European Target 5 aims at reducing communicable disease:

> *By the year 2000 there should be no indigenous cases of poliomyelitis, diphtheria, neonatal tetanus, measles, mumps and congenital rubella in the region and there should be a sustained and continuing reduction in the incidence and adverse consequences of other communicable diseases, notably HIV infection* (World Health Organization, 1991).

Vaccination against eradicable disease in European countries would appear to be a realizable goal. The technology is long established, simple and inexpensive. Field management practices of proven efficacy were established in WHO's smallpox eradication campaign - immunization coverage; surveillance of target disease; outbreak investigation and response. Yet the Region faces a vaccine crisis in 1994 and a recrudescence of diphtheria in Russia and other republics of the former Soviet Union. Thus instead of progress towards the desired state of the future, Europe appears to be reverting—at least in Target 5—to the situation of the past. This reversal has less to do with medical technology than with unforeseen political and social changes—perhaps the most profound geopolitical changes seen in Europe since the 19th Century. However, when historians come to write the history of the 20th Century, they will marvel not only at human ingenuity in developing effective vaccines, but also that there was an international will and structure to bring this technology to all humankind. Efforts towards achieving zero poliomyelitis incidence in the 50 countries of the WHO Region for Europe continue and are especially focussed on the Transcaucasian and Central Asian Republics of the former Soviet Union, where the great majority of cases occur:

Indigenous and Imported Poliomyelitis in the WHO Region for Europe, 1991-93

	1991	1992	1993
Balkans	74	11	2
Transcaucasus	61	48	92
Central Asia	160	31	85
Other European	23	91	17

Source: Oblapenko, G. WHO Region Office for Europe, March 1994.

HEALTH SCENARIOS

WHO's current strategy for advancing the health of Europeans therefore pays attention to possible trends in society, as well as to future trends in demography, health status and health technology. These broader analyses, in 1990 and 1992 (World Health Organization, 1990; 1992), have provided a basis for framing areas of activity that the Organization foresees for the 6-year period from 1996 to 2001, which will extend WHO's health strategy for Europe beyond the existing horizon into the 21st century.

WHO's Member States in the European region have themselves been defining alternative pictures and possible futures in society, in public health and in health care. Most notable has been the "scenario" studies of health care technologies, cancer, cardiovascular disease, accidents, AIDS, etc. reported by the Netherlands. The Netherlands year 2000 scenario for progress in care of the elderly (Hollander CF and Becker HA (eds.) 1985) is envisaged by extrapolating demographic trends, which point to:

- increasing numbers, higher expectations and level of education among the elderly; and
- reduced proportions of children and young people.

THE ROLE OF WOMEN IN HEALTH ADVANCES

Health care advance is contingent upon social change in every part of the world. One societal development that has key importance for family planning and child survival is the role and educational opportunities of women. A "futures" perspective on the contribution of women to health and socioeconomic development is being analyzed by the WHO Region of the Americas. That region also showed that health objectives could be achieved, despite civil conflict and economic hardship: Zero incidence of poliomyelitis—Europe's Target 5—was realized in the hemisphere of the Americas by 1991.

THE CENTURY OF HUMAN SURVIVAL

Our zest to preserve human existence has made the twentieth century a landmark in human existence. For the first time man, and especially woman, have begun to live out their life spans. It is an irony that historians may come to celebrate the twentieth century as the century of human survival. The twentieth century will surely be seen as the century in which human beings asserted the universal solidarity of humankind and directed their technological abilities to freeing the species from suffering which hitherto killed children and adults by the million. The health agenda of the 21st Century will be to consolidate this historical progress in human existence and to confront the consequences of it.

WHEN THE BELL DOES NOT TOLL

In Europe and the United States, the medicine of the twenty-first century will increasingly focus on the quality of life of the disabled and of the "old old", as long life becomes certain and very long life increasingly probable. Because of our success as a species, more and more persons are transiting their eighth and ninth decades. This biological success began when cave dwellers, who needed to hunt to survive, nevertheless gave food, clothing, shelter and care to their disabled brethren. The mortal remains of Shanidar give us insight into what we must do to carry this success into the Twenty-first Century. Many more of us will, in our eighth decade, enjoy a level of health that will allow us to lead a productive life. The price of our collective survival is that the frailer members of society will become more numerous and will need to be cared for. When the bell does not toll, our involvement in mankind becomes even greater.

INTO THE 21ST CENTURY

The concept of making investments for health gain (World Bank, 1993) has forced health policy makers to take a longer view of the impact of their decisions. Like financiers making long-term investments, those who are making decisions that will impact on tomorrow's health are doing so against some vision of the 21st Century. The field of vision is broad and gives equal attention to possible political, social and technological developments. Is there a methodology that can help make these "health futures" studies less speculative? This is a question addressed in a recent WHO Consultation on Health Futures (World Health Organization, 1993, WHO / HST 93.4; WHO Notes and News, 1994). Health futures methodology proceeds first with a process of *visioning,* that is to say establishing a shared commitment to some desirable future state, such as described above in the aspirational objectives for the year 2000. Next is the process of *scanning*. This is a health intelligence process which involves data analyses and projection of trends, emerging issues and technologies—similar to the scientific foundation laid for the WHO European health strategy. The final stage in the process is the development of alternative *scenarios*. It is this last stage that brings a practical application to the health future exercise, since it helps define pathways in the direction of a desired future, as well as mileposts for assessing progress.

The relevance of future studies for the United States is apparent, even if one only considers the decisions that would need to be taken to change the mix of human resources for health care provision. Policies to reduce the supply of physicians and / or to change the primary care / specialist mix have enormous potential for reducing the costs of care, when the direct and indirect expenditure generated per physician is estimated at $1 million. The relevance of future studies is even more apparent if the "scan" is extended to emerging technological development. Expert systems will readily provide the clinician of the 21st century with practice guidelines via her practice computer. Emerging technologies may reduce the disease frequency of highly prevalent conditions, such as diabetes, and vaccination possibilities against HIV infection may exist by the turn of the century. Between 1987 and 2015, a two-thirds reduction is predicted in heart disease mortality in the United States, half the fall attributable to therapeutic advances (World Health Organization, 1993, WHO/HST93.4, pp. 9-10).

Visions for 21st century health systems and on the future of public health are being catalogued by the International Health Futures Network, which publishes a newsletter and a compendium. The electronic "information superhighway" will be the future route by which such studies and their results are made accessible worldwide. As these studies become better known, health futures studies may feature in graduate degree programmes in public health and health policy. *Objectives for the Nation for the Year 2000* was a milestone in public health which has a profound and continuing impact outside the United States. A current reform proposal aims to bring health security with comprehensive health coverage to all Americans. Extrapolation of trends in health expenditure, without reform, project these rising to $1,631 billion (18.9% of Gross National Product) by the Year 2000. Defining how such very large expenditures might bring about a desired state of the nation in the year 2010 is the next task for people, health care providers and policy makers in the United States.

REFERENCES

Clark, G. and S. Piggott. 1965. Prehistoric Societies. Penguin, England.

Department of Health. 1992. The Health of the Nation, A Strategy for Health in England. Her Majesty's Stationary Office, London.

Editorial Proceedings of Royal College of Physicians of Edinburgh. 1989. 19, 3, p. 261-262.

Hollander, CF and HA Becker (Eds.) 1985. *Growing old in the future: Scenarios on health and aging.* Steering Committee on future health scenarios, Utrecht: Martinus Nijhoff.

Sherrington, CS. 1953. *Altruism in Man on his Nature.* Doubleday, New York, 262-298.

Solecki, R.S. Shanidar. 1971. *The First Flower People.* Knopf, New York, p. 212.

United States Public Health Service. 1989. *The Year 2000 National Health Objectives.* Department of Health and Human Services, Washington.

vanLawick-Goodall, J. 1971. *In the Shadow of Man.* Houghton Mifflin, Boston, p. 204-211.

WHO. Notes and News. 1994. *Probing Health Futures.* World Health Forum, Vol. 15, p. 100.

World Bank. 1993. *Investing in Health: World Development Report, 1993.* Oxford University Press.

World Health Organization. 1989. *Global Strategy For Health For All By The Year 2000 Second Report on Monitoring Progress.* Geneva, A62/4.

World Health Organization. 1990. *Future Trends in Society and the European Health for All Strategy, Report of a WHO Consultation, 19-20 February.* Copenhagen, (ICP/HSC 013(6)/BD/2).

World Health Organization. 1991. *Targets for health for all: The health policy for Europe.* Copenhagen, September.

World Health Organization. 1992. *Future Trends in Society and the European Health for All Strategy, Report on the Second Consultation.* Copenhagen, (EUR/ICP/HSC 013(b)).

World Health Organization. 1993. *Health for all: How it looks now.* World Health Forum, Vol. 14.

World Health Organization. 1993. *Health Futures in Support of Health for All: Report of an International Consultation 19-23 July.* Geneva, WHO/HST93.4.

Medicine and Health Care Into the Twenty-First Century. Edited by S.K. Majumdar, L.M. Rosenfeld, D.B. Nash and A.M. Audet.

Chapter Nine

ROLE OF GOVERNMENT IN SETTING STANDARDS OF CARE THROUGH CLINICAL PRACTICE GUIDELINES

RISA LAVIZZO-MOUREY, M.D.
Deputy Administrator
Agency on Health Care Policy and Research
U.S. Public Health Service
2101 East Jefferson Street, Suite 600
Rockville, MD 20852

INTRODUCTION

As America enters the twenty-first century, health care providers will come under increasing pressure to deliver better health care, for more people, in ways that are more efficient and cost-effective. Reform of the nation's health care system will result in much broader health coverage—with benefits available to all Americans. However, no one will tolerate a compromise in quality. Therefore, health care providers must continue making improvements in the appropriateness and effectiveness of the services they offer—in effect, to provide greater value for the expenditure of health care dollars.

To function successfully in such an environment, providers and health care administrators will have to work "smarter," not necessarily harder. It is increasingly evident that a key to working smarter in medicine involves making better use of a clinical and scientific knowledge base. Providers will have to rely less on "the rules of thumb," "professional pearls" or "the latest findings", and rely more on comprehensive syntheses of the best scientific evidence to know what works best and guide their clinical decisions.

In approaching this new and more demanding health care future, it is important to make full use of all available tools and resources. Among these, none offers

Obviously, no individual practitioner could review and pass informed judgment on such a vast body of scientific literature on a regular basis. Panel members, bringing a variety of professional perspectives and expertise to the task, evaluate the quality of evidence from the scientific literature. In cases where the scientific evidence is unclear or lacking, just as in real clinical situations, recommendations are based on the expert judgment and collective experience of panel members.

AHCPR-sponsored practice guidelines are *not* rigid, prescriptive documents. They recommend treatments or suggest a course of action where evidence of effectiveness exists, or where the most effective course has been scientifically determined; but they also make full allowance for legitimate differences of clinical opinion (7, 8, 9, 10, 11, 12, 13, 14). For example, the guideline on acute pain management outlines strategies for assessing pain intensity, but acknowledges that after implementing these strategies, if there remains uncertainty, a diagnostic trial of analgesics is often appropriate. The guidelines on detection, diagnosis and treatment of depression clearly indicates that although depression can almost always be treated successfully with medication, psychotherapy, or a combination of both, all patients do not respond to the same therapy. Algorithms for selecting optimum modes of treatment for depression are presented, but the provider is encouraged to try alternate treatments, or combinations of treatments, for patients who do not respond to the initial intervention.

Moreover, AHCPR-sponsored guidelines are designed to facilitate active participation by patients and consumers in the process of medical decision making, especially by encouraging patients to engage in informed discussion of treatment options with their health care provider. For example, as the practice guideline on management of cataract in adults makes clear, a decision in favor of surgery for the cataract should not be made by the physician alone. Rather, the patient should be fully informed of all available treatment options by the physician, including associated risks. But the final decision regarding surgery should be the patient's alone, based on subjective criteria concerning the degree to which the presence of the cataract impairs personal autonomy and quality of life.

To facilitate consumer involvement in decision making, a consumer version of each guideline is available in English and Spanish. The goal of the consumer version is to inform consumers about the issues and controversies, to raise questions that they should discuss with their provider and, most important, to correct misperceptions. They are short, and are designed for a typical rather than a sophisticated consumer.

All AHCPR-sponsored guidelines undergo critical peer review and testing before they are released to practitioners and the public. This process helps ensure that the language in each document is clear to intended users, and that information is presented in a useful format. All AHCPR-sponsored clinical practice guidelines will be updated periodically—as often as necessary—to reflect advances in medical knowledge, development of new technology, and changes in the appropriateness or clinical utility of recommendations.

In summary, AHCPR has endeavored to establish a process for the development of guidelines that will serve as a model and assure scientifically rigorous, multidisciplinary guidelines.

INFORMATION DISSEMINATION

Traditional means of disseminating guidelines, include announcing the availability of clinical practice guidelines through the general media and trade press, direct mailing to appropriate providers, medical libraries and other user groups, and re-printing the guidelines in appropriate medical journals or membership publications. In addition, AHCPR is strongly committed to making computerized versions of guidelines available on-line. It has been estimated that by the year 2000 fully 85 percent of the world's information will be in electronic format; a mere 15 percent will be available in print form only. AHCPR is on the "leading edge" of this trend toward electronic means for information dissemination.

AHCPR-sponsored clinical practice guidelines are already available in CD-ROM format—a product which will be marketed through the National Technical Information Service (NTIS). The AHCPR is also cooperating with the private sector on several projects which will make its clinical practice guidelines available through subscription services, in CD-ROM format. For example, the American Medical Association (AMA) is placing all AHCPR guidelines in the AMA *Directory of Practice Parameters,* a CD-ROM data source. Teton Data Systems has included AHCPR-sponsored guidelines in its commercially-available compact disc product (STAT!-Ref), which offers a medical library, on disc.

The agency is working with the National Library of Medicine (NLM) to develop a full-text electronic retrieval system for clinical practice guidelines. The goal of all these efforts is to make guidelines truly available to all, to assist in clinical decision making. As computers become more compact and powerful, hand held computers with the capability to store a library of guidelines are just around the corner. This hand held, readily accessible library, will promote the use and impact of guidelines.

IMPLICATIONS OF PRACTICE GUIDELINES FOR THE NATION'S HEALTH CARE SYSTEM

The use of clinical practice guidelines will almost certainly become more widespread as health care providers look for ways to eliminate ineffective or inappropriate treatments and intensify their efforts to optimize the services they deliver. Increasingly, managed care organizations will seek to manage treatment prospectively, or at the "front end." Already, some health maintenance organizations (HMOs) are depending less on retrospective utilization reviews to determine the appropriateness of medical procedures, and are moving toward decision making that is based on practice guidelines (15).

For example, in 1989, a Minneapolis-based HMO, an affiliate of Blue Cross / Blue Shield of Minnesota, began using a commercially-available computer software program to help review the medical appropriateness of some 30 medical procedures; the program is based on clinical practice guidelines developed by medical specialists, as well as extensive review of the medical literature. When a specialist employed by the HMO recommends surgery, he or she must run the patient's clinical indicators and outcomes research bring greater science to medical decision making, the benefits will accrue to patients and health care providers in the twenty-first century.

REFERENCES

1. Chassin, M.R., Kosecoff, J. and R.E. Park, et al. 1987. Does inappropriate use explain geographic variations in the use of health care services?: a study of three procedures. *JAMA*. 258:2533-2537.
2. Wennberg, J. and A. Gittleson. 1973. Small-area variation in health care delivery. *Science*. 182:1102-1108.
3. Wennberg, J., Freeman, J.L. and W.J. Culp. 1987. Are hospital services rationed in New Haven or over-utilized in Boston? *Lancet*. 1:1185-1189.
4. Lu-Yao, G.L. and D. McLerran et al. 1993. An assessment of radial prostatectomy: time trends, geographic variation, and outcomes. *JAMA*. 269:2633-2636.
5. Omnibus Budget Reconciliation Act of 1989 (P.L. 101-239).
6. Field, M.J. and K.N. Lohr, eds. 1990. *Clinical practice guidelines: directions for a new program.* Institute of Medicine, National Academy Press. Washington, D.C. 160 pp.
7. Woolf, S.H. *Interim manual on clinical practice guideline development.* US Department of Health and Human Services, Public Health Service, Agency for Health Care Policy and Research Pub. No. 91-0018.
8. *Acute pain management: operative or medical procedures and trauma.* Clinical practice guideline. 145 pp. (AHCPR 92-0032).
9. *Pressure ulcers in adults: prediction and prevention.* Clinical practice guideline. 63 pp. (AHCPR 92-0047).
10. *Urinary Incontinence in adults.* Clinical practice guideline. 125 pp. (AHCPR 92-0041).
11. *Cataract in adults: management of functional impairment.* Clinical practice guideline, number 4. 226 pp. (AHCPR 93-0542).
12. *Depression in primary care: volume 1, detection and diagnosis.* Clinical practice guideline, number 5. 124 pp. (AHCPR 93-0550).
13. *Depression in primary care: volume 2, treatment of major depression.* Clinical practice guideline, number 5. 175 pp. (AHCPR 93-0051).
14. *Sickle cell disease: screening, diagnosis, management, and counseling in newborns and infants.* Clinical practice guideline, number 6. 97 pp. (AHCPR 93-0562).
15. Webb, L.Z. and D.H. Kuykendall, et al. 1992. The impact of status asthmaticus practice guidelines on patient outcome and physician behavior. *Quality Review Bulletin.* Dec. 18 (12):471-476.
16. ACP (American College of Physicians). 1986. *Clinical efficacy assessment project: procedural manual.* Philadelphia, PA: The College.
17. Eddy, D. (in collaboration with the Council of Medical Specialty Societies). 1991c. *A manual for assessing health practices and designing practice policies: the explicit approach.* Philadelphia, PA: American College of Physicians.
18. Monrad-Aas, I.H. Malpractice. 1991. *Quality Assurance in Health Care.* 3(1):21-39.

Medicine and Health Care Into the Twenty-First Century. Edited by S.K. Majumdar, L.M. Rosenfeld, D.B. Nash and A.M. Audet. © 1995, The Pennsylvania Academy of Science.

Chapter Ten

THE FEDERAL ROLE IN TECHNOLOGY ASSESSMENT

SEAN R. TUNIS, M.D. and **ELAINE J. POWER**
Health Program
Office of Technology Assessment
U.S. Congress
Washington, D.C. 20510-8025

INTRODUCTION

When the federal government created the Medicare program in 1965, few policymakers thought that within a decade it would become the dominant payer for health care services in the country. Rapid increases in outlays for this program naturally stimulated inquiry into the factors driving the increases, and in particular greater attention to what was being purchased.

It soon became clear that in fact relatively little was known about the risks, benefits and costs of most medical practices (1), and further evidence of the poor objective basis for many medical practices has continued to accumulate over the years. At the same time, health care spending has stubbornly refused to slow its steady climb. Both trends have repeatedly underscored the need to develop methods for making more rational and defensible choices regarding medical technology.

The role of the federal government in medical technology assessment however has been an uneasy one. The purpose of this paper is to examine the forces promoting and opposing federally sponsored health technology assessment, particularly clinical practice guidelines, and to place federal technology assessment in historical perspective. In doing so, we highlight some potential barriers to the performance and application of technology assessment, including the political dynamics of evaluating medical technology, the challenges presented by the inevitable role of uncertainty and value judgments in health care decision making, and the difficulty of changing clinical practice. Awareness of these issues will be important in setting reasonable expectations for technology assessment, and it may provide direction for increasing the ultimate impact of this activity on health care.

DEFINITIONS

In this paper "health care technology" includes drugs, devices, procedures, and the organizational and supportive systems within which health care is delivered (2). The inclusion of "organizational and supportive systems" is an acknowledgment that the implications of a health intervention depend on its context, and that clusters of individual technologies organized in a specific way can themselves become a more complex technology—e.g., an intensive care unit. There are two important implications of defining technology in this way. First, in common usage, "technology" has come to be equated with medical devices, and general discussions of technology assessment may inadvertently overemphasize principles that are not easily applicable to drugs, procedures, or other medical technologies. Second, the broader definition reflects the view that most of the decisions made in the health care system involve medical technology.

We use the term "health technology assessment" to refer to a structured analysis of a health care technology that is performed for the purpose of providing input to a policy decision (3). Requisite components of a health technology assessment include the collection or generation of information about a technology, a synthesis and critical analysis of that information in the context of the policy decision to be made, and presentation of the result in language that is relevant to the decision. Analytic methods such as clinical trials, decision analysis, and cost analysis are not in themselves technology assessments, but rather tools that provide information that may be used in such an assessment. Examples of policy decisions—decisions that establish general rules and usually affect a group rather than only an individual—include the insurance coverage determinations, hospital equipment purchasing decisions, institutional drug formulary selections, and community vaccination program policies. The individual clinical decision to advise vaccination for a particular patient may make use of information about safety, efficacy, cost, patient preferences, and other factors, but these would not constitute a technology assessment according to the definition used here.

The recent policy statement of the US Preventive Services Task Force (USPSTF) on home uterine monitoring (HUM) for pre-term labor illustrates several of the important features of a technology assessment. The intent of that report was to provide a basis for both individual- and group-level policy decisions regarding use of this new technology. Information collected and synthesized as part of that assessment included all clinical trials on HUM, an interpretation of the individual trials based on study design and selection of study endpoints, consideration of potential harmful effects and resource requirements of HUM, and a survey of other organizations' assessments of this technology.

The analysis performed for Medicare coverage on its decisions liver transplants is another example of a technology assessment. Based on survival rates following liver transplant for individual causes of liver failure, that assessment recommended coverage for transplants for patients with chronic active hepatitis and other non-malignant liver diseases, while declining to pay for transplants for patients with hepatic malignancies who had only 5% survival at 5 years (4). Medicare ultimately decided against coverage for transplants for patients in the poor prognosis group, while covering other transplants, suggesting at least implicit use of cost-effectiveness in the decision.

In coming to that conclusion, the report explicitly considered issues other than safety and effectivenesss of the procedures, including organ supply, ethical concerns, and other considerations. This broad perspective is an important characteristic of technology assessments performed in conjunction with social policy decisions. It derives from the need for the analysis to be responsive to the broader needs of the population affected, in addition to the risks, costs and benefits for individuals.

HISTORY OF FEDERAL HEALTH TECHNOLOGY ASSESSMENT

The roots of technology assessment, as originally conceived, lie not in the field of medicine but in the political debates of the 1960s over the social consequences of scientific and technological advances. Early uses of the term specifically required that technology assessments should identify indirect effects of technological innovations and assess these effects for the purpose of improving decisions regarding the social use of technology (5). The term "technology" was clearly intended to be broadly defined; an early report by the National Academy of Sciences identified as potential candidates for assessment such technologies as acupuncture for pain relief, prenatal tests for fetal deformities, and outpatient clinic treatment for heroin addicts (6).

Several developments of the mid-1970s are commonly associated with the rise in interest in health care technology assessment. The development of breakthrough technologies such as renal dialysis and CT scanning, which promised great benefits at enormous costs, coincided with rising concern about national health care spending. During the same decade, there was growing documentation of the major gaps in evidence that existed in medical decision making, (7, 8) supporting the view that money was being spent on ineffective use of health care technology. Health economists dubbed this care as 'flat-of-the-curve' medicine (9), a reference to the shape of the cost vs benefit curve at increasing levels of expenditure for which there was no measurable benefit. The economic and clinical importance of this systematic failure to evaluate technology was documented in a 1978 congressional report from the health program at the Office of Technology Assessment (OTA) (7), providing a strong rationale for a more prominent role for the federal government in conducting or promoting systematic evaluations of technologies.

In 1978, the National Center for Health Care Technology (NCHCT) was created by Congress (Public Law 95-623) to address the need for better information about costs, risks and benefits of medical technology. The Center was located in the

Office of the Assistant Secretary for Health, within the Public Health Service. Operating with an annual budget of $4 million, the role of the Center was to provide advice to the Medicare and Medicaid programs on coverage decisions, to meet the information needs of health planning agencies and programs, to establish priorities for technology assessment, and to help develop improved methods for evaluating safety and efficacy of medical technology (10, 11). The Center was directed to broader consider some implications of new and existing medical technologies, including their legal, ethical and social aspects. Although one participant believed NCHCT to have provided tens of millions of dollars in savings to Medicare (10), it was eliminated when the Reagan administration did not request funds for the Center in the 1982 budget. Opposition to the center from the medical profession, device manufacturers and the National Institutes of Health, along with the Reagan administration efforts to decrease government size and regulatory oversight, all may have played a part in the center's demise (12). Responsibility for advising Medicare on technology issues was transferred to the Office of Health Technology Assessment (OHTA) within the National Center for Health Services Research (NCHSR).

Concerns about the implications of medical technology and the potential value of a coherent mechanism for assessments persisted after the NCHCT was discontinued (2, 13, 14). In 1984, Congress passed legislation directing the Institute of Medicine (IOM) to establish a public-private technology assessment consortium to address a range of medical technology issues (Public Law 98-551). This body, known as the Council on Health Care Technology (CHCT), focused primarily on conceptual and methodologic issues in technology assessment (15-19). The CHCT was hampered throughout its operations by the requirement that it obtain private funds in order to qualify for federal support, and a lack of consensus among council members about how it should operate (12). As a result, the IOM did not seek further public funds for the Council after 1989, and its statutory authorization was allowed to expire.

Because the CHCT had a limited ability to conduct specific technology assessments, the primary organizations conducting such assessment for the federal government during most of the 1980s were the OHTA (in the Publich Health Service), the NIH (through its consensus development program), and the OTA (a congressional support agency). Each of these, however, had its own limitations as a source of health technology assessments for federal policy making.

The OHTA conducts technology assessments to provide coverage recommendations for Medicare and health services funded by the Department of Defense (DOD). Funding for the office has been stable in the past decade at about $1 million per year, which supports 6 full time staff and about 15 assessments annually (Table 1). In general, the assessments are conducted by individual staff members who collect published literature and literature provided by manufacturers on effectiveness of the technology. The staff synthesize this literature, consult with the Food and Drug Administration (FDA), NIH and other relevant federal agencies as needed, and arrive at a conclusion as to whether the technology is supported by adequate evidence.

Consensus conferences on medical practice and technology issues have been an ongoing activity at NIH since 1977. They are two day events, in which the first day is devoted to presentations on the latest knowledge regarding a particular condition or technology, and the second day devoted to open public input followed by an expert panel issuing a summary statement based on the information presented. They rarely have the opportunity for extensive research or formal literature reviews, relying instead primarily on input from experts in the field. Recent conferences have addressed treatment for obesity, the role of HDL cholesterol in heart disease, and laparoscopic cholecystectomy. These conferences are considered primarily a vehicle for professional education and research agenda setting, rather than a source of information for setting Medicare or other federal health program policies.

The health program at the OTA conducts broad studies of major issues associated with medical technology at the request of Congress. Examples of assessments include studies of the impact of regulation on the medical device industry, the role of physician payment on use and costs of medical technology, measuring the quality of medical care, and potential issues associated with providing home infusion therapy to Medicare beneficiaries. While these large studies often include assessments of some individual technology assessments as case studies, the OTA does not routinely assess specific medical technologies. In addition, its agenda is determined by Congress, rather than by the specific administrative

TABLE 1

Technology Reviews and Assessments Conducted in 1992 and 1993
Office of Health Technology Assessment

REVIEWS
HOME UTERINE MONITORING
PLATELET-DERIVED GROWTH FACTOR FOR TREATMENT OF WOUNDS AND CHRONIC SKIN ULCERS
COMBINED LIVER-KIDNEY TRANSPLANTS
OUTPATIENT SURGERY FOR COCHLEAR IMPLANTATION
COMBINED LIVER-KIDNEY TRANSPLANTS
DRUG DELIVERY DEVICES
THE LYMPHEDEMA PUMP
SMALL BOWEL AND LIVER-SMALL BOWEL TRANSPLANT
IMPLANTABLE BONE STIMULATOR FOR SPINAL FUSION
INTRADIALYTIC TOTAL PARENTERAL NUTRITION
ASSESSMENTS
REASSESSMENT OF CARDIAC OUTPUT MEASUREMENT BY BIOIMPEDANCE
PATIENT AND INSTITUTIONAL SELECTION CRITERIA FOR HEART-LUNG TRANSPLANTATION
BONE MINERAL DENSITY STUDIES
ROUTINE TESTING REQUIREMENTS FOR DIALYSIS PATIENTS
EXPERT CONSENSUS ON THE APPROPRIATE USES OF ULTRASOUND
PLETHYSMOGRAPHY
MAGNETIC RESONANCE ANGIOGRAPHY
PANCREAS-KIDNEY TRANSPLANTATION
REFRACTIVE KERATOPLASTY

the "outcomes, effectiveness and appropriateness of health care services and procedures" (Public Law 101-239, 42 USC 1320b-12). Each term in this phrase from the legislation has a historical context and meaning derived from specific bodies of research, associated with particular investigators and policy makers. 'Outcomes research', associated with the work of Dr. John Wennberg and colleagues, was initially distinguished by its focus on using functional status, patient preferences and other patient-centered information in evaluating the impact of health services (27). The term "effectiveness research," promoted by William Roper, refers to the effects of treatment under ordinary circumstances (in contrast to the limited generalizability of the results of many traditional clinical trials) (26). Motivation for this initiative derived in part from an inability to project the results of many clinical trials to treatment for elderly patients, the existence of a large Medicare database available for analysis, and a perceived need to provide some form of reassurance that recent changes in the way Medicare paid for hospital inpatient care would not result in Medicare patients being consigned to poor quality care (12). Finally, 'appropriateness of care' was explored extensively by a group at RAND, which used expert groups to develop ratings of the appropriateness of treament when performed for various medical indications (23, 25). The prevalence of inappropriate care identified in RAND studies forms one of the justifications for arguments of significant cost savings potentially resulting from these areas of research (25).

Although the three terms initially designated different lines of research that tended to emphasize somewhat different methodological techniques, all are now used with such abandon as to be virtually indistinguishable in common usage.

In accordance with the enthusiasm for applying these techniques and lines of research more broadly, the AHCPR legislation outlined in some detail the expectation that the agency would pursue the use of existing data and previously published research as an inexpensive and rapid approach to begin to fill in gaps in medical knowledge (Richard Greene, personal communication). The appeal of alternatives to randomized trials is usually justified based on the expense of prospective trials, the perception that they do not represent actual practice and therefore may have limited applicability or impact on clinical decisions, the increasing availability of large databases, and the wider availability of computing power to process that information.

The centerpiece of AHCPR's effectiveness research agenda is a set of 14 multi-disciplinary, multi-site Patient Outcomes Research Team (PORT) projects, each funded at $1 million per year for 5 years (Table 3). Each PORT is devoted to a specific clinical condition and addresses diagnosis, treatment, long-term management, and prevention issues related to that disorder. Methods of study for these projects included extensive literature reviews and meta-analyses, database studies of geographic variation and other patterns of care, targeted primary data collection, decision analyses, and dissemination activities (Sanford Schwartz, personal communication). Four PORTS entered their 5th year of operation in 1993 (cataract, myocardial infarction, low back pain, and prostrate disease). They have produced a considerable number of publications, some of which have generated important hypotheses concerning the clinical conditions under study.

There is yet no firm evidence to suggest that practices have changed specifically as a result of work done by these research teams, but studies to look at this issue are underway.

In early 1993, AHCPR invited PORT investigators to a workshop to review their experiences to date and make suggestions for how the program may be modified in future grants. Based on the discussion at this workshop, AHCPR staff concluded that greater flexibility of methodologies was needed, that less emphasis on comprehensive meta-analysis may be justified when literature is deficient, that emphasis on administrative data should be decreased, and that new efforts to develop better data bases should be supported (Richard Green, personal communication). For the next generation of PORTs, it is expected that more emphasis will be directed to primary data collection, although the agency's effectiveness research program is still expected to continue exploring the utility of administrative data to study clinical effectiveness.

TABLE 3

Agency for Health Care Policy and Research
Current Patient Outcomes Research Team Projects (PORTs)

	PRESENT PROJECT PERIOD	
GRANTS	**START DATE**	**ENDING DATE**
BACK PAIN OUTCOME ASSESSMENT TEAM U. of Washington, Seattle, WA	9/01/89	8/31/94
CONSEQUENCES OF VARIATION IN TREATMENT FOR ACUTE MYOCARDIAL INFARCTION (AMI) Harvard Medical School, Boston, MA	9/07/89	8/31/94
VARIATIONS IN CATARACT MANAGEMENT: PATIENT AND ECONOMIC OUTCOMES - Johns Hopkins U., Baltimore, MD	9/07/89	9/29/94
ASSESSING THERAPIES FOR BENIGN PROSTATIC HYPERTROPHY AND LOCALIZED PROSTATE CANCER Dartmouth College, Hanover, NH	9/07/89	8/31/94
ASSESSING AND IMPROVING OUTCOMES: TOTAL KNEE REPLACEMENTS - Indiana U., Indianapolis, IN	4/01/90	3/31/95
VARIATIONS IN THE MANAGEMENT AND OUTCOMES OF DIABETES - New England Medical Center, Boston, MA	6/01/90	9/29/95
OUTCOME ASSESSMENT PROGRAM IN ISCHEMIC HEART DISEASE - Duke U., Durham, NC	7/01/90	8/01/95
OUTCOME ASSESSMENT IN PATIENTS WITH BILIARY TRACT DISEASE - U. of Pennsylvania, Philadelphia, PA	8/01/90	8/31/95
ANALYSIS OF PRACTICES: HIP FRACTURE REPAIR & OSTEOARTHRITIS - U. of Maryland, Baltimore, MD	9/01/90	9/29/95
ASSESSMENT OF THE VARIATIONS AND OUTCOMES OF PNEUMONIA - U. of Pittsburgh, PA	9/30/90	9/29/95
CONTRACTS		
VARIATIONS IN MANAGEMENT OF CHILDBIRTH AND PATIENT OUTCOMES - The Rand Corporation, Santa Monica, CA	9/28/90	9/27/95
SECONDARY AND TERTIARY PREVENTION OF STROKE Duke U. Medical Center, Durham, NC	8/01/91	8/01/96
SCHIZOPHRENIA PATIENT OUTCOMES RESEARCH TEAM U. of Maryland, Baltimore, MD	9/30/92	9/29/97
PATIENT OUTCOMES RESEARCH TEAM (PORT) ON LOW BIRTHWEIGHT IN MINORITY AND HIGH RISK WOMEN U. of Alabama, Birmingham, AL	9/30/92	9/29/97

THE ROLE OF STAKEHOLDER OPPOSITION

Through the 1980s, medical technology assessment has made a great contribution to health care and health research through its continual emphasis on the need for better evidence regarding the costs, risks, and effectiveness of medical interventions (3). But the vision of many in the medical technology assessment field in the early 1980s that this endeavor would enable government policy makers to rationalize the use of scarce and expensive health care resources, has not materialized. Certainly examples can be found of individual technologies for which payment was denied by Medicare or other payers, and practices have changed accordingly. Broad effects, however, have not been observed.

A major reason for this limited impact is that technology assessment, like any activity of the federal government, is heavily influenced by the participation of the "stakeholders" who would be affected by the conduct of this activity. Because one purpose of technology assessment is to guide national policy decisions that would potentially affect the flow of resources in many areas of health care, the stakes are high, and the involvement of stakeholders is substantial. Medical professionals, medical product manufacturers, and the public are groups for whom technology assessment may have major consequences.

Historically, the medical profession has been strongly opposed to greater involvement by the federal government in evaluating technology. Opposition from this group was important in the failure to reauthorize the NCHCT (10, 12). Much of the opposition related to the fear that formal government-sponsored assessments would be used to substitute for, rather than support and supplement, medical judgment. The American Medical Association (AMA) testified at congressional hearings in 1981 that federal technology assessment was unnecessary because:

> Clinical policy analysis and judgments are better made—and are being responsibly made—within the medical profession. Assessing risks and costs, as well as benefits, has been central to the exercise of good medical judgment for decades. The advantage the individual physician has over any national center or advisory council is that he or she is dealing with individuals in need of medical care, not hypothetical cases (10).

The highly sensitive issue of the federal government playing a role in defining appropriate medical practice goes back to the original establishment of the Medicare program. The Social Security Act of 1965, which established Medicare and Medicaid, stated explicitly that "nothing in this title shall be construed to authorize any federal officer or employee to exercise any supervision over the practice of medicine . . ." (section 1801). The AMA viewed the functions of the NCHCT as a move in the direction of greater federal involvement in medical decision making, made particularly uncomfortable by the NCHCT's role in providing payment recommendations to enforce these government-sponsored judgments.

The medical device industry, represented by the Health Industry Manufacturers Association (HIMA), has also consistently raised concerns about a prominent federal role in assessment of medical technology. They too testified against continuation of the NCHCT, raising as their strongest objection the potential impact of the list of emerging technologies generated by the Center, which they argued could lead to premature assessments that could stifle medical innovations. They also argued that assessment activities could be undertaken by numerous other federal entities (e.g., the NIH), and that the Center was therefore redundant. Finally, in their view, a flawed assessment by a single, central assessment body could have serious consequences for public health and for the manufacturers of the device evaluated (10, 12).

While the drug industry might be expected to have concerns similar to those of the device industry, through most of the 1980s, it was not highly visible in technology assessment issues. This may be due to the more prominent role of the FDA in the approval process for drugs as compared to devices. The high evidence standard imposed by the FDA on drugs has led most payers, including Medicare, to offer coverage for any FDA approved product. Such coverage is not automatic for devices, many of which are held to less stringent data requirements for FDA approval (28).

Patients also have a major stake in the conduct and application of technology assessment. Because patients often become involved in health care policy discussions only when they need care that is difficult to obtain, the consequence of patient activism for technology assessment has tended to be inhibitory. Particularly in the context of life-threatening or serious disease, when existing therapies are not adequate, patients may demand access to new technologies more quickly than evaluation of those technologies can be completed. In such situations, patients may be willing to sacrifice clear proof of safety and efficacy in order to avoid delay in the approval and broad availability of the product (29). Much of the pressure for modification of FDA approval procedures came from the AIDS community, in a quest to hasten access to new therapies (30). The intense perceived need for approval of some effective therapy for Alzheimer's disease may have been a factor in the recent FDA approval of tacrine (Cognex), despite divergence of opinion as to whether the small observed benefits justified the relatively frequent toxicity of the drug. Denial of access to therapies that appear promising but are not yet proven, or technologies that are proven but are not considered to be cost-effective, are likely to encounter resistence from potential recipients and their families.

One of the most prominent examples of the tension between evaluation and pressure for access to therapy is the case of high-dose chemotherapy and bone marrow transplant for advanced breast cancer. There exists professional disagreement about whether this relatively new technology has been proven to be effective. Several independent panels of experts have, however, concluded that the procedure should be considered experimental. Despite this, many insurance companies have decided to pay for the treatment, in part because many who refused to pay eventually lost their case in court (31). (The courts tend to resolve disputes involving health insurance contracts in favor of the patient, because they are seen as having the least bargaining power). In a novel approach to addressing the need to collect more data and make a potentially useful technology available, the National Cancer Institute has collaborated with Blue Cross / Blue Shield and other payers to conduct several clinical trials of the procedure, with the insurer having agreed to pay as long as the patient was enrolled in a trial. Although these trials are accruing patients, those who insist on the new therapy outside of the trials are still often allowed to have it.

THE CONSTRAINTS OF EVIDENCE, VALUES, AND CLINICAL IMPLEMENTATION

The enthusiasm for medical technology assessment derives in part from the expectation that it can provide clear answers to difficult questions about which health care services are worth providing. But technology assessment synthesizes and analyzes information to help policy makers; it does not by itself make decisions. Nor does it implement those decisions (although the feasibility of implementation can be part of the analysis). For all its usefulness, the impact of technology assessments—and particularly assessments that take the form of structured, systematic practice guidelines—are constrained by the evidence upon which they rest, the value judgments that they cannot replace, and the malleability of the medical care systems they hope to affect.

The limited number of good quality studies for most clinical problems has always been one of the problems faced by technology assessors, and it continues to be so. Without reliable data on the basic issues of safety and effectiveness, the ability to provide information in support of policy decisions is compromised. Yet expert opinion holds that only a small fraction of clinical practices are supported by results of controlled clinical trials (7).

The experience of guideline development panels has highlighted this problem, as the panels encounter few good quality studies available to support many clinical recommendations they are trying to make. For example, in developing the AHCPR-sponsored cataract surgery guideline, none of the 48 articles reviewed concerning indications for cataract surgery provided evidence to support a clinical recommendation: "The search of the literature did not reveal any information helpful in elucidating precise indications for surgery" (32). All of the articles on preoperative medical evaluation for cataract surgery were noted to have serious methodologic flaws. Similarly, of 119 published articles on visual tests for contrast sensitivity, commonly used to evaluate the need for cataract surgery, the panel found fewer than 10 studies relevant to the question, most of which were inadequate in methods or content (32). In a recent appropriateness study, 38% of coronary angioplasty procedures were determined to be of uncertain value, reflecting a lack of clear published evidence on the use of this common procedure (33). These examples are fairly representative of the quality of evidence available for many procedures and practices.

The lack of high quality evidence from clinical trials on many existing medical technologies, and the expense of conducting such trials, was a major impetus behind the desire to explore the research potential of existing administrative databases in the federal government's "effectiveness initiative." This approach has a number of problems when used to assess the comparative effectiveness of medical interventions, including the problems with the type and quality of the data in these databases, and the potential bias resulting from comparisons of treatments to which patients were not randomly assigned (34). At the same time, however, well controlled clinical trials themselves are viewed with skepticism by some clinicians and researchers. The use of rigorous patient entry criteria and the specialized setting in which trials are often conducted frequently raise questions about the relevance of results to the "average" patient (Richard Greene, personal communication). The effort to fill information gaps by relying on expert opinion applied to best available evidence—the method underlying AHCPR practice guidelines, RAND appropriateness guidelines, and NIH consensus conferences—is also hampered by questions about the optimal means of controlling bias and conflict of interest in these group processes (35).

Lack of is information on effectiveness is not the only missing element for decision making. Reliable information on cost also hampers the evaluation on cost-effectiveness, an important component of many technology assessments. Because there has been considerable debate about the appropriateness of considering cost as an explicit factor in decision making, exploration of the methodologic hurdles in considering costs are only beginning to be addressed. The Medicare program, for example, has not yet acted on regulations proposed in January 1989 that would allow cost-effectiveness to be used as an explicit criterion for making coverage decisions, and it therefore does not currently have the legal authority to do so.

In contrast, federally sponsored guidelines panels have had strong reservations about considering costs. In recent meetings, for example, the UPSPSTF has begun to discuss use of cost-effectiveness analysis in their preventive care recommendations, but it does not plan to include costs in its 1994 edition of its guidelines (Marthe Gold, personal communication). Similarly, formal efforts to estimate the economic impact of different clinical practices have not been part of the methodology followed by the AHCPR guideline panels. The 1992 reauthorizing legislation of AHCPR contains more explicit language about inclusion of cost information in guidelines and technology assessments (Public Law 102-410), and the Agency has organized several workshops and contract studies to explore how cost information might be incorporated (Jill Bernstein, personal communication).

When good evidence regarding the effectiveness and costs of a technology does exist, translating that evidence into a policy decision can require painful and controversial value judgments. As long as a technology is associated with some net benefit, the answer to the question of whether or not it is worth using (or paying for) is a matter of subjective value attributed to that benefit (36). If the political and social consequences of making decisions that permit costs to be a deciding factor are sufficiently explosive, policy makers may find little use for the information.

For example, recent studies on the use of thrombolytic therapy after heart attack suggest that a drug that is 10 times more expensive than its alternative might save 1 more life for every 100 patients treated. Whether a health plan or insurer pays for this product can only be decided based on weighing the cost against the benefit. The most problematic aspect of the decision—whether actions that improve one's chances of surviving should be denied simply because they're expensive—can actually be heightened, rather than resolved, by having the evidence and knowing the tradeoffs.

The need to balance benefits and costs arises not only in assessments comparing two different technologies but when considering the appropriate use of a given technology among different patients and clinical circumstances. Abdominal CT scanning, an expensive diagnostic technology, may be both highly beneficial and cost-saving when selectively used as a substitute for exploratory surgery (29). The same test, however, is of marginal value when routinely used to diagnose vague complaints of abdominal pain, and the test may actually result in harm if unsuspected abnormalities are discovered that then require further testing to be proven insignificant. Similarly, new treatments such as lithotripsy for kidney stones, minimally invasive surgery for gallstones, and balloon dilation for narrowed peripheral arterial have been shown highly cost-effective in a subset of patients, but possibly cost-raising to the health care system when they are eventually used in a much broader range of patients (37-39).

Whatever the tradeoffs that are applied at the population level for the purposes of policy making, individuals facing a particular treatment or test make their own tradeoffs based on their personal preferences as well. These individual considerations sometimes interfere with the ability to make simple policy decisions regarding technologies, and the inability of technology assessment to resolve these issues neatly may decrease the enthusiasm for such assessments. Some clinical guidelines have successfully taken both population-level tradeoffs and personal preferences into account. For example, recent guidelines by AHCPR cataract surgery should be offered to state that patients who find that they are dissatisfied with the lifestyle limitations imposed upon them by their visual impairment. Objective vision tests alone, however, are not valid for selecting surgical candidates (32).

Finally, even when underlying evidence is of good quality, the impact of guidelines and other technology assessments on clinical practice often seems to be very small. Lomas and colleagues studied the effects of a national guideline on Cesarean section that, if fully implemented, would have decreased rates of this procedure. Despite widespread knowledge of and agreement with the guideline, clinical practices were apparently unaffected by it (40). Similarly, NIH guidelines developed through consensus conferences have generally not been associated with changes in clinical practice (41). Even intensive implementation efforts, involving direct contact with physicians, frequent reinforcement, or specific recommendations on individual patient charts, have in many cases resulted in few changes in practice (42-44).

While changes in practice are often slow to occur, many new technologies are adopted rapidly despite lack of evidence that they are effective, and often with considerable reason to believe that they are not. A recent case in point is the rapid increase in use of an antigen test to detect prostate cancer. There is as yet no evidence that testing improves outcomes, and a good chance that it results in considerable needless diagnostic testing and therapeutic interventions with high rates of expected complications. The increased use in this test has come after widespread press coverage and corresponding consumer demand (45).

CHANGING PERCEPTIONS AND NEW DIRECTIONS

Despite the apparent potential of technology assessment, in the past there has been only modest willingness to fund it in the public sector. Since the end of the 1980s, however, medical technology assessment at the federal level has gained increasing acceptance and political support.

A substantial factor in this acceptance has been the highly visible support given by the American Medical Association to the new AHCPR, particularly the program to develop practice guidelines. Given the AMA's history of strong objections to government-sponsored assessments and guidelines, this about-face might at first appear surprising. Several factors underlie the new willingness to accept a greater federal role in creating guidelines.

First, there is accumulating evidence of wide variation in clinical practices, which has tended to undermine the argument that experienced physicians usually know by experience what treatments are best. There is also a greater appreciation within the medical profession of the value of objective evidence from primary data. Federal support of clinical evaluation may be seen as more acceptable given the increasing appreciation of this evidence. It has also been suggested that the prospect of government cost-containment through greater control over physician payment, particularly expenditure caps, may have motivated the medical profession to embrace guidelines and effectiveness research as a relatively more attractive policy response to the rising urgency of containing costs (46). Finally, an important factor has been AHCPR's explicit attempt to include a majority of clinicians on its guidelines panels, and to reassure clinicians that its guidelines are intended primarily to supplement rather than replace medical judgment.

The changing health care environment, in which managed care is becoming increasingly pervasive, has affected stakeholders other than physicians as well. Pharmaceutical manufacturers, for example, have historically been relatively disassociated from discussions of medical technology assessment. Recently, however, increasing discussion of cost-effectiveness as a criterion for including drugs in hospital, managed care, and government program formularies has led pharmaceutical manufacturers, too, to take a great interest in the topic of technology assessment. The discussion is no longer theoretical, even at the highest levels; the first public draft of the Clinton administration's health reform proposal would have included cost-effectiveness as a criterion for drug coverage under the Medicare program.

HIMA, representing the medical device manufacturers who once mustered such strong opposition to technology assessment in Washington, proposed that technology assessment be performed by multiple entities, institutions or individual providers. The federal role, under this proposal, would be to provide a central clearinghouse of technology assessment reports which could be referred to by individual decision makers. The proposal specifies that both peer-review and "gray" literature reports (studies not indexed in most literature databases, such as those produced by consulting firms) be included, and that the clearinghouse make no attempt to synthesize or evaluate the quality of the information it collects (Tom Long, personal communication). Consumers of this information, health plans and physicians, would be responsible for drawing their own conclusions from the accumulated evidence. HIMA's proposal reflects its discomfort with a central decision mechanism for medical technology and its stake in discouraging a process that might inhibit the diffusion of some technologies.

The vision for a system of decentralized technology assessment has been challenged by the payer community, who favor a more coordinated, centralized approach to making insurance coverage decisions. In their view, it is expensive and inefficient for numerous providers and payers to collect and interpret the same body of evidence, when such functions could be performed in a collaborative process. As expressed by one insurance consultant, "the notion that payers should continue to guide technology diffusion through individual decisions affecting their own markets is inherently destabilizing to any national attempt to control health care costs" (47). Acting on these views, representatives from the major payer organizations developed a plan to contribute $1 million to support a public-private collaboration for technology assessment that would have been overseen by AHCPR (47). Although there is little formal documentation of discussion of this initiative, representatives from HIMA and individual device manufacturers testified against it at a public hearing in March 1992, and the AMA did not support the initiative. Following this hearing, there were no further discussions between AHCPR and insurer groups concerning shared financial support of technology assessments.

In the absence of centralized federal technology assessment for general use, several large payers have substantially increased their own commitment to technology assessment activities. The largest of these efforts is a collaboration between Blue Cross / Blue Shield Association, of which individual Blue Cross and Blue Shield plans are members, and Kaiser Permanente, a national managed health care provider. This collaboration will perform about 40 technology assessments per year (more than double the number produced annually by OHTA), and the sponsors plan to make their products available on a subscription basis to other providers and payers. Other insurers are investing in this activity as well. Prudential, for example, recently committed to a budget of $20 million over 5 years to establish an "outcomes institute" (to be directed by former Health Care Financing Administration's Administrator William Roper), which will provide an analytic foundation for coverage and policy decisions by this insurer.

Thus, at the same time that the government has been more willing to find a permanent place for ongoing clinical guidelines and individual technology assessment, the private sector's thirst for these assessments, and its willingness and capability of producing them, is growing as well. The ultimate appropriate federal role—whether it should be a coordinator or central producer of assessments and guidelines—is still unclear.

What is clear is that the political and health environment that made federal technology assessment anathema to many stakeholders has changed dramatically. It is no longer primarily the federal government but private insurers and health care organizations that are seeking to manage medical technology. The pressures on these organizations to restrain cost increases show no signs of slacking, and medical technology assessment is likely to continue to gain in importance and use. The constraints of insufficient evidence, a reticence to make painful value judgments, and competing pressures on clinicians and patients that have limited the impact of clinical guidelines in the past will not disappear, however. Rather, they may come to the fore, as the pressures on insurers and managed care providers to constrain costs by the way they manage medical technology increasingly clash with the concerns of clinicians and patients who desire access to promising but untested technologies.

There is no policy approach that will allow for the findings generated by technology assessment to relieve insurers, clinicians and patients of the need to make complex decisions, with large amounts of intrinsic uncertainty and a substantial element of judgment. What technology assessment can do is to compile the best objective evidence available, identify the aspects of a decision in which values, preferences, and uncertainty play a role, and examine the consequences of policy choices. Whether a public or a private sector endeavor, medical technology assessment is likely to play a significant role in the health care decisions of the future.

REFERENCES

1. U.S. Congress. 1976. Development of medical technology: opportunities for assessment. Washington, DC: U.S. Government Printing Office.
2. U.S. Congress. 1982. Strategies for medical technology assessment. Washington, DC: U.S. Government Printing Office.
3. Power, E.J., Tunis, S.R. and J.L. Wagner. 1994. Technology assessment and public health. Ann Rev Publ Health. 15:561-79.
4. Hotta, S.S. 1990. Assessment of liver transplantation. Washington, DC: U.S. Department of Health and Human Service. AHCPR publication-90-8.
5. U.S. Congress. 1973. Office of Technology Assessment: background and status. Washington, DC: U.S. Government Printing Office. Committee print-No. 99-672.
6. National Science Foundation O, Research Applications Directorate. 1973. Candidates and priorities for assessments, volume IV: an approach to priorities. Washington, DC: U.S. Government Printing Office. IRT-310-R.
7. U.S. Congress. 1978. Assessing the safety and efficacy of medical technologies. Washington, DC: U.S. Government Printing Office.
8. Eddy, D.M. and J. Billings. 1988. The quality of medical evidence: implications for quality of care. Health Affairs. 7:19-32.
9. Fuchs, V.R. 1972. Health care and the United States economic system: an essay in abnormal physiology. Milbank Mem Fund Q. 50:211-37.
10. Perry, S. 1982. The brief life of the National Center for Health Care Technology. N Engl J Med. 307:1095-100.
11. Fineberg, H.V. 1985. Technology assessment: motivation, capability, and future directions. Med Care. 23:663-71.
12. Rettig, R.A. 1991. Technology assessment - an update. Invest Radiol. 26:165-73.
13. Bunker, J.P., Fowles, J. and R. Shaffarzick. 1993. Evaluation of medical technology strategies: proposal for an institute for health care evaluation. N Engl J Med. 306:687-92.
14. Institute of Medicine. 1983. A consortium for assessing medical technology. Washington, DC: National Academy of Sciences.

Medicine and Health Care Into the Twenty-First Century. Edited by S.K. Majumdar, L.M. Rosenfeld, D.B. Nash and A.M. Audet. © 1995, The Pennsylvania Academy of Science.

Chapter Eleven

THE MINNESOTA CLINICAL COMPARISON & ASSESSMENT PROGRAM
Bridging the Gap between Clinical Practice Guidelines and Patient Care

CATHERINE BORBAS, Ph.D., DANIEL B. McLAUGHLIN, M.P.A. and **ALVIN SCHULTZ, M.D.**

2550 University Avenue West,
Suite 223 North
St. Paul, MN 55114

INTRODUCTION

The need for accessible, effective and efficient health care services has become a national priority in the United States. However, few attempts to change the health care delivery system or clinicians' practice style have been successful (Eisenberg, 1986; Lomas, 1991). Currently, many believe that clinical practice guidelines and outcomes research will significantly improve the effectiveness and efficiency of health care services. But, are these ideas any different from many others that have been tried and failed?

Research (Eisenberg, 1986); (Williamson, 1982); (Soumerai, 1990); (Lomas, 1989, 1991) has shown that information-based programs, such as guideline publication and feedback of information, have had limited success with changing clinicians'

Reprinted with permission from the Hospital Research and Educational Trust.

behavior. Researchers (Eisenberg, 1986); (Lomas, 1989); (Mittman, 1992) have suggested that new strategies must be developed that incorporate ideas from the social sciences and adult education that have been associated with successfully motivating human behavior change. This paper describes a program in Minnesota that is attempting to do this.

The Minnesota Clinical Comparison & Assessment Project (MCCAP) was initiated to improve the appropriateness, effectiveness, and efficiency of health care delivery in Minnesota. MCCAP offers a collective strategy which links, in an iterative manner, clinical practice guidelines with outcome data reported back to clinicians. The methods and materials developed by the program are non-proprietary and could be adapted by other communities. Since its inception, the MCCAP consortium has grown to include 53 Minnesota hospitals. Hospitals range in size from 19 to 788 beds, representing approximately sixty percent of the licensed beds in Minnesota. Member hospitals include multi-specialty, academic institutions and community hospitals in urban and rural areas. Most aspects of MCCAP could be replicated by both health care providers and purchasers in other communities (See Figure 1).

Origins of a Collective Strategy

In 1988, the Healthcare Education & Research Foundation (HERF), a non-profit, applied research foundation in St. Paul, Minnesota, evaluated the usefulness of severity of illness systems (e.g. Medisgroups) for Minnesota hospitals and found that existing severity systems had technical merits but that clinicians had difficulty trusting and using the systems. Therefore, it was recommended that hospitals delay purchasing severity systems and, in the interim, establish a collective program to improve hospitals' and clinicians' ability to use comparative clinical information. Subsequently, the MCCAP was developed to address this need.

Rationale for a Collective Strategy

Many of the hospitals in MCCAP are competing for market share; however, they choose to join together to accomplish their "quality of care" objectives in order to undertake projects that are usually beyond the capability or resources of any one hospital and in order to benefit from economies of scale.

At the community level, MCCAP provides the organizational structure necessary to unify the duplication and fragmented quality improvement programs initiated by individual health care institutions, medical specialty societies and state medical and hospital associations. This has forced and conserved community resources and funds.

Sponsors and Participants

In 1989, the Minnesota Clinical Comparison & Assessment Project (MCCAP) was formally implemented under the auspices of the Healthcare Eduation and

Research Foundation (HERF). The program was co-sponsored with six other organizations (See Figure 2).

Funding

Core funding for MCCAP is provided by the sponsoring organizations and the member hospitals and their medical staffs. Funding for specific projects also have been provided by outside sources, including the Pew Charitable Trusts and the Bush Foundation. Beginning in the fall, 1992, the MCCAP began receiving funds as a subcontractor to Harvard Medical School for two guideline dissemination studies—

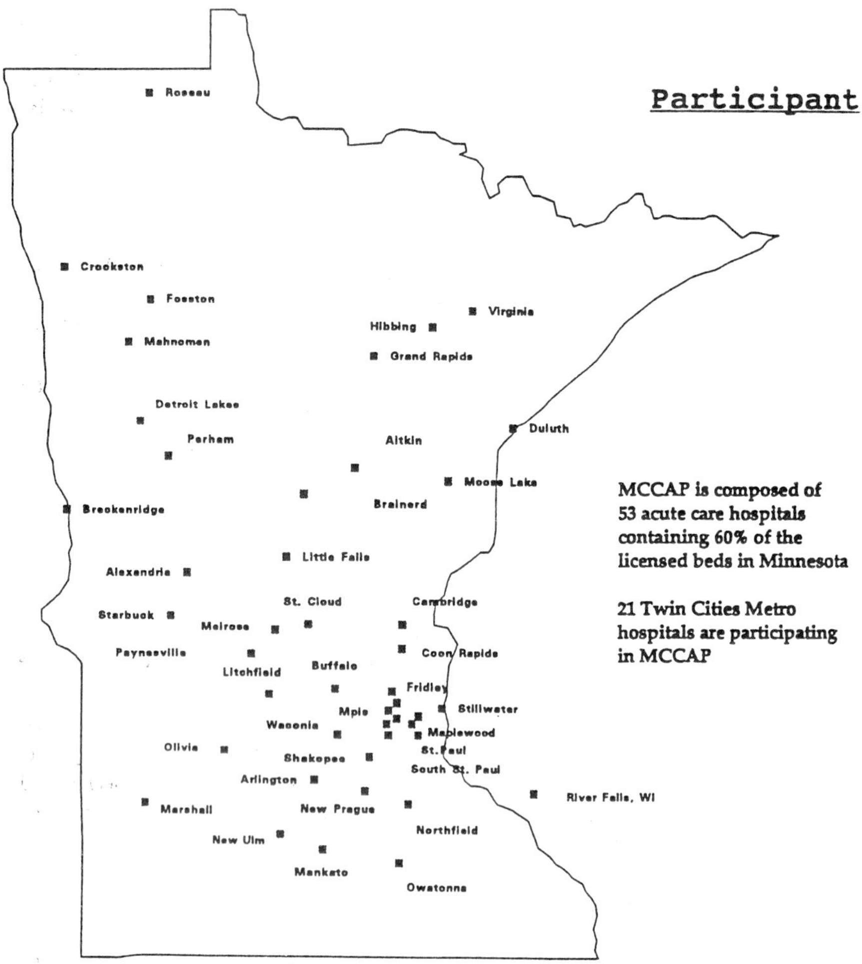

FIGURE 1. MCCAP. Minnesota Clinical Comparison & Assessment Program.

one with Stephen Soumerai, Sc.D., Associate Professor, as Principal Investigator, funded by the Agency for Health Care Policy and Research (AHCPR) and the other funded by the National Cancer Institute (NCI) with Edward Guadagnoli, Ph.D., Assistant Professor, as Principal Investigator.

Role of Practice Guidelines

Clinical practice guidelines serve a central role in the MCCAP but only as one part of a broader strategy. Guidelines are viewed as a necessary, but not sufficient, means to change clinical behavior and ultimately improve patient care. A broad iterative framework was implemented with four integrated sets of activities:

1. development of clinical practice guidelines
2. acquisition and analysis of appropriateness and outcomes data
3. feed back of information to clinicians at the participating hospitals, and
4. revision of clinical guidelines based on outcomes findings.

MCCAP uses guidelines to *predispose* clinicians to focus on specific treatment methods and expected patient outcomes for a defined patient population. Then, data are collected, analyzed and presented to clinicians. This allows clinicians to compare their treatment methods and patient outcomes to those of their colleagues and to the guideline recommendations. Through this process, MCCAP attempts

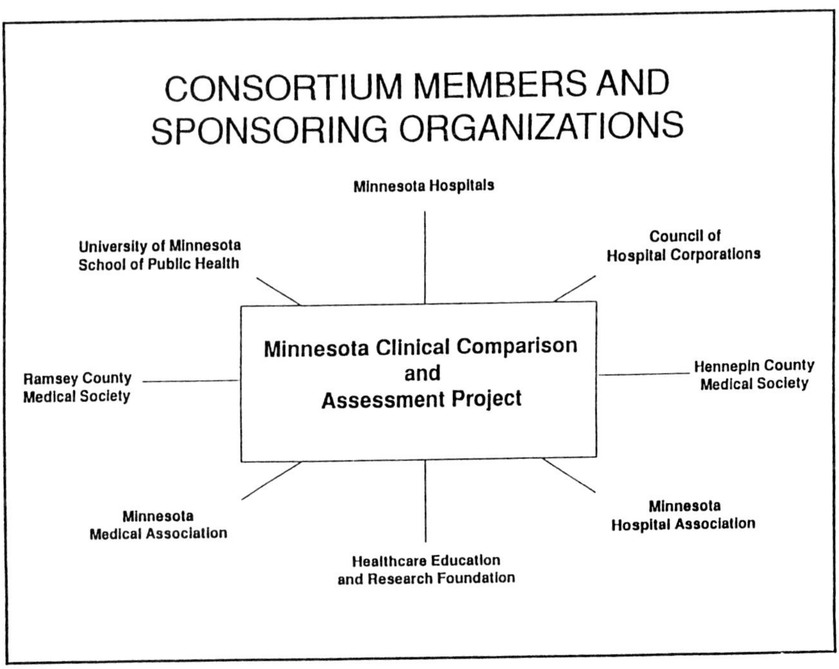

FIGURE 2. Consortium Members and Sponsoring Organizations.

to *enable* clinicians to evaluate their practice style and patient outcomes and, if appropriate, change their treatment methods. Finally, the aggregate outcomes information is used to revise and strengthen the original guidelines. After this, another cycle of data collection and feedback will begin. Theoretically, after each cycle of this process, MCCAP guidelines will be improved with outcome-based data which could be used to evaluate and improve health care in Minnesota. See Figures 3 & 4—MCCAP CYCLE: PROCESS.

This very broad strategy was chosen because it had been repeatedly demonstrated and reported by researchers that programs which relied solely on information-based strategies did not change clinical behavior (Eisenberg, 1986, Lomas, 1991). It has been suggested that the publication of guidelines was a necessary but not sufficient means to change organizational and individual clinical behavior (Lomas, 1991) and that clinicians' fundamental values and attitudes also need to be addressed and incorporated into behavior change strategies (Lomas, 1989, 1991; Mittman, 1992). Therefore, MCCAP attempts to enhance traditional information-based programs (i.e. guideline publication, audit and feedback programs) with a strategy that incorporates principles from the social sciences and management theory. For example, it was assumed that clinicians, like other groups, were affected by significant social influences such as significant reference groups, familiar traditions, values and attitudes. Therefore, involvement in MCCAP was sought from local clinical opinion leaders and significant reference groups for clinicians such as local professional medical societies and associations. In order to motivate clinicians to participate, they were asked to voluntarily join the program for personal and

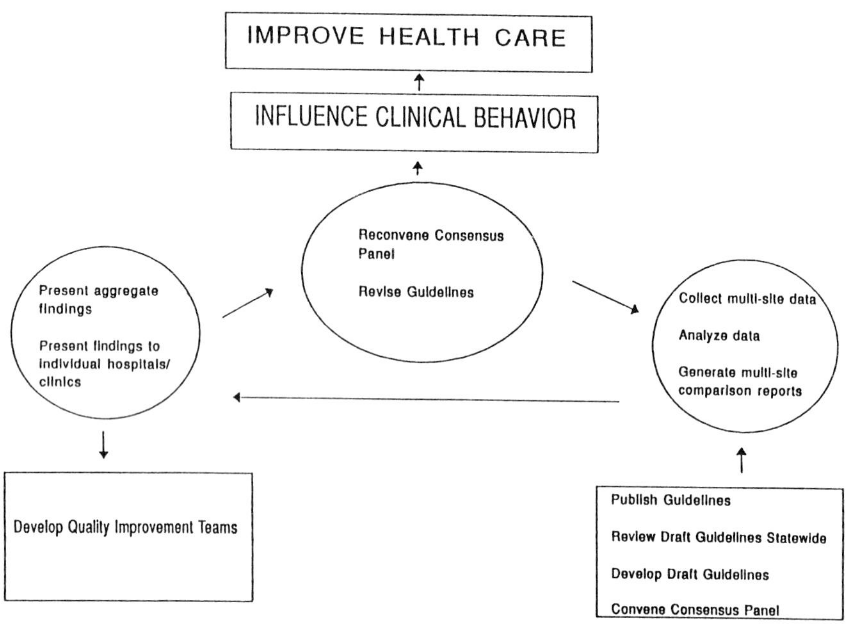

FIGURE 3. MCCAP Model for Quality of Care Evaluation & Improvement.

professional reasons. In order to reduce clinicians' and institutions' anxiety about possible public disclosure or unintended uses of MCCAP data, strict data policies were mutually established. Finally, a broad, representative governance structure was developed to provide an outgoing vehicle to address the concerns of the participants.

MCCAP Objectives

The initial objecties for MCCAP (1989-1992) were to:

1. Develop a governance structure for MCCAP which addressed the individual and mutual concerns and interests of the sponsoring organizations and participating institutions;
2. Develop a guideline development and review program which could be used by Minnesota health care institutions and practicing clinicians;
3. Develop a centralized data acquisition and analysis program; and,
4. Develop an information feedback program for the consortium hospitals.

Beginning in 1993, the program will also attempt to:

5. Determine the effectiveness of its feedback program in changing clinical decision-making and behavior, and eventually patient care;
6. Bridge the gap between nationally developed guidelines and outcomes research and their local application within Minnesota health care settings; and,
7. Continuously improve and automate the data acquisition and presentation methods.

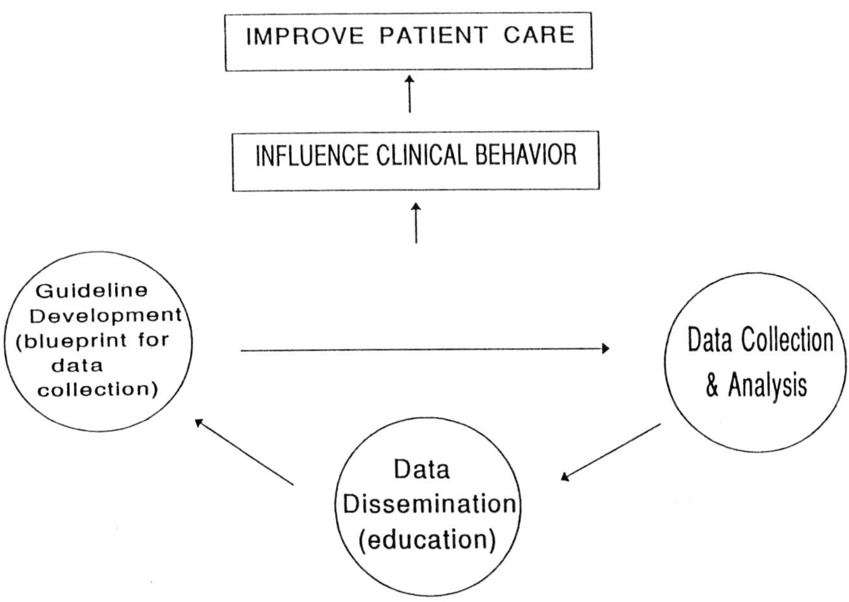

FIGURE 4. Overview of the Minnesota Clinical Comparison and Assessment Project.

PROGRAM IMPLEMENTATION

Barriers to a successful implementation of MCCAP were identified based on the experiences of the participants, a review of similar programs elsewhere and an evaluation of available research. Subsequently, strategies were devised to address these issues. Tables 1 through 5 outline the MCCAP strategies for dealing with: the concerns of individual clinicians and institutions, about guideline development and clinical performance evaluation, and technical barriers to a multi-site data acquisition, analysis and feedback program.

The MCCAP planners needed to address the concerns raised by sponsors and participants as a first priority. Concerns were raised about MCCAP being yet "another quality" program. There was great skepticism about the validity and reliability of clinical information systems already on the market. Performance information was already being generated from a variety of hospital departments, various hospitals, and multiple managed care programs. Clinicians voiced concerns about the use of clinical practice guidelines as "cookbook medicine." Dealing with these concerns quickly and directly was essential to the successful implementation of MCCAP.

TABLE 1

Individual Clinicians' Concerns About Implementation of MCCAP

The following concerns of clinicians were identified as potential barriers to MCCAP implementation:

INDIVIDUAL CLINICIANS' ISSUES	MCCAP RESPONSE
1. Performance review raises anxiety for most individuals and groups.	1. MCCAP has developed an educational and respectful educational environment in order to reduce anxiety about performance evaluation and improvement. Participation in MCCAP is voluntary.
2. Physicians feel targeted by the growing number of clinical review programs.	2. Clinical opinion leaders and other practicing physicians, hospital medical staffs and state medical associations were recruited to insure that MCCAP was implemented in a positive manner and for purposes related to improving patient care.
3. Clinicians distrust data systems with "black boxes."	3. All MCCAP materials and analyses plans are nonproprietary, collaboratively developed and openly reviewed.
4. Clinicians fear that invalid or unreliable data will be publicly disclosed.	4. MCCAP has a strict data policy. No data are publicly disclosed with physician or institution identifiers.
5. Clinicians fear that data will be used prematurely to establish reimbursement levels.	5. MCCAP's data policy and contracts with the hospitals state that MCCAP data are to be used for quality improvement activities only.
6. Physicians fear the loss of the patient/MD relationship, physician autonomy, and loss of the peer review process. They also feel conflicts between their patient advocacy and gatekeeper roles.	6. Hospital medical directors and staff, medical associations and specialty society leaders are heavily involved in MCCAP to ensure physician concerns are addressed. MCCAP stresses professional incentives for participation, especially patient care improvement possibilities.

An ongoing process of communication between MCCAP and its sponsors and participants was established to recognize the traditional values of local professional and clinical communities. In order to be responsive to the organizational cultures and interests of the participants, MCCAP communications stressed the voluntary nature of the program, its educational approach, and the mutual goals of MCCAP and the member hospitals. A reporting schedule was developed with the participating hospitals and associations to encourage coordination of overlapping projects.

In a very structural way, participation was built into the project's governance and operations. A highly participatory governance structure includes representation from member hospitals, medical staffs and state health care associations. Key hospital and association leaders were asked to join the HERF board in order to fully participate in the oversight of MCCAP. Executive directors and boards from the state hospital, metro hospital, and medical associations were approached for support prior to program implementation. Similarly, preliminary support was gained from CEOs and executive medical staff of each member hospital.

Advisory committees composed of medical directors, quality management directors, medical records directors and nursing directors were established in order to encourage integration of MCCAP activities and ongoing hospital activities.

Program Scope

Since 1989, MCCAP has published guidelines for five topics, chosen due to their high volume, treatment cost, suspected variation in treatment, suspected variation in patient outcomes, or clinical controversy regarding use of the procedure or treatment options. Guidelines address: total hip replacement, elective cholecystectomy, Cesarean birth, treatment of pediatric asthma and uncomplicated myocardial infarction.

TABLE 2

Institutional Concerns About Implementation of MCCAP

INSTITUTIONAL AND SYSTEM ISSUES	MCCAP RESPONSE
The following problems were identified as concerns of the member institutions:	
1. Health care institutions have difficulty determining how to evaluate and improve clinical care. This is a complex task; therefore, hospitals have had difficulty implementing effective quality evaluation and improvement programs.	1. MCCAP hospital CEOs, department leaders and excecutive medical staffs bring a great deal of collective expertise to the development of all aspects of the MCCAP. Extensive outside consultation and research expertise also have been sought.
2. Quality of care programs are undertaken by hospital CME, QA, QI, individual clinical departments, "study groups," and hospital administration but are poorly integrated.	2. MCCAP attempts to coordinate and focus hospital "quality of care" programs on specific topics.
3. A plethora of "quality" programs exist inside and outside hospitals. Clinicians and hospital staffs are overwhelmed and confused.	3. MCCAP attempts to coordinate the "quality" programs sponsored by local hospitals, medical societies and professional societies.

MCCAP guidelines were developed to serve the following functions:

1. To provide a mechanism in Minnesota to review and consolidate generally accepted indications for treatment, methods of treatment, and expected patient outcomes for specific clinical conditions and procedures.
2. To encourage clinician "buy-in" to the MCCAP process as a means to evaluate and improve clinical services.

TABLE 3

Barriers to Guideline Development and Dissemination

GUIDELINE DEVELOPMENT PROBLEMS	MCCAP RESPONSE
MCCAP needed to address the following issues in order to implement a guideline development program:	
1. Clinicians fear that the guidelines represent prescriptive "cookbook medicine."	1. MCCAP guidelines do attempt to standardize and codify local clinical practice. However, MCCAP emphasizes that these guidelines will be continually revised based on new research and outcome data. MCCAP also stresses that clinicians must take a lead in directing evaluation and improvement of patient care.
2. Clinicians fear that guidelines will become rigid standards and used for reimbursement and legal purposes.	2. All MCCAP guideline documents state that they are *not* standards and should be used as recommendations only.
3. Clinicians fear that guidelines will impede clinical advances and new technology and that they will become quickly outdated.	3. MCCAP guidelines are revised and updated regularly. Infusion of new information into clinical practice currently is a slow process and MCCAP provides a method to improve this process.
4. Clinicians criticize guidelines that summarize only processes of care and do not also include outcomes of care.	4. MCCAP guidelines not only discuss processes of care, but also include a section on "anticipated outcomes" at discharge and post-discharge.
5. Clinicians criticize guidelines that are developed by academics and don't relate to all practicing clinicians.	5. MCCAP panels are broadly representative of practicing and academic clinicians statewide. In the future, data from actual practice in Minnesota will be used to update the guidelines.
6. Clinicians distrust guidelines developed through the "consensus" panel process and prefer to use guidelines based on controlled trials or outcomes research.	6. MCCAP not only develops consensus guidelines but also collects outcomes data and appropriateness data from actual practice to modify and improve the original guidelines.
7. Clinicians distrust guidelines that are developed by large consensus groups and, therefore, can become very general and broad.	7. MCCAP guidelines are tied to an information system which is used to tighten and improve the specifications of the guidelines.
8. Clinicians and many others are critical of locally developed guidelines and believe they are "recreating the wheel" and are duplicating the work of national groups.	8. MCCAP guidelines rely on existing guidelines whenever possible and only add sections not available in other guidelines, especially sections on "anticipated outcomes." MCCAP stresses that local review of national guidelines is an essential step to facilitate local application.

3. To serve as the broad foundation or "logic statement" for MCCAP's clinical evaluation program.
4. To provide a framework to specify needed patient outcomes information required to improve future treatment recommendations.

The MCCAP research director, medical director, and quality assessment director attended all guideline panel meetings. They provided the majority of staff support for the panel, synthesized the materials and meeting discussions into the initial draft guideline documents and developed the corresponding data collection tools. The MCCAP staff also supervised a statewide review of all guidelines prior to publication and worked with the panel chair to synthesize the review comments and the draft guidelines for final publication.

TABLE 4

Barriers to Development of a Multi-Site Data Acquisition Program

DATA ACQUISITION PROBLEMS	MCCAP RESPONSE
In attempting to collect data across hospitals, the following problems were identified and strategies developed:	
1. It is difficult to design a data collection program for evaluation purposes since there is not clinical consensus (local or national) on appropriate treatments and expected outcomes for many clinical conditions and procedures. Therefore, it is difficult to determine what information is needed to evaluate the appropriateness, effectiveness or efficiency of the care provided.	1. MCCAP developed five sets of clinical practice guidelines to serve as the starting point for clinical evaluation and improvement. Thus, data collection forms were developed in conjunction with the guidelines.
2. Information is inconsistently recorded by physicians and other clinicians within and across institutions.	2. Nursing patient assessment instruments were enhanced and standardized across all MCCAP sites to include necessary baseline information and other information routinely not well documented. Detailed data abstracts and dictionaries were developed and tested at each hospital. Extensive data integrity checks also were implemented.
3. Existing proprietary data collection and analysis systems were evaluated. Several problems were found. All systems were expensive and none collected all of the information required for MCCAP, especially baseline and outcomes data. Also, clinical resistance to "black box" proprietary systems has been well documented.	3. MCCAP worked with hospitals to develop a standardized data collection system. The guideline panel members and other hospital clinicians participated in the development of the data collection tools and the analysis plan. Statistical modeling was used to "adjust" the outcomes information. Clinicians reviewed and suggested "adjuster" information to be used in the analysis process.
4. Patient outcomes data post-discharge and the corresponding patient baseline data at admission are often missing in medical records.	4. Nursing assessments at the MCCAP hospitals were developed to capture baseline information which corresponds to patient outcomes surveys completed six months post-discharge.

Barriers to Guideline Development

Barriers to guideline development and dissemination were identified on two levels—technical and emotional. The technical issues related to limitations of the

TABLE 5

Barriers to Effective Data Analysis and Presentation

DATA ANALYSIS AND PRESENTATION PROBLEMS	MCCAP RESPONSE
In attempting to analyze and present clinical information in a way that is useful to clinicians, the following problems were identified and strategies developed:	
1. Presentations to clinicians often use data grouped by ICD-9 or DRG. These groupings are not familiar to most clinicians and do not capture information in a clinically useful or familiar way.	1. MCCAP information is collected for narrowly defined, homogenous patient populations that correspond to clinical practice and, therefore, the information is clinically useful and relevant.
2. Due to the small sample sizes for specific conditions typically available within one hospital, the following types of information are presented to clinicians: • Data unadjusted for differences among patients (i.e. case-mix, risk, severity). • Non-comparative data. • Descriptive data. • Processes of care data, not outcomes data. • Data that emphasize variations around the group mean for specific issues (e.g. average length of stay, average use of certain drugs, therapies). Clinicians are often encouraged to comply with these group means.	2. MCCAP collects large sample sizes from multiple hospitals in order to do the following: • MCCAP data are adjusted for differences among patients. • MCCAP data are presented in a comparative format. • MCCAP collects and links appropriateness and outcomes information. • MCCAP recognizes that the group mean may be wrong and stresses the importance of patient outcomes information and outcomes-based guidelines to evaluate care. • MCCAP data attempt to focus on both compliance with guideline indications and actual practice. Where the two differ, further investigation is undertaken to determine if the guidelines should be altered, clinical practice changed or both.
3. Data are often presented by hospital staff, not clinical colleagues or practicing clinicians.	3. Practicing physicians are centrally involved involved in MCCAP data presentations.
4. Hospital programs are not coordinated with other professional programs and do not offer professional incentives for participation.	4. State medical associations and specialty societies are encouraged to become involved with MCCAP and collaborate on projects.
5. Proprietary data acquisition and analysis systems are often used which prevent open demonstration of the algorithms used to analyze the data.	5. MCCAP data acquisition and analysis processes are open and non-proprietary. Therefore, severity adjustment and other analysis methods can be fully disclosed.
6. Clinicians receive a plethora of information from health care payers, hospital quality management departments, and many other sources which are often contradictory and confusing to them.	6. MCCAP attempts to coordinate the "quality of care" programs within the participating hospitals in order to avoid duplicative and conflicting programs.
7. Information is often presented in a way that focuses on "outlier" physicians only, not the	7. MCCAP presents system-wide information and stresses opportunities for group improvement.

guidelines themselves such as their broad, general nature and narrative style and the difficulty of translating them into a measurement and evaluation system. See Table 3 for specific details.

Clinicians' deep feelings and resentments about guidelines also were identified as potential barriers to the implementation of the program. Clinicians voiced concerns about guidelines contributing to the standardization and de-personalization of health care. In response to concerns about "cookbook medicine", MCCAP leadership worked closely with medical associations, hospital executives and medical staffs to encourage physicians to take a proactive, leadership role in guideline development and to view this as an extension of their professional role and responsibility. Also, local clinical leaders were recruited to chair and be members of the guideline panels.

MCCAP guidelines were not represented as standards of care but rather the authors' and reviewers' best statement at a certain time about the appropriate and effective treatment for certain clinical conditions. Also, MCCAP guidelines were developed specifically to be used in conjunction with a data acquisition, analysis and presentation program. It was planned that MCCAP guidelines would be revised after MCCAP data are analyzed and clinical innovation occurs.

Guideline Scope and Format

In order to not "recreate the wheel" and to build on existing knowledge, MCCAP staff reviewed and evaluated a wide variety of guidelines for content and format. When the program began in 1989, however, no existing guidelines were found to completely meet the needs of the program. Therefore, sections from several existing guidelines were combined and expanded. For instance, for the MCCAP Cesarean Birth guidelines, we were able to use sections from the American College Obstetrics & Gynecology (ACOG), (1991) guidelines on Induction and Augmentation of Labor were used. Also, several guidelines from the "Clinical Efficacy Assessment Project" (C.E.A.P.) published by the American College of Physicians (ACP), (1987) were used.

In general, however, limitations were found with most existing sets of guidelines. Many guidelines related to processes of care with no information on outcomes of care. Due to their lack of outcomes information, the guidelines that were examined generally did not easily lend themselves to evaluations of the "effectiveness" of care. Patient risk or severity adjuster information (e.g. comorbidities) to modify patient outcomes was not found. Many guidelines outlined indications for procedures or treatments, especially diagnostic procedures such as endoscopy, but did not specify expected patient outcomes.

Research support for existing guidelines was limited. Many guidelines failed to clearly state the basis for their recommendations or rate the quality of the support for the recommendations (i.e. random controlled trials, research and/or clinical experience of panel members). Well-documented research to support guidelines development has been limited due to a variety of problems with research design and generalizability of findings. Particularly difficult to find was research related to the expected outcomes of treatment. In the future, the outcomes research and the guidelines being developed by the AHCPR and other national specialty societies should correct these problems.

Originally, an algorithm format similar to that used by the Harvard Community Health Plan Algorithm Program (Gottlieb, 1990) was presented to panel members to use as a model for guideline development. However, the panel criticized the algorithms for resembling recipes which did not capture the complexity of patient care. The review group also resisted taking the time to learn the algorithm formatting.

Getting Started on Guideline Development

The guideline format eventually chosen was adapted from a draft THR guideline developed by the American Academy of Orthopedics. The physician review panel judged this format to be concise but adequately inclusive. The section which specified the study population definitions was particularly valuable. See Figure 5 for the format and information included in MCCAP guidelines.

FIGURE 5. MCCAP Guideline Format

	Data Element	Data Source
I. Condition or procedure Population Definition/Description (codes)		
II. Indications for Hospitalization or Procedure a) Admission functional status/previous medical management b) Admission/procedure appropriateness		
III. Processes of Care a) Procedure appropriateness b) Process measures/management issues		
IV. Anticipated Outcomes a) Mortality ALSO Disposition Functional status - at discharge and post-discharge Patient satisfaction - post-discharge Complications Other condition - specific measures b) Modifiers (case-mix, risk, severity adjusters)		
V. Supporting Evidence		
VI. Recommendation Grading System a) **Grade A** *Large randomized control trials* with clear-cut results and with a low risk of false-positive or false-negative error. b) **Grade B** *Small randomized control trials* with less certain results and with a moderate to high risk of false-positive and/or false-negative error. c) **Grade C** *Non-randomized cohort and historical comparisons,* the subjects of which did and did not receive the therapy under question, as well as uncontrolled case series.		

In order to be representative of practice styles in a variety of settings state-wide, letters were sent to the Medical Directors or Chiefs of Staff, Nursing Directors, and Quality Management Directors at all Minnesota hospitals requesting names of candidates to serve on the guideline panels as well as the state and county medical associations and specialty societies. Consequently, the guideline panels consisted of academic and practicing physicians, nurses and quality management representatives from rural and urban areas, and from large, multi-specialty institutions and small community hospitals. Family practitioners as well as specialists and surgeons and referring physicians, as appropriate, were recruited for all panels.

The panels were led by a chair and co-chair who assumed responsibility for the structure of the panel meetings, assignment of the workload between meetings, final approval of the guidelines prior to publication, and updating of the guidelines after publication. The panel chair and co-chair also assisted with analysis of the data related to the guidelines and presentation of the aggregate data to the participating hospitals. In the near future, the guideline panels will be reconvened to review the aggregate data to determine if the guidelines need revision.

The THR Consensus panel was the first to meet. All guideline meetings were held in the evening with dinner since panel members were all practicing clinicians recruited from institutions statewide. The number and duration of meetings required to complete the final guideline draft varied from panel to panel. One group finished a guideline draft after two four-hour meetings within a six-week period. Others met for three hours on a monthly basis for six to nine months.

The THR panel influenced, to a great degree, the work of the other panels. Initially, MCCAP staff proposed that the guidelines cover broad conditions and procedures. However, the THR panel discussed, at length, whether they should attempt to write guidelines for all THR patients or a subset of the group. As was to be the case with all of the other MCCAP panels, the THR panel chose to concentrate on a fairly narrowly defined homogenous THR patient group*. The clinicians stated that this grouping of patients was treated in a similar way which allowed them to specify how they typically treated their patients. The clinicians said they could "relate to" or "visualize" this group of patients. The clinicians were adamant that DRG or ICD-9 groupings were unfamiliar to them and did not represent how they mentally grouped patients. Therefore, the surgeons were able to outline clear indications and treatment options for this patient group. Prior to this decision, the group had trouble focusing their discussion since they had difficulty developing recommendations that were applicable to all subsets of THR patients. The other four guideline panels had similar experiences. All groups agreed that it was much easier and more clinically useful to them to develop separate sets of guidelines for subsets of patients within a broad patient population. Thus, we developed guidelines for non-acute elective cholecystectomies rather than all cholecystectomies and uncomplicated myocardial infarctions instead of all acute myocardial infarctions.

---

*Replacement of the articular surfaces of the acetabulum and femoral head with appropriate fixation of components to bone on the pelvic and femoral side of the hip joint, or in certain cases, "bipolar" femoral-acetabular arthroplasty.

This information was very helpful to MCCAP staff not only in terms of improved skills at guideline development, but it also provided important insights later about analysis and feedback of this information. We concluded that if clinicians had difficulty outlining indications for treatment and expected patient outcomes for broad categories of patients, they also would probably have difficulty applying and using feedback information about these same broad grouping of patients.

Concurrent with developing guidelines, the panel members and MCCAP staff also developed data collection tools to acquire key information such as treatment and procedure indications, patient outcomes and severity adjusters which corresponded to the guidelines. MCCAP staff worked concurrently with the panel to identify data elements and sources for this key information.

Once each of the guideline drafts was completed, it was prepared by the MCCAP quality assessment director for statewide review. The draft guidelines were sent with a review form to appropriate departments at all Minnesota hospitals. Family practioners reviewed all guideline sets. Phone interviews also were conducted with selected groups to gain further in-depth reviews. The review comments were synthesized for the review panel and the draft guidelines were revised and published. The guidelines were sent to the offices of all specialists and referring physicians in the study areas and to all Minnesota hospitals.

Associated Costs of Guideline Development

The typical expenses related to guideline development included: panel member consultant fees; staff salaries and expenses (quality management, nurses, research staff, physician); literature searches; meeting rooms and meals; travel expenses; duplicating and mailing expenses; and guideline review by survey or phone interviews.

MCCAP guidelines have required approximately $40,000 per guideline to develop plus the volunteer effort of the panel members and review groups. As part of a grass roots effort, MCCAP panel members volunteered their time and travel expenses. This often involved two to three-hour travel time plus the meeting time. MCCAP's largest guideline development expenses were those required to support one full-time quality assessment person for a nine-month period and a part-time physician to assist the panels. Duplicating and mailing expenses associated with statewide review and publication of the guidelines were the other major expense areas.

Data Acquisition, Analysis and Presentation

Clinical practice guidelines are the focus of this chapter; however, a description of the MCCAP guidelines program would not be complete without some information on the data collection and presentation components of MCCAP.

In planning for the collection of data from multiple hospitals throughout Minnesota, several barriers to successful implementation were identified and addressed. See Table 4 for specific details.

Hospital cooperation with MCCAP was extraordinary allowing data acquisition to begin with few start-up delays or unforeseen events. This has been attributed to the following:

- The MCCAP organization and governance structure had developed a tremendous sense of "ownership" of MCCAP among the consortium members which encouraged them to make MCCAP work.
- Extensive hospital executive level and clinician support encouraged hospital staffs to implement the program.
- MCCAP employed medical record abstractors to collect data rather than adding to the work of existing hospital staffs. Staff reciprocated with extensive cooperation with MCCAP.
- Extensive prior planning with key staffs which resulted in close working relationships between MCCAP and consortium staffs throughout implementation.

In 1991, data collection—medical record abstraction and post discharge patient surveys—began at thirty-six hospitals for all patients who fell within the scope of the MCCAP guidelines on elective cholecystectomy (3,500 patients including laparascopic), total hip replacement (2,500 patients) and Cesarean birth (2,700) patients). Presentation of MCCAP data analysis findings began in January, 1993 at each of the participating hospitals.

MCCAP data analysis and presentation were planned collaboratively with the member hospitals and research consultants. Certain commonly used data analysis and presentation methods that are commonly used by hospitals and health plans were identified by MCCAP as barriers which may interfere with effective evaluation and improvement programs. See Table 5 for specific details.

Hospital Appications of MCCAP

MCCAP has provided the member hospitals with many essential tools for quality of care evaluation and improvement (See Figure 6). Member hospitals have used MCCAP in various ways, but primarily as their collective resource for comparative "quality of care" information. Most hospitals have coordinated their internal quality improvement programs around the topics chosen for evaluation by MCCAP. Beginning in the summer 1993, hospitals are expected the use of MCCAP data to their external audiences including patients, health plans and large purchasing groups.

Use of MCCAP Guidelines

In general, MCCAP Guidelines have served a key role for member hospitals. Clinicians who participated in MCCAP studies stated that the guidelines provided an opportunity for their input prior to the MCCAP evaluation of care at their hospitals; therefore, the guidelines provided the basis for an open, "fair" and respectful evaluation program. The guidelines also provided a clear statement of the clinical logic that supported treatment recommendations and expectations for the overall evaluation process.

The HealthSpan hospitals in Minnesota have been involved in all MCCAP studies. John Kleinman, M.D., Vice President, Medial Affairs, Unity Hospital, says, "Our hospital has benefitted from using the locally developed MCCAP guidelines because guidelines that are not tested locally are similar to the recent

treatment methods and their impact on patient outcomes were linked. For example, at the feedback sessions, surgeons questioned MCCAP guideline recommendations for prophylactic antibiotics prior to performing an elective cholecystectomy. However, the MCCAP staff was able to compare patients who received antibiotics and those who did not and demonstrated that the two did not have a significantly different wound infection rate (See Figure 9). With this additional information, the guideline recommendations were taken much more seriously and quality improvement groups at many hospitals were formed to consider changing antibiotic use. John Kleinman, M.D., Vice President Medical Affairs, Unity Hospital, says, "The MCCAP information is useful in that it has enabled us to ask the 'why' questions. The MCCAP information has shown us that outcomes of elective cholecystectomy patients who receive prophylactic antibiotics are not different from the outcomes of patients who do not receive prophylactic antibiotics. We are now asking ourselves 'Why are some of us ordering prophylactic antibiotics in all cases of elective cholecystectomies?' " Paul Bowlin, M.D., Corporate Medical Director, Fairview Hospital and Healthcare Services, a multi-hospital system in Minnesota, says, "We have just begun to know and extract information from this data. We need to identify whether the guidelines need to be revised based on the outcomes analysis or evaluate ourselves, specifically in the areas of prophylactic antibiotics, when surgery should be done and the use of cholangiograms. Either way, this analysis will lead to patient care improvement and significant cost savings."

FIGURE 7

Persistence of Most Distressing Symptom at 6 Months After Elective Cholecystectomy

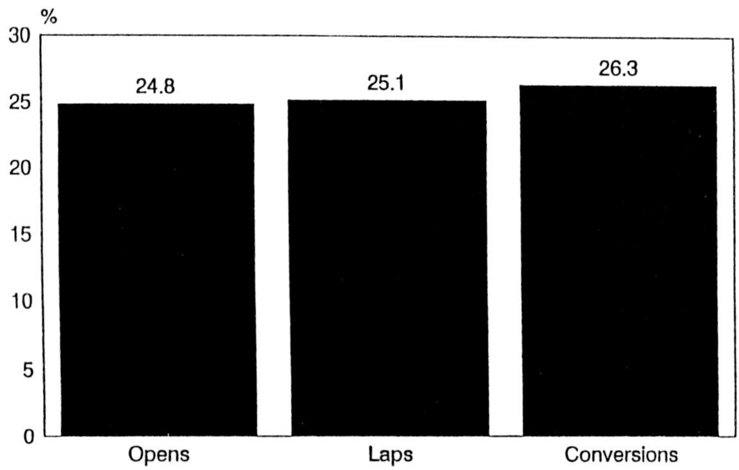

not significant n=2397

Finally, the use of guidelines with outcomes information enhanced hospitals' routine quality assessment activities and raised questions about some traditional quality assurance methods. In most cases, quality assessment programs tend to look at "average" occurrences (i.e., average length of stay, average resource use, etc.) and attempt to bring "outliers" closer to the average. But, MCCAP has demonstrated that the average is not always the ideal. Figure 10 shows the average use of cholangiograms and what it should be if cholangiograms were performed for the indications suggested by MCCAP guidelines and outcomes information. Note the marked difference between the two rates (i.e. hospital average and hospital appropriateness). It is estimated that the difference between the two rates involves approximately $900,000 in health care expenditures. This type of analysis has assisted the quality assurance departments at MCCAP hospitals, but also has underscored the limited value of "averages" and the importance of using guidelines and outcomes information.

MCCAP Evolution

Although MCCAP was initially developed for hospitals' internal quality improvement purposes, many hospitals have broadened its application. For example, Fairview Hospital and Healthcare Services and the HealthEast hospitals in St. Paul, Minnesota will be using their findings from the MCCAP Elective Cholecystectomy, Total Hip Replacement and Cesarean Birth studies to form clinical pathways teams to address identified improvement opportunities. These pathways programs will serve internal purposes but also will be part of a collaborative venture with the Employers Association Health Care Buyers Coalition, a local business coalition, and the Prudential Plus Program in Minnesota.

FIGURE 8

Hospital XYZ: Post Surgery Return to Work Days

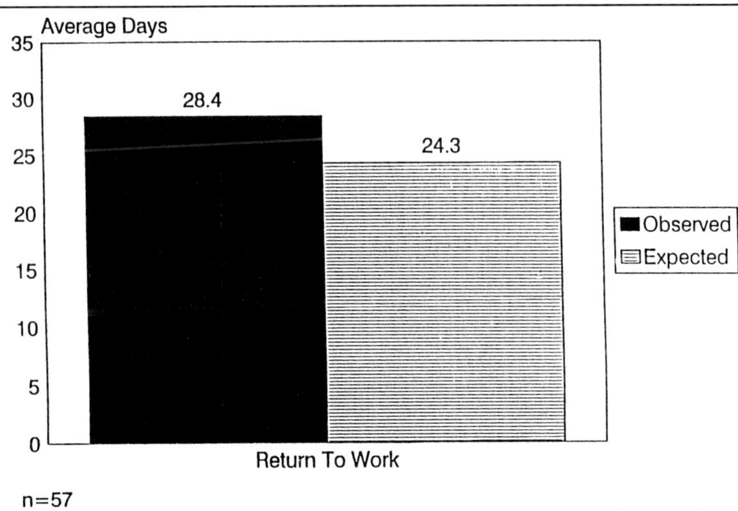

LESSONS LEARNED

Four years ago, many were very skeptical that a voluntary, grass-roots quality improvement program could be effectively implemented or sustained by a consortium of competing health care institutions. Contrary to this, the size of the MCCAP consortium has doubled and a guideline development, outcomes research and feedback program are operational across fifty-three Minnesota hospitals and clinics.

Since 1989, MCCAP has functioned as a "natural laboratory" to test the feasibility of implementing an effective program which incorporates clinical guidelines, analysis of patient outcomes information and information dissemination to clinicians. Hopefully, the MCCAP experience will be helpful to assist in the current national health care debate which often cites guideline development and outcomes management as key "quality improvement" tools.

Guideline Effectiveness

The usefulness of MCCAP guidelines is being evaluated on two dimensions:

1. Are the MCCAP guideline recommendations valid and therefore, does compliance with these recommendations improve patient outcomes?
2. Do MCCAP guidelines influence clinical decision-making and behavior change ultimately, patient care?

To date, our experience with evaluating the validity of MCCAP guidelines has been limited to our Elective Cholecystectomy guidelines and our success is mixed. The validity of these guideline recommendations varies and points to the value of

FIGURE 9

Incidence of Postop Wound Infections by Use of Prophylactic Antibiotics

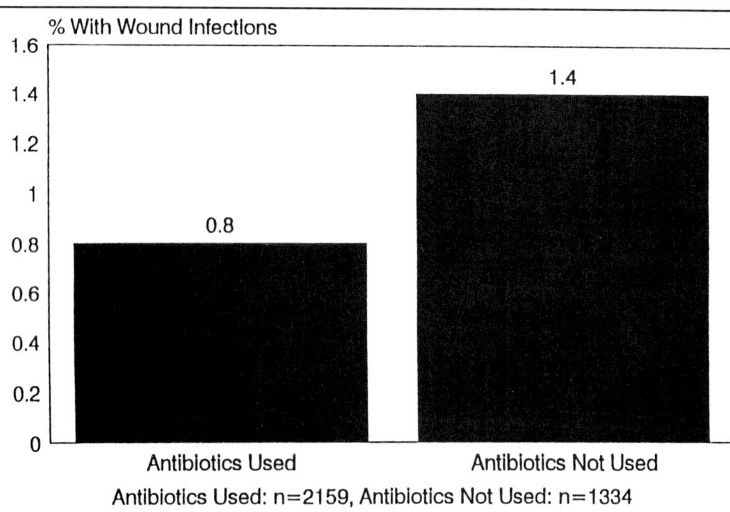

patient outcomes data for evaluating and improving recommendations. After analyzing the MCCAP Elective Cholecystectomy outcomes data, we have found that some MCCAP guidelines recommendations are effective at linking processes of care and positive patient outcomes and others are not. For example, the MCCAP indications for cholangiograms and prophylactic antibiotics appear to be valid; however, the recommendations on indications for cholecystectomies need to be improved based on our outcomes findings. Figures 11 and 12 illustrate these findings. Figure 11 shows that where cholangiograms were undertaken in compliance with MCCAP guideline recommendations, the reported clinical findings (e.g., presence of gallstones, bilary stricture) warranted the procedure. However, very few clinical findings were found to warrant the cholangiograms that were performed and did not comply with MCCAP recommendations.

Overall compliance with MCCAP guideline indications for Elective Cholecystectomy was 88%. However, unlike previous guideline programs, MCCAP was able to evaluate these guideline recommendations with patient outcomes data. Figure 7 shows that almost 25% of the Elective Cholecystectomy patients reported significant post-surgery symptoms that resembled pre-surgery symptoms. Compliance with MCCAP recommendations for Elective Cholecystectomy did not improve the chances that patients would not report significant symptoms post surgery (See Figure 12). We are now studying in depth the patient population with significant post-surgery symptoms in order to revise MCCAP recommendations for appropriate use of Elective Cholecystectomy.

We also will evaluate whether the publication of MCCAP guidelines influenced or changed clinical behavior in Minnesota. Unfortunately, we can not completely answer this question at this time since we do not have firm evidence that any changes

FIGURE 10

Use of Cholangiograms by Hospital

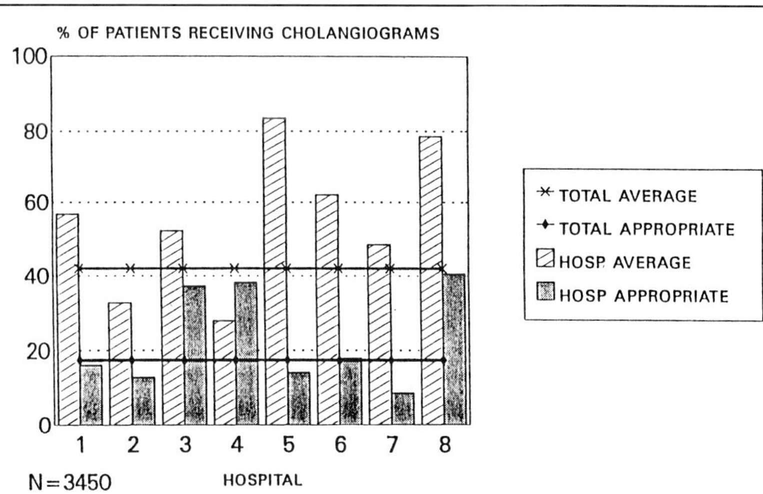

in local clinical practice patterns were attributable to the publication of MCCAP guidelines. We hope to answer this question with our two new federal grants which are currently underway. However, we do have some experience and antedotal findings. Our initial skepticism about the effectivenss of guidelines alone in changing clinical behavior was confirmed. We sought extensive clinical review and input to the MCCAP guidelines before publication. Few changes were suggested to the draft guidelines and most clinician input suggested a great deal of consensus with the guidelines. After this statewide review we sent a copy of the guidelines to all Minnesota hospitals and physicians' offices. However, a year later when we went to the hospitals to present MCCAP data, we discovered that few practitioners had read the guidelines in depth and many did not remember receiving them at all. Therefore, it is doubtful that the publication of MCCAP guidelines had much impact on local practice. However, as noted earlier, MCCAP guidelines did serve a very important role in the over-all MCCAP program since they were viewed by clinicians as the basis for an open and "fair" evaluation program. This experience reinforced our original commitment to linking guidelines to a data collection and feedback program.

Currently, we are presenting Elective Cholecystectomy and Cesarean Birth data to the medical staffs at the participating hospitals. In order to review and reinforce the guidelines and link them to clinical evaluation, we are presenting sections of the guidelines in an algorithmic format with the corresponding data that has been analyzed in aggregate and hospital-specific groupings. Thus, when we present appropriateness information on Elective Cholecystectomy patients, we first outline the guideline indications for the procedure and then present our findings for each hospital compared to the others. This appears to be an effective way to review and reinforce the guidelines with clinicians.

FIGURE 11

Operative and Pathological Findings by Adherence to Cholangiogam Guidelines

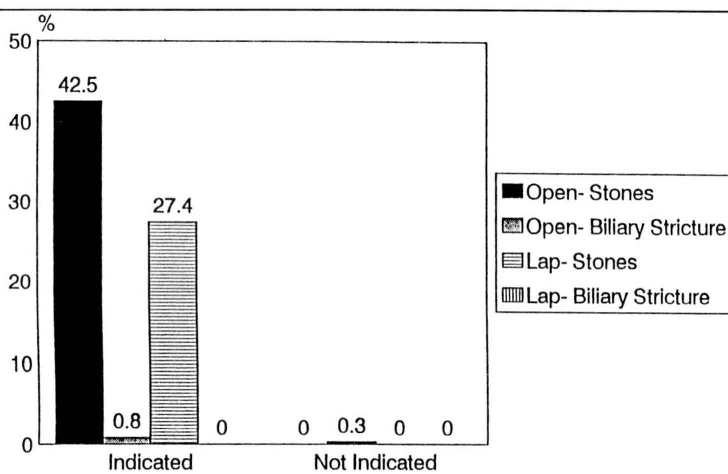

Indicated: open n=254, laps n=106 Not Indicated: open n=376, laps n=612

The amount of compatibility of nationally developed guidelines with locally developed guidelines was surprising to us. The MCCAP Uncomplicated Myocardial Infarction consensus panel was near completion of its work before the members had access to the Myocardial Infarction guidelines developed by the American College of Cardiology (ACC) and the American Heart Association (AHA) (1990). However, the recommendations in both documents were almost identical. We had a similar experience with the MCCAP Pediatric Asthma guidelines and those published by the National Heart, Lung and Blood Institute, (1991). Like others, we had assumed that we would find more differences than we did. This experience has reinforced our intention to de-emphasize development of guidelines and instead, focus on applying and/or endorsing guidelines developed by national organizations and the federal government.

However, the importance of local guideline review and endorsement should not be minimized. Even when we used nationally developed guidelines, we still found it important to have local clinical opinion leaders associated with the guidelines to not only lend their authority but also act as informal advisors to practicing clinicians about the guideline recommendations. For example, MCCAP developed guidelines for the treatment of "uncomplicated" Myocardial Infarction patients but did not form another panel to develop guidelines for the remainder of the MI population. Instead, we asked a local panel to simply review and endorse the guidelines developed by the ACC and the AHA (1990). We are now evaluating any differences in local acceptance of these guidelines without other locally developed guidelines.

The costs and amount of work, however, needed for "outcomes" evaluations are often underestimated. Also, the importance of two grops of data—1) patient functional status ad admission and 2) outcome, risk-adjustment data—are often

FIGURE 12

Persistence of Most Distressing GI Symptom at 6 Months by Adherence to Guidelines

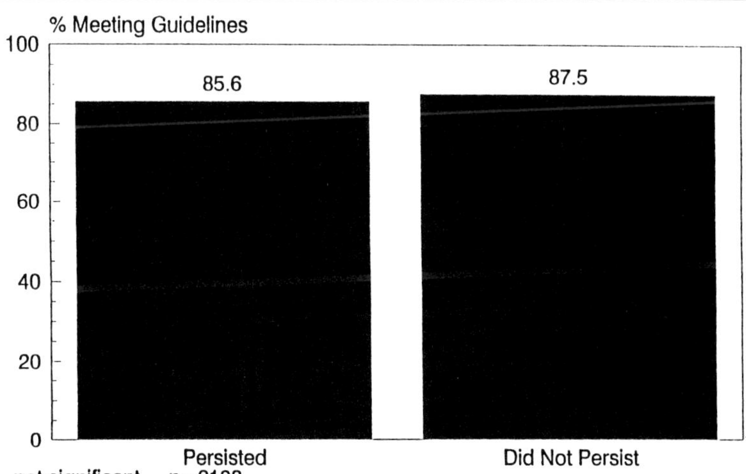

minimized or overlooked. However, this information is essential for outcomes analysis. We must know the functional status of patients at the time of hospital admission in order to evaluate the impact of hospital treatment on the patient after discharge. In other words, if we expect a patient to play the piano after discharge, we must know if he could play prior to the hospitalization. In order to evaluate the effectiveness of the hospital intervention, we must know what patient "risk" factors (i.e. age, co-morbidity) are present which may interfere with the expected outcomes for "average" patients treated in a similar manner. However, this information is not routinely documented in medical records. Therefore, we have had to change and standardize nursing admission assessment tools and require nursing staffs to interview patients.

In order to gain post-discharge "outcomes" information, we are collecting outcomes data from patients through surveys and interviews in the hospital and after discharge. Tracking patients for surveys after discharge often becomes cumbersome and costly since 1) only sixty percent of our patients returned surveys after two requests and we had to phone thirty percent for interviews; and, 2) certain patient populations are transient and difficult to track. Finally, most risk-adjustment information also is costly to acquire since it not only usually requires medical record abstraction but also, it is not routinely documented in a standardized way in the medical record and, therefore, often requires development and use of a "new" form or protocol. The costs and difficulty of evaluating the appropriateness of care also are underestimated. In order to do this type of evaluation, we must know if and what kind of medical treatment was undertaken prior to hospitalization or to a procedure. This usually requires information from a sophisticated claims system, medical record or clinic record. This information also is not routinely in the medical record or not recorded in a standardized manner. Again, in order to acquire this information, we have had to introduce new protocols or standardize existing assessments which has been difficult to do and was costly.

Unfortunately, at this time guidelines can rarely be literature based and clinical experience must be used as the basis for many guideline recommendations. However, if this is done, recommendations should be differentiated by their level of support (i.e. findings based on random-controlled trials, large studies but not randomized, or the clinical experience of panel) in order to allow the reader to evaluate the strength of the recommendation. Also, it is important to state on the guideline documents the sources and time frames for the recommendations since most guidelines represent "best care" at a certain point in time and will need revisions to remain current.

Certain important aspects of guideline development are often underrated. The process of guideline development itself must be carefully undertaken since many decisions about the process itself do effect the final guideline. In particular, panel leadership and panel composition are key components of the guideline development process. A committed panel leader is essential. Ideally, the panel leader should have good interpersonal skills to encourage participation and good management skills to complete the work required. A mix of specialists, referring physicians and family practitioners on the panel is essential to address issues of procedure and appropriateness and effectiveness of treatment options. For example, the family practitioners on the Total Hip Replacement panel were very interested in the indications for the procedure such as types of medical management to be tried prior to a total hip replacement. The surgeons focused heavily on the procedure itself. A mix of panel members helps to insure that full continuum of care for specific conditions is considered. Non-physicians also serve critical roles on guideline panels. Nurses are extremely helpful at outlining patient care after surgery and patient education. Quality Assessment staff played a key role on MCCAP panels by integrating the guidelines with clinical evaluation and improvement activities. MCCAP research staff was required to assist the panel members evaluate research findings and journal publications. The research staff also helped insure that the panel developed guidelines which could be incorporated into clinical evaluation and improvement programs.

The time, effort and expense required for guideline development are usually grossly underestimated by program participants and organizers. The panel members and especially the panel chairs committed more time and effort to the guideline process than they expected. Several panel members had participated in hospital quality management programs which usually require a limited time commitment and minimal work for clinicians. Contrary to this, each MCCAP panel member was asked to assume primary responsibility for a section of the guidelines. This included undertaking a literature search, writing a guideline section and presenting it to the other panel members. On average, members had to commit up to nine months of time with monthly meetings and a significant amount of work between meetings. The panel members also had to commit to reconvene and update the guidelines in the future. Finally, the work itself was unfamiliar to the panelists. Many panel members had limited experience with evaluating research and literature for the guidelines and required a great deal of staff support.

Overall, guidelines for procedures were far easier for the panels to develop than guidelines for clinical conditions. Panel members had the least amount of trouble developing guidelines for how to do a procedure or how to diagnose and treat a condition. They encountered more difficulty specifying the indications for a procedure or treatment and the most difficulty in specifying patient outcomes and risk adjusters for patient outcomes. MCCAP staff had to provide a great deal of assistance to the panel in order to complete these sections of the guidelines. The MCCAP staff also assumed primary responsibility for linking the guidelines to data collection (i.e. data sources and elements) and analysis.

As noted earlier, guidelines were much easier for clinicians to develop if the topics were narrowly defined and if the patient groupings resembled those clinicians recognized as "typical patients." Now that we're feeding back data to physicians, this experience has been repeated. Quite often when we have encountered resistance to our data, we have alleviated the problem by reminding the group of the defined study population. This appears to provide a great deal of clarity for the physicians and enables them to identify what they typically do for these types of patients and then evaluate their methods more precisely. Thus, we have found it very important to remind ourselves about the direct relationship of guidelines to data analysis and presentation if clinical behavior change is our goal.

Currently, the costs of data collection/analysis and presentation are approximately $50 per case. Costs include specific analysis costs, extensive data integrity checks, patient tracking and other expenses not routinely calculated in "average costs" per patient by proprietary systems. The major cost components are the patient surveys and interviews and the medical record abstraction. These two activities account for approximately $35-$40 on average per patient. We have not found any ways to reduce these costs either through increased automation or use of current proprietary data collection systems. We have considered using the Uniform Clinical Data Sets (UCDS), currently under development by the Health Care Financing Administration (HCFA), and have been impressed with its potential as a data collection system for MCCAP. At this time, however, we would need to augment the UCDS with our own data monitoring and integrity program and patient survey program.

Consequently, we are currently recommending that MCCAP and other clinical evaluation programs be implemented using a combination of health plan claims data, medical record information and patient-generated information. Increasingly, we will be using claims data to monitor, evaluate and identify opportunities for improvement in a certain covered populations. When improvement opportunities are identified which will require intensive study and probably require clinical behavior change, MCCAP or a MCCAP-like program will be implemented. Thus, the use of MCCAP-like programs will be reserved for focused priority areas where intensive clinical information is required. This may be the best way to benefit from MCCAP's strengths and conserve and focus future resources.

FUTURE CHALLENGES

In order to be relevant in today's health care environment, MCCAP is evolving to address the urgent need of health care consumers and purchasers for publicly disclosed clinical evaluation information. Currently, the MCCAP board is addressing this issue by revising the original data policy to allow broader disclosure of data. Also, the Healthcare Education and Research Foundation (HERF), the originator and coordinating organization for MCCAP, has attempted to address the need for clinical evaluation information by developing a new and separate program which builds on the MCCAP experience and methodology but is explicitly developed to evaluate and publicly disclose clinical performance information.

The ultimate question for MCCAP will be whether the program can influence clinical decision-making and improve the appropriateness, effectiveness and efficiency of patient care. In three years after the completion of our two studies with Stephen Soumerai, Sc.D. and Edward Guadagnoli, Ph.D., we will be able to answer this question with much more certainty.

Ultimately, the benefits of programs like MCCAP must be weighed against their costs. At this point, we are attempting to conserve resources by prioritizing and focusing our study areas and by building, to a greater degree, on the work currently underway by national groups and the federal government. Over-all, our experience with MCCAP has convinced us that changing health care delivery is possible, but that often expectations are inappropriately raised about single "new" strategies. We believe programs should be built on what has been learned by not only health researchers, but also by others in related fields. In particular, that new and more sophisticated information systems alone are not what are required to improve health care. Improved information systems must be used in combination with strategies that focus on the interpersonal and organizational forces that affect health care delivery. A combination of technical, interpersonal and organizational considerations must be recognized and addressed in order to not just evaluate but, in fact, improve health care delivery.

ACKNOWLEDGEMENTS

We would like to thank the following organizations and individuals for their continued support of the MCCAP: the 53 participating health care institutions and medical staffs, the Minnesota Hospital Association and Metropolitan Healthcare Council, the Minnesota Medical Association, Hennepin and Ramsey County Medical Societies (the Minneapolis and St. Paul Societies) also provided extensive assistance and consultation. Robert Kane, M.D., Professor, School fo Public Health, University of Minnesota and Nicole Lurie, M.D., Assistant Professor, Division of Health Service Research and Policy, University of Minnesota, Edward Guadagnoli, Ph.D., Assistant Professor and Stephen Soumerai, Sc.D., Associated Professor who have provided research expertise. Finally, none of this work would be possible without the dedicated MCCAP liaisons, panel members, task forces and, very importantly, the MCCAP staff—Lynda Dent, Joanne Engwer, Shannon Flood, Shirley Germann, Barbara McLaughlin and Nora Morris.

REFERENCES

American College of Physicians. 1987. "Clinical Efficacy Assessment Project."

American College of Gynecologists, "Induction and Augmentation of Labor, *ACOG Technical Bulletin,* July, 1991: Number 157.

Berwick, D.M. 1989. "Sounding Board: Continuous Improvement As An Ideal in Health Care?" *New England Journal of Medicine*; 320(1):53-56.

Borbas, Catherine. 1988. "Comparison of Patient Illness Severity Systems - Implications for Hospital Implementation and Assessment of Medical Practice, June, 1988.

Eddy, D.M. 1990. "Anatomy of Decision," *JAMA,* 263:441-443.

Eddy, D.M. 1990. "Practice Policy—What are They?" *JAMA,* 263:877-880.

Eddy, D.M. 1990. "Guidelines for Policy Statements: The Explicit Approach," *JAMA,* 263:2493-2505.

Eisenberg, J.M. 1986. *Doctors' Decisions & The Cost of Medical Care,* An Arbor, MI: Health Administration Press Perspectives.

Ellwood, P.M. 1988. "Shattuck Lecture - Outcomes Management: A Technology of Patient Experience," *New England Journal of Medicine,* (318):1549-56.

Gottlieb, L.K., Margolis, C.Z. and S.C. Schoenbaum. 1990. "Clinical Practice Guidelines at an HMO: Development and Implementation in a Quality Improvement Model," *Quality Review Bulletin,* 16:80-86.

Lomas, Jonathan. 1989. "Promoting Clinical Policy Change: Using Art to Promote the Science in Medicine," in Anderson, T.F. Mooney (eds.): *The Challenge of Medical Practice Variations,* London: MacMillan Press.

Lomas, Jonathan, et al. 1989. "Do Practice Guidelines Guide Practice," *New England Journal of Medicine,* (321):1307-1311.

Lomas, Jonathan, et al. 1989. Do Practice Guidelines Guide Practice," *New England Journal of Medicine,* (321):1307-1311.

Mittman, B., Tonesk, X. and P. Jacobson. 1992. "Implementing Clinical Practice Guidelines: Social Influence Strategies and Practitioner Behavior Change," *Quality Review Bulletin,* (18:12) 413-422.

Roper, W.L., Winkenwerder, W., Hackbarth, G.M. and H. Krakauer. 1988. "Effectiveness in Health Care. An Initiative to Evaluate and Improve Medical Practice," *New England Journal of Medicine,* (319):1197-202.

Soumerai, S.B. and J. Avorn. 1990. "Principles of Educational Outreach (Academic Detailing) to Improve Clinical Decision Making," *Journal of the American Medical Association,* (263):549-556.

Thomas, J. William, Ph.D., Ashcraft, Marie, Ph.D. and Janet Zimmerman, M.P.P. 1986. "An Evaluation of Alternative Severity of Illness Measures for Use by University Hospitals." Prepared for the University Hospital Consortium, December 29, 1986. The University of Michigan, Ann Arbor, Michigan.

Williamson, J.W. et al. 1982. *Teaching Quality Assurance & Cost Containment in Health Care: A Faculty Guide* (San Francisco: Jossey BASS).

Medicine and Health Care Into the Twenty-First Century. Edited by S.K. Majumdar, L.M. Rosenfeld, D.B. Nash and A.M. Audet. © 1995, The Pennsylvania Academy of Science.

Chapter Twelve

PRACTICE PROFILES AND PHYSICIAN FEEDBACK: The Mount Sinai Experience with a Cesarean Section Reduction Initiative and Physician Credentialing

STEPHEN A. MYERS, D.O.
Chairman, Maternal/Fetal Medicare
Department of Obstetrics and Gynecology
Mount Sinai Hospital
California Ave. at 15th St., Rm. F208
Chicago, IL 60608

INTRODUCTION

While not revolutionary, the changes currently taking place in delivery of health care, and those anticipated to occur, should certainly be described as being an "accelerated evolution." And one small component of that process is the current trend of analyzing the effectiveness of care; the "outcomes movement."

This work will describe one Department's experience with "keeping track of what we do." The description will focus primarily on the process and the journey, rather than on the medical specifics of what was accomplished. The process which began as simple data collection, evolved into a comprehensive physician feedback system, will be presented associated with our *initial* goal of a cesarean section reduction initiative. But also presented will be the further application by this Department of these principals to a broader-based quality assurance system and the subsequent development of practice profiles and their use for credentialing and reappointment. This journey has taken seven years (so far). To be sure, it is not presented to represent either a "final product" or as the "only way," but rather as simply one example of what can be done.

BACKGROUND

Experience with physician feedback and, more importantly, its effect on modifying physician behavior is surprisingly limited. Compared to the explosive growth in the medical literature over the past several decades, there are a paucity of published reports. Perhaps the fact that the subject lacks significant scientific background, offers no high technology, and deals with illusive notions that are generally difficult to quantitate, have contributed to the comparative lack of published experience.

Indeed, not until more than a decade after tonsillectomy, for example, had ceased becoming a common pediatric operation, did the first links related to physician feedback begin to appear. In 1977, Wennberg, et al. reported that physician feedback in tonsillectomy rates played a significant role in the decreased utilization in a five year period between 1969 and 1973 (1). In their discussion, they note that only two previous reports existed linking physician feedback to changing surgical practices; one from 1959 related to pelvic surgery (2), and a Canadian experience related to hysterectomy audits from 1977 (3). They prophetically wrote that "the hypothesis that feedback of data on incidence of procedures can lead to a reduction in variation . . . needs further testing" (1). Three years later, the same conclusion regarding the effect of feedback on tonsillectomy was published by Moore and Pratt (4). They conclude that education of physicians, including comparative rates of the procedure had its own effect on utilization.

Similar experiences were beginning to be reported, particularly in the area of cost containment. In 1974, Buck and White found reviewing billing claims and charges resulted in changes in physician practice (5). In 1979, Lawrence identified the role of physician education in Cost Containment by use of identifying individual utilization (6). Paris, et al. in 1980 demonstrated the impact of a surveillance program on practice patterns in an ambulatory setting (7). In 1980, Martin, et al. found that physician feedback had a dramatic effect on test-ordering behavior of medical residents while financial incentives had no effect (8). And by 1981, Eisenberg and Williams reviewed several strategies related to changing physician practice pattern and emphasize the importance of feedback as an element of "education" (9). They conclude that, "A broader definition of education might include feedback to the physician about his pattern of practice." (9) They note that such feedback, ". . . plays on the physicians sense of achievement and desire to excel. Feedback, therefore, inevitably involves a more subtle reinforcement or admonition for current behavior" (9).

Physician Feedback and Cesarean Section

The obstetrical literature is replete with articles related to route of delivery and obstetric outcome, as well as it should be. But by 1981, the National Institutes of Health had already expressed concern over increasing cesarean utilization, (10) a concern echoed by the obstetrical staff at Mount Sinai (11). At the same time, several authors began to explore the role of the physician in the cesarean phenomenon and the possible role of physician feedback in controlling cesarean rates. In 1982, Rosenberg et al. observed a drop in cesarean section rates contemporaneously with the onset of a cesarean section audit in Glasgow (12). In 1983, Williams and Chen are the first to suggest that simply disseminating hospital specific rates would effect the rise of cesarean utilization (13). In 1985, Anderson and Lomas suggest that "wider exposure of clinicians to this [cesarean] information would presumably decrease the variability in clinical policies and improve the quality of care" (14). They go on to conclude that such information plays a central role "in the provision of effective care." Similarly, Goyert, et al. in analyzing the effect of individual physician practice styles in cesarean rates, also emphasized the potential role of physician feedback in order to address what they call the "either under-appreciated or under-reported . . ." physician factor in cesarean utilization (15).

MT. SINAI AND PHYSICIAN FEEDBACK

Since 1988, the published experience of the Mount Sinai Hospital Cesarean section reduction initiative has focused with not only what it is possible to achieve with a concerted departmental effort, but importantly with the methodology utilized in order to make it work; i.e., the "tools". The results of our first two years experience focused on obstetric and neonatal outcome (16). The experience after six years has remained virtually unchanged, with only larger numbers added to support the validity of the approach (17). The six year experience again focused on the obstetric outcome and what is possible. During this period, in part as a result of continuing queries regarding *precisely* what it was that we really did at Mount Sinai (of course, implicit in the question was the knowledge that we invented *no new* obstetrics), we began to critically evaluate, from a functional perspective, the entire approach that was taken. That approach, characterized by effective peer review, integrated into an effective quality assurance process which includes comprehensive feedback to physicians about not only their cesarean section utilization, but includes a total activity profile is reported in considerable detail elsewhere (18, 19, 20). While many different strategies have been suggested, reviewed nicely by Stafford, (21) it has become clear that the single most important element in the success of the Mount Sinai Cesarean Section Program is the means, the approach, and the effect that physician feedback had on modifying behavior. By providing practitioners details not usually known even to themselves about their practice, effective peer pressure is exerted without the need for more public process.

CESAREAN SECTION REDUCTION - THE MOUNT SINAI EXPERIENCE

Background

By 1984, cesarean delivery had become the most common surgical procedure performed in the United States (22). Rates peaked by 1988 when 24.7 percent of all women in labor were delivered by cesarean section, (23) with nearly one million such procedures performed. By 1991, with rates declining slightly to 23.5%, there were still nearly one million cesarean deliveries (24). More than a decade after a National Institutes of Health (NIH) consensus report questioned the rising cesarean birth rate, (10) little effort has been made to effectuate substantive reductions in cesarean utilization.

While recent national cesarean rates may be plataeuing at 24% to 25%, (23, 24, 26) national trends still seem somewhat disappointing in that significant reduction has yet to be realized. Individual success stories have been published, and a few broad-based programs have emerged. Even a recent large scale, state wide effort in New York, using a quality assurance approach, seemed to define success as merely holding hospitals to a 25 to 28% cesarean rate (27).

The NIH consensus report went virtually unnoticed when published in 1981 (11), but the Mount Sinai Department of Obstetrics and Gynecology saw it as an opportunity. Rather than perpetuating the cesarean debate by some form of literature review or by recommendation, in 1986 we prospectively implemented a cesarean section reduction initiative with the specific intent of both lowering cesarean utilization and also reporting our actual experience (16).

In November of that year 1986, President Reagan signed the Health Care Quality Improvement Act, representing Congressional action to protect the bolster peer review (28). Peer review is one of the several possible strategies for controlling the rising cesarean section, (21) and effective peer review using a computer-assisted data collection and analysis system was an integral element of the successful cesarean section reduction program implemented at Mount Sinai Hospital Medical Center in Chicago (16, 18, 19, 20).

The Cesarean Polemic

The point has often been made that cesarean section rates could be reduced to zero if we wanted, but that we would not like the outcome if we did. So clearly then, the effort which must be made is to continue with the essential cesarean operations while trying to reduce only the unnecessary ones. There is considerable resistance from obstetricians when such goals are proposed, however.

First, there is an implied assumption that it is better to "err on the safe side", even if a cesarean section may not be entirely indicated. While the general principle is correct, the wider and looser application of it related to cesarean section has resulted in an implied safety when often none has been demonstrated.

A variety of other explanations have been offered to attempt to explain physicians' resistance. Fear of medical-legal actions for a poor outcome is often mentioned, but rigorous scientific evaluation of any care and effect is lacking. Physician convenience, (29) practice style, (30) service status, (31) have all been found to be related to cesarean utilization. A "time bias" (31) is easy to criticize. However, such criticism is not necessarily accurate. While the golf course is usually mentioned as competing with the obstetricians' time, other patients in the office, patients in the operating room, and administrative responsibilities also legitimately compete with the obstetrician's time. Moreover, as our patients come to expect a more humanistic approach to care, they need to recognize that it is human to become fatigued after 18 or 24 hours of work, and human to want to be with family if separated for an evening or two. And to all these competing interests, a simple fact must be factored in, it's just so much easier to do a 30 minute operation than to sit with a patient for hours. And so the complexities of the polemic become apparent.

Mount Sinai's Successful Program: Necessary Structure

The cesarean section reduction program implemented at Mount Sinai consisted of peer review based on analysis of detailed, relevant data. Pivotal to the successful implementation of the program was the coming together of three crucial elements:

- authorization,
- support, and
- expertise.

In the case of Mt. Sinai, authorization came in the form of the Department Chairman of Obstetrics deciding, in conjunction with the Director of Maternal-Fetal Medicine (MFM) to establish such a program. Not uncommonly, such authorization can come from hospital management, or risk management or quality assurance leaders. Importantly, although authorization can come from outside a department, successful *acceptance* is far more likely when the physician leader, such as Department Chairman, is the authorizing body. The inherent independence of physicians puts the authorization by individuals other than the Chairman or a recognized physician leader in a most difficult light.

Importantly at Mount Sinai, it was stated from the onset by both the Chairman and the MFM Director that it was their belief that cesarean utilization could and should be lowered. This stated goal to reduce cesarean became the belief of the entire team representing the authority, support and expertise for the process. Through our experience, we believe that unless the authorizing body can credibly support the goal, successful implementation will be difficult.

Support is necessary not only for acquisition of initial materials, but also for ongoing needs. The Mount Sinai program required the purchase of a relational data base with personal computer. A full-time experience perinatal coordinator was trained to become a full-time system support individual responsible for data acquisition, data entry, report writing, and generalized support. But clearly the development and the direction of all the activities were under the supervision of the Director of Maternal-Fetal Medicine; the key expertise figure of the group.

Setting a Goal for Mount Sinai

While many authorities correctly could argue that it is impossible to prove which cesarean rate is "correct", it seemed for quite some time that the many centers interpreted that position as almost any cesarean rate is acceptable. Consequently, we felt it was desirable to formulate a "target cesarean rate" (16) specific to Mount Sinai. This rate was based on several straight forward assumptions based on current all practitioners, it was clear that not only was the comparison accurate, but that no individual had been singled out.

Feedback to Practitioners

Perhaps the most powerful peer review tool is sharing with physicians their individual data. At the end of each calendar year, each attending physician within the department receives a comprehensive summary of this or her obstetric and gynecologic activities. Small numbers make individual tabulations less useful if done more frequently. Each physician also receives an accompanying letter and graphs, depicting how his/her performance compares with the other members of the department.

Obstetricians who are identified as "outliers" receive a different type of communication inviting them to a private review of their data with the division director. For example, a physician with a 17½ percent cesarean section rate in 1988 was noted to have performed more cesareans for dystocia than his peers. Naturally, a possible explanation is that the cesareans were attributed to a disproportionate number of larger-than-normal babies. The flexibility of the perinatal database allows us to verify this, providing the practitioner actual data on his practice. In fact, his patients delivered by cesarean for dystocia had infants of the same average birth weight as the rest of the department, yet twice as many received cesarean sections. We presented to this physician the case of a baby he delivered by cesarean because he thought it too large when, in fact, it weighed only five pounds. Following the discussion, this physician's cesarean rate fell to 15 percent the following year, and to 13 percent in 1990.

The form in which the data are utilized is as important as the data themselves. The tone of communication with physicians is presented in the letter to a physician with one of the highest departmental cesarean section rates. The final paragraph states:

> "Please accept these data in the context in which they are intended: as information for your own use, and as a comparison to your peers."

By providing individual practitioners with details about their own obstetric practice, not usually known to even themselves, they are given the opportunity to compare their own practice to that of their peers. Effective peer group pressure is thus exerted without the need to enlist a more public review process. Since nobody wishes to be perceived as an outlier, affected physicians usually modify their practice patterns. It has not been necessary to take any punitive action in the department related to cesarean performance. The approach has demonstrated that when practitioners are given information about their own activities, that it provides physicians with the opportunity to modify their own behavior.

If Mt. Sinai had it to do all over again, there is little that would be done differently. Some important lessons were learned along the way. The exact target is not as important as setting a target. The avoidance of searching for, buying, or developing the perfect tool allowed for extremely rapid implementation. We did not get bogged down in that search, or did we attempt to please everyone. We avoided the committee approach to almost everything. Perhaps the only modification at our institution would be to disconnect the entire monitoring and QA function from being identified with only the goal of the cesarean section reduction program. In that way, long-term continuation of the process would become less dependent on a single clinical issue.

The Take Home Message

Based on our experience with cesarean section, successful change in physician practice patterns can be accomplished by adhering to the following principles:

- authority, support, and expertise are needed for any program to succeed
- peer review of total activity profiles based on detailed data is essential
- the ability to observe details of practice and outcome are likely more valuable than attaining the original goal of an improvement project
- data collection must be transparent to patient care, i.e., it happens automatically with little, if any effort
- as hospitals attempt to track and improve performance the key specifics are:
    - A. Identify a goal. Goal must be held by position of authority and team.
    - B. Put together a team. (authority, support, and expertise)
    - C. Collect the least amount of essential data necessary.
    - D. Hospital leadership should prepare and stick to an attitudinal response when physicians exhibit "fight or flight" response.
    - E. Assume change will take time and be prepared to be patient.

Since the cesarean section reduction initiative is highly adjustable to a specific institution, it lends itself to implementation elsewhere. Successful reduction of cesarean utilization will, however, depend on such factors as current cesarean utilization (a reduction of cesarean utilization will, however, depend on such factors as current cesarean utilization (a reduction from 50 percent to 15 percent), local practice patterns (i.e., attitudes toward vaginal births and after c-section), and most important, the recognition that a cesarean section rate above 15 percent is almost always excessive. *Unless this attitude is held by some individual(s) of authority in a department, successful or effective cesarean reduction is unlikely to be achieved.* The approach had become so successful on the obstetric service that a comparable program was implemented on the gynecology service. Once again, an integrated, automated data collection and analysis system is the centerpiece of the program. Such data enables effective and focused peer review that in time, will effectuate changes in practice patterns in a fashion similar to the one observed on the obstetrics service.

CREDENTIALLING AND REAPPOINTMENT THE MOUNT SINAI EXPERIENCE

Background

As the "outcome" movement developed from an occasional isolated article prior to the 1980's, to a more generalized recognition of its importance by the mid 1980's, several key articles appeared which served to focus the attention of the medical profession and well as indicate the future direction for the "outcomes movement". In 1987, Roberts, et al., reviewed the history of the Joint Commission of Accreditation of Hospitals (JCAH now known as the Joint Commission on Accreditation of Health Care Organization, JCAHO) (32). In that review, they cited the *1924* "minimum requirement" that the medical staff "review and analyze at regular intervals their clinical experience" (32). Just one year later, in August of 1987, Dennis O'Leary drew an unequivocal standard by which the JCAHO would follow (33). In that work, he recognized that Medical practice requires the clinician to be "skilled in pattern-and-trend analysis" and to act on these probabilities when caring for patients. He explained that performance parameters must be selected to yield "meaningful information" and that, "the volume of data must be limited to ensure that the data produced are manageable and can be effectively used in the quality assurance process" (33). In 1988, Dr. Arnold S. Relman, the Editor-in-Chief of the prestigious New England Journal of Medicine states, "we can no longer afford to provide health care without knowing more about its successes and failures. The Era of Assessment and Accessibility is drawing at last" (34). Perhaps it should not be surprising, then, if by 1992 the JCAHO would require as a part of its survey guidelines for *credentialling of medical staff* some notable additions to the usual information. Those new guidelines now require that "reappraisal of professional performance" and "current competence" be part of the credentially/re-credentialling process (35). While not specifically using the term, it is clear that a detailed *practice profile* on each practitioner would be necessary in order to comply with not only the letter, but the spirit of the requirement as well.

Another Opportunity

By the early 1990's, the Department of Obstetrics and Gynecology had developed a considerable experience in tracking activities within the Department. The details of these efforts have already been reported (18, 19). Key to the success of this activity was the evolution of these activities into a cohesive, integrated quality assurance system within the department (see Figure 1). As depicted by the figure, two automated and two manual systems are used to tabulate data which results in a "total activity profile". While this is done for the Department as a whole at regular intervals, it is done for each individual practitioner on an annual basis. An example of an individual annual report which accompanies the more detailed profile is also presented (see Figure 2). It was apparent, that incorporating these individual practice profiles, into a comparative individual (peer) departmental practice profile credentialling function would be a logical next step.

The Mt. Sinai Reappointment Profile

As a result of the composite individual and Departmental activity profiles, the JCAHO credentialling requirements could be easily satisfied. Importantly, rather than focusing on individual adverse outcomes, adverse outcome rates could be easily calculated and compared to others in the department. This can only be accomplished if data is collected for 100% of activities; allowing for the "numerator" as well as the "denominator" to be determined. In this way, Mt. Sinai was able to determine a critical piece of information; not if any adverse outcome had occurred but if any EXCESS amount of adverse outcome occurs.

This point is easily demonstrated by comparing perinatal morbidities to perinatal mortality rates; the later being the usual parameter. As the number of deliveries increases, the number of mortalities rise, but the *rate* should be expected to remain constant. Moreover, by comparing such rates to the "peers" (the rest of the department) or by tracking such rates longitudinally for individuals, clear and compelling inferences can be made regarding practice.

This was taken one step further at Mt. Sinai by developing Specialty-specific data (Obstetrics an Gynecology) and looking at "deficiency rates" (short for deficiency in care - the euphemistic term for a mistake) for each specialty. Remarkably, at Mt. Sinai, this was reasonably consistent by specialty; about one in 200 cases for the department.

A reappointment form was developed (see Figures 3 and 4). As can be seen from these forms, several key elements became evident; 1) detailed data must be collected for all, 2) the process must be on-going and not sporadic, 3) individual clinical areas (like cesarean rates, for example) individual physicians *are not* singled out for analysis, and 4) this process takes time and considerable support. *Importantly, since*

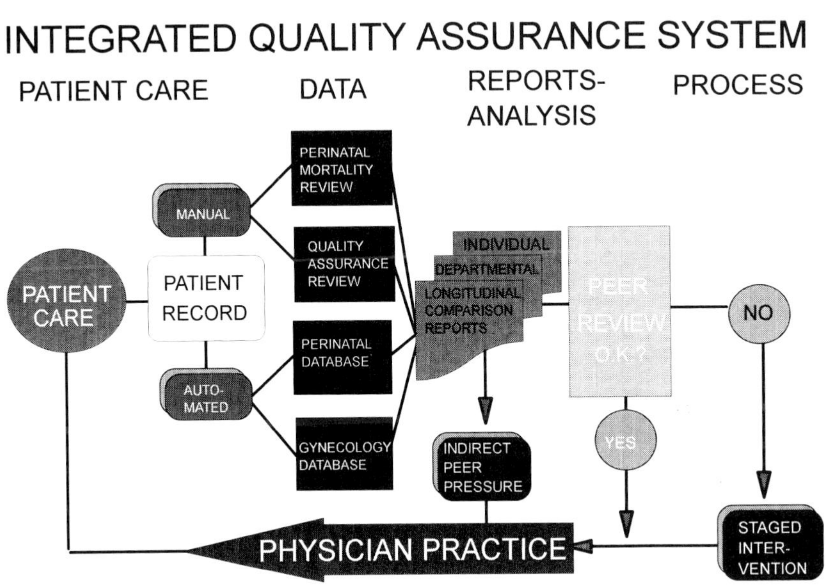

each practitioner is receiving the composite information that goes into the Credentialling process on an annual basis, the physicians have been incorporated into, rather than excluded from the process. This later point is essential in order to maximize not only the influence of this process on altering physician behavior but also to enhance physician acceptance of the process as well. It is clear that without such acceptance, such efforts will not only be more difficult, but likely be much less effective as well.

SAMPLE ANALYSIS OF DEPARTMENT- AND PHYSICIAN-SPECIFIC PERFORMANCE DATA AT MOUNT SINAI HOSPITAL MEDICAL CENTER

Dear Doctor:

The Department of Obstetrics and Gynecology is sharing with you a confidential summary of your annual obstetrical and gynecological activities. Along with your annual obstetrical report and departmental data, we have included additional information not previously collected. This new information contains your gynecological activities and a comparative summary of the QA Committee's yearly assessments.

Moreover, several specific quality of care data are presented. For obstetrics, this includes the total Cesarean rate, primary Cesarean rate, percentage of elective repeat Cesarean sections, and total operative obstetrics rate (Cesarean and operative vaginal deliveries). Fetal death rate and a summary of potential avoidable deaths are also presented.

For gynecology, the percentage of all patients receiving diagnostic laparoscopy are presented along with the number of cases in which the preoperative diagnosis for hysterectomy did not match the postoperative diagnosis, the number of cases in which the clinical indication for a hysterectomy was listed as "other," and the number of cases in which there was major operative morbidity (injury, return to OR, wound dehiscence).

Total deficiency of care (DIC) cases, as determined by the QA Committee, and specialty-specific DIC rates for both obstetrics and gynecology are also presented.

For your practice, the following data are presented. An asterisk (*) represents significant deviation from your peers and a focused audit is recommended.

As always, please accept these data in the context in which they are presented—for your personal use and to serve as a comparison with your peers. Identification of significant deviations from departmental/peer patterns offers the best opportunity we all have to focus efforts at avoiding future problems. Your participation in the departmental quality assurance efforts is appreciated.

Sincerely,

Stephen A. Myers
Director, Maternal/Fetal Medicine

Edmond Confino, MD
Director of Gynecology

OBSTETRICS

C-Section Rate	Primary C-Section Rate	% Elective Repeat C-Sections	Total Operative Obstetrics Rate
9.8	7	2	12

Fetal death rate (per 1,000 patients): 10
Potential avoidable perinatal deaths: 2

GYNECOLOGY

% All Patients With Diagnostic Laparoscopy	# Hysterectomy Preop Diagnosis ≠ Postop Diagnosis	# Hysterectomy Indications = Other	# Major Operative Morbidity
5	0	0	1

QUALITY ASSURANCE SUBCOMMITTEE

Department-Specific Data

Obstetrics	Gynecology
20 DICs/2,816 cases (.67)	9 DICs/1,681 cases (.53)

Practitioner-Specific Data

# DICs	DIC Rate	# DICs	DIC Rate
5*	1.23	0	0

Specific Deficiencies:
1. Traumatic delivery
2. Late genetic diagnosis
3. Abnormal fetal heart tone (FHT), unrecognized
4. Abnormal FHT, no paper
5. Undiagnosed pregnancy with adverse morbidity

* Review of cases indicates suboptimal resident supervision.

FIGURE 2. A sample "physician letter" of the author. Reprinted with permission from Myers, S.A. and C. Izui. 1993. Reflections on Clinical Improvement: The Questionable Role of Clinical Practice Guidelines. *Quality Letter for Health Care Leaders,* June 1993, 5(5):22-27. Published by Baden & Associates, Inc. Rockville, MD.

Past Experience/Future Possibilities

The effectiveness of the approach at Mount Sinai Hospital is unquestioned. Not only was our initial, limited goal of reducing cesarean utilization achieved on a long term basis (as a result of a legitimate change in attitudes by physicians) but the expansion and evolution of the monitoring activities to encompass *all* Departmental activities accomplished benefits not originally anticipated. By tracking details of all practice activities within the Department, true practice profiles were established long before they were required. To the credit of the entire Department, who as a group understood and accepted the value of this activity, the process has been fully integrated into department activities and is actually taken for granted.

Now, as the "outcome movement" becomes more firmly established, details regarding either Department or individual practice profiles can be presented longitudinally for a period of several years. The importance of avoiding the "snap-shot" approach has been discussed nicely by Plume (36). He also emphasized that even when sophisticated statistical analysis accompanies "snapshot observation", that the accuracy achieved by more longitudinal observations allows for more acurate decision making. While data collection necessary for such longitudinal reporting is necessarily more complex, there is really no other alternative. Simply saying that it is too difficult is not an option.

Unless physicians understand the benefit of such self-analysis, and institute

Obstetrics and Gynecology
Physician Reappointment Profile

APPOINTEE: Myers — Year Ending: 7/92 — Appointment Date: 1985
Privileges: Level II GYN
Level III OB Subspecialty — STATUS: Attending

A. Activity Profile

GYNECOLOGY	Indiv.	Dept.	OBSTETRICS	Indiv.	Dept.
# Gynecology Admits	99	2249	# Obstetric Admits		5180
Medical	10	85	Mothers	940	5180
Surgical	89	2164	Babies	953	5259
Major Morb. Rate	22/1000	5/1000	PMR Rate	27.3	31.9
# of Deficiency	0	6	# of Deficiency	3	15
DEF Rate	0	3/1000	DEF Rate	3.1/1000	3/1000

B. Attending Annual Staff Meeting	Yes	No
1. Attending Annual Staff Meeting		x
2. Attending 25% of Department Meetings	x	
3. Attending 25% of Department Meetings	x	
4. Evidence of CME of File	x	
5. Annual Dues Paid	x	
6. Current Medical License on File	x	
7. Current DEA License on File	x	

C. CLINICAL INFORMATION
1. Average length of Stay/Dept. Average 2.50/3.16
2. Medical Record Suspensions
3. # of Documented Patient/Hospital Complaints
4. # UR Denials 3
5. # UR Denials 3

FIGURE 3. The reappointment profile of the author for the latest year it was required.

Today, health care consumers are becoming better educated, better organized, less tolerant and increasingly vocal. Their voices are more and more in unison and they are being heard clearly. They are demanding better, more universal health care with a greater emphasis on efficency, consistency and cost controls; a 21st-century health care system that will deliver quality care to everyone at reasonable costs.

HEALTH CARE QUALITY: An Evolving Concept

Quality is an elusive concept. Most agree that, like a beautiful butterfly, it is difficult to capture. It is subjective, abounding with adjectives, right-brained, seen and appreciated differently by all of us. That interpretation, that very vagueness, while perhaps pleasing to most of us, tends to inhibit meaningful discourse on the subject.

Therefore, to enjoy a reasonable dialogue and to establish a common language, Philip Crosby's operational definition of quality shall be employed in this paper: Quality is, quite simply, conformance to requirements (9). He refers to the requirements of a product or a service, the outcome or result of a process; the delineation of those factors that meet the expressed needs and desires of the consumer and have been agreed upon by the provider of the product or service.

The emphasis here is upon the customer. It was not always that way.

QUALITY BY CHANCE

In the early 1900s, it was the reputation of the physician or the hospital that provided the only assurance that the patient-consumer would receive reasonably good care. In retrospect, it was, by anyone's standard, a "buyer-beware" market, requiring faith in the healer, sprinkled with a generous pinch of resignation. There was medical education and credentialing of a sort, but for the most part, health care was the purview of the physician, a black box, a supplier-oriented paternalistic system whose secrets were unshared and guarded jealously.

QUALITY BY CHECK

The advent of peer review (physicians examining the performance of other physicans) brought a dramatic change to that elitist medical fraternity. Now, care of the patient was subjected to scrutiny by others. That function was still guarded jealously by the profession, but it did at least provide the first opportunity for clinicians to compare processes and outcomes, to learn from, and on occasion, to discipline one another.

Quality Assurance (QA), which is still very much operational today, added a new dimension to the improvement of quality: a systematic method of looking at and comparing health care processes and outcomes. QA continues to identify the outlier, the unusual case, the exception to the rule, separating, as Donald Berwick has said, "the bad apples from the good apples" (10).

Utilizing predetermined criteria, the examiner identifies what is considered to be unacceptable care. The cause of that unacceptable care is then attributed to an individual, most commonly a physician, who is then censured/disciplined in some manner. Although QA has many drawbacks and remains internally oriented, it has moved quality out of the hands of the immediate provider and into a more universal, although still confidentially and legally protected, environment (Figure 2).

Certainly, quality assurance focused health care's attention on its own performance and has identified some "bad" doctors. But, one may argue that the improvements have been obtained at a very high price—the resentment of "quality" by practitioners and others who either perceived that they were (or were in fact) victimized by flawed criteria and overzealous review.

FIGURE 2. Characteristics of Quality Assurance

Weaknesses of QA	*Strengths of QA*
Depends on inspection after the fact.	Provides an organizational approach to quality.
Applies criteria arbitrarily and irregularly.	Is based on measurement.
Directs corrective action to outliers while leaving flawed processes in place.	Applies review criteria objectively and systematically.
Targets people as the cause of problems.	Establishes a comparative data base.
Assigns quality responsibility to a non-participant department.	

QUALITY BY CAUSE

Today, Total Quality Management (TQM) is replacing Quality Assurance and Peer Review. Some call TQM a total quality revolution since its basic philosophy differs radically from the chance-and-check activities of the past. But it is not revolution; it is reformation (11), building upon the very best element of QA—the measurement function; employing strategic identification of problems, measurement of process inputs, evaluation of problem resolution and continuous monitoring of processes to maintain the gain. More importantly, it differs from its predecessors in that problems are attributed primarily to processes and not to individuals.

The primary tenet of quality management is prevention; examining and testing processes before the fact rather than depending on inspection after the fact. TQM assigns responsibility for quality to everyone in the system and not to an add-on department (Figure 3).

QUALITY BY CONTINUOUS IMPROVEMENT

In order to meet the ever-increasing demand for quality and cost in an ever-more complicated health care marketplace, providers today have turned to industry for guidance. They have adopted the Continous Quality Improvement (CQI) teachings of Deming, Juran and Crosby, and are using their theoretical prescriptions to identify the needs of the customer (health care purchasers and consumers), to reduce variation in, and outcomes of, care. Moreover, they want to limit, or even eliminate, waste.

	Quality Assurance	Continuous Quality Improvement
Focus	Inspection	Prevention
Problems	People	Processes
Responsibility	Department	Everyone

FIGURE 3. Quality Assurance Versus Continuous Quality Improvement.

Often, the terms Continous Quality Improvement (CQI) and Total Quality Management (TQM) are used interchangeably. While it is convenient, it's also inaccurate.

Why?

While CQI is a process, TQM is the management method employed to make CQI occur. Neither are static concepts. Both may be improved continuously to accomplish the goal of quality outcomes at quality costs.

TOTAL QUALITY MANAGEMENT

Total Quality Management (TQM or Quality Management, QM) is a strategic management system designed to accomplish one goal—universal continuous improvement in the processes that produce the products and services of an organization (Figure 4).

FIGURE 4. Operational Steps to Institute Quality Management

- Management Commitment - Establish a Quality Policy, express personal commitment and provide resources.
- Quality Improvement Team - Plan, implement and manage CQI.
- Measurement - Identify key processes and provide objective data for improvement.
- Cost of Quality - Identify the price of doing things wrong as a measure of non-conformance and improvement.
- Quality Awareness - Keep personal and organizational focus on quality.
- Corrective Action - Appoint teams and individuals sytematically to identify, correct and improve performance.
- Quality Celebration - Establish a day to celebrate quality progress and reaffirm commitment.
- Education - Train everyone to actively carry out their roles in quality improvement.
- Goal-Setting - Encourage individuals to establish improvement goals for themselves and their work groups.
- Error Cause Removal - Provide every individual with a method of communicating problems to management.
- Recognition - Publicly appreciate those who participate.
- Quality Councils - Bring together individuals to share QM information on a regular basis.
- Do It All Over Again - Make certain CQI never ends.

QM has been defined by Crosby as "a systematic method of guaranteeing that organized activities will happen the way they are planned," (12) and those activities consistently will produce products or services that meet customer requirements. Beeler Gausz, a disciple of Crosby's teachings, opines that "A routine value in the (QM) culture must be that services and products will be carried out on time and will be right the first time and every time" (13).

FEATURES OF QUALITY MANAGEMENT

The number of sociological and scientific measurement tools employed by TQM are not only extensive, but also are changing constantly. The following discussion summarizes only some of its more important activities.

ALL WORK IS A PROCESS

A process is an activity or a series of activities that change something. It has an input and an output. The latter is the result of a change in the input brought about by the process. The outputs of clinical processes are patient outcomes, and when they are unacceptable, as with all outputs, quality management looks to the process.

This is not merely a philosophical approach to quality, it also is a practical one. Experts agree that more than 80 percent of problems may be traced to the process while less than 20 percent are caused by individuals. Because QM does not look to the physician or some other individual as the cause of poor performance, it promotes a culture in which everyone is free to participate in eliminating problems without fear of reprisal. "Drive out fear in the organization," Dr. Deming says (14), and allow employees to attack the process rather than each other.

PROCESSES FORM SYSTEMS

No process stands alone any more than any of us exist without the influence of our forbearers. We are their product as our children are of us. So it is with processes; the output of one becomes the input to the next and so on. Taken together, processes form a universal system—a continuum, if you will—while the boundaries of any given system are arbitrarily set by designation of its initial input and final output.

Hospitals are systems—the interaction of many disciplines, bounded by patients entering the system (input) and patients exiting the system (output). The entire health care industry also is a system—an organization of component systems—hospitals, clinics, health-maintenance organizations (HMOs), third-party payers, insurance companies, government programs, and so on.

Keep in mind that a system is holistic. In other words, the whole is greater than the sum of its parts (15).

This philosophy suggests that:

1. Processes that comprise systems are highly interrelated and interdependent, and when (and only when) addressed in relationship to the whole, contribute synergistically to the function of that whole.
2. The output of a system is the product, directly or indirectly, of every process comprising that system.
3. The quality of a system's output is dependent upon the quality of every component of that system.

Hence, maximum performance only will occur if all components are designed, continuously improved and maintained to be appropriate and capable of meeting their individual requirements every time—and are integrated synergistically.

The following is an example of a process addressed holistically and producing synergism:

> Caring Memorial Hospital improves its admitting, transfer and discharge processes by introducing new software that requires the interaction of many employees. New and longtime employees are trained in the use of this software. Follow-up measurement reveals a decrease in admission time, earlier posting of intrahospital patient transfers, and planned discharges that result in improved bed utilization and reduced costs. Additionally, patient and employee satisfaction levels, as measured by surveys, are increased.

The following is an example of a process addressed independently resulting in negative synergism:

> The patient transportation department (PTD) spends two employee hours each morning locating wheelchairs. Corrective action is undertaken. All wheelchairs are returned to the department at 5 p.m. and chained. The PTD problem is solved. All chairs are available in the department each morning and two employee hours are saved. However, the hospital transportation system after 5 p.m. is thrown into chaos.

Successful health care organizations of the 21st century will be highly integrated and will address all processes holistically, but today we are not there yet. Still, many health systems have produced impressive results.

> Community Hospital investigated and improved care for pneumonia, reducing hospital length of stay by three days, reducing costs, freeing up beds and making resources available for other services (16).

> A hospital system investigated cause of postoperative infection, instituted antibiotic administration within two hours of surgery and reduced infection rate from 1.8 to 0.4 percent, improving care of the patient and saving $720,000 in one hospital over six years (17).

> A hospital reduced average drug delivery time from three hours to less than 15 minutes (18).

CUSTOMER ORIENTATION

Quality management centers around the customer. Its processes are performed for the customer and it is the customer's requirements, as agreed by the provider, that determine the product or service to be delivered. Ah, you ask, but who is the customer in health care? Is it the patient, the family, employers, third-party payers, the government, the community, others?

In fact, it is all of these, but the primary customer, the ultimate customer, the one for whom all of medicine is practiced is . . . the patient. David Eddy insists that patients and their advocates must be the ones to set requirements for their care, not only by stating their desires regarding the outcome of that care but also by learning, understanding and then deciding upon which processes are to be used to accomplish that goal (19). Wennberg practices that philosophy through the Foundation for Informed Medical Decision Making. Using interactive video programs, patients are informed about the benefits and risks of alternative treatments and are encouraged to determine their preferences for treatment. As informed consumers, they have made dramatic changes in the practice of medicine as exemplified by the experience in Washington state where prostate surgery rates dropped 50 percent and at the Kaiser Foundation Health Plan in Colorado, where rates fell 20 percent (20).

SUPPLIER/CUSTOMER (S/C) RELATIONSHIPS

Each process has a supplier who performs the process and a customer who receives the output of that process. Such relationships may be internal (i.e., employee to employee, department to department) or external (i.e., hospital to patient, pharmaceutical company to hospital pharmacy). It is the S/C relationship, bounded by the requirements of the outcome and often, the process, that is the basic tenet of Quality Management. When requirements are 1) clearly set by the customer and 2) negotiated and agreed upon by the supplier and then met each and every time, quality has by definition, been served. There is no hassle, no confusion, no wasted time or misused materials. Moreover, there is no need to repeat the acitivity or pay the consequences because it was incorrectly chosen or improperly performed. As there is no gap between the expectations of the customer and those of the supplier, neither need be disappointed. The setting of clear, well-communicated requirements is fundamental to establishing wholesome, productive relationships in a quality system.

> An example of poorly communicated requirements: An intravenous antibiotic is ordered by phone for a patient in the emergency room. Pharmacy ships the medication to the emergency room, not being informed, however, that the patient has been sent to intensive care. Hours later, intensive-care personnel receive the written order and call the pharmacy for medication.

THE PRICE OF NON-CONFORMANCE (PONC)

An unnecessary cost occurs when things are not done right the first time, when the decision of what to do is improper or the requirements of the process are not met. This unnecessary cost is called the price of non-conformance (PONC). It may consist of rework, overtime, duplication of efforts, extended lengths of stay, DRG denials, waste, excess inventory, and so on. And, it often is significant. The PONC in service industries has been repeatedly calculated to affect 25-35 percent of sales, (9, 14) while estimates in health care, including performing incorrect and unnecessary procedures, is frequently calculated at 35 percent of income and has been estimated by some to be as high as 50 percent (21). Conversely, when tasks are carried out correctly the first time, the cost of doing those things right, termed the price of conformance (POC), is minimal. The truism "as quality goes up, costs go down" is analogous to "an ounce of prevention is worth a pound of cure."

When key indicators identify a potential problem that needs to be addressed, the consequences of that problem to the organization (and often times to the customer of that problem) can be identified and clearly communicated in a very common language—money. As such problems are resolved, the savings in terms of recaptured PONC also can be easily identified and communicated. Therefore, as the quality strategy captures an organization, costs begin to decrease. Quality is never free but it can pay for itself many times over—and, it can resupply precious resources to improve access to the health care system for those who might otherwise go without it.

The PONC is not necessarily confined to the provider side of the S/C relationship. Often, consumers suffer from it as well by way of their pocketbooks or, worst yet, their health and survival.

> An example of the PONC being shared with the customer: A 33 year old woman was examined for outpatient surgery. Inexplicably, she was not asked the routine question, "Did you have breakfast?"
>
> She had.
>
> Immediately after the induction of anesthesia, she vomited, aspirated stomach contents, was admitted and received intensive care for 12 days.

In the aforementioned case, the PONC in terms of dollars equates to the cost of care rendered minus the expected routine outpatient charges, not to mention potential liability. The cost to the patient cannot be estimated but may be set by the courts.

TEAMWORK

Although small intradepartmental problems may be solved at a local level, solving big problems that impact many departments and many people requires the attention and cooperation of all the stakeholders. But most stakeholders are sequestered in comfortable vertically-oriented areas of expertise, reporting to their boss and denying allegiance to the horizontal, cross-functional orientation of processes performed for their internal and external customers.

We are all too familiar with the expression, "That's not my department" ringing through the corridors of a dysfunctional organization. Such counterproductive relationships hold little chance of survival in the 21st century. Teamwork will be the code of conduct, the sociologic equivalent of process integration. Teamwork will strategically unite departments, disciplines, companies or diverse interests and will provide the forum for the coordination, integration and simplification of processes while at the same time improving outcomes and reducing costs. The operational steps of quality management, meanwhile, are devoted to creating a culture of teamwork and cooperation.

MEASUREMENT

In order to get where we are going, it's essential that we understand where we have been and where we are so we can plot the course of the future (9). Measurement, says William Scherkenbach, is the voice of the process (22). Simply put, it replaces subjectivity with objectivity and tells us what is happening so we may respond or restrain wisely.

Today, health care organizations are becoming more and more like big industry. Charts and graphs cover the walls from accounting and dietary to obstetrics and intensive care, recording indicators of activity and monitoring key processes. Many are penned in a statistical control format, much as manufacturing and chemical processes are graphed, watching for trends or drifts in processes that prompt corrective action before outcomes are affected, thus practicing the highest form of prevention.

In the 21st century, measurement will be systematized throughout health care. Indicators will follow hundreds of key processes. Outcomes only will be examined occasionally as continuously-monitored processes will result in a high degree of conformity to preestablished requirements.

FACILITATIVE MANAGEMENT

As quality management integrates processes in order to profit from the synergistic contributions of each area, management must integrate employees and also allow them to contribute synergistically. Under TQM it is the responsibility of management to remove barriers to teamwork and integration, to educate, expand roles and encourage employees initiatives. It will be the philosophy of management to be diametrically opposite of the controlled, compartmentalized and job-delineated autocratic organization of the past.

EMPOWERMENT

Recently, a manager was heard to say, "The employees of this organization don't give a darn about anything. They're lazy. No wonder we're not competitive." "Well," someone asked, "why do you hire lazy, don't give-a-darn people in the first place?"

"Oh," he said, "We don't."

Frankly, it's the organization and not the people.

People rarely go to work to do a poor job. Quality management builds upon the concept that workers want to be successful. It empowers people to do the right thing right the first time and if they do not know what that is, ask before acting. It encourages continuous education, establishes recognition systems, supplies appropriate equipment and working conditions, and celebrates employee success.

Crosby says that cooperation, consideration, understanding, encouragement and respect are the management tools of tomorrow. They will allow all of the players in that system to contribute maximally, not only to improve system performance but to enjoy it as well.

Empowerment provides individuals that right.

COMMITMENT

There is more talk than action concerning top leadership's commitment to quality. In fact, quality experts say that failure to institute a full-blown cultural quality change most frequently results from the fact that top management becomes uncomfortable with the pursuit of quality.

Leaders must mold a vision for the organization, encourage quality cultural values, strategically plan quality efforts, encourage employees to set goals and then assist them in meeting those goals. They must provide unrelenting evidence to everyone in the organization that quality will be first among equals with regard to schedule and cost. Employees and physicians in those organizations must be convinced that their efforts will be supported, that this is not just another fleeting management scheme. Quality will not happen, says Tom Peters "without perpetual, enthusiastic, visceral commitment to the new quality culture." He also says that all employees are boss-watchers (23). As leadership goes, so goes the organization.

INVOLVING PHYSICIANS

Physicians, as major players in clinical processes, order more than 80 percent of health care resources, often without any significant fiscal responsibility. Most are independent of major organizations and, therefore, do not fall under the control of management. In fact, it is that very fact that differentiates the business of health care from other industries and creates a conundrum for organizational planners.

However, physicians are good managers. They respond to sound data and are becoming educated and skilled in the disciplines of management and leadership. This is leading to a new relationship between health care management and clinicians. Doctors are being appointed to positions of leadership in the health care industry. Additionally, doctors are organizing to address quality issues and are responding to data and improving clinical outcomes while reducing process variation and costs.

Today, there is abundant evidence that physicians, as they become educated in the principles of TQM/CQI, will become leaders and significant participants in the quality culture of the 21st century.

Some examples of physician participation in QM:

Knee surgery outcomes improved while reducing length of hospitalization by three days. Costs decreased (24).

Coronary Artery Bypass Grafting with angiography mortality reduced to 2.2 percent, length of stay shortened and costs reduced to half of average (25).

Provided with outcomes data, physicians have reduced Medicare patients' cost of care 37 percent in one year with no change in quality indicators (26).

CONCLUSION

Today, health care is under siege and the winds of change will continue to blow because society is demanding more. More, that is, for less. The monies are limited and demands increase. In such a scenario, there is no room for inappropriate care; and certainly no room for inefficient care.

Requirements must be carefully set and met every time. New innovative systems of care must be devised, old processes re-engineered, and rigid management systems replaced by flexible, people-empowered organizations. The cost of poor quality must be eliminated and the freed-up resources applied elsewhere.

Health care leaders of the future will produce maximum performance through teamwork and superior communications. They will extend supplier-customer relationships beyond the artificial walls of today's health care centers deep into the society in which they serve. Custom-oriented, they will take health services into the community rather than waiting for the community to seek that care.

Prevention will be the focus of future health care spending, removing the spotlight from after-the-fact, dramatic but very expensive acute tertiary care. And, by forming a more perfect union among patients, buyers, providers and insurers, the leaders of tomorrow will position health care to not only meet, but to exceed the expectations of all of its stakeholders.

Continuous Quality Improvement will be the process, Quality Management will provide the method.

REFERENCES

1. Gilbreath, R.D. 1987. *Forward Thinking,* New York: McGraw Hill Book Company.
2. Friedman, E. 1991. "The Eternal Triangle: Cost, Access and Quality." *Physician Executive* 17(4):3-9, July-Aug.
3. Hughes, J.M. 1992. "Reducing Health Care Costs: A Case for Quality." *Physician Executive* 18(4):9-15, July-Aug.
4. Bennett, G. 1993. "Florida Hospitals Graded and Compared for Cost-Efficiencies." Healthcare Business Services, Inc. July 29.
5. Wennberg, J.E., et al. 1989. "Hospital use and mortality among Medicare beneficiaries in Boston and New Haven." *New England Journal of Medicine,* Oct. 26, p. 1168.

in medical settings. In addition, we discuss the basics of decision analysis, a technique for explicitly combining information and patient preferences to help physicians and patients make better decisions.

THE INFORMATION EXPLOSION

Dissemination of Information

In the last thirty years, biomedical research has produced an explosion of information which physicians must now synthesize to practice state of the art medicine. Physicians can no longer expect to read even a fraction of the relevant clinical research papers from primary sources, and given the lag in publishing, traditional textbooks cannot always summarize truly current knowledge. Timely compendia of journal articles with critiques (such as the Yearbook series and Journal Watch) have been available for a number of years, but recently, electronic decision support has become increasingly important. This can take several forms:

1. Literature databases: These allow rapid bibliographic searches, provide abstracts on line and sometimes link to full electronic text for rapid access to published data (1).
2. Electronic textbooks and journals: A number of standard textbooks and journals have been encoded onto electronic media, such as compact or floppy discs. More recently "textbooks" that exist only for electronic distribution have been "published", allowing for more rapid updating and providing for interactive use (1, 2).
3. Expert systems: The principles of medical informatics and artificial intelligence can produce expert systems that accept patient-specific information and combine that information with knowledge in its database and provide advice regarding clinical strategies for a particular patient (3).
4. Clinical information systems: These systems can examine patient specific data and match these data against rules to identify exceptions, potential interactions, omissions, and errors.

Synthesizing Information

Information is not only being disseminated in new ways but is also being synthesized in new ways. Studies can be pooled by meta-analysis, particularly when the power of the individual studies is limited by their sample size (4). This is particularly useful for relatively uncommon diseases or events: one or even several hospitals may have difficulty mounting a study large enough to have the power to identify statistically significant effects, even in the face of a treatment with fairly substantial benefits.

Clinicians must often synthesize a constellation of clinical findings and offer some estimate of the likelihood of certain outcomes, such as probability of survival or operative mortality. Clinical prediction rules and logistic regressions have been developed to provide a quantitative or qualitative estimate of probabilities of diagnoses or events given constellations of findings in a number of clinical settings (5). For example, clinical prediction rules are available to estimate operative complications based on cardiac status and other factors (6, 7, 8).

INFORMED CONSENT

Although the basic legal concept of consent in medical practice arose in the early 20th century, it was not until 1957 that the disclosure of information was required as part of the consent process and the term "informed consent" was applied. In a crucial case, the California Court of Appeals stated that physicians were required to inform patients of "any facts which are necessary to form the basis of an intelligent consent . . . to proposed treatment" (9). Today, informed consent is generally held to serve to foster autonomy and promote shared rational decision making (10, 11). Thus, the physician needs to present the relevant clinical information to her patients in a way that enables the patients to make rational decisions based on their own preferences. This may require a more detailed and current knowledge of the relevant literature than can be obtained from medical textbooks or review articles and also presupposes an understanding of the psychology of decision making.

WHEN DO THE BENEFITS EXCEED THE RISKS?

Most clinical decisions involve weighing potential benefits against risks. That "the benefits exceed the risks" is a phrase often used both day to day in obtaining informed consent and in developing formal practice guidelines for particular diagnostic or therapeutic interventions. The judgement that the benefits of a course of action exceed its risks is subjective and, for the same clinical scenario, may vary substantially from physician to physician and patient to patient. In particular, the course of action that produces the best average survival is not necessarily the preferred course of action for an individual patient, because patients vary both biologically (e.g., in co-morbidities) and in their preferences (e.g., they may have different tolerances for risk and different attitudes towards states of less than perfect health).

A broad definition of risk is the perception of the possibility of adverse events occurring. As most medical choices entail the possibility of morbidity or mortality related to either an intervention or to natural processes, medical decision making falls under the category of decision making under risk and involves both adverse outcomes and uncertainty. There are a number of theories of how decisions are or should be made under risk. One can distinguish descriptive from prescriptive models of decision making. There is little *a priori* reason to expect the two perspectives to coincide, unless one believes either that intuitive decisions are optimal or that more explicit or formal methods cannot inform clinical judgments. In most of these models, the optimal choice is a function of the probability distribution of possible outcomes produced by each possible choice. To make a truly informed decision, a doctor and patient should want a complete enumeration of the possible outcomes of each strategy under consideration, with quantitative estimates of their relative likelihoods, based on objective data, but tailored to the individual patient. Unfortunately, such detailed information tailored to a specific patient is generally not available. The lack of objective probabilities is common to decision making in many domains, not only medicine, and where some objective information is available to use as a starting point, formal decision making can reflect subjective probabilities which represent a personal degree of belief in the likelihood of a given event.

There is some evidence that most physicians do not use explicit quantitative probabilities in their day to day clinical judgments. Many decisions seem to be based on some internal estimate of likelihoods, and the more these intuitions can be made explicit and communicated to the patient, the more likely it is that patients will understand the risks involved in proposed interventions. This should help to minimize the ubiquitous simple errors observed when either patients or physicians use implicit judgment or heuristics to combine likelihoods (12).

Expectation and Risk Attitude

Clinical decision making, analogous to decision making in other spheres, must reflect the idea the strategy that produces the best *average* or "expected" outcome is not necessarily the preferred strategy for everyone who is making a *one time* decision. The "one shotter" must accept the consequences of a single "role of the dice", rather than the average return of many rolls. A monetary example may make this clearer. A lottery or a gamble that offers a 50% chance of winning $1000 and a 50% chance of winning $0 has an average or expected value of $500, i.e., if the lottery were played a large number of times, the average return would likely be very close to $500. This expected value is calculated by taking each possible prize, multiplying by the probability of winning that prize, and summing over all possible prizes. For this lottery, 0.5 times $1000 plus 0.5 times $0 gives the expected value $500. But someone paying the lottery once will either receive $1000 or $0, not $500. Given the option of receiving $400 for sure, without any risk, or playing this lottery only once, many people would opt for the sure $400, even though on average, the lottery would return more money. Such behavior suggests that decisions under uncertainty may not be based solely on the average outcome of the lotteries or gambles involved. A person who is willing to take the sure $400 in preference to the lottery is said to be risk averse. The difference between the "risk free" $400 and the risky expected return of $500 can be viewed as an insurance premium, also termed the risk premium ($100 in this simple example), which someone might be willing to pay to avoid the risk of losing the lottery.

An analogous situation holds in medicine when dealing with options that offer different risks of dying. Consider one strategy that will avoid perioperative death in 400 patients compared to a second strategy that might succeed or fail, with a probability of 50%. If the second strategy succeeds, perioperative death will be avoided in 1000 patients, but if it fails, perioperative death will be avoided in none.

Some people are risk averse and would not take the gamble, which on average would avoid 500 deaths, but would rather settle for avoiding 400 deaths for sure.

A similar phenomenon occurs when dealing with risks for different lengths of survival. We often consider therapies that, on average, offer increased average survival (or life expectancy) at the expense of a risk of immediate death. Many surgical treatments fall in this category of trade-off. In a study of patients with lung cancer (13), formal assessment of attitudes toward various lengths of survival led to the conclusion that some patients would prefer radiation therapy to surgical therapy to avoid the immediate risk of mortality due to surgery, even though on average, life expectancy would be greater with surgery.

Quality of Life

Trade-offs between quality of life and survival, between different kinds of morbidity, or both are common when physicians and patients make clinical decisions. Prostatectomy for early prostatic cancer may prolong average survival, but at the risk of impotence or incontinence. Beta blockers for angina or hypertension may cause depression or sexual dysfunction. Electroconvulsive therapy offers the opportunity to improve severe depression at the risk of permanent cognitive impairment. McNeil et al. studied the attitude of a group of healthy volunteers toward normal speech and survival using formal techniques of decision analysis (14). They integrated those attitudes with survival data in patients for stage T3 laryngeal cancer treated with laryngectomy versus radiation therapy. Although laryngectomy offers longer average survival than radiation, radiation therapy preserves speech, and in that study approximately 20% of the volunteers said they preferred radiation to laryngectomy. Similarly, Barry et al. have shown that choice of management of benign prostatic hypertrophy depends largely on patient preferences regarding the symptoms of prostatism and the complications of surgery (15).

But involving patients in medical decision making and understanding our patients' preferences requires getting patients to appreciate fully what their quality of life might be in states they have not experienced. The paradigm of "shared decision making" supplemented by a videodisc presentation featuring a number of patients who had prostatectomy and some who have been treated conservatively is now being tested (16). Similar modules are being developed for other medical decisions. Preliminary results indicate that resource utilization may be decreased when patients are given a balanced understanding of the benefits and risks of invasive therapies. Modern information intensive media, such as the videodisc controlled by a microcomputer program, also afford the opportunity for interactive decision support for both patients and clinicians.

Decision Making with Ambiguous Data

As discussed above, when some objective data or experience are available, decisions are sometimes made using subjective probabilities based on these data or experience.*

*In intuitive decision making conscious numerical values may not be assigned to the likelihoods of events but such numerical values can sometimes be inferred from observed choices.

such preferences dates back to the 17th century (28): people choose among monetary lotteries based on the expected utility of the lottery, rather than expected true monetary value, where the utility represents the perceived worth to them of a given amount of money. Economists have always assumed that, in general, a given increment in wealth has less perceived value for a wealthy person than for a poor person. The marginal utility of money (the utility of an additional increment of wealth) decreases as wealth increases. If the utility of $1000 is less than twice the utility of $400, someone who chooses among lotteries based on expected utility would prefer a sure gift of $400 to a 50:50 lottery between $1000 and $0, because its utility is greater than the expected utility of the lottery.

The theoretical basis for the idea that decisions under risk should be made based on expected utility has been the dominant theory of decision making since the 1940's (29), although it still remains controversial (30). Under this theory, choices between lotteries can be used to measure utility, i.e., relative value with attention to attitude toward risk. If we now ask someone who prefers the $400 to the 50:50 lottery what probability of winning $1000 would make her indifferent between the lottery and the $400, she might say 0.7, for example. Indifference implies that the expected utilities of the two options are equal. The values assigned to the best and worst outcomes can be chosen arbitrarily, so we can assign $0 a utility of 0 and we can assign $1000 a utility of 1. The expected utility of the indifference lottery (a 70% chance of winning) is then 0.7*1 + 0.3*0 = 0.7, which must then be equal to the utility of $400 because the decision maker said she was indifferent at that probability of winning. The utility of any monetary value can be found by setting up other choices between lotteries. Conversely, we might ask how much money ($400, $300, $200, etc.) would be just equivalent to a 50:50 lottery between $1000 and $0. For example, one individual might find $300 equivalent to the 50:50 lottery, while someone else who is more risk averse might find $200 just equivalent. Such an indifference value is the "certainty equivalent" of the lottery for that person, and the difference between the certainty equivalent and the expected value of the lottery is the so-called "risk premium", alluded to earlier.

Utilities for Time

The utility concept can be applied to life years to capture a patient's preferences for risks involving survival. Utilities for different lengths of survival can be measured using a similar approach to that described for assessing utilities for monetary values. For example, a patient is presented with two hypothetical therapies: therapy A which offers certain survival for exactly 4 years, and therapy B in which the probability of immediate death is p, but those who survive the immediate post-therapy period live 10 years. The decision maker can then be asked to specify the value of p that makes therapy A and therapy B equally attractive. If they said 0.2, for example, then we can equate the utility of 4 years with the utility of a lottery offering a 0.2 chance of immediate death and 0.8 chance of surviving 10 years. We can again arbitrarily assign 10 years a utility of 1, and 0 years a utility of 0. The utility of living 4 years can be found by calculating the expected utility of the lottery: 0.2*0 + 0.8*1 = 0.8. This person is indifferent between the sure 4 years and a lottery with average or expected survival of 8 years. This is risk aversion with respect to time, and the difference (8 years minus 4 years) is the risk premium. By presenting a set of such choices, a utility curve for a range a survival time can be constructed. The information from this utility curve can then be combined with the survival curve associated with each option to calculate the expected utility of survival. In general, the utility of the average survival figure should not be used since survival curves with different shapes but identical average survival will, in general, have different expected utilities of survival.

Utilities for Intermediate Health States

The utility of intermediate states of health could also be measured using a lottery based approach (31), but is most often done using the time trade-off method, assuming that the trade-off between quality of life and survival for any given patient is a relatively fixed proportion (32). In this approach, a patient is offered the hypothetical choice of remaining in an intermediate state of health for a specified amount of time, for example, having moderate angina for ten years followed by death, or undergoing a hypothetical new therapy that would restore them to good health but would shorten their remaining life span to less than 10 years. They are asked to specify the minimum life span in perfect in health that the therapy must provide for them to be indifferent between the new therapy and remaining in the intermediate health state (moderate angina) for ten years. In other words, they are asked to specify the proportionality constant which governs their trading improvements in quality of life for a decrease in survival. The ratio of the life years in good health to life years in the intermediate health state at the indifference point defines the quality adjustment factor for that state. When certain conditions are met, this quality adjustment factor can be multiplied by the number of years spent in that state to give the utility of time spent in that intermediate health state (33).

For example, the patient may be told to assume that he would survive for another 10 years but would be blind for that entire period. He might then be asked to consider a therapy which could restore his sight but would shorten his life. He is then asked to specify the minimum survival without blindness he would accept rather than living 10 years with blindness. If the patient answered 8 years the quality adjustment factor for blindness would be $8/10 = 0.8$.

DECISION MODELS

The simplest model used in decision analysis is the decision tree, in which all decisions to be made, all chance events, and all final outcomes are represented in temporal sequence. The strategies available to the decision maker at any point are denoted as branches of a decision node, represented by a square; all possible subsequent events then become branches of a series of chance nodes, each represented by a circle; the final outcomes are scenarios or terminal nodes, represented by rectangles.

An example is shown in Figure 1. This tree represents a simplified version of the following clinical scenario:

> A 72 year old white male presents with an ischemic right foot. The patient developed angina 6 months ago. Because of his history of claudication, a dipyridamole thallium myocardial perfusion scan, rather than an exercise thallium scan, was performed, and showed a significant area of redistribution on thallium imaging, but no changes on electrocardiogram. Cardiac catheterization revealed 70% stenosis of the left anterior descending coronary artery but a tiny distal vessel that was felt to be unapproachable by either angioplasty or coronary artery bypass surgery. He has no history of myocardial infarction. Physical exam, echocardiogram, and laboratory tests are otherwise normal. An angiogram is performed and the patient is found to have a tight occlusion of his right iliac artery and moderate femoral-popliteal disease.

It is felt that there are two principal options for this patient:

1. Below knee amputation.
2. Revascularization surgery (aorto-femoral bypass).

There are the two braches at the square decision node at the left (root) of the tree (Figure 1). If amputation is performed, the patient may die in the operating room (with probability pDieAmp, shown in italics), or may survive with a below knee amputation. These mutually exclusive chance events are represented by the circular chance node in the Amputate branch of the decision node. The value of the

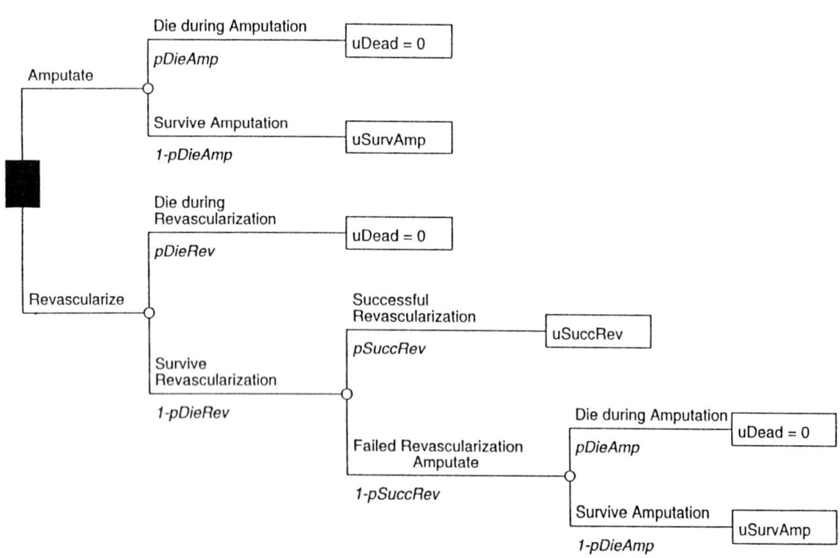

FIGURE 1. Decision tree representing the clinical example. The square is the decision node. Each circle is a chance event. Probabilities are shown in italics. Utilities of outcomes are shown in rectangles.

outcomes of this chance node are represented by the utilities Dead (defined as 0) and uSurvAmp. The latter must capture the patient's preference for life with a below knee amputation for the duration of his life expectancy. Utilities measure the value of the outcome (or the strength of preference for the outcome) were this event to occur. The assignment of these utilities will be discussed below. If revascularization is performed, there is a chance of dying in the operating room (with probability pDieRev), or surviving the revascularization surgery. If the patient survives this riskier operation, a second chance node represents the chance that the revascularization procedure is successful. The chance of success is pSuccRev and its utility uSuccRev, which is presumably greater than the utility of life after amputation. If the revascularization fails, the patient will then have to undergo amputation, and in the branch denoting that sequence of events a third chance node represents the chance of dying during amputation. If the patient survives, the utility is again uSurvAmp.

Using the index of Goldman et al. (6), we can estimate the complication rate for the two types of surgery contemplated. For the amputation, this patient is in Goldman's class I, with an average ischemic event rate of 1%, and for the revascularization, he falls in class II, with an event rate of 7%. Although the numbers in Goldman's study were too small to calculate mortalities rates given an ischemic event in each class, to get an estimate, we can pool the data for the three lower risk classes (class IV appears to have a much higher rate than the others) to get an approximate rate of 25%. Thus, the operative mortality for this patient for the amputation is estimated to be about 0.25%, and for the revascularization, about 1.75%. We can compare this estimate for the operative risk for the revascularization with that calculated from the study of Eagle et al. (8). That study takes into account the history of angina and the result of the dipyridamole thallium test. The predicted cardiac event rate using Eagle's logistic regression is 24%. Using their overall mortality rate of 20% in those who had a cardiac event, we can estimate operative mortality to be approximately 5%. The overall operative mortality rates reported for aortofemoral bypass are about 2%, but the results in these studies were not stratified according to the result of thallium imaging (34). By using the higher value of 5% as our base case value, we will be if anything, biasing the analysis in favor of amputation. Similarly maintaining our bias, the operative mortality rates reported for below knee amputations are generally considerably higher than 0.25%, but patients in these series are generally much higher risk than this patient (35). Finally, the chance of successful revascularization in this setting is about 80% (34, 36).

Assume that survivors of amputation or revascularization have the same life expectancy as a 72 year old male with single vessel disease who has not undergone surgery. One currently popular technique for estimating this life expectancy is to assume a declining exponential curve and add the average mortality rates related to the patients age, sex and race plus any comorbitities present, thereby producing an effective compound force of mortality (37). Although survival curves have a more complex shape in general, this is often a reasonable approximation where a disease process, rather than aging, dominates mortality. This approach uses effective average mortality rates, so the errors tend to cancel, overestimating mortality in the near term and underestimating it in the far term. In this simple survival model, the overall average mortality rate (time constant of the declining exponential) is the sum of the average mortality rates attributable to the patient's demographics, his disease, and each comorbidity. The approximate mortality rates due to comorbidities can be estimated from the literature, again using the declining exponential approximation and by assuming the separate forces of mortality to be independent. The patient's life expectancy can be calculated as the reciprocal of this overall mortality rate. The life expectancy for a typical 72 year old white man, taken from life tables, is 10 years (38), giving an average mortality rate of 1 death per 10 years, or 0.1 per year. The excess mortality rate for patients with one vessel disease has been estimated to be between 0.012 and 0.019 per year (39). We shall use 0.015, a value in the middle of this interval as the base case value. Summing these gives the overall mortality rate of 0.115 per year; the reciprocal 1/0.115 gives the expected survival, 8.70 years. Although this value will only represent the utility of survival if the patient is risk neutral, i.e., if his utility curve for time is linear, we assume risk neutrality in this example, for simplicity. Thus we take uSuccRev to be 8.7.

The calculation so far has assumed survival in good health, which at best would be applicable only to the survivors of peripheral revascularization. (For simplicity sake we will assume that the patient is angina free on medication and ignore the side effects of that medication.) In the amputation branch, we must also consider the disutility of life with a below knee amputation. As discussed above, this is assessed by the time trade-off approach. The patient would be asked to specify the minimum survival in good health he would accept as a trade for 10 years survival with a below knee amputation. (We use 10 years as a "round" number approximately appropriate for this patient.) If he answered eight and one half years, then below knee amputation would be assigned a quality adjustment factor of 8.5/10, or 0.85, and the utility of survival (expressed in units termed "quality adjusted life years" or QALY's) after a below knee amputation would be found by multiplying the utility of survival in good health (8.70) by 0.85, producing a utility of 7.40 quality adjusted life years. We have ignored the pain and suffering associated with surgery in assigning the utilities to the survivors of both operations. Short term morbidities can be accounted for by subtracting an appropriate amount of utility whenever the procedure or event occurs.

In Figure 2, the tree is shown with the values of all variables displayed. The probabilities are shown in italics. The expected utility of each chance (circular) node is calculated by "averaging out", i.e., by multiplying the utility of each branch by its probability, and summing over all branches. This effectively calculates a weighted average utility, using the branch probabilities as weights. The expected utility of amputation is 0.0025*0 + 0.9975*7.40 = 7.38 QALY's, as shown in the top oval in Figure 2. To calculate the expected utility of revascularization, we start at the distal end of the tree and work backward, sequentially averaging out each chance node. As shown in the oval at the lower right of Figure 2, the expected utility of the chance node describing amputation after a failed revascularization is identical to the value calculated above (7.38 QALY's**). The expected utility of the chance node describing surviving revascularization (shown in the middle of Figure 2) is 0.8*8.70 + 0.2*7.38 = 8.44 QALY's. Finally, the expected utility of revascularization, calculated by averaging out the remaining chance node (shown in the oval at the lower left of Figure 2), is 0.05*0 + 0.95*8.44 = 8.02 QALY's. Thus, the expected utilities of the two strategies are:

Amputation	7.38 quality adjusted life years
Revascularization	8.02 quality adjusted life years

so that revascularization appears to be the preferred strategy by a modest margin of almost 8 quality adjusted months. This model ignored the pain and suffering associated with the surgical procedures. Short term morbidities can be accounted for by subtracting an appropriate amount of utility whenever the procedure or event occurs. Such factors might make revascularization slightly less attractive, but unless the short term morbidity of revascularization exceeded the short term morbidity of amputation by 8 months, revascularization would still be preferred.

Sensitivity Analysis

Initially the decision model is run using the best estimates for the probabilities and utilities in the decision tree, but there is often uncertainty as to the true value

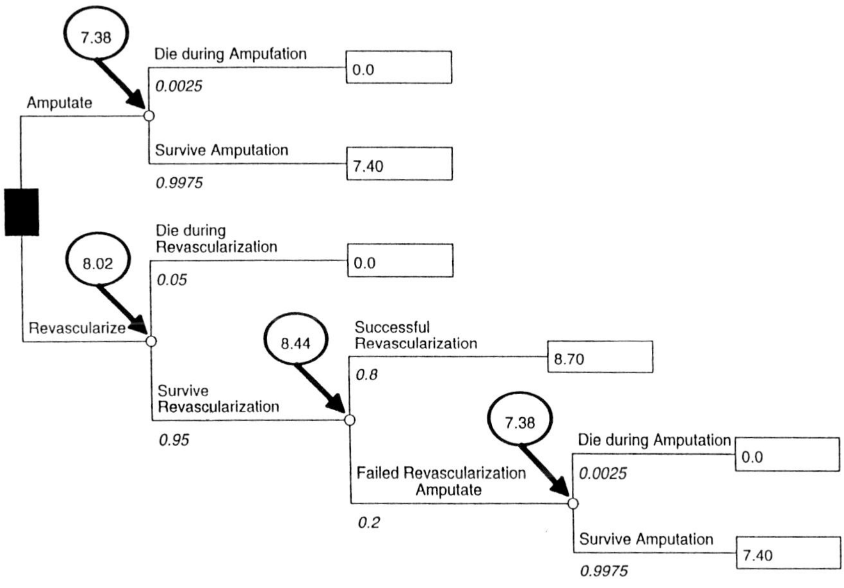

FIGURE 2. Decision tree with all variable values displayed. Expected utilities are shown in the ovals.

**Again, for simplicity, we ignore the extra short term morbidity of the second operation.

of these variables. As discussed above, when that uncertainty is due to disparate results in different clinical trials because of small sample size, studies can be pooled formally using a statistical technique called meta-analysis. Pooling studies essentially generates a larger sample size, providing statistical power and perhaps a more reliable estimate of variables. But uncertainty frequently still remains either due to a lack of literature or to specific patient characteristics that distinguish the individual patient at hand from the average patient in a clinical trial. In sensitivity analysis, a variable is systematically varied over a specified range, and the expected utility and ranking of strategies is recalculated at several points along that range. If the ordering of strategies does not change as a variable changes throughout its plausible range, one can be confident in these rankings, even though there was uncertainty in that variable. This demonstration of the robustness of the rankings of strategies to changes in these variables may be effective cognitive support that will help minimize ambiguity avoidance.

In our example, revascularization has greater expected utility than amputation by a comfortable*** margin, using the base case estimates for probabilities and utilities, even though some of these values were somewhat biased in favor of amputation. We might feel more confident that revascularization is indeed the preferred strategy, however, if this ranking is unaltered by a change in the most uncertain of those variables. In a one-way sensitivity analysis, the value of one variable is varied over a specified range and the expected utility for each strategy is recalculated over that range. The results can be displayed graphically. The value of that variable at which the two strategies produce the same expected utility is called the "threshold" value of that variable. If the true valuable is unlikely to approach the threshold value, we can be more confident in the ranking of strategies. In Figure 3, a one-way sensitivity analysis of the operative mortality for revascularization surgery is plotted. The threshold value is about 0.13, i.e., all other things being equal, the revascularization strategy is preferred if the risk of dying during that operation is less than 0.13. Using two different clinical prediction rules we estimated the operative mortality to be substantially less than 13%, so our conclusion that revascularization is better holds within the plausible range of operative risk. In Figure 4, a one-way sensitivity analysis of the quality of life after amputation is shown. The threshold value is about 0.94, i.e., as long as that quality of life is less than 0.94, revascularization is preferred. Again, the threshold value seems likely to be well above the true value for most patients.

In a so-called two-way sensitivity analysis, one variable is varied over a specified range, and the threshold value of a second variable is calculated for two strategies for each value in that range. This produces a graph showing the optimal strategy for all combinations of the two variables, with the calculated threshold lines forming the border between the regions. Figure 5 displays a two-way sensitivity analysis of the operative mortality for revascularization surgery and quality of life after amputation. Amputation is preferred for all combinations of operative mortality

***Forgive the pun.

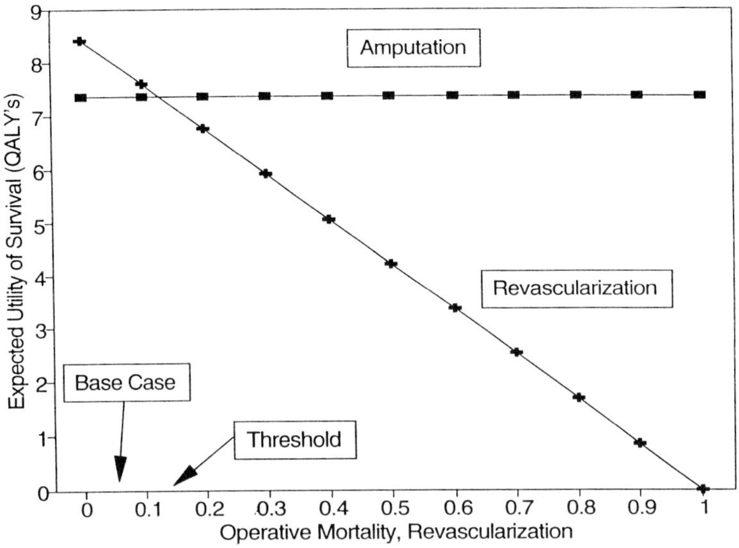

FIGURE 3. One-way sensitivity analysis of operative mortality rate for revascularization surgery. Each line corresponds to a strategy. The intersection is the threshold value.

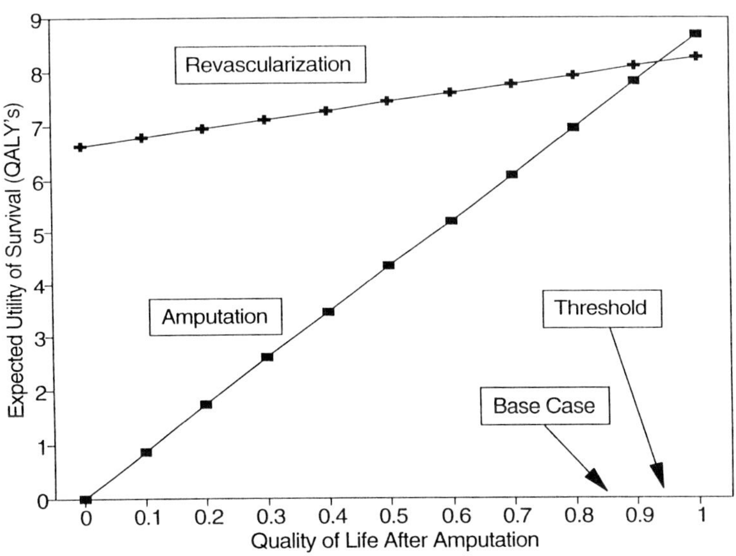

FIGURE 4. One-way sensitivity analysis of quality of life after amputation. Each line corresponds to a strategy. Note that both strategies are affected by the quality of life after amputation, as that outcome can occur in both strategies, albeit far less likely after revascularization surgery.

for revascularization and quality of life after amputation above the line, and revascularization is preferred for combinations below the line. Our base case assumptions correspond to point X. Because amputation is only preferred at combinations of these two variables that are felt to be unlikely, we can be confident that revascularization is the preferred strategy.

This example was kept simple for didactic purposes, but even here the calculation of expected utilities and thresholds was becoming time consuming if done "by hand" and, in fact, was facilitated by using a computer program that allows construction and evaluation of decision trees (40). Many clinical scenarios are considerably more complex. Although it is often difficult to capture all aspects of a clinical scenario in a model, the use of such software allows one to build and analyze quite complex models that represent the most important clinical aspects that are relevant to a decision. In particular, Markov models, rather than decision trees, are useful where there are ongoing risks, when events may occur more than once, and when the timing of events is important (41, 42).

SUMMARY

The knowledge underlying medical practice and the process of clinical decision making are changing dramatically. The amount of information a clinician must absorb and process has grown exponentially, but the development of a number of

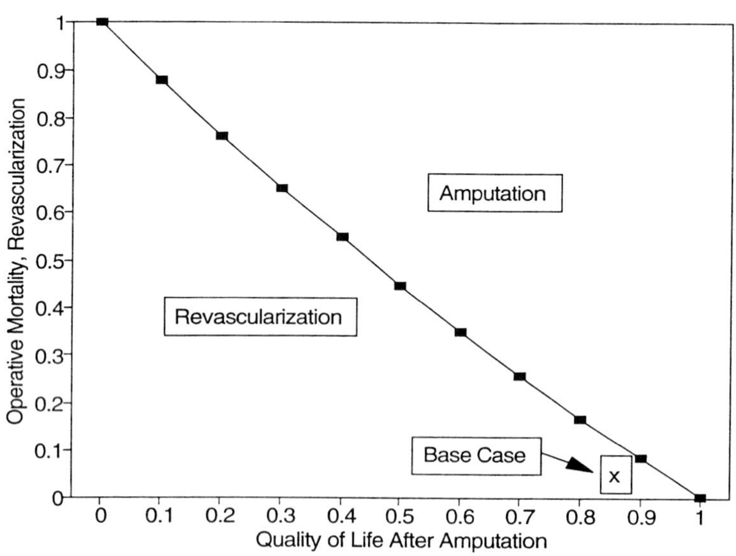

FIGURE 5. Two-way sensitivity analysis of the relation between operative mortality for revascularization surgery (vertical axis) and quality of life after amputation (horizontal axis). Each combination of these two factors corresponds to a point on the graph. (The base case values correspond to the point X.) Revascularization surgery is preferred for all points lying in the region below the curve.

computer-based tools has made the task of acquiring and using this information easier. Simultaneously, the concept of informed consent and models of shared decision making have emerged, so the clinician must be prepared to present to her patients the relevant clinical data in such a way that they can participate in choosing the clinical strategy that fits their preferences. If decision making is to be truly a shared process, the clinician will need a thorough familiarity with the relevant literature and an understanding of the psychology of decision making. Decision analysis offers a formal method by which prognostic data from the literature, from databases, and from prediction tools, can be combined with quantitative representations of the patient's preferences. Because of explicit problem representation, quantitative representations of outcome probabilities and preferences, and the ability to ask "what if?" by doing sensitivity analyses, decision analysis can often provide additional insight into clinical decisions, particularly by identifying and quantifying the trade-offs involved. The judicious use of these tools should improve and inform the choices which physicians and patients must make.

REFERENCES

1. Cox, J.J., Dawson, K.J. and K.E.F. Hobbs. 1992. The electronic information revolution and how to exploit it. Br J Surg; 79:1004-1010.
2. Kassirer, J.P. 1992. Journals in bits and bytes: electronic medical journals. New Engl J Med; 326:195-197.
3. Shortliffe, E.H. Clinical decision-support systems. In: *Medical Informatics: Computer Applications in Health Care.* E.H. Shortliffe, L.E. Perreault, eds., Reading:Addison-Wesley, pp. 466-502.
4. Sacks, H.S., Berier, J., Reitman, D., Ancona-Berk, V.A. and T. Chalmers. 1987. Meta-analyses of randomized controlled trials. New Engl J Med; 316:450-455.
5. Wasson, J.H., Sox, H.C., Neff, R.K. and L. Goldman. 1985. Clinical prediction rules: Applications and methodologic standards. New Engl J Med; 313:789-793.
6. Goldman, L., Caldera, D.L. and S.R. Nussbaum, et al. 1977. Multifactorial index of cardiac risk in noncardiac surgical procedures. New Engl J Med; 297:845-850.
7. Detsky, A.S., Abrams, H.B. and J.R. McLaughlin, et al. 1986. Predicting cardiac complications in patients undergoing noncardiac surgery. J Gen Intern Med; 1:211-219.
8. Eagle, K.A., Coley, C.M. and J.B. Newell, et al. 1989. Combining clinical and thallium data optimizes preoperative assessment of cardiac risk before major vascular surgery. Ann Intern Med; 110:859-866.
9. Katz, J. 1984. The Silent World of Doctor and Patient. New York:Free Press, pp. 60-62.
10. Annas, G.J., Glantz, L.H. and B.F. Katz. 1977. Informed Consent to Human Experimentation. Cambridge:Ballinger, pp. 33-38.
11. President's Commission for the Study of Ethical Problems in Medicine and Biomedical and Behavioral Research. 1982. Making Health Care Decisions. Washington: Government Printing Office, pp. 2-3.

12. Tversky, A. and D. Kahneman. 1982. Judgment under uncertainty: Heuristics and biases. In: *Judgment Under Uncertainty: Heuristics and Biases.* D. Kahneman, P. Slovic, A. Tversky, eds. Cambridge:Cambridge University Press, pp. 3-20.
13. McNeil, B.J., Weichselbaum, R. and S.G. Pauker. 1978. Fallacy of the five-year survival in lung cancer. New Engl J Med; 299:1397-1401.
14. McNeil, B.J., Weichselbaum, R. and S.G. Pauker. 1981. Speech and survival: Tradeoffs between quality and quantity of life in laryngeal cancer. New Engl J Med; 305:982-987.
15. Barry, M.J., A.G. Mulley and F.J. Fowler, et al. 1988. Watchful waiting vs. immediate transurethral resection for symptomatic prostatism: The importance of patients' preferences. JAMA; 259:3010-3017.
16. Kasper, J., Mulley, A.G. and J.E. Wennberg. 1992. Developing shared decision making programs to improve the quality of health care. QRB; 18:183-190.
17. Fellner, W. 1961. Distortion of subjective probabilities as a reaction to uncertainty. Quart J Econ; 75:670-689.
18. Ellsberg, D. 1961. Risk, ambiguity, and the Savage axioms. Quart J Econ; 75:643-669.
19. Ritov, I. and J. Baron. 1990. Reluctance to vaccinate: Omission bias and ambiguity. J Behav Decis Making; 3:263-277.
20. Cohen, B.J. and S.G. Pauker. 1994. How do physicians weigh iatrogenic complications? J Gen Int Med.; 9:20-23.
21. Spranca, M., Minsk, E. and J. Baron. 1991. Omission and commission in judgment and choice. J Exp Soc Psych; 27:76-105.
22. McNeil, B.J., Pauker, S.G., Sox, H.C. and A. Tversky. 1982. On the elicitation of preferences for alternative therapies. New Engl J Med; 306:1259-1262.
23. Bell, D. 1982. Regret in decision making under uncertainty. Oper Res; 30:961-981.
24. Raiffa, H. 1968. Decision Analysis: Introductory Lectures on Choices under Uncertainty. New York:Random House.
25. Weinstein, M.C. and H.V. Fineberg. 1980. Clinical Decision Analysis. Philadelphia:Saunders.
26. Pauker, S.G. and J.P. Kassirer. 1987. Decision analysis. New Engl J Med; 316:250-258.
27. Kassirer, J.P. Moskowitz, A.J., Lau, J. and S.G. Pauker. 1987. Decision analysis: a progress report. Annals Int Med; 106:275-291.
28. Jorland, G. 1987. The Saint Petersburg Paradox 1713-1937. In: *The Probabilistic Revolution, Volume 1:Ideas in History.* L. Krüger, L.J. Daston, M. Heidelberger, eds. Cambridge:MIT Press, pp. 157-190.
29. vonNeumann, J. and O. Morgenstern. 1944. Theory of Games and Economic Behavior. Princeton:Princeton University Press, pp. 15-31.
30. Allais, M. and O. Hagen, eds. 1979. Expected Utility Hypothesis and the Allais Paradox. Dordrect:Reidel.
31. Mehrez, A. and A. Gafni. 1989. Quality-adjusted life years, utility theory, and healthy-years equivalents. Med Decis Making; 9:142-149.

32. Torrance, G.W. 1986. Measurement of health state utilities for economic appraisal. J Health Econ; 5:1-30.
33. Pliskin, J.S., Shepard, D.S. and M.C. Weinstein. 1980. Utility functions for life years and health status. Oper Res; 28:206-224.
34. Mannick, J. Whittemore, A.D. and M.C. Donaldson. 1987. Aortofemoral bypass for atherosclerotic aortoiliac disease. In: *Current Therapy in Vascular Surgery,* 2nd edition. C.B. Ernst, J.C. Stanley, eds. Philadelphia: B.C. Decker, pp. 391-394.
35. Malone, J.M. and J. Goldstone. 1986. Lower extremity amputation. In: *Vascular Surgery,* 2nd edition. W.S. Moore, ed. Orlando:Grune & Stratton, pp. 1139-1206.
36. Brewster, D.C., Perler, B.A., Robison, J.G. and C. Darling. 1982. Aortofemoral graft for multilevel occlusive disease. Arch Surg; 117:1593-1600.
37. Beck, J.R., Kassirer, J.P. and S.G. Pauker. 1982. A convenient approximation of life expectancy (the "DEALE"). Am J Med; 73:883-888.
38. Sox, H.C., Blatt, M.A., Higgins, M.C. and K.I. Marton. 1988. Medical Decision Making. Boston:Butterworths, p. 376.
39. Wong, J.B., Sonnenberg, F.A., Salem, D.N. and S.G. Pauker. 1990. Myocardial revascularization for chronic stable angina. Annals Int Med; 113:852-871.
40. Sonnenberg, F.A. and S.G. Pauker. 1986. Decision maker. In: *MEDINFO '86: Proceedings of the Fifth Conference on Medical Informatics.* R. Salamon, B. Blum, M. Jorgensen, eds. Amsterdam:North Holland, p. 1152.
41. Beck, J.R. an S.G. Pauker. 1983. The Markov process in medical prognosis. Med Decis Making; 3:419-458.
42. Sonnenberg, F.A. and J.R. Beck. 1993. Markov models in medical decision making: a practical guide. Med Decis Making; 13:322-338.

Medicine and Health Care Into the Twenty-First Century. Edited by S.K. Majumdar, L.M. Rosenfeld, D.B. Nash and A.M. Audet. © 1995, The Pennsylvania Academy of Science.

Chapter Fifteen

A REVIEW OF THE BIOTECHNOLOGY INDUSTRY AND ITS PROSPECTS FOR THE FUTURE

MARC KRAMER
Executive Director/Chief Operating Officer
Eastern Technology Council
435 Devon Park Drive, Suite 803
Wayne, PA 19087-1945

THE BUSINESS OF BIOTECHNOLOGY

"Biotechnology—the use of data and techniques of engineering and technology for the study and solution of problems concerning living organisms" (1).

INTRODUCTION

Over the past three decades, with basic fundamental research support from the Federal government, the United States has become the international leader in biotechnology research, development, and commercialization. The business of biotechnology is younger than any other technology business. Its roots only trace back to the early and mid-1970s, with the birth of Agrigenetics, Cetus, Centocor, and Genentech.

Number and Location of U.S. Biotechnology Companies

There are, according to the Biotechnology Industry Organization (BIO), approximately 1,231 companies in the U.S. engaged in some aspect of biotechnology, an

11 percent increase over 1991. Two hundred and twenty-five are publicly held, which is a 16 percent increase over 1991 (2). Genentech was the first biotechnology company to go public with a successful offering in 1980.

The areas with the highest concentration of companies: (3)	
San Francisco Bay	181
New York	136
Boston	128
Washington, DC	115
San Diego	100
Los Angeles	68
Texas	52
Pennsylvania	51
Seattle	48
North Carolina	46
Market segments served	
Therapeutic	38 percent
Human Diagnostics	28
Supplier	16
Agricultural	10
Chemical/Environmental	8
Profile by size	
Small (1-50 employees)	76 percent
Mid-Size (51-135)	16
Large (136-299)	6
Top tier (300 plus)	2
Employment	
Total number of employees	79,000
Projected employment year 2,000	200,000

Biotechnology promotes health and environmental advances, its two main uses.

Health

Advances in health-related biotechnology are of enormous value in containing spiraling health care costs through new diagnostic, prevention, and treatment techniques. More than 1,000 clinical trials are currently in progress using biotechnology-derived pharmaceuticals; 400 biotechnology-derived clinical diagnostic devices exist that are currently being used in clinical practice (4). The recent successful cloning of blood clotting factors VIII and IX may possibly lead to the development of better therapy for hemophiliacs, realizing a significant cost savings over the life of these patients. Health related biotechnology encompasses a broad spectrum of basic and applied research, including (5):

Diagnostics
DNA manipulation
Drug delivery systems
Food-borne contaminants and toxins
Food nutrition
Instrumentation
Medical devices
Substance abuse
Therapeutics
Tissue engineering
Transgenic animal model development
Vaccines

Biotechnology has also resulted in the newly emerging field of gene therapy. Gene therapy trials have recently been approved in the U.S. for the treatment of cystic fibrosis and other inherited disorders, cancer, and AIDS. The possibilities for the prevention and treatment of disease through the use of biotechnology are enormous (6).

According to the Clinton 1994 budget plan, strong federal research programs would stimulate industry to develop new products. More innovative product development will require the emergence and enhancement of new interdisciplinary research areas at the interface of biology and engineering (7). The Clinton proposal, as laid out at the time this book is being written, is to lower the cost of some drugs and freeze the price of others.

Environmental

Environmental technologies need to take full advantage of the tools of molecular biology that can be used to reduce, manage, or remedy problems of environmental pollution, cleanup, and prevention. Even more fundamental, however, is the use of biotechnology research to provide a basis for new approaches for determining complex ecological relationships and for managing ecosystems. Bioremediation, expected to be a $300 million industry by 1995, relates both to ecosystem management and to reduction of human health risks (8).

New technologies are needed for the full potential of bioremediation to be realized, however, biotechnology promises the development of efficient and effective biotreatment systems. It will also provide methods to elucidate the environmental fate of biological agents used in treatment systems, to identify the metabolic products of treatment processes, and to determine environmental factors that promote bioremediation (9).

Given the well-known problems associated with oil spills and multiple contaminants at hazardous waste sites, further research is essential for successfully scaling the scientific and engineering barriers to the remediation of remote and complex waste mixtures. Understanding the fundamental aspects of safe application of biotechnology products, including the development and use of environmentally benign alternatives to chemical presticides, will allow federal regulatory agencies to insure appropriate oversight without impeding technology development and commercialization (10).

Negative Side

This will undoubtedly affect both the bottom line of drug companies and possibly discourage private and institutional investment in the industry. If this should happen the industry will downsize and contract.

Positive Side

The Clinton administration recognizes the fact that drugs cut the amount of time people spend in hospitals and seeing specialists. With greater use of drugs, companies won't feel the sting of lower drug prices as much, because of the increase in volume sales. The administration has increased the amount the federal government is investing in biotechnology by seven percent and has worked on speeding up the approval process for drugs.

Overview on the Types of Research Being Conducted for Commercialization

Industry participants are still debating what constitutes the biotechnology industry. Biotechnology is actually several technologies, applied to a wide range of existing industries. The markets identified for both public and private companies are the following (11)

- *Human health care-diagnostics*—designs clinically important, innovative tests which are highly accurate and whenever possible simple to use (12).
- *Human health care-therapeutics*—are complex pharmaceutical products subject to extensive testing and clinical trials in a regulatory environment administered by the Food and Drug (FDA). The industry is working on AIDS, heart disease, cancer, viral infection, arthritis, diseases of the immune system, and other areas (13).
- *Plant and animal genetics and health care*—encompasses products to treat plant and animal disease, products to strengthen resistance to environmental factors (e.g. frost, herbicide), and improve seeds and seedlings, and more productive livestock (14).

There are smaller segments, which include special contract services, food processing, energy/petroleum, bioremediation, software and other fields.

In most cases, biotechnology applications are the end product basic research. Much of this research is in the subs-disciplines of biology such as cell and structural biology, genetics, neuroscience, biochemistry, and, to a growing extent, ecology. Other disciplines normally not thought to be associated with the biological sciences, such as computer science, physics chemistry, engineering and materials science, are also key to the expanding research base fueling the biotechnology industry (15).

RESEARCH AND DEVELOPMENT

More than any other industry, biotechnology is driven by research and development and its finances are driven by the need to fund R&D. While traditional businesses either start with revenues, or revenues that are less than a few years away, revenues for a biotechnology company can be five to 10 years away. Other industries regard research and development (R&D) as a luxury item, whereas biotechnology relies solely on R&D to get a product to the marketplace and thereby generate profits.

The reason for the high cost of product development stems from the amount of money needed to build the right research facilities, hiring a high level of educated professionals and running pre-clinical and clinical trials. A 1986 study performed by then Arthur Young, called "Biotech 86: At the Crossroad," the study reported that the industry was R&D intensive, but that the amount of money going into R&D would go down and be funneled into manufacturing and marketing (16). With the exception of a few companies like Genentech and Amgen, the industry has not changed in the last seven years in regards to where it uses its money—it still goes heavily into R&D.

The results of the research that has been performed has yielded significant results. In 1986, according to Arthur Young, the industry realized approximately $9 million in sales. Today that number is $10 billion as of June 30, 1993, according to Ernst & Young's eighth annual survey of the industry's 450 chief executives (17). That figure covers the sales of 1,272 biotechnology companies (18).

A 1994 report released by President Clinton's Office of Science and Technology, entitled "FCCSET Initiatives in the FY 1994 Budget," estimates sales at $50 billion and employment of over 250,00 people by the year 2,000 (19).

Right now that seems a long way off. The pharmaceutical's largest company, Merck had $8.6 billion in 1992 alone (20).

Additional facts on research and development, according to BIO:[21]

- Total biotechnology industry R&D expenses were $4.9 billion.
- An average of $259 million over 10 to 12 year period was spent for each approval.
- R&D expenditures as a percentage of revenue were 74 percent.
- R&D expenditures as a percentage of total expenditures were 38 percent.
- Average R&D expenditures per employee are $62,000.
- Total federal biotech R&D per year is $4.9 billion.

The following is a sampling of the research of various biotechnology companies:

IBAH Affinity Biotech, Inc.,—applies its proprietary microemulsion technology to the development of oral dosage forms of protein and peptide therapeutic agents and a new generation of perfluorocarbon-based synthetic blood. Drawing on its expertise in surface chemistry, Affinity also formulates a variety of taste-masked liquid and chewable drugs, including analgesics, antibiotics, and anti-ulcer drugs (22).

Apollon, Inc.—was founded with a primary focus in the area of nucleic acid-based pharmaceuticals. Through collaborative research programs, Apollon has also spawned two peptide-based products candidates, one conventional small molecule pharmaceutical product, and a genetic vaccine. Apollon has focused a large portion of its resources on the development of this genetic vaccine, directed at the potential therapy and/or prophlaxis of AIDS (23).

Applied Technology Genetics Corporation (ATGC)—develops, manufactures and markets leading genetic screening products to diagnose genetic disease, predisposition to disease, and toxic environmental events. An ATGC proprietary product called Mutation Detection Enhancement (MDE) technology provides efficient and reliable screening of large regions of DNA, with a unique ability to identify hundreds of mutations.

Centocor, Inc.—develops, manufactures, and markets diagnostic and pharmaceutical products for human health care. Centocor's products are based on monoclonal antibodies and are primarily intended for use in the management of patients with infectious, cardiovascular, and autoimmune diseases, and cancer (25).

Cephalon, Inc.—a neuropharmaceutical company, whose primary focus is on neurodegenerative diseases which are characterized by the death of neurons, the specialized conducting cells of the nervous systems. Cephalon has concentrated its research programs on the prevention of neuronal death in several disorders such as amyotropic lateral sclerosis Alzheimer's disease, head and spinal cord inury, stroke and peripheral neuropathy (26).

DNA Plant Technology Corporation (DNAP)—applies a spectrum of technologies to develop and specialize plant-based products and environmental diagnostics for consumer and industrial markets. DNAP addresses commercial opportunities in three major markets: premium fruits and vegetables; specialty edible oils; and environmental diagnostics related to the detection of pesticide residues and environmental contaminants (27).

DNX Corporation—researches and develops therapeutic products and biological testing services based on transgenic animals. DNX uses its proprietary microinjection process to insert genetic material, including human genes, into an animal's permanent genetic makeup, resulting in the development of transgenic animals with new commercially valuable traits (28).

Magainin Pharmaceuticals Inc.—is engaged in the research and development of a new class of therapeutic products for the treatment of infections and certain cancers and the promotion of healing. Magainin's most advanced class of products under development are 'magainins' which are peptides that kill certain pathogens and cancer cells by puncturing the membrane of the cell (29).

Zynaxis Inc.—applies proprietary technologies to the development of new therapeutic drug delivery systems and laboratory diagnostic products. Zynaxis has focused its research and development efforts primarily in two areas, the development of a variety of cell linker molecules for the delivery and retention of therapeutics drugs and radiopharmaceutical to disease sites; and the development of cellular diagnostic systems for the measurement of a variety of cell types found in blood and other body fluids (30).

Financing Biotechnology Companies

According to a November 9, 1993 *Wall Street Journal* article, the cost of developing one drug can be as low as $125 million, if developed by a small company, and has high as $500 million, if developed by a major pharmaceutical company. The cost differences are due to size of overhead, length of time to develop the drug, and location of the company (31).

Past History: 1970 to 1990

When biotechnology first arrived on the scene in the late 1970's, financing was difficult because the industry had no track record. Funds for startup companies came from well-heeled "investor angels" and venture capitalists. Once Amgen and Genentech launched successful commercial products in the late 1980's and early 1990's, the industry became the new "Gold Rush."

Money was poured into the industry by venture capitalists. Over the last 12 years, $3 billion in venture capital, according to the Office of Science and Technology in 1993, has been invested in approximately 300 biotechnology companies. The report states that 22,000 people are associated with the biotechnology-based human therapeutics industry alone. During the 1980s, an average of 75 new biotechnology companies were established each year (32).

Companies with no products but huge promise went public within three years. A company like Centocor with no drug sales was trading for $120 plus a share, before splits, and its market capitalization was over $1 billion. The computer giant Unisys had $9 billion in sales and its market capitalization was two-thirds less than Centocor.

Present to Future: 1990 Forward

When companies like Centocor, U.S. Bioscience and Synergen couldn't get flagship drugs approved, the treasure chests of money being thrown at biotechnology companies dried-up, almost overnight. The price of publicly traded biotechnology stocks have dropped as much as 80 percent in the past two years and the market for new public offerings has been closed.

There are two things that have saved the industry and are consequently propelling it today:

- Successes of companies such as Amgen, Genentech and Chiron that were able to get Federal Drug Administation (FDA) approval and have products pending approval.
- The pharmaceutical industry's need for new products. Because of their small size relative to fully-integrated pharmaceutical firms, biotechnology companies tend to be more "entrepreneurial" in the research process. As a result, discoveries are made at a more rapid pace. These biotechnology discoveries are fueling the pharmaceutical companies' pipelines, via licensing agreements and joint collaborations—both being long-term sources of financing for biotechnology companies.

Below is a chart showing the various financing alternatives that were featured in Ernst and Young's "Biotech 93 Accelerating Commercialization" (33).

Type	Amount ($ millions)	Co. Age	Co. Stage	Advantage	Disadvantage
Grants/Gifts	$0-$5	Inception to 5 years	Pre-seed	"Free-money"	Limited availability and size. Some grant-specific requirements.
Venture capital	$1-$10	1-5 years	Pre-clinicals	Availability. Substantial VC Involvement.	Lower valuations. Substantial VC Involvement.
Private Placements	$1-$35	1-10 years	Preclinical-Advanced Clinicals	Higher Valuations	Limited Ability
Strategic Alliances	$1-$40	Unlimited	Clinical to matureity	Sub. for integration. Sub. size.	"Futures" can be the most expensive financing.
Initial Public Offering	$15-$100	3-10 years	Incubation	Large financing cash serv. required.	Markets highly cyclical; public valuation not completely manageable.
Secondary	$20-$150	3 years +	Start-up to	Same as IPO, but often at higher valuations.	Infrastructure requirement
SWORDs	$20-$50	Sponsor must be public	Preclinical to clinical trials	"Off balance sheet." Theoretically, avoids dilution.	Repurchase can be costly. Technical difficulties.
R&D Partnership	$1-$50	1 to unlimited	R&D Some tax.	Same as SWORDS, but ability is limited leverage,	Same as SWORDS-liquidity and transfer.
Debt:					
Convertible	$1-$100	1-10 years	Clinical to maturity	Usually "cheap." Sold based upon convertability. Generally not based on yield.	Debt service requirements.
Asset based	$1-$50	1 to unlimited	Developmental	No dilution.	Initially for buildings and equip., then receivables inventory.
Unsecured	$1-$10	Over 5 years	Operational	No dilution.	Generally unavailable.
Operations	Limited	1 to unlimited	Operational	Cheapest form of financing.	Limited source of cash.

Venture capital, according to BIO, has committed over $100 million since 1991. BIO also reports that stock offerings over the past 10 years have raised over $5.5 billion and $3.2 billion has been raised since 1991 (34).

Another source of funding is the federal government. According to the Office of Science and Technology in 1993, federal support for biotechnology in fiscal year 1993 was approximately $4 billion (35).

Seventy percent of the federal dollars committed to biotechnology comes from the U.S. Department of Health and Human Services, which contains the National Institutes of Health (NIH). Other federal agencies supporting the industry are the Departments of Agriculture and Energy and the National Science Foundation (36).

Following are comments by industry chief executive officers on the future of industry financing:

Dr. Phillip Schein, co-founder and chairman/CEO U.S. Bioscience in Conshohocken, PA, feels the future of financing biotechnology companies is in question.

> "The uncertainties associated with the direction which our health care system will take, as well as some notable product failures during the past two years, has dampened the enthusiasm of Wall Street to provide unlimited source of capital," said Schein. "The alternative is to seek an alliance with a large and established corporate partner. However, the traditional American pharmaceutical industry is undergoing a significant period of retrenchment and consolidation as it attempts to respond to the changing horizon in managed health care.
>
> "Cuts are likely to take place in their R&D budgets before their marketing programs are affected. This could result in either greater opportunities for biotechnology companies, who will serve as seedbed R&D organizations for the large pharmaceutical corporations, or an overall reduced national effort in R&D, which will include reduced opportunities for relationships with large companies in the future" (37).

Dr. Frank Baldino, co-founder and chairman/CEO of Cephalon, West Chester, PA, has a more positive view of future financing than Dr. Schein.

> "Traditional avenues of financing will continue to be available to the industry," said Baldino. "Public equity markets will likely remain the primary source of capital for public biotech companies. Recently the capital markets have become more selective than usual, but this reflects changing market dynamics and legislative uncertainty, rather than a shift in attitude about the prospects of biotech industry.
>
> "Recent changes in capital gains tax legislation will provide incentive for patient capital investments into small cap, less than $50 million, companies. The hope of course is that similar incentives will be made available for the public companies whose capital requirements exceed those available from the venture industry" (38).

Dr. George Rathmann, founder of Amgen and co-founder and chairman/CEO of ICOS, Seattle, Washington, is one of the original pioneers of the industry. His first company, Amgen, was one of the two most successful biotechnology companies in the industry's history. He believes recent and future successes will finance future growth.

> "The various types of partnerships as well as consolidations can reduce the requirement that each single company finance its own factory and its own sales force," said Rathmann. "It seems likely that continued technical and commercial successes should be sufficient to sustain a reasonable level of financing in the coming 10 years" (39).

Another pioneer, Dr. Hubert Schoemaker, co-founder and chairman of Centocor, West Chester, PA, said "If you have a good organization, excellent technology and products, captial will flow to you either from industrial partners or Wall Street; the cost of capital does vary over time" (40).

The Effect of Health Care Reform on Biotechnology

The future of biotechnology is uncertain because there have been few major success stories to date. There isn't a chief executive officer in the industry that doesn't think numerous major product success aren't just around the corner. What is of concern is the Clinton Administration's threat of drug price-controls.

Comments from industry CEOs on upcoming health care buying changes:

Frank Baldino of Cephalon:

"Biotechnology should have a bright future under health care reform. Biotech companies are developing novel diagnostic and therapeutic products to treat disease more effectively and less expensively than current medical practice. We are not about "me-too" products; we are about discovery and innovation. If successful, biotechnology companies will be providing significant medical benefits to patients with significant savings to the health care system.

"For example, current research into the underlying cause of Alzheimer's disease and stroke may produce significant new products to treat these conditions, not just their symptoms. The implications of this for health care are enormous because if we can treat diseases like Alzheimers early on, we can preserve a reasonable quality of life for patients, help them avoid hospital or nursing home care for many years, and save billions of dollars in health care expenditures" (41).

George Rathmann of ICOS:

"If we limit the question to whether biotech will continue to produce profound changes in human health care, I think the answer is a clear yes. If we must consider the uncertainties introduced by health care reform and general business trends, the crystal ball gets a lot cloudier. In other words, I can't predict the stock value of the biotechnology index any better than anybody else. General business trends (fewer third party payers and stronger buying groups) may soon be capable of controlling prices where multiple brands of pharmaceuticals are available. This change could make me-too directed R&D obsolete" (42).

Phillip Schein of U.S. Bioscience:

"The proposed changes in the health care system, both those initiated by the private sector as well as by government, have two principal goals: reduced costs and the provisions of medical care to individuals who are being underserviced by our current system. Profits will be increasingly driven by volume considerations, rather than the ability to premium price a new product. It is therefore difficult to determine how the final result will impact on the pharmaceutical industry, and biotechnology specifically.

"This may have a significant impact on biotechnology products that are not viewed as 'breakthrough,' since they are typically produced using more expensive technologies than the traditional manufacturing processes required for more simple chemicals. Therefore, they may have to show more than simple equivalency in order to be accepted into formularies developed by government agencies or large purchasing groups, such as HMO's. In essence, success can be ensured only if products in the pipeline are envisioned to have a profile of efficacy and safety exceeding that of drugs already in the market, or if they respond to disease states that are currently inadequately treated by existing drugs, such as AIDS and cancer" (43).

Hubert Schoemaker of Centocor:

"Biotechnology represents a major part of the solution to solving the health care problems in terms of providing cost effective health care. Societies want more health care at a low cost. This can be accomplished only through prevention of disease, early detection and improved efficiency of drugs. Biotechnology will impact all of these areas and is the most promising approach" (44).

Robert Serenbetz, president and CEO of DNA Plant Technology, Cinnaminson, NJ:

"The proposed changes in the health care system should have little effect on the agricultural biotechnology sector. One potential positive is that through greater participation in the health care system, lower income groups may be encouraged to consume more nutritious foods, which would be a benefit to the agricultural sector" (45).

When Will the Pay-Off Begin?

Over the past 15 years, billions of dollars have been poured into the nation's biotechnology companies with only a few commercial successes to claim. According to BIO, the following are current and projected sales and revenues for U.S. biotechnology companies (46):

- Total revenues of public and private companies are $8.1 billion.
- Total product sales are $5.9 billion
- Total market capitalization is $50 billion.
- Total assets are $50.6 billion.
- Export sales of U.S. biotechnology products are $640 million.

Health Care

Currently, the world's top pharmaceutical and agricultural companies, but with a much greater emphasis on health care, are teaming with biotechnology companies throughout the country.

Companies like Eli Lilly, SmithKline Beecham and Hoffman LaRoche believe their investments in companies like Centocor, Cephalon and Genentech will develop blockbuster drugs that will take the place of their current star drugs that are coming off patent.

In the health care arena, the following companies have had drugs approved:

Biogen/Schering Plough—a drug to treat hepatitis B called Intron A.

Genentech—a drug called Kogengate for hemophilia A.

Chiron/Berlex—a drug called Betaserson that deals with multiple sclerosis.

Agricultural

In the agricultural arena, companies like Monsanto, American Cyanamid, Genzyme and DNX are developing potential products that will lead to decreasing the spoilage of tomatoes, virus resistant crops, and infant formula.

The following is a small sampling of three new products approved this year in bio-agricultural area:

Crop Genetics—Spod-X bioinsecticide, a protein-encapsulated virus used to protect vegetables and flowers against beet worms.

EcoScience's Bio-path, which uses a naturally occurring soil fungus to kill cockroaches.

Myogen's third genetically-engineered bioinsecticide, M-Peril, which is used against the European corn borer.

Following are comments by industry CEOs on a timetable for commercialization of products:

Philip Schein of U.S. Bioscience believes the industry is still developing. "In general, the vast majority of the biotechnology industry is at an early stage of validating research concepts in terms of their ability to deliver safe, effective, and commercially viable products," said Dr. Schein. "Nevertheless, there are sufficient examples of success so that companies should be encouraged to take on the challenges associated with the drug development process, although they may need to prioritize more carefully and support only those drugs that have the highest probability of success and acceptance in the market" (47).

The amount of revenue currently being generated, according to Frank Baldino of Cephalon, is starting to become significant. "This is a rapidly maturing industry that generated $6 billion in product sales in 1992," said Dr. Baldino. "There are now 21 therapeutic biotechnology products and more than 600 diagnostic products on the market.

"Sixteen additional products are currently awaiting Food and drug Administration approval, and nearly 90 percent of biopharmaceutical companies which do not currently have products on the market expect to do so by 1996. After 20 years of development, biotechnology is delivering on its promise" (48).

One of the few chief executive officers and founders of a company to see his company develop a spectacularly successful drug is George Rathmann, founder of biotechnology star Amgen and up and coming star, ICOS. Dr. Rathmann believes new commercially viable products are around the corner.

"We should certainly expect an acceleration in the commercialization of biotechnology products," Dr. Rathmann said. "There will be many products of more modest commercial value in contrast to the high proportion of blockbusters during the past 10 years. But we will see something else.

"There will be increasing examples of products which are forerunners to broad families of products where the first member validated a basic new insight to human physiology. For example, a cure for multiple sclerosis might lead more or less directly to cures for lupus, glomerular nephritis and even arthritis" (49).

Chiron, one of the major biotechnology companies out of Emeryville, California, is on the verge of commercializing a huge blockbuster drug called Betaseron, the first new treatment for multiple sclerosis in a generation. Chiron is on the verge of developing a vaccines for genital herpes, which afflicts an estimated 25% of U.S. adults, and for the hepatitis C virus that infects about 150,000 Americans each year (50).

CONCLUSION

The future of biotechnology—its evolution into a mature industry—may be in question, because of the new health care reforms and agricultural Federal Drug Administation concerns currently being reviewed in Washington, D.C. The issue which needs to be addressed is the potential value biotechnology adds to both health care and agriculture, leading to a better quality of life for everyone.

Clearly, the biotechnology industry has begun its quest of gaining both investor and general public support. Despite some disappointments, potential drugs on the horizon, such as Genentech's Activase or Centocor's 7E3, blood clot dissolving drugs, will hopefully prove the viability and great need to maintain this industry.

The general public's concern over giant vegetables and two-headed pigs will disappear through the educational efforts of the media. Genetic engineering is therefore resulting in improvements in yield, hardiness and resistance to disease of crop plants, and may lead to the introduction of new kinds of plant foods. The quality and quantity of food will provide the country with great exporting opportunities to countries like China, Russia and India, who have large populations to feed.

Although the Clinton health care proposed reforms are of great concern to the industry, Clinton's promise to speed up the patent and drug approval process will decrease costs in developing drugs. Currently, according to BIO, biotechnology patents take 27 months to be issued compared to 18 months for all other patents. This is crucial to the success of the industry because biotechnology patent applications have grown at an annual rate of 15 percent since 1990.

It is doubtful the current White House administration, which purports to be the "technology administation" will let this industry slip into the hands of foreign competition. The stakes are too high. The jobs created by the biotechnology industry are high paying, challenging and improve the quality of life and lower the costs of health care.

Medical doctors, tired of the constraints put on them by the federal government and lured by the challenge and lucrativeness of the field, will turn to working as researchers and business leaders in biotechnology in increasing numbers.

Aside from health care, biotechnology in time will make a significant positive impact on agriculture and the environment. The ripple effect for other industries such as commercial and residential construction, retail and leisure will be significant. The intellectual jobs developing in this industry will help absorb jobs lost in the defense and electronics industries.

The political bottom line is that no administration wants to be held responsible for selling off the future of the country. The current and future administations will be more focused on development than pure research, because it is the politically correct thing to do. The average voter doesn't understand that the building blocks of future drugs are built by basic resarch. Tax payers only understand finished products that impact them and their families.

Science education and improving the quality of life driven by biotechnology, are going to be the slogans for the rest of this decade and into the new century.

REFERENCES

1. Burril, Steven G. and Kenneth B. Lee. 1986. Biotech 86: At the Crossroad, p. 8. Arthur Young, San Francisco, CA.
2. Office of the Biotechnology Industry Organization, 1992-1993. State Of The Industry Report, p. 2.
3. Ibid, p. 3.
4. Ibid, p. 5.
5. Ibid, p. 4-5.
6. Office of Science and Technology, *FCCSET Initiatives In The FY 1994 Budget*, p. 31.
7. Ibid, p. 31.
8. Ibid, p. 34.
9. Ibid, p. 34.
10. Ibid, p. 35.
11. Burrill, Steven G. and Kenneth B. Lee. 1986. Biotech 86: At the Crossroad, p. 8. Arthur Young, San Francisco, CA.
12. Ibid, p. 9.

Medicine and Health Care Into the Twenty-First Century. Edited by S.K. Majumdar, L.M. Rosenfeld, D.B. Nash and A.M. Audet. © 1995, The Pennsylvania Academy of Science.

Chapter Sixteen

THE IMPACT OF CLINICAL PRACTICE GUIDELINES ON THE FUTURE OF MEDICINE

STEPHEN H. KING, M.D.
District Health Director
Georgia Department of Human Resources
Division of Physician and Mental Health
2011 Eisenhower Drive
P.O. Box 14257
Savannah, GA 31416-1257

INTRODUCTION

The future of medicine depends on improving the certainty of outcomes. This expectation is especially characteristic of patients and payers. Medicine in the future must increase accuracy in decisions, until now served well by intuition alone. The widespread confusion over the differences of the ability of medicine to provide care and to effect a cure make it necessary for medicine in the future to develop a clear understanding of what it means to make valid clinical decisions. Conversely, when there is not a satisfactory scientific base, medicine in the future must be able to say that cure is uncertain. An early English language use of the word *guideline* referred to a rope used to guide miners through labyrinthine turns in the mine. Each decision made on their way involved enough uncertainty that success in their returning was unlikely without assistance. The use of clinical practice guidelines will increase the certainty of a satisfactory future.

Why the Current Interest in Clinical Practice Guidelines?

Were it not for powerful economic interests concerned about uncontrolled increase in tax revenues necessary for health care, and the rapidly increasing cost to industry of health insurance, the issue of health care reform and the interest in clinical practice guidelines would not have surfaced. The concern is not so much over the absolute amount that is spent on health care as is the rapid and uncontrolled rise in that amount. Most physicians are not aware of the frustration and anger that exists in the political and business community over this issue. Every governor in every state, a generation of presidents and every corporate leader competing internationally has seen their public agendas and their competitive edge destroyed by unanticipated health care obligations. In the late 80s, this frustration led to the real possibility of expenditure caps for physicians services reimbursed by Medicare. Organized medicine suggested the use of clinical practice guidelines to contain costs as an alternative to expenditure caps. In 1989, that compromise created the Public Health Service Agency for Health Care Policy and Research and the beginning of the Federal initiative in practice guidelines.

Variability in practice and the management issues associated with variability also occupy the attention of policy makers at all levels. For officials responsible for resources used for the medical care of others, recent research showing wide variation in practice patterns has increased their concerns about the basic value of health care—a concern already brought into focus by uncontrolled increases in costs. Practice variations that are not driven by differences in disease patterns and that do not lead to differences in outcome give the appearance of a system that is not in control. To the manager, control of variability at least offers the opportunity to help with control of growth in costs. Clinical practice guidelines appear to offer a basis for the policies and procedures necessary to build management control into the legislative appropriation process.

Policy making bodies are also frustrated by research that is of little help in forming a basis for policy; by an inability to evaluate the claims of competing interests; by difficulty with coverage and payment decisions; by the fact that policy decisions to use or not use medical intervention are generally unrelated to outcomes; and by the current irrational process governing liability. For all of these reasons, it seems intuitive that clinical practice guidelines may be of help.

HISTORY OF CLINICAL PRACTICE GUIDELINES

Statements about the process of care have been around for as long as there has been a written record. Early Egyptian hieroglyphics contain a number of examples of what could pass as a modern practice guideline. One example is the admonition to immobilize the head and upper body when attempting to move someone with a broken neck.

Some of the best collection of practice guidelines may be found in nurse practitioner protocols. Though they originally were developed to satisfy the concerns of practicing physicians, they have become excellent tools for standardization of best practices in systems of care which provide ambulatory community based primary care. These protocols are also quite useful as an aid to programs of ambulatory quality assurance/quality improvement and as a basis for continuing education.

Recommendations about the care of patients with sexually transmitted diseases, tuberculosis, the prevention of immunizable diseases, and different degrees of prevention that may be used in the care of chronic diseases are examples of practice guidelines developed by public health agencies that are commonly used by the medical community. These guidelines are used as the basis for community-based programs of health protection and promotion.

The National Institute of Health has a long tradition of providing advice to the medical community through the promulgation of recommendations developed by a consensus panel of recognized experts.

The Academy of Pediatrics Red Book is widely used by the pediatric community and others who provide medical care to children. These guidelines are extensive and regularly updated, representing current medical information about common clinical conditions found in children.

The Clinical Efficacy Assessment Project of the American College of Physicians regularly produces clinical guidelines that serve a variety of purposes, including the use of the laboratory, screening, and general medical care. This effort was one of the first to attempt to tie recommendations to the scientific evidence that is available in the literature.

In 1989, the United States Preventive Services Task Force published a Guide to Clinical Prevention Services. This book considered the evidence for the use of 169 clinical preventive services. For the first time, the importance of the methodologic vigor used in guideline development was described. They related a taxonomy of qualities of evidence to the strength of the recommendation, borrowing heavily from previous efforts by a similar task force in Canada.

CHARACTERISTICS OF CLINICAL PRACTICE GUIDELINES

At the beginning of the Federal effort to develop clinical practice guidelines, the Institute of Medicine in the National Academy of Science was engaged by the Public Health Service to provide advice on how it might approach its new responsibilities for practice guidelines. Their work included definition of terms and the development of important attributes or characteristics of guidelines.

The work of the Institute of Medicine has had an important influence on the development of clinical practice guidelines. The definition and attributes of practice guidelines described here are taken from this work.

Definition:

> Practice guidelines are systematically developed statements to assist practitioner and patient decisions about appropriate health care for specific clinical circumstances.

Attributes:

VALIDITY: Is the guideline a true statement? Practice guidelines are valid if, when followed, they lead to clearly projected health and cost outcomes. A valid guideline is supported by a scientific base, considers the health outcomes and cost of alternative courses of action, requires a relationship between the evidence and the recommendations, uses an explicit and rigorous analysis of the strength of the scientific and clinical evidence cited, discusses the means used to evaluate the evidence, and is explicit about the use of expert judgement. Finally, the guideline is peer reviewed for face validity, scientific content and accuracy of literature analysis.

RELIABILITY/REPRODUCTIBILITY: Practice guidelines are reliable and reproducible if, given the same evidence and methods for development, another group of experts produce the same statements; and, if given the same circumstances, the guidelines are interpreted and applied consistently.

CLINICAL APPLICABILITY: Practice guidelines are as inclusive of defined patient populations as scientific and clinical evidence and expert judgement permit, and they explicitly state the populations to which statements apply. Clinical practice guidelines are no more inclusive of populations than can be supported by evidence or explicit judgement.

CLINICAL FLEXIBILITY: The clinical practice guideline clearly identifies situations that lead to exceptions in its use.

CLARITY: The clinical practice guideline uses unambiguous language, defines terms precisely, and uses a logical, easy to follow mode of presentation.

MULTIDISCIPLINARY PROCESS: The clinical practice guideline is developed by a group process that requires contribution and investment from representatives of affected persons—including patients, payers and providers. Participation may include serving on panels that develop guidelines, providing evidence and viewpoints to the panels, and reviewing draft guidelines.

SCHEDULED REVIEW: Practice guidelines include statements requiring review to determine whether new clinical evidence or changing professional consensus warrant redevelopment.

DOCUMENTATION: The procedures followed in developing guidelines, the participants involved, the evidence used, the assumptions and rationales accepted, and the analytic methods employed are meticulously documented and described.

METHODOLOGIC PRINCIPLES IN GUIDELINE DEVELOPMENT

Guideline development depends on a mixture of subjective judgement, findings in the literature, evidence based on the results of careful outcomes studies and patient preferences.

but it does serve the same kind of assurance of completeness that a checklist used by a pilot to determine readiness prior to flight. As organizations begin to develop guidelines the use of a guide such as this (guidelines for guidelines, so to speak) forces the process to operate in an open and explicit manner. This format is very useful when used in a teaching activity.

A. Short version of guideline.
B. Amplification of statement. Include detailed information for clinical implementation, including:
    1. Description of condition being addressed.
    2. Type of patients and clinical presentations for which guideline applies.
    3. Elements of care that are appropriate, inappropriate, or of intermediate or uncertain appropriateness in specific clinical situations.
    4. Information to give patient.
    5. Decisions that need to be made based on patient preferences.
    6. Confidence limits. Identify and provide rationale for major foreseeable exceptions and alternate management strategies. Specify intended flexibility (or strictness) of use.
C. Methods
    1. How topic was selected.
    2. How panel and chair were selected. Provide names, specialties, affiliations, and brief biographies of panel members and others responsible for guideline.
    3. Clarification of purpose. Each of the following parameters should be discussed from a methodologic perspective, describing with each parameter the scope of relevance (e.g., which types of patients, interventions, settings, etc. were considered relevant to the panel and which types were not) and the methodologic rationale for those selections.
        a. Target condition.
        b. Patient/clinical presentation.
        c. Interventions, alternative treatments in current use, and interventions not considered.
        d. Setting (type of provider, practice setting).
        e. Outcomes to be changed.
        f. Intended users.
    4. Assessment of clinical benefits and harms.
        a. Evidence Model. Provide a graphical or tabular listing of the outcomes (benefits and harms) that were identified by the panel as important for study in assessing the effectiveness of the interventions and the specific linkages for which evidence was sought. Outcomes of interest should be defined as clearly as possible (e.g., "five-year survival rate"). Outcomes not considered, and the reasons for these decisions, should also be documented.
        b. Types of evidence reviewed. Define the types of evidence that the panel considered relevant and that served as the basis for the literature search. Also describe the types of literature or data that were excluded.

c. Reviewer(s). Document the names and qualifications of the person(s) who performed the literature search and those who evaluated the quality of the evidence.
d. Retrieval methods. Describe the search strategy (e.g., bibliographic sources, keywords) for locating relevant studies and for eliminating irrelevant studies.
e. Methods for judging quality of the evidence. Describe the criteria that were used to evaluate the internal and external validity of studies examined by the panel.
f. Summary reports for each linkage in Evidence Model. For each linkage, provide narrative reviews, summary tables, and other methods for synthesizing the data (e.g., meta-analysis) that describe the magnitude and probability of the outcome(s) of interest, the degree of uncertainty surrounding the estimates, and the limits of the generalizability of the evidence.
g. Summary of overall benefits and harms. Use "balance sheets" or other methods to describe the overall benefits and harms based on the total body of evidence for all linkages.
h. Group judgement decisions and rationale. Describe components of the model for which evidence was lacking and for which subjective judgements such as expert opinion were used to estimate benefits and harms. The rationale for the group judgement, the methods used to reach consensus, and the degree of panel agreement should be made explicit.
i. Patient preferences. Describe the extent to which patient preferences were considered in assessing the importance of benefits and harms, the methods that were used to assess patient preferences, and how this information was incorporated into the group's decision-making process.

5. Assessment of public policy issues.
   a. Costs, impact on other health care resources, and other social choices. Describe the projected costs of the interventions, how these costs relate to health outcomes, and other overall public policy implications of the guideline.
   b. Feasibility issues that present barriers to implementation (e.g., concerns of patients, practitioners, and payers).
   c. Written and verbal testimony from open forum.
   d. Panel discussion of open forum testimony.
6. Peer review and pretesting. List the names and affiliations of the reviewers, the processes used by the reviewers in judging the document and by the panel in interpreting review comments, and the process used in pretesting the document. Review comments and pretesting data should be summarized.
7. Final rationale for guideline. Include criteria used to draw conclusions from the evidence and the extent to which factors other than clinical benefits and harms (e.g., costs) influenced the guidelines.
8. Recommendation of others. Include suggested reasons for discrepancies with other groups.
9. Disclaimers.

a. Medicolegal statement.
b. Recommend mechanism for periodic review, updating, or predetermined revision date.
c. Technical developments or current research that may call for a change in the guideline in the near future.

10. Research priorities. Identify gaps in the evidence for which expert opinion was needed and for which additional research is indicated to provide objective information on effectiveness.
11. Follow-up Activities. Recommendations for dissemination (including potential formats for different users), quality assurance (e.g., recommendations on whether the guideline should be used as a standard of quality or for utilization review purposes), and formal evaluation of impact (including potential settings and approaches for evaluating impact). Recommendations on strategies for using the guideline in clinical training and continuing professional education, and other methods to improve compliance with the guideline should be outlined.
12. References.
13. Author(s) of document.

UTILITY OF PRACTICE GUIDELINES

Theoretically, practice guidelines have a role in health care delivery because of the presumption that their scientifically valid base increases benefit and decreases cost of health care services that are variably provided. In a New England Journal of Medicine editorial, Louise Russell recently described two goals for a reformed health care system. She stated that the care provided should be proved effective by good science and that those effective services that bring the most health for the sources spent should be given the highest priority. The policies needed to implement such a system are in essence practice guidelines developed by a rigorous methodology.

However, for guidelines to work, they must be useful to managers. They must be able to strengthen management control of the effectiveness, value and cost of health care.

Management uses. For managers of systems of care the uses of guidelines in cost considerations become their most important value. Guidelines can accommodate the inclusion of costs in clinical decisions in the following ways:

When resources are fixed and time is immediate, such as triage in the emergency room, available resources and outcomes drive decisions.

When benefits and harms of a common intervention are unclear, it can be reasonable to omit the practice.

When evidence supports more than one treatment of similar costs, each with different effects, the patient can reasonably make a choice.

When evidence supports more than one treatment of similar effects, each with different costs, the patient can understand paying the difference or receiving the less costly option.

When evidence shows that alternative interventions produce similar clinical and perceived patient effects, there may be an ethical obligation to use the less costly treatment.

Other uses include the ability to control costs with coverage and payment decisions, to reduce the system inefficiencies of practice variability, define benefit packages, clarify and enable patient choices and consent and to eliminate the payer's "mystical black box."

Uses of guidelines in clinical decisions. In the majority of instances, guidelines are currently used as an aid to clinical decision making. Examples of guidelines used as policies in organized systems include practice management policies, protocols for physicians and physician extenders and in specialized sites such as emergency rooms and orthopedic cast rooms, drug formularies and system policies to protect against defensive medicine.

Risk management/medical liability. General counsel for the American Medical Association has concluded that clinical practice guidelines have the potential to rationalize court decisions where much unfortunate health policy is now developed.

"Good" guidelines should carry more weight in court. By "good" the law is increasingly coming to mean guidelines that are based on evidence rather than expert testimony. Courts may increasingly come to expect guidelines to be clear and specific (explicit) and that they are developed by a reputable process.

The law is coming to view bad guidelines as vague and non specific and that they lack documentation and that they lack careful reasoning. Some states are trying specific statutory recognition of guidelines. That could be desirable, but only for "good" guidelines. So far, legislatures have been unable to determine what "good" means.

Uses for policy development. For many years national guidelines have served public health purposes well. The medical community has been able to utilize best practices in the management of community problems such as tuberculosis, sexually transmitted diseases, immunizations in both children and adults, and more recently, HIV infection. This is the best example to date of a national utility for practice guidelines.

Resolution of conflict using practice guidelines. What does a manager do when faced with guidelines that are in conflict? The answer usually is revealed when the guidelines are evaluated for methodologic strength. As examination of their target, their objectives, and their methodology of development should help identify sources of disagreement between guidelines—as well as providing an excellent educational experience.

Does the conflict involve a specific health condition?

Does the conflict involve similar patients?

Does the conflict involve similar providers?

Does the conflict involve similar settings?

Does the conflict involve methodologic principles, including the use of evidence?

Do parties to the conflict share similar objectives such as patient outcomes, saving money, protecting territory, promoting technology, achieving personal or financial gain?

Total quality management uses of guidelines. With the TQM focus on systems problems, strong customer-supplier relationships, improvement of average performance and reduction in variability, the actual policies that are developed to implement these activities are guidelines. The only way to assure that the policies accomplish their intended purpose is for the process for their development be valid.

Changing average performance requires benchmarks which delineate the expectations of the processes of care as well as identify system problems. Guidelines serve these purposes.

Staff development uses. Medical specialty groups that have invested staff time and resources in guideline development activities find that the organized knowledge base developed by this exercise serves well in specialty certification curriculum development. In the same manner, there is increasing expectation that licensure means understanding and use of best practices for commonly encountered conditions. Additionally, the accreditation of an institution may increasingly be dependent on a demonstration of policies and procedures that meet explicit standards of validity.

Medical staff that work together in guideline development often report that the process clearly enhances clinicial decision making for the group. In addition, the effect of this activity seems to exercise the intellect in a way that is helpful to decision making in other activities in the medical care setting or elsewhere in their personal lives.

Uses in ethical dilemmas. Could the decision of whether to do or not do a thing for a patient be clarified by the scientific basis for its use? Is it ethical to consider costs and the potential loss of resources for others when considering an intervention for an individual patient? If resources are restricted, what criteria do we use in their allocation? Is the individual or the society to be considered first? Is the guideline the property of the provider or the patient?

Facilitate equity in the use of best practices. On the political scene there is a great deal of discussion about issues of access to health care. At the heart of the issue, however, is concern over equity in which access is only part of the problem. With the advent of practice guidelines the realization that best practices can be described and that they are even more uneven than access will bring much more attention to finding ways to describe basic benefit packages. Benefit packages that contain at a minimum those practices that are deemed to be effective will form the basis of successful health care reform. Practice guidelines form the heart of that process.

DISSEMINATION/IMPLEMENTATION

There are a few principles that have great influence on the successful adoption and use of the guidelines.

Practitioner knowledge of guidelines and acceptance of validity are key to success.

However, they are not by themselves the key to provider behavior change or change in patterns of practice.

Other problems at work include the need to overcome information overload, habitual practice patterns, malpractice fears, and economic disincentives. There is a need to change from a focus on provider behavior to a focus on environment in which care is delivered.

EVALUATION

In the final analysis, for the guidelines to have value they must do what they were intended to do. After all, it is the purpose of the guideline to try to be, among all possible recommendations, that one which is correct. It might be said that only mother nature knows which one that is. Modern and future medicine places its reason for existence on a concept called scientific validity, and that may be the way to her heart. So, if the guideline is valid, we believe it is the one that mother nature already knows to be right.

When the guideline is based on subjective judgement, then it is necessary to measure patient outcomes as science is unavailable to support claims of guideline validity. However, when the guideline is science based, then it may be necessary to only look for changes in provider and patient behavior. In this case it is more likely that the recommended actions are, in fact valid.

Since, in most cases, it is not yet known whether guidelines will do what they are intended to do, an evaluation of methodologic rigor becomes a surrogate for an evaluation of the guideline itself.

CONCLUDING POINTS

Certainly guidelines are not a solution to everything that might be considered wrong with health care. But it is reasonable to say that they should—no*must*—be a part of the fabric of any reasonable reform as well as a major tool to force change for the good.

Guidelines can improve the quality and measurement of clinical care.

Guidelines can reduce the cost of inappropriate, unnecessary, ineffective or dangerous care.

Guidelines can improve patient decisions about the choices they have and make informed consent mean what it says.

Guidelines can help rationalize political decisions about health and social policy. In any environment that policy is developed, the use of guidelines should help develop an emphasis and expectation of effective medical care.

The development and use of guidelines should improve clinical decision making.

The development and use of guidelines should help in resolving conflict within medicine and between medicine and other groups, such as administrative and fiscal interests.

Medicine and Health Care Into the Twenty-First Century. Edited by S.K. Majumdar, L.M. Rosenfeld, D.B. Nash and A.M. Audet.

Chapter Seventeen

LACK OF PRIMARY CARE PHYSICIANS: A Challenge into the Next Century

GANG XU, Ph.D. and J. JON VELOSKI, M.S.[1]
Center for Research in Medical Education and Health Care
1025 Walnut Street
Philadelphia, PA 19107

INTRODUCTION

One of the most pervasive challenges facing the United States health care system has been and continues to be that of specialty distribution (1). A maldistribution of physicians has been noted for more than 50 years and has been a concern of medical educators and governmental policymakers for much of this century (2, 3, 4, 5, 6). In recent years, this issue has become increasingly urgent as the number of primary care physicians continues to decrease, which contributes significantly to the national health care crisis: the difficulty of accessing health care, particularly in rural and inner city areas, and the raising cost. As the Nation is stepping into a new century, to slow or reverse this trend is increasingly gaining public support and health care reform is becoming a top priority of the national agenda of the Clinton administration (7).

Through the years and decades, policy makers and medical educators interested in the area of physician work force, career choice in particular, have made great efforts to understand this issue. Yet, a significant portion of this area remains to be studied. The purpose of this chapter is to examine what we know—and what we

---

[1]Dr. Xu is research associate and Mr. Veloski is director, Medical Education Division, Center for Research in Medical Education and Health Care; both are faculty members of Department of Psychiatry and Human Behavior, Jefferson Medical College, Philadelphia, PA.

have yet to learn—in this broad and important area in medical education research.

Primary care physicians are defined in the chapter as those who specialize in general/family practice, general internal medicine and general pediatrics. They were usually referred to as "generalists" in primary medical care (8).

The chapter has two parts. The first part provides an overall view of the current status of physician distribution in the nation. It presents a historical perspective of this issue and identifies factors that have been documented in years of research that have influenced such pattern of change in physician distribution. The second part summaries the proposals and suggestions that have been made on this issue, raises the questions that need to be answered and the actions yet to be taken.

OVERALL VIEW OF CURRENT STATUS OF PHYSICIAN MANPOWER

History

Confluent forces have acted to structure U.S. medicine in a way favoring specialism since World War II (9). This has largely resulted from the enormous growth of medical knowledge and by substantial and increasing financial support for biomedical research through the National Institutes of Health. Concurrently, the percentage of medical doctors engaged in primary care has decreased two fold, from over 88 percent in 1931 to about 40 percent in the 1970s (3).

In the early 1970s, a significant change took place in graduate medical education, particularly in family practice after it was approved as a medical specialty in 1969. That action eventually affected the number of practicing physicians engaged in primary care by increase of Federal and State funding for primary care training programs. The percentage of physicians engaged in primary care training increased from 34 percent in school year 1971-72 to 48.6 percent in school year 1976-77, with the largest percentage increase occurring in family practice (3). Primary care specialties in the 1976-77 school year accounted for a greater percentage of filled graduate medical training positions than at any time in the previous 27 years (3).

The goal of producing more primary care physicians was largely unsuccessful in the 1980s. Title VII of the Health Professions Educational Assistance Act, for instance, was intended to support the development of undergraduate and residency training in primary care specialties. It was the major program in the 1980s which used federal resources to target the specialty choices of American medical school graduates and further development of primary care education. About $50 million in grants were awarded to medical schools annually, between 1977 and 1985, with most schools receiving some funds under the program. However, the Title VII primary care grant programs did not lead to the anticipated changes in the composition of the physician work force (10).

Accompanied by this decreasing number of generalists was the fact that the supply of physicians in the U.S. has doubled during the past 20 years. It has continued to outpace population growth for several decades (8). There is now one physician for every 500 Americans, and the number of physicians is increasing at a rate three times faster than the population. However, the ratio of primary care physicians to the national population has decreased since 1963. This trend has been especially pronounced in rural areas and impoverished urban communities (11, 12). It was estimated by the Department of Health and Human Services of the Health Resources and Services Administration that this would be worse by the year 2000 (13).

In order to reverse this trend, medical leaders have set a national goal that the proportion of medical students entering primary care specialties of family medicine, general internal medicine, and general prediatrics should be 50% by the next century (14).

National Trend of Physician Distribution

Seniors' choice of specialty: The interest expressed by graduating seniors in primary care specialities has declined at an alarming rate throughout most of the 1980s and further in the 1990s (15). The actual percentage of seniors choosing primary care in the period from 1982 to 1992 dropped from 15.5 to 9.0 for family practice, from 14.4 to 3.2% for general internal medicine, and from 6.2 to 3.4 for general pediatrics, for a total primary care drop from 36.1% in 1982 to 14.6% in 1992 (16, 17).

Although a proportional change of students interested in certain specialties does not necessarily mean a change of quality and credentials of those students, some recent studies (18, 19) reported a significant decrease in the percentage of top students choosing careers in primary care specialties.

Residents' choices: The number of U.S. medical graduates entering residencies in internal medicine, family practice, or prediatrics, fell by 19 percent from 1986 to 1992 (30). A large and increasing proportion of residents entering internal medicine and pediatrics intend to subspecialize (21). About two thirds of recent residents in internal medicine have entered subspecialty careers (22). Of 1991 and 1992 graduates who began residencies in internal medicine, about 85 percent intend to enter subspecialty fields (23). The percentage of students entering pediatrics who intend to become subspecialists has risen from 30 percent in 1986 to 70 percent in 1992. If 1992 graduates of U.S. medical schools persist in their plans, only about 16 percent will become primary care practitioners (11 percent in family practice, 3 percent in general internal medicine, and 2 percent in general pediatrics) (23).

Rural and some inner city areas: Rural communities continue to have problems in gaining access to basic health care services, a problem exacerbated by persistent shortages of physicians, financially threatened rural hospitals, and weak local economies. There are about 30 physicians per 100,000 population in the counties with a population smaller than 2,500 compared with a physician/population ratio of 175/100,000 in metropolitan areas (24). Furthermore, a disproportionately large number of medical school applicants intend to practice in mid-size communities; a disproportionately low number of applicants in rural areas (25). During the medical school years, the overall percentage of students declaring interest in rural practice dropped from 6.2% of matriculation to 5.0% at graduation (26).

Factors that Influence Choice of Specialty

Medical students' career choice and physician's choice of specialty and location are affected by a number of factors, among them are (1) School's structure; (2) Student's characteristics; (3) School environment; (4) Residency program; (5) Characteristics of health care system, and (6) other.

School's Structure

Medical school's structure is related to the proportion of its graduates entering primary care. It has been known that public schools generally produce more generalists than private schools (27) and establishment of a department of family medicine has a positive impact on the number of family doctors it produces (27). The geographic location of the school is another factor related to the production of medical school graduates entering primary care. The mountain region, for instance, usually reports the highest percentage of medical school graduates who are first-year residents in family practice programs and the Middle Atlantic and New England regions had the lowest percentage (28).

Student's Characteristics

Gender and racial status: Racial-ethnic background in itself appears to be related to senior medical students' specialty selection. Women students and nontraditional students (second degree, older, some prior experiences before matriculation into medical school) were more likely than their respective classmates to choose primary care fields (29, 30). Underrepresented minority students defined as Black, Hispanic, and American Indian were more likely than their white counterparts to serve in underserved areas (31). Asian-Americans, comprising 2.9% of the total population and 12.3% of the total medical school graduates in 1992, had a relatively low percentage of graduates who went into primary care specialties in comparisons with their classmates (29, 32).

Rural background and interests: Students who entered medical school with an interest in family practice were almost three times as likely to choose family practice as a career upon graduation than matriculants who were interested in other specialties (33). Those who remained in family medicine were more likely than their counterparts to come from small towns, and have graduated from a public college (34). Medical students with rural ties are also more likely than urban students to practice in a rural area of the state (35, 36) and to seek certification in one of the generalist specialties (more commonly family practice) and to plan rural practices (26, 29). During the time period of 1982-1992, medical students with rural background were four times more likely than students with non-rural ties to plan rural practice at matriculation (16.2% versus 4.1%) and at graduation (13.2% versus 3.2%) (26).

Debt: The relationship between indebtedness and students' choice of specialty is not clear, although such a relationship might exist. Debt could be a factor for those choosing highly remunerative specialties (37). However, in some other studies little correlation was found between debt and specialty choice (38). It seems that a number of other variables need to be taken into consideration such as types of medical school attended (public or private) (29, 39), hometown (29), expected income and students' marital status (40), or the opportunity to "moonlight" during residency (40). It also suggests that the inappropriateness of combining several specialties into non-primary care may diminish the impact of indebtedness on students' specialty choice. One economic study using national data indicated that a $10,000 increase in indebtedness raises the probability of choosing anesthesiology by approximately 3.6%. In a similar fashion, the probability of choosing radiology falls approximately 7.2% (40).

A thorough study of 1992 graduates (17) indicated that debt played only a minor part in determining career choice. The median debt of all graduating seniors in 1992 (81.2% of whom graduated with debt) was $50,000. However, about the same amount of debt was seen among those who choose primary care and those choosing medical subspecialties or orthopaedic surgery. At high debt levels (greater than $75,000), the graduating seniors were somewhat more likely to choose high-earning specialties. It was also shown that factors such as clerkship experiences, the intellectual content of the specialty, and role models were rated more important than debt (17). It was suggested that students might not attribute importance to the amount of their educational debt as influencing their choice of specialty, even though it might exist (41).

Personality: Whereas medical schools use a variety of personality tests in educational research, the one that is frequently reported in recent years as related to specialty selection is the Myers-Briggs personality profile. The personality types of the general practitioners of the 1950s were greatly different from that of the early family practice residents of the 1970s, who preferred to see the world in terms of the immediate facts of experience and to make decisions objectively (42). The personality profiles for surgeons were unique, whereas distinctive personality profiles did not emerge for internists or family practitioners (43). Use of other personality profile instruments was not significantly associated with students' specialty selection (44). However, the match of personality and specialty choice was often cited as one of the important factors in the medical students' career decision (29).

Medical School Environment

Curriculum: While most medical students make their final choice of specialty during or after their clerkship year (45), the structured curriculum and the timing of the clerkship may have an important influence on students' choice of primary care (46). Students who attended medical schools with a required third-year clerkship in family practice were signficantly more likely to enter family practice residency training than students who attended school with a required fourth-year clerkship, or who attended a school with no required family practice clerkship (47). The amount of time devoted to required training in family practice (27) or in ambulatory care (48) has also been cited as the important factor related to graduates' decision to enter primary care.

Students who had clerkship experiences in rural areas would be more likely to practice in rural areas. Experience in a family medicine clerkship may be associated with changes in attitudes that represent development of a more informed image of primary care (49). Negative clerkship experiences influenced students' choice of that specialty (45) and a year-long experience in the clerkship of family practice is highly associated with their choice of residency in the specialty (50).

Residency program: The content and emphasis of the curriculum and location of residency were regarded as more important for those switching to primary care than those switching to non-primary care (51). Residency training in small communities may influence physicians' location in rural communities (36).

Characteristics of Health Care System

A recent and exhaustive analysis by Stimmel (52) argues that the health care system exercises the most powerful determinants of students and physicians' ultimate career choice. Several factors related to the career choice have been identified. Among them are increases in reimbursement for primary care physicians and funding for the national Health Service Corps program.

Income: Income has been shown to be associated with physicians' satisfaction/dissatisfaction with their work (35), public perception of specialty prestige (53), students' choice of family practice (54), of technology-oriented specialties (55), of primary care/non-primary care (56), and graduates' residency choice (57). Income was rated more important for non-primary care than primary care (56). The largest factor inhibiting the supply of family physicians appears to be the relatively lower income of family practice compared to other specialty fields (54). Students' expected income, combined with some other factors such as marital status (37) and debt (58), has been an important factor influencing graduates' choice of primary care disciplines. For instance, those with both high debt and high income expectations are more likely than others to choose a non-primary care specialty (58).

Funding from federal and state government: It would be difficult to assess the impact of federal funding on students' choice of career, holding other factors constant. In one study of Title VII programs, it was found that federal funding had only a little, if any, direct impact on students' career choice of primary care (10). The amount of financial support to school through Title VIII programs was deemed too small compared to other financial rewards schools obtained such as research grants from the National Institutes of Health.

Other

Controllable lifestyle: In recent studies, controllable lifestyle was listed as one of the most important factors attracting more well-qualified students into technology-oriented specialties such as anesthesiology, pathology, radiology (59), and emergency medicine (60). Long working hours influenced physicians' decision to switch away from general internal medicine (45), and from general surgery (61).

state's continued funding is crucial, at least in maintaining primary care education programs, in supporting through loans those needed and most-likely future generalists, and in promoting activities in primary care education research. The issue of imbalance of financial reward between primary and non-primary care has to be addressed. Compared with other countries, such as Canada where the income of general practitioners is 80 percent or more of that of most specialists (82), primary care physicians in the U.S. earn only about 40 to 60 percent as much as specialists (83). For instance, the income gap between family doctors and all doctors in the U.S. is $102,000 versus $171,000 in 1992 and comparative figures are $85,000 and $102,000 in Canada and $76,000 and $80,000 in Germany (84). Under the current pressure of cost containment, it is not reasonable to increase the patients' charges for primary care. However, redistribution of national medical expenditures between generalists and specialists will not add to health care costs. The resource-based relative value scale has been implemented and it will change to some extent the income differences between primary and non-primary care physicians, assuming most of primary care physicians involved in cognitive services areas. In an economic study (85), it was concluded that a 1 percent increase in anticipated income increases the number of those choosing that specialty by 0.5 percent. This relation predicts that even the full adoption of the new Medicare Relative-Value Scales for payment by all payers would increase the entry of U.S. students into primary care by less than 6 percent.

Although a reduction of number of subspecialty training positions is suggested, such a forced regulation "would not resolve the issues of the quality of the recruits or the satisfaction of practitioners unless economic reforms simultaneously brought the relative incomes of generalists and specialists closer together" (73).

Secondly, we need goals. A national goal was established for medical schools to produce 50% of its graduates, entering primary care, by the year 2000. American Academy of Family Physicians (AAFP) sets a goal of 25% of seniors entering the family practice residency program by the next century. Unless each medical school has its own goal this national goal would not be possibly achieved. What is more important and crucial was that specific goals of medical schools have to be based on a thorough understanding of this issue, taken into account of its own circumstances where strategies are to be taken and policies to be implemented. This leads to the third category: research.

We need research because only by doing so can we have solid support for our implemented policy. From pre-matriculation through practice we have come a long way to understand this issue of specialty selection and change of career. Yet, we still have a long way to go. For instance, at the point of admission, we need to know what are the factors that influence entering students who are interested in primary care at the entrance to medical school? Are there significant differences between those who are interested in primary care and their classmates in terms of prior experiences, family backgrounds, personality types, and motivation to become a doctor? And what is the stability rate from the first year to the fourth year of medical school, and more specifically, whether such stability rates vary with race, gender, age or other demographic characteristics of students? For instance, if women students are more favorably inclined toward caring for the medically indigent than men, and the former are also less likely to change this attitude toward providing care for the underserved during the years of medical school (86), what we need to know is why this gender effect occurs, and to what extent a medical school's environment has brought such a difference about gender. In a broad sense, we need to assess more precisely the relationship between a school's environment and the percentages of graduates entering primary care, holding other factors constant.

The American Academy of Family Physicians stated that emphasis should be on the first-year graduate (residency) positions needed to provide more physicians in primary care, with the inference that a comparable number of physicians will remain in the field of primary care at the end of graduate medical training (3). It has been reported that roughly 3.5% net of physicians between training and practice changed their career from primary care to nonprimary care specialties (87). However, research is obviously lacking in fully addressing the pattern of change in physicians' careers among specialties and within primary care in particular.

Another area of research which demands attention is graduates of osteopathic medical schools and of foreign medical schools. Osteopathic physicians account for only 3.9% of the physicians in the U.S. but they represent 9.3% of the physicians in the primary care specialties and 12.2% of those in family and general practice (12). About 57% of all osteopathic medical school graduates are in general practice with a total primary care being 65% (88). As seen in the pattern of change of students' career choice in the allopathic schools, a general decrease of the percentage of graduates from osteopathic medical school interested in primary care was noted in the recent decade (89). Owing mainly to a declining interest in primary care by young allopathic medical school graduates, allopathic postdoctoral program directors, particularly in primary care specialties, began to actively recruit osteopathic physicians. It has reached the point where two out of every three osteopathic medical school graduates currently training in a primary care residency can be found in an allopathic program (90). In each of the primary care specialties (family medicine/general practice, pediatrics, and internal medicine), the number of osteopathic residents in allopathic programs is higher than that in osteopathic program (91).

Another trend was seen as more graduates from foreign medical schools start their residency training in the U.S. The first year residency position demonstrates a 31.6% increase between 1989-1990 by graduates from foreign medical schools, most of this increase (63.4%) occurred among noncitizens of the U.S. (92). How this increase of osteopathic school graduates and international medical graduates will impact on the distribution of the physician work force is yet to be seen? More specifically, will the quality of primary care physicians remain the same as the result of this? And what is the best estimate of this trend in the next century? And what are the characteristics differences between allopathic and osteopathic medical schools which directly attribute to the producers of primary care physicians?

CONCLUSION

The reform of the health care system increasingly receives public attention. In recent issues of the *Philadelphia Inquirer*, the most circulated newspaper in the state of Pennsylvania, a mini-series of reports in March 1993 on health care reform raised a great concern among the public about the present system. More and more people are becoming aware of this issue. A general consensus seems to be emerging that we need changes, we need more generalists and we need to do some things which are new.

This chapter summariezes the historical development of the physician work force and career choice in this country, identifies factors that influence students' specialty choice, lists proposed models and suggestions made to change physician distributions and outlines potential future actions. Only 6 years remain before the next century, and the goal of 50% of graduates entering primary care is a tough task within this relative short period of time. However, with determination, courage, and well-planned strategies, we can meet the challenge.

ACKNOWLEDGEMENT

This research was supported in part by contract number 240-91-0059 from the Division of Medicine, Bureau of Health Professions, Department of Health and Human Services.

REFERENCES

1. Kindig, D.A. and H. Movassaghi. 1989. The adequacy of physician supply in small rural counties. *Health Affairs.* 8:63-76.
2. U.S. Department of Health and Human Services. 1992. *Health Personnel in the United States. Eighth Report to Congress, 1991.* Health Resources and Service Administration, Bureau of Health Professions, DHHS Pub. No. HRS-P-OD-92-1. September.
3. United States General Accounting Office. 1978. *The Comptroller General, Report to the Congress of the United States. Are enough physicians of the right types trained in the United States?* HRD 77.92, May 16.
4. Health Resources and Services Administration. 1991. *Primary Care 2000: HRSA's Long-Range Plan for Health Professionals.* Unpublished manuscript, Health Resources and Services Administration. January 11.
5. Nutter, D.O., Helms, C.M. , Whitcomb, M.E. and W.D. Weston. 1991. Restructuring health care in the United States: a proposal for the 1990s. *Journal of the American Medical Association.* 265:2510-2516.
6. Griffin, W.O. Jr. 1990. A national health service. *Archives of Surgery.* 125:534-4.
7. *Health Security Act.* 1993. The President's Request to the American People: The White House Domestic Policy Council.

8. *Health Personnel In the United States.* 1992. Eighth Report to Congress, 1991. U.S. Department of Health & Human Services, Bureau of Health Professions, DHHS Pub. No. HRS-P-OD-91-1. September.
9. Ginzberg, E. 1989. Do we need more generalists? *Academic Medicine.* 64:495-497.
10. Rosenblatt, R.A., Whitcomb, M.E., Cullen, T.J., Lishner, D.M. and L.G. Hart. 1993. The effect of federal grants on medical schools' production of primary care physicians. *American Journal of Public Health,* 83:322-328.
11. Rosenblatt, R. and D. Lishner. 1991. Surplus or shortage? Unraveling the physician manpower conundrum. *Western Journal of Medicine.* 154:43-50.
12. Barnett, P.G. and J.E. Midtling. 1989. Public policy and the supply of primary care physicians. *Journal of the American Medical Association.* 262:2864-2868.
13. Singer, A.M. 1989. Projections of physician supply and demand: A summary of HRSA and AMA studies. *Academic Medicine.* 64:235-240.
14. Kindig, D.A., Culltice, J.M. and F. Mullan. 1993. The elusive generalist programs: Can we reach a 50% goal? *Journal of the American Medical Association.* 270:1069-1073.
15. Barnett, P.G. and J.E. Midtling. 1989. Public policy and the supply of primary care physicians. *Journal of the American Medical Association.* 262:2864-2868.
16. *1992 Graduating Student Survey Results: All Schools Summary.* 1992. Washington, D.C.: Association of American Medical Colleges, Section for Educational Research.
17. Kassebaum, D.G. and P.L. Szenas. 1992. Relationship between indebtedness and the specialty choices of graduating medical students. *Academic Medicine.* 67:700-707.
18. Golden, W.E. Initial careeer choices of medical school honors graduates in the early 1970s and 1980s. *Academic Medicine.* 64:616-21.
19. Jarecky, R.K., Donnelly, M.B., Rubeck, R.F. and R.W. Schwartz. 1993. Changes in the patterns of specialties selected by high and low academic performers before and after 1980. *Academic Medicine.* 68:158-160.
20. Levinsky, N. 1993. Recruiting for primary care. *The New England Journal of Medicine.* 328:656-660.
21. Stein, J.H. 1991. Grand cru versus generic: different approaches to altering the ratio of general internists to subspecialists. *Annals of Internal Medicine.* 114:79-82.
22. Anderson, R.M., Lyttle, C.S., Kohrman, C.H., Levey, G.S. and M.M. Clements. 1992. National study of internal medicine manpower: XIX. Trends in internal medicine residency training programs. *Annals of Internal Medicine.* 117: 243-250.
23. Kassebaum, D.G. and D. Green. 1992. Interest in generalist careers continues to wane. *AAMC Reporter.* 2:1.
24. Rosenblatt, R.A. 1991. The potential of the academic medical center to shape policy-oriented rural health research. *Academic Medicine.* 66:662-667.
25. Head, R. and D. Harris. 1987. Characteristics of medical school applicants: implications for rural health care. *Family Medicine.* 21:187-190.

26. Rosenblatt, R.A., Whitcomb, M.E., Cullen, T.J., Lishner, D.M. and L.G. Hart. 1992. Which medical schools produce rural physicians? *Journal of the American Medical Association.* 268:1092-1094.
27. Campos-Outcalt, D. and J.H. Senf. 1989. Characteristics of medical schools related to the choice of family medicine as a specialty. *Academic Medicine.* 64:610-615.
28. Schmittling, G. and R. Graham. 1989. Entry of U.S. medical school graduates into family practice residencies: 1988-1989 and eight-year summary. *Family Medicine.* 21:132-138.
29. *Trends Plus. U.S. Medical School Applicants, Matriculants, Graduates 1992.* 1993. Division of Educational Research and Assessment, May.
30. Mobray, R.M. 1989. Research in choice of medical specialty: a review of the literature 1977-87. *Australia and New Zealand Journal of Medicine.* 19:389-399.
31. Geiger, H.J. 1993. Why don't medical students choose primary care? *American Journal of Public Health.* 83:315-316.
32. Babbott, D., Baldwin, D.C. Jr., Killian, C.D. and S.O. Weaver. 1989. Racial-ethnic background and specialty choice: A study of U.S. medical school graduates in 1987. *Academic Medicine.* 64:595-599.
33. Rabinowitz, H.K. 1990. The change in specialty preference by medical students over time: An analysis of students who prefer family medicine. *Family Medicine.* 22:62-63.
34. Rezler, A.G. and S.G. Kalishman. 1989. Who goes into family medicine? *Journal of Family Practice.* 29:652-656.
35. Movassaghi, H. and D. Kindig. 1989. Medical practice and satisfaction of physicians in sparsely populated rural counties of the United States: results of a 1988 survey. *The Journal of Rural Health.* 5:125-136.
36. Jarratt, L.G., Leonardson, G.R. and W.J. Nord. 1989. Practice location factors influencing South Dakota school of medicine graduates (1977-85). *South Dakota Journal of Medicine.* December, 15-21.
37. Petersdorf, R.G. 1991. Financing medical education. *Academic Medicine.* 66:61-65.
38. McLaughlin, M.A., Daugherty, S.R., Rose, W.H. and L.J. Goodman. 1991. The impact of medical school debt on postgraduate career and lifestyle. *Academic Medicine.* 9:S43-S45.
39. Fox, M. 1993. Medical student indebtedness and choice of specialization. *Inquiry.* 30:84-94.
40. Bazzoli, G.L. 1985. Does educational indebtedness affect physician specialty choice? *Journal of Health Economics.* 4:1-19.
41. Xu, G. and J.J. Veloski. 1993. Factors influencing physicians' decisions to remain in emergency medicine. *Academic Medicine.* 67:413.
42. Taylor, A.D., Clark, C. and A.E. Sinclair. 1990. Personality types of family practice residents in the 1980s. *Academic Medicine.* 65:216-218.
43. Zelow, P.B. and S.R. Daugherty. 1991. Personality profiles and specialty choices of students from two medical school classes. *Academic Medicine.* 66:283-287.
44. DeForge, B.R. and J. Sobal. 1991. Investigating whether medical students'

intolerance of ambiguity is associated with their specialty selections. *Academic Medicine.* 66:49-51.
45. Babbott, D., Levey, G.S., Weaver, S.O. and C.D. Killian. 1991. Medical student attitudes about internal medicine: a study of U.S. medical school seniors in 1988. *Annals of Internal Medicine.* 114:16-22.
46. Senf, J.H. 1990. Specialty selection: trend over time in one medical school. *Journal of Family Practice.* 30:217-218.
47. Rabinowitz, H.K. 1988. The relationship between medical student career choice and a required third-year family practice clerkship. *Family Medicine.* 20:118-121.
48. Rucker, L. Morgan, C., Ward, K.E. and B.B. Bell. 1991. Impact of an ambulatory care clerkship on the attitudes of students from five classes (1985-1989) toward primary care. *Academic Medicine.* 66:620-622.
49. Duerson, M.C., Grandall, L.A. and J.W. Dwyer. 1989. Impact of a required family medicine clerkship on medical students' attitudes about primary care. *Academic Medicine.* 64:546-548.
50. Ellison, M.J., Cummings, D.M., Worthington, R.C. and C.C. Bremmer. 1990. Clinical pharmacology and therapeutics in primary care: an elective for fourth-year medical students. *Journal of Clinical Pharmacology.* 30:489-493.
51. Markert, R.J. 1991. Why medical students change to and from primary care as a career choice. *Family Medicine.* 23:347-350.
52. Stimmel, B. 1992. The crisis in primary care and the role of medical schools. *Journal of the American Medical Association.* 268:2060-2065.
53. Rosoff, S.M. and M.C. Leone. 1991. The pubic prestige of medical specialties: overviews and undercurrents. *Social Science Medicine.* 32:321-326.
54. Bowman, M.A. 1989. Family physicians' supply and demand. *Public Health Report.* 104(May-June):286-93.
55. Lieu, T.A., Schroeder, S.A. and D.F. Altman. 1989. Specialty choices at one medical school: recent trends and analysis of predictive factors. *Academic Medicine.* 64:622-629.
56. Roger, L.Q., Fincher, R.M.E. and L.A. Lewis. 1990. Factors influencing medical students to choose primary care or non-primary care specialties. *Academic Medicine.* 65:S47-S48.
57. Choice of specialty: it's money that matters in the U.S.A. 1989. *Journal of the American Medical Association.* 267:1921.
58. *Debts and career plans of osteopathic medical students in 1990.* 1990. Rockville, M.D. American Association of Colleges of Osteopathic Medicine. AACOM Debt Survey.
59. Schwartz, R.W., Jarecky, R.K., Strodel, W.E., Haley, J.V., Young, B. and W.O. Griffen Jr. 1989. Controllable lifestyle: a new factor in career choice by medical students. *Academic Medicine.* 64:606-609.
60. Xu, G. and J.J. Veloski. 1991. A comparison of Jefferson Medical College graduates who chose emergency medicine with those who chose other specialties. *Academic Medicine.* 66:366-368.
61. Wolfson, P.J., Robeson, M.R. and J.J. Veloski. 1991. Medical students who enter general surgery residency programs: A follow-up between 1972 and 1986. *The American Journal of Survery.* 162:491-494.

Medicine and Health Care Into the Twenty-First Century. Edited by S.K. Majumdar, L.M. Rosenfeld, D.B. Nash and A.M. Audet. © 1995, The Pennsylvania Academy of Science.

Chapter Eighteen

PREPARING UNDERGRADUATES FOR MEDICAL SCHOOL

BARBARA Y. STEWART, Ph.D.
Associate Professor of Biology and Health Sciences Advisor
Department of Biology
Swarthmore College
500 College Avenue
Swarthmore, PA 19081-1397

INTRODUCTION

The preparation of undergraduates for medical school was addressed by Thomas Huxley in 1869 to members of the Liverpool Philomathic Society in an after-dinner speech in which he decried the fact that medical students in England had to spend the first eighteen months of their medical school training on the subjects of physics, chemistry, botany, and physiology as well as the subjects of anatomy, pharmacy and therapeutics, all of which "are absolutely and entirely strange to him" (1). He suggested that the principles of physics, chemistry and biology should be studied and required *before* entering medical school in order for students to gain both information in these areas and practice in inductive reasoning and logic. The first years of medical school then could be devoted entirely to the study of medicine.

Huxley also advocated the use of laboratories in training undergraduates in the physical sciences, even though they involved "a good deal of expenditure of time without always an obvious result" (1). He cautioned instructors that they should be certain that what a student "learns, he learns of his own knowledge" (1). In physics, for example, a pupil should not be told that a magnet attracts iron, but should see and feel the pull of the magnet on the iron filings (1). Indeed, students should be taught to doubt information until they have verified it in the laboratory.

The medical student, especially, should be one who is able to make observations, take data and draw conclusions, so that he or she in the future, will be able to determine what is wrong with a patient and if possible remedy the situation (1).

Today, medical schools in the United States require premedical students to understand the principles of physics, chemistry, biology and mathematics before they enter medical school and to have a grasp of English literature as well as a background in other humanities. In 1984, the Association of American Medical Colleges (AAMC) published a report on the "General Professional Education of the Physician and College Preparation for Medicine" and stated that "A broad and thorough baccalaureate education is an essential component of the general professional education of physicians" (2).

ACADEMIC REQUIREMENTS

Formal Course Requirements

Most medical schools in the United States require a year of biology, a year of physics, a year of mathematics and two years of chemistry which must include a year of organic chemistry. Laboratories must be included with the science courses. However, the specific course requirements for admission to each medical school vary considerably. In fact, eight of the 123 medical schools in the United States (University of Cincinnati, University of Illinois, Southern Illinois University, University of Missouri-Kansas City, Northwestern University, University of Pennsylvania, Medical University of South Carolina, and Wayne State University) do not indicate specific course requirements, although they may recommend them (2). These institutions rely more heavily on performance on the Medical College Admission Test (MCAT) or American College Test (ACT) and a baccalaureate degree from an accredited college or university to indicate competence in the physical and natural sciences.

Other medical schools have quite specific requirements. Some like Harvard, Duke University, Johns Hopkins University, University of Minnesota-Duluth, the University of Texas at Galveston, Houston and San Antonio, University of South Carolina, Texas A&M and Washington University require either integral and/or differential calculus to satisfy the mathematics requirement, while other medical schools will accept algebra or statistics as well as calculus (2). Expository writing is listed as a requirement of such schools as the University of Colorado, Robert Wood Johnson, Albany, Case Western Reserve, Louisiana State University in New Orleans, University of Missouri-Columbia and Harvard. Biochemistry is recommended by many medical schools but required by Mayo Medical School. Spanish is highly recommended at the University of California, Los Angeles (2).

The premedical student is well-advised to purchase a copy of the latest *Medical School Admission Requirements, United States and Canada* (2) in his or her freshman year of college and read it carefully to plan for inclusion of the required courses during the undergraduate years.

Grade Point Average

Grade point averages (GPAs) are determined by assigning a 4.00 to an A, a 3.67 to an A –, a 3.34 to a B +, a 3.00 to a B, etc. and are often divided into a science GPA, a non-science GPA and a total GPA. The total GPA for matriculants in medical schools in the United States from 1983 to 1993 has changed very little from a high of 3.49 in 1983 to a low of 3.40 in 1989. In 1993 the total grade point average was 3.47, the average science grade was 3.41 and the average non-science grade 3.55 (3). The competitive premedical student, therefore, must have an average between an A – and a B +. Some medical schools report much higher grade point averages, for example the total GPA at the University of California at San Francisco and the University of Florida in 1993 was 3.7 (2). Other medical schools have total averages closer to 3.2. In any case, medical schools view the GPA as one of the most important indications of academic achievement and motivation.

Medical College Achievement Test

The Medical College Achievement Test (MCAT) is given twice each year, on the third Saturday in April and now on the third Saturday in August. Before 1994, the exams were administered in April and September, but the increasing number of applicants (See "Applications to Medical School" below) prompted the exam to be given earlier so that medical schools would have more time to process the applications. The morning examination session includes a multiple choice Verbal Reasoning test which covers diverse topics in the social sciences, humanities and the natural sciences and a multiple choice Physical Science test based on physics and physically-related chemistry. In the afternoon there are two essays required for a Writing Sample exam and a multiple choice Biological Science test based on biology and related organic chemistry. The Verbal Reasoning, Physical Sciences and Biological Sciences are graded on a 15 point scale from 1 (low) to 15 (high) and the Writing Sample is graded on an alphabetical scale from J (low) to T (high) (2).

Students prepare for the MCAT in a variety of ways. First and foremost, mathematics and all of the science courses—biology, chemistry and physics, should be completed before taking the exam. In addition, students need to review all the course material and become acquainted with the test mechanics and question format. The AAMC publishes two sets of materials, a *MCAT Student Manual* which describes the four sections of the test (Verbal Reasoning, Writing, Physical Science and Biological Science) and a *MCAT Practice Test I* and a second set of materials which includes practice items in all four areas to be tested and a *MCAT Practice Test II* (2). In addition, most students feel they need either a commercial review book such as *A Complete Preparation for the MCAT, 6th Edition by James L. Flowers, M.D., M.P.H.* (4), or a commercial course such as the Stanley H. Kaplan Review Course for the MCAT.

The average MCAT score for medical school matriculants for the spring and fall tests in 1993 in Verbal Reasoning was 9.4, in the Physical Sciences 9.4 and in the Biological Science 9.5. The average alphabetical grade for the Writing Sample was "O". Except for the Writing Sample grade, all of the means for 1993 were higher than the 1992 scores of 9.2 for Verbal Reasoning, 9.2 for Physical Sciences and 9.3 for the Biological Sciences (3). Students who score below the average usually retake the examination.

OTHER EXPERIENCES WHICH PREPARE UNDERGRADUATES FOR MEDICAL SCHOOL

Extracurricular Activities

Premedical students are encouraged to participate in extracurricular activities while in college, primarily because of the opportunity to learn to work and communicate with others. Participation in activities outside the classroom also teaches a student how to manage a complex time schedule, learn about organizational hierarchy and develop leadership skills (5). Medical schools feel it is far better for students to be deeply involved in two or three activities in which they invest considerable time and energy than to dabble in a large number of activities.

Most premedical students choose athletics, sororities or fraternities, social or political action groups, international relations clubs, student government or religious organizations (5). Students who commit themselves to two or three activities and emerge as leaders of these groups indicate to medical school admissions committees that they can manage their time efficiently, are involved but not overloaded and have learned valuable interpersonal skills.

Research

Research experiences are valuable in many ways. They introduce the student to new information, important laboratory techniques, experimental design, the analysis of data, critical thinking, working with a research team and, perhaps, preparation for publication. Sometimes small research projects or independent studies can be done with a professor as part of the academic program in a science major and appear on the college or university transcript.

One of the most beneficial research experiences can be obtained at a university or national laboratory offering an undergraduate summer research program. In 1994, the University of Cincinnati College of Medicine, the New York University Medical Center, the American Heart Association, the Mayo Clinic, the University of Pennsylvania, the Brookhaven National Laboratory and Baylor College of Medicine were some of the organizations that offered research experiences with stipends to qualified undergraduates (6, 7). These summer fellowships are competitive and winning one can benefit the undergraduate premedical student both from the laboratory experience and the additional information which usually helps in studying for the MCAT. Directors of admission look with favor on students who have been awarded these summer fellowships.

Health Care Related Experiences

Medical schools are looking for individuals with a strong sense of personal responsibility, honesty, emotional maturity, compassion and sensitivity to the feelings of others. Students who volunteer either during the school year or the summer in health care related facilities show they are motivated and committed to helping people.

Today there are many opportunities for involvement in the health of the community. Premedical students can volunteer in emergency rooms in a hospital, care for the elderly, the handicapped, the deaf, the visually impaired, the learning disabled, the mentally retarded or the terminally ill (5). Abortion clinics, homeless shelters and AIDS programs will gladly accept any willing, hard-working students and these valuable experiences help the premedical student decide whether he or she wants to spend his or her life in the field of medicine.

The Generalist Physician Project

There is, at present, an imbalance in the number of physicians who are generalists (defined as general internists, general pediatricians and family physicians) and those who are specialists (8). In 1961, 50% of the practicing physicians in the United States were generalists; by 1988 that number had dropped to 33% (8). The AAMC Office of Generalist Physician Programs (OGPP) is sponsoring a National Primary Care Day in the fall of 1994 to raise students' awareness of generalist medicine (9).

It is also clear that there is an inadequate number of generalists entering the profession. In 1993, a Generalist Physician Task Fore of the AAMC developed a policy statement to address this problem and to motivate more students to pursue generalist careers (8). One of the proposals suggested that medical school admission committees seek those students who show genuine interest in primary care medicine, public and community service or practicing in a rural area (8). It is clear that undergraduates seeking admission to medical school today should show evidence of health care related experiences as that an important non-academic factors used by admissions committees in choosing among the many academically outstanding candidates.

ROLE OF THE PREMEDICAL ADVISOR IN PREPARING UNDERGRADUATES FOR MEDICAL SCHOOL

Most undergraduate colleges or universities have a member of the science faculty of Dean's Office who counsels each premedical student, provides information on different kinds of medical schools and prepares a composite letter of recommendation which includes evaluations from several faculty members, research mentors and athletic or job supervisors. The committee letter of recommendation is probably the most important responsibility of the premedical advisor because it can inform the medical schools of such personal attributes as intellectual curiosity, interactive skills and judgment and social and political awareness, all of which are important for medical students to possess (10).

Advising

Over the past few years the duties of the premedical advisor have increased largely because the applicant pool has increased and become more diverse and the application process more complicated. The most time-consuming job of the advisor is that of counseling students from the time they enter as freshmen to the time when as seniors or as alumni they have applied to medical school and have been placed on a waiting list, accepted to more than one medical school, or have been unsuccessful in gaining admission to medical school. In the latter case, the premedical advisor must help students reassess their motivations in a humane and compassionate manner, advise them about post-baccalaureate programs, graduate schools and foreign medical schools and sometimes counsel the parents as well (10).

Special Meetings with Undergraduates

During freshman orientation the premedical advisor usually meets with all first-year students interested in a possible career in medicine to discuss the courses which satisfy the medical school requirements and introduce himself or herself to the students. In the junior year, the premedical advisor discusses the current admissions outlook, factors affecting the application to medical school, the MCAT exam and provide evaluation forms to be distributed to faculty and non-faculty for letters of recommendation. At this time students are requested to fill out a questionnaire which asks about extracurricular activities, medically related experiences, awards, summer jobs. In addition, the student is asked to write a one page essay explaining the reason for wanting a career in medicine. Often in the spring of the junior year a group meeting is held with those students who were interviewed and accepted at medical schools the previous fall and those students who are applying next summer. All of these activities help prepare the undergraduate for medical school.

Source of Information

The premedical advisor is also the source of information about special programs for undergraduates, summer jobs, summer fellowships, Medical Scientist Training Programs and alternatives to medical school such as Masters Programs in Public Health, Physicians Associate Programs or Podiatry. He or she is expected to keep up in the field of medical education by reading the *Journal of the American Medical Association (JAMA), Academic Medicine, Journal of the Association of American Medical Colleges (AAMC) and the AAMC Reporter.* The National Association of Advisors to the Health Profession publishes both *The Advisor* and *Between Issues*, and the Office of Statewide Health Planning and Development of the State of California publishes an excellent newsletter of the Health Professions Career Opportunity Program entitled *Health Pathways* (10). Often the success of students gaining admittance to medical school is directly related to the efforts of the premedical advisor at their institution.

7. Brochures received in the Health Science Office at Swarthmore College, Swarthmore, PA. 1993-94.
8. Greer, David S., Bhak, Karyn N. and Bernarda M. Zenker. 1994. Comments on the AAMC Policy Statement Recommending Strategies for Increasing Production of Generalist Physicians. *Academic Medicine, Journal of the Association of American Medical Colleges.* 69:245-260.
9. Frase-Blunt, Martha, Editor. 1994. Medical Schools to Celebrate National Primary Care Day. *AAMC Reporter,* Vol. 3, No. 9. May 1994.
10. Stewart, Barbara Y. 1992. The Role of the Premedical Advisor at Small Undergraduate Institutions. *The Advisor, Publication of the National Association of Advisors for the Health Professions.* Campaign, IL, Vol. 13, No. 1:10-14.
11. *Facts - Applicants, Matriculants and Graduates 1987-1993.* AAMC, Washington, D.C.
12. Secondary School Science Minority Achievement Registry, Vol. I. Project 3000 by 2000. 1994. AAMC, Washington, D.C.
13. Frase-Blunt, Martha, Editor. 1994. Another Record Applicant Year. *AAMC Reporter,* Vol. 3, No. 7 March 1994. p. 1.
14. Jones, Harry S., Etzel, Sylvia I. and Barbara Barzansky. 1993. "Educational Programs in US Medical Schools." *JAMA*. 270:1061-1068.

Medicine and Health Care Into the Twenty-First Century. Edited by S.K. Majumdar, L.M. Rosenfeld, D.B. Nash and A.M. Audet.

Chapter Nineteen

MEDICAL EDUCATION'S RESPONSE TO PRIMARY CARE

SARENA D. SEIFER, M.D.[1] and
EDWARD H. O'NEIL, M.P.A., Ph.D[2]

[1]Medical Education Research and Policy Fellow
[2]Executive Director
Institute for Health Policy Studies and
Center for the Health Professions
University of California
1388 Sutter St., Suite 805
San Francisco, CA 94109

INTRODUCTION

There is growing recognition that regardless of the particulars of health care reform in the U.S., there is a woefully inadequate supply of primary care providers to deliver the care. With uncommon agreement, the nation's health care and educational establishments have rallied around the call for a "50-50" balance between the supply of the nation's generalist and specialist physicians (1-3). The movement, though broad, has only a few sources of inspiration: the perception that primary care physicians provide more cost effective care and more patient oriented care, international comparisons of other health care systems and their balance of physician workforce compared to costs and outcomes, and the role that primary care physicians now play in existing managed care operations in the U.S. (4-6). This said one would think it an easy task to change the array of schools, training programs, financing mechanisms and overseeing bodies that inform the physician production process. Nothing could be further from the truth. The "black box" that produces each new year's crop of residency trained physicians contains a confusing mix of institutional prerogatives, professional and sub-specialty jealousies, misdirected federal subsidies, state's rights, student's preferences and the ever present workforce needs of the teaching hospital (7).

If the goal of physician workforce policy is to achieve a balance between generalists and specialists, then the nation falls far short, as specialists now represent 70 percent of practitioners and fewer than one in five students express a preference for a career in primary care medicine (8). The medical school and its dean and faculty are a convenient whipping boy for this state of affairs. While medical schools bear some, perhaps the majority of the responsibility, it is essential that the rich set of factors influencing this process be understood if we are to have any hope of reaching a better balance between specialists and generalists. This paper seeks to put this discussion in some historical context, examine the influences that shape career choice in medicine and looks at leverage points for change that policy makers and medical schools have available. Medicine and medical schools will necessarily play a part in how the nation responds. This paper focuses on one type of provider, the primary care physician, defined as family practitioners, general pediatricians, and general internists. The authors also recognize the important and growing contribution that other health care workers contribute in the delivery of primary care, particularly certified nurse mid-wives, nurse practitioners and physician assistants, but one beyond the scope of this paper, is how these professional communities can more effectively work together to redefine the ways we organize and deliver primary care.

BACKGROUND

As difficult as it may be to imagine today, the health care world was not always so specialty- and technology-focused. It is only in the past half century for a host of reasons that health care and medicine in particular have moved so rapidly and forcefully in this direction. The Second World War serves as a useful historical watershed. It generated many of the forces that eventually translated themselves into the movement to specialization. Of particular importance were the expansion of knowledge related to health care, the growth of the health care enterprise and the change in the nation's attitude about higher education.

The final act of hostility of WWII, the dropping of the atomic bombs on Hiroshima and Nagasaki, was also the culmination of the single largest federal investment in general and applied research to date, the Manhattan Project. Just as the bombs changed for ever how we think about energy and war, the project itself changed the way we think about research, its support, its efficacy and its role in national policy. Prior to the war, research on all fronts of the university was carried out with a smattering of public and private support, but was essentially the by-product of what one did as a member of a University faculty. After 1945, research became a conscious part of federal and to some extent state public policy. This translated into a steady and significant growth in the size and scope of the National Institutes of Health, changing the way in which the academic community organizes, conducts and values basic biomedical research. Fully half of the Institutes were founded between 1945 and 1955 and the NIH budget grew from .02 percent of GNP in 1950, to its peak of .15 percent in 1965. There were corresponding developments in clinical research. Throughout the war there was an active clinical research effort aimed at improving the chances of those wounded in battle. Following the war, this same interest in improving clinical technique expanded throughout the health care system (9, 10). The war also brought millions of soldiers into the pattern of regular health care. As poor as it may have been, military health care was better than what many people had readily available to them in their community. This raised the expectations about access to health care as a part of a quality of life. In the years following the war, the veterans also found that they had more resources with which to pay for additional health care. As other needs were met, the three decades following the war witnessed a steady growth in the number of people covered by insurance and the total dollars spent by the nation on health care. This trend in more care, coupled with the preceding trend of more specialized knowledge led to a proliferation of specialists and specialized knowledge throughout the health care system (11).

Finally, the educational enterprise grew during this period spurring the growth in research, specialized patient care and training programs to produce new specialists. Immediately following WWII there was a rapid increase in the number of medical schools and teaching hospitals to accommodate the new demand for care. With passage of the Serviceman's Readjustment Act of 1944, there was a broader change in the public attitude about higher education, what it should do, who should suport it and who should attend. Thus, the educational enterprise, confronted with a growing demand for more specialized research and more physicians, particularly specialists, found itself with a resource base to accommodate growth. Along the way the continued growth in research funding, expansion of patient care through Medicare and Medicaid, and the spiraling income of medical specialists became a defining reality of the academic health center by the beginning of the 1990's (12).

These and other social and economic changes have altered the ways medical education is organized and financed. The number of medical students doubled between 1960 and 1990, but these students were taught by a faculty that grew fourfold during the same period (13). This growth was fed by a dramatic shift in the ways in which medical schools and their accompanying training programs received their funding. The first figure compares medical school revenue from the period 1960-1990. Clearly, the financial framework of the medical education enterprise is now driven by two sources: clinical income of faculty and research support. These sources of income have dramatically increased the size of the operation. In 1991-1992, the nation spent 23 billion dollars on medical education (14). Any notion that a budget of this size could be financed exclusively by the states, private endowments or student tuition is simply unimaginable.

While medical schools depend less on student fees for the financing of the operation of medical education (declining as a proportion of total medical school operation during the 1980's from 5.4 to 4.2 percent), they nonetheless increased significantly as a burden to students paying the tuition. In 1991-92, the median annual tuition of private medical schools was $19,038 and of state public schools was $6,600 (15). To finance this tuition and other related expenses, the medical student community has increasingly turned to loans to finance education. During the decade of the eighties, the mean indebtedness of medical student grew from $20,000 to over $50,000. As students approach indebtedness of $75,000, they will find it necessary to make incomes in excess of $145,000 to service the indebtedness. Few primary care careers offer such levels of compensation during the first five years of graduation (16).

The support of primary care or generalist training comes principally from Title VII of the Public Health Service Act. Between 1977 and 1985, Title VII provided over $450 million in support to medical schools and teaching hospitals to support primary care training. However, an analysis showed that the level of changes in funding for primary care was unrelated to changes in graduates practicing in primary care settings (17). Obviously, the predominance of faculty practice revenue that is obtained through specialist practice and the overwhelming influence of research support from the National Institutes of Health overwhelms the capacity of the Title VII resources to make a fundamental difference in the culture of the medical school and teaching hospital environment.

Moreover, the number of practicing primary care physicians, the current level of training in primary care and the expression of student interests in primary care careers is far short of the "50-50" goal. In 1991, less than one third of the practicing allopathic physicians were in primary care fields (18). Generalist residency positions were 40 percent of all available positions in that year, but none of the categories of primary care positions filled (19). Finally, less than 15 percent of the 1992 graduating medical school seniors indicated a preference for a generalist career (20). This current state of affairs has led one analysis to conclude that even if half of all training programs were converted to primary care in 1993, something that has not happened, more than half of all physicians would remain specialists as late as the year 2040 (21).

INFLUENCES ON PRIMARY CARE CAREER CHOICE

Clearly, the problem of primary care training and service is daunting. An amazing array of research has been conducted on those factors that contribute to medical students decisions about careers. It is important to give this research due consideration before we explore what might be done by medical schools and policymakers to remedy this situation.

There are various ways of conceptualizing the process medical students undergo before ultimately settling on a practice specialty. Ernst and Yett, in their comprehensive and critical review of the literature up to 1982, identify three non-competing hypotheses for medical student career choice: the "personality hypothesis," where personal characteristics, including background factors as well as personality type, predispose individuals to particular choices; the "experiential hypothesis," where the medical education process itself molds and shapes students' preferences; and the "economic hypothesis," where market forces and the individuals' attempts to maximize earnings affects career choice (22). We believe that all three of these theories are needed to explain such a complex process.

The resurgence of a primary care-based system as the solution to problems of health care cost, access and quality has generated a flurry of articles and commentary on why medical student interest in the field continues to decline. Despite more than 170 articles, two literature reviews and a selected bibliography on medical specialty choice in the last decade, the determinants of physicians' specialty choices are still not well understood (22-26).

The methodological flaws of existing studies of medical student specialty selection have been well described (27-29). Many studies are conducted within a single institution and do not involve multiple predictors of specialty choice, limiting the generalizability of the results. Most have been descriptive and not tied to an explicit theoretical framework. Finally, career preference during medical school or at the time of the residency match is often the study endpoint rather than actual career attainment.

Despite these limitations in the literature, factors influencing the choice of a primary care career do appear to fall into the following broad categories: student sociodemographics, student personality and attitudes, medical school and residency program characteristics, and the practice environment of medicine (actual and perceived). In reviewing what is known, we will focus our discussion on those influences most amenable to policy intervention and actions undertaken by the medical education system.

Student Sociodemographics

Race and Sex. A sizeable body of evidence indicates that women and underrepresented minorities disproportionately choose primary care specialties (20, 30-40). Annual surveys of medical school graduates find that women respondents consistently plan to pursue primary care medicine at higher rates than men (35). Other studies have shown that of students entering internal medicine and pediatrics, women have lower rates of subspecialization (36). Among young practicing physicians, a higher proportion of women than men are in primary care practices, despite no gender differences evident in their specialty plans at graduation from medical school (34).

A now classic study of the medical school class of 1975, demonstrated that a significantly higher percentage of minority graduates chose primary care specialties has been substantiated more recently (32). Underrepresented minorities, particularly Mexican-Americans, appear to have the highest proportion of any group in primary care (31). Among young physicians, Blacks and Hispanics are overrepresented in the primary care specialties (34).

Several explanations have been proposed for these findings. As a group, women are felt to be drawn toward primary care practice, which is often seen as more humanistic and accommodating of family choices and flexible schedules than other specialties. A desire to help people, particularly to serve the needs of their own communities, has been shown to be a strong motivator of underrepresented minorities choosing primary care. The inclination of minority graduates toward practice in socioeconomically deprived communities is four times that of non-minorities (37). Sexism and racism have been raised as plausible explanations for the underrepresentation of women and minorities in certain specialties, but there has been little empirical evidence to support these claims (41, 42).

Unfortunately, minority medical graduates in recent years appear to be following the subspecialty trend of their non-minority counterparts. Although higher percentages of minority physicians are actually practicing in primary care fields, minority medical student interest in primary care had declined significantly in the last five years. In 1987, 30.2 percent of minority medical graduates planned certification in a primary care specialty, a number that has fallen below that of non-minority students to 13.5% in 1992 (37). This may be partly explained by minority students' greater sensitivity to rising medical school tuition and educational debt, which we discuss below.

Hometown size. Hometown size may influence specialty choice and preference of practice community. As hometown size increases, there is an apparent increase in the percentage of students who choose a specialty practice (43). Medical students who have spent a considerable amount of time living and working in rural communities are more likely to become primary care physicians and return to such areas to practice (44-46).

Student personality and attitude. Ernst and Yett reported that more than a dozen different measures of personality characteristics have been used in studies of medical student career choice (26). Since no systematic efforts have been made to compare the findings or evaluate the methods, it is difficult to summarize the results and determine their meaning. Medical students contemplating primary care careers often give greater weight to the desire to help people as a career motivation, are more oriented toward considering the psychosocial context of patients' problems, and are more likely to perceive a need for change to improve health care in the U.S. (43). Students inclined toward specialty practice tend to be more technology-oriented, enjoy doing procedures and value higher incomes and degrees of diagnostic certainty (47, 48). Nevertheless, it is safe to say that no personality profile for students attaining primary care careers has been identified, and it is difficult to imagine how one could be operationalized from a recruitment/admissions or policy perspective.

Institutional Characteristics of Medical Schools and Residency Programs

Academic health centers argue that the practice environment and a reimbursement system that favors subspecialty care may confound their ability to alter their students' specialty choices (49). The timing and stability of medical student career decisions suggest otherwise. Only 14% of entering medical students have made a firm specialty choice before matriculating, but by the senior year, 72% have made a firm decision and another 19% are strongly considering a particular specialty (50). As many as 80% of medical students change their specialty choice between the time of the Medical College Admission Test and graduation (51), with most deciding on a specialty while in their third or fourth year of medical school.

During medical school, students' interest in primary care generally wanes in favor of other specialties (52). A review of fifteen studies of medical student career stability and change found that the specialty choice of 39% of medical students remained stable, with a marked preference for internal medicine subspecialties and a dramatic decline in interest in family medicine during the four years of medical school (52). While 30% to 40% of students enter medical school with a preference for family medicine, only about one-third of these actually enter family medicine residencies (51-53).

Whether this disaffection with primary care is primarily due to the medical school experience, culture or other institutional characteristics, one cannot be sure. Again, the timing of these decisions indicates that medical schools can influence these choices. It is difficult to tease out the effects of a student's unfamiliarity with other fields, his or her level of student debt, or perceptions of the practice environment after graduation. Students starting out with particular specialty preferences seem to be affected by the medical school experience differently. Students who enter medical school with an interest in family medicine are almost three times as likely to choose family practice as a career than matriculants who were interested in other specialties (54), indicating that despite any institutional factors, initial preference does matter. In a study of graduates of state schools choosing family medicine residencies, graduates with little or no interest in family medicine prior to entering medical school were found to be influenced by educational curricula and faculty role models. Those beginning medical school already interested in family medicine were found to be most influenced by personal issues and practice characteristics (55).

The Culture of the Medical School. More than three decades ago, Snyder described the concept of the "hidden curriculum" communicated to students through informal discussions and certain behaviors that are not easily quantified or documented (56). Anecdotal examples of this abound, and are often revealed during focus groups of medical students: the medical school curriculum committee dominated by turf-protecting subspecialists, the faculty member who expresses surprise and dismay at his top student's decision to become a family physician, the students who speak disparagingly about the long hours and short rewards of primary care. Faculty and student attitudes, combined with an American society enamored with the latest technological discoveries and subspecialty care, do little to nurture medical student interest in primary care.

Informally, the medical education process exposes students to faculty role models in different fields, concepts of specialty status and prestige, sense of professional identity and career options based on hands-on experience in a relatively limited number of clinical settings. The emphasis in medical schools on memorizing details, recalling obscure disease entities and etiologies and learning not what is commonly seen but what is commonly asked on board exams, does not encourage generalist skills and attitudes. As medical students face the realities of medical practice and a seemingly infinite growth in medical knowledge, it is understandable that students gravitate toward specialties that have a defined and narrow skills set and patient population. In the medical school environment, generalists are either portrayed as unattractive gatekeeper/case managers, or as physicians who are faced with the daunting task of mastering all that is known.

Having reviewed the sources of medical schools revenue and the external influences impacting the academic health center, it is easy to imagine how these could reinforce a culture that values subspecialty and tertiary care, biomedical research and isolation from the broader community. This culture underlies the mission of the medical school and is manifest in every aspect of its functioning, from its admissions policy to its curriculum development to its policies for promotion and tenure.

The revenue sources of a medical school contribute to its institutional culture. A clear relationship exists between financing streams and graduates' specialty choices. Public medical schools have consistently produced more primary care physicians than private medical schools. In 1992, graduates from publicly funded medical schools were more than twice as likely as those from privately funded medical schools to be in family medicine residencies (57, 58). Many public schools were founded with an explicit mission to meet their state's health care needs. Their clearer sense of purpose with respect to producing primary care physicians is often translated into admissions policies and curricular innovations (46).

Whitcomb and his colleagues examined the institutional influences on career choice by comparing twenty-five medical schools that were "high producers" of primary care physicians with the same number that were "low producers" (59). Their findings demonstrate important differences between the two groups in terms of their revenue sources, commitments to primary care education, research programs, and complement of required clinical clerkships. High-producer schools were mainly public schools with smaller class sizes, less emphasis on biomedical research, and affiliations with community-based family medicine teaching sites. All had departments of family medicine, compared with only nine of the low-producing schools. An inverse relationship was found between the production of primary care physicians and receipt of federal support in the form of either NIH funding to the school or Medicare direct medical education payments to the school's major teaching hospital. These findings led the authors to conclude that a research-intensive, specialty-oriented environment will influence students to choose non-primary care careers, although a strong commitment to a primary care curriculum may negate this influence in some schools.

Other studies of institutional revenues predictive of medical student specialty choices have revealed similar patterns (60). Categorical funds aimed at promoting primary care practice simply cannot be expected to reverse the subspecialty-oriented training environment associated with funds derived from patient care revenue and biomedical research grants (17). Federal research support for medical schools is a hundred times greater than federal support for primary care education and departments (60).

The Curriculum. The length, quality, nature and timing of student exposure to primary care are important influences on medical student career decisions. For the most part, voluntary courses have not been shown to significantly influence specialty choices because students choosing to participate are already more likely to match in a primary care field (61). On the other hand, a required clinical experience in family medicine during the third year of medical school has a profound effect on student interest in the field (58, 59, 62-64). Putting family medicine on par with the other medical specialties emphasized in the third year may be a marker of a school's commitment to primary care and respect of family medicine as a career choice. As of 1992, only 59% of the nation's 126 medical schools had required third year clerkships in family medicine. On average, students from these schools are twice as likely as other students to pursue family medicine training (58).

It is unclear whether the timing and length of the primary care clerkship or its content is more important in influencing student choices. One medical school's ten year experience with a required ambulatory clerkship in the fourth year appears to have helped maintain their level of graduates entering primary care residencies (65). Other analyses of curricular influences on family medicine career choice found the number of weeks of required family medicine training to be the most significant (66).

Interestingly, required first year generalist courses have a negligible impact on career decisions (67). These courses are often fragmented approaches to teaching selected aspects of generalism, such as bioethics or psychosocial health, which may appear to students as "add-ons" and afterthoughts to the curriculum. Schools that offer a required first year clinical experience in primary care were associated with a 2% increase in the number of graduates entering family practice, controlling for type of medical school and family medicine administrative structure (67). This suggests that adding a few lectures into an already burgeoning didactic curriculum does little to interest medical students in primary care, but that early exposure to primary care practice in a clinical setting may have a positive effect.

The recognition of family medicine as an academic department and its presence in the required curriculum of the medical school seem to be important to medical student career decisions. Medical schools with departments of family medicine consistently produce graduates who are more likely to enter family medicine residencies than those with only a family medicine division, section or none at all (57, 59). In 1992, 12.6% of graduates from the 99 medical schools with family medicine departments began family medicine residencies, compared with 3.5% of graduates from the 18 medical schools without a department (57).

The curricular characteristics and focus of residency training programs are also associated with certain career outcomes. Graduates of primary care residency training programs pursue generalist careers significantly more often than graduates of traditional tracks in both internal medicine and pediatrics (68-70).

Faculty Role Models. Role models and mentors are critical to the career development of physicians-in-training, and may in large part determine the range of specialty choices that students consider (71-75). Role models and the opportunity to view the practice of primary care medicine in an ambulatory setting are often cited by medical students as important to their consideration of a primary care career (74, 75). The paucity of community-based role primary care role models in most medical schools leaves many students unaware of the viability of this practice option for themselves.

Tuition and Financial Aid. During the 1980s, rising student educational debt levels paralleled a declining interest in primary care (76). The effect of this debt on primary care career choice has been much debated in the literature, and is often raised in the context of anecdotal examples and intuitive beliefs. Several studies have reported that high indebtedness is associated with a tendency to choose non-primary care careers and careers in teaching, research and administration (76-79). Debt due to unsubsidized student loans (e.g., Health Education Assistance Loans) appears to be the true culprit when sources of debt are disaggregated (78). Information from first and second year medical students suggests that anticipated debt may influence their consideration of certain specialties (80).

The implications of student indebtedness are particularly worrisome among minority students. Since 1985, the median educational debt of minority medical graduates has exceeded that for non-minority graduates by about $8,000 for private schools and $2,400 for public schools, with more than one-fourth of minority graduates owing more than $75,000 in 1992 (37). The high cost of medical education may deter minority college students from seriously considering a medical career, and the debt accumulated may undermine their commitment to practice primary care.

The Issue of Self-Selection. It is unclear to what extent students "self-select" which medical schools they apply to and eventually attend, based on factors such as the school's mission, tuition level, curricular characteristics or graduates' career tendencies. Studies of interventions are often difficult to interpret, because many curricular changes are voluntary. Students already interested in primary care may be the ones who tend to select elective clerkships, primary care residency tracks and schools known for their community-oriented philosophy. Forced-choice responses to the AAMC 1992 matriculating student survey, completed by almost 91 percent of the entering class, indicate that the general reputation of the school, teaching methods of the school and geographic location are roughly equally important factors in selecting a particular medical school (81). Given the competitiveness of medical school admission and rankings of medical schools in the popular press based on levels of prestige and research funding, it is difficult to imagine that students base their decisions on the subtleties of the medical school's mission and curricular details. Students entering medical school in 1992 on average applied to 8.4 medical schools and only had a choice between 2.2 medical schools (81).

The Practice Environment of Medicine (Actual and Perceived)

As the environment of medicine changes, so do student expectations of what their lives should be like as physicians. Students seem to be placing a growing emphasis on the desire to have a "controllable lifestyle", one which will accommodate family obligations, outside interests, and a comfortable income. For many physicians-in-training, medicine is viewed as a career and not a life. In the last decade, the search for a "controllable lifestyle" seems to explain in part the declining interest in primary care (82). Unlike radiologists, anesthesiologists and surgical subspecialists, primary care physicians are often perceived by medical students to be overworked, over-stressed and undervalued in both societal and economic terms.

Attitudes about their career options and particular fields of medicine almost certainly influence medical student career decisionmaking. National surveys have shown that compared with other specialties, internal medicine is seen as being more stressful during residency, more demanding of time and workload as a career, and less rewarding financially (82). Medical school graduates switching their career preference away from internal medicine cite the type of patient seen (e.g., chronically ill, alcohol abusers) as well as dissatisfaction and stress among residents as important influences (83, 84). Of the 15 percent of physicians who make major specialty changes after graduation, more of them leave than enter primary care specialties (86). The reasons for these changes frequently involve financial and lifestyle considerations that became more prominent in career decisionmaking over time, such as working hours, location and financial remuneration.

Perceptions of specialties are often formed and reinforced during medical school and residency, and may in part derive from institutional factors, such as the opportunity to interact with generalist role models or the on-call schedule of the residents. Students' lack of awareness of the lifestyle of a particular specialty may be a significant factor in students' declining interest in primary care. On the other hand, many elements of the practice environment (e.g., the reimbursement system, the value society places on high-technology) may be beyond the influence of medical schools. Exposure to general internists may do little to reverse medical student perceptions of the field when many of these physicians are dissatisfied with their careers for exactly the same reasons (82, 86).

MEDICAL EDUCATION'S RESPONSE

Given the complexity of medical student career decisions, it may not be reasonable to hold medical schools fully accountable for the career choices of their graduates, yet they must take responsibility for influences within their own sphere: their institutional missions, admissions and recruitment policies, curriculum and faculty role models. Given the repeated calls for an increase in the production of primary care physicians, and warnings of an oversupply of many medical subspecialties, it is unethical for schools and residency programs to promote fields that may become obsolete, or for which there is little or no need.

Any set of recommendations for change in medical or health professional education must be chastened with the reality that the calls of reformers have gone unheeded for over a century. Given the fundamental orientation of the health care system during much of this period to specialization and biomedical research the lack of success of these proposals for change are not surprising (87, 88). Nonetheless, it is encouraging that the current round of health care reform pays substantial attention to the necessity of changing health professions education and workforce policies as a part of overall health care system reform. The report of the President's Task Force on Health Care Reform contains a detailed description of plans to reduce the number of specialty training programs, improve funding for primary care education, encourage primary care oriented research and further reduce the disparity between the payment to specialists and generalists (89). These reforms propose to redirect substantial public subsidies for medical education (both explicit and implicit) to achieve socially responsible outcomes, including increasing the supply of primary care physicians. Successful reforms depend on major changes in the financing streams which now offer medical schools strong disincentives to promote primary care. While the final form of the reform is not known at this writing, it seems safe to assume that proposals contained in the report are reflective of broader trends that will eventually take hold.

Already there are substantial changes occurring at the state level. In the last three years, 31 state legislatures have introduced at least one bill to expand the supply and encourage a more appropriate distribution of primary care physicians, including mandating curricular reform in state-funded medical schools (90). Increasingly, states are calling on publicly funded health professions schools to achieve community-responsive outcomes. The comprehensive health care reform bill passed by Minnesota last year includes a requirement that the University of Minnesota's medical school increase the number of graduates who practice primary care by 20% annually over the next eight years. Tennessee now requires its two state universities to jointly develop and implement a plan that will increase the number of graduates entering primary care by 10%. Similar proposals holding medical schools accountable for their graduates' career decisions are pending in other states (90).

CONCLUSION

In light of these reforms and the review of the literature as to what has proven effective in reforming medical education for primary care, we propose the following recommendations to the leadership of medical schools.

Refine institutional mission—Every school in the nation does not need an overarching commitment to primary care education, research and training, although most will need to make primary care a fundamental part of their mission if they are to survive in the patient care market place, respond to regulations from federal and state governments and truly serve the professional interests of their students. A realignment of institutional mission with a proactive affirmation of primary care is an essential place to begin, but only if the institution can genuinely make such a commitment. According to the Liaison Committee on Medical Education, less than half of the seventy-six medical schools with goals or objectives relating to the training of primary care physicians give admission preference to students experessing an interest in primary care or have required ambulatory care experiences (91).

Recruit students with an active interest in primary care—Medical schools must undertake more aggressive recruitment efforts to reach students with demonstrated interest in primary care, and revise their admissions policies accordingly. Although we concede that our own literature review has failed to identify essential characteristics predictive of students who become primary care physicians, it seems reasonable to ask medical schools to give special weight to students from rural areas, minority backgrounds, and those with extracurricular activities and stated preferences consistent with primary care. Greater representation of primary care physicians on medical school admissions committees may serve to reinforce this focus.

Institute and elevate the status of primary care-focused curricula—The evidence is clear that early exposure to a substantive primary care experience is essential to keeping students open to the possibility of a primary care career. This initial acquaintance should be reinforced by other primary care components to the medical school curriculum; required third-year clerkships in each of the generalist specialties that include an ambulatory component, community-based primary care clinical experiences and opportunities to form mentor relationships with primary care physicians. In creating ongoing ways to interact with the changing health care delivery

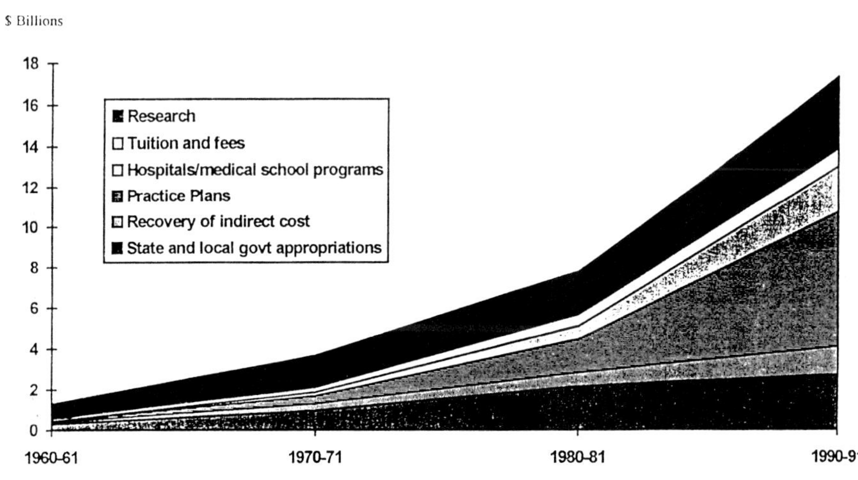

FIGURE 1. Major revenue sources for US medical schools, adjusted to constant 1991 dollars. Source: JAMA, Medical Education Issues, 1962, 1991, 1981, 1991. Adapted with permission of JAMA, 1995.

system, medical schools will expose students to the "real world" of primary care practice in health maintenance organizations, community clinics and physicians' offices. To ensure that proposed changes are not undermined by other aspects of their educational program, medical schools must reexamine their entire curriculum and its objectives, methods of instruction and evaluation. Medical schools need to assess and reform their "hidden curricula" before lasting change can be made in their formal ones.

Create a generalist oriented faculty—Students learn how to become a professional by observing senior members of the profession practice. If the dominant role models in terms of numbers or prestige are of one sort the majority of students will follow this lead, regardless of how other parts of the overall educational program are changed. If the nation needs a primary care workforce, then it must have a primary care faculty at many if not most of its medical schools. To accomplish this, medical schools will need personnel policies that can accommodate primary care faculty. This will mean changing the appointment, promotion and tenure processes in most schools. There will also need to be ways to build the generalist part of the faculty practice. Most faculty practices have emerged in just the opposite direction of highly specialized tertiary care. To have a primary care faculty practice will require creativity and tenacity on the part of medical school leadership. Related to the creation of building a more primary care oriented faculty is expanding the opportunities for community-based generalists to be a part of the educational program. This development would underscore the critical linkage between education and the changing care delivery system.

Establish financial incentives to enter primary care—Medical schools need to take a more active role in educating students about financial aid, debt management and loan repayment options, and aggressively seek alternative sources of financial assistance, such as alumni contributions or work-study programs which involve students in research and teaching. With tuition making up a small and declining percentage of medical school revenue, schools should consider placing ceilings on tuition levels and student indebtedness.

Develop research initiatives around primary care themes—The investment in research in medical schools has produced an abundance of biomedical knowledge that has improved the well-being of the nation. A similar investment must now be made in understanding how that knowledge is incorporated into clinical practice and how it influences patient and population outcomes. This and related subjects of inquiry are the legitimate research domain of the primary care faculty. In addition, support for research on medical education related to program effectiveness and its impact on the care system must be a part of the response from medical education to the primary care shortage.

ACKNOWLEDGEMENT

The authors wish to acknowledge the contribution of Jeff Kahn in the research and design of Figure 1.

This investigation was supported in part by the AMSA Foundation and by the National Research Service Award T32 HS00044 from the Agency for Health Care Policy and Research.

REFERENCES

1. Council on Graduate Medical Education. 1992. *Improving Access to Health Care Through Physician Workforce Reform: Directions for the 21st Century.* Bureau of Health Professions, Health Resources and Services Administration, US Public Health Service, Rockville, MD.
2. Physician Payment Review Commission. 1993. Reforming Graduate Medical Education. In: *1993 Annual Report to Congress.* Physician Payment Review Commission, Washington, D.C.
3. Pew Health Professions Commission. 1993. *Primary Care Workforce 2000: Federal Health Policy Strategies.* Pew Health Professions Commission, San Francisco, CA.
4. Ginzberg, E. 1992. Health Care Reform: Where Are We And Where Should We Be Going. *N Engl J Med.* 327:1310-1312.
5. Starfield, B. 1992. *Primary Care: Concept, Evaluation and Policy.* Oxford, New York.
6. Altman, S. 1992. The Mix of Physician Manpower and Its Effect on US Health Care Expenditures: the US versus Other Industrialized Nations. Presented at the National Primary Care Conference, March 30, Washington, D.C.
7. O'Neil, E. 1992. Education as Part of the Health Care Solution. *JAMA.* 268:1146-1148.
8. Rivo, M. and D. Satcher. 1993. Improving Access to Health Care Through Physician Workforce Reform. *JAMA.* 270:1074-1078.
9. Smith, Bruce L. 1990. *American Science Policy Since World War II.* Brookings, Washington, D.C, pp. 36-72.
10. Boniface, Zoe E. and Rebecca W. Rimel. 1987. *US Funding of Biomedical Research.* Pew Charitable Trusts, Philadelphia, PA, pp. 5-21.
11. Starr, P. 1982. *The Social Transformation of American Medicine.* Basic Books, New York.
12. Kerr, C. 1990. Higher Education Cannot Escape History: the 1990's. In Jones, L., Nowotony, F. (Eds.) *An Agenda for the New Decade.* Jossey-Bass, San Francisco, pp. 13-17.
13. Jolin, et al. 1992. US Medical School Finances. *JAMA.* 268:1149-55.
14. Krakower, J., Jolly, P. and R. Beran. 1993. US Medical School Finance. *JAMA.* 270:1087.
15. Jones, R. 1992. *American Medical Education-Institutions, Programs and Issues.* American Association of Medical Schools, Staff Report, Washington, D.C.

16. Petersdorf, R. 1991. Financing Medical Education. *Acad Med.* 66.
17. Rosenblatt, R. and M. Whitcomb, et al. 1993. The Effect of Federal Grants on Medical Schools Production of Primary Care Physicians. *Am J Public Health.* 83:322-27.
18. American Medical Association. 1993. *Physician Characteristics and Distribution in the US.* American Medical Association, Chicago, IL.
19. American Medical Association. 1993. Graduate Medical Education. *JAMA.* 270:1116-1119.
20. Kassebaum, D. and M. Szenas. 1992. Specialty Preference of Graduating Medical Students: 1992. *Acad. Med.* 67:800-806.
21. Kindig, D., Cultice, J. and F. Mullan. 1993. The Elusive Generalist Physician. *JAMA.* 270:1069.
22. Ernst, R.L. and D.E. Yett. 1984. Physician's Background Characteristics and their Career Choices: A Review of the Literature. Medical Care Review 41(1):1-36.
23. Davis, W.K. and P.A. Bouhuijs, et al. 1990. Medical Career Choice: Current Status of Research Literature. *Teach Learn Med.* 2(3):130-138.
24. Mowbray, R.M. 1989. Research in Choice of Medical Specialty: A Review of the Literature 1977-87. *Aust NZ J Med.* 19:389-399.
25. Colquitt, W.L. 1993. Medical Specialty Choice: A Selected Bibliography with Abstracts. *Acad. Med.* 68(5):393-433.
26. Ernst, R.L. and D.E. Yett. 1985. *Physician Location and Specialty Choice.* Health Administration Press, Ann Arbor, Michigan.
27. Woodward, CA. 1990. Developing a Research Agenda on Career Choice in Medicine. *Teach. Learn. Med.* 2(3):139-140.
28. Campos-Outcalt, D. 1991. Family Practice Specialty Selection: A Research Agenda. *Fam. Med.* 23(8):609-619.
29. Pathman, D.E. and C.R. Agnew. 1993. Querying Physicians' Beliefs in Career Choice Studies: The Limitations of Introspective Causal Reports. *Fam. Med.* 25(3):203-207.
30. Bowman, M.A. 1986. Specialty Choice of Black Physicians. *Journal Nat. Med. Assoc.* 78:13-5.
31. Haynes, R.A. and C.D. Killian. 1990. *Practice Patterns of Young Physicians: Outcomes of Graduates' Plans in Three Areas-Primary Care, Geographic Location, and Socioeconomically Deprived Areas.* Final report to the Robert Wood Johnson Foundation, grant no. 13430. Washington, D.C: Association of American Medical Colleges.
32. Keith, S.N., Bell, R.M., Swanson, A.G. and A.P. Williams. 1985. Effects of Affirmative Action in Medical Schools: A Study of the Class of 1975. *N Engl. J. Med.* 313:1519-1524.
33. Weisman, C.S., Levin, D.M., Steinwachs, D.M. and G.A. Chase. 1980. Male and Female Career Patterns: Specialty Choices and Graduate Training. *J. Med. Educ.* 55:813-825.
34. Cohen, A.B., Cantor, J.C., Barker, D.C. and R.G. Hughes. 1990. Young Physicians and the Future of the Medical Profession. *Health Affairs.* 9(Winter): 138-148.

35. Haynes, R.A. 1991. *Primary Care: Ethnicity, Gender and Undergraduate Major.* AAMC, Washington, D.C.
36. Weisman, C.S., Levin, D.M., Steinwachs, D.M. and G.A. Chase. 1980. Male and Female Career Patterns: Specialty Choices and Graduate Training. *J. Med. Educ.* 55:813-825.
37. Kassebaum, D.G., Szenas, P.L. and K. Caldwell. 1993. Educational Debt, Specialty Choices and Practice Intentions of Underrepresented-minority Medical School Graduates. *Acad. Med.* 68:506-511.
38. Petersdorf, R.G., Turner, K.S., Nickens, H.W. and T. Ready. 1990. Minorities in Medicine: Past, Present and Future. *Acad. Med.* 65:663-670.
39. Adams, E.K. and G.J. Bazzoli. 1986. Career Plans of Women and Minority Physicians: Implications for Health Manpower Policy. *J. Am. Med. Women's Assoc.* 41:285-292.
40. Johnson, D.G., Lloyd, S.M. and R.L. Miller. 1989. A Second Survey of Graduates of a Traditionally Black College of Medicine. *Acad. Med.* 64:87-94.
41. Cohen, M., Woodard, C.A. and B.M. Ferrier. 1988. Factors Influencing Carer Development: Do Men and Women Differ? *J. Am. Med. Women's Assoc.* 43:143-154.
42. Pinn, V.W. 1984. The Underrepresented in Graduate Medical Education and Medical Research. *Journal Nat. Med. Assoc.* 76:857-862.
43. Burkett, G.L. and M.H. Gelula. 1982. Characteristics of Students Preferring Family Practice/Primary Care Careers. *J. Fam. Prac.* 14:505-512.
44. Kegel-Flom, P. 1977. Predictors of Rural Practice Location. *J. Med. Educ.* 52:204-209.
45. Black, Ross R., Schmittling, G. and Thomas L. Stern. 1980. Characteristics of Family Practice Residency Graduates in the United States. *J. Fam. Pract.* 11:767-778.
46. Roberts, Allan, Foster, Robert and Margaret Dennis, et al. 1993. An Approach to Training and Retaining Primary Care Physicians in Rural Appalachia. *Acad. Med.* 68:122-125.
47. Lieu, T.A., Schroeder, S.A. and D.F. Altman. 1989. Specialty Choices at One Medical School: Recent Trends and Analysis of Predictive Factors. *Acad. Med.* 64:622-629.
48. Fincher, R.E., Lewis, L.A. and L.Q. Rogers. 1992. Classification Model that Predicts Medical Students' Choices of Primary Care or Non-Primary Care Specialties. *Acad. Med.* 67:324-327.
49. Association of American Medical Colleges. 1993. AAMC Policy on the Generalist Physician. *Acad. Med.* 68:1-6.
50. Swanson, A.G. 1989. Commentaries: Specialty Choice. *Acad. Med.* 64:583.
51. Babbott, D., Baldwin, D.C., Jolly, P. and D.J. Williams. The stability of early specialty preferences among U.S. medical school graduates in 1983. *JAMA.* 259:1970-5.
52. Markert, R.J. 1983. Change in Specialty Choice During Medical School. *J. Fam. Prac.* 17:295-300.

53. Babbott, D., Baldwin, D.C., Killian, C.D. and S.O. Weaver. 1989. Racial-Ethnic Background and Specialty Choice: A Study of U.S. Medical School Graduates in 1987. *Acad. Med.* 64:695-699.
54. Rabinowitz, H.K. 1990. The Change in Specialty Preference by Medical Students Over Time: An Analysis of Students Who Prefer Family Medicine. *Fam. Med.* 22:62-63.
55. Godkin, M. and M. Quirk. 1991. Why Students Chose Family Medicine: State Schools Graduating the Most Family Physicians. *Fam. Med.* 23:521-526.
56. Snyder, Benson, R. 1971. *The Hidden Curriculum.* Knopf Books, New York.
57. Kahn, Norman B., Graham, Robert and Gordon Schmittling. 1993. Entry of US Medical School Graduates into Family Practice Residencies: 1992-1993 and Three-year Summary. *Fam. Med.* 25:502-510.
58. Kahn, Norman B. and Stephen Jackson, et al. 1993. Results of the 1993 National Resident Matching Program. *Fam. Med.* 25:511-516.
59. Whitcomb, M.E., Cullen, T.J., Hart, L.G., Lishner, D.M. and R.A. Rosenblatt. 1992. Comparing the Characteristics of Schools That Produce High Percentages and Low Percentages of Primary Care Physicians. *Acad. Med.* 67:587-591.
60. Campos-Outcalt, D. and J.H. Senf. 1992. Medical School Financial Support, Faculty Composition, and Selection of Family Practice by Medical Students. *Fam. Med.* 24:596-601.
61. Herold, Arthur H., Woodard, Laurie J. and Rubens J. Pamies, et al. 1993. Influence of Longitudinal Primary Care Training on Medical Students' Specialty Choices. *Acad. Med.* 68:281-284.
62. Erney, S.L., Allen, D.L. and K.F. Siska. 1991. Effect of a Year-Long Primary Care Clerkship on Graduates' Selection of Family Practice Residencies. *Acad. Med.* 66:234-236.
63. Kassebaum, D.G. and R.A. Haynes. 1992. Relationship between Third-year Clerkships in Family Medicine and Graduating Students' Choices of Family Practice Careers. *Acad. Med.* 67:217-219.
64. Rabinowitz, H.K. 1992. Sixteen Years' Experience with a Required Third-year Family Medicine Clerkship at Jefferson Medical College. *Acad. Med.* 67:150-156.
65. Shore, W.B. and J.E. Rodnick. 1993. A Required Fourth-year Ambulatory Clerkship: A 10-year Experience with Family Practice and Primary Care Internal Medicine Sites. *Fam. Med.* 25:.
66. Campos-Outcalt, D. and J.H. Senf. 1989. Characteristics of Medical Schools Related to the Choice of Family Medicine as a Specialty Choice. *Acad. Med.* 64:610-615.
67. Mengel, M.B., Davis, A.B. and E.D. Barton. 1992. Generalist Courses in U.S. Medical Schools and Their Relationship to Career Choice. *Fam. Med.* 24:234-237.
68. Crain, L.S., Dienst, E.R. and M.J. Malloy. 1981. The Effects of Primary Care Versus Traditional Training on Career Choice in Pediatrics. *West. J. Med.* 135:248-251.

69. Noble, J., Friedman, R.H., Starfield, B., Ash, A. and C. Black. 1992. Career Differences between Primary Care and Traditional Trainees in Internal Medicine and Pediatrics. *Ann. Int. Med.* 116:482-487.
70. Rosenthal, Thomas C., Maudlin, Robert K. and Michael Sitorius, et al. 1992. Rural Training Tracks in Four Family Practice Residencies. *Acad. Med.* 67:685-691.
71. Osborn, Emilie H.S. 1993. Factors Influencing Students' Choices of Primary Care or Other Specialties. *Acad. Med.* 68:572-574.
72. Colwill, J.M. 1988. Primary Care Education: A Shortage of Positions and Applicants. *Fam. Med.* 20:250-254.
73. Taggart, M.P., Wartman, S.A. and A.F. Wessen. 1987. An Analysis of Medical Students' Residency and Specialty Choices. *Soc. Sci. Med.* 25:1063-1068.
74. Rogers, L.Q., Fincher, R.E., Lewis, L.A. and L.D. Nance. 1989. A Survey to Determine Factors Influencing Medical Student's Career Choices. *Acad. Med.* 64:417.
75. Gruppen, L. and D. Brown. 1981. Longitudinal Change in Specialty Preferences: Sex Differences. In *Research in Medical Education: Proceedings of the Twentieth Annual Conference.* Association of American Medical Colleges, Washington, D.C., pp. 101-105.
76. American Medical Student Association/Foundation. 1991. *Financing Medical Education: Conference Proceedings.* AMSA Resource Center, Reston, Virginia.
77. Dial, T.H. and P.R. Elliott. 1987. Relationship of scholarships and indebtedness to medical students' career plans. *J. Med. Ed.* 62:316-324.
78. Bazzoli, G.J. 1985. Medical Education Indebtedness: Does It Affect Physician Specialty Choice? *Health Affairs.* 4:98-104.
79. Geertsma, R.H. and J. Romano. 1986. Relationships Between Expected Indebtedness and Career Choice of Medical Students. *J. Med. Educ.* 61:555-559.
80. Hafferty, F.W. and J.G. Boulger. 1986. A Look by Medical Students at Medical Practice in the Future. *J. Med. Educ.* 61:359-367.
81. Association of American Medical Colleges. 1992. *1992 Matriculating Student Survey Results: All Schools Summary.* AAMC, Washington, D.C.
82. Schwartz, R.W., Jarecky, R.K. and W.E. Strodel, et al. 1989. Controllable Lifestyle: A New Factor in Career Choice By Medical Students. *Acad. Med.* 64:606-609.
83. Schwartz, M.D., Linzer, M., Babbott, D., Divine, G., E. Broadhead and the Society of General Internal Medicine (SGIM) Interest Group on Carer Choice in Internal Medicine. 1991. Medical Student Interest in Internal Medicine: Initial Report of the Society of General Internal Medicine Interest Group Survey on Factors Influencing Career Choice in Internal Medicine. *Ann. Int. Med.* 114:6-15.
84. Babbott, D., Levey, G.S., Weaver, S.O. and C.D. Killian. 1988. Medical Student Attitudes About Internal Medicine: A Study of U.S. Medical School Seniors in 1988. *Ann. Int. Med.* 114:16-22.
85. Tardiff, K., Cella, D., Seiferth, C. and S. Perry. 1986. Selection and Change of Specialties by Medical School Graduates. *J. Med. Educ.* 61:790-795.

flood of biologic discovery which continues unabated. The resulting knowledge has laid the groundwork for advances in health care, with the prospect of new pharmaceutical products and medical practices that will have major impacts on the prevention, diagnosis, and treatment of human disease.

These sweeping changes have led to corresponding adaptations in graduate biomedical education, the system for maintaining the necessary replenishment of trained research personnel. With these changes in mind, our purpose in this chapter is twofold. First, we describe currrent approaches to research training—not only of those who will generate the underlying knowledge that ultimately determines tomorrow's medical practice, but of the next generation of physician-scientists who will apply the emerging concepts and tools to problems of human disease. Second, looking beyond the discovery and clinical application phases of biomedical investigation, we provide an overview of health services research, including the workers who will extend and refine our understanding of the processes by which health services are made available and of how they may be provided more effectively, efficiently, and at lower cost.

RETROSPECTIVE LOOK

A generation ago, biomedical research was mainly clinical and, to a large extent, directly translatable into the care of patients. A physician-patient relationship was a key characteristic of the research, and hence, the investigator almost always held an MD degree. The emphasis on organ and human biology in biomedical research at that time made receipt of the MD degree an adequate preparation for an investigative career. Most MD researchers had little formal training in science beyond that offered in the medical school curriculum or acquired through fellowship in specialty divisions of departments of medicine, pediatrics, neurology, etc. As described by Smith, problems were observed, characteristically at the bedside, and ". . . then pursued to whatever depth the investigator was able to penetrate from previous experience or from technologies acquired for that specific purpose" (1). While that approach could be fruitful in the hands of a particularly gifted researcher, most investigators were ill-equipped for studies requiring a level of "sustained scholarship".

Diminished MD Role in Research

In contrast to that period, physician participation in biomedical research has declined, as evidenced by a progressive decrease in percentage of MD investigators holding NIH research grants. For example, the share of grant awards, exclusive of program project and center grants, fell for MDs from 31 percent in 1977 to 25 percent in 1992, compared to an increase from 67 percent to 74 percent over the same period for PhD investigators (2). That trend is a cause for concern. Continuation of the downturn has the potential for undermining the transfer of laboratory advances to clinical practice, while research itself might be denied the unique insights arising from expertise in human pathology. This concern is explored later in the chapter under the heading of TRAINING OF PHYSICIAN-SCIENTISTS.

Numerous reasons have been given to explain the declining level of physician participation in research. The effect of cumulative student indebtedness, the uncertainties of academic life, the instability of research funding, a perception of greater financial rewards in clinical practice, the paucity of suitable role models, the rigidity of Board requirements for specialty certification, etc. have been cited as deterrents to attracting the brightest young physicians to careers in research medicine.

Without discounting the influence of these factors, a more compelling reason, based on the changing relationship of science and medicine, may be at work here. Clinical faculty in American medical schools have been finding it ever more difficult to fulfill the triple role of clinician, teacher, and scientist that was characteristic of an earlier day. The increasing complexity of contemporary medical practice and the growing sophistication of modern biomedical research have made each of these functions virtually a full-time job. The roles of well-qualified clinician and first-rate scientist have become so demanding that only an unusual combination of circumstances and talent permits an individual to exercise both functions with distinction. Briefly stated, the academic physician can no longer devote a day or two to the laboratory and hope to perform meaningful investigation. Nor, in Petersdorf's view, will academic physicians devoting less than half-time to clinical medicine be able to compete effectively with their peers in the care of patients (3).

Moreover, changes in the organization of research at the cutting edge have left even less room for the part-time investigator. Several writers, for example, believe that ". . . medical research requiring the tools of molecular biology will be done by teams working full-time in the laboratory, . . . concentrating entirely on their research and in close and rapid communication with others in similar laboratories . . ." (4, 5). Using investigation of oncogenes as a model, Littlefield anticipates that members of these teams will be mostly PhDs, plus those few MDs or MD/PhDs who are thoroughly trained in the new biology and can devote at least 90 percent of their time and effort to the laboratory.

In an interesting commentary on demands of research in the new era, Petersdorf has proposed a two-platoon medical school faculty (3). One would consist of practitioners/teachers with highly honed clinical skills. The other, a team of investigators/teachers, would be engaged virtually full-time in the laboratory in order to remain technically up-to-date and productive in today's competitive research climate.

Under these circumstances, to avoid a "painful straddling of divergent ambitions", top-rank students, for whom the prospect of caring for patients had been a primary motivation for attending medical school, have opted in great numbers for careers as clinical specialists (6).

Changing Locus of Clinical Research

At the same time, clinical research has moved from the bedside, where patient contact and research were closely linked, toward the basic science laboratory with its emphasis on biochemistry, cell biology, and genetics (7, 8). According to Gill,

". . . animal and cellular model systems became the norm, not the exception: and with the use of such model systems, variables could be more tightly controlled, answers more unequivocally formulated, and concepts transposed to the next higher order of organization" (5). This changing face of clinical investigation was first documented by Feinstein et al. in a survey of topics, sources, and sites of the research abstracts associated with the annual Atlantic City "Spring Meetings" of the American Federation for Clinical Research, the American Society for Clinical Investigation, and the Association of American Physicians (9, 10, 11). Their findings indicated that the proportion of "clinical" topics, evidenced by research that was patient-centered, disease-oriented, or concerned with human material, had consistently declined. Concurrently, the proportion of "basic" investigations, using materials that were neither of human origin nor diseased, increased steadily.

The shift to laboratory-oriented science as the focal point of clinically relevant research presents today's physician-researcher with the prospect of a rapidly changing body of knowledge, increasingly removed from current medical practice. The new scientific frontiers are exemplified by molecular biology,[1] an expanding body of expertise that can no longer be covered by a medical school curriculum in which laboratory courses have been curtailed or eliminated and which has been increasingly geared to the specialized requirements of clinical practice. Therefore, physicians who select a research career must devote time and effort in laboratory training virtually equivalent to a PhD program, over and above the previous seven or eight years of medical school and housestaff experience. Combined MD/PhD programs are seemingly an excellent alternative. Based on research retention, grant success, publication performance, and rate of academic advance, the integrated MD/PhD pathway has been enormously successful. Those programs, however, are relatively costly and their output too limited to meet current or projected needs for basic biomedical researchers.

The foregoing factors, plus the certainty that breakthroughs in biomedical science will continue to depend on expertise in molecular biology, as defined, make it almost inevitable that PhD scientists will constitute the core of biomedical researchers well into the 21st century. There may be a need, therefore, for changes in PhD training of a sort that will broaden their perspectives in human biology and stimulate their interest in clinically relevant research.

TRAINING OF BASIC SCIENTISTS

Since a substantial fraction of graduate students in biomedical science are enrolled

---

[1]The term *molecular biology*, as used in this chapter, is broadly defined. In addition to mechanisms of DNA replication, recombination, and gene expression, it focuses on: membranes, receptors, and signalling; cell cycle control; enzyme reaction mechanisms; protein sorting and trafficking; and, the organelles and cytoskeleton that serve as "machinery" of the cell. A principal goal of the research is to determine relationships between molecular structure and physiologic function, which are of fundamental importance for understanding all interactions within biologic systems.

in doctoral programs at U.S. medical schools, the reader may question the need for special efforts to point their training more directly to problems in human health and disease. The answer is that most PhD programs in medical schools, despite their physical proximity to hospitals and clinics, offer training essentially similar to that of their counterparts in university divisions of the arts and sciences. As these programs have developed at academic health centers, faculty have tended to establish independent curricula that often bear little relationship to medical courses at the same institution. The design of separate courses has permitted faculty to articulate their teaching more closely to their own research interests. It is also possible that faculty may have organized, consciously or subconsciously, graduate programs that replicate those in the arts and sciences where they themselves were trained. The disconnection between graduate and medical school curricula leaves little opportunity for instruction of students in human pathophysiology. It may even result in training that actually deemphasizes clinical relevance. Selection of a dissertation topic, for example, is usually based on its tractability and general interest, rather than on its clinical implications and importance. While this may enhance scientific rigor, it also shields students from medically oriented research experience.

Interest in Clinically Relevant Research Wanes

Prospective PhD students frequently express an interest in human disease and health-related research. In that context, an overwhelming majority of graduate students indicated in interviews that such interest was an "important factor" in their decision to matriculate in a doctoral program at a medical school (12). As in all graduate programs, however, the laboratory years represent an intense and consuming period of concentration, with students frequently isolated in their thinking from the ambience of the medical center. Consequently, after some six years in that atmosphere, they are likely to graduate with little understanding of problems unique to the clinic, no experience in collaborating with physician-researchers, and a lack of familiarity with the medical lexicon.

PhD Contributions to Clinical Research

Despite these deterrent factors, a number of non-physician scientists have conducted research of significant clinical importance. Lipsett identified some 20 PhD members of the Endocrine Society in 1980 as the "moving force" behind highly original and productive clinical investigations. Included were Yalow for her work on metabolism of parathormone and gastrin physiology, and Tait for his discoveries in steroid dynamics and aldosterone physiology (13). The annual reports of research activities of the Howard Hughes Medical Institute contain examples of achievement that is possible when outstanding bench researchers are motivated to probe areas related to human disease. Not atypical is the abstract of a PhD geneticist in whose laboratory the human phenylalanine hydroxylase gene was isolated by molecular cloning, and the cloned gene used to analyze the cellular DNA of normal and PKU-affected individuals (14). That work subsequently led to the development of a prenatal diagnostic procedure for PKU in families with previously affected children. The procedure is now widely used in the United States and Western Europe. Illustrative of the same point are two major advances in our understanding of neurologic disease—the isolation of the gene that is defective in muscular dystrophy and the demonstration that myasthenia gravis is an autoimmune disease involving the acetylcholine receptor—that came from laboratories directed by PhD scientists, one working in a clinical and the other in a basic science setting.

New Pathways for PhD Training

To train basic scientists whose work will be oriented to medical problems, new educational approaches have been launched by a number of graduate schools at leading academic health centers, such as Stanford, University of Alabama, and University of Chicago. The goals of these innovations are: (a) to sharpen sensitivity to the clinical ramifications of basic scientific research; (b) to produce a cadre of PhD investigators who will bring concepts and technologies of the biological revolution to bear on the study of disease-related problems; (c) to increase the frequency and intensity of scientific interactions between basic and clinical science researchers; (d) to prepare PhD scientists to discharge effectively the teaching responsibilities associated with faculty appointments in medical school clinical departments[2]; and, (e) to enrich and diversify PhD training by capitalizing on the unique resources of the medical school environment.

While conforming to no unitary model, these new approaches share, to varying degrees, the following characteristics and points of emphasis:

- *Institutional environment.* One of the defining aspects of the new biology has been a blurring of boundaries between traditional disciplines. This emerging synergism among disciplines has given rise to a heightened emphasis on interdepartmental initiatives in graduate teaching. The administrative organization of several of the parent institutions, for example, includes a committee structure. In that system, graduate faculty are aligned not only in departments that focus on discrete disciplines, but concomitantly in committees which cross departmental lines and, in some instances, have degree-granting authority. Composed of basic and clinical scientists, the committees serve as a mechanism for fostering interdisciplinary research, while offering graduate students a perception of the integrated nature of biological science.
- *Curriculum.* Coursework varies according to the PhD program to which the student has been admitted. Typically included are biochemistry, genetics, and cell/molecular biology, plus other classes and laboratory rotations specific to the particular program. In addition to existing offerings, new graduate-level courses are being developed to introduce students to the fundamentals of

---

[2]The PhD component of clinical department faculty of medical schools has risen steadily since the early 1970s (15, 16). Now comprising some 17 percent of full-time faculty in those departments, funding for these positions could become problematic in an increasingly price-conscious market for health services.

human biology, principles of pathology and mechanisms of underlying disease states, and an overview of major diseases. A variety of teaching methods are utilized, such as lectures and reading materials, discussion sessions including actual case histories and patient presentations by clinicians, and demonstrations of diagnostic procedures.

- *Mentorship.* A pedagogical mechanism common to most of these programs is the dual-mentorship. One mentor, a basic scientist, works with the student to design an individualized program, and is responsible for integrating the technical and theoretical material taught in laboratory courses with the work in faculty laboratories during the research years. The second, a clinical scientist, is appointed to oversee and coordinate the student's contacts with the clinical arena throughout the latter years of the traineeship.
- *Research phase.* Selection of the thesis topic is considered crucial to success of the endeavor. Students will conduct their thesis research in the laboratories of faculty scientists whose own investigations are strongly oriented toward human disease processes and interventions. Further, a frequent characteristic of dissertation committee membership is the inclusion of a clinical scientist.
- *Other experiences.* A variety of experiences are built into the research years to preserve and nurture the focus on human disease. This is accomplished through participation in appropriate Grand Rounds, journal clubs, clinical conferences, departmental seminars, off-campus retreats, and annual poster sessions.

Other Training Formats

In addition to a degree-related program, new approaches at some graduate schools include establishment of a free-standing course in pathobiology. For example, an innovative one-semester course in pathobiology for basic scientists was launched in 1984 at an academic health center in Boston (12). The enrollees—graduate students, postdoctoral fellows, and junior faculty—meet twice weekly at 2.5 hour sessions. Participants are given the opportunity to study gross and microscopic tissue specimens, observe major diagnostic procedures, and participate in presentations of patients. In addition to the course director who is a physician-scientist, a faculty expert in the underlying biologic process for the particular disease to be considered interacts with the students in a Socratic format that emphasizes mechanisms, hypotheses, and experimental approaches.

Offered as an elective, the course has been increasingly oversubscribed. Of interest in this connection is the fact that applications have been received from graduate students at nearby universities. Evidence of its effectiveness is already apparent, such as questionnaire responses indicating instances where participation in the course had influenced choice of a thesis research topic. In addition, an appreciable number of former course participants have subsequently selected laboratories in clinical departments as the site of their postdoctoral training.

In summary, there is reason for optimism that PhDs of outstanding promise can be attracted to clinical research by giving them a better understanding of human disease during their graduate studies. Above all, novel ways must be found to project

Subspecialty Route

Research training has traditionally been intermixed with clinical specialty preparation for most physicians with investigative interests. Accordingly, graduating residents with research inclinations move directly into subspecialty programs with the expectation of pursuing certification and beginning research training at the same time. This reasonable intent frequently results in compromising either the clinical or research component, most often the latter. Training for today's research is a lengthy and demanding process. It is unlikely that a part-time experience of one or two years in a locus where research is not the dominant goal can equip the individual for a research career. Moreover, the science taught in subspecialty divisions, with few exceptions, has been faulted for being superficial and limited in scope (1, 18).

The intense competition for research support has increasingly taken its toll of the undertrained investigator. The professionalization of research has steadily selected against the MD investigator who, as indicated earlier, had at one time enjoyed a better prospect of success in obtaining grant support than the PhD applicant. An important manifestation of this professionalization has been a lengthening of the training required to prepare physicians for independent research careers. At the root of the MD's reduced competitiveness in the research grants arena has undoubtedly been an insufficiency of training in relation to the increasingly complex demands of modern biological science.

Analyses in a 1989 report of an NIH Task Force underscored the strong relationship between duration of post-residency research training and later success in receiving NIH research support (19). Where the median length of training was 12 months or less, only 20 percent of former MD trainees ever applied for NIH grants and a mere 10 percent of the total ever received a grant. By contrast, 43 percent of those with more than 24 months of training sought NIH grants, and 70 percent of the total were successful. Further, the proportion of applications from, and awards to, physicians was found to have dropped in the past 15 to 20 years from one in three to approximately one in four. These and similar observations prompted the Task Force, and its consultants, to recommend that training awards be made for no less than two years, with possible extensions to three or four years in order to prepare most participants for independent research careers. Compared to that recommendation, more than 60 percent of individuals with a professional doctorate had been appointed in 1986 to NIH training grant programs for periods of 12 months or less.

Other Post-Residency Training Formats

As alternatives to the subspecialty pathway, a variety of opportunities now exist for physicians who need a concentrated transition period to acquire the skills to compete with their PhD colleagues for research support. One such program, which aptly reflects the growing influence of the graduate education model of doctoral training, has been proposed by Ganem and subsequently described by Martin (20). These newer initiatives are targeted to a dual clientele.

The first, and larger, group is comprised of MD graduates who have completed a general residency, with or without a subspecialty sequel, but who have had no significant research experience. Located at centers with a record of excellence in research and training, these programs generally have multidepartmental breadth. They offer a curriculum of graduate-level courses, including intensive laboratory modules in cell/molecular biology techniques, as well as resources for an in-depth and mentored research experience. In addition, mentors, through informal advising and formal seminars, assist trainees in developing a clear sense of responsibility and ethical standards of conduct in research and scholarship. Among the critical assets of these programs is an opportunity for the post-MD trainee to interact on a day-to-day basis with graduate students and postdoctoral fellows, thereby engendering a sense of identity with the community of biomedical scientists.

Although the training sequence in these programs is free of competing clinical service obligations, allowance for some clinical time, depending on the nature and needs of the research project, may be made for recruitment of research subjects, conduct of ambulatory studies, or follow-up of patients on metabolic wards. The objective, character, and limits of such involvement, however, are clearly defined and circumscribed. In most cases, three years are required to accomplish the coursework, seminar participation, and independent study and research necessary to produce a new physician-scientist.

In the second group, physicians will have had significant exposure to research in the form of summer or off-quarter traineeships, year-out fellowships, or in dual-degree (MD/PhD) programs.[4] It is also worth noting in this connection that completion of a research thesis is a curriculum feature at several medical schools—either as a requirement for graduation or as an elective for attaining special recognition such as the degree of Doctor of Medicine with Distinction in Research (21). Individuals in this category are for the most part at a stage of development where a structured academic environment is no longer necessary. They can therefore participate advantageously, as postdoctoral fellows, in an apprenticeship/preceptorship type of training in the laboratory of a single faculty member.

TRAINING HEALTH SERVICES RESEARCHERS

The aim of health services research is to study the organization and performance of health care delivery systems. Specifically, its focus is on such variables as cost, quality, access, and medial effectiveness of health care received by individuals. The information and analyses resulting from health services research can illuminate the cost and effectiveness of alternative organizational or program proposals, provide

---

[4]Most dual-degree graduates enter residency training. To qualify for a faculty position in a clinical department, many will also complete subspecialty training. Consequently, such individuals may spend as much a five years in residency and clinical fellowship programs. The pace of conceptual and methodologic change is now so swift that even the most gifted MD/PhD may lose touch with the leading edge of his/her discipline during those years. Reentry into laboratory research after this discontinuity often requires a basic science postdoctoral fellowship of one or two years.

has increasingly emphasized interdisciplinary training programs. By producing scientists who are not locked into insular disciplines, those programs can help significantly to avoid premature obsolescence of PhD scientists. The basis for that belief is twofold: (a) that major advances tend often to occur at the common boundaries between disciplines as we know them today; and, (b) that since scientific requirements cannot accurately be foreseen 5 to 10 years in the future, broadly grounded pre-PhD training, with specialization left to the postdoctoral years, is a prudent strategy for ensuring responsiveness to changing national research needs.

To sustain the momentum of the scientific revolution, it is necesary to find new ways of teaching that encourage interdisciplinary approaches, particularly at the interface between the basic and clincial sciences. This is exemplified by recent innovations aimed at broadening graduate students' knowledge of human biology and disease.

Physician-Scientist Training. Although the drop in MD market share of NIH grants has been noted (25), data from the Association of American Medical Colleges' annual surveys of graduating classes suggest a growing interest, on the part of medical students, in research in the choice of career paths. For example, the percentage of respondents who indicated an expectation to be "exclusively or significantly involved in research" rose from 9 percent in 1979 to 15.6 percent in 1989. Concurrently, the percentage of medical school seniors stating a "primary preference for full-time research or academic activities" increased from 20 percent to 31 percent over the same period.

These findings should perhaps be interpreted with a degree of caution, inasmuch as the time for decision on fulfillment of the respondents' expressed plans is some three years in the future. Nevertheless, in the face of a seemingly clear trend, but keeping in mind the extent of commitment needed to excel in modern laboratory investigation, it is reasonable to ask about career options that are feasible for a young physician intent on cultivating a research interest while maintaining a meaningful role in clinical medicine.

Role of the Intermediary. For medical graduates unable to devote their energies undividedly to bench research, Littlefield has suggested as a career option the role of intermediary between "bench and bed" (26). Progress in clinical research requires a constant dialogue between laboratory and clinic, which in turn needs an interpreter who understands both worlds and speaks both languages—a physician who is capable, as stated earler, of functioning not only as a clinical investigator, but as a more fundamental scientist, depending on where the problem leads. The physician-scientist, for example, can play a key role in enabling the rapid and efficient discovery of disease genes by helping to develop family pedigrees and well-defined phenotypes. Moreover, the physician-scientist is able to study patients intensively, permitting the clinical situation to guide the nature of the questions, as well as the manner of seeking the answers. Described by one observer as an "amphoteric existence" (1) calling for compromise with excellence in both areas of activity, the physician-scientist's role of intermediary could nevertheless provide a satisfactory career for those interested in combining research and patient care.

Outlook for Health Services Research. The current infrastructure for health services research cannot support the volume of monitoring, analysis, and feedback that will be required by policymakers to test and implement various strategies for health care reform. The outlook for increased funding and sponsorship of health services research, however, is extremely favorable over the short-term.

The proposed Health Security Act, released by the Administration in late 1993, projects increases in authorization for health services research from a base of $150 million in 1995 to $400 million in 1996; $500 million in 1997; and $600 million for the years 1998 through 2000. While the precise dollar figures will undoubtedly change, the trend is unmistakable. Enlarged research support will in turn generate an increased demand for well-qualified investigators, and provide the means for academic institutions to expand their graduate training for the field.

REFERENCES

1. Smith, Lloyd H. 1989. "Training of Physician/Scientists." National Research Council. Report of the Committee on Biomedical and Behavioral Research Personnel. Vol. III: Commissioned Papers. National Academy Press. Washington, D.C.
2. Personal Communication, Robert F. Moore, Division of Research Grants/, National Institutes of Health, January 14, 1994.
3. Petersdorf, Robert G. 1984. "Managing the Revolution in Medical Care." Journal of Medical Education, vol. 59, February, pp. 79-90.
4. Littlefield, John W. 1984. "On the Difficulty of Combining Basic Research and Patient Care." American Journal of Human Genetics, vol. 36, pp. 731-735.
5. Gill, Gordon N. 1984. "The End of the Physician-Scientist?" The American Scholar, vol. 53, no. 3. Summer, pp. 353-368.
6 Fredrickson, Donald S. 1981. "Biomedical Research in the 1980s." Special Article, New England Journal of Medicine, vol. 304, no. 9, February 26, pp. 509-517.
7. Daly, Walter J. 1982. "A Personal Testament—Reflections on the Tower of Babel." Journal of Laboratory and Clinical Medicine, vol. 99, no. 1, January, pp. 10-14.
8. Warren, James V. 1983. "The Evolution of the Clinical Investigator." Journal of Laboratory and Clinical Medicine, vol. 101, no. 3, March, pp. 335-350.
9. Feinstein, A.R., Koss, N. and J.H.M. Austin. 1967. "The Changing Emphasis in Clinical Research: I. Topics Under Investigation. An Analysis of the Submitted Abstracts and Selected Programs at the Atlantic City Meetings During 1953-1965." Annals of Internal Medicine, vol. 66, pp. 396-419.
10. Feinstein, A.R. and N. Koss. 1967. "The Changing Emphasis in Clinical Research: II. Sites and Sources of the Investigations." Annals of Internal Medicine, vol. 66, pp. 420-434.
11. Feinstein, A.R. and N. Koss. 1970. "The Changing Emphasis in Clinical Research: III. Follow-Up Report for the Years 1965-1969." Archives of Internal Medicine, vol. 125, pp. 885-891.

clinical integrity" in the managed care world of the future (3). Thus we expect a continuing demand for physician management education.

In this chapter we will explore five questions related to physician management education. First, why is there a need for more physicians in managerial roles? Second, in what settings will physician managers work and what roles will they play? Third, what motivates physicians to pursue management education? What types of physicians are interested in administration? Fourth, what skills do they need? In what ways, if any, do their educational needs differ from other managers? Fifth and finally, when in a physician's clinical training should a management education be considered?

WHY WILL WE NEED PHYSICIAN MANAGERS?

Two key issues have confronted the United States health care system for the last two decades—costs and quality. These will remain important challenges into the next century. We believe physician managers are uniquely qualified to meet those challenges.

Physicians are central to any cost containment effort in health care. We know, for example, that physicians' clinical decisions determine about 60-80 percent of all health expenditures (4). We also know that physician involvement in hospital decision making can impact costs. Sloan and Becker found that hospitals with physicians on the governing board tended to have lower costs (5). Other empirical findings suggest that physician managers could play key roles in cost containment activities. Custer et al. analyzed hospital and physician responses to prospective payment and concluded that cost minimization requires cooperation between hospital administrators and medical staffs (6). Physician managers may provide the link that is necessary for effective cost containment.

Historically, economists have conceptualized the hospital as an entity with two separate firms (7). One firm is controlled by the hospital administrator and supplies inputs to the other. The second firm, controlled by the medical staff, combines inputs from the first firm with physician inputs to produce health care. However, Shortell argues that the distinction between the two firms, between "clinical" and "administrative" decision-making, has become blurred (8). New types of decisions that require the participation of managers and clinicians have emerged. Consequently, the traditional two-firm, dual authority model of many health care organizations may have become outmoded. Shortell suggests it should be replaced by a model of shared authority. Physician executives may be those who are best able to manage that shared authority. Shortell also advocates introducing physicians to management concepts early in their training to prepare them for their new collaborative roles (9).

Schneller believes that medical informatics will profoundly change the health care landscape and require a new paradigm for managerial roles. Like Shortell, he believes that separation of medical and managerial decision-making structures will no longer be feasible. However, "for physicians to be credible collaborators, greater investments in physician executive training will be necessary" (10).

Physician managers may also affect quality of care. A number of studies have shown that more extensive physician participation in hospital decision making is associated with higher quality patient care (11). Palmer et al. note that the success of a quality improvement program depends on its credibility with practicing physicians (12). Physician managers may provide that credibility.

There is good evidence that physician involvement in managerial decision-making can contain costs and improve quality. Some would argue it is easy to implement cost control programs when quality is not a consideration or start quality improvement programs when money is no object; the real challenge is to contain costs without sacrificing quality. That has been the prevailing paradigm in health care—that cost and quality must be traded one for the other. The most important task for physician managers in the future may be to evaluate that paradigm. Administrators who lack clinical experience could take on this task; however, it is more appropriately assumed by physician administators. "The value added by the experienced physician will be commonality of frame of reference with practitioners, insight into implications for individual behavior and, more importantly, the likelihood of a high level of trust" (13).

WHAT ROLES WILL PHYSICIAN MANAGERS PLAY?

The idea of physician managers is not new to health care. Most hospitals in the United States were originally headed by a physician superintendent. It was not until the 1930s and 40s that management of hospitals was gradually turned over to lay administrators. Physicians retained leadership roles within the medical staff but administrative leadership was assumed by non-physicians (14). However, physicians in administation were often targeted to handle roles with which non-physician managers were uncomfortable or which they perceived as marginally important (15). Some were not even considered part of the management team (16). In fact, at one time, physicians in management were assumed to be merely in a transition from active clinical practice to retirement. The management roles they were in lacked substantive authority (17).

The changes in payment mechanisms that characterized the 1980s prompted the re-emergence of full-time physician executive positions within hospitals and other health care organizations. Surveys of physician managers have confirmed that most function in the liaison role between clinicians and senior administrators (18). Physician managers have been utilized to evaluate and improve patient care, to mediate with other physicians, and to recruit new physicians. Kindig characterizes them as boundary spanners, Schneller as buffers (19, 20).

Regardless of the label, the role seems to require someone who understands and speaks the language of both medicine and management. In the minds of many administrators, this has meant that the physician executive's job was to carry messages from management to medical staff, to translate managerial issues in terms physicians would understand and respect. Regrettably, there has been less consideration of the need for physician executives to carry messages from medical staff to management, to translate clinical issues in terms managers would understand and respect, perhaps because non-physician managers have been slow to acknowledge the value of the physician manager's perspective. Schneller observed that non-physician executives have been concerned that physician managers will base decisions on the professional norms of physicians rather than the norms of professional managers (21). Nonphysician managers have slowly gained a greater appreciation for the talents of physician managers. This appreciation is sure to be enhanced as these types of managers co-mingle in graduate health administration programs.

Some physicians will continue to serve in these more traditional liaison roles. However, others will move beyond the interface role to general management positions where they can exert even more influence over the shape of health care delivery in the future. As physicians assume chief executive positions, we will come full circle back to the days of the physician superintendent (22).

The growing emphasis on cost containment in the health care field has prompted other roles for physicians in administration. Health care organizations are merging clinical and financial information to evaluate the cost effectiveness of specific treatments and the performance of physicians. Physician managers are needed who can interpret both types of data (23). Filerman identified a number of administrative functions that are being shaped by new knowledge and new technology that will be best implemented by drawing upon clinical expertise (24). These include the following: (1) outcomes management, in which the use of unnecessary inputs is limited; (2) interpreting the validity and organization-specific applications of health services research, particularly those that impact on physician ordering patterns; (3) managing clinical technology assessment and acquisition processes.

Physician managers will have opportunities to work in a variety of settings. In the past, most opportunities have been in hospitals and large, multi-specialty group practices. Those opportunities will expand, but a growing number of physician executives will work in managed care and other insurance companies, employer settings and consulting firms (25).

Academic health centers have always offered many opportunities for physicians to assume leadership roles in hospital, practice plan, medical school or university administration. Typically, physicians have assumed leadership roles in academic medicine by virtue of their clinical reputations. Most department chairs, for example, lack any formal management education (26). Merry notes that physician leadership in the future can not be limited to clinical competence but must include "the ability to motivate a group of peers to achieve particular organizational purposes" (27). This will be a critical skill for physician leaders in academic health centers since the teaching and research roles of these institutions may threaten the financial viability of their patient care activities in the future. Thus, the need for well-trained physician managers in leadership positions will become even more essential.

As we noted earlier, all physician managers will need to address issues of cost and quality. However, nowhere will this role be more critical than in managed care organizations. Leider and Bard argue that physician executives are needed to manage the inevitable tension between the orientation of these organizations and the orientation of physicians (28). As a consequence, Filerman predicts we will see more physicians serving as chief executives in managed care companies (29).

WHO WANTS TO BE THE BOSS?

Physicians today have a variety of motivations for pursuing a management position. Many find themselves in administrative positions with no formal background (30). A 1985 survey of physician managers demonstrated that only 13 percent had management degrees, but 62 percent thought it was advisable for physician executives to have a management education (31). While many more physician managers have management training today, it is still common for physicians to move into management positions without a management degree.

Other physicians want to move into management out of a desire to have a broader impact than is possible through one-on-one patient care (32). Hodge and Nash draw an analogy to physicians who want to serve as chief residents out of a desire to improve the training experience for others. "Physician executives are interested in achieving the same goal of improving health care, but on a larger scale" (33).

Some physicians would like a management degree but not a management job. They are full-time clinicians who feel a need to better understand the management and policy issues that affect their daily lives (34). They believe management training can help put physicians and administrators on an equal footing (35).

Some physicians consider a management career because of dissatisfaction with private practice. In Kindig's survey only 18 percent reported dissatisfaction with clinical practice as a reason for moving into administration (36). However, more recent anecdotal evidence from health administration educators suggests that number is growing. Ironically, it is frustration with the bureaucracy of health care that drives some physicians to consider leaving patient care to assume positions within the bureaucracy. These physicians need to be realistic about the role of management. Sources of satisfaction are quite different for clinicians and administators. Being the boss won't necessarily solve their problems.

WHAT WILL PHYSICIAN MANAGERS NEED TO KNOW?

Management education may help some physicians be better managers; it may help others be better clinicians. In a 1992 report on health profession education, the Pew Health Professions Commission outlined the skills and attitudes that will be needed by various health occupations in the year 2000 (37). Analysts at Pew assumed we would have a continuing environment of constrained resources and an even larger reliance on managed care forms of organization and financing. In that world, they argued, physicians will need skills not currently cultivated by most medical schools. These include a population perspective of health care needs that relies on the tools of epidemiology and planning, an information emphasis that allows physicians to evaluate practice and improve patient care, as well as skills in outcomes research and technology assessment. Many of these are skills routinely developed in health administration education programs (38).

Hillman, Nash and others have identified certain skills that will help physician executives meet the challenges of the future, including some of the skills discussed in the Pew Report (39, 40). These include skills in financial analysis, cost accounting, decision science, marketing, strategic planning, health policy and law. Once again, these are content areas typically associated with accredited programs in health services administration.

Goldfield and Nash have argued that we will have two different types of physican leaders in the future (41). One type will design the interventions necessary to assure cost effective care. They are the physicians who will conduct or direct outcomes research, craft practice guidelines, evaluate physicians' practice patterns, and advise on economic credentialling of medical staff members. The other type of leader will communicate those interventions to rank and file physicians. They will be the boundary spanners of the future. These two types of physician leaders may need very different skills and very different types of education.

We agree there will be different types of physician executives with differing educational needs. Those who are actively involved in outcomes research, guideline development and analysis of physician practice patterns will need stronger backgrounds in statistics, decision science, and epidemiology than the offerings of most management degree programs. Those who will work with practicing physicians to communicate and enforce new practice standards will need strong backgrounds in organizational behavior, management of professionals, financial management and law. Their needs might be well served by a health administration or business administration degree program.

Most of the skills identified as important by industry observers are skills we associate with generic management education. Courses in a Master of Business Administration program that is accredited by the American Assembly of Collegiate Schools of Business would certainly include organization behavior and design, strategic management, finance, accounting and economics (42). If management in the health care field is not that different from management in any other industries, a generic management degree would be perfectly appropriate (43). Yet there may be some unique attributes of the health care industry that require specialized management education. Shulkin et al. argued that business schools often do not understand the health care system. "By divorcing management education from medicine, these training programs and the physicians who participate in them lose much of the opportunity to integrate clinical and management disciplines into a broad understanding of how best to operate medical organizations" (44).

There are other compelling reasons for specialized training for physician managers. First, to work effectively with practicing physicians, physician executives must have clinical credibility (45). Physicians often move into leadership roles because they are well-regarded clinically; most physician managers believe they need to maintain their clinical credentials by spending part of their time in practice. In one study, physician managers reported they spent about 20 percent of their time in patient care. Those in hospitals and HMOs spent even more (46). Hodge and

Nash suggest that maintaing a clinical practice can also be very rewarding; it adds diversity to the manager's work and provides a different source of work satisfaction (47). Since most physician executives will have both clinical and management roles, Kindig and Lastiri argue physician management education should parallel those dual roles (48).

Specialized programs can also help physicians deal with the very different perspectives of clinicians and administators. Clinicians usually work one-on-one with patients. They have considerable autonomy and can make many decisions on their own. Their orientation is typically short term. In contrast, administrators usually work and make decisions in groups and have a longer term perspective. The culture of individual autonomy that physicians learn in medical school conflicts with an organizational culture that emphasizes teamwork and shared decision-making (49). These differences can make the transition from clinician to administator a difficult one. Physician management education should recognize those differences and help prepare physicians for the transition.

The differences in orientation between physicians and managers can create organizational tension between the two groups. Physicians in organizations may feel they have divided loyalties (50). Managers' loyalties rest with the organization and its viability. Physicians loyalties are to their profession and their patients. Physician managers need to know how to manage this tension between organizational needs and professional standards (51).

The question that remains is whether these issues require physicians to have separate management education programs. Kindig and his colleagues at the University of Wisconsin believe a program targeted to physicians is appropriate given the need to develop both management skills and clinicial evaluation skills (32). They offer a Master of Science in administrative medicine that is only for physicians. Others feel the issues of divided loyalties and different perspectives apply to all clinicians in management roles, not just physicians. For this reason, New York University offers a separate program for clinician managers that includes physicians, nurses, pharmacists and so forth (53). Schneller has stated that physician management training should "be sufficiently unique to avoid physician executives being forced to suppress their commitment to the clinical enterprise. Because physician executives should be charged with the integration of clinical data into the mainstream of management and organizational assessment techniques, it would also be a mistake to isolate the entire training of physician executives from the broader management classroom" (54).

We believe physician managers need education that focuses on the health care field and that recognizes the managerial and clinical issues that are unique to that field. However, we think physicians benefit from studying with other health professionals. We agree with Filerman's assertion that health care institutions are not well served if their physician and non-physician executives "go in different directions to advance the same knowledge and skills" (55).

Our program at Widener University is designed primarily for the health care professional who wants to pursue a graduate health administration degree while continuing to work full-time. Consequently, our students come to class with a

17. Leider, Harry L. and Marc A. Bard. 1994. Leadership in Managed Care Organizations: The Role of the Physician Manager. In: D.B. Nash (Ed.) *The Physician's Guide To Managed Care.* Aspen: Gaithersburg, MD.
18. Betson, Carol. 1989. Physician Managers: A Description of Their Job in Hospitals. *Hospital and Health Services Administration.* 34(3):353-369.
19. Kindig, David A. 1989. Background and Issues. *The Journal of Health Administration Education.* 7(4):677-682.
20. Schneller, Eugene S. 1989. Role Design for the Physician in Management: The Mandate of Managed Care. *The Journal of Health Administration Education.* 7(4):683-693.
21. Schneller, Eugene S. 1991. The Leadership and Executive Potential of Physicians in an Era of Managed Care Systems. *Hospital and Health Services Administration.* (36)1:43-55.
22. Kissick, William L. 1989. Health Care Management According to Ben Franklin. *The Journal of Health Administration Education.* 7(4):723-737.
23. Hodge, Jr., Robert H. and David B. Nash. 1993. The Physician Executive. In: D.B. Nash (Ed.) *Future Practice Alternatives in Medicine.* IGAKU-SHOIN, New York, NY, pp. 237-266.
24. Filerman, Gary L. 1991. The Future of Medicine and Management Education. AUPHA Annual Meeting, Washington, DC.
25. Ibid.
26. Minogue, William F. (Ed.). 1992. *Managing In An Academic Health Care Environment.* American College of Physician Executives (ACPE), Tampa, FL. 159-167.
27. Merry, Martin D. 1993. Physician Leadership for the 21st Century. *Quality Management in Health Care.* (1)3:31-41.
28. Leider, Harry L. and Marc A. Bard. 1994. Leadership in Managed Care Organizations: The Role of the Physician Manager. In: D.B. Nash (Ed.) *The Physician's Guide To Managed Care.* Aspen: Gaithersburg, MD.
29. Filerman, Gary L. 1991. The Future of Medicine and Management Education. AUPHA Annual Meeting, Washington, DC.
30. Shulkin, David J., Kronhaus, Alan K. and David B. Nash. 1992. A Privately Financed Fellowship Model for Management Training of Physicians. *Academic Medicine.* 67(4):266-270.
31. Kindig, David A. and Santiago Lastiri. 1986. Administrative Medicine: A New Medical Specialty? *Health Affairs.* Winter:146-156.
32. Filerman, Gary L. 1989. Toward a Future of Consequence: The Education of a Health Service Administrator. *A Future of Consequence.* The Association of University Programs in Health Administration (AUPHA), Arlington, VA.
33. Hodge, Jr., Robert H. and David B. Nash. 1989. The Physician Executive. In: D.B. Nash (Ed.) *Future Practice Alternatives in Medicine.* IGAKU-SHOIN, New York, p. 244.
34. Brown, Gordon D. 1989. Physician Executives, or Management Training for Physicians. *The Journal of Health Administration Education.* 7(4):694-701.
35. Bloomberg, Mark. 1992. Management Training for the Physician Executive. *Physician Executive.* 18(2)10-14.

36. Kindig, David A. and Santiago Lastiri-Quiros. 1989. The Changing Managerial Role of Physician Executives. *The Journal of Health Administration Education.* 7(1):33-46.
37. *Health Professions Education for the Future: Schools in Service to the Nation.* 1993. The Pew Health Professions Commission, San Francisco, CA.
38. *Criteria for Accreditation.* April 1992. Accreditation Commission on Education for Health Services Administration, Arlington, VA.
39. Hillman, Alan L., Nash, David B., Kissick, William L. and Samuel P. Martin. 1986. Managing the Medical-Industrial Complex. *New England Journal of Medicine.* 315(8):511-513.
40. Schneller, Eugene S. 1991. The Leadership and Executive Potential of Physicians in an Era of Managed Care Systems. *Hospital and Health Services Administration.* (36)1:43-55.
41. Goldfield, Norbert and David Nash. 1989. *Physician Leaders: Past and Future Challenges.* The American College of Physician Executives (ACPE), Tampa, FL.
42. American Assembly of Collegiate Schools of Business (AACSB) Accreditation Criteria. 1993. St. Louis, MO.
43. Sheldon, Alan. 1975. *Organizational Issues in Health Care Management.* Spectrum Publications, New York.
44. Shulkin, David J., Kronhaus, Alan K. and David B. Nash. 1992. A Privately Financed Fellowship Model for Management Training of Physicians. *Academic Medicine.* 67(4):267.
45. Ashley, John T. 1989. Physicians in Administration: Working at the Medicine and Management Interface. *A Future of Consequence.* The Association of University Programs in Health Administration (AUPHA), Arlington, VA.
46. Kindig, David A. and Santiago Lastiri-Quiros. 1989. The Changing Managerial Role of Physician Executives. *The Journal of Health Administration Education.* 7(1):33-46.
47. Hodge, Jr., Robert H. and David B. Nash. 1993. The Physician Executive. In D.B. Nash (Ed.) *Future Practice Alternatives in Medicine.* IGAKU-SHOIN, New York.
48. Kindig, David A. and Santiago Lastiri. 1986. Administrative Medicine: A New Medical Specialty? *Health Affairs.* Winter: 146-156.
49. Merry, Martin D. 1993. Physician Leadership in the 21st Century. *Quality Management In Health Care.* 1(3):31-41.
50. Goldfield, Norbert and David Nash. 1989. *Physician Leaders: Past and Future Challenges.* The American College of Physician Executives (ACPE), Tampa, FL.
51. Ibid.
52. Kindig, David A. 1989. Administrative Medicine at the University of Wisconsin-Madison. *The Journal of Health Administration Education.* 7(4):734-737.
53. Rodwin, Victor C. and Anthony R. Kovner. 1989. New York University's Advanced Management Program for Clinicians (AMPC). *The Journal of Health Administration Education.* 7(4):702-710.

54. Schneller, Eugene S. 1991. The Leadership and Executive Potential of Physicians in an Era of Managed Care Systems. *Hospital and Health Services Administration.* (36)1:52.
55. Filerman, Gary L. 1991. The Future of Medicine and Management Education. AUPHA Annual Meeting, Washington, DC, p. 9.
56. Hilsenrath, Peter E., Levey, Samuel, Weil, Thomas P. and Robert Ludke. 1993. Health Services Management Manpower and Education: Outlook for the Future. *The Journal of Health Administration Education.* (11)3:407-419.
57. Ibid. p. 418.
58. *Health Professions Education for the Future: Schools in Service to the Nation.* 1993. The Pew Health Professions Commission, San Francisco, CA.
59. Couch, James B. 1993. Educating Physicians for the 21st Century. In: D.B. Nash (Ed.) *Future Practice Alternatives in Medicine.* IGAKU-SHOIN, New York.
60. Daugird, Allen J. and Donald C. Spencer. 1990. The Perceived Need for Physician Management Training. *The Journal of Family Practice.* 30(3):348-352.
61. Wholey, Michael H. and John E. Capman. 1990. Business and Managerial Education in the Medical School Curriculum. *Southern Medical Journal.* 83(2):204-205.
62. Couch, James B. 1993. Educating Physicians for the 21st Century. In: D.B. Nash (Ed.) *Future Practice Alternatives in Medicine.* IGAKU-SHOIN, New York.

Medicine and Health Care Into the Twenty-First Century. Edited by S.K. Majumdar, L.M. Rosenfeld, D.B. Nash and A.M. Audet.

Chapter Twenty-Two

ROLE OF ALLIED HEALTH IN HEALTH CARE

KEVIN J. LYONS, Ph.D.[1] and
LAWRENCE ABRAMS, Ed.D.[2]

[1]Associate Dean, College of Allied Health Sciences
Director, Center for Collaborative Research
and
[2]Dean, College of Allied Health Sciences
Vice President for Student Affairs
Thomas Jefferson University
130 South 9th Street, Suite 810
Philadelphia, PA 19107

INTRODUCTION

The American health care delivery system is in a period of rapid and accelerating change. Political, economic, technological and social forces are interacting in such a way that fundamental change in the current system is highly likely. As the health care system is in transition, so are the allied health professions. This diverse group of occupations, who are involved in almost all aspects of health care, will be susceptible to the outcomes of these competing forces. However, because of the great diversity of these professions, determining how the forces will touch the allied health professions, as a group, is impossible. These forces will affect each of the professions in different ways. What can be said, however, is that the allied health work force will look differently, 10 or 20 years from now, than it looks today. This chapter will provide a description of the allied health professions, a discussion of the problems they are currently facing and the steps being taken to address these problems. It will conclude with some tentative predictions of the outcomes of these steps.

What are the Allied Health Professions?

Defining allied health has proven to be a challenge, and lists of the allied health professions vary. Generally, however, the term "allied health" has been used to encompass a cluster of health professions, numbering as many as 100 occupational titles, exclusive of physicians, nurses and a handful of others. Allied health personnel constitute the majority of the health care work force. Mostly women, they work in all types of care; primary, acute, tertiary and chronic and in all types of settings, including physicians' and dentists' offices, HMOs, laboratories, freestanding facilities offering special services, ambulances, home care, and hospitals (6). Among the major areas of responsibility of allied health professionals are the delivery of health or related services pertaining to the identification, evaluation and prevention of diseases and disorders, dietary and nutrition services; rehabilitation and health system management. In these capacities, the professionals work with widely varied degrees of autonomy, dependence on technology, and regulation.

Because of the comprehensive nature of the responsibility of allied health professionals, individuals admitted to a hospital often receive the largest share of services from these personnel. For example, a victim of a serious automobile accident may receive immediate treatment at the scene from an emergency medical technician or paramedic, then brought to a trauma center where a phlebotomist draws blood for a medical technologist in the clinical laboratory to analyze. If surgery is necessary, a respiratory therapist, perfusionist or surgical technologist may be involved. A hospital stay means a nutritionist has a role to play in recovery. If post-surgical rehabilitation is necessary, this might be provided by a physical therapist, occupational therapist, or a speech therapist. In addition to these individuals, it is also likely that countless other allied health professionals, from medical records technicians to vocational counselors, have been part of the health care team that served this patient.

As the health care reform movement puts more emphasis on prevention, a larger variety of allied health practitioners will have important roles to play. The dental hygienist working to prevent tooth and gum disease as well as detect oral cancer; the radiographer taking vital mammograms for early breast cancer detection; the cytotechnologist screening Pap smears for signs of cancer are but a few of the many allied health professions that will provide preventive and diagnostic services.

The following is a partial list of the over 100 allied health professions.

TABLE 1

Audiology	Physical therapy
Corrective therapy	Physician assistance
Dental hygiene	Psychology
Dietetics	Radiologic technology
EKG/EEG technology	Recreation therapy
Health care administration	Rehabilitation counseling
Health education	Respiratory care
Medical technology	Social work
Microbiology technology	Speech-language pathology
Nutrition	Surgical technology
Occupational therapy	

There are no exact figures of the number of allied health professionals in the United States. Estimates from various sources put the number from two to three million or between 50%-60% of the health care work force (1, 6). The training of allied health professionals is as diverse as the care they provide. The educational preparation of those seeking to become allied health professionals varies considerably. Some enter the profession through hospital-based programs, spending one or two years in clinical training. Others attend university-based programs which culminate in associate, baccalaureate or master's degrees (6).

What are the Major Trends in Allied Health?

All of the allied health professions are in a period of growth and change. The typical pattern of growth seen in the professions is an evolution from clinical specialties, concerned solely with providing services to physicians or dentists, through a number of intermediate stages where they strive for increased autonomy, to full professions, capable of providing a wide variety of services independently of physicians or dentists.

One notable trend in allied health education is the desire of many of the professions to seek higher educational requirements for entry to the profession. Prior to 1960, the primary mode of preparing allied health professionals was on-the-job training. At that time, there were less than 15 colleges of allied health sciences in the country. The decade of the 1970s saw sharp increases in the number of these academic units, so that today almost all major universities have programs in allied health in one form or another (5). Each of the professions has followed the pattern of developing college-based programs, some to a greater degreee than others. For example, while medical technology is still primarily a hospital-based program, there are numerous programs that provide baccalaureate level training in medical technology. Occupational therapy requires a baccalaureate degree, either from an accredited program or with a degree in another field and a period of specialized training in occupational therapy. In physical therapy, training beyond a bachelor's degree is necessary. To become a speech pathologist, a master's degree is required.

Increased educational preparation brings with it improved approaches to practice. As the knowledge base in each of the professions expands, the potential of professionals to provide more comprehensive patient care improves. As a result, many of the allied health professions are seeking greater autonomy. Most states still require some form of physician supervision of allied health activities, a practice that increases health care costs and severely limits the scrope of the services that allied health professionals can provide. In many of the more established professions, particularly those that provide rehabilitation, preventive or primary care services such as physical therapy, occupational therapy, dental hygiene or speech and language pathology, significant efforts are being made to gain the right for professionals to practice and be reimbursed for their services without physician or dentist referral. For example, now, in most states, dental hygienists can perform many services with only general supervision of a dentist. General supervision is interpreted as supervision which does not require the physical presence of a dentist. In over

There are few doctoral programs in any of the fields further reducing supply and driving up salaries. This lack also requires those seeking a terminal degree to take doctoral work in fields outside of allied health. The result is a small supply, a large demand and even higher salary requirements.

Even among doctorally-prepared faculty, there are relatively few highly skilled researchers. A real need exists for enhancing the research skills of allied health faculty. While some of the allied health professions are now beginning to take systematic steps to train investigators, these projects are long term efforts and are not expected to have any immediate results.

There is also a need to investigate the way practice is conducted. As new treatments are developed, serious research must be conducted to assess the effectiveness of these treatments since, too often, clinical interventions are guided by convention rather than empirical assessment and research. Finally, there remains the need in many of the professions to build a body of knowledge linked to a theoretical framework. Withouth this effort, their knowledge base and, consequently, their practice will lack organization and direction.

The education of allied health professionals is an expensive proposition, particularly in those programs such as dental hygiene and some of the laboratory science programs, that require training in the use of advanced technology. One estimate of the average costs, in 1993 dollars, for educating selected allied health students, is about $14,000. This includes approximately $19,000 in lab sciences, $18,500 for a dental hygienist, $14,500 in physical therapy, $13,500 in occupational therapy and $12,500 for diagnostic imaging (3).

Recruitment and retention of allied health professionals is difficult and made more so by the absence of opportunities for career advancement in many jobs. While entry level salaries are relatively high, averaging about $32,000 annually, the wage scale is compressed, and opportunities for significant promotions are absent. Therefore, most professionals quickly reach a peak in earnings and must move into administrative or supervisory positions if they expect to progress in their careers.

Efforts to gain significant increases in support for programs to train new allied health professionals is hindered by the lack of public awareness regarding the existence of many of the fields. Allied health can truly be called an invisible majority. For example, the public knows what a physician is, but relatively few know anything about professions such as cytotechnology. This lack of public perception makes gaining widespread support difficult, particularly on Capitol Hill, where Congress makes important funding decisions that could help alleviate many of the problems. There is also inadequate recognition of allied health professionals on the state and Federal level. For example, while allied health professionals represent between 50%-60% of the health care work force, there is no agency that deals solely with allied health issues or that provides sufficient funding for allied health research.

External Influences on the Utilization of Allied Health Professionals

The Seventh Report to the President and Congress (March, 1990) identified major demographic changes that will effect allied health professionals in the decades ahead. These changes are those that are driving the demand for the professions and will require them to be more effectively used. The first of these is the projected increase in the number of elderly persons, by far the largest users of health care services. The number of elderly individuals are increasing more rapidly than the rest of the population. This growth is expected to continue well into the 21st century, particularly between 2010 and 2030, when those born immediately after World War II reach age 55. With increases in life expectancy of the population and efforts to reduce hospital length of stay, the need for rehabilitation and home health care professionals such as occupational therapists, physical therapists, respiratory therapists and audiologists will continue to rise. The U.S. Bureau of Health Professions estimates that 3,800 additional full-time equivalent physical therapists and 7,200 full-time equivalent occupational therapists will be needed to serve persons 65 and over in the year 2000.

A second more immediate concern is linked to the health care reform movement. There are approximately 37 million people without health insurance in the United States. Almost all health care reform proposals will seek to provide some form of health insurance for these individuals. There is also expected to be a growing emphasis on programs of health promotion and disease prevention which are integral components of the education of many allied health professionals. This huge growth of those seeking services will increase the load on an already overburdened health care system, one that is already experiencing shortages of health care providers, particularly allied health professionals. Other influences, such as changes in methods of payment for medical services, emphasis on cost containment, advances in technology, increased attention to quality of care concerns, and changes in the case mix and treatment methods, will also have a major impact on the structure and delivery of services of the health care industry.

What Steps are being Taken to Address these Problems?

While the number of challenges facing the allied health professions are significant, there are efforts underway which may help to alleviate some of these difficulties. The current emphasis by the Clinton administration on health care reform, with its focus on primary care, will begin to direct attention to the potential roles of allied health professionals in the support or provision of cost-effective health care. Attention is being drawn to alternative strategies and models of care as policymakers search for solutions to the high cost of health care and to find ways to provide care to those millions of people without care or with inadequate care. The PEW Commission and the Institute of Medicine, in their studies, recognized the importance of allied health in this environment (6, 8). The Bureau of Health Professions, stimulated by this attention, arranged with the College of Allied Health Sciences at Thomas Jefferson University to conduct a national workshop, in March, 1994, to address the role of allied health in the delivery of primary care. The purposes of this workshop were to describe the roles of allied health professionals in the direct provision and support of primary health care, to identify key research questions and develop recommendations to address educational, regulatory and professional issues related to this role. Finally, the U.S. Department of Health and Human Services recently charted a National Commission on Allied Health to address the pressing issues facing the professions. This commission, although a temporary advisory committee, is the first Federal recognition of allied health in a formal way. It has been charged with making recommendations to the Secretary of the U.S. Department of Health and Human Services and to Congress regarding three important issues. These are: supply and distribution of allied health personnel, current and future projected shortages, particularly in underserved and rural areas, and the identification of the priority research needs within the allied health professions. The commission is also charged with making recommendations concerning Federal policies which need to be developed with respect to shortage areas, changes in educational programs that will need to be undertaken to increase the supply and develop a research base and improvements in the data bases required to overcome current information deficiencies relating to the roles and functions of the allied health professionals. This commission is expected to begin its work in the summer of 1994 and terminate in the summer of 1995.

The emphasis on health care reform is also calling into question the way that the nation thinks about and delivers health care (4). The Pew Health Professions Commission has noted that, "One result [of the reform movement] will be the capacity to expand from a system focused solely on the provision of individual care to a system that also addresses overall population health . . . and a diversification in the mix of providers and their roles as these new systems seek to deliver care in the least expensive and most appropriate manner" (7). If the health care system in the United States shifts to a more population-based approach, it will have a far-reaching impact on the role of allied health professionals. By focusing on risk factors in the physical and social environments, the center of care could become the community rather than the individual (8). If so, then allied health professionals, with their focus on health promotion and disease prevention, will take on increasingly responsible roles in the delivery of primary health care.

Many of the professions themselves are recognizing the potential power that exists in numbers and are banding together into organizations which may have greater influence on health policy issues. For example, the American Physical Therapy Association, the American Occupational Therapy Association and the American Speech-Language-Hearing Association have formed a group called the Tri-Alliance, in an attempt to present a unified response to the health care reform movement from the perspectives of three professions. A second new group, called the Coalition for Allied Health Professions, is a broader-based group. A steering committee, comprised of 17 representatives, from two and four-year colleges and universities, laboratory fields, physical therapists, dental hygiene, government agencies, health care administrators, and private companies, met for the first time in Washington, D.C., on September 12, 1993 to "address the magnitude of health care reform issues and to ensure the adequate supply of allied health care professionals, [and to] formulate strategies which enhance allied health's contribution to the national health care agenda at all levels, local, state and federal" (2). Whether these coalitions will become a viable force representing the interests of allied health or whether each group will try to promote their own narrow self interest in the name of the group remains to be seen. What is important is that these organized endeavors represent a significant movement, among a large segment of the allied health work force, to work together in the face of what many perceive is a crisis.

In addition to these attempts at cooperation among the professions regarding health policy issues, there appears to be an increased interest in cooperation in research and the delivery of care. The major stimulus for this interest comes from Federal and foundation funding agencies and is most obvious in calls for proposals which stress collaboration among health care professionals in research, training and demonstration projects. Of great importance in these efforts are that they stress collaboration, not only among allied health disciplines, but between allied health and others such as nursing and medicine.

What are the Likely Outcomes?

Speculation regarding the outcome of the health care reform movement on the future roles of allied health professions is precarious. However, there appear to be four areas in which change can be expected. The first is that there will probably be significant changes within the professions themselves. Some will become larger and more influential, others may become smaller or go out of existence, while still others may reorganize and/or combine their functions with others. For example, many of the larger professions such as physical therapy, occupational therapy or speech and language pathology, will grow stronger. These groups are devising theoretical frameworks to define the profession, developing a strong research base to inform practice, increasing their communication efforts with policymakers, and reorganizing some of their functions to be more responsive to a wider range of clients. Other professions, particularly some of the smaller, more technology driven ones, may cease to exist. Advances in technology may make these professions obsolete or their functions may be absorbed by some of the larger ones. Still others may reorganize or merge with related fields. The concepts of "clustering," or multicompetency, where professionals in two or more related fields such as cytotechnology and medical technology, gain skills in the other's discipline may gain more widespread acceptance and result in entirely new professions.

The second area of change is that there will be more involvement of the allied health professions in the provision of primary care. With the anticipated addition of 37 million people to the health insurance rolls, the tremendous expansion of the geriatric population and the large underserved segment of the population in rural and urban areas, there will be an increased need for the provision of primary care services to these groups. Many of the allied health professions will focus their efforts on ways in which they can provide care to these groups.

The impact of technological change upon the allied health professions is difficult to fully assess. Among factors to be considered are the following: automation in clinical laboratories, increased use of computer-based technologies and other advances that permit more health care to be delivered in outpatient settings. While these can have a positive impact on the delivery of patient care, they may have varying effects on the allied health professions. For some, it may mean the need to conduct research on the effectiveness of the technology or gain advanced education in its use. For others, it may have a negative impact, if it allows for faster, more accurate and cost-effective services than that presently being provided by practitioners.

Shortages of allied health professionals will continue. Although hospitals and other health care institutions may find alternative ways to acquire the services supplied by allied health practitioners, all projections predict a significant demand for allied health professionals into the foreseeable future. While the Clinton health care reform proposal does not, as yet, articulate specific needs for allied health manpower, providing the additional health care required will ultimately necessitate a substantial expansion in the allied health work force.

What are the Recommendations for Greater Impact on Health Care?

In order for the allied health professions to have a greater impact on the delivery of effective health care, there are at least three major initiatives that must be undertaken. These are: 1) a more systematic examination of allied health, particularly regarding issues of cost, quality of care, allied health practices, supply, demand and utilization, and cross-cultural comparative studies of the allied health professions, 2) greater cooperation among the disciplines in such areas as informing health policy, team approaches to care and increasing the visibility of the allied professions to the general public, and 3) continued emphasis on collaboration among the professions in research, education and patient care.

The systematic study of allied health issues is a critical undertaking. There are at least four areas of research that need to be pursued. Particularly important are studies which address the cost and quality of services provided by allied health professionals. One focus of these studies should be on the cost-effectiveness of allied health services. The outcome of these studies will provide information to justify the increased use of allied health professions in providing services to those most in need. Studies which assess the effectiveness of procedures used by allied health professionals will be necessary in order to validate these practices and further the development of a scientific base of the various professions. Supply, demand and utilization studies are also important. These studies will provide the needed information to help policymakers make effective decisions regarding the most appropriate utilization of the current work force. Data from these studies will also be useful to educators in helping them determine future training needs. Finally, cross-cultural studies which assess the roles and functions of allied health professionals in other countries can provide data that might suggest more effective ways to organize allied health care delivery in the United States.

In order to effectively conduct the needed research, attention must be paid to the training of allied health researchers. To develop a cadre of competent allied health researchers, specific faculty development programs should be developed at the university level which focus on research training. Money should also be earmarked at the Federal level to support this much needed training.

The current efforts at cooperation among the various allied health disciplines needs to continue. Two areas are particularly important. The first is in the area of health policy. The allied health professions make up close to 60% of the health care work force, but have very little influence in setting health policy. While many of the large professional associations have their own legislative affairs office devoted to articulating the needs of the profession, a more effective approach would be to organize on a much broader scale, with a larger representation of allied health professionals. These cooperative efforts will be even more effective if they include interactions and cooperaiton with other disciplines such as nursing, medicine and osteopathy and if they also focus on other initiatives which will increase the viability of the allied health profession, particularly to the general public.

Cooperation and collaboration should be expanded beyond the health policy and public relations arena. This cooperation should extend to individuals providing care. Many of the health problems faced by those seeking care are multifaceted and can better be provided by teams of professionals working together. This will require many of those in the allied health professions to learn to work collaboratively with physicians, nurses and other health care professionals.

This need for collaboration has implications for both allied health educational programs and for research endeavors. Educational programs will need to stress team-oriented approaches to care and develop programs which will provide prospective allied health professionals with the skills needed to work in groups. Because of the overlap in knowledge among many of the health professionals and the ever-expanding educational requirements, there will need to be more attention paid to the development of core learning experiences which involve both common areas of knowledge among the various professions and joint clinical training. These experiences will not only provide allied health professionals with a better understanding of the potential contributions of other disciplines, but it will contribute to the more efficient organization of many educational programs. Finally, as knowledge expands in all the fields, there will be an increased need to engage in collaborative approaches to research. Interdisciplinary teams, organized to address important health care problems, have the potential to lead to more innovative and effective solutions than narrowly focused, discipline-specific approaches. More attention will need to be given to these approaches in the future.

SUMMARY

The allied health professions are a large and diverse group of health care providers, constituting approximately 60% of the health care work force in the United States. This group of professionals is involved in almost all aspects of care, yet is an "invisible majority" when policymakers consider issues of health care. The professions are in a period of growth and change but, as they continue to mature, have the potential to make a major impact on the delivery of health care in the 21st century. The professions are experiencing a number of challenges, most of which are related to their relatively recent development as important players in health care delivery. These challenges include a lack of adequate data regarding the characteristics, numbers or functions of allied health personnel, shortages of both faculty and practitioners which are projected to continue for the foreseeable future, and an immature research base. As the health care reform movement gains momentum, these problems are beginning to be recognized in both the public and private sector and the first steps toward their resolution have begun. The outcome of these steps, and the future of the allied health professions appear to be very promising, particularly because of the potential contributions they can make to cost-effective health care. However, before they can realize this bright future, they will have to undergo a number of changes and will be faced with continued uncertainty. The professions will also have to realize they have control over their destiny and take the necessary steps to realize their potential. These steps include the systematic study of their practices, increased cooperation among the various disciplines and more emphasis on collaboration in research, education and patient care.

REFERENCES

1. Association of Schools of Allied Health Professions. 1993. *Allied Health and Health Care Reform.* Position Paper. Washington, D.C.
2. Coalition for Allied Health Professions. 1993. *Enhancing Allied Health Involvement in Health Care Reform.* Position Paper. Bethesda, MD.
3. Collins, J. 1993. *Impact Analysis of the Loss of the State Appropriation on the College of Allied Health Sciences.* Philadelphia, PA. Thomas Jefferson University.
4. Elwood, T. 1993. Director of Government Relations and Policy Research for the Association of Schools of Allied Health Professions. Washington, D.C. Personal Correspondence.
5. Hamburg, J. (Ed.) 1974. *Review of Allied Health Education, I.* Lexington, KY. The University Press of Kentucky.
6. Institute of Medicine. 1989. *Allied Health Services: Avoiding Crises.* Washington, D.C. National Academy Press.
7. Shugars, D.A., O'Neil, E.H. and J.D. Bader. (Eds.) 1991. *Healthy America: Practitioners for 2005, An Agenda for Action for U.S. Health Professional Schools.* Durham, NC: The Pew Health Professions Commission.
8. O'Neil, E.H. and D.M. Hare. (Eds.) 1990. *Perspectives on the Health Professions.* Durham, NC. The Pew Health Commission.
9. U.S. Public Health Service. 1990. *Seventh Report to the President and Congress on the Status of Health Personnel in the United States.* Washington, D.C. Department of Health and Human Services.

Medicine and Health Care Into the Twenty-First Century. Edited by S.K. Majumdar, L.M. Rosenfeld, D.B. Nash and A.M. Audet.

Chapter Twenty-Three

NURSING: Key Issues for the Twenty-First Century

CYNTHIA FLYNN CAPERS, Ph.D., R.N.*

Director, Undergraduate Progams and Associate Professor
School of Nursing
LaSalle University
Philadelphia, PA 19141

INTRODUCTION

The health care system is experiencing a revolution. There is widespread dissatisfaction with the service provided with public complaints of fragmented, depersonalized, and inadequate care. There are cries and accounts of geographical and cultural barriers to care. Consumers and providers heatedly debate the economics of health care. Technological and scientific advances in treatment of diseases make headline news. Ethical dilemmas of clinical decision making are discussed in hollowed halls of universities while families sit in hospitals and question the "rightness" of prolonging the life of technologically dependent loved ones. All of this is occurring when people are getting sicker, the general population is getting older, inflation skyrockets, and individual resources become more sparse.

In response, proposals for changing the health care system abound; special interest groups scurry to protect their turf; and the argument about the status of health care as a privilege or right is revisited time and time again. So what is the answer? Clearly no one knows for sure, but surely, everyone has an opinion.

Consequently, the health care literature is replete with articles addressing health care trends, problems, and issues. Since nurses make up the largest group of health care providers, many of these publications specifically address the nursing profession. The purpose of this brief chapter is to discuss key issues for nursing in the

---

*At the time of the writing of this chapter, Dr. Capers was completing her sixth year as a gubernatorial appointee to the Pennsylvania State Board of Nursing. She is now on the Board of Directors of the Pennsylvania Nurses Association.

21st century. It is not intended to be duplicative of other publications. Instead, a selective view of nusing in Pennsylvania will be provided because of the author's professional affiliations and activities. Particular attention is directed to educational and practice trends.

NURSING AND NURSING ROLES

As a backdrop to addressing nursing in the 21st century, the meaning of nursing and the multiple roles of nurses are provided. This information will then be used as a reference point for further discussion.

Caring has been identified as the "essence of nursing and the distinct, dominant, central and unifying focus" (Leninger, 1991) Most nursing theorists provide definitions of nursing that show the centrality of *caring* to the discipline, and terms such as "helping" and "nurturing," are used to explain and define nursing. Nursing is also characterized as a unique profession; a profession that provides a service; a profession that is both an art and a science.

In more specific terms, the American Nurses' Association defines nursing with respect to the realm of phenomenon of which nurses are concerned, i.e., "the diagnosis and treatment of human responses to actual or potential health problems" (ANA, 1980). From a legal perspective, nursing is defined by the practice acts of each state. The Pennsylvania State Board of Nursing defines the practice of professional nursing as "diagnosing and treating human responses to actual or potential health problems through such services as case finding, health teaching, health counseling, and provision of care supportive to or restorative to life and well-being, and executing medical regimens as prescribed by a licensed physician or dentist" (Commonwealth of Pa., 1985).

The roles of nurses span the areas of *practice, administration, education, research,* and *entrepreneurship.* The *practice* arena is commonly associated with the provision of direct nursing care to individuals, families, groups, and communities. Staff nurses, clinical nurse specialists, and nurse practitioners provide direct care to clients/patients. Nursing *administration* focuses on managerial and administrative responsibilities associated with the delivery of care to clients/patients within various health care agencies. Vice presidents for nursing, nursing coordinators, supervisors, nurse managers, and head nurses are titles that have been used to indicate nursing administrators. Nursing *educators* are most commonly seen as the faculty that has the primary responsibility of providing instruction to undergraduate and graduate nursing students. Teaching roles are implemented by professors and instructors, whereas deans, directors, and departmental chairs have administrative responsibility. The educator role can be expanded to include those nurses who have responsibility for staff development and continuing education of nurses within health care facilities and other organizations.

Within the past decade, *researchers* and *entrepreneurs* have received credibility as nursing roles. Nurses have developed programs of research that build and test theories; delineate significant practice interventions; and specify managerial and administrative strategies. The funding for this research comes from public and private sources. The establishment of the National Institute of Nursing Research in 1993 marks the significance that nursing research has to health care delivery.

Nurse entrepreneurs have developed businesses that provide health and nursing services to clients. The businesses are diverse and may focus on providing staffing to larger health care agencies to the provision of professional services such as primary care, counseling, and support groups. Nurses also have roles and responsibilities associated with organized nursing. The organizations have goals and responsibilities that span local, state, and national levels. Examples include the Pennsylvania Nurses Association, the American Nurses Association, and the National League for Nursing. In these organizations nurses are executive administrators, advisors, educators, and researchers.

EDUCATIONAL TRENDS

It has been speculated that the need will increase for nurses at all levels—baccalaureate, masters, and doctoral. National trends describing enrollment in basic RN programs show an upward trend that began in 1988 (NLN, 1991). Total enrollments are documented at approximately 200,000 students. This total remains shy of the 225,000 enrollees of 1980. However, the number of baccalaureate enrollees have increased over the ten year period while the number of diploma and associated degree enrollees declined. Despite this trend, there is concern that by 2005 ". . . the numbers of individuals interested in nursing, the number of nursing educational programs, and the opportunities for graduate and special training will not be adequate to meet demand" (O'Neil, 1993).

The specific manner in which this trend will influence the number of nurses in Pennsylvania is unclear. Pennsylvania's trend for enrollment in basic RN programs was similar to that of the nation's. In 1980, there were 15,898 enrollees. Following a period of decreased enrollment, in 1988, there was an upward trend with 14,159 enrollees in 1989. For years, it has been apparent that Pennsylvania schools of nursing graduate an adequate *number* of nurses to meet the needs of Pennsylvanians, however, many of these graduates choose to practice in neighboring states. Because of this trend, Pennsylvania has been dubbed a "feeder" state.

Presently, there are a number of nursing education initiatives throughout the state. Some of them have met with controversy. Pennsylvania has more diploma programs than any other state (NLN, 1991). Preparing nurses for the practice of professional nursing through hospital-based programs is viewed to be out-of-step with current professional and educational trends. In an effort to move these nursing education programs to a baccalaureate level, the Hospital Association of Pennsylvania (HAP) proposes to establish an educational institution that has HAP as the sole member. This institution would then be the umbrella under which diploma programs could continue to exist and offer their hospital based nursing programs. Among nursing educators, the HAP approach to nursing education has received no reported support, outside of the diploma educators' group in Pennsylvania. A more favorable strategy has been the development of articulation agreements that enable licensed registered nurses from diploma and associate degree programs to move into RN completion programs for the purpose of obtaining a baccalaureate degree in nursing. This trend has received wide support within the nursing community, with several nursing programs demonstrating years of success with RN-BSN programs (e.g. La Salle University, School of Nursing in Philadelphia, PA).

In addition, there are several nurse practitioner programs in the state, but they are located on the far eastern and western urban centers of the state. It is timely then, that in October of 1993, the Pennsylvania Department of Health placed a call for applications for mid-level primary health care practitioner demonstration grants. This funding source was "designed to demonstrate that institutions of higher education working with a wide variety of organizations can make significant, innovative, and replicable changes in mid-level primary care education and training which will measurably increase the supply and distribution of primary care practitioners serving in underserved areas" of Pennsylvania (Grant Application, Commonwealth of Pennsylvania, Department of Health, October 1993). Also, calls and proposal submissions to the Pennsylvania State Board of Nursing and discussions at professional meetings across the state indicate that several new nurse practitioner programs are in various stages of development.

PRACTICE TRENDS

The practice settings offer different and more colorful illustations of the health care revolution. There is no easy way to describe the kaleidoscope of factors that are shaping the practice area. The clinical realities are astounding. Clearly, however, nurses are required to care for sicker patients with less resources and often for less rewards.

Nurses receive mixed messages. Multiple reports and trends analyses show that there is an urgent need for nurses, but yet, new graduates can not always get positions. Staff nurses are over worked; but yet, hospitals focus on downsizing professional staff and hiring lesser prepared personnel for the delivery of highly specialized care.

Patients are coming into the hospital sicker due to lack of funding for preventative health care. This situation is confounded by patients being discharged from the hospital before resolution of their health problems. Consequently, skilled nursing facilities are becoming the hospitals of yester years. Homes are the place where sub-acute, post-surgical, restorative, and rehabilitative care is provided.

Hospitals are closing at a time when care needs are increasing. The focus of health care today does not appear to be on quality care, but instead—cost savings and time efficiency disguised in the language of "best buy health care". Is this the trend we want to be carried into the twenty-first century?

Where, then, are Caring, Holism, and Continuity of Services that are Associated with the Essence of Nursing?

Nurses who value these qualities are expressing their discontentment with the current health care system. There is concern that patients will not get the requisite care needed while hospitalized. There is fear that they, the licensed nurses, will be held accountable for care that was given by unlicensed personnel who were working with the same group of patients. There is frustration with the need to provide more teaching and supportive care in situations where there is not time or resources.

The most treasured resource for the provision of health care is manpower resource. It is known that nurses comprise the largest group of health care providers. The composition of nursing is ever changing. The number of licensed registered nurses has been estimated at anywhere from over 1.7 million (O'Neil, 1993) to over 2.2 million (ANA, 1993). The national statistics on number of advanced practice nurses including: nurse practitioners, clinical nurse specialist, and nurse widwives. Nurses who are educationally prepared to be advanced practicing nurses do not always practice in these specialized roles. Finally, there is often a disparity in the numbers of certified registered nurse practitioners, possibly because of the lack of uniformity in counting from state to state (Safriet, 1990). It is known, however, that the active licenses in Pennsylvania include: 1,719 certified registered nurse practitioners; 184,302 licensed registered nurses; and 55,499 licensed practical nurses. These nurses are concentrated in the urban areas of Pennsylvania with noted shortages in the rural counties (Commonwealth of Pennsylvania, Bureau of Professional and Occupational Affairs, October, 1993).

A number of strategies have been used to resolve the myriad of nursing concerns in practice settings. Many of these originate from health care and nursing administrators and nursing management. For example, *shared governance* is stated to be a way of enabling nurses to control their practice settings. With this model of management nurses have circumscribed control of nursing practice on their units. This control includes things such as decision making about continuing educations, protocols for delivery of care, interviewing nurses for potential employment, maintaining appropriate coverage for staffing, and problem resolution on unit related issues. Shared governance has been seen by some as a way to promote professionalism. Others see the practice of shared governance as putting more responsibility for nursing management on to the staff nurse, at a time when they are over worked with patient care. In addition, because of cost control some nurse executives and managers have limited overtime and removed financial work incentives (e.g. shift differential, Baylor plan of 36 hours on weekends for 40 hours of pay, etc.). These examples illustrate some of the perplexing situations of practice and managment which currently exist in hospitals. As a consequence, some staff nurses express feelings of frustration with the clinical demands, and of being devalued by the hospital and its administators. Nevertheless, nursing administrators continue to deliberate and make decisions that are in keeping with their administrative charge to keep their health care agencies solvent. But what happens to providing safe, quality services? Is the priority safe, quality care or cost savings? As the current health care revolution goes on, all seek win-win solutions, but they continue to elude detection.

For the past twenty years, collective bargaining has been effectively used to improve the practice of nursing. Even though these strides continue to be a positive force for the practice of nursing, there has always been debate about the appropriateness of unions in a profession. Now the issue is revisited with questions raised about the role and emphasis which collective bargaining should have in the 21st century. Some say "more" and others say "less". In some situations, the phrase "economic and general welfare of nurses" has been reduced to mean union. This indeed was not the intent when the language was initiated several years ago. Today the primary activities of collective bargaining units address salary and work conditions of staff nurses. This positions nursing managers and administrators in opposition to staff nurses. This positioning is divisive to the nursing profession.

The collective bargaining units that represent most nurses are housed within the state nursing associations (e.g. Pennsylvania Nurses Association) of the American Nurses' Association. Thus, discord associated with the union arm of the associations spills out into all areas of the state and national organizations. State nursing associations that have recently experienced challenges pertaining to collective bargaining include California, New Jersey, Maryland, Washington, and Pennsylvania. It is impossible and inappropriate to belabor all of the perspectives pertaining to collective bargaining. Suffice it to say that through unionization quality care has been enhanced, advocacy for workplace environments has received attention, and economic and general welfare of nurses have been addressed. But, in some way, there has also been an impediment to unity of professional nursing throughout the states. Division is not needed for the twenty-first century; unity is!

Analysis of current state practice acts and regulations, and the development of model language for national use are additional ways to address nursing practice. In the twenty-first century, the advanced nurse practitioners will be more frequently available as primary care providers. Nursing has continually voiced the merits of nurse practitioners as health care providers. (Safriet, 1992). Data addressing the cost savings and quality care of nurse practitioners have been available for decades. In collaboration with other nursing organizations, the National Council of State Boards of Nursing has developed model language for regulatory boards regarding the licensing of advanced practice nurses to provide primary care. In Pennsylvania, nurse practitioners receive certification from the Board of Nursing. However, practice is jointly regulated by Nursing and Medical Boards. Prescriptive privileges for certified registered nurse practioners (CRNPs) is the most pressing issue of today. Clear regulations addressing prescriptive privileges are *essential* for CRNPs to make a more significant contribution as primary care providers in Pennsylvania.

The Pennsylvania State Board of Nursing has acted on several topics of revelance to the practice of nursing in the twenty-first century. The three topics to be collectively addressed here are: (1) expanding the scope of practice of *licensed practical nurses* to enable the administration of intravenous medications; (2) putting forth the legal opinion that when appropriate protocols have been established, staff nurses can take written orders for care from *physician assistants, certified registered nurse practitioners,* and *certified nurse midwives*; and (3) initiating language for regulations that will enable nurses to delegate nursing activity to *unlicensed personnel* who have appropriate training and skill to implement the activity assigned. Each of these actions by the Board was taken with the intention of providing reasonable and safe boundaries for the delivery of safe care in multiple home and health care settings in Pennsylvania. Currently, it was thought that the changes would empower nurses to take charge of their practice. The changes addressed areas of practice that would be *allowed* by regulations; not areas of practice that *must occur*. In other words, LPNs do not have to give intravenous medications, but with proper education they can do so. Licensed nurses do not have to take orders from PAs, CRNPs, or CNMs but with appropriate protocols, they can do so. The caveat: in private circles nurses are stating that the "*empowering*" intent of the Board has or will become administrative "*mandates*". If this does evolve, then the intentions of the Board will be misused.

Today, there are opportunities for nurses to practice in homes, nursing centers, school based clinics, coporations/businesses, colleges, skilled nursing facilities, nursing homes, and community centers, *and* hospitals—not *just* hospitals. Preparing nurses for changes in care delivery settings requires re-socialization of graduates, changes in curricular approaches to education of nurses, and changes in the public image of nursing.

Hospitalized patients have specialized needs. The advanced nurse and nurses prepared in critical care will be needed to provide this specialized care. Why then are hospitals downsizing by removing professional staff, particularly the clinical nurse specialists? It seems that a *mix of professional nurses* is needed to provide appropriate and safe care in the hospital. This staff mix could include critical care nurse specialists with skills and knowledge to provide direct care; clinical nurse specialists to serve as case manager for patients while hospitalized; and nurse practitioners to provide primary care and management of health problems *before* hospitalization and *after* discharge from the hospital. The specialized knowledge held by professional nurses seems to be the best match for the broad based clinical and family needs of hospitalized patients. *In preparation for the twenty-first century, the use of unlicensed assistive personnel as the most frequent provider of direct care in hospitals and homes needs to be curtailed.* As stated by the President of the American Nurses Association, Virginia Betts, JD, RN "registered nurses are the best buy for quality safe care" (Presentation, Pennsylvania Nurses' Associaiton Convention, Pittsburgh, PA November 3, 1993).

CHALLENGES

With rampant changes in the health care arena, the *need* for nurses today is unquestioned. The multiple settings for delivery of nursing care will continue to challenge nurses to examine how they can best serve clients in those settings. It will be different. The hospital will not be the place to give detailed teaching—the home, nursing centers, and extended care facility will be. Holistic care can be provided if nurses work collaboratively with other health care professionals. For example, clinics housed within public schools, e.g. school based clinics, may become sites for case finding and health promotion. Knowlege about family nursing and cultural diversity will be essential if patient adherence to health care suggestions is to be realized. Yes, nurses can continue to care, to nurture, to help, to do case finding, to offer restorative care. Nurses will continue to be nurses. But there are challenges.

These challenges are not new; they are however different. Different because the times are different, the environment is different, the resources are different, and the needs are different. Most nurses today are individually and collectively pushing in the following directions:

(1) *Re-evaluating the process for preparing nurses for practice*—Educational programs are addressing curriculum revisions for care of clients in community settings and care of underserved populations; use of preceptors from clinical areas as faculty; faculty practice groups that serve as a way of educating students; preparing advanced practicing nurses; and core curriculum to focus on critical thinking and clinical decision making.

(2) *Examination of clinical skills required for delivery of care to clients/patients in hospitals and homes*—Proficiency of practicing nurse is continually under scrutiny. Nursing administrators and educators are collaborating about ways to best prepare nurses for clinical practice. Nursing extern and intern programs are seen as practical ways to enhance clinical proficiency. Continuing educational programs are encouraged for all licensed nurses.

(3) *Socialization of nurses as leaders and change agents*—the centrality of nursing leadership to issues associated with the 21st century is clear. Nurses are speaking out, the visibility of nursing leaders is explicit, the role of nurses as primary care providers is being addressed. However, empowerment remains underplayed. Nurses must authentically believe that they (we) are agents of change. Individual and collective empowerment is foundational to effective and meaningful change.

(4) *Political action associated with health policy initiative and third-party reimbursements*—Nurses have been positioning themselves as forces to be heard. The American Nurses Association often speaks for nursing. However, in the late 1980s a coalition of nursing organizations evolved to jointly oppose the creation of a health care worker then labelled "registered care technician (RCT)". Nursing was successful as a coalition and halted the RCT activity. The coalition of nursing organizations continues to speak with unity on a number of political issues. Continued action of this sort is essential for the twenty-first century. Leaders with health care policy expertise will be necessary to further position nursing for the twenty-first century. Presently leaders such as Virginia Trotter Betts, JD, RN (President of the American Nurses Association) and Claire Fagin, PhD, FAAN (Past President of the National League for Nursing and Interim President of the University of Pennsylvania) are forging the way.

(5) *Collaborative models of care*—As the health care delivery system changes the need for interdisciplinary collaborative models becomes more evident. Joint professional approaches are required to provide individual, families, and communities with health care services that address their unique needs. Through collaboration there can be better utilization of services, a holistic approach to care needs, and improved follow-through. Ultimately, the outcomes could be improved and health care status of citizens elevated.

To act on the challenges of today and tomorrow the nursing discipline needs the collective wisdom that represents knowledge of the paths tread; vision about the roads that are ahead with definitive options that can be exercised to traverse the roads; and patience, but vigilent participation in the revolution of today. With revolutions comes change! Nurses need to influence the direction of this change. Through leadership, thoughtful deliberations, coalitions, and innovative approaches this can be done.

ACKNOWLEGEMENTS

Acknowlegements to Jessie Rohner, Dr. P.H., RN, Executive Administrator, Pennsylvania Nurses' Asociation; and Marguerite Ambrose, RN, MSN and Helene Nawrocki, RN, MSN (Faculty of La Salle University, School of Nursing) for their candid input and critique.

REFERENCES

American Nurses Association. 1980. *A social policy statement.* Kansas City, MO (Now Washington, DC).

American Nurses Association. 1993. News release 10/6/93. 600 Maryland Avenue, SW. Suite 100 West, Washington, DC 20024-2571.

Commonwealth of Pennsylvania. 1985. *The professional nursing law* (Act of 1951, P.L. 317, No. 69). Harrisburg, PA: Bureau of Professional and Occupational Affairs, Department of State.

Leininger, M. 1991. *Cultural care diversity and universality: A theory of nursing.* New York: National League for Nursing Press.

National League for Nursing (NLN). 1991. *Nursing data review 1991.* Division of Research, New York: National League for Nursing Press.

O'Neil, E.H. 1993. *Health professions education for the future: Schools in service to the nation.* San Francisco, CA: Pew Health Professions Commission.

Safriet, B. 1992. Health care dollars and regulatory sense: The role of advanced practice nursing. *Yale Journal on Regulation. 9*(2), New Haven, CT: Yale Law School.

Medicine and Health Care Into the Twenty-First Century. Edited by S.K. Majumdar, L.M. Rosenfeld, D.B. Nash and A.M. Audet.

Chapter Twenty-Four

SEARCHING FOR THE LOST KEY UNDER THE LIGHT OF BIOMEDICINE: A Triangular Biopsychosocial Paradigm May Cast Additional Light on Medical Education, Research and Patient Care

MOHAMMADREZA HOJAT, Ph.D., STEVEN SAMUEL, Ph.D. and TROY L. THOMPSON II, M.D.

Center for Research in Medical Education and Health Care
Department of Psychiatry and Human Behavior
Jefferson Medical College
1025 Walnut Street
Philadelphia, PA 19107-5083

INTRODUCTION

Health, according to the World Health Organization Constitution, is defined in relation to physical, psychological and social dimensions, and the *WHO Constitution* defines "health" as "a state of complete physical, mental and social well-being and not merely the absence of disease or infirmity" (WHO, 1948). This definition is at odds with the currently often dominant "biomedical" paradigm in which "disease" is reduced to a unidimensional concept defined only in terms of somatic parameters, and in which the psychological and social aspects of health and disease may be overlooked. Instead, a balance should be maintained in the emphasis on the three determinants (somatic, psychological, and social) of health and disease.

Total adherence to a confined biomedical model is not adequate to balance the scientific task, social responsibility, and public accountability of medicine (Engle, 1977). Inappropriate utilization of this model has contributed to the current crisis in medicine.

The restricted view of health and disease through only the window of the biomedical paradigm does not encompass other important aspects of the etiology and treatment of many diseases, as well as illness prevention and maintenance of health measures (Genest and Genest, 1987). Although the often prevailing biomedical view of health and disease has shed bright and promising light on the pathophysiological and preventive aspects of many illnesses, the constraints of the model have sometimes obscured the clinical vision of its disciples. There are many illness conditions that do not lend themselves to formulations derived from just a biomedical paradigm (Kimball, 1981).

SEARCHING FOR THE LOST KEY UNDER THE LIGHT

As a result of the prevalent attachment to the biomedical paradigm, medical issues are often primarily addressed under the light of laboratory data. Recent findings strongly suggest that the search for the key to some medical issues should be carried out in yet unlighted spots outside laboratory walls. This situation is like the story of a man who came home in the darkness of night, dropped his key at his doorstep, and began to search for it across the street under the only light pole in that area. When asked why he was looking there, he replied "the light is much better here". It may seem most reasonable to search for the key to solve most medical problems primarily through examining associated laboratory data, where admittedly the light has been brightly shed on many previously dark spots of medicine. However, ongoing changes in lifestyle, in social and cultural values, in environment and ecology, and the emergence of some new diseases (e.g., AIDS) demand our "lights" be focused on some typically "dimmer spots", where important keys to some increasingly complex medical issues may be hidden.

THE BIOMEDICAL PARADIGM

The concept that each disease is caused by a specific pathogenic agent probably existed to some degree in antiquity, as is evident by the ancient policy of isolating leprosy patients in tightly guarded sanitariums. However, the scientific basis of the "germ theory" model was not established until the second half of the 19th Century when Louis Pasteur substantiated that paradigm by postulating the idea of specific interactions between microorganisms and host immunity (Susser, 1973). Pasteur's postulations, supported by Robert Koch's discovery of the role of the tubercle bacillus in the etiology of tuberculosis, shed new light on many medical mysteries of that period. The crux of the new idea, the exclusive causal relation between a specific germ (a microorganism) and a specific disease, helped to precipitate a major scientific paradigm shift, which was a prelude to the biomedical model (White, 1991). The primary emphasis on laboratory data for diagnosis in this model suggested to many that disease etiology was synonymous with bacteriology and, as a result, many other potentially fruitful areas for research were placed in limbo (White, 1991). New technological and scientific developments and advancements provided further support for the paradigm, which came to be viewed by some as the panacea to solve all human health problems and suffering. The long-term consequences of over-emphasis on the biomedical model began to limit the breadth of medicine's vision.

An essential factor that was overlooked by those focusing solely on the biomedical model was that not all diseases, then or now, involve germs or pathogenic agents. A germ could be a necessary, but not a sufficient condition in the genesis of some illnesses. In fact, much human illness cannot be conceptualized or treated by a single factor-single disease approach (Kimball, 1981). Illness often depends on a multiplicity of factors involving somatic and psychological processes of individuals in relation to their environment. Many of the "human factors" have not been brought "into the light" because they lie outside of the boundaries of the purely biomedical scientific paradigm in which "proximal" causes of illness are the focus of attention and "distant" causes are overlooked.

THE IRONY OF THE BIOMEDICAL PARADIGM

It seems ironic that when it comes to health maintenance and patient care, the biomedical paradigm is often largely incognizant of psychosocial factors, yet in the design and conduct of medical research, the role of the psychosocial factors has received considerable acknowledgment. For example, in clinical trials, control for a psychophysiological response, the "innocuous" response known as the *placebo effect*, is of prime concern. This indicates an acceptance of the notion that psychosocial variables may contribute significantly to many physiological responses. The well-established fact that a pharmacological inactive ingredient can produce physiological effects similar to that of an active pharmacological agent supports the proposition that not only in research settings, but in educational and clinical settings, the phenomenon of health and illness may be most productively viewed beyond the boundaries imposed by the biomedical paradigm alone.

Related to the well-known placebo effects in research are measurable physiological effects produced by psychosocial elements in clinical settings. For example, neurochemical reactions to *transcendental meditation*, or its western relative, the *relaxation response*, have long been observed in clinical settings, but have often not been considered important by medical researchers, probably due in part to their apparent discordance with a "pure" biomedical paradigm. The effects of psychosocial processes on somatic healing also often seem so distant from mainstream medical thought that they have been labeled "factor x," an unknown factor, in alternative therapeutic modalities (White, 1991).

CONDITIONS INCONGRUENT WITH THE BIOMEDICAL PARADIGM

While the biomedical model seems to explain etiology, treatment, and prevention of many medical conditions, it is less suitable or cogent in explaining many others. For example, the influences of social support systems, including human bonding, on the maintenance of general health (Blanc, et al., 1980; Irwin, et al., 1986; Pashko, Deturck & Vogel, 1980) and on the immune system in particular have been well documented (Antonovsky, 1979; Bartrop, et al., 1977; Berkman & Syme, 1979; Riley, 1981,; Schliefer, et al., 1983). Epidemiological studies have shown a significant increase in morbidity and mortality, including the phenomenon of sudden death, following a disruption of human bonding by separation or bereavement (Jacobs & Ostfeld, 1977; Parkes, 1972; Kaprio, Koskenvuo & Rita, 1987). A solely biomedical model is not optimal for explaining these and several other conditions that will be discussed later.

On the one hand, VanEgeren and Gellman (1992) indicated that cardiovascular disease is partially caused by hyperfunctioning of the cardiovascular system in response to everyday events and elevated blood pressure and essential hypertension as a function of individual behavior and personality variables in response to routine interactions have been extensively studied (Johnson, Gentry, & Julius, 1992). Personality factors, such as competitiveness, sense of urgency, accelerated pace of activities, aggressiveness—and particularly hostility and cynicsm—which are defined as the constellation of the Type A behavior pattern, have been identified as risk factors associated with cardiovascular reactivity and coronary artery disease (Friedman & Rosenmann, 1959; Rosenmann, 1992). In a meta-analytic study, Harbin (1989) indicated that during cognitive challenges, individuals with Type A behavioral pattern often showed greater systolic blood presure reactivity and greater increase in heart rate than others. Moreover, anxiety, hostility, and difficulty in managing personal stress have been implicted in the pathogenesis of hypertention (Rosenmann, 1992).

On the other hand, the health promoting effects of a supportive interpersonal network in achieving and maintaining general health have also been well-established (Berkman & Syme, 1979; Lynch, 1977; Parkes & Stevenson-Hinde, 1982; Mechanic, 1974; Cobb, 1976; Heller, 1979; House, 1981). But, possible health promoting functions of such psychosocial variables have received relatively little attention in medical research *per se*. For example, the positive effects of the following factors in the prevention of illness and maintenance of health have been demonstrated, mostly by research in behavioral sciences disciplines: social support systems (Berkman & Syme, 1979; Jones & Moore, 1989; Sarason, Sarason & Sherin, 1986), cohesive and functional families (Berkson, 1962), peer relations (Hojat, 1982; Sullivan, 1953), coping mechanisms (Selye, 1976; Lazarus & Folkman, 1984; Garber & Seligman, 1980), personality traits of hardiness and resiliency (Kobasa, 1979; Kobasa, Maddi & Kahn, 1982; Kobasa & Puccetti, 1983), other adaptive personality types and behavioral styles (Johnson, Gentry & Julius, 1992; Friedman & Rosenmann, 1959; Rosenmann, 1990, 1992), life activities and perceptions of health (Jenkins, Rosenmann & Zyanski, 1972), and mother-infant bonding or attachment and feeding styles as related to the general health of infants and mothers (Klaus, et al., 1972; Klaus & Kennell, 1982; Reite & Field, 1985; Oseid, 1979). The relevance of the research findings in these areas to individual and public health strongly suggest that they should be included more vigorously as subjects of focused attention within medical education, practice, and research.

ILLNESS AS A FUNCTION OF DISRUPTED AFFECTIONAL TIES

The onset of a number of medical illnesses following psychosocial disturbances has also been well documented. A growing body of evidence in psychosomatic medicine suggests a frequent causal link between psychosocial factors and the onset or exacerbations of some forms of asthma, autoimmune conditions, cancer, congestive heart failure, diabetes mellitus, infectious hepatitis, leukemia, lupus erythematosis, peptic ulcer, hyperthyroidism, and rheumatoid arthritis (Hojat & Vogel, 1989; Jacobs & Charles, 1980; Henoch, Batson & Baum, 1978; Lynch, 1977; Morillo & Gardner, 1979; Reite & Field, 1985; Reite & Short, 1983).

A 1977 study by Bartrop and colleagues was probably one of the first in humans to show that an experience of separation and loss could lead to a defect in immune system functioning. Henoch, Batson, and Baum (1978) reported that social events, such as divorce, separation from parents, and adoption, often played important roles in relation to the onset and course of juvenile rheumatoid arthritis. Jacobs and Charles (1980) found that certain life events, such as maternal separation, death of a close family member, and changes in residence and school, occurred with greater frequency just prior to the onset of cancer in children who developed the condition than with other children. Bereavement has been associated with depressed immune functioning and the onset and progression of cancer in both sexes (Bartrop, Lazarus & Luckhurst, 1977; Irwin, Daniels & Weiner, 1987; Kaprio, Kaskenvuo & Rita, 1987; Schliefer, et al., 1983). Susceptibility to some infectious diseases, presumably due to immune system inhibition, has also been associated with psychosocial factors (Jemmott & Locke, 1984). Causal connections between emotional events and impairment of the immune system have also been described by other researchers (e.g., Rogers, Dubey, & Reich, 1979; Kiecolt-Glaser, et al., 1984a, 1984b; Reite, Harbeck & Hoffman, 1981; Vogel, 1985; Chrousos & Gold, 1992).

Lynch (1977) proposed that loneliness can "break the human heart," and living alone has been found to be related to increased recurrence of major cardiac events (Case, et al., 1992). The individual's perception of loneliness experiences can be even more detrimental to the functioning of the human heart than actual physical isolation (Hojat, 1992). Loneliness may function as a type of "social immunodeficiency virus" that is detrimental to the young and old of both sexes (Hojat, 1989; Hojat, 1982; Hojat & Vogel, 1989).

ILLNESS IN RESPONSE TO STRESSFUL EVENTS

Both heart disease and cancer, the two major causes of death in this country, have been linked to environmental stressors of modern life (Fox, Temoskok & Dreher, 1987; Rahe, Meyer, Smith, Kjaer & Holmes, 1964; Taylor, 1978). Stressful life events, including occupational stress, unsatisfactory interpersonal relations in the occupational environment, lack of job security, and breakdown of the family and family values, have at times been linked to the development of both cancer and heart disease (Berkson, 1962; Levenson & Bemis, 1991).

Furthermore, a phenomenon known as mass psychogenic illness (Colligan, Pennebaker & Murphy, 1982) suggests that psychosocial stressors may not only influence an individual's health but may also contribute to medical symptoms in a group of individuals who work or live in the same environment (Alexander & Fedoruk, 1986; Colligan & Murphy, 1979; Small & Borus, 1983). This kind of illness may be "contagious" among those in the group, yet no biomedical reason has been found to explain the outbreak of such an illness (Colligan, Pennebaker & Murphy, 1982; Maguire, 1978; Mayou, 1975). However, chronic stressful working or living conditions, mediated by inadequate personal coping skills, have been found to contribute to the outbreak of such illness (Colligan, et al., 1982).

ILLNESS AS A FUNCTION OF ENVIRONMENTAL FACTORS

Environmental and social dimensions have been noted recently in the etiology of environmental hypersensitivity reactions, which have been increasing substantially in prevalence. Although the biomedical model is often capable of explaining some cause-effect relations between physical environment (e.g., pollution) and these conditions, there are other symptoms that cannot yet be thoroughly explained. Environmental hypersensitivity has become known as the "20th Century disease" (Stewart & Raskin, 1985) and appears to be a mass allergic reaction that is triggered in some individuals by exposure to air, water, foods, synthetics and other common environmental substances (Stewart, 1990). However, because these illnesses do not appear to fit the biomedical paradigm, leading to the lack of usual scientific evidence for their causes, some reseachers have used what may be the psychological defense mechanism of denial of what is not yet understood, and raised questions about the very existence of such conditions (Stewart, 1987; Terr, 1986; Lum, 1982).

A CASE IN POINT: Somatization Disorder

It is evident that many conditions cannot be explained by a biomedical paradigm and their effects on individuals as well as public health, utilization of health care resources, and the resultant financial burden on society could be decreased to a large extent by expanding the scientific paradigm in medicine. As an example, one such illness condition, somatization disorder, will be discussed to portray the negative effects of constraining the scientific medical paradigm by placing psychosocial factors outside medicine's typical focus of attention. This disorder includes a group of somatic symptoms that suggest a physical abnormality, but for which no organic etiology can be demonstrated (Smith, 1991; Rasmussen & Avant, 1989), and it often develops in the presence of psychogenic distress. It was known in the 1800's as hysteria and neurasthenia, and was later also called Briquet's Syndrome after the French physician who identified patients who had multiple physical symptoms but no demonstrable medical disease.

This condition will be discussed for several reasons. A considerable number of patients with somatization disorder frequently seek medical treatment from primary care and subspecialist physicians and consume a considerable amount of health care resources, often with poor outcomes. And, due to the common inaccurate belief that somatic symptoms must have some underlying organic etiology, medical educators as well as clinicians often do not adequately understand and recognize this disorder, therefore, many cases are misdiagnosed. Consequently, health care professionals as well as laboratory resoures are often misdirected, with no positive outcome. Also, somatization disorder does not lend itself to explanation by the biomedical model of disease. Frith and Knowlden (1992) described somatization as an "undifferentiated illness" and reported that 50% to 70% of medical encounters with patients with this condition had been precipitated by psychosocial rather than biomedical problems. Consequently, physicians who are overly devoted to the biomedical paradigm are less likely to be vigilant for this condition in their evaluations and more likely to mismanage patients with this illness (Smith, 1991).

According to the NIMH Epidemiologic Catchment Area (ECA) studies, somatization disorder in the community is estimated to have a prevalence of from one person in a thousand to 20 in 100 and to be more common in women (Swartz, Landerman, George, Blazer & Ecobar, 1990; Swartz, Hughes, Blazer & George, 1987; Escobar et al., 1989; Escobar & Canino, 1989). The prevalence among patients of primary care physicians is high. Smith (1991) reports that as many as 6% of patients in primary care practices have somatization disorder and that they are almost uniformly unrecognized, undiagnosed, and consequently mismanaged. Kirmayer & Robbins (1991) estimated that 26% of patients in family medicine clinics met the criteria for some form of somatization disorder. Bridges and Goldberg (1985) found that 56% of primary care patients with psychiatric problems had somatized presentations. These patients are also over represented in subspecialty practices (Smith, 1991). According to Martin, Roberts, and Clayton(1980), more than a quarter of women receiving noncancer-related hysterectomies had somatization disorder.

It should be noted that somatization is different from malingering and psychosomatic illnesses. Malingering involves faked physical symptoms that are *intentionally* produced for some form of personal benefit or gain. Psychosomatic disorders, on the other hand, are precipitated by psychosocial stressors and, unlike somatization, an associated physical abnormality (such as peptic ulcer) can be identified (DSM-IIIR, 1987).

Patients with somatization disorders typically have a multitude of somatic complaints, long and complex medical histories, have seen an inordinate number of physicians, and change their physicians frequently due to frustration and lack of satisfactory results. A phenomenon known as "doctor shopping" (Ketterer & Buckholtz, 1989) or "doctor hopping (Smith, 1991), a behavior which involves repeatedly switching from one physician to another, is a common feature of patients with somatoform disorders. These types of patients, therefore, have extraordinary health care utilization (Smith, 1991), including a high number of office visits and unnecessary surgical procedures. Obviously, these costs could be reduced if the patients were correctly diagnosed and appropriately managed. However, due to the underestimation by many physicians of the importance and frequency of psychological and social factors in producing these types of symptoms, physicians are often not adept at identifying and managing patients with somatization disorders (Smith, 1991; Stewart, 1990). Physicians may also not know how, and may be uncomfortable, in the management of patients with somatization disorders, so they are likely to be reluctant to identify these conditions. A physician's vigilance and empathic consultation and follow-up with patients with these types of somatic complaints have been found to more effective in improving patients' health status than any form of biomedical treatment (Thomas, 1987).

A TRIANGULAR MODEL: The Biopsychosocial Paradigm Revisited

Some physicians have felt, or at least behaved as though, medicine should only be the science of the structure and function of the body organs (Engle, 1977). As a result, defective organs of patients rather than the patients themselves have become the primary focus of attention of some medical caregivers. The misplaced emphasis of the biomedical paradigm as a comprehensive model for clinical care is on the somatic aspects of disease rather than the human elements of illness. Disease by itself is an empty term until a patient suffers from it. Sir William Osler said that it is as important to know what kind of patient has a disease, as it is to know what kind of disease a patient has (cited in White, 1991). A patient, and for that matter any human is greater than the sum of healthy and unhealthy cells or the sum of ill- or well-functioning organs. From a general systems theory viewpoint (Churchman, 1979), a patient or a healthy human is an active element in a macrosystem in which there are constant interactions with other factors in the system, including somatic strengths and vulnerabilities. From this perspective, psychosocial factors, such as personality, perceptions, sensations, interests, emotions, memory, values, attitudes, beliefs, cultural stereotypes, relationships and social supports, independently and interactively may contribute, in many different ways, to the health and illnesses of each member of the system.

Engle (1977) stated, "medicine's crisis derives from logical inference that since disease is defined in terms of somatic parameters, physicians need not be concerned with psychosocial issues which lie outside medicine's responsibility and authority." That is, this crisis in medicine stems not only from its over-adherence to a biomedical paradigm, but also from its divorce, or at least frequent separations, from the psychosocial companions of health and illnesses. Medicine will optimally serve the public when patients rather than diseases are the primary focus of its activities.

Kimball (1981) has noted that many illnesses have psychosocial aspects that may influence their cause, precipitation, manifestation, course, and outcome. The disciplines of medicine, psychology, and sociology have sometimes been unfriendly and even hostile to one another. This is unfortunate because their relative separation greatly diminishes their combined potential (White, 1991). Therefore, it seems desirable to build on and expand the biomedical model by incorporating more psychological and social considerations into it and encouraging more collaboration between various health care related disciplines. Such collaboration might yield productive research on many aspects of patient care (Engel, 1977; Taylor, 1978) and promote improved interactions between physicians and patients (Kimball, 1981). If the various disciplines that could shed light on understanding health and illness behaviors do not actively communicate, the story about a group of blind individuals who each tried to describe an elephant by touching a different part of its body could continue to be recreated in health care. Their individual understanding of what an elephant looks like was, of course, incomplete due to their inability to experience the whole, that is, how the various parts fit together to form an elephant. But a somewhat different version of this story by Mowlavi, a classical Persian poet, may also reflect some of the present situation in medicine. In this story, a group of keen-sighted individuals encountered a strange animal in the darkness. Their argument around recognizing the animal proved to be null when someone arrived with a light (cited in Gharajedaghi, 1981). A parallel of the later version of the story to the current situation in medicine is that keen-sighted medical educators, researchers, and clinicians should more actively adopt the biopsychosocial paradigm, where it could cast light in areas where such light is needed to improve investigator's vision to more comprehensively view the problems under investigation. With a more "englightened" view, health care professionals can gain a better understanding of health and disease in an integrated or "holistic" manner, to use the term introduced more than 60 years ago by Jan Smuts (cited in White, 1991).

In the biospychosocial paradigm, the biomedical aspects of health and illness have an important and essential place as a supporting pillar. However, the more encompassing biopsychosocial model offers the means whereby medicine can coalesce its maturity as a human science. The heart of the biopsychosocial model involves a physician who has been educated to view health and disease from a broad perspective, to establish and maintain dialogue with patients, and to apply intuition and introspection in addition to medical knowledge and other clinical skills. Such an approach is essential for optimal medical education and practice. Adoption of the biopsychosocial paradigm involves thoughtfulness about the overall illness process and sensitivity to the ongoing interactions between patients, their families, and support systems, including health care professionals and the health care system.

CONCLUSIONS

Medicine might further benefit patients by assuring that its scope integrates the psychological, social, and biological determinants of health and illness in a triangular model. The foundation of this approach should be laid in the medical school education. Awareness of the importance of psychological and social factors in matters of health and illness contributes to developing a more comprehensive vision of the complex issues of health and illness, including understanding patient's behavioral motivations.

Physicians implicitly play three roles in patient care as clinician, patient educator, and resource manager (Gonnella, Hojat, Erdmann & Veloski, 1993b). More effective doctor-patient communication and better adherence to therapeutic interventions usually results when physicians effectively perform their roles as patient educators and resource managers. Performance in these roles can be enhanced by medical school and resident education on relevant psychosocial and social-cultural knowledge and understanding (Gonnella, Hojat, Erdmann & Veloski, 1993a, 1993b). Such knowledge gained in medical school has been found to positively influence clinical practice after formal education ends (Hojat, Gonnella, Veloski & Erdmann, 1993; Gonnella & Hojat, 1983). Therefore, a triangular, biopsychosocial paradigm, in addition to broadening medicine's scientific vision, may also contribute to better doctor-patient relationships and enhanced patient care.

Many efforts to educate medical students and residents in the theory and practice of the biopsychosocial approach have been reported (Engle et al., 1957, Engel, 1967). These include dissection of medical interviews via the clinical case method (Kimball, 1975; Kimball, 1981; Kimball, 1983), videotaped patient interviews (Roeske, 1979; Silverman, et al., 1983), interviews of family members (Wehlage, 1987), teaching the model at medical grand rounds (Frankel and Rosenblum, 1983) and to medical residents in outpatient clinics (Rosenblum and Frankel, 1984), utilizing the Patient Evaluation Grid to obtain a medical history (Leigh, et al., 1981), Blackwell's fictional biography prepared by medical students for their cadaver (Blackwell, 1985), and educational models implemented not by physicians, psychiatrists, or psychologists but by social scientists, sociologists, and social workers (Reiker and Begun, 1980; Hunsdon and Clarke, 1984; Rivara and Wasserman, 1984). Further implementation of such programs into medical education will depend upon the commitment and persistence of medical educators who, despite increased awareness of the importance of the biopsychosocial model amongst today's students and faculty, continue to face considerable resistance by those who would prefer to maintain the *status quo*. However, the clinicians, teachers and researchers who seek to further study and utilize the biopsychosocial model will be moving further toward the WHO's definition of achieving and maintaining optimal health for our patients.

ACKNOWLEGMENTS

The authors thank Joseph S. Gonnella, M.D., Daniel Z. Louis, M.S., David M. Macfadyen, M.D., Howard K. Rabinowitz, M.D., and Leonard M. Rosenfeld, Ph.D., for reviewing this chapter and Hooshang Rahnama for providing some of the nonmedical literature cited.

REFERENCES

Alexander, R.W. and M.J. Fedoruk. 1986. Epidemic psychogenic illness in a telephone operators' building. *Journal of Occupational Medicine, 28,* 42-45.

American Psychiatric Association. 1987. *Diagnostic and statistical manual of mental disorders* (3rd edition revised). (DSM-IIIR), Washington, D.C.: American Psychiatric Association.

Antonovsky, A. 1979. *Health: Stress and coping.* San Francisco: Jossey-Bass.

Batrop, R.W., Lazarus, L., Luckhurst, E., Kiloh, L.G. and R. Penny. 1977. Depressed lymphocyte function after bereavement. *Lancet, 1,* 834-836.

Berkman, L.F. and S.L. Syme. 1979. Social network, host resistance and mortality: A nine year follow-up study of Alameda County residents. *American Journal of Epidemiology, 109,* 186-215.

Berkson, J. 1962. Mortality and marital status. *American Journal of Public Health, 52,* 1318-1329.

Blackwell, B. 1985. Medical education and modest expectations. *General Hospital Psychiatry, 7,* 1-3.

Blanc, G., Herve, D., Simon, H., Lisoprawski, A., Glowinski, J. and J.P. Tassin. 1980. Response to stress of mesocortical-frontal dopaminergic neurons in rats after long-term isolation. *Nature, 284,* 265-271.

Bridges, K.W. and D.P. Goldberg. 1985. Somatic presentation of DSM-III psychiatric disorders in primary care. *Journal of Psychosomatic Research, 29,* 563-569.

Case, R.B., Moss, A.J., Case, N., McDermott, M. and S. Eberly. 1992. Living alone after myocardial infarction: Impact on prognosis. *Journal of American Medical Association, 267,* 515-519.

Chrousos, G.P. and P.W. Gold. 1992. The concept of stress and stress system disorders: overview of physical and behavioral homeostasis. *Journal of American Medical Association, 267,* 1244-1252.

Churchman, C.W. 1979. *The systems approach revisited and updated.* New York: Dell Publishing.

Cobb, S. 1976. Social support as moderator of life stress. *Psychosomatic Medicine, 3,* 300-314.

Colligan, M.J. and L.R. Murphy. 1979. Mass psychogenic illness in organizations: An overview. *Journal of Occupational Psychiatry, 52,* 77-80.

Colligan, M.J., Pennebaker, J.W. and L.R. Murphy (eds.). 1982. *Mass psychogenic illness: A social psychological analysis.* Hillsdale, NJ: Lawrence Erlbaum.

Engel, G.L. 1967. Medical education and the psychosomatic approach: A report on the Rochester Experience, 1946-1966. *Journal of Psychosomatic Research 11,* 77.

Engel, G.L. 1977. The need for a new medical model: A challenge for biomedicine. *Science, 196,* 129-136.

Engel, G.L., Greene, W.L., Reischman, F., Schmale, A. and N. Ashenburg. 1975. A graduate and undergraduate teaching program on the psychological aspects of medicine. *Journal of Medical Education, 32,* 859-870.

Escobar, J.I. and G. Canino. 1989. Unexplained physical complaints: Psychopathology and epidemiological correlates. *British Journal of Psychiatry, 154,* 24-27.

Escobar, J.I., Rubino-Stipec, M. Canino, G. and M. Karno. 1989. Somatic Symptom Index (SSI): A new and abridged somatization construct. *Journal of Nervous and Mental Disease, 177,* 140-146.

Fox, B.H., Temoshok, L. and H. Dreher. 1987. Mind-body and behavior in cancer incidence. *Advances, 5,* 41-56.

Frankel, B. and S. Rosenblum. 1983. Teaching a biopsychosocial approach on medical attending rounds. *General Hospital Psychiatry, 5,* 133-140.

Friedman, M. and R.H. Rosenmann. 1959. Association of specific overt behavior pattern with blood and cardiovascular findings. *Journal of American Medical Association 169,* 1286-1296.

Frith, J. and S. Knowlden. 1992. Undifferentiated illness. *The Medical Journal of Australia, 156,* 472-476.

Garber, J. and M.E.P. Seligman. 1980. *Human helplessness: Theory and application.* New York: Academic Press.

Genset, M. and S. Genset. 1987. *Psychology and health.* Champaign, IL: Research Press.

Gharajedaghi, J. 1981. *On the nature of management of the social system.* Published by the Social Systems Sciences Department of the University of Pennsylvania, Philadelphia. (Available from the Social Sciences Dept., University of Pennsylvania).

Gonnella, J.S. and M. Hojat. 1983. Relationship between performance in medical school and postgraduate competence. *Journal of Medical Education, 58,* 679-685.

Gonnella, J.S., Hojat, M., Erdmann, J.B. and J.J. Veloski. 1993a. A case of mistaken identity: Signal and noise in connecting performance assessments before and after graduation from medical school. In J.S. Gonnella, M. Hojat, J.B. Erdmann & J.J. Veloski (Eds.). *Assessment measures in medical school, residency and practice: The Connections.* (pp. 17-34). New York: Springer.

Gonnella, J.S., Hojat, M. Erdmann, J.B. and J.J. Veloski. 1993b. What have we learned and where do we go from here? In J.S. Gonnella, M. Hojat, J.B. Erdmann & J.J. Veloski (Eds.). *Assessment Measures in medical school residency and practice: The Connections.* (pp. 155-173). New York: Springer.

Harbin, T.J. 1989. The relationship between the Type A behavior pattern and physiological responsivity: A quantitative review. *Psychophysiology, 26,* 110-119.

Heller, K. 1979. The effects of social support: Prevention and treatment implications. In A.P. Goldstein & F.H. Kanfer (Eds.), *Maximizing treatment gains: Transfer enhancement in psychotherapy.* (pp. 353-382). New York: Academic Press.

Henoch, M.J., Batson, J.W. and J. Baum. 1978. Psychosocial factors in juvenile rheumatoid arthritis. *Arthritis and Rheumatism, 21,* 229-233.

Hojat, M. 1982. Loneliness as a function of parent-child and peer relations. *The Journal of Psychology, 112,* 129-133.

Hojat, M. 1989. A psychodynamic view of loneliness and mother-child relationships: A review of theoretical perspectives and empirical findings. In M. Hojat, & R. Crandall (Eds.). *Loneliness: Theory, research, and impliations* (pp. 135-144). Newbury Park, CA: Sage.

Hojat, M. 1992. Social and economic factors in patients with coronary disease. *Journal of American Medical Association, 268,* 195-196.

Hojat, M. and W.H. Vogel. 1989. Socioemotional bonding and neuorobiochemistry. In M. Hojat & R. Crandall (Eds.). *Loneliness: Theory, research and applications.*

(pp. 135-144). Newbury Park: Sage.

Hojat, M., Gonnella, J.S., Veloski, J.J. and J.B. Erdmann. 1993. Is the glass half full or half empty? A reexamination of the associations between assessment measures during medical school and clinical competence after graduation. In J.S. Gonnella, M. Hojat, J.B. Erdmann, & J.J. Veloski (Eds.). *Assessment measures in medical school, residency, and practice: The Connections.* (pp. 137-152). New York: Springer.

House, J.S. 1981. *Work stress and social support.* Reading, MA: Addison Wesley.

Hunsdon, S. and S. Clarke. 1984. The impact of illness on patients and families: Social workers teach medical students. *Social Work in Health Care, 10,* 41-52.

Irwin, J. Ahluwalia, P. Zacharko, R.M. and H. Anisman. 1986. Central norepinephrine and plasma corticosterone following acute and chronic stress: Influence of social isolation and handling. *Pharmacology, Biochemistry and Behavior, 24,* 1151-1154.

Irwin, M. Daniels, M. and H. Weiner. 1987. Immune and neuroendocrine changes during bereavement. *Psychiatric Clinic of North America, 10,* 449-465.

Jacobs, S. and A. Ostfeld. 1977. An epidemiological review of the mortality of bereavement. *Psychosomatic Medicine, 39,* 344-357.

Jacobs, T.J. and E. Charles. 1980. Life events and the occurrence of cancer in children. *Psychosomatic Medicine, 42,* 11-24.

Jemmott, J.B. and S.E. Locke. 1984. Psychosocial factors, immunologic mediation, and human susceptibility to infectious diseases: How much do we know? *Psychological Bulletin, 95,* 78-108.

Jenkins, C.D., Rosenmann, R.H. and S.J. Zyzanski. 1972. *The Jenkins activity survey for health prediction.* Boston: Authors.

Johnson, E.H., Gentry, W.D. and S. Julius (Eds.). 1992. *Personality, elevated blood pressure, and essential hypertension.* Washington, D.C.: Hemisphere.

Jones, W.H. and T.L. Moore. 1989. Loneliness and social support. In M. Hojat & R. Crandall (Eds.). *Loneliness: Theory, research and applications.* (pp. 145-156). Newbury Park, CA: Sage.

Kaprio, J. Koskenvuo, M. and H. Rita. 1987. Mortality after bereavement. *American Journal of Public Health, 77,* 283-287.

Ketterer, M.W. and C.D. Buckholtz. 1989. Somatization disorder. *Journal of American Osteopathic Associations, 89,* 489-490.

Kiecolt-Glaser, J.K., Garner, W., Speicher, C., Penn, G.M., Holliday, J. and R. Glaser. 1984. Psychosocial modifiers of immuno-competence in medical students. *Psychosomatic Medicine, 46,* 7-14.

Kiecolt-Glaser, J.K., Garner, W., Speicher, C., Penn, G.M., Holliday, J. and R. Glaser. 1984b. Urinary cortisol levels, cellular immunocompetency, and loneliness in psychiatric inpatients. *Psychosomatic Medicine, 46,* 15-23.

Kimball, C. 1975. The clinical case method in teaching comprehensive approaches to illness behavior. *Psychosomatic Medicine, 35,* 454-467.

Kimball, C. 1981. *The biopsychosocial approach to the patient.* Baltimore: Williams and Wilkins.

Kimball, C. 1983. Psychosomatic education: The University of Chicago's program

in liaison psychiatry. *Journal of Psychosomatic Research, 27,* 5-8.
Kirmayer, L.J. and J.M. Robbins. 1991. Three forms of somatiztion in primary care: Prevalence, co-occurrence, and sociodemographic characteristics. *Journal of Nervous and Mental Disease, 179,* 647-655.
Klaus, M.H. and J.H. Kennell. 1982. *Maternal-infant bonding.* (2nd ed.). St. Louis, MO: Mosby.
Klaus, M.H., Jerauld, R., Kreger, N.C., McAlpine, W., Steffa, M. and J.H. Kennell. 1972. Maternal attachment: Importance of the first postpartum days. *New England Journal of Medicine, 286,* 460-463.
Kobasa, S.C. 1979. Stressful life events, personality and health: An inquiry into hardiness. *Journal of personality and Social Psychology, 37,* 1-11.
Kobasa, S.C. and M.C. Puccetti. 1983. Personality and social resources in stress resistance. *Journal of Personality and Social Psychology, 45,* 839-850.
Kobasa, S.C., Maddi, S.R. and S. Kahn. 1982. Hardiness and health: A prospective study. *Journal of Personality and Social Psychology, 42,* 168-177.
Lazarus, R.S. and S. Folkman. 1984. *Stress, appraisal, and coping.* New York: Springer.
Leigh, H., Feinstein, A. and M. Reiser. 1981. The patient evaluation grid: A systematic approach to comprehensive care. *General Hospital Psychiatry, 2,* 3-9.
Levenson, J.L. and C. Bemis. 1991. The role of psychological factors in cancer onset and progression. *Psychosomatics, 32,* 124-132.
Lum, L.C. 1982. "Total allergy syndrome" or fluctuating hypocarbia? *Lancet, 1,* 516.
Lynch, J.J. 1977. *The broken heart: The medical consequences of loneliness.* New York: Basic Books.
Maguire, A. 1978. Psychic possession among industrial workers. *Lancet, 1,* 376-378.
Martin, R.L., Roberts, W.V. and P.J. Clayton. 1980. Psychiatric status after hysterectomy. *Journal of the American Medical Association, 244,* 350-353.
Mayou, R. 1975. The social setting of hysteria. *British Journal of Psychiatry, 127,* 466-469.
Mechanic, D. 1974. Social structure and personal adaptation: Some neglected dimensions. (pp. 32-44). In G.V. Coelho, D.A. Hamburg and J.E. Adams (Eds.), *Coping and adaptation.* New York: Basic Books.
Morillo, E. and L.E. Gardner. 1979. Bereavement as an antecedent factor in thyrotoxicosis of children: Four case studies with survey of possible metabolic pathways. *Psychosomatic Medicine, 41,* 545-555.
Oseid, B. 1979. Breast-feeding and infant health. *Seminars in Perinatoloty, 3,* 249-254.
Parkes, C.M. 1972. *Bereavement.* New York: International Universities Press.
Parkes, C.M. and J. Stevenson-Hinde, (Eds.). 1982). *The place of attachment in human behavior.* New York: Basic Books.
Pashko, S., DeTurck, K.H. and W.H. Vogel. 1980. Use of the catherized rat in studies on social interactions and plasma catecholamines. *Pharmacology, Biochemistry and Behavior, 13,* 471-473.
Rahe, R.H., Meyer, M., Smith, M., Kjaer, G. and T.H. Holmes. 1964. Social stress and illness onset. *Journal of Psychosomatic Research, 8,* 35-44.

Rasmussen, N.H. and R.F. Avant. 1989. Somatization disorder in family practice. *American Family Physician, 40,* 206-214.
Reiker, P. and J. Begun. 1980. Translating social science concepts into medical education: A model and a curriculum. *Social Science & Medicine, 14,* 607-612.
Reite, M. and T. Field (Eds.). 1985. *The psychobiology of attachment and separation.* New York: Academic Press.
Reite, M. and R. Short. 1983. Maternal separation studies: Rationale and methodological considerations. (pp. 219-253). In K.A. Miczek (Ed.), *ethopharmacology: Primate Models for neuropsychiatric disorders.* New York: Liss.
Reite, M., Harbeck, R. and A. Hoffman. 1981. Altered cellular immune response following peer separation. *Life Sciences, 29,* 1133-1136.
Riley, V. 1981. Psychoneuroendocrine influences in immuno-competence and neoplasia. *Science, 212,* 1100-1109.
Rivara, F. and A. Wasserman. 1984. Teaching psychosomatic issues to pediatric house officers. *Journal of Medical Education, 59,* 45-53.
Roeske, N. 1979. The medium and the message: Development of videotapes for teaching psychiatry. *American Journal of Psychiatry, 136,* 1391-1397.
Rogers, M.P., Dubey, D. and P. Reich. 1979. The influence of the psyche and the brain on immunity. *Psychosomatic Medicine, 41,* 147-164.
Rosenblum, S. and B. Frankel. 1984. Teaching the biopsychosocial model to medical residents in an outpatient clinic. *Psychosomatics, 25(10),* 751-759.
Rosenmann, R.H. 1990. Type A behavior: A personal overview. *Journal of Personality and Social Psychology, 55,* 1-24.
Rosenmann, R.H. 1992. Type A behavior pattern and cardiovascular reactivity: Is there a relationship with hypertension. In E.H. Johnson, W..D Gentry, & S. Julius (Eds.). *Personality, elevated blood pressure, and essential hypertension* (pp. 87-111). Washington, D.C.: Hemisphere.
Sarason, I.G., Sarason, B.R. and E.N. Sherin. 1986. Social support as an individual difference variable: Its stability, origins and relational aspects. *Journal of Personality and Social Psychology, 50,* 845-855.
Schleifer, S.J., Keller, S.E., Camerino, M., Thornton, J.C. and M. Stein. 1983. Suppression of lymphocyte stimulation following bereavement. *Journal of the American Medical Association, 250,* 374-377.
Selye, H. 1976. *The stress of life* (revised edition). New York: McGraw-Hill.
Silverman, d., Gartrell, N. Aronsen, M. Steer, M. and S. Edbril. 1983. In search of the biopsychosocial perspective: An experiment with beginning medical students. *American Journal of Psychiatry, 140,* 1154-1159.
Small, G.W. and J.F. Borus. 1983. Outbreak of illness in a school chorus: Toxic poisoning or mass hysteria? *The New England Journal of Medicine, 308,* 632-535.
Smith, G.R. 1991. *Somatization disorder in the medical setting.* Washington, D.C.: American Psychiatric Press.
Stewart, D.E. 1987. Environmental hypersensitivity disorder, total allergy, and 20th century disease: A critical review. *Canadian Family Physician, 33,* 405-410.
Stewart, D.E. 1990. The changing faces of somatization. *Psychosomatics, 31,* 153-158.

Stewart, D.E. and J. Raskin. 1985. Psychiatric assessment of patients with "20th Century disease" (total allergy syndrome). *Canadian Medical Association Journal, 133,* 1001-1006.

Sullivan, H.S. 1953. *The interpersonal theory of psychiatry.* New York: Norton.

Susser, M. 1973. *Causal thinking in the health sciences.* London: Oxford University Press.

Swartz, M., Hughes, D., Blazer, D. and L. George. 1987. Somatization disorder in the community: A study of diagnostic concordance among three diagnostic systems. *Journal of Nervous and Mental Disease, 175,* 26-33.

Swartz, M. Landerman, R., George, L., Blazer, D. and J.I. Escobar. 1990. Somatization disorder. In L.N. Robins & D. Regier (Eds.). *Psychiatric Disorders in America* (pp. 220-257). New York: Free Press.

Taylor, S.E. 1978. A developing role for social psychology in medicine and medical practice. *Personality and Social Psychology Bulletin, 4,* 515-523.

Terr, A. 1986. Environmental illness: A review of 50 cases. *Archives of Internal Medicine, 146,* 145-149.

Thomas, K.B. 1987. General practice consultations: Is there any point in being positive? *British Medical Journal, 294,* 1200-1202.

VanEgeren, L.F. and M.D. Gellman. 1992. Cardiovascular reactivity and everyday events. In E.H. Johnson, W.D. Gentry, & S. Julius (Eds.). *Personality, elevated blood pressure and essential hypertension.* (pp. 135-150). Washington, D.C.: Hemisphere.

Vogel, W.H. 1985. Coping, stress, stressor and health consequences. *Neuropsychobiology, 13,* 129-135.

Wehlage, D. 1987. Use of a family member interview to teach the biopsychosocial model. *Psychosomatics, 28,* 371-377.

White, K.L. 1991. *Healing the schism: Epidemiology, medicine, and the public's health.* New York: Springer-Verlag.

World Heatlh Organization (WHO). 1948. *World Health Organization Constitution: Basic documents.* Geneva: World Health Organization.

Medicine and Health Care Into the Twenty-First Century. Edited by S.K. Majumdar, L.M. Rosenfeld, D.B. Nash and A.M. Audet.

Chapter Twenty-Five

TOWARDS A NATIONAL POLICY ON PHYSICIAN SUPPLY

JAMES P. NOLAN, M.D.

Professor and Chairman
Department of Medicine
University of Buffalo
State University of New York
Buffalo, New York 14215

INTRODUCTION

In the United States, a rational way to match workforce needs to output has always been strongly resisted for any professional group. Teachers, lawyers, Ph.D. scientists, and engineers, have experienced periods of significant oversupply and times of shortage. Without any formal planning, the lack of positions after graduation has led to declines in the number of students enrolling in those disciplines. Physician supply until recently never seemed to reach any significant degree of market place saturation because of the poor relationship between demand and need. With the cost of health care rising at unacceptable rates, and with the perceived imbalance of specialists and generalists, a number of proposals have been put forth in association with the President's Health Reform Plan to regulate supply based on need. In this chapter, the history of this supply imbalance will be reviewed, and the present proposals for physician supply regulation into the 21st Century will be discussed.

HISTORY OF POLICY ON PHYSICIAN SUPPLY

Before the Second World War, most practicing physicians were generalists, and were expected to care for the entire age spectrum, perform surgery and did not consider themselves expert in just one area. Graduate medical education usually was one year, and in many states an internship was not necessary for licensure. Beginning in the late 1940's, spurred by the rapid development of the National Institutes of Health, specialization became the rule in Academic Medical Centers. Subspecialty divisions flourished, both for focussing research problems and for providing increasingly complex tertiary care. Such specialization was true not only in Departments of Medicine, but surgical specialties began to break away from Departments of General Surgery as well. However, the seeds of the major problem in the subsequent lack of generalist physicians were sown in Departments of Internal Medicine which traditionally have been the largest departments in medical schools. Overspecialization received a further major stimulus in the 1960's with the passage of Medicare and Medicaid.

In the mid 1960's, the first attempt was made to seriously address the inadequate supply of generalists in the workforce, as well as the mal distribution of physicians in rural and inner-city areas. The Federal Government through construction grants and capitation payments encouraged the creation of a number of new medical schools. In the early 1970's direct support was provided for training in family medicine, general internal medicine and general prediatrics. Through the National Health Service Corp and Area Health Education Centers, generalism was fostered, as well as the need to place physicians in geographic areas of need. Unfortunately, these inducements to generalist careers had little effect as student choice accelerated toward careers in specialties. Indeed, the expansion of medical school graduates that resulted from the Federal initiatives in the 1960's and 70's had the perverse effect of creating an oversupply of medical specialists that will have a profound effect on workforce projections for the next several decades. In addition to the increased number of U.S. Medical Graduates with their propensity to specialize, two other developments occurred that significantly exacerbated the problem. One was the steady and significant growth in the number of International Medical Graduates entering residency positions in this country (1). To a large part, this influx was in the generalist specialties and internal medicine absorbed the majority of these physicians. As the attractiveness of internal medicine declined as a career choice for U.S. Medical Graduates, there was no decline, and indeed an increase in the number of preliminary and categorical slots available in internal medicine programs (2). Over the years, the service needs of hospitals coupled with the reluctance of many practicing physicians to use hospitals without a resident staff have stalled any efforts to downsize the number of trainees. While the international graduates have often been of high quality, they have tended to specialize at an even higher rate than their U.S. counterparts, further exacerbating the maldistribution (3). A second development in the 70's and 80's was the increased number of U.S. students obtaining medical degrees from either abroad or off-shore (4). These trends made any significant decrease in medical enrollment in U.S. schools difficult considering the almost endless supply of residents available from outside the country.

Since demand cannot be equated with need in the delivery of health care, the result of overspecialization has had effects over and above drawing needed providers from careers in generalism. Specialists contribute to the escalating cost of medical care that now threatens to limit necessary government expenditures in other sectors. Even when handling primary care problems, specialists order more tests and consultations compared to generalists, and without obvious benefit to the patient (5). A new and powerful imperative has entered the marketplace which adds urgency to the need for rapid development of a policy on physician supply. The emergence of large managed care organizations and their increasing penetration in all areas of the nation has further reduced the need for the large number of specialists being produced and already in practice. It is estimated that HMO membership will grow from 42 million in 1991 to 55 million in 1994. Under any national reform scenario, this trend will accelerate dramatically. The need for primary care physicians in managed care settings is increasing at the same time that the proportion of U.S. medical graduates entering primary care is declining. While presently almost 70% of practicing physicians designate themselves as having a specialty and 30% do not, the number of graduating seniors in 1992 entering family medicine, general internal medicine and pediatrics was less than 15%. Since it is estimated that HMO's use significantly less specialists in their organizations, we are clearly turning out a workforce not in synchrony with present and future needs. Indeed in areas of the country today, specialists are not able to maintain a patient base when not needed by a local managed-care network.

FAILURE OF INCENTIVES

If as described, a number of historical and social factors have conspired to create a workforce that fails to meet the needs of our citizens, what steps have been taken to redress the imbalance, and have these initiatives failed. While some might argue that enough time has not been given to allow educational and financial incentives to shift the incoming provider workforce toward primary care specialties, the argument can be made that we no longer have the time to wait. If the elusive goal of 50% primary care practitioners is to be reached within an achievable time frame, it is clear that incentives alone may not be sufficient, and that a more deliberate and encompassing workforce policy on a national level may be necessary.

Educational incentives have been developed over the past 15 years to attract more students into family medicine, general internal medicine and pediatrics. Through Title VII grants, increased faculty support has been obtained by schools and training programs in the primary care disciplines. In addition, significant state support has been devoted to the development and strengthening of Departments of Family Medicine with mandates for increased curricular time in the training of medical students. A number of educational organizations and private philanthropies have joined the governmental groups in proposing programs to increase the primary care provider workforce. The Association of American Medical College through its Generalist Initiative has called for a significant restructuring of medical education at all levels to increase student interest and preparation for generalist careers (6). The Robert Wood Johnson Foundation has developed directed grant programs to foster desired workforce changes. In addition to developing generalist faculty, all proposals have in common the need to move the bulk of training out of the tertiary care centers and into ambulatory settings. The lack of role models of generalists in the hospitals, and the mix of chronically-ill, dying patients has been felt to reduce medical students appreciation of the joys of generalist practice. The move to attractive ambulatory, "real-life" sites for instruction has been hampered by several factors. Most notably, resources have been lacking to develop ambulatory practice sites in the number necessary to accommodate large numbers of students and residents. Since most of the teaching must be on a one to one faculty-student basis, it is expensive of time, space and faculty effort. The in-patient team of attendings, residents and clerks has been judged, particularly in internal medicine, to be the most cost-effective educational modality. Despite some promising new programs to increase training in amulatory sites (7) most training in internal medicine and pediatrics remains hospital based. In internal medicine departments, there has been a significant increase in the size and quality of Divisions of General Internal Medicine. With guidance and support from the Society for General Internal Medicine, role models have increased dramatically, and generalist faculty are occupying more key positions in the training of students and residents. Unfortunately, despite this activity, only 3.5% of U.S. seniors in 1992 were headed toward careers in general internal medicine.

If educational incentives have not changed the generalist-subspecialist mix, what about financial incentives? Clearly, the great disparity of income between the cognitive generalists, and the procedural specialists has been the major factor in shifting students preferences away from the primary care disciplines. In no other Western Country is the compensation differential so wide. Students leave medical school with an average indebtedness of close to 60,000 dollars and many have debts well above that level. It is not surprising, that a recent study showed a strong correlation between the earning potential of various specialties and the fill rate in the match (8). Since esteem and respect are often reflected by annual compensation, it is understandable why the primary care specialties have held such little allure despite the educational incentives to make such careers more attractive. Loan forgiveness programs have failed to alter the balance and are unlikely to do so as long as certain specialties receive such a high proportion of the physician payment dollars. An attempt to address this disparity was implemented by the Health Care Financing Administration in their Resource Based Relative Value Scale for Medicare Payments. While full implementation will lower the reimbursement for precedurealists, the calculation has proven to be disappointing for many generalists particularly in the face of increasing fixed costs of practice.

In seems fair to summarize that at the present time the current mix of educational and financial incentives, in combination with public policies and cultural perceptions have failed to overcome the dysfunctional provider mix of generalists and specialists. While it is true that market reform is making some headway in decreasing the need for specialists and increasing the rewards for generalists, it seems unlikely that incentives will work within a time frame necessary for the health needs of the nation.

THE REGULATORY APPROACH

While some would argue that the incentive approach will work given enough time, the momentum toward serious restructuring of the health delivery system has led to serious proposals to regulate the size and specialty distribution of the physician workforce. Perhaps no single outcome speaks more to the failure of the incentive system than the continued reluctance of senior students to choose generalist disciplines that continues in the latest National Residency Matching Program. While studies have looked at why senior medical students do not go into general internal medicine (9), lifestyle issues continue to predominate. In addition to long hours, relatively low pay and perceived lack of respect, the enormity of the knowledge base in the field remains a deterrent to bright, conscientious students.

Because of these factors, much support has been marshalled for a national policy on physician supply that would allocate training program slots to achieve a desired workforce balance. The general consensus seems to be that a 50-50 split between the generalist disciplines and medical, surgical and support subspecialties would be a suitable distribution. Even in the highly unlikely event that such a 50% split could be implemented immediately, it is estimated that it would take until the year 2040 for a 50-50 mix to be achieved in the physician population in practice (10). While many argue that our output in Family Medicine, General Internal Medicine and Pediatrics should be at least 70% to allow for a faster equilibration in the workforce, most believe that such a radical change in a short period of time is unrealistic. Rather, it has been suggested that specialists, particularly those in internal medicine who have had a basic generalist training experience may be re-trained to assume primary care responsibilities as specialty opportunities disappear.

That some action on a national policy to regulate physician supply is near can be seen by the number of proposals for such regulation that are now on the table. While it is unlikely that any one of the current proposals will be adopted in its entirety, there are enough similarities that allow a general outline to be seen. In all plans of regulation, it is recognized that geographic maldistribution is a problem regardless of total physician numbers, and that special attention must be given to significantly increasing in the physician workforce the number of underrepresented minorities (11).

PROPOSALS

While significant differences exist in the various Workforce proposals put forth, certain common themes are addressed. These issues of general concern include:

1. Limits on the overall number of training positions
2. The desired ratio of generalist/specialist physicians
3. A definition of the generalist or primary care physician
4. The creation of a body(s) to oversee medical education
5. Establishment of a method for financing medical education
6. Specification of the recipient of medical education funds

7. Methods/criteria for evaluating training programs
8. Encouragement to training in ambulatory settings
9. Provision of funds for retraining of the existing workforce
10. Provision of transitional relief funds for teaching hospitals.

All plans recognize both the need and difficulty of accurately projecting primary care and specialty needs decades in the future. While the necessity to limit the future size of the workforce seems clear, how to reduce medical school classes and limit training opportunities for International Medical Graduates is not always clearly addressed. Further complicating all proposals is the need to assess the numbers, and responsibilities of non-physician providers in primary care and the specialties, and their effect on physician numbers and mix.

The Council on Graduate Medical Education (C.O.G.M.E.) was authorized by Congress in 1986 to provide to Congress and the Secretary for Health and Human Services an ongoing assessment of physician supply trends, and to recommend appropriate efforts to address identified needs. In its first several reports, C.O.G.M.E. expressed concern about specialty and geographic mal distribution despite an ever-growing overall pool of physicians. The third and most recent report addresses Workforce Reform and outlines steps to make reform a reality (12). In its report, C.O.G.M.E. would restrict the aggregate number of residency training positions to 110% of U.S. Medical Graduates, and would define a 50/50 allocation of slots between family medicine, general internal medicine, general pediatrics and all other specialties (allopathic and osteopathic). A Physician Workforce Advisory Committee would be established and be staffed by Health and Human Services. C.O.G.M.E. establishes a G.M.E. funding pool that would be administered by HHS, and all third party payors would be taxed for its support. For any institution to receive G.M.E. funding, it must be part of a consortium, and the HHS Secretary would establish the eligibility criteria for funding from the pool, with the provision that all consortia must achieve the 50-50 ratio. C.O.G.M.E. encourages greater training in ambulatory sites through the use of consortia containing such institutions. They also propose the establishment of a new authority under Title VII of the PHS Act for retraining non-generalists in comprehensive primary care competencies.

The Physician Payment Review Commission (PPRC) in its 1993 Annual Report to Congress (13) proposes a similar regulatory approach. It differs in relying on the Accreditation Council on Graduate Medical Education to determine need and allocation of residency positions based on educational quality. The PPRC recommends transitional funds be made available to hospitals losing residents who have a disproportionate share of indigent patients. Other organizations such as the Association of Professors of Medicine and the Association of American Medical Colleges have made detailed recommendations to support the assessment and allocation of physician manpower (14).

The proposal from the Clinton Administration in their comprehensive Health Security Act proposal has similar provisions but is different in some key areas. While the HHS secretary determines the number of training positions in each specialty, the aggregate number of 110% U.S. medical graduates is not present. Further, the training slots for primary care specialties would be increased to 55% with the

York State and local carriers for a demonstration project to develop innovative sites and programs to increase the residency output of generalists to 50% within three years. Thus, as with the reforms proposed to ensure universal health coverage, options in developing and implementing physician supply policy will undoubtedly encourage a state role where appropriate. It seems likely that New York State, for example, will want to continue the considerable progress already made in rationalizing the supply of physicians within its borders.

A major unknown in the development of a National Policy on Physician Supply is the role and numbers of non-physician providers. Both physician-assistants and nurse practitioners have been utilized in ever-increasing numbers not only as providers of primary care, but to provide services in the acute hospital and subspecialty areas as well. Under the Clinton Plan, funds will be earmarked to significantly increase the output of such providers. It is also appartent that major nursing associations believe that 80% of primary care can be delivered as effectively by nurse-practitioners as by physicians. Further they believe that these care givers should be allowed independent practice without physician supervision. If such non-physician providers assume a major role in the provision of care, the numbers of general physicians needed in the next century may be considerably fewer than now projected.

Significant opposition presently exists to the concept of a National Workforce Commission, and the allocation of training positions. Medical students resent the notion that career choices will be severely restricted in the future. It should be pointed out, however, that choice has always been restricted, with positions in specialties such as opthalmology being many fewer than applicants from our schools. Nevertheless, there is little question that what is being proposed will be a quantum change in the level of competition. The American Medical Association also vigorously opposes any federal limitation of specialty choice. Their position is that students forced arbitrarily into generalist careers will be unhappy, and therefore less satisfactory providers. Those in opposition believe that market forces, and better financial incentives will solve the generalist/subspecialist mismatch without the necessity of a cumbersome, federal bureaucratic approach.

Thus as a major component of the restructuring of the entire health care system, the number and type of physicians in the workforce will be critical to the success of any plan. Most observers believe that the educational and financial incentives already in place or proposed, will not work in time. Further, many educators feel that we are doing our medical students a great disservice by offering them career choices that may not lead to professional employment. It seems clear, therefore, that the growing concensus for a national policy on physician supply will lead to the changes necessary to provide the health care needed in the 21st century.

BIBLIOGRAPHY

1. Mick, S.S. and J.L. 1984. Worobey. Foreign medical graduates in the 1980's: trend in specialization. AM J Pub Health; 74:698-703.
2. Kletke, P.R., Schleiter, M.K. and A.R. Tarlov. 1987. Changles in the supply of internists, the internal medicine population from 1978 to 1998. Ann Int Med; 107:93-100.
3. Andersen, R.M., Lyttle, C.S. and C.H. Kohrman et al. 1992. National study of internal medicine manpower: XIX Trends in internal medicine residency training programs. Ann Int Med; 117:243-250.
4. Woodroffe, F.J. 1982. Offshore medical schools. Lancet; 2:546-547.
5. Greenfield, S., Nelson, E.C. and M. Zubkoff et al. 1992. Variations in resource utilization among medical specialites and systems of care: results from the medical outcomes study. JAMA; 267:1624-1630.
6. Association of American Medical Colleges. 1993. Increasing the number of generalist physicians. Acad Med.; 68:1-6.
7. Nolan, J.P. and T.S. Inui. 1992. Tinkering or real reform? The choice is ours. Ann Int Med.; 116:S 1042-1045.
8. Colwill, J.M. 1992. Where have all the primary care applicants gone? New Eng J Med.; 326:387-393.
9. Babbott, D., Baldwin, D.C., Killian, C.D. and S.O. Weaver. 1989. Trends of evolution of specialty choice. Comparison of U.S. medical school graduates in 1983 and 1987. JAMA; 261:2367-2373.
10. Kindig, D.A., Cultice, J.M. and F. Mullan. 1993. The elusive generalist physician, can we reach the 50% goal. JAMA; 270:1069-1073.
11. Shea, S. and M.T. Fullilove. 1985. Entry of black and other minority students into U.S. medical school. N Eng J Med; 313:933-940.
12. Rivo, M.L. and D. Satcher. 1993. Improving access to health care through physician workforce reform. JAMA; 270:1074-1078.
13. Schwartz, A., Ginsburg, P.B. and L.B. LeRoy. 1993. Reforming graduate medical education. Summary report of the physician payment review commission. JAMA; 270:1079-1084.
14. Luke, R., Terwilliger, J. and T. Ibrahim. 1993. Developing a strategy for providing federal GME support. Am J Med.; 95:1-6.
15. Report of the New York State Commission on Graduate Medical Education. 1986. Department of Health, Albany, New York.

his or her own goods. Given this ideological disposition, it is not surprising that American ethicists dealing with rights issues have focused primarily on "rights in" rather than "rights to" medical care. Issues related to the individual, both the rights of the patient and the prerogatives/responsibilities of the health care provider, have been the subject of bioethics, and not wider justice issues related to the allocation of resources or access to health care.

Modern conceptions of human rights formulated at the end of World War II have a much broader conception of the nature of rights and the role of government than the eighteenth century liberal interpretation still current in the United States. The single most authoritative standard, the Universal Declaration of Human Rights, adopted unanimously by the United Nations General Assembly in 1948, replaces John Locke's three generic rights—to life, liberty, and property—with nearly two dozen specific rights. These rights fall into two categories—civil and political rights, much like the rights guaranteed in the U.S. Bill of Rights, and social, economic, and cultural rights, including the rights to health and health care, education, adequate standard of living, security during illness and disability, availability of a job, and participation in the cultural life of the community. Together these rights are considered to establish minimal standards of decent social and governmental practice[5].

RATIONALE FOR A RIGHT TO HEALTH

In designating health as a basic human right, the framers of the Universal Declaration of Human Rights and the International Covenant on Economic, Social and Cultural Rights recognized that health care and health protection are essential for the individual and community development and well-being in a modern society. Technological development, population growth, and societal complexity have made it difficult, if not impossible, for the individual in contemporary societies to assure his or her well-being apart from a societal commitment to provide access to health services and government action to protect public health.

The central importance of the impact of health status on our personal lives and the concomitant influence of the health care system on our common lives was a theme of the 1983 report issued by the President's Commission for the Study of Ethical Problems in Medicine and Biomedical and Behavioral Research. Given a mandate in 1980 to study the ethical and legal implications of differences in the availability of health services, the Commission concluded that "society has an ethical obligation to ensure equitable access to health care for all"[6]. Refraining from using rights language, the Commission's recommendations approximate many of the elements of a right to health care. Equitable access, according to the Commission, requires that citizens be able to secure an adequate level of care without excessive burdens. While the Commission stated that individuals have an obligation to pay a fair share of the cost of their own care, it vested ultimate responsibility for ensuring equitable access with the federal government. The Commission also argued that the goal of cost containment should not focus on limiting the attainment of equitable access for those less well served by the current arrangements[7].

According to the Commission, access to health care is a fundamental ethical issue, a matter of equity and justice, for four reasons. First, health care makes a central contribution to promoting personal well-being. Second, health care can broaden a person's range of opportunities, "that is the array of life plans that is reasonable to pursue within the conditions obtaining in society"[8]. Third, health care "has the ability to relieve worry and enable patients to adjust to their situation by supplying reliable information about their health"[9]. Finally, "health care expresses and nurtures bonds of empathy and compassion"[10].

The Commission's conclusion that securing equitable access to health care is a societal rather than a merely private or individual responsibility rested on three lines of reasoning. First, the Commission characterized health care, especially scientific health care, as a social product requiring the investment, skills, and efforts of many individuals. Second, the need for health care is unevenly distributed among persons and highly unpredictable. Third, differences in health status, and hence differences in health care needs, are largely out of an individual's control and are therefore undeserved. Therefore, the Commission did not consider it appropriate or in most cases even feasible to apply the notion of personal responsibility to health care in a fair way[11].

The proposed conceptualization of a right to health in this chapter also includes broad provisions for health protection, including claims on all levels of government to achieve a safe environment adequate for human health and well-being, to promote health lifestyles, and to assure safe working conditions. A more narrowly formulated right to health care has significant limitations. Clearly there are regions of the world in which the most valuable steps toward improvement of health are not medical services but public health protection. Poor countries with limited resources would better improve health standards by investing scarce resources in clean water and environmental clean-up rather than by offering curative health care to a small fraction of the population. Moreover, even within an advanced industrialized country, health status will continue to deteriorate and health care costs will continue to escalate unless there is greater attention paid to promoting more favorable health conditions. As a recent publication of the American Public Health Association points out, improvements in the standard of health depend on preventing health problems before they arise. Investments in curative health care make little sense unless they are accompanied by policies that deal with the roots of public health problems. Moreover, the failure to do so contributes to the escalating cost of health care. For example, federal crop subsidies for the cultivation of tobacco persist despite the fact that smoking is the leading known cause of cancer and a major factor in heart disease[12].

Realizing that the severity of environmental problems in many areas threatens the health and well-being of many people, some environmentalists and human rights theorists have proposed recognition of a human right to a safe environment that would protect human health and safety. Actual and potential threats to health are the primary focus of this proposed right. One proponent, philosopher

James Nickel, who is the author of major text on international human rights, argues that few human rights violations other than programs of mass extermination can cause such widespread and substantial damage to the health and welfare of a community as environmental threats. In defining the scope of a proposed right to a safe environment, he recommends that the level of safety from environmental risks be reduced to a level satisfactory or adequate for health. Acknowledging that this formulation is somewhat vague and imprecise, he assumes that this norm will then be specified into concrete risk standards through democratic legislative and regulatory processes, in light of current scientific knowledge and fiscal realities[13].

The American Public Health Association identifies five basic determinants of health: access to medical care, a healthy environment, healthy neighborhoods, healthy behaviors, and community health services. Components of a healthy environment include clean air, safe drinking water, fluoridation of the water supply, and the reduction of avoidable work place accidents. Healthy neighborhoods refer to places where young people can grow up well educated and free from crime and drugs, where governments provide basic services for all their constituents, and where families have resources to care for their children. Healthy behavior means lifestyles and conduct calculated to reduce or eliminate unnecessary risk to one's own health and that of others—proper eating habits, regular exercise, use of seat belts, avoiding drugs, tobacco, and alcohol. Community health service incorporates basic health and sanitary programs[14].

A rights approach imposes duties on both individuals and governments. In the case of a recognized legal right, relevant government authorities assume primary responsibility to achieve realization of a right. The duty of governments has several distinct components, including to respect, protect, and fulfill. These obligations are both negative—not to violate—and positive—to uphold or implement. The responsibilities of government encompass formulating a framework or plan through which to achieve progressive realization, as well as undertaking specific policies and actions intended to achieve that goal. In addition, legal recognition means that the content of the right should be used as a standard of evaluation for all public policies. Finally, government has the duty to set a framework conducive to private individuals and groups contributing to implementation.

The duty to respect the equality of all persons, which is intrinsic to a human right, is associated both with a responsibility not to discriminate and a positive component, to remove obstacles or barriers. Where there is legacy of discrimination or inequities related to a right, governments have a particular responsibility to rectify and redress this pattern. Given the U.S. context, this translates into the need for a vigorous affirmative action policy with regard to health care, one component of which would be to give minority health issues and the problems of the poor priority in funding. Another component would be to evaluate systematically whether proposed public policy changes would have a beneficial impact on these communities. It would also necessitate addressing toxic waste disposal issues since toxic waste sites tend to be located in poor and minority communities. Concerted efforts to address and compensate for the unequal distribution of health care facilities, particularly the lack of qualified professionals and good quality facilities in many urban centers and remote rural areas would constitute a fourth requirement.

COMPONENTS OF A RIGHT TO HEALTH

Recognition of a right to health would acknowledge that all persons, without regard to their purchasing power, social status, gender, race, or personal merit are entitled to basic health services and comprehensive health protection. Reciprocally, it would underscore the ethical responsibility of society to provide for the health of its members. A human rights approach would also confer a priority on meeting the needs of the groups most disadvantaged by the legacy of unequal access to health care and patterns of exposure to toxic substances. While legal recognition would not automatically guarantee the right to health, it would create an obligation for both federal and state governments to establish a broad framework and enact specific policies to promote the goal.

It should be noted that the proposed right to health is not an unlimited entitlement. Economic constraints make it more appropriate to recognize a right to a limited scope of health care than an entitlement to all possible beneficial care. This formulation acknowledges that society has a responsibility to provide health care to all members but lacks sufficient resources to address all of their potential health needs. By linking limits with rights, a rights-based approach to health care reform offers a framework through which to seek a national consensus on a cost-conscious standard of medical care that would be provided to all citizens and residents. In this trade-off of rights and limitations, the government would provide the security of an entitlement to basic health care that does not depend on financial or employment status and that cannot be lost because of health disabilities. In exchange, members of society would accept a series of obligations: the duty to respect and be sensitive to the health care needs of others, individual responsibility to adopt healthy lifestyles, the collective obligation for meeting the needs of the most vulnerable members of society, and the duty to recognize individual limits on claims to a reasonable level.

Because the proposed right to health includes a broad commitment to health protection along with an entitlement to health care, it would be consistent with a new health care paradigm focussing on preventive and primary care. Public policy and social investments would seek to prevent illness rather than treat its effects. Such a paradigm shift away from curative health care would both improve health status and hold down costs. Consistent with this paradigm, limitations in available resources for health would primarily affect the range of curative services that are included in the basic health care package. Savings would be sought through rationing high cost diagnostic techniques and operations, like organ transplants, as well as controlling investments in technology.

The following are the central characteristics and components of a right to health consisting of a right to basic and adequate health care and a right to health protection:

- a universal legal entitlement to a basic health care package that is guaranteed equally to all citizens and residents and cannot be withdrawn;
- structural reforms to rectify inadequacies and inequities in the current health care system so as to assure that all persons and groups have equal access to quality health care;
- affirmative action measures are taken in order to bring the health status of the most disadvantaged and vulnerable communities up to mainstream standards;
- effective monitoring of access to health care and the health care status, particularly of currently underserved communities and groups, so as to modify health care policies to meet their needs;
- health care is treated as a social good to be distributed according to principles of justice rather than a commodity to be distributed by market forces for the financial benefit of health care providers;
- the health paradigm and investment patterns stress preventive and primary care rather than curative health services;
- there is meaningful public participation in setting priorities and shaping health care reform;
- health care is affordable to all and publicly financed;
- simple and effective means of recourse exist for those whose right to health is violated;
- priority is accorded and commensurate investments made in public policies to provide health protection, including reducing exposure to toxic substances, improving the quality of air and water, offering incentives for healthy life styles, and assuring work place safety.

INTERNATIONAL RECOGNITION OF A RIGHT TO HEALTH

Several major international human rights instruments recognize the right to health. The United Nations Declaration of Human Rights (1948), the principal standard by which human rights are identified today, states that "everyone has a right to a standard of living adequate for the health and well being of himself and of his family, including food, clothing, housing, and medical care and necessary social services . . ."[15]. Article 12 of the International Covenant on Economic, Social and Cultural Rights (1976), a treaty intended to make more specific and binding the obligations of governments to protect the social, economic, and cultural rights enumerated in the Universal Declaration, "recognizes the right of everyone to the enjoyment of the highest attainable standard of physical and mental health," and to that end, mandates that state parties to the Covenant (governments which have ratified the instrument) undertake the following steps to achieve full realization of this right:

(a) The provision for the reduction of the stillbirth rate and of infant mortality and for the healthy development of the child;
(b) The improvement of all aspects of environmental and industrial hygiene;
(c) The prevention, treatment and control of epidemic, endemic, occupational and other diseases;
(d) The creation of conditions which would assure to all medical service and medical attention in the event of sickness[16].

The World Health Organization (WHO) has also recognized a right to health. Language in the preamble of its Constitution states, "The enjoyment of the highest attainable standard of health is one of the fundamental rights of every human being without distinction of race, religion, political belief, economic, or social condition." The WHO defines health as a "state of complete physical, mental and social well-being and not merely the absence of disease of infirmity"[17]. In 1977, the World Health Assembly reaffirmed that health is a basic human right and a world-wide social goal essential to the satisfaction of basic human needs and the quality of life. It set the goal of "Health for All" by the year 2000, the attainment of a level of health that will permit all citizens to lead a socially and economically productive life. Two years later, the Declaration of Alma-Ata further linked the "Health for All" goal with efforts to rectify inequalities in health status of people both within and between countries[18].

Constitutions of a number of countries include a right to health or health protection. A constitiutional right to health or to health protection, however, is rarely an individual, immediately enforceable right. It is more likely to be a programmatic or policy right that articulates goals[19]. While not as broad as a right to health, protection encompasses attention to the public health context of curative medicine. Thus a right to health protection goes beyond medical intervention to include preventive measures, such as the provision of potable water and improvement of environmental conditions. Sometimes the distinction is articulated as the right to health care when one is sick and the right to health protection to prevent the population from becoming sick.

RIGHT TO HEALTH IN THE UNITED STATES

Although Americans have a disposition to frame claims in the language of rights, the United States is the only major democracy that fails to recognize a universal entitlement to health care. That there is no mention in the Constitution or Bill of Rights is not surprising. Modern concepts of human rights, particularly of economic and social rights, emerged in response to World War II and the holocaust. Moreover, until the development of modern medicine and public health measures in the late nineteenth and early twentieth centuries, there was little that governments could do to improve health or health outcomes.

In contrast with other societies in which health care is considered to be a social

Recently the language of rights has reemerged, albeit haltingly, in the American health reform debate. President George Bush spoke about a right to health care in his 1991 State of the Union Address, and the 1992 Democratic platform had a provision advocating a right to health care. In January 1993, Rep. Ed Pastor (D-Ariz.) introduced a nonbinding concurrent resolution resolving that it is the sense of Congress that "access to health care services is a fundamental human right" and that all legislative proposals by the President and Congress concerning national health care reform should be based upon recognition of this fundamental right[29].

Much like the 1983 report of the President's Commission, the 1993-1994 Clinton administration proposals for health care reform incorporated some of the substance of a right to health care while refraining from using rights language. Consistent with a human rights approach, the draft Health Security Act proposed comprehensive health benefits for all American citizens and legal residents, regardless of health or employment status[30]. To create security, one of its fundamental goals, these benefits would provide a full range of medically necessary or appropriate services. The health plan also precluded any health plan denying enrollment to an applicant because of health, employment or financial status, or charging some patients more than others because of age, medical condition or other factors related to risk[31].

The defeat of the Clinton health plan and the inability to formulate a bipartisan compromise measure in the 1994 session of Congress appears to have undermined the momentum for significant health care reform. There is a declining commitment to universality. Current proposals lack provisions for assuring comprehensive benefits to all Americans. The mobilization of the medical-industrial complex in favor of the status quo has apparently defeated possibilities for adopting a new health care paradigm emphasizing preventive and primary services. Thus prospects for recognizing a right to health or health care are once again very poor, at least in the short run.

ADVANTAGES OF A HUMAN RIGHTS APPROACH TO HEALTH CARE REFORM

A human rights approach focuses on the ethical and normative foundations of health care reform. Currently the health care policy debate is being centered on economics, particularly on the narrow issues of reducing health care costs and increasing efficiency. Health care reform, however, raises fundamental questions about what we owe to one another as human beings and members of a common society. Recognition of a right to health would clarify the moral claims of individuals and help resolve issues of societal obligations and goals related to health.

By stressing the importance of health policies and institutions responding to the needs of the most disadvantaged and vulnerable communities, a human rights approach can help counter the influence of affluent and powerful constituencies in shaping public policy. A reform process oriented toward the goal of improving the health status of "have nots" would be very different from a middle class standard. The goal would be to craft a health care system and standard of health protection capable of being as responsive to the needs of the disadvantaged as the current system is to the middle class. These efforts would result in greater justice and equity, to the benefit of all members of society.

If health is viewed as a right, rather than as a contingent benefit, it would improve the prospects for a more fundamental health care reform. It is a political fact of life in this country that the most important political issues are framed in the language of rights.

The recognition of health or health care as a basic right protects principles of universality and equality of benefits. It is likely that health care reform will phase in coverage of currently unprotected individuals. By acknowledging the right of all persons to an entitlement to basic health care, universality and equality would have priority over other goals, like cost containment. It would also protect these entitlements from being reduced or eliminated by future administrations less committed to health security.

A human rights approach translates into a series of clear and compelling government obligations that go far beyond cost containment or increasing the efficiency of the health care system to assuring appropriate and available basic health care and protecting the public's health. A secure and meaningful right to health would require the federal and state governments to undertake structural reforms that rectify inadequacies in the health care system, empowerment strategies to enable rights holders to exercise their claims, and public policies that seek to protect and promote the public's health.

A human rights approach as conceptualized here provides meaningful linkages between rights and responsibilities. It assumes a trade-off in which the political system provides a secure entitlement in exchange for the people's acceptance of limits on the benefits that are publicly funded, the responsibility to care for themselves and the collective duty to provide for the health needs of the vulnerable and disadvantaged. Right holders' responsibility to be sensitive to the constraints imposed by limited societal resources may mean tolerance for waiting period for non-emergency care, controls over investments in and use of high technology medicine, and lack of public financing for at least some high cost organ transplants, experimental techniques, and cosmetic surgery.

By establishing clear individual entitlements to health care and health protection, a human rights approach would empower individuals and groups to assert their claims as well as offering potential recourse for those whose rights are violated.

Recognition of a right to health linking health protection, preventive services, and primary care has a much greater potential for improving the health care status of the population at a more reasonable cost than health care reform that focusses on curative health services.

REFERENCES AND FOOTNOTES

1. Portions of this paper are adapted from the author's *Exploring a Human Rights Approach to Health Care Reform* (1993, American Association for the Advancement of Science, Washington, D.C.). The latter publication is an interpretation of the findings from four consultations on the right to health care sponsored by the American Association for the Advancement of Science with the assistance of The Robert Wood Johnson Foundation. The proposed formulation of the right in this paper is broader than the right to health care and reflects the views of the author.
2. Freeden, Michael. 1991. *Rights.* University of Minnesota Press, Minneapolis, p. 7.
3. Donnelly, Jack. 1992. Establishing a Right to Health Care in the United States: An International Human Rights Perspective, Paper prepared for the American Association for the Advancement of Science Consultation on the Right to Health Care: Scope and Limitations of the Right, December 4.
4. Shapiro, Ian. 1986. *The Evolution of Rights in Liberal Theory.* Cambridge University Press, Cambridge, England.
5. Nickel, James W. 1987. *Making Sense of Human Rights: Philosophical Reflections on the Universal Declaration of Human Rights.* University of California Press, Berkeley and Los Angeles, p. 4.
6. President's Commission for the Study of Ethical Problems in Medicine and Biomedical and Behavioral Research. 1983. *Securing Access to Health Care: The Ethical Implications of Differences in the Availability of Health Services,* Vol. I, U.S. Government Printing Office, Washington, D.C., 1983, p. 4.
7. *Ibid.,* pp. 3-5.
8. *Ibid.,* p. 16.
9. *Ibid.,* p. 17.
10. *Idem.,* p. 17.
11. *Ibid.,* pp. 22-25.
12. American Public Health Association. 1992. *America's Public Health Report Card: A State-by-State Report on the Health of the Public.* APHA, Washington, D.C., pp. 1-3.
13. Nickel, James W. The Human Right to a Safe Environment. 1993. *The Yale Journal of International Law,* Vol. 18, No. 1, pp. 281-295.
14. American Public Health Association, *op. cit.,* pp. 3-4.
15. Universal Declaration of Human Rights, *The International Bill of Rights,* United Nations, New York, 1985, p. 8.
16. *Ibid.,* p. 14.
17. World Health Organization, Preamble to the Constitution, in *The First Ten Years of the World Health Organization,* WHO, Geneva, 1958, p. II.
18. Pinet, Genevieve. 1993. "Human Rights and the WHO Health for All Indicators," paper prepared for the American Association for the Advancement of Science Consultation on Standards and Indicators to Monitor the Achievement of the Right to Health Care, 26 February, Washington, D.C.

19. See for example, Hernan Fuenzalida-Puelma and Susan Scholle Connor, eds., *The Right to Health in the Americas: A Comparative Constitutional Study.* Pan American Health Organization, Washington, D.C., 1989, 9.608.
20. On these developments, see Arnold S. Relman, M.D., The Shattuck Lecture - The Health Care Industry: Where Is It Taking Us? 1991. *The New England Journal of Medicine,* Vol. 325, pp. 854-859.
21. O'Keefe, Janet. 1993. "Financing Reform and Access to Health Care: Extending and Ensuring a Right to Comprehensive Health Care," paper prepared for the American Association for the Advancement of Science Right to Health Care Project.
22. Marmor, Theodore R. 1991. In: Thomas J. Bole III and William B. Bondeson (Eds.) *Rights to Health Care.* Kluwer Academic Publishers, Dordrecht, the Netherlands, pp. 26-27.
23. O'Keefe, *ibid.*
24. Taylor, Timothy. 1992. The Needs of Native Americans. Presentation at the American Association Right to Health Care Consulation: Defining a Minimum Adequate Standard of Health Care, November 13.
25. President's Commission, *ibid.*, pp. 146-154.
26. Including the Poor, Health Policy Agenda for the American People: The Final Report of the Ad Hoc Committee on Medicaid. 1989. Cited in Health Care Crisis in American Fact Sheet. 1989. Bioethics Consulation Group, Minneapolis.
27. Bovbjer, Randall R., Griffin, Charles C. and Caitline E. Carroll. "U.S. Health Care Coverage and Costs: Historical Development and Choices for the 1990's," *The Journal of Law, Medicine & Ethics,* Vol. 212 (Summer 1993): p. 142.
28. President's Commission on the Health Needs of the Nation. 1953. U.S. Government Printing Office, Washington, D.C., p. 3.
29. House Concurrent Resolution No. 56, 103rd Cong., 1st Session.
30. *Health Security: Preliminary Plan Summary.* 1993. U.S. Government Printing Office, Washington, D.C., p. 1.
31. *Ibid.,* pp. 2-3.

Medicine and Health Care Into the Twenty-First Century. Edited by S.K. Majumdar, L.M. Rosenfeld, D.B. Nash and A.M. Audet.

Chapter Twenty-Seven

THE EPIDEMIOLOGY OF INJURIES AND VIOLENCE: A Public Health Perspective on Violence Prevention

CHUKWUDI ONWUACHI-SAUNDERS, M.D., M.P.H.* and **ROBERT K. ROSS, M.D.**

Deputy Health Commissioner of Philadelphia
Department of Public Health
1600 Arch Street, 7th Floor
Philadelphia, PA 19103

INTRODUCTION

The mission of public health is to prevent unnecessary morbidity and mortality and to promote health. Tuberculosis, Measles, Hepatitis, AIDS, and Influenza are all considered public health issues of importance because they significantly impact on morbidity and mortality, and are largely preventable. But none of these has taken a greater toll on as many persons in the United States as the epidemic of violence. Consequently, federal public health leadership has recently proclaimed "injuries" in general, and violence, more specifically, as an issue of public health importance. Currently, federal, state, and local public officials are grappling with how to implement violence prevention programs at the community level. This chapter reviews the scope of the violence problem in the United States, and provides an example of a community-based approach to reduce and prevent interpersonal violence.

---

*Dr. Saunders is Deputy Health Commissioner, with the Philadelphia Department of Public Health. Dr. Ross is currently the Director of Health Services in San Diego County and was formerly Commissioner of Public Health in Philadelphia.

EPIDEMIOLOGY AND BACKGROUND

Injury is a major problem in the United States (1). In public health, injury can be divided into two categories (Table 1): intentional (such as, homicide and suicide) and unintentional (motor vehicle crashes, falls, poisoning, burns and drownings). It has long been thought that the unintentional injuries are "accidents", random, uncontrollable acts of fate. But injuries are predictable and largely preventable. After heart disease and cancer, injuries are the third leading cause of death in the United States (1, 2). Each year over 150,000 people in the United States die from injuries. Moreover, injuries are the leading cause of years of potential life lost and of premature death (death before the age of 65) (Table 2) (1, 2, 3). Injuries account for more years of potential life lost than cancer, diseases of the heart, congenital anomalies and HIV infection combined. Injuries disproportionately affect the young, and are the single greatest killer of people in the United States between the ages of 1 and 44 (1). Researchers have shown that injuries also have a disproportionate impact on people of color in this country—particularly African-Americans, Hispanics, and Native Americans (4, 5, 6). Death rates due to injury for African-American males are high not only for homicides, but also for other injuries—such as residential fires, and pedestrian mishaps (Table 3) (5, 6).

The common term for intentional injuries is violence. But, injuries are merely a physical manifestation of violence. More than one third of injury deaths are intentional (Table 4) (2). In the field of public health, violence is defined as the threatened or actual use of physical power against another person, against oneself or against a group or community which either results in or has a high likelihood of resulting in injury, death or deprivation. (Secretary's Blue Ribbon Panel on Violence Prevention, Jan. 15, 1993).

TABLE 1
Unintentional and Intentional Injury

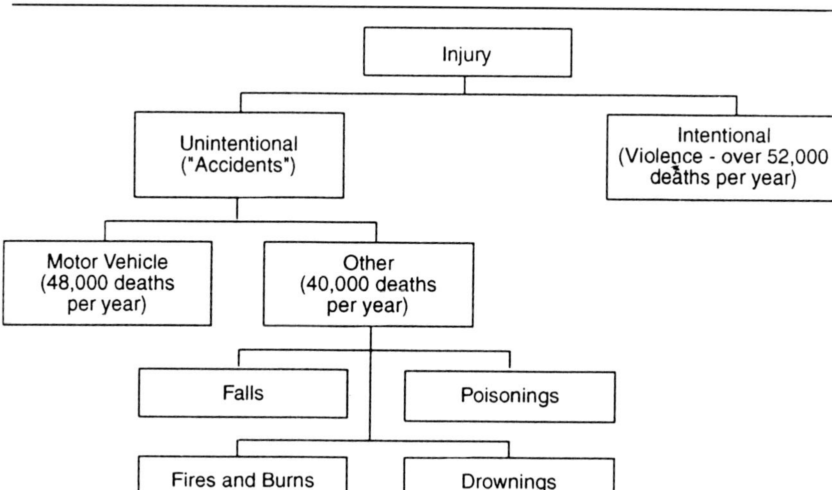

TABLE 2

*Estimated Years of Potential Life Lost Before Age 65 Per 100,000 Person, United States, 1991**

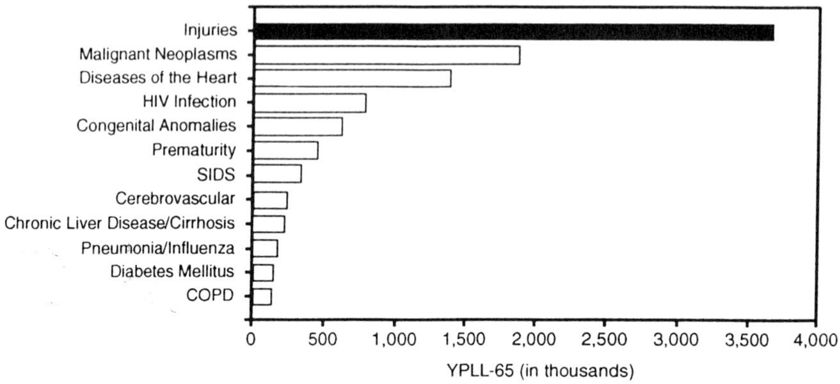

*Provisional Data

TABLE 3

Disproportionate Impact of Selected Injuries on Blacks, 1987

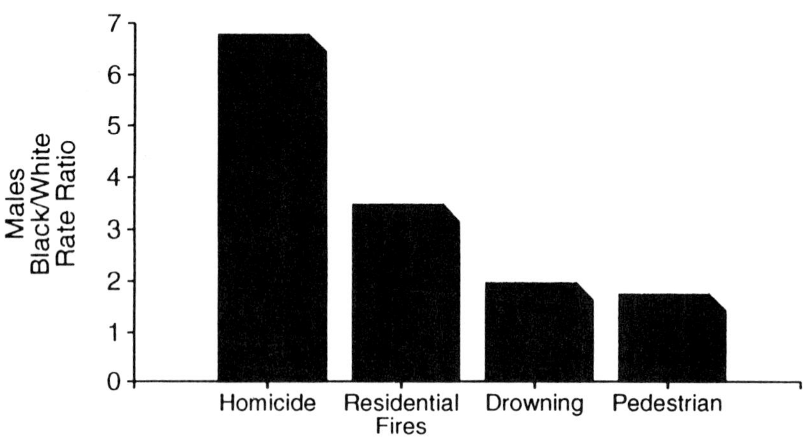

Violence includes homicide—an example of interpersonal violence—and suicide, an example of self-directed violence. Each is the most severe outcome of that type of violence.

In 1992, according to the National Center for Health Statistics (provisional data) 26,570 persons in the United States died as a result of homicide and legal intervention. However, each year more than 2.2 million people suffer nonfatal injuries and disabilities from violent and abusive behavior (2).

Homicide appears to be more common as a cause of death in the United States than anywhere else in the world. Therefore, violence is a U.S. societal problem. The U.S. homicide rate for males 15-24 years of age is unmatched among other nations such as Scotland, Canada, England, and Japan (7, 8). There is a disproportionate affect on young adults in the U.S., with homicide as the second leading cause of death among youth 15-24 years of age. Unintentional injuries represent the leading cause of death in this age group (9). Although homicide occurs among all racial and ethnic groups living in the United States, it disproportionately affects African-American youth.

Because of the manner in which the data are collected, (by "race" instead of by "ethnicity"), there is little available information regarding ethnic variations in homicides. However, previous research has indicated that Hispanic males are also at high risk for homicide (7, 10, 11, 12).

Homicide is the leading cause of death for both young African American males and females 15-34 years and the problem is worsening. Homicide rates since the mid eighties have risen dramatically for young African-Americans, while the rates for whites have essentially remained stable (11). In 1987, homicides accounted for 42 percent of all deaths to African-American males 15-24 years old. By 1992 this figure

TABLE 4
The Various Forms of Violence

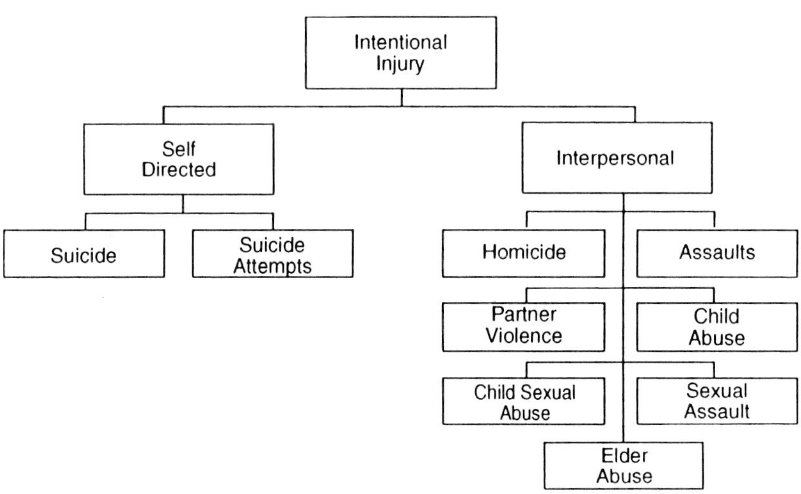

had risen to 57 percent. For young African-American females in 1987, 26 percent of all deaths were attributable to a homicide; by 1992 this figure had risen to 30 percent.

Previous epidemiological research has identified "suggested factors" associated with homicides (7, 10, 11, 14). Homicide rates serve as the most "convenient" but limited indicator of the level of violence. The data on homicides are more accessible than data on nonfatal assaults. Most of the available data are derived from criminal justice reports.

Criminal justice data provide some valuable information regarding the demographic characteristics of offenders, the circumstances of the death and the specific type of weapon used. However, social scientists warn that homicide statistics should be used with caution due to variability in the quality and reliability of data collection (13).

What is known about most homicides? Consider the following:

- Most homicides are committed by males on males. This represent more than 50 percent of the homicides that occur in the United States.
- Most homicides are intraracial, that is they occur between people of the same race/ethnicity (i.e. African-Americans killed African-Americans, whites killed whites and Hispanics killed Hispanics). Less than 10 percent of the homicides that occur in the U.S. are interracial (9).
- The majority of homicides occur between family members or acquaintances (Table 5). If the acquaintance and the family categories are added together, more than 50 percent of homicide victims knew their offenders. This relationship between the victim and the offender does not differ by race.
- A large proportion of homicides occur as the result of conflict or arguments. A study that analyzed U.S. homicides from 1979-1988 found one third or 35% were due to a conflict (11).
- Firearms are the leading method used. The recent increase in homicide among young African-American males is in large part attributable to firearms. When weapon use is considered by race, no obvious differences exist.
- Homicide rates are highest in the western and southeastern parts of the U.S. (11, 13, 15). Although some northeastern urban centers have higher homicide rates than some states.
- Studies have shown that socioeconomic status or social class, plays a role in determining risk of death by homicide (13, 16).

It is important to note that suicide, or self-directed violence, is an integral part of violence in society. Suicide rates have increased threefold for white and black males since the 1950's. As in homicide, firearms are also the weapons of choice in suicide for both males and females.

The Need for Data

Violence, a complex psychosocial problem, is having an enormous impact on the public health. The public health definition of violence as "the use of physical force" however is limited. Analyzing criminal justice data highlights only the physical outcomes, or the "injuries" sustained, as a result of violent acts. Clearly, the effects of violence go beyond those of physical injuries when defined broadly. Violence also has profound negative psychosocial effects. Research has highlighted the adverse impact of merely viewing violence (17, 18, 19, 20, 21). The use of a broad definition of violence allows for a more complete physical, psychosocial and political view of the total impact of this problem.

Data about homicides are readily available, but, nonfatal assaults and suicide attempts can not be ignored as we explore the universe of the violence problem. Homicide and suicide are merely fatal outcomes of violence, and, as such represent only the tip of a very large iceberg of intentional injuries.

Above and beyond the number who die, many more persons are hospitalized, bedridden or suffer some degree of restricted activity or emotional scarring as a result of violence.

TABLE 5

The Context in Which Most Homicides Occur

- Among Persons Who Know Each Other

- As the Result of Firearms

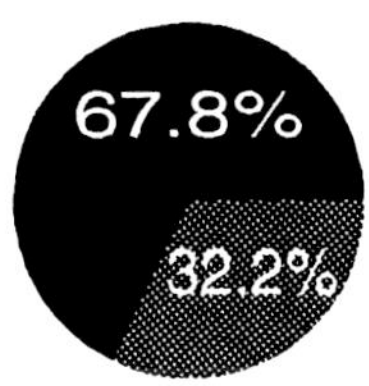

- Among Minority Males

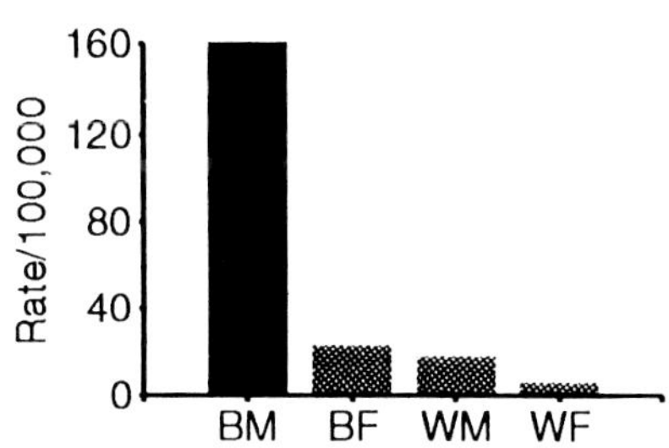

CDC

The 1993 percentage of homicides that occur as a result of firearms is higher than 60%.

- Media (print/TV/radio) may feature positive teen role models as "ambassadors" of violence prevention;
- Hospitals, emergency rooms, and trauma departments can report violent assaults to local health departments, as they would any "reportable" communicable disease. This would advance the purposes of data collection/risk factor identification, etc;
- The medical examiner's office may provide grief assistance counseling to families of victims and elicit their involvement in the coalition;
- Business leaders/Service organizations (Kwanas, fraternities, etc.) may initiate/expand mentoring programs for youth.

5. Experts in the field of public health, as well as academic-based clinical researchers, can help develop rigorous and innovative evaluation efforts for the initiative. Through the development of these new methodologies, research and evaluation as it relates to violence prevention can be enhanced.

OBSTACLES

A variety of obstacles exist that interfere with the ability to institutionalize violence prevention activities at the community level. The following problem areas must be addressed:

1. *Acceptance of violence as "nonpreventable", thereby relegating solutions to the criminal justice arena.* The community must relinquish the notion of the inevitability of interpersonal violence. Society's traditional approach to the problem has been through a criminal justice orientation. No longer can solutions be limited to building more jails and detention centers.
2. *Negative Perceptions of the Public Health and Medical Community.* There is ample distrust of the public health system by communities of color. Some of this stems, for example, from the well known U.S. Public Health Service-conducted 35-year "Tuskegee' syphilis study in southern blacks. The AIDS crisis, needle exchange programs, and family planning controversies (e.g. Norplant use in low income women) have all been fueled by misperceptions and misunderstanding of the role of government in crafting solutions and research efforts by academic institutions. Public health and medical professionals should anticipate a healthy skepticism from target communities and their leadership about a "public health approach" to violence prevention, particularly on issues of research and evaluation.
3. *Fragmentation of Human Service Delivery Systems.* Health and Human Service delivery systems are categorical, program oriented, and not family-centered. Since violence prevention efforts require a comprehensive approach, the need is critical for health, human service, education, law enforcement, recreation and other agencies to communicate and collaborate. Moreover, there is a need to establish leadership roles for extra-governmental institutions such as the church, business community and the foundation/philanthropic communities.
4. *Resource Starvation.* State and local governments throughout this nation are struggling to maintain fiscal solvency, with budgets for health, human services, education

and recreation being trimmed at the local level. Resources for new (as well as existing) programs are being tightened, often leaving inner city and rural communities with diminished health and human service infrastructure and delivery capacity.

5. *Monolithic View of Violence Prevention.* Interpersonal violence is a multi-faceted problem. Not only are there a variety of forms of interpersonal violence (random, gang-related, domestic, etc.), but, in a multi-ethnic and multicultural society, approaches must be tailored to the demographics of the community. What may be crafted as an approach for African-American youth may not necessarily translate into a workable solution for Latino, Asian-American, or Native American youth. Thus, the inclusion of "grassroots" community leadership is essential to generate effective violence prevention strategies.

A COMMUNITY COALITION AS A VEHICLE FOR A VIOLENCE PREVENTION PROGRAM

The Philadelphia experience reveals that the aforementioned challenges are most effectively met by a community-wide coalition of appropriate and concerned leadership. The role of the public health community and medical leadership in convening this coalition is defined in the following paragraphs.

Step One: Involving Political Leadership, and Identifying Community Leadership

The interest, involvement and support of local political leadership must be obtained. The top elected official for the jurisdiction must establish a visible leadership role in preventing violence involving youth. Such individuals include mayors, members of county boards of supervisors, city councilpersons, state senators and representatives and other elected officials. This first step is essential to the success of coalition-building, for the following three reasons: 1) Elected officials must enhance the visibility of interpersonal violence as a major, but preventable, societal issue. Violence prevention is a ready-made campaign issue. 2) Elected officials have access to a wide-ranging group of community-based constituencies, and their leaders, who can be accessed through the "sponsorship" of such officials. There is no "yellow pages" directory of community leadership, but that leadership is well known to officials who direct election campaigns every two to four years. 3) Health and Human Service policy initiatives have been reduced to budget issues. A budget is a political document—no more, no less—that reflects the will of an electorate and its political leadership. In order for violence prevention activities to be realized, they must emerge as budget items at the federal, state and local levels.

Step Two: Building the Coalition

After consultation with, and the elicitation of support from political leadership, elected officials (and/or their aides) should be polled as to suggestions for coalition involvement. The goal of the coalition should be clearly defined: to craft a community-wide strategy to reduce interpersonal violence. The size of the coalition is not nearly as important as its representation. The coalition at a minimum should include both public and private sector leadership, as follows:

PUBLIC SECTOR

- Health Department
- Human/Social Services Department
- Local School District(s)
- Recreation Deparment
- Police Department and Criminal Justice Agencies
- Juvenile Justice Agency

PRIVATE SECTOR

- Clergy/Churches/Synagogues
- Chamber of Commerce/Business Community
- Community-Based Civic and Neighborhood Organizations
- Foundation/Philanthropic organizations
- Health Professional organizations
- Youth Employment Agency or Jobs Programs Youth/Recreation Agencies
- Professional Sports Teams
- Universities/Professional Schools/Schools of Public Health
- Media Representatives
- Any Organizations Committed to Mentoring/ Role Model Activities

The previous list of agencies and organizations, at first glance, will appear foreboding. But each organization has a vital role to play, and this list is by no means exhaustive. In order to shape violence prevention as a community-wide problem with community-wide solutions, each organization must recognize the critical roles of other organizations, as well as its own role. Coalition conveners and leadership should be well aware of the resource and fiscal constraints faced by many of these organizations, and the need (early on) to recommend "low cost" or "no cost" activities.

The coalition should meet regularly to commit to a process for establishing work plans, deadlines, committees and subcommittees, and strengthening communication and collaboration. Early activities should be simple, definable, and low cost. These may include radio appearances by coalition leadership, editorial writing in local newspapers, and well publicized youth/clergy/health conferences and "retreats" committed to violence prevention. The Coalition will build momentum from early, simple successes.

It is recommended that work groups and committees be comprised of concerned citizens from vastly differing backgrounds. The Philadelphia experience indicates that there is much to be learned from the interaction of a psychiatrist, a youth counselor, and a Baptist minister during strategic development.

Teen and youth involvement is critical to the success of the coalition. Recruitment is recommended of former and/or current gang leaders, youth offenders, and youth civic leadership. A youth "violence prevention" retreat or conference is suggested, with recommendations brought back to the general coalition membership.

Step Three: Developing the Plan

The development of a community wide strategy should be documented in the form of a written plan which can be presented to the senior elected official(s) of the country or municipality. The plan may be complex, and might consist of dozens of activities from a multitude of agencies and organizations. Many plan activities and programs will be multidisciplinary and collaborative, and some will be limited to the efforts of a single group. For this reason, an "action team" or "work group" format is suggested.

The action teams consist of multi-disciplinary smaller groups of concerned citizens—perhaps five to ten individuals—that can craft defined segments of the comprehensive plan. In the Philadelphia model, these "teams" were divided as follows:

1. ACADEMIC COMMUNITY
2. ALTERNATIVES/LEGISLATION
3. BUSINESS COMMUNITY
4. EARLY INTERVENTION
5. INCARCERATED YOUTH
6. INTERFAITH
7. LONG-TERM SURVIVORS
8. MEDIA/ARTS
9. NEIGHBORHOODS
10. SCHOOLS
11. TEENS
12. VICTIMS/WITNESSES/ PERPERTRATORS

Educational, socioeconomic, and ethnic representation should be broad among the team members. Action Teams should have a chair and a co-chair. The chair/co-chairs should periodically report to the coalition on the progress of the action plan segment until its completion.

Action Teams should have a common deadline for completion of their workplans. Upon completion, work plans are submitted to coalition leadership for review and consolidation.

Development of the plan may take 12 months or longer. It is assumed that the plan is always in "draft" form, since the need for constant and continous community input is critical.

IMPLEMENTING THE PLAN

The plan, with its many elements, should be shared with local political leadership. Financing of plan segments must be addressed by coalition leadership through the identification of existing sources of public and private support, as well as new sources at the federal, state and local level. Financing strategies must be shared with elected officials to gain insight on opportunities for funding, and to win timely support.

A press event should be held so that the coalition can unveil programmatic details and activities to the community-at-large. Broad-based media coverage is critical, as is the involvment of top elected officials. The temptation to portray violence prevention as a short-term fix must be avoided. The reduction of interpersonal violence resembles a consistent marathon effort rather than a sprint.

ROLE OF PUBLIC HEALTH AND THE PHYSICIAN

It is critical that public health professionals, the physician community and academic medicine play a central role in convening a violence prevention effort, for three reasons: 1) physician involvement crystallizes violence as a public health, and not just a criminal justice problem; 2) a public health strategy is inherently prevention focused, collecting and using morbidity/mortality data to define at-risk communities, and to develop and target outreach and educational activities; 3) a public health approach should assume a rigorous and well defined evaluation; and 4) clinical researchers skilled at obtaining public and private sector grant funding can assist the coalition in competing successfully for resources.

The following are examples of medical roles in violence prevention in conjunction with coalition activities:

A. Physicians

Physicians need to familiarize themselves with risk assessment for victims, perpetrators, and witnesses of violence. These same physicians serve as a crucial link in the referral of these patients to fundamental multi-disciplinary support services (27).

Physicians must also keep abreast of relevant statistics so that they can help to correct the misconceptions and myths that are associated with misunderstanding violent behavior (e.g. The myth that homicides are perpetuated by violent strangers).

Physicians need training in the recognition of health related problems that may arise secondary to violence (28).

B. Hospitals/Emergency Rooms/Outpatient Clinics

These entities can begin to institute surveillance systems that will collect accurate data on nonfatal assaults so as to better identify risk factors, develop interventions and evaluate their impact.

C. Medical Schools

Academic medical centers must call for multidisciplinary curriculum development to enhance physician and medical student knowledge and skills related to the recognition and screening of patients who have violence related health problems. They can also assist in the development of protocols for counseling of victims, perpetrators, and witnesses of violence.

D. Schools of Public Health

Faculty, students, and fellows can assist the coalition in developing evaluation and assessment tools.

CONCLUSION

Interpersonal violence is a U.S. societal problem that must be addressed from all levels of the society. It is largely "preventable", and must be deemed as "unacceptable" by the community. Just as M.A.D.D. catalyzed a community-based response which influenced public policy, the public health and medical communities have a central role to play in convening a community-wide response. That response must be comprehensive, multidisciplinary and community-based.

Violence prevention is a longterm effort, of which at least one to two years may be required for community-wide planning. Involvement of grassroots community leadership and affected youth is critical to a successful planning effort. The political leadership and the media should be well invested at the front end of the initiative in order to maximize community investment.

REFERENCES

1. Sciences, National Research Council, and the Institute of Medicine. 1985. *Injury in America: A Continuing Public Health Problem.* The National Academy Press. Washington, DC. 1-24.
2. Public Health Service. 1991. Healthy People 2000: National Health Promotion and Disease Prevention Objectives. *DHHS.* (PHS 91-50212). Washington, DC: U.S. Department of Health an Human Services.
3. Rice, D.P., Mackenzie, E.J. and Associates. 1989. *Cost of Injury in the United States: A Report to Congress.* San Francisco, CA: Institute for Health and Aging, University of California, and Injury Prevention Center, The Johns Hopkins University. 1-35.
4. U.S. Department of Health and Human Services. August 1985, Report of the Secretary's Task Force on Black and Minority Health. Washington, DC.
5. Gulaid, J., Onwuachi-Saunders, E.C., Sacks, J. and D. Roberts. 1988. Differences in Death Rates Due to Injury Among Black and Whites, 1984, MMWR. (NOSS-3). 25-31.
6. Onwauchi-Saunders, E.C. and D. Hawkins. Black & White Differences in Injury: Race or Social Class. Ann Epidemiol 1993; 3:150-153.
7. Rosenberg, M.L. and J.A. Mercy. 1991. Assaultive Violence. In: M.L. Rosenberg and M.A. Fenley (Ed.) *Violence in America: A Public Health Approach.* Oxford University Press. NY. 2-19.
8. Fingerhut, L.A. and J.C. Kleiman. 1990. International and Interstate Comparisons of Homicide Among Young Males. JAMA. 263:3292-3295.
9. Centers for Disease Control. 1986. Homicide Surveillance: High Risk Racial and Ethnic Groups-Blacks and Hispanics, 1970-1983. Atlanta, GA: Centers for Disease Control, 1986.
10. O'Carroll, P.W. and J.A. Mercy. 1986. Patterns and Recent Trends in Black Homicide. In: D.F. Hawkins (Ed.) *Homicide Among Black Americans.* Lanham, Maryland: University Press of America. 1986. 29-42.

This paper considers professionalism in medicine in the context of health care reform. After reviewing some of the writings of physicians, ethicists, and sociologists, a working definition of medical professionalism and the need for physicians to reaffirm its elements will be discussed. I then will describe some of the barriers to and opportunities for medical professionalism under health care reform.

Proposed means for preserving professionalism in medicine include creating a health care system that minimizes physicians financial conflicts of interest and maximizes their accountability and responsibility to patients and society as well as upholds their commitment to excellence in work and clinical judgment. Physicians should set high standards of professional conduct and maintain them through various strategies, including medical licensure, quality initiatives, and peer and patient assessments. Additionally, reform of the curricula of physicians-in-training is necessary to educate them in the delivery of cost effective services, and the values, attitudes, and behaviors fundamental to medical professionalism.

DEFINITION

Many lawyers, physicians, and academicians have written on the characteristics of a profession. Justice Louis Brandeis believed a profession had three features: the preliminary training was intellectual, involving knowledge, as distinguished from skill; work that was pursued primarily for others and not for one's self; and the amount of financial return was not the only measure of success (1). Building on the writings of Abraham Flexner, a well-known leader in medical education in the early twentieth century, Richard Foa, a physician, summarized professionalism in medicine as a set of distinct activities. First, it was intellectual and embodied virtues (e.g., honesty, courage, justice, creativity) essential to the achievement of excellence. Second, it was practical and characterized by sets of skills and values that were further developed by life-long learning and that were taught to novices. Third, the activity was autonomous, complex, and absorbing, yet lead to the formation of collegial organizations. Lastly, it received the acknowledgement of society because it furthered goals set for it by society (2, 3).

Talcott Parsons, a medical sociologist writing in the 1950's, argued that medicine was and deserved to be a profession because generally physicians responded to a high moral calling, adhered to a code of ethics, assumed a fiduciary role with patients, and mastered a technical body of knowledge. Appropriately, society granted medicine professional status and accordingly, autonomy over work and the right of self-regulation (4). Elliot Friedson, a medical sociologist writing several decades later, argued instead that medicine was a profession because it had been successful in convincing the elite segment of society that there was value in its work. Arguments used to justify medicine's privileged position included 1) that physicians had to master an unusual degree of skill and knowledge; 2) that they could be trusted to work conscientiously without supervision; and 3) that they would undertake the proper regulatory action to maintain competence. The elites then secured medicine as a profession through political and economic influence. As such, medicine was granted autonomy, including the exclusive right to determine who could legitimately do its work and how the work should be done (5).

More recently, Larry Churchill, an ethicist, argued that maintaining medicine as a profession in modern times was dependent upon physicians' reaffirmation of a distinctive medical ethic. This ethic would be composed of moral elements and high standards of behavior. The benefit of reestablishing such a moral tradition included developing among physicians a sense of critical distance—a perspective from which to view change. Failure to do so would permit physicians to continue to succumb to whatever economic forces were most powerful. Second, a distinctive medical ethic would allow both physicians and patients to know with greater clarity why the practice of medicine had larger meaning in society. Third, a distinctive medical ethic would help maintain trust in the fiduciary role of physicians in serving the interest of patients (6).

I define medical professionalism as a set of values, attitudes, and behaviors that result in serving the interests of patients and society before one's own. Values essential to professionalism are honesty and integrity. The professional physician has an attitude of humility, and also accountability to colleagues, patients, and society. Professional behaviors include a non-judgmental and respectful approach to patients, the pursuit of specialized knowledge and skills with a commitment to excellence and life-long competency, and a collegial and cooperative approach to working with members of the health care team in the delivery of patient care. The professional physician refrains from financial conflicts of interests, meets standards set by the profession, and provides community and public leadership. In exchange for putting the interests of the patient and society first, physicians are afforded trust, respect, and the confidentiality of patients (7).

BARRIERS TO MEDICAL PROFESSIONALISM

The lack of explicit professional standards that are taught and reinforced throughout medical education, and a strong medical licensure system able to enforce these standards among practicing physicians, has contributed to a loss of professionalism in medicine. Equally important, physician reimbursement and financial incentives within the health care system often has facilitated physician self-interest (8, 9). Physicians now are accused of making too much money, of publishing fraudulent research, and of advertising a false level of expertise (10-13). There is less public acceptance of physicians' refusal to treat patients with AIDS or the elderly and uninsured, particularly when many of the uninsured and underinsured are middle class citizens employed in full-time occupations (14, 15). Unwillingness to tolerate abuses of power has resulted in increasing furor regarding sexual harassment of patients by physicians (16, 17).

Other players in the health care system are also under attack for greed, fraud and breaches of the public's trust. Americans want to prohibit insurance companies from discriminating against patients with serious illnesses or pre-existing medical conditions, and from raising premiums beyond the ability of most citizens to pay.

Pharmaceutical companies face criticism from charging more for drugs in this country than they do abroad, and for advertising and marketing schemes directed at physicians and other health care professionals. Health maintenance organizations that serve predominantly healthy Americans as a means of increasing income and minimizing costs also are seen as forfeiting a responsibility to the larger community and, may not survive under health care reform.

The major barriers to medical professionalism under health care reform are the economic incentives designed to increase competition under a system of cost containment within a society that continues to expect the availability of advanced technology and therapeutics without regard to cost and social benefit. Competition will intensify in the short run between physicians for income, and in the long-run between managed care plans in efforts to drive down costs. Fee-for-service practice will fade away as a dominant model of health care delivery and be replaced by managed competition with health systems, with groupings of health insurance companies, hospitals, managed care organizations, and physicians (18). Physicians will enter group practices and health maintenance organizations, and increasingly become salaried employees. Within limits, patients will be able to choose physicians and physicians will be able to participate in several insurance plans.

While competition may improve efficiency, it may lead to a loss of professionalism through undermining collegiality among physicians, increasing financial incentives to limit medical services, and weakening the doctor-patient relationship (19). Under managed competition specifically, the doctor-patient relationship could suffer. Development of trust and commitment between patients and doctors requires time and continuity of medical care which could be difficult, if not impossible, to establish if patients and providers change regularly. Patients may be forced to change physicians because their employers switch managed care plans, or because their insurance company changes physician provider groups. Physicians may change to another managed care plan which does not insure patients previously cared for. My concern is that physicians' fiduciary role for patients, or their sense of responsibility to always work for the patient's benefit, will be compromised unless attention is directed at preserving the doctor-patient relationship and the attitudes of accountability that are built into it.

Another potential barrier to medical professionalism under health care reform is cost containment. To preserve medicine as a profession, physicians must meet both the demands of patients and the needs of society. On the one hand, serving the patient's interests by performing more and more services runs counter to societal efforts to control health care costs. On the other hand, physicians must learn how to deliver high quality medical services more conservatively and cost effectively. In truth, physicians are not trained to make medical decisions based on economic factors. Ultimately, the problem of delivering medical services within a system of constrained resources will need to be recast into medical terms with the development of standards of medical care that incorporate economic reality into medical judgment. In other words, therapies that are determined to be medically appropriate and included in a comprehensive benefits package should be based on science, tested in a clinical context, and evaluated in terms of cost effectiveness (20). To preserve medical professionalism, physicians will need to feel that they are using their best medical judgment in recommending a treatment strategy, that treatment already having been evaluated independently in terms of its cost effectiveness.

Lessons from England regarding the rationing of health care services reveal several patterns of responses among physicians that are instructive as this country moves forward with health care reform (21, 22). Researchers noted that British physicians recognized they worked within a system of limited resources. As a means of rationalizing the limitation, if a given therapy was not available, physicians would communicate to patients that the treatment would not be of medical benefit, would be painful, or would lead to a poorer quality of life, even if prolonged. Recently as health care services in Britain have become more limited, physicians have begun to speak out concerning their inability to serve the patient's medical needs within a system that traditionally has guaranteed access to effective treatment (personal communication, Duncan Forrest, MD). Second, to preserve professionalism, British physicians demanded freedom in clinical judgment. The tenacity with which physicians in England, Canada, and America demand clinical autonomy, I believe, reflects the professional's need for control over his or her work. For physicians, this is providing health care to patients on an individual basis. Third, the general practitioner in England, because of a close and long-standing relationship with a patient and family, was often spared attack when he or she did not offer a life-prolonging therapy, in part because of the respect that patients had for physicians. In the latter case, societal values and expectations for end-of-life support and trust in the doctor-patient relationship were critical in allowing physicians both to serve the interests of the patient and society without undermining a sense of professionalism.

Conflicts of interest are emerging as another important barrier to medical professionalism because of the danger that the interests of society and patients may come after financial self-interest (23). Researchers consistently demonstrate that contracts which generate income change physician behavior. Physician-owned facilities have higher utilization rates. Physicians prescribe medications more often after attending a pharmaceutical sponsored education conference or social event. Profit-sharing arrangements consistently alter physician referral patterns (8). Moving the health care system toward a model of market competition may promote more greed and self-interest—those behavior among physicians and provider institutions that the public characterizes as most unprofessional.

ACHIEVING MEDICAL PROFESSIONALISM UNDER HEALTH CARE REFORM

To serve the needs of patients and society, a fundamental principle of medical professionalism, we must ensure that all Americans have universal access to comprehensive, high quality medical care. The challenge is to do so in ways that strengthen the economy, improve the security and stability of individuals and families, enhance the quality of services, and foster professionalism in all aspects of health care delivery. Physicians have a critical role to serve as public leaders

Based on experience teaching and lecturing on medical professionalism to medical students, residents, and faculty, I offer some suggestions. The case examples should reflect the daily practice of medicine either on the wards, in the clinics, or in the doctor's office to make the ideas personally and professionally relevant. Didactic sessions combined with small group discussions and use of critical incidents along with structured readings help to provide a theoretical context and an enriched understanding of the barriers to and importance of medical professionalism. Lastly, a curriculum also should be an experiential one which includes community service initiatives (7).

Another means to strengthen professionalism in medicine is the establishment of high standards of conduct by the profession itself, and empowerment of state medical licensing agencies to hold physicians accountable to such standards. The Federation of State Medical Boards has developed a "model medical practice act" for use in drafting state laws on physician licensure. The model act specifies unprofessional conduct as fraud in billing, chart documentation and reporting of personal identification and professional qualifications; mental impairment and incompetence in the practice of medicine; sexual misconduct or other forms of exploitation of patients; substance abuse; violation of patient confidentiality; and representing to patients that an incurable condition is curable (33). While several states have incorporated language similar to the model act, (34) generally physicians only lose their licenses for serious cases of substance abuse and billing fraud. Self-regulation by the profession for less offensive acts is not the rule.

A final strategy to maintain professional values and behaviors is to minimize physicians' financial conflicts of interest (8, 9, 23). Physicians, when making clinical decisions should not be tempted by financial incentives that increase income either by using more or limiting services to patients. Fee splitting and kick-backs should be eliminated and physician ownership in medical facilities reduced. Reliance on physicians alone has not solved problems of conflict of interest. Thus, regulation, either through incorporation of conflict of interest guidelines into state medical licensure statutes or passage of federal legislation, may be necessary (8).

I foresee that the greatest challenge to medical professionalism under health care reform is preserving a commitment to excellence and regard for the patient as a person. As physicians become salaried employees, every effort must be expended to preserve the highest standards of a profession and at the same time prepare physicians to practice in a reformed health care environment. To preserve medicine as a profession, physicians will need to retain clinical autonomy and the right to use their best medical judgment in the care of patients without micro-management by external reviewers. Cost containment does not imply mediocrity, and yet the American public has become accustomed to very expensive highly specialized health care with state of the art medical technology and therapeutics. A health care system that pays more attention to preventive medicine and public health as well as primary care will look profoundly different than what we are accustomed to now. So how do we preserve a commitment by physicians to serve the patients's needs? How do we ensure that physicians will continue to strive for superior clinical competency? How do we foster among physicians and other health care professionals an attitude of collegiality and cooperation in the care of patients? How do we guarantee that physicians will refrain from exploitation of patients and maintain their honesty and integrity? These are not easy questions, but failure to address them forthrightly and strive to preserve medical professionalism in the context of health care reform will only create more problems in the future because ultimately patients want a competent compassionate physician whom they can trust to act in their best interest.

SUMMARY

Medical professionalism is a set of values, attitudes, and behaviors that result in serving the interests of patients and society before one's own. Values essential to professionalism are honesty and integrity. The professional physician has an attitude of humility, and also accountability to colleagues, patients, and society. Professional behaviors include a non-judgmental and respectful approach to patients, the pursuit of specialized knowledge and skills with a commitment to excellence and life-long competency, and a collegial and cooperative approach to working with members of the health care team in the delivery of patient care. The professional physician refrains from financial conflicts of interest, meets standards set by the profession, and provides community and public leadership. In exchange for putting the interests of the patient and public first, physicians are afforded trust, respect, and confidentiality of patients.

Under health care reform, patients and physicians face more challenges preserving medicine as a profession. The greatest threat will come with the economic incentives designed to increase competition under a system of cost containment within a society that continues to expect the availability of advanced technology and therapeutics without regard to cost. To maintain an old professional value, that of putting the patient first, within a system of constrained resources will require a shift in attitude, a change in the paradigm of defining "best" from all that is possible for the individual, to that which is medically appropriate and cost effective and of benefit to society at large.

Health care reform also offers the opportunity to guarantee universal access to high quality, cost effective, and comprehensive health care, and in doing so, serve the needs of patients and society. Medical professionalism may be further enhanced through increasing accountability of the system to the public for overall costs, of the academic medical establishment for educating adequate numbers of generalist physicians, and of physicians themselves for maintaining competency and strengthening the doctor-patient relationship. Physician education at all levels should incorporate curricula on medical professionalism as well as strategies designed to enhance quality patient care. To reinforce professional values, attitudes, and behaviors, medical students, residents, faculty, and physicans could be evalted on their professional conduct throughout the continuum of training and practice of medicine.

Lastly, to preserve medicine as a profession, reform of the health care system must diminish physicians' conflicts of interest and at the same time retain physicians' clinical autonomy, their ability to use their clinical judgment in the patient's best interest, and their rights of self-regulation. Medicine as a trade will benefit no one. Affirmation by physicians of a high professional calling and a commitment to serve the collective good of society is neccessary. Similarly, the public must decide that maintaining medicine as a profession rather than as an occupation represents the larger social benefit.

ACKNOWLEDGEMENTS

I thank I. Kathryn Hill, MEd, for information on the Federation of State Medical Boards modern practice act, and the Robert Wood Johnson Foundation - Veterans Affairs for support as a Clinical Scholar. Copies of "Medical Professionalism: Reaffirming a Healing Art: A Learning and Teaching Guide for Physicians-in-Training", can be obtained by writing to P. Preston Reynolds, M.D., Ph.D.

REFERENCES

1. Brandeis, Louis D. 1933. *Business—a Profession.* Boston: Hole, Cushman, and Flint.
2. Foa, Richard D. 1986. Are Physicians Professionals? *Pharos.* Summer: 21-3.
3. Flexner, Abraham. 1915. Is Social Work a Profession? In: *Proceedings of the National Conference of Charities and Corrections: 42nd Annual Meeting,* Baltimore, May 12-19.
4. Parsons, Talcott. 1951. *The Social System.* Glencoe, IL: Free Press.
5. Friedson, Elliot. 1988. *Profession of Medicine.* Chicago: University of Chicago Press.
6. Churchill, Larry R. 1989. Reviving a Distinctive Medical Ethic. *Hastings Center Report.* May/June:28-34.
7. Reynolds, P. Preston. 1994. Reaffirming Professionalism through the Education Community. *Ann. Intern. Med.* 120:609-14.
8. Rodwin, Marc C. 1993. *Medicine, Money and Morals: Physicians' Conflicts of Interest.* New York: Oxford University Press.
9. Relman, Arnold S. and Uwe Reinhardt. 1986. An Exchange on For-Profit Health Care. *Health Affairs.* 5:5-31.
10. Johnson, Timothy G. Restoring Trust Between Patient and Doctor. *N. Engl. J. Med.* 22:195-7.
11. Petersdorf, Robert G. 1986. The Pathogenesis of Fraud in Medical Science. *Ann. Intern. Med.* 104:252-4.
12. Friedman, Paul J. 1993. Integrity in Biomedical Research. *Acad. Med.* 68: Supplement.
13. Reade, Julia M. and Richard M. Ratzan. 1987. Yellow Advertising: Advertising by Physicians in the Yellow Pages. *N. Engl. J. Med.* 316:1315-8.
14. Gerbert, Barbara, Maguire, Bryan, Bleecker, Thomas, Coates, Thomas and Stephan McPhee. 1991. Primary Care Physicians and AIDS: Attitudinal and Structural Barriers to Care. *JAMA.* 266:2837-42.

15. Miles, Steven H. 1992. What Are We Teaching About Indigent Patients? *JAMA*. 268:2561-2.
16. Gartrell, Nanette K., Milliken, Nancy, Goodson, William, Theimann, Sue and Bernard Lo. 1992. Physician-Patient Sexual Contact: Prevalence and Problems. *West. J. Med.* 157:139-43.
17. Wolinsky, Howard. 1991. Public, Medicine Showing Growing Concern Over Doctor-Patient Sexual Relationships. *Amer Coll Phys Observer.* December: 1-4.
18. Emanuel, Ezekiel J. and Allan S. Brett. 1993. Managed Competition and the Patient-Physician Relationship. *N. Engl. J. Med.* 329:879-82.
19. Spivey, Bruce E. 1990. Professionalism, Specialization, and Competition. *Amer. J. Ophth.* 110:688-95.
20. Weiner, Janet. 1994. Towards a Uniform Health Benefit Package. In: Health Care Reform: A Human Rights Approach. Edit. Audrey R. Chapman. Washington, DC. Georgetown University Press:197-210.
21. Schwartz, William B. and Henry J. Aaron. 1984. Rationing Hospital Care: Lessons From Britain. *N. Engl. J. Med.* 310:52-6.
22. Grumbach, Kevin and John Fry. 1993. Managing Primary Care in the United States and in the United Kingdom. *N. Engl. J. Med.* 328:940-45.
23. Thompson, Dennis F. 1993. Understanding Financial Conflicts of Interest. *N. Engl. J. Med.* 329:573-6.
24. Mirvis, David M. 1993. Physicians' Autonomy—The Relationship Between Public and Professional Expectations. *N. Engl. J. Med.* 328:1346-9.
25. Schroeder, Steven A., Jane S. Zones, Johnathan A. Showstack. 1989. Academic Medicine as a Public Trust. *JAMA*. 262:803-12.
26. Schroeder, Steven A. and Lewis G. Sandy. 1993. Specialty Distribution of U.S. Physicians—The Invisible Driver of Health Care Costs. *N. Engl. J. Med.* 328:961-2.
27. Berwick, Donald M., Godfrey, A.B. and J. Roessner. 1990. *Curing Health Care: New Strategies for Quality Improvement.* San Francisco, CA: Jossey-Bass.
28. Delbanco, Thomas L. 1992. Enriching the Doctor-Patient Relationships by Inviting the Patient's Perspective. *Ann. Intern. Med.* 116:414-17.
29. Ramsey, Paul G., Wenrich, Marjorie D., Carline, Jan D., Inui, Thomas S., Larson, Eric B. and James P. LoGerfo. 1993. Use of Peer Ratings to Evaluate Physician Performance. *JAMA*. 269:1655-60.
30. Freymann, John G. 1989. The Public's Health Paradigm Is Shifting: Medicine Must Swing With It. *J. Genl. Intern. Med.* 4:313-9.
31. The American Academy of Physician and Patient was established in 1993 and is dedicated to enhancing the doctor-patient relationship.
32. Will Health-Care Reform Affect Physician-Patient Relationships? 1993. *Intern. Med. World. Rep.* June 15:4.
33. Federation of State Medical Board of the United States. 1991. *A Guide to the Essentials of A Modern Medical Practice Act.* Sixth Edition: 12-3.
34. States which have similar language include Delaware, Idaho, Louisiana, Minnesota, New York, and South Dakota.

Medicine and Health Care Into the Twenty-First Century. Edited by S.K. Majumdar, L.M. Rosenfeld, D.B. Nash and A.M. Audet.

Chapter Twenty-Nine

HUMAN RIGHTS: Health Concerns for the Twenty-First Century

VINCENT IACOPINO, M.D., Ph.D.
Physicians for Human Rights, Western Regional Director
Survivors International of Northern California, Medical Director
312 Sutter St., Suite 606
San Francisco, CA 94108

INTRODUCTION

Throughout our history, society has charged healers with the duty of understanding and alleviating causes of human suffering. As we enter the twenty-first century, the nature and extent of human suffering has compelled health providers to redefine their understandings of health and the scope of their professional interests and responsibilities. In the past century, we have witnessed ongoing epidemics of armed conflicts and human rights abuses, epidemics which have devastated and continue to devastate the health and well-being of humanity. Armed conflicts have claimed the lives of more than ninety million people in the twentieth century, and increasingly, civilians have become the victims of war (1). Eighty-five percent of war related deaths in the nineteen eighties were civilians (1). Today, nearly fifty countries are engaged in armed conflict (2). Torture, forced disappearance and political killings are systematically practiced in more than ninety countries (3); rape is used as an instrument of war (4, 5), and more than ninety million landmines threaten the lives and limbs of ordinary people (6). Over the past twenty years, armed conflicts and human rights violations have created 43 million refugees and displaced persons (7). This represents about one in every 130 inhabitants of the globe. Also, with the advance of technology has come the persistent threat of global destruction by nuclear and chemical weapons. Despite a century of technological progress, social inequities, interpersonal violence and environmental threats continue to plague the health of the world community.

Health professionals are ill-equipped to address suffering caused by armed conflcts and human rights abuses because medical and health concerns in the twentieth century have focused almost excusively on the diagnosis, treatment and prevention of disease. In recent years, health professionals have begun to recognize the importance of the protection and promotion of human rights as necessary preconditions for individual and community health (8, 9, 10). However, nascent human rights concerns among health professionals have been limited to avocational interests, rather than professional ones, and have not yet been integrated into health education, services, research or policy.

As health professionals redefine their interests to include human rights, a number of complex, related issues need to be addressed. How do we define and understand human rights? What is the basis for human rights concerns among health professionals? What is the scope and depth of the issues relevant to health professionals? How can health professionals improve individual and community health by protecting and promoting human rights? This chapter examines the origins of health and human rights concerns and outlines a conceptual basis for human rights concerns among health professionals. It suggests a variety of strategies to integrate human rights concerns into health practice and considers potential barriers to adopting such concerns.

ORIGINS OF HEALTH CONCERNS

Historically, healing has reflected practitioners' understandings of suffering. Healers interpret the experiences of those who suffer and through their knowledge of cause and effect, intervene to alleviate and prevent suffering. The validity of healers' knowledge is rooted in the world view of the communities in which they practice. In Western cultures, healers' knowledge has been based largely on rational and empirical traditions which are manifest in science and technology. Fundamental to empirical and rational modes of thinking is the assumption of a dichotomy between subject and object. Science and technology assert claims of objective knowledge, independent of subjective experience (11). Consequently, science and technology appear to achieve authoritative status over, and freedom from, historically contingent beliefs, values and traditions, as well as the vicissitudes of human emotions, conscious and unconscious. Scientific methods intentionally aim to reduce contextual understandings of everyday life to context-free explanations. Thus, scientists attempt to reduce complex phenomena to objective knowledge by proving the null hypothesis, or that which is not true (12).

These reductionist concepts increasingly have come under attack (13, 14, 15). Contemporary philosophers have argued that human endeavors are inherently based on history and tradition (16), and that all claims to truth rest on interpretation within that context (15). Kuhn pointed out the necessity of interpretation in science during the process of forming questions, taking measures, analyzing results and assessing the meaning of findings (17). He proposed that paradigms of scientific knowledge are historically contingent and shift once new paradigms supplant outdated ways of thinking. Critics of reductionism also have suggested that the concept of objectivity in science and technology masks human interests which attempt to dominate nature (18) and establish social control (11).

In the case of medicine and health care, science has largely reduced the complex phenomenon of suffering to the concern of disease (19, 20, 21). The concept of diseases as objective, knowable entities disconnected from the context of subjective, unknowable experiences has failed to acknowledge individuals' personal suffering (22, 23). More recently, alternative views of sickness, such as the "biopsychosocial model" (24), have attempted to acknowledge the role of individual psychosocial factors unaccounted for by the disease paradigm. Others have used personal accounts of illness experiences to assess individual meanings of illness (25, 26, 27). While trends to focus attention on illness rather than disease brings health professionals closer to addressing personal suffering, it does little to address the social conditions that cause suffering or the personal interests of health professionals that may contribute to one's suffering (28).

By decontextualizing and reducing suffering to pathophysiology, healers have neglected social conditions which affect health and well-being, and thereby have marginalized their own roles in society. In the course of medical encounters, patients present to their doctors a variety of personal troubles that are often rooted in social issues (28); however, these issues generally do not receive critical attention. Instead, medical discourse typically cuts off contextual social issues and redirects the focus of the encounter to technical concerns (29). Consequently, the processing of social issues with technical concerns trivializes and ignores human suffering. By medicalizing suffering, doctors unintentionally maintain dominance in their encounters with patients, encourage conforming social behavior and attitudes and marginalize patients' concerns and social problems (30).

Finally, the seemingly objective and apolitical enterprise of curing diseases has not only neglected issues of personal suffering and their social causes, but has also formally excluded recognition of the vested interests of health professionals. Increasingly health professionals have been criticized for their preoccupation with financial interests and control over practice conditions while neglecting the problems of access, quality assurance, cost effectiveness, technology assessment and professional incompetence and malfeasance. These criticisms are beginning to be addressed under pressure of the present health care crisis. However, as we prepare to cross the threshold of the next century, redefining the course of medicine and health care should reflect insight and leadership and not simply reactionary and idiosyncratic conditions in the midst of crisis. The health care crisis simultaneously presents the opportunity and need for health professionals to re-examine their definitions of health and the scope of their professional responsibilities. Human rights violations are among the most urgent social causes of human suffering for healers to consider given their devastating health consequences. However, addressing the health consequences of human rights violations presumes some understanding of human rights concepts.

ORIGINS OF HUMAN RIGHTS CONCERNS

Contemporary concepts of human rights were not formally articulated until after the Second World War. The notion of individual rights, undiminished by the claim of the divine rights of kings, can be traced to the Magna Carta (1215) and later the English Bill of Rights (1689), the French Declaration of the Rights of Man and the American Declaration of Independence (31, 32). With growing beliefs in natural law and universal order in the seventeenth and eighteenth centuries, John Locke (1632-1704) introduced the idea of inalienable rights of life, liberty and estate, as natural entitlements by reason of being human. An individual had the natural right to follow the dictates of his or her own will. Jean Jacques Rousseau (1712-1778) later distinguished between such natural rights and civil rights. Individuals living within the state forfeited their natural rights in exchange for a set of civil rights, and government had the responsibility of protecting these civil rights. According to Immanuel Kant (1724-1804), the dignity of man, which is intrinsically linked with his irreducible status as a subject, means that he always has to be recognized as an "end in himself" (33). Kant's formulation of the ontological status of the subject is reflected in the Universal Declaration of Human Rights of 1948, which states in its preamble that "recognition of the inherent dignity and of the equal and inalienable rights of all members of the human family is the foundation of freedom, justice and peace in the world."

Although the concept of natural law subsequently played an important role in the abolition of slavery, improving working conditions, education, and movements for universal suffrage and unionism, it was not until the fall of Nazi Germany that the idea of human rights found its contemporary expression (32). During the Nazi reign of terror, state laws authorized arbitrary police search and seizure, imprisonment, torture and execution of Jews and other minorities without public trial. Six million Jews, two-thirds of all European Jews, were systematically exterminated (34). As a result, the United Nations Declaration of Human Rights in 1948, and the numerous covenants and conventions derived from it, recognized beyond the pale of any utilitarian law, regardless of its ideological grounding, that certain actions were unconditionally wrong. Although declarations of international human rights have conceptual roots in the theory of natural rights, the justification of human rights was rhetorical, not philosophical (32); such rights were expressions of moral identity in the context of the Holocaust and the Second World War; they were self-evident and derived from common societal goals of peace and justice and individual goals of human dignity, happiness and fulfillment. In effect, human rights prescribed conditions for physical, psychological and social well-being by attempting to prevent and alleviate suffering.

The principles of the 1948 Universal Declarations were eventually transformed into two legally binding treaties in 1976. The first, the International Covenant on Civil and Political Rights, recognizes the rights of every human being to life, liberty and security of persons from torture and other forms of cruel, inhuman or degrading treatment. It prohibits slavery, guarantees the rights to a fair trial and protects persons against arbitrary arrest or detention. It recognizes freedom of thought, conscience and religion, freedom of opinion and expression, the right of peaceful assembly and of emigration, and freedom of association. The second, the International Covenant on Economic, Social and Cultural Rights, acknowledges the state's responsibility to promote better living conditions for its people. It recognizes everyone's right to work, to fair wages, to social security, to adequate standards of living, health and education and freedom from hunger. It also undertakes to ensure the right of everyone to form and join trade unions.

Since the end of the Second World War, many human rights doctrines have been set forth, including the Four Geneva Conventions of 1949, and their two Additional Protocols which outline measures protecting civilians, the sick and the wounded, and medical services in times of armed conflict. A variety of additional treaties address other problems such as genocide, torture, slavery, discrimination, and the rights of women, children and indigenous persons. Recently, there has been substantial debate over the issues of universal application of human rights, accountability of human rights violators and the priority of certain rights relative to others. Because protecting and promoting human rights has direct bearing on the health of individuals and communities, health professionals should be active participants in debates on human rights issues. However, health concerns traditionally have not included human rights. To suggest now that human rights are relevant health concerns and should influence the course of health practice in the next century requires conceptual justification.

HUMAN RIGHTS AND HEALTH PROFESSIONALS

For centuries, principles contained in the Hippocratic Oath (35) such as beneficence, non-malfeasance, and confidentiality have guided health professionals in the art of healing. These principles, together with more recent bioethical concepts of patient autonomy and informed consent, represent the foundations of one of the fastest growing curricular studies in undergraduate and graduate medical education, medical ethics. Such principles have been complemented by a trend of humanism in medical training, a trend that distinguishes illness concerns from disease processes (25, 36). However, health professionals' conceptual notions of disease and illness have not yet included the health consequences of human rights violations; nor have there been substantial efforts to teach human rights in medical education (37). Although human rights and health concerns have distinctly different origins, they share the common purpose of preventing and alleviating suffering.

Clearly, crimes of war and violations of fundamental civil and political rights have devastating health consequences (38). Political killings, forced disappearances and torture, including rape, not only aim to destroy the bodies and minds of individuals, but to destroy the health and well-being of entire communities. According to Scarry (39), the purpose of such violence is the establishment of power of one group over another by juxtaposing its ideology with the reality of death and injury it inflicts upon an opposing group. Death and injury caused by armed conflict and political violence are compounded by impairment of infrastructure. Deteriorations in supplies of food and water and effective sanitation frequently trigger massive dislocations of people and widespread disease and starvation. Health services may be overwhelmed by increased health needs in these circumstances, and although international laws safeguard medical neutrality during war, health professionals and services are often targets of abuse.

Perhaps the most devastating health consequences of political violence is that of long-term psychological trauma. Following extreme trauma, feelings of trust and hope and the sense of order and meaning are often displaced by fear and mistrust, feelings of rage, shame and guilt (40). The lives of survivors of torture and other human rights abuses are forever changed. Nightmares, flashbacks, problems with memory, concentration, anxiety and depression challenge and complicate everyday living (41). Such trauma not only affects survivors, but also their families (42) and members of the community. In fact, anyone who is exposed to the trauma of survivors, including clinicians, may experience a vicarious form of trauma (43).

Armed conflicts and systematic violations of human rights also have great impact on social organization and cooperation. Refugees and those living in exile often lose everything that is familiar to them, such as their language and customs, their homes and social supports. Family dynamics and financial status may change radically. Many refugees have no housing, means of income or transportation, and may in fact be incarcerated on their arrival to a country of asylum. Access to medical or psychological care may be limited or non-existent, and when legal status is in question, work and education opportunities are also precluded.

As health professionals' understandings of causes of suffering begin to shift from disease to illness, and from disease and illness to social conditions such as human rights violations, so too must efforts to prevent and alleviate suffering. It is common wisdom among human rights organizations that prevention of human rights violations involves full and impartial investigations, the prosecution of those responsible, and the implementation of adequate reforms to guard against future violations. Health professionals' unique knowledge and skills enable them to document evidence of violations of international human rights and humanitarian law and to hold violators of human rights responsible for their actions. Through the exemplary work of Physicians for Human Rights, Amnesty International, Human Rights Watch, the American Association for the Advancement of Science and others, health professionals have documented the widespread practice of extrajudicial execution, torture and rape in armed conflicts (4, 5, 44, 45), conducted forensic examinations and exhumations of mass graves (46, 47, 48, 49), documented the effects of armed conflicts on health care delivery, including violations of medical neutrality (5, 45, 50, 51), assessed health conditions in refugee camps (52, 53) and prisons (54, 55, 56), and campaigned for the release of detained health professionals.

Education is another critical element to preventing human rights abuses. By educating the public and government, health professionals may successfully promote health. In their capacity as educators, health professionls have the responsibility of informing the public and government of the considerable health effects of human rights abuses and prescribing action to prevent the suffering it causes. Professional leadership and advocacy for health, through protecting and promoting human rights, is commensurate with health professionals' duty of alleviating and preventing suffering, as long as it remains non-partisan. Human rights education should involve ongoing research on the relationship between health and human rights as well as the teaching of human rights to health professionals and others.

powerlessness. The very common responses of numbness, apathy, disinterest and avoidance among potential human rights advocates often precludes the development of human rights concerns. Becoming an effective healer not only involves understanding, preventing and treating social causes of human suffering, but also recognizing the context of one's own personal and emotional considerations. While working to prevent human rights abuses and to address the health needs of survivors may represent extraordinary challenges, such work also may be a source of exceptional meaning and fulfillment.

HUMAN RIGHTS IN THE TWENTY-FIRST CENTURY

Before any strategy of implementing human rights concerns may be realized in the next century, human rights must first become an issue of concern. The development of human rights concerns among health professionals in the twenty-first century will depend largely on the degree to which health professionals recognize the health consequences of human rights violations and leaders begin to respond to the problem. Meaningful dialogue within the profession will ultimately guide the development and expression of human rights concerns in medicine and health care. However, as a prelude to such dialogue, it may be worth considering how human rights concerns may develop and be manifest in the general domains of education, research, health services, policy and advocacy in the future.

For health professionals to effectively respond to social causes of human suffering in the next century, human rights concerns should be integrated into curricular studies and research activities. The subject of human rights and notions of understanding, preventing and treating social causes of suffering have largely been unexplored by health professionals. Although problems such as violence, poverty, education, discrimination and others, have increasingly captured the interests of health professionals, such interests generally define social problems in relation to the presence or absence of disease, rather than states of well-being provided by the protection and promotion of human rights. Health professionals need to begin to question and redefine their definitions of health and suffering; they need to study and articulate the relationship between health and human rights and learn to improve present documentation methods and treatment interventions. Academic discourse on human rights may be facilitated by undergraduate and graduate courses in schools of medicine, public health and nursing, fellowship and graduate research programs in human rights, and greater emphasis on international health experiences. Educational training for clinicians may be initiated through continuing medical and health education courses and symposia on the subjects of prevention and treatment. Publication of original research, books, and news articles relevant to human rights would increase awareness and understanding of human rights issues.

Health professionals also have the responsibility of educating the public and official representatives of government on important health issues. Documentation of human rights abuses would be futile if the public and government representatives were not apprised of their consequences. Similarly, treatment efforts to alleviate the suffering caused by human rights abuses would remain only marginally effective without broad support from government and the public. Human rights educational campaigns are critical not only because they are essential to raising awareness, but because they are essential to overcoming the tremendous resistance inherent in confronting painful issues. Advocating for health is both a political and professional responsibility; it calls attention to the physical and psychological consequences of deliberate and systematic acts of violence which aim to destroy individuals and communities. However, advocacy to prevent and alleviate suffering must remain non-partisan to be credible and effective.

Efforts to integrate human rights concerns into health education and research will be influenced by the issues of leadership, organization, funding and policy. Leaders in medicine and health care may help to initiate human rights concerns among health professionals by participating in educational training, research and advocacy. They may help to improve organization and communication between health professionals and human rights organizations. Together with human rights activists, health professionals may identify areas of common interest and articulate clear and consistent positions on the protection and promotion of human rights, which may serve as the basis for future policy. The development of human rights policy will need to be supported by further research on the relationship between health and human rights, and on the efficacy of specific initiatives. Adequate funding for such research will undoubtedly depend on the success of generating awareness of the importance of preventing and alleviating suffering by protecting and supporting human rights.

Specific skills and knowledge of health professionals enable them to recognize and document the health consequences of human rights violations and to advocate the abolition of such causes of human suffering. The extent of armed conflict and violation of human rights today clearly underscores the need for health professionals to participate in the documentation process. Improving quantitative and qualitative methods of documentation and education should be a component of such participation. In addition to documenting the health consequences of armed conflicts and violations of basic human rights, health professionals have not yet begun to address the health consequences of hunger, poverty, discrimination, interpersonal violence, illiteracy, pollution, and unemployment from a human rights perspective. These issues and documentation of unethical experimentation and conduct of health professionals deserve greater attention.

Documentation of abuse also has therapeutic effects. For example, survivors of torture who leave their country may need to demonstrate a "well founded fear of persecution" to gain refuge from their perpetrators. By documenting physical and psychological evidence of torture, health professionals may provide the safety that survivors need to begin the process of rebuilding their lives. In the process of providing medical testimony for political asylum cases, clinicians also have the opportunity to educate members of the judicial system who may have limited understandings of the problem of torture and may be under pressure to reject such cases.

Testimony of human rights violations, whether expressed in the court room, before Congress, in medical literature, or in the media, validates the reality of what may otherwise have seemed unbelievable experiences of suffering. As Eli Wiesel has said: "What hurts the victims most is not the cruelty of the oppressor, but the silence of the bystanders." Testimony becomes a part of our historical consciousness and it compels us to act. Inaction and impunity for perpetrators has profound psychological effects that exacerbate the trauma of human rights violations (71).

More than two million documented refugees and asylum seekers have come to the United States in the past twenty years (72, 73), many of whom have experienced torture and other traumatic human rights abuses (57). These figures most likely underestimate the true prevalence of survivors since they do not account for undocumented residents and because of the substantial barriers to the recognition of survivor status. Although estimates of the number of survivors of torture in the United States appear large, most health problems of survivors are not widely recognized by health professionals, and at present, there are only a handful of treatment centers that provide care for survivors. Treatment centers provide more than integration and consolidation of services; they provide professional expertise in dealing with complex emotional issues of survivors and providers alike, a safe and structured environment and the ability to carry out much needed research. Unfortunately, development of treatment centers has been limited by lack of recognition of the problem of torture and a critical lack of funding. Consequently, the vast majority of survivors have not been identified, nor engaged in treatment. Presently, there are approximately forty treatment centers worldwide. Given limited resources, many facilities have had to limit the duration of treatment, the indications for therapeutic intervention and the range of available services. Many treatment centers depend on funding from the United Nations Voluntary Fund for Victims of Torture. In 1992, that budget was about eight million dollars. The United States has contributed a mere six hundred and sixty thousand dollars between 1982 and 1992 (74). Efforts to treat survivors in the future will depend as much on funding as it does now.

In the course of clinical practice, health professionals have the unique opportunity to recognize the physical, psychological and social health consequences of human rights abuses, and with some training, to participate in appropriate treatment interventions. Improving present treatment efforts calls for the development of additional services, including specialized treatment centers, health services research, and collaboration between health providers in the United States and other countries.

Health services for refugees in developing countries address basic health needs, such as food and water, shelter, sanitation and medical care. However, such services generally do not reach the current twenty-five million people who are internally displaced. Although the basic health needs of refugees are often addressed in some capacity, health consequences of gross human rights violations are not. Death and injury from ongoing exposure to war, victimization by security forces whose duty it is to protect refugees, psychological effects of prolonged confinement and intentional policies of maintaining austere camp conditions to prevent new arrivals, have profound physical, psychological and social health consequences. In their efforts to address the health needs of highly traumatized and vulnerable populations, health professionals need to examine and begin to address the health consequences of human rights violations. The incompatibility of health and human right abuses highlights the need for the health professionals of today and tomorrow to participate in international public health initiatives.

CONCLUSIONS

Worldwide abuses of human rights have reached epidemic proportions in the twentieth century. Armed conflicts and violations of basic human rights, such as extra judicial executions, torture, rape and forced disappearances, have devastated the health of millions of individuals and the communities in which they live. This intentional plague of human destruction has been amplified by concomitant starvation and disease, the destruction of life-sustaining infrastructure and massive dislocations of people.

Traditional disease concerns have failed to recognize the physical, psychological and social health consequences of violations of basic human rights and other social causes of suffering. The duty of understanding the causes of human suffering and the professional responsibility of preventing and alleviating suffering, requires healers of the twenty-first century to re-examine their medical and health concerns. Because the protection and promotion of human rights aim to alleviate social causes of suffering, health providers have a well founded, professional interest in human rights concerns. Human rights documentation organizations and treatment centers for survivors of torture have undertaken important initial prevention measures. However, human rights concerns that aim to prevent and alleviate suffering must eventually be integrated into health education, research, services and policy.

Health professionals face immense challenges in addressing human rights concerns. The extent of human rights violations, the complexity of their causes and enormity of their consequences make for extraordinarily difficult and emotionally challenging work. Despite such challenges, and the intransigent financial and ideological interests of the present health care system, healers can no longer afford to limit their interests to disease and subsequently marginalize their role in society. Health professionals cannot stand by as silent witnesses to the incalculable human suffering that is caused by armed conflicts and human rights violations. What is at stake is not only the individual and community well-being and our professional credibility as healers, but the safeguarding of our humanity for centuries to come.

REFERENCES

1. Sivard, R.L. 1987. *World Military and Social Expenditures, 1987-1988*. WMSE Publications, Leesburg, VA, pp. 28-31.
2. 1992. United Nations High Commissioner for Refugees. Focus: Emergency. *Refugees.* 91:4-35.
3. 1992. Amnesty International. *Amnesty International Report, 1992.* Amnesty International Publications, London, England.
4. Swiss, S. and J.E. Giller. 1993. Rape as a Crime of War: A Medical Perspective. *JAMA* 1993. 270:612-615.

5. Gossman, P. and V. Iacopino. 1993. *The Human Rights Crisis in Kashmir: A Pattern of Impunity.* Physicians for Human Rights and Human Rights Watch, Boston, MA and New York, NY, pp. 214.
6. *Landmines: A Deadly Legacy.* 1993. The Arms Project: A Division of Human Rights Watch and Physicians for Human Rights, New York, NY and Boston, MA, pp. 510.
7. Toole, M.J. and R.J. Waldman. 1993. Refugees and Displaced Persons: War, Hunger and Public Health. *JAMA.* 270(5):600-605.
8. Nightengale, E.O. and E. Stover. 1986. A Question of Conscience: Physicians in Defense of Human Rights. *JAMA.* 255:2794-2797.
9. Nightengale, E.O. 1990. The Role of Physicians in Human Rights. *Law Medicine and Health Care.* 18(2):13209.
10. Geiger, H.J. and R.M. Cook-Deegan. 1993. The Role of Physicians in Conflicts and Humanitarian Crises: Case Studies From the Field Missions of Physicians for Human Rights, 1988-1993. *JAMA.* 270:616-620.
11. Habermas, J. 1970. Technology and Science as "Ideology," pp. 81-122. In: *Toward a Rational Society: Student Protest, Science and Politics.* Beacon Press Boston, MA, pp. 132.
12. Popper, K. 1959. *Logic of Scientific Discovery.* Basic Books, New York, NY.
13. Rabinow, P. and W.M. Sullivan. 1987. The Interpretive Turn: A Second Look, pp. 1-30. In: P. Rabinow, and W.M. Sullivan (Ed.) *Interpretive Social Science: A Second Look.* University of California Press, Berkeley and Los Angeles, CA. pp. 395.
14. Kuhn, T.S. 1970. *The Structure of Scientific Revolutions.* The University of Chicago Press, Chicago, IL, pp. 210.
15. Derrida, J. 1970. Structure, Sign and Play in the Discourse of the Human Sciences, pp. 247-264. In: D.E. Macksey (Ed.) *The Structuralist Controversy: The Languages of Criticism and the Sciences of Man.* Johns Hopkins Press, Baltimore, MD.
16. Gadamer, H.G. 1976. On the Scope and Function of Hermenuetical Reflection, pp. 18-43. In: *Philosophical Hermeneutics.* University of California Press, Berkeley and Los Angeles, CA, pp. 243.
17. Kuhn, T.S. 1977. The Function of Measurement in Modern Physical Science, pp. 178-224. In: *The Essential Tension Selected Studies in Scientific Tradition and Change.* The University of Chicago Press, Chicago, IL, pp. 366.
18. Marcuse, H. 1966. *One Dimensional Man: Studies in the Ideology of Advanced Industrial Society.* Beacon Press, Boston, MA, pp. 260.
19. Foucault, M. 1975. *The Birth of the Clinic: An Archaeology of Medical Perception.* Vintage Books, New York, pp. 215.
20. Taussig, M.T. 1980. Reification and the Consciousness of the Patient. *Social Science and Medicine.* 14:3-13.
21. Cassell, E.J. 1991. *The Nature of Suffering and the Goals of Medicine.* Oxford University Press Inc. New York, NY, pp. 254.
22. Sullivan, M. 1986. In What Sense is Contemporary Medicine Dualistic? *Culture Medicine and Psychiatry.* 10:331-350.

23. Eisenberg, L. 1981. The Physician as Interpreter: Ascribing Meaning to the Illness Experience. *Comprehensive Psychiatry.* 22(3):239-248.
24. Engel, G.L. 1977. The Need for a New Medical Model: a Challenge for Biomedicine. *Science.* 196:129-136.
25. Kleinman, A. 1988. *The Illness Narratives.* Basic Books, New York, NY, pp. 284.
26. Williams, G. 1984. The Genesis of Chronic Illness: Narrative Reconstruction. *Sociology Health and Illness.* 6(2):175-200.
27. Bury, M. 1982. Chronic Illness as Biographical Disruption. *Sociology Health and Illness.* 4(2):167-182.
28. Waitzkin, H. 1991. Theoretical Approaches to Medical Encounters, pp. 11-26. In: *The Politics of Medical Encounters: How Patients and Doctors Deal With Social Problems.* Yale University Press, New Haven, CT, pp. 311.
29. Mishler, E.G. 1984. *The Discourse of Medicine: Dialectics of Medical Interviews.* Ablex, Norwood, NJ, pp. 224.
30. Waitzkin, H. 1991. Theoretical Approaches to Medical Encounters, pp. 19-21. In: *The Politics of Medical Encounters: How Patients and Doctors Deal With Social Problems.* Yale University Press, New Haven, CT, pp. 311.
31. Weston, B.H. 1992. International Human Rights: Overview, pp. 14-30. In: R.P. Claude and B.H. Weston (Ed.) *Human Rights in the World Community: Issues and Actions.* University of Pennsylvania Press, Philadelphia, PA, pp. 480.
32. Henkin, L. 1990. Introduction: The Human Rights Idea. pp. 1-10. In: *The Age of Rights.* Columbia University Press, New York, pp. 224.
33. Kochler, H. 1990. *Democracy and Human Rights.* International Progress Organization, Vienna, Austria, pp. 31.
34. Dawidowicz, L.S. 1986. The War Against the Jews 1933-1945. Bantam Books, New York, NY, pp. xxxvi.
35. 1974. Hippocratic Oath. *Dorlands Illustrated Medical Dictionary, Twenty-Fifth Edition.* W.B. Saunders, Philadelphia, PA, pp. 715.
36. Cassell, E.J. 1976. Disease As "it": Concepts of Disease Revealed by Patients' Presentation of Symptoms. *Social Science and Medicine.* 10:143-146.
37. Geiger, H.J. 1993. The American Medical Establishment: an Absent Partner, pp. 159-172. In: K.M. Cahill (Ed.) *A Framework for Survival: Health, Human Rights, and Humanitarian Assistance in Conflicts and Disasters.* Basic Books, New York, NY, pp. 352.
38. Zwi, A. and A. Ugalde. 1989. Towards an Epidemiology of Political Violence in the Third World. *Social Science and Medicine.* 28(7):633-642.
39. Scarry, E. 1985. *The Body in Pain: The Making and Unmaking of the World.* Oxford University Press, New York, NY, pp. 385.
40. Somnier, F.E. and I.K. Genefke. 1986. Psychotherapy for Victims of Torture. *British Journal of Psychiatry.* 149:323-329.
41. Goldfeld, A.E., R.F. Mollica, B.H. Pesavento and S.V. Faraone. 1988. The Physical and Psychological Sequelae of Torture: Symptomatology and Diagnosis. *JAMA.* 259(18):2725-2729.

42. Slotkoff, N. 1992. The Holocaust: Survivors and Their Children, pp. 136-148. In: Basoglu, M. (Ed.) *Torture and its Consequences: Current Treatment Approaches.* Cambridge University Press, New York, NY, pp. 527.
43. Fishman, Y. 1991. Interacting With Trauma: Clinicians' Responses to Treating Psychological Aftereffects of Political Repression. *American Journal of Orthopsychiatry.* 61(2):179-185.
44. Fuller, A., Wilentz, A. and S. Oliver. 1992. *Return to the Darkest Days: Human Rights in Haiti Since the Coup.* Americas Watch, Physicians for Human Rights and the National Coalition for Haitian Refugees, New York, NY and Boston, MA, pp. 20.
45. Iacopino, V. and S. Jones. 1992. *Bloody May: Excessive Use of Lethal Force in Bangkok.* Physicians for Human Rights and Asia Watch, Boston, MA and New York, NY, pp. 50.
46. Miguel, A. and E. Stover. 1991. *Guatemala: Getting Away With Murder.* Americas Watch, Physicians for Human Rights and the National Coalition for Haitian Refugees, New York, NY and Boston, MA, pp. 85.
47. Stover, E. 1992. *Unquiet Graves: The Search for the Disappeared in Iraqi Kurdistan.* Middle East Watch and Physicians for Human Rights, New York, NY and Boston, MA, pp. 41.
48. Stover, E. 1991. *The Search for Brazil's Disappeared: The Mass Grave at Dom Bosco Cemetery.* Physicians for Human Rights, Boston, MA, pp. 19.
49. 1991. *Medical Testimony on Victims of Torture: A Physicians Guide to Political Asylum Cases.* Physicians for Human Rights, Boston, MA, pp. 20.
50. Geiger, H.J., Eisenber, C. and S. Gloyd, et al. 1989. A New Medical Mission to El Salvador. *New England Journal of Medicine.* 321:1136-1140.
51. Sirkin, S. 1991. *Iraq-Occupied Kuwait: The Health Care Situation.* Physicians for Human Rights/Denmark and Physicians for Human Rights/USA, Boston, MA, pp. 35.
52. de Waal, A. and J. Leaning. 1992. *No Mercy in Mogadishu: The Human Cost of the Conflict and the Struggle for Relief.* Physicians for Human Rights and Africa Watch, Boston, MA and New York, NY, pp. 25.
53. Sandler, R.H., Epstein, P.R., Cook-Deegan, R.M. and A. Shukri. 1991. Initial Medical Assessment of Kurdish Refugees in the Turkey-Iraq Border Region. *JAMA.* 266:638-640.
54. Shansky, R. and K. Thorburn. 1990. *Health Care in Detention: A Study of Israel's Treatment of Palestinians.* Physicians for Human Rights, Boston, MA, pp. 46.
55. Naier, P.A. and R. Shansky. 1991. *Hidden From View: Human Rights Conditions in the Krome Detention Center.* Minnesota Lawyers Committee and Physicians for Human Rights, Minneapolis, MN and Boston, MA, pp. 81.
56. Traver, J., Cranberg, L., Stover, E. and N. Forbes. 1993. *Cruel and Inhuman Treatment: The Use of Four-Point Restraints in the Onondaga County Public Safety Building, Syracuse, New York.* Physicians for Human Rights, Boston, MA, pp. 100.
57. Baker, R. 1992. Psychosocial Consequences for Tortured Refugees Seeking Asylum and Refugee Status in Europe, pp. 82-106. In: M. Basoglu (Ed.) *Torture*

and its Consequences: Current Treatment Approaches. Cambridge University Press, New York, NY, pp. 527.
58. Galeano, E. November 11, 1987. Los Uruguayos Firmamos a Contramano, a Contramiendo. *El Pais.* Montevideo, Uruguay, pp. 13.
59. Lifton, R.J. 1988. *The Nazi Doctors: Medical Killing and the Psychology of Genocide.* Basic Books, New York, NY, pp. 576.
60. Stover, E. and E. Nightingale. 1985. Codes of Ethics and Declarations of Abuse, pp. 253-279. In: E. Stover and E. Nightingale (Ed.) *The Breaking of Bodies and Minds: Torture, Psychiatric Abuse, and the Health Professions.* W.H. Freeman and Company, New York, NY, pp. 319.
61. Proceedings of an International Meeting, Copenhagen, August 1986. 1987. Doctors, Ethics and Torture. *Danish Medical Bulletin.* 34(4):185-216.
62. British Medical Association. 1992. Medical Involvement in Torture, pp. 33-63. In: *Medicine Betrayed: The Participation of Doctors in Human Rights Abuses.* Zed Books Ltd., Atlantic Highlands, NJ, pp. 234.
63. Rasmussen, O.V. 1990. Medical Aspects of Torture. *Danish Medical Bulletin.* 1(1)1-88.
64. Jones, J.H. 1993. *Bad Blood: The Tuskegee Syphilis Experiment.* Free Press, New York, NY, pp. 300.
65. Beecher, H.K. 1966. Ethics in Clincial Research. *New England Journal of Medicine.* 274:1354-1360.
66. Rothman, D.J. 1987. Ethics and Human Experimentation: Henry Beecher Revisited. *New England Journal of Medicine.* 317(19):1195-1199.
67. Weinstein, H. 1991. *Psychiatry and the CIA: Victims of Mind Control.* American Psychiatric Press, New York, NY, pp. 300.
68. Bandura, A. 1990. Mechanisms of Moral Disengagement. In: W. Reich (Ed.) *Origins of Terrorism: Psychologies, Ideologies, Theologies, States of Mind.* Cambridge University Press, New York, NY, pp. 304.
69. Staub, E. 1990. The Psychology and Culture of Torture and Torturers, pp. 49-76. In: P. Suedfeld (Ed.) *Psychology and Torture.* Hemisphere Publishing Corporation, New York, NY, pp. 207.
70. Randall, G.R. and E.L. Lutz. 1991. Approach to the Patient, pp. 55-69. In: *Serving Survivors of Torture: A Practical Manual for Health Professionals and Other Service Providers.* American Association for the Advancement of Science, Washington, DC, pp. 199.
71. Kordon, D.R. 1991. Impunity's Psychological Effects: Its Ethical Consequences. *Journal of Medical Ethics.* 17:29-32.
72. 1991. The Situation of Refugees, pp. 13-24. In: *Working With Refugees and Asylum Seeker: A Handbook for Red Cross/Red Crescent Staff and Volunteers.* League of Red Cross and Red Crescent Societies, Geneva, Switzerland, pp. 187.
73. December 31, 1992. *Refugee Reports,* Washington, DC, 8(12):5-13.
74. United States Economic and Social Council. January 8, 1993. *Consolidated Reports on Ten Years (1982-1992) of the United Nations Voluntary Fund for Victims of Torture.* E/CN. 4/1993/23:1-66.

Medicine and Health Care Into the Twenty-First Century. Edited by S.K. Majumdar, L.M. Rosenfeld, D.B. Nash and A.M. Audet. © 1995, The Pennsylvania Academy of Science.

Chapter Thirty

PHYSICIAN WELLNESS PROGRAMS: Coping With Health Care Change

ABRAM M. HOSTETTER, M.D.,[1]
PENELOPE P. ZIEGLER, M.D.[2] and
ROBERT L. LAMB, M.A.[3]

[1]Chairman
[2]Medical Director, Physicians Health Program
[3]Project Associate
The Educational and Scientific Trust of the Pennsylvania Medical Society
777 East Park Drive, P.O. Box 8820
Harrisburg, PA 17105-8820

INTRODUCTION

Concern for the well-being of physicians in the turbulent 90s is well founded and must become the subject of considerable discussion within the profession.

Traditionally, physicians have expected to work long hours, digest large quantities of technical information and sometimes make split-second life and death decisions. To the long-recognized demands associated with the practice of medicine have been added new stressors stemming from anticipated system-wide change and lack of work-environment control. Today, as practice outcomes are thrown about like batting averages of professional baseball players, the security of anonymity, similar to the security of tenure in education, is disappearing.

In the face of these growing pressures, thousands of men and women have succeeded in serving their patients competently. Until recently, unless their conduct was outrageous and/or their results disastrous, the precision of their clinical skills remained largely unknown, nor did anyone demand a more exact accounting. Behind closed doors, nurses used anecdotal information to establish their own informal quality networks and colleagues, as assistants at surgery and consultants, could see tell-tale signs of sloppy practice. Tissue committees acted as a deterrent to those few surgeons who might be tempted to unethical surgery. And utilization review and audit committees responded to the requirements of the Joint Commission, but by and large the efficiency and effectiveness of physicians was unmeasured. Most physicians, if they completed a residency, passed their "Boards," and subsequently used due diligence, were "home free."

Increasingly, the rules by which medicine has been practiced are changing. For example, the financial consequences of clinical decisions made by physicians have become so great that even the prerogatives of mastering high tech knowledge no longer protect the physician from outside interference in his or her clinical judgments. Concern over the use of resources and achieving measurable outcomes has escalated to the point where the collective wisdom of specialists has laid out critical pathways which ostensibly achieve the best result at the lowest cost. For the physician who is used to doing it "my way," practice parameters and guidelines take much of the fun out of his or her work, and at the least, impinge on clinical autonomy.

Moreover, the demographics of the physician workforce are changing as the percentage of female medical graduates rises, bringing internal pressures to a profession already buffeted by external change. As the profession moves from male domination closer to a 50-50 split, issues unique to women will necessarily come to bear on medical education and practice, such as their higher suicide rate, and child care and other family-influenced issues.

Small wonder that physicians report being stressed.

STRESSORS INTERNAL TO THE PROFESSION

Training

Historically, stress for physicians begins with prepping for the MCAT. Once within the hallowed walls of medical school, the pressures increase, as formerly exceptional students find themselves surrounded by equally exceptional students, all of whom struggle to keep up with the deluge of information. From the first day of classes, a medical student is "behind in my reading."

The characteristic strengths of a typical medical student—hard work, perfectionism and dedication to medicine, become liabilities when pushed to the extreme. The image of strength and stability, the model sought by medical students, also becomes a prison of isolation which prevents them from sharing the pain, apprehension, doubt, disappointment, and uncertainty which may be undermining their emotional health.

Judith Samkoff, MD, ScM, a researcher for the Keystone Peer Review Organization in Harrisburg, writing in the July 1993 issue of PENNSYLVANIA MEDICINE cites a figure of 13 to 50 percent of medical students who develop psychological problems and may need counseling, support, and additional coping mechanisms (1).

The intern and residency years bring the added stresses of clinical experiences, including overwork, dealing with failure, long hours, sleep deprivation, and changing shift disorientation. Critical decisions must be made on less than adequate information. Often immediate action is necessary and risks mount. Among those risks are the possibility of violent assault, exposure to hepatitis and drug resistant tuberculosis, and the constant knowledge that the just admitted patient may be HIV-positive. By mid 1993, 37 health care workers, through work related accidents, had become infected with the HIV virus from HIV positive patients (2).

While idealism may propel a student into medical school, the harsh realities of school politics and the inevitable hazing reinforce the need to postpone recreation and relaxation until the MD degree is earned and residency completed. This postponement of self-care activities needed to maintain emotional balance takes a heavy toll (3).

Changing Demographics

Formerly a predominately male profession, medicine today is becoming increasingly popular to females. In 1993, the number of female medical graduates in Pennsylvania reached an all time high of almost 500 or 40 percent of the graduating classes. At Temple University, 53 percent of the graduating class were women (4).

As reported in JAMA in the September 1, 1993 issue, more than half the residents in family practice in the United States are female. The number of males and females in internal medicine and OBGYN residencies is roughly evenly divided, while in pediatrics, women outnumber men two to one (5).

The impact of increasingly large numbers of women physicians entering the workforce is a subject for future study. Women physicians, because of child rearing responsibilities, often look for more predictable schedules. There are also reports in the social psychology literature that women appear to excel at nurturing relationships and networking. Therefore, some health care analysts believe that women physicians will adapt more easily to a managed care environment than their male counterparts.

J.C. Richings, writing in the British Journal of Psychiatry in 1986, found a fourfold increased risk of suicide among women physicians as compared to a similar cohort of non-physician women. Subsequently in 1991, British researchers Firth-Cozens found that 46% of a sample of women house officers fulfilled the criteria for clinical depression (6).

Data on two-physician families while sketchy, seems to indicate that the female physician usually assumes a larger responsibility for home and child management. The other option exercised most frequently by dual medical families is that of paid child care. During the child rearing years, if clinical skills are to be retained, female physicians often do so through part-time practice (7).

In an interview with *The New York Times,* Esther J. Nash, MD, who with her husband David Nash, MD, founded a support group for physician couples in 1981 called Dual Doctor Families (DDF) (8) said, "A man may meet many female hospital staff, but for a woman, the men she meets happen to be doctors."

There is no consensus as to whether doctor-doctor marriages have a higher than expected divorce rate. Certainly future physician wellness programs need to recognize the increasing incidence of two-physician families and how that trend relates to physician stress and wellness (9).

STRESSORS EXTERNAL TO THE PROFESSION

During the sixties and seventies, physicians in training expected medical science to change, but the business rules of the Blues, commercial insurers, Medicare and Medicaid, seemed constant and predictable.

In this comparatively stable business environment a generation of entrepreneurial medical specialists flourished. These physicians, seemingly free to set their own time schedules, perceived themselves to be the masters of their own destinies. Most patients held them in awe and in the office, the hospital, and the community, many physicians enjoyed wide respect.

The prevailing physician reimbursement system—usual, customary and reasonable UCR—was user (physician) friendly. Meanwhile, hospitals continued to be the physician's workshop and administrators generally complied with physician requests. The media spotlighted every technical breakthrough and raised the public's expectations to miracle levels.

Changes in Health Care Delivery and Payment Structure

Today, the health care delivery and reimbursement environments are changing rapidly. Soaring demands by Medicare beneficiaries have led the federal government to impose defacto cost control by regulation. Physicians call this the "hassle factor" whereby increasing and ever-changing Medicare regulations gradually strip physicians of their independence and control, and actually interfere in the doctor-patient relationship. The hassle factor has also increased the cost of care inasmuch as a typical internist often must hire two office assistants to process the paperwork associated with his or her patients (10).

Malpractice Litigation

Hints of a new source of trouble and stress for physicians appeared as the nation became increasingly sensitized to individual rights during the mid 1970s. Physicians saw both the frequency of malpractice actions against them and the size of awards and settlements increase. Nor were interns and residents adequately prepared by their training institutions for the litigious environment which they were about to enter.

For physicians seeing patients, the number one practice concern during those years was the liability issue. It permeated doctor "shop talk" and dominated the agenda of physician organizations, thus amplifying its effect as a stressor. It led to a further proliferation of orders for studies and procedures, a trend which came to be known as "defensive medicine."

In the years since the medical liability crises of the 70s, most physicians expect to be sued sometime during their medical career, many, more than once. For example by the early '90s, eight out of ten Fellows of the American College of Obstetrics and Gynecology had been sued (11).

PARADIGM SHIFT

In the transition from the 80s to the 90s, ownership of health care in the United States passed from providers to payers. The delivery of health care became public business, rather than a private doctor-patient matter. The principal cause of this hostile takeover by payers, both public and private, was the inability of providers to rein in persistent double-digit medical inflation (12).

In Pennsylvania this frustration manifested itself in legislation (Act 89 of 1986) creating the Health Care Cost Containment Council. Dominated by business and labor, with only token seats for providers, this government-funded independent agency set about collecting uniform data on hospitals and physicians. It assumed that focusing a public spotlight on hospital and physician performance would marshal marketplace forces to help slow medical inflation (13).

At first its reports placed additional stress on hospital medical staffs by making public allegedly comparable statistics on specific procedures and diagnoses performed at various hospitals. Later that stress was transferred directly to individual physicians with the release of the coronary artery bypass surgery report which was hospital and physician specific (13).

In Pennsylvania and then nationwide, Democratic candidates discerned that health care was an issue which could be translated into votes. The first evidence of this came in 1991 with the victory of Senator Harris Wofford over Richard Thornburgh in Pennsylvania.

While as of this writing, the final shape of a national health program is not known, certain system-wide changes have already begun as hospitals, physicians and insurers position themselves for the future. The common denominator of all this activity is change—a synonym for stress (14).

THE AGE OF MANAGED CARE

Based on White House rhetoric, the assumption is that under national health care reform, eventually all citizens will be part of a managed system. The dominant physician paradigm in Pennsylvania and other Northeast states has been one of relatively small, usually single-specialty groups, ranging from five to 25 doctors. But the expected managed care groups will probably be five to ten times that size (15).

Empirical evidence available from the downsizing of American industry and current research on physician job satisfaction all point to a probable period of high stress for physicians as the American health care system is restructured. For most physicians, becoming a member of a large managed care organization will require a cultural shift of tectonic proportions.

It is possible then to speculate on the likelihood of additional stress for U.S. physicians as thousands of them hastily form unique service structures with no other motivation than survival as practicing physicians. Not only will collegial behavior be altered to fit a "corporate" medical culture, but medical decisions will be compelled to meet cost-effectiveness criteria (16). Picture the reaction of these champions of personal/professional freedom as they read the medical and surgical practice guidelines handed to them by a group medical director. Imagine their feelings as they gradually realize that their incomes and retirement savings hinge both on patient satisfaction, which will be continuously monitored, and on their ability to stay within the resource guidelines of the organization. Peer over their shoulder as they review the formulary from which they must prescribe.

Lack of control over one's environment is a key element in creating stress. M. Allison in a paper entitled "Signs of Stress" given at the Society of Public Health conference, London, England, in 1991 reported stressors related to physicians in the organizational structure and climate of the British health service:

"Lack of autonomy or control;
Level of involvement in decision-making;
Poor communication at all levels;
Lack of opportunity for interaction with colleagues;
Closed, negative policies;
Rapid, substantial change;
Lack of feedback. (6)"

Since coping satisfactorily with any threat or stress is enhanced by developing a realistic cognitive perception of the dangers, there will be a much greater need for physicians to have arenas in which they can openly share and discuss their problems. As the current physician marketplace switches from a network of individual and small group referral patterns to one of large competing entities, opportunities for communication between physicians outside "the organization" are likely to dwindle, as are the present forums for "networking" and "sharing", such as within county and specialty medical societies. Physicians need an outlet for their irritation and frustration that stems from trying to balance patient advocacy with the newly-foisted role of "resource allocator"; for example, how does one deal with the rules regarding permissible laboratory studies or frequency of patient visits, withheld until after doctors have signed their contracts? Such unethical post-contract surprises contribute to both physician paranoia and stress (17).

The specter of rejection, last experienced by many physicians when they competed to enter medical school and residency, will likely be revisited as managed care entities select their panel of "cost effective, quality physicians." The stress of rejection by the managed care plan will be followed by the equally traumatic experience of losing long-time and valued patients whose insurance will reimburse only those visits to "preferred" physicians (18). (The term "preferred provider" is a euphemism used by insuring organizations to describe the selection process through which they deny access by their beneficiaries to physicians who perform costly operations or procedures.)

In the hospital setting physicians are seeing the customary uncontested renewal of their privileges come under a different kind of scrutiny. To the pre-DRG, often pro forma review of privileges by the credentials committee, are being added print-outs of outcomes, hospital revenue and resource use, in short a box score (from the hospital's point of view) on each physician. The implication is that eventually, appointment or reappointment may depend on more than clinical qualifications and medical staff support. "Economic credentialing" will present a major challenge to ethical decision making in medicine (19).

Stress Within the Nursing Profession

If physicians are perceiving additional stress in the hospital, they are not alone. Nurses, responding to a Service Employees International Union's "National Nurse Survey" in 1993 said that increased workloads are outpacing salary increases. The survey's main findings:

- Seven out of 10 nurses report staffing levels are often inadequate.
- Nurses increasingly must absorb more non-nursing assignments.
- Because nurses have less time to spend with patients, there are more errors.
- To fill scheduling gaps, nurses are given assignments for which they may not be trained.
- Stress-related illness—hypertension, back injuries, depression—is increasing.
- Two-thirds of the nurses surveyed say they have thought of leaving their current job or the profession as a whole.

Because of the high cost of inpatient care, only patients with serious conditions are allowed by payers to remain in hospital beds. Less ill patients are redirected to ambulatory settings, and same day surgical units. This means that virtually all the patients for whom a nurse is responsible are seriously ill and require close monitoring, often necessitating support from high technology equipment.

Physicians perceive stress problems for themselves in relation to nursing as lack of adequate staffing, errors in communications, and a decline in the quality of nursing care. Problems in nursing almost always impact on physicians (20).

Coping With Reform

For physicians, accustomed to great autonomy and authority, the transition to teamwork and consensus will assuredly be stressful (8). "Environmental control" looms large as a major ingredient of job satisfaction and wellness for many physicians. The perception that freedom of choice for both patient and physician may be lost in a managed system is a growing source of anxiety.

In the transition from solo practice and small groups to large managed care entities, some physicians will experience fewer traumas than others. They are the doctors who by choice already practice in large organizations. Examples include staff HMOs, such as Kaiser Permanente, and clinics such as Henry Ford and Mayo, not to mention the many large groups in the mid-west and California. In Pennsylvania, large group practices include Geisinger and Robert Packer (Guthrie Clinic), as well as the faculty practice plans at the state's medical schools. Nevertheless, the great majority of the 33,500 physicians in Pennsylvania do not practice in large groups (15).

A 1991 survey by the American Medical Association looked at the question of internal discipline within a "group." This question is important because the term "managed care" implies a practice culture geared to agreed-upon standards. The

(AMA) survey, however, found that most physicians in groups enjoyed a large amount of autonomy. Only 38.2% used practice parameters from a specialty society or any other protocol to influence group member clinical behavior. The other clinically restrictive device, used by 25.9% of the groups surveyed, was a peer review mechanism established by the group itself. Only 18% required members to adhere to hospital length of stay guidelines and only 12.6% required their doctors to prescribe according to a formulary (21). Clearly any major consolidation of physicians and groups will create the need for numerous adaptive skills, including learning to:

- Adjust to more careful internal and external monitoring;
- Get along with colleagues;
- Forego some ego gratification for the good of the group;
- Reach consensus on business matters;
- Reach consensus on clinical matters;
- Accept criticism;
- Function as a member of a team;
- Accept non-physicians with equal voice in team decisions;
- Accept responsibility for patient care without full authority;
- Become comfortable with computer data and usage;
- Serve both the patient and the corporate bottom line; and
- Accept reduced remuneration (22).

Future wellness programs will need to help physicians adapt successfully to these demands.

As medicine begins to mirror a corporate culture, physician stress symptoms mimic those of corporate middle management. In a recent Pennsylvania case, the "stress" on managed care physician gatekeepers and specialists to conserve resoures prevented any of them from venturing beyond the narrowest interpretation of their authorized responsibilities. Their perceived loss of overall control manifested itself as a nascent "That's not my job" attitude. The result was that critical information, lurking in the patient's various files, lay unobserved until a plaintiff's attorney put the pieces together and was successful in recovering monetary damages for the maltreated patient.

Under the traditional fee-for-service paradigm the physician was free to advocate as much care as called for by his or her medical judgment. Under a managed care system the physician serves two masters, the patient and the bottom line of the organization, with the organization's first interest being to use the fewest resources possible. This intrusion into the traditional doctor-patient relationship will likely increase stress for physicians in managed systems and be one that physician wellness programs need to address (17).

A Robert W. Johnson Foundation funded 1990 poll conducted by the AAMC, the AMA and Georgetown University, of physicians under the age of 40 who had been in practice between two and six years, found that one in three of the physicians sampled would not go to medical school again. This reinforces anecdotal perceptions of physician attitudes and adds credence to the assertion that physician wellness will become increasingly important in the future (22).

Daniel E. Ford, MD, assistant professor of medicine, epidemiology and health policy, Johns Hopkins Health Institutions, Baltimore, MD, conducted a study among 550 physicians who graduated from Johns Hopkins from 1948 to 1964, all white and 93% male, with a mean age of 57.

Ford found that:

- Satisfaction rankings increased, the longer physicians had been out of medical school.
- Physicians working for HMOs "tend to be less satisfied with their jobs, with less control, less physician resources and less social support."
- Younger physicians said their jobs were more demanding than did older physicians, and they also complained of less job control and fewer resources.
- "The best predictor of job satisfaction among physicians was a sense of control over the work environment (24)."

John-Henry Pfifferling, PhD, Director of the Center for Professional Well-Being, Durham, NC, in an August, 1993 interview, reported that in his practice, he is seeing physicians over 40 years of age exhibiting greater pain, frustration, anger, and a heightened sense of "gloom and doom." Used to being in control, they increasingly are asking, "Who's in charge? Who's calling the shots?"

Behaviors which result from mounting stress include:

- Poor estate planning;
- Abandonment of personal future goals;
- Passive suicide (Self-destructive and dangerous behaviors);
- Feelings that events are out of one's control; and
- A sense of depression.

His reading of many younger physicians is that they will have an easier time adjusting to some facets of health care reform. He sees them more prepared for change, comfortable with computers and the stream of emerging quality and outcome data.

One phenomenon he and his associates at the Center have observed is a growing frustration on the part of house staff and medical students. These physicians in training, anticipating the changes about to occur, expect their faculty to help prepare them for the new medical world order. Instead, they perceive the faculty practicing "business (science) as usual." This appears to anger and alienate students and house staff from faculty and gives rise to more "we-they" behavior.

As the stress level rises in mature physicians, Dr. Pfifferling and his colleagues at the Center find increased demand for career counseling. More physicians are exploring sabbaticals, downsizing, ways to slow down, and ways to take early retirement. A related issue, needing research, is, what quality of care does a physician with low morale give (22)?

Recent physician focus groups conducted by The Educational and Scientific Trust of the Pennsylvania Medical Society have shown a growing level of anger in physicians. Researchers heard this anger focused upon the national organization which represents all physicians, in what appears to be a classic example of "scapegoating."

Physician support programs, such as the "Physicians' Health Programs" sponsored by The Educational and Scientific Trust of the Pennsylvania Medical Society, know that physicians tend to self-talk themselves into believing that, "I am responsible for everyone's happiness" and "I am not responsible for my unhappiness." Operating on an "I am totally responsible for what goes on here" premise, physicians quickly isolate themselves into believing, "if anything can go wrong, it will, 'Murphy's Law' and "No one understands my special needs." Their isolationist mind-set nurtures a distorted self-concept which has been characterized as either "I am superior/perfect" or "I am inferior/worthless." These distorted beliefs are worrisome because they provide the base for future behavior. This behavior, rooted in a flawed belief system, can range from that of a "difficult, disruptive" person to one who is withdrawn and self-destructive.

The world's finest medical education system which prepares its students to provide unparalleled technical medical care, also leaves them with a set of unwritten personal behavior rules which can be remarkably unhealthy. The positive state to which medical students aspire is that of being "professional." The outward manifestation of "professional" is a calm composed demeanor which is able to move from the bedside of a new mother and her healthy baby to that of a terminal cancer patient, to that of an aged patient in need of a death pronouncement, to the emergency room where life is ebbing from a mangled and broken body, all without becoming emotionally involved in any of these human dramas. On this journey to "professionalism" students often adopt their own set of survival rules. These dysfunctional rules can be described as:

- Don't trust, don't talk, don't feel;
- Don't rock the boat;
- Don't communicate directly;
- Don't be selfish; and
- Don't have fun (3).

Are physicians under stress identifiable? Are there telltale signs and symptoms? Yes. Symptoms of unsuccessful stress management include:

- Change in work habits and/or appearance;
- Loss of interest;
- Distant from friends and family;
- Talks about quitting medicine; and
- Temper outbursts (3).

Traditional programs for impaired physicians, such as the Physician's Health Programs in Pennsylvania, report increasing numbers of physicians exhibiting unhealthy coping strategies. These include:

- Denial and avoidance;
- Increased alcohol use;
- Self-medication with other drugs;
- Burnout;
- Angry outbursts;
- Passive-aggressiveness;
- Stress-related physical symptoms, such as back ache, high blood pressure, and GI troubles;

- Self-destructive acting-out behaviors;
- Apathy; and
- Nihilism (3).

All too often, those closest to a physician are not trained to identify these markers and are not prepared to offer a source of stress management techniques for the doctor. A goal for the future must be the education of the physician family in how to identify the symptoms of poor stress management and to have effective techniques available with which to cope.

A NECESSARY COMPONENT OF HEALTH CARE REFORM: Physician Wellness Programs

In the 70s and 80s, as the nation broadened its response to alcoholism and drug abuse from one of incarceration to one also embracing rehabilitation, the concept of restoring impaired physicians took root. Today, physicians' health programs are generally accepted in the medical community with some programs including the medical family and a few moving into stress and wellness. Given the magnitude of anticipated change in medicine, it would appear that a major physician wellness effort is justified.

While rehabilitation and long term recovery from addiction are acceptable concepts to most physicians today, such was not always the case. An earlier school of thought decreed that doctors who became addicted to alcohol and drugs were (and should be) lost to the profession. Medicine was similar to a boot camp in which only the strong survived. Impaired physician programs were not yet politically correct and physicians who sought help were viewed as weak.

Today, that belief has faded. Hospital medical staffs, county medical societies, state medical societies, and the American Medical Association (AMA) all recognize the need for programs to which physicians can turn for help. Most have responded with physicians' health committees. And while some programs have expanded to embrace the entire medical family, the broader issue of physician stress and wellness is largely uncharted. In the academic environment, problems of medical students, residents and faculty may be addressed through programs modeled after Employee Assistance Programs (EAPs). However, most such programs attempt at best, secondary prevention. Few medical schools or residency training programs specifically include stress management/wellness concepts in their curricula.

Typical stress management and burnout prevention programs advise individual physicians to:

- Reexamine life priorities and values;
- Engage in regular physical exercise;
- Develop hobbies, sports, travel;
- Accept the importance of recreation time and take action on that belief;
- Develop a support network;
- Examine negative self-talk;
- Reserve some quiet time and use it;
- Repair self-esteem with help;
- Identify stressors and corrective choices;

- Deal with grief and failure especially cumulative loss, etc.;
- Learn to say, "I don't know";
- Learn to say "no";
- Deal with sensuality in healthy ways;
- Relearn to laugh. Use humor as creative retraining; and
- To adapt (25).

Formal Programs Address Litigation Stress

The increased frequency of allegations of malpractice has given rise to a new syndrome, "litigation stress," a phenomenon now handled by formal physician support programs across the nation, including one in Pennsylvania sponsored by the Physicians' Health Programs (PHP) and administered by The Educational and Scientific Trust of the Pennsylvania Medical Society (26).

Physician Family Wellness

While concern for the practitioner caught in these changes moves to center stage, professionals in the field know that it is not just the physician who is buffeted, but the entire medical family and even the office staff. Physician wellness means attention to the needs of the "extended family."

Over the past ten years, efforts, often growing out of impaired physician programs, have emerged to address the broader question of physician family wellness. These programs have developed after therapists have dealt separately with impaired parents and disturbed children. The findings of higher than expected anger and violence in medical families have led therapists to experiment with medical family support systems. Much of the data in this field has come from the physician family workshops of the Menninger Clinic and the work in Georgia of the Medical Society of Georgia and the auxiliary of the medical society (27).

These therapists have found that the stresses in a medical family are qualitatively different from those in non-medical families. Spouses and children often engage unknowingly in major enabling behavior to allow the physician to pursue medicine with an intensity that is self imposed. While the family would probably not use the term "enabling," spouse and children would admit to rearranging their own priorities and behavior in ways to assure that the physician can make an unlimited commitment to the practice of medicine. The result can be the withholding of anger and resentment by family members until in some instances, it explodes with devastating results.

Among the most effective responses to these needs have been physician family workshops in which, with the help of facilitators, physicians and their wives or significant others, spend time with other physician couples communicating honestly and openly about their feelings and the problems they are experiencing. This sharing opens lines of communications between physicians and their significant others.

Intimate communication, which requires active listening on the part of the physician, does not come easily for doctors. The revelation of inner feelings, which leaves one vulnerable, has usually been "cauterized" through at least seven years of formal medical education and subsequent years of "professional" behavior (27).

- Are continuing education resources allocated for personal growth and enhancement of leadership?
- Is the ancillary staff included on the designated leadership team and is their input valued?
- Does the group give sabbaticals (28)?

CONCLUSION

Job changes, along with marriage, divorce and deaths are among the greatest stressors in people's lives. As this century draws to a close, U.S. physicians are witnessing the death of entrepreneurial practice of medicine. The subsequent transition to managed care can be expected to create an extraordinary, if temporary, stressful period in the lives of many physicians. Later, in the managed care environment, new stresses can be anticipated as physicians are torn between being the patient's advocate and simultaneously being at financial risk for over-utilizing system resources. Hopefully, clinical guidelines and critical pathways will help reduce these ethical dilemmas.

Just as business and industry find employee wellness a critical component of cost control, so managed care organizations will find physician wellness critical to patient satisfaction and organization profitability. The best managed care organizations will provide physician wellness programs for their doctors.

APPENDIX A

Examples of Physician Wellness Programs in Existence

1. The Center for Physician Development, Beth Israel Hospital, Boston
2. Office of Resident and Fellow Support at Children's Hospital, Boston
3. Jefferson Medical College, "Stress Management for Residents," Timothy Brigham, PhD., Coordinator Research and Special Projects, Graduate Medical Education, Philadelphia, 1025 Walnut Street, Philadelphia, PA 19107-5083 (215) 955-8067
4. The Center for Professional Well-Being, John-Henry Pfifferling, PhD, Director, 21 W. Colony Place, Suite 150, Durham, North Carolina 27705 (919) 419-0011
5. The Quality of Life Task Force available to physicians working in the Kaiser Permanente system, San Francisco, CA. Director: Martha Snider, MD
6. Harvard Community Health Plan, orientation program for primary care physicians, Cambridge, MA
7. The Institute for Stress Medicine, Robert S. Eliot, MD, FACC, Director, P.O. Box 2618, Littleton, CO
8. The Menninger Clinic "Physician Family Workshops" and the "Workshops for the Children of Physicians," Martin Leichtman, PhD, 5800 W. Sixth St., Box 829, Topeka, Kansas 66601
9. The American Academy on Physician and Patient, 3000 Chestnut Avenue, Suite 320, Baltimore, MD 21211
10. Univesity of Louisville Medical School, Joel Elkes, MD and Leah Dickstein, MD, Louisville, KY
11. Michigan State Medical Society, State-wide Physician Wellness Program, Chairman: Carl Hammerstrom, MD
12. The Well Physician Course, Mary R. McBean, MD, FCFP, Assistant Professor, Department of Family Medicine; Janet L. Wright, MD, FRCP, Clinical Assistant Professor, Department of Psychiatry - University of Calgary College of Physicians and Surgeons

APPENDIX A *(continued)*

13. C.W. Metcalf & Company - Humor Prescription "Care for the Care Giver," 2801 S. Remington Suite 2, Fort Collins, CO 80525
14. "Creating Your Health," Robert A. Partridge, MD, Health Press, 1017 Foss Avenue, Drexel Hill, PA 19026.
15. Mary Ann Contogiannis, MD, president, AMA Physicians Health Foundation, 515 N. State Street, Chicago, IL 60610
16. Practice Conflict Resolution Services, Society for Professional Well-Being, 21 West Colony Pl, Durham, NC 27705

APPENDIX B

Examples of Resources Available to Physicians and other Health Care Professionals for the Management of Stress and Maintenance of Well-being.

Newsletter Being Well - Newsletter of the Society for Professional Well-Being, 21 West Colony Place, Durham, NC 27705.

Audio cassettes - (a popular communication media among physicians which can be used during drive time).

Stress Talk - Whole Person Associates, 210 West Michigan, Duluth, MN 55802-1908, (800) 247-6789.

Stress Management for Professionals - by Roger Mellott, Career Track Publications, 3085 Center Green Drive, Boulder, CO 80301-5408, (303) 440-7440.

Power Under Pressure - Robert Kriegel, PhD., Nightingale Conant, 7300 North Lehigh Avenue, Chicago, IL 60648, 1-800-525-9000.

Stress For Success - Peter G. Hanson, MD, Nightingale Conant Audio, IL 60648, 1-800-525-9000.

The Well Physician Course - The American Medical Association International Conference on Physician Health, Scottsdale, AZ, January 28, 1993, First Tape, Inc., 770 N. Lasalle St. - Suite 301, Chicago, IL 60610, (312) 642-7793/Fax (312) 642-9624.

Medical Family Well Being - The American Medical Association International Conference on Physician Health, Scottsdale, AZ, January 28, 1993, First Tape, Inc., 770 N. Lasalle St. - Suite 301, Chicago, IL 60610, (312) 642-7793/Fax (312) 642-9624.

VIDEO

Managing Stress - CRM Films, 2215 Faraday Avenue, Carlsbad, CA 92008, 1-800-421-0833, 25 minutes.

Stress: You're in Control - American Media Incorporated, 4900 University Avenue, West Des Moines, IA 50266-6769, 1-800-262-2557; Fax: 515-224-0256.

Stress Illustrated - (23 minutes) Creative Media, Films Incorporated, 5547 N. Ravenswood Ave., Chicago, IL 60640, 1(800)323-4222; Fax (312) 878-0416.

REFERENCES

1. Samkoff, J.S., MD, ScM. 1993. 1993. Pennsylvania Medicine, 96, 34-37.
2. House, A.C. 1993. (Centers for Disease Control).
3. Ziegler, P., MD. 1993. The Physicians' Health Programs, The Educational and Scientific Trust, PA Medical Society, Stress Management in Medical Practice.
4. Montesano, M. 1993. Pennsylvania Medicine, 44-45.
5. Anonymous. 1993. Journal of the American Medical Association. 270:1116-1117.

6. Morgan, D.R., Eds. 1992. Stress and the Medical Profession (British Medical Association, London).
7. Phelan-Adams, A., M.D. 1993. "Child care crisis especially acute for women doctors," American Medical News, May 10, pp. 24.
8. Saxena, V., MD. 1993. "Putting out the flames that threaten medicine," American Medical News, March 22-29, pp. 21-22.
9. Wadman, M.K. 1992. "Often Belittled by Their Male Colleagues, Women Doctors Also Find Pay Disparity," Wall Street Journal, The, November 25, pp. B1.
10. Mcllrath, S. 1992. "Red tape doctor's top complaint in Medicare reform," American Medical News, October 12, pp. 6.
11. Gable, G.K. 1989. Allegheny County Medical Society Bulletin, 108-109.
12. Page, L. 1991. "HHS: Health spending still outpaces economy," American Medical News, October 28, pp. 9.
13. Galewitz, P. 1991. "Hospital costs irregular," Evening News, April 24, pp. 1.
14. Lake, F. 1993. "Preview old reform plan in recent media reports," This Week, September 13, pp. 2.
15. M. Department. 1993. (Pennsylvania Medical Society, Harrisburg, PA).
16. Goldfield, N. 1991. QRB Quality Review Bulletin 11, 343-8.
17. Hostetter, A. 1993.
18. Penna. Medical Society. 1993. Division of Policy and Programs, Pennsylvania Medicine 96, 1-12 (Blue insert).
19. Bolsen, B. 1992. "Stamp out economic credentialing," American Medical News, June 15, pp. 21.
20. Noble, B.P. 1993. "Pushing Nurses to a Breaking Point," Sunday New York Times, The, January 10.
21. Mitka, M. 1993. "Survey studies physician autonomy, control in groups," American Medical News, February 22, pp. 5.
22. Pfifferling, J.H., PhD. 1993. (The Educational & Scientific Trust of the Pennsylvania Medical Society).
23. A.A.M. Colleges. 1990. "AAMC Participates in RWM Foundation Study of Physician Practice Patterns," Weekly Report, August 8, pp. 1.
24. Skelly, F.J. 1993. "Building Better Doctors," American Medical News, March 1, pp. 27-29.
25. Pfifferling, J.H., PhD. 1991. Center for Professional Well-Being, Things I Wish They Had Taught Me in Training.
26. A. Office of Public Information. 1993. (American College of Obstetrics & Gynecology).
27. Talbott, G.D., Goetz, K. & R., MD and M. Leichtman, PhD. 1993. Medical Family Well-Being, International Conference on Physician Health, 1993 (American Medical Association, Federation of State Medical Boards, Canadian Medical Association Federation of Medical Licensing Authorities of Canada, Scottsdale, Arizona, 1993).
28. Beck, L.C., LLB, CPBC and P.W. Smith, CPBC. 1993. Pennsylvania Medicine 96, 38-39.

Medicine and Health Care Into the Twenty-First Century. Edited by S.K. Majumdar, L.M. Rosenfeld, D.B. Nash and A.M. Audet. © 1995, The Pennsylvania Academy of Science.

Chapter Thirty-One

MEDICINE AS HUMANITIES

JOHN D. ENGEL, Ph.D.[1] and
DEBORAH L. JONES, Ph.D.[2]

[1]Northeastern Ohio Universities, College of Medicine
4209 State Route 44, P.O. Box 95
Rootstown, OH 44272
[2]Accreditation Council for Graduate Medical Education
Chicago, IL

Medicine is the most humane of sciences
and the most scientific of the humanities
Edmund D. Pellegrino

Why in particular do physicians require art?
And what has this to do with medical ethics?
The reason is that, if the enjoyment of art is a
defense against indifference, apathy, and the
erosion of the soul produced by stress, then
medicine is obliged to care for itself through art.
Josef Kovacs

INTRODUCTION

As the title of this chapter suggests, we hold a particular conceptualization of the relationship between the humanities and medicine. This conceptualization, in turn, frames our idea of what constitutes the abstract and practical connections between medicine and humanities, i.e., *medical humanities.*

Our perspective has evolved over combined careers of some 37 years at all levels of medical education. Our assessment of medical humanities emerges from our experiences as a social psychologist and an educational sociologist working in departments of Internal Medicine, Family Medicine, and Psychiatry. In addition to our faculty responsibilities, one or the other of us has been a director of research in medical education at a large midwestern medical school, a director of medical education for a community hospital, an administrative associate at the Association of American Medical Colleges, and a director of educational programs at the American College of Surgeons. In addition to our teaching responsibilities, one of us has served as director of a program in medical humanities and social sciences and the other has served as director of continuing medical education. As a result of our practicing in a variety of academic and clinical settings, our view of the relationship between the humanities and medicine has shifted. We once saw the medical humanities as a branch of applied humanities and social sciences; we now see them as a hybrid field woven through the fabric of medicine to create a distinctive pattern. This particular viewpoint was foreshadowed by Pellegrino as early as 1979 (1) and further articulated by Thomasma several years later (2). Thomasma's argument is particularly instructive.

> If the problems we address arise from medicine, and the questions are framed by the medical context, the insights we offer are relevant to its employment, the strategies we use are molded by its educational framework, and clinical relations are necessitated by its practice, then we ought to critically question whether medical humanities are a branch of applied humanities at all . . . if their origin, goal, and matter are in medicine, they are best seen as a second order reflection on medical theory and practice which are themselves a branch of the humanities. As such, the medical humanities are a form of meta-medicine . . . (pp. 72-73).

This way of contextualizing the relationship of the humanities and medicine suggests a particular sensitizing definition for the field. Modifying Thomasma's thoughts about medical humanities, we believe that *medical humanities are disciplined social critiques of the forms of thinking and acting required by health professionals to nurture a human perspective on medical theory, practice and delivery in an age characterized by rapidly changing social, economic, and technological features.* When we refer to the *medical humanities,* we have in mind a wide variety of disciplines including history, philosophy, and literature as well as those areas of the social sciences that have strong humanistic traditions. More generally, we regard the relationship between the humanities and medicine as a specific instance of what ought to be the relationship between liberal education and professional education. In addition, we believe and will argue later that the best work in medical humanities takes place where the humanities and medicine intersect intellectually and practically and where an interdisciplinary perspective guides the work.

This chapter presents a review of medical humanities in four separate though related parts. The first section describes the modern historical relationship between medicine and the humanities in Western societies, but emphasizes the engagement of the two fields in the United States during the late 19th and 20th centuries. The next section surveys recent connections between specific disciplines in the humanities and medicine. The third portion of the chapter describes the establishment, growth and development of medical humanities programs at various levels of the medical education system. Part four both critiques and speculates about the formal engagements between medicine and the humanities.

HISTORICAL CONNECTIONS BETWEEN THE HUMANITIES AND MEDICINE

The present day intimate connection between science and medicine and the popular idea (among the lay public as well as many physicians) that the practice of medicine is applied science are recent events in the history of medicine. In a longer view, medicine has been referred to as one of the oldest *learned* professions. In Western traditions, the roots of the relationship between medicine and the humanities can be traced to Greek thought in the fifth and fourth centuries B.C. While the development of this relationship is beyond the scope of this chapter, it may be said (at the risk of oversimplification) that education in the humanities was of practical value and intimately connected with the practice of medicine (3). In this regard, Cassell notes that from Maimonides to Lewis Thomas, the history of the medical profession has been punctuated by people of broad and liberal education (4).

From the late 19th century through the early part of the 20th century, distinguished physicians in American medicine proclaimed the importance of the humanities in educating physicians. Cassell, referring to a graduation address by Dr. William Fussell at the Women's Medical College in 1857, notes that in the mid-nineteenth century, "... it was believed that the physician's knowledge should include 'literature of the past and present; history ancient and modern; politics, and religious beliefs of the times'" (4). In 1909, S. Weir Mitchell, the famous Philadelphia physician-writer, wrote that physicians should develop their literary and artistic talents, concluding that:

> Few men in early life can do much more than is needed to learn our art and its sister sciences; but, as time goes on, there are many who can add to it other pursuits which greatly benefit them in a wide sense, and enlarge and strengthen their mental powers, or pleasantly contribute to the joys of life, and so even to the growth of a man's moral nature (5).

So strongly did Sir William Osler believe in the value of a liberal education that he outlined a course of reading for all medical students that could be covered in short periods of time at the beginning and at the end of each day (6) (See below)

OSLER: "BEDSIDE LIBRARY FOR MEDICAL STUDENTS"

A LIBERAL education may be had at a very slight cost of time and money. Well filled though the day be with appointed tasks, to make the best possible use of your one or of your ten talents, rest not satisfied with this professional training, but try to get the education if not a scholar, at least of a gentleman. Before going to sleep read for half an hour, and in the morning have a book open on your dressing table. You will be surprised to find how much can be accomplished in the course of a year. I have put down a list of ten books which you may make close friends. There are many others; studied carefully in your student days these will help in the inner education of which I speak.

I. Old and New Testament	VI. Epicteus (2)
II. Shakespeare	VII. *Religio Medici* (2)
III. Montaigne (1)	VIII. *Don Quixote*
IV. Plutarch's *Lives* (1)	IX. Emerson
V. Marcus Aurelius (2)	X. Olive Wendell Holmes - Breakfast-Table Series

(1) The Temple Classics, J.M. Dent & Co. (2) Golden Treasury Series, MacMillan Co.

THE HUMANITIES AND MEDICINE: Recent Connections

Cassell has referred to the connection between the humanities and medicine as "Putting living persons back into medicine" (4). As he sees it, ". . . the problem arises because physicians are trained from the first days of medical school to disregard the knowledge they bring with them of everyday life and human function as irrelevant to medicine. Another obstacle is that doctors are not trained to include in their decision making the kind of "soft" and often subjective information that is relevant to the everyday life and function of sick persons" (16).

If medical humanism is to be one component of an education system which assists in the growth and development of physicians who are not burdened with the characteristics noted by Cassell, then, to understand how this is to be facilitated we should first ask, What is medical humanism? Thoughtfully, though conservatively, Edmund Pellegrino (13) has spoken of two important strands of humanism, strands, in our view, that are woven together at a practical level and can (or should) be disentangled only for analytical purposes. Pellegrino's ideas deserve serious attention:

> The first strand is humanism as a *literary and educational ideal.* This is the most traditional conception of humanism. It is based in, and on, a familiarity with the Judeo-Christian and the Greco-Roman classical tradition, especially in its seminal texts. In medicine its prototypes in the West are physicians like Thomas Linacre, John Caius, Thomas Percival or William Osler. These were men educated in classical languages and literature. They were men noted for their lifelong scholarship, their bibliophilia, and their eloquence in writing and speaking. The disciplines most pertinent to this kind of humanism were the classical liberal arts—history, literature, language, and philosophy . . .
>
> The second sense in which medical humanism is used is as an *affective and behavioral ideal.* This concept emphasizes humanitarianism, humaneness and sensitivity to the patient's needs as a person. It centers on empathy, warmth, receptivity, and openness to the human and personal dimensions of illness. This concept is thought by many to be exemplified in a concern for the psychosocial dimensions of illness, and for treating the patient "as a person." The relevant disciplines are held to be sociology, psychology, economics, communication and interviewing skills. Much attention is also directed to a "humane" concern for the emotional health of the medical student, to the potential dehumanizing effects of the process of education itself. The affective strain emphasizes *the physician as a well adjusted, emotionally mature, secure and caring person* (p. 82).

Pellegrino's comments are an apt preamble to the next section of this chapter, which discusses the connections between medicine and specific areas of the humanities. In addition, we would also add two caveats. First, while we discuss the various humanities disciplines separately, we recognized that, in practice, there is considerable overlap across the fields. Also, as we noted previously, we have chosen to limit our review to three disciplines—philosophy, history, and literature.

PHILOSOPHY

Philosophy as a discipline connects with medicine at two broad levels of involvement. One is at the level of having something important to say about the understanding of moral dilemmas in clinical situations. The other level of engagement concerns the logic, epistemology, and metaphysics of problems peculiar to medicine. (It is beyond the scope of this chapter to consider the area of ethics as it relates to biomedical research) In this review, because of the disproportionate attention it receives both in the professional and lay communities, we will concentrate on medical ethics. However, we want to note in passing the very important questions addressed in this other area. Philosophers of medicine are concerned with questions such as:

(a) What is the purpose and nature of medicine as a profession?
(b) What is the nature of important concepts such as health, disease, illness, treatment, morbidity, cure, etc.?
(c) What is the relationship between biomedical science and medical practice?
(d) How do values enter the practice of biomedical science and medicine?
(e) What is the nature of the authority of the physician?
(f) What is the relationship between theories of medicine and clinical practice?

Here, medicine and philosophy deal with fundamental though historically and contextually framed issues concerning the language and concepts of medicine as well as the methodology of clinical judgment and decision making. The interested reader will find a comprehensive review of these areas written by Englehardt and Erde (14).

In recent times, medical ethics has become enormously popular both within the profession and the lay public. Until the 1960s, the dominant mode of thinking in medical ethics was influenced by the Hippocratic ethic (15). Beginning in the 1960's, this large body of work received increasingly strong critique as part of the general intellectual, political, and organized consumer unrest of the time. Pellegrino (15) notes:

> Concomitantly, the character of medicine was being altered by the specialization, fragmentation, institutionalization, and depersonalization of health care. At the same time, the number and complexity of medical ethical issues expanded as the power of medical technology presented new challenges to traditional values (p. 1159).

During this decade, philosophers began to enter the field of medicine and brought with them a systematic/analytic process grounded in moral philosophy for thinking about ethical dilemmas in medical environments. The content of this thinking was usually some variation of deontology or consequentialism. Ross (16) had developed a theory of prima facie principles which became the dominant mode of engaging in ethical decision-making. In 1989, Thomas Beauchamp and James Childress published *Principles of Biomedical Ethics* (17). This text quickly became one of the standard references for academic medicine. In their work they chose prima facie principles which seemed particularly appropriate in medical contexts—*nonmaleficence, beneficence, autonomy,* and *justice.* As explained by Pellegrino, these two philosophers, when trying to apply principles to a real clinical situation involving a moral dilemma (15), were well aware of the practical limitations in Ross's theory. In the complex particulars of a clinical case, abstract and equally weighted principles of bioethics were inevitably in conflict with each other. According to Pellegrino (15), Beauchamp and Childress tried to overcome this problem in the following manner:

> [They] proposed four requirements that must be met to justify infringement of a prima facie principle or obligation: (1) the moral objective sought must be realistic, (2) no morally preferable alternative is available, (3) the least infringement possible must be sought, and (4) the agent must act to minimize the effects of infringement. In this way, the authors hoped to steer a course between the absolutism of principles and the relativism of situation ethics. Their guidelines are helpful, but do not eradicate the inherent limitations of any set of prima facie principles that is not lexically ordered (p. 1160).

In our view, the attempt intellectually to correct the problems encountered in applying abstract principles to concrete particular situations could not succeed because of what Alfred North Whitehead referred to as the *fallacy of misplaced concreteness,* i.e. mistaking the abstract for a complete representation of all concrete instances of a phenomenon (18).

The weaknesses of principlism as the dominant form of medical ethics has been criticized widely (19, 20, 21, 22). While the particulars of the organized criticisms are varied, ultimately they hold to the belief that a strong form of principlism cannot help us understand complex clinical situations and many are doubtful that even a weak form of these theories will survive. While it would be foolhardy to speculate about the outcome of these debates, there is reason to be optimistic about the positions and understandings which could result from this exchange of viewpoints. But what are the most popular competing viewpoints? We will mention four: *virtue ethics, casuistry, feminist ethics,* and *narrative ethics.*

In the recent past, the characteristics of virtue-based theories have been articulated by Alasdair McIntyre (23, 24). Fundamental in this view is a focus on the proper character of physicians—those human qualities which will allow physicians to perform their socially allotted functions. McIntyre argues that virtue ethics (which characterized much of ethics until the 1960s) cannot be recovered—it was too private and too idiosyncratic. Pellegrino contends that virtue ethics, in order to contribute to any theory of medical ethics, "must be anchored in some prior theory of the right and good and of human nature in terms of which virtues can be defined. It also requires a community of values to sustain its practice . . . This will require a conceptual link with duties, rules, consequences, and moral psychology, in which the virtue of prudence plays a special role" (p. 1161).

Casuistry, a technique of practical reasoning for the ethicist, has great appeal for physicians because it is based on clinical cases, the coin of the clinical realm (25). Jonsen and Toulmin define casuistry as

> . . . the interpretation of moral issues, using procedures of reasoning based on paradigms and analogies, leading to the formulation of expert opinion

> about the existence and stringency of particular moral obligations, framed in terms of rules or maxims that are general but not universal or invariable, since they hold good with certainty only in the typical conditions of the agent and circumstances of action (p. 5).

One finds cases that are clear examples of some principle and then, through a comparative method, one moves from these cases to less clear cases, ordering them by a process of analogy. This reasoning process does not discard principles but makes them secondary to the particulars of the case and thus is an attempt to move back and forth between case and principle in such a way as to deny the absolute character of principles.

The ethics of caring and social justice have received emphasis within a *feminist* movement in medical ethics (26, 27). While medical ethics is a relatively new discipline, feminist ethics is even a more recent discipline. Sherwin (26) notes: "Feminist ethics . . . derives from the explicitly political perspective of feminism, wherein the oppression of women is seen to be morally and politically unacceptable . . . it incorporates a critique of the specific practices that constitute their oppression" (49).

Within feminism, it is more accurate to talk of *feminisms,* recognizing the intellectual, social, and cultural variety characterizing the movement. Nevertheless, the strength of the collective viewpoint is in (a) the recognition of multiple and interrelated sources of oppression that exist in society, and (b) the explicit use of race, class and gender as key features in the analysis of moral dilemmas in clinical medicine. What is of interest here is the relationship of these features to everyday clinical decision making and to macro issues of health policy. A feminist perspective sensitizes ethicists and health professionals to the ways in which the practice of medicine reinforces dominant viewpoints about race, class, and sexual preference which disadvantage those who are subordinate in a given situation. Further, feminist ethics forces consideration of social context and the individuality of experience, thus rejecting the reliance on abstract reasoning that is seen in other forms of ethics (26). Among other things, these viewpoints have opened up discussion of a new set of issues, including viewing as disease normal features of female reproduction and patterns of dominance and power in clinical decision-making.

Narrative ethics places emphasis on the patient's life story as the context in which ethical judgments ought to be made (28). By taking a narrative stance toward ethical analysis, one includes a time dimension and historical sequence as critical features. Howard Brody makes a distinction between the *old medical ethics,* a Hippocratic or beneficence-centered ethics, and the *new medical ethics,* a patient-centered, autonomy-centered ethics. According to Brody, the old ethics focuses on how to decide what is best for the patient and then how to act to support this decision. In this view, there is no special obligation to gain the patient's cooperation in the decision process. The new medical ethics, on the other hand, has a special focus on the processes involved in promoting patient autonomy and in guarding against physician paternalism (29).

The point of Brody's critique is that both views are partial and extreme in their own way. This situation, he argues, opens the discussion to examining additional moral dimensions of the physician-patient relationship, including one that he and several other ethicists favor, namely that of *power.* Brody maintains that an important task for medical ethics is to recognize formally the use of physician power in the relationship with patients so that physicians, patients and others vested in this type of relationship can collectively come to a way of thinking about and perhaps even of setting guidelines for the use of power, so that the physician shares with the patient both information and the moral responsibility for deciding among treatment alternatives. Given this position, Brody then offers an epistemology to support a different kind of theory about medical ethics.

Conceptually, Brody argues for two forms of moral reasoning - *formal* and *narrative.* By formal reasoning he has in mind reasoning that moves from axioms to conclusions in a prescribed and logical fashion (deductive reasoning, if you prefer). An important feature of this type of moral reasoning is its claim to be independent of content. The product of such reasoning is offered as ahistorical and decontextualized knowledge. Narrative moral reasoning, for Brody, is reasoning "... that makes sense of events and yields further conclusions, primarily by placing those events in a broader life context and then viewing the relationship among all the events that seem relevant" (p. 248). In contrast to formal moral reasoning, narrative reasoning occurs in context and is primarily informed by the cultural, historical, and practical relationships embedded in the person's context. For Brody, formal moral reasoning has been more characteristic of both the old and new medical ethics and, consequently, socio-cultural and political dimensions of the physician-patient relationship do not and cannot become an explicit part of this type of moral reasoning. If one allows such practical dimensions into the discussion of theories of medical ethics, then one also allows into the conversation an active role for narrative moral reasoning as a way of identifying and transacting moral dilemmas. On this point, Brody (29) states:

> Narrative reasoning would proceed differently. When we have a momentous decision to make, we often ask ourselves how that decision would fit within our unfolding life story. Would it cohere in a meaningful and authentic way as the sort of action that the principal character of this narrative would be likely to perform? Or does it stick out as an incoherent and unexplainable aberration? Given that most of us want to view ourselves as people who care about our close associates and the opinion they have of us, it seems unlikely that we would finally make such a decision without checking their reactions. We normally do this by extended conversations, over time, in which we can verbally try on various alternative decisions to gauge the reactions of those we care about. It is not until we can assemble those reactions—and until we can practice *owning* the various decision options by hearing the words come out of our mouths—that we can decide what our true preferences are. Our preferences and values emerge from the narrative process; they are not "facts" that can be known prior to the process and independently of it (p. 249).

Finally, it is interesting to note that both narrative and feminist medical ethics share common values in terms of the importance of context, power, gender, race, social class and the particulars of a person's life story to ethics deliberations.

HISTORY

History has long been acknowledged as a means for providing a sense of continuity, grounding our current experiences in the past, and broadening our range of experiences. Regardless of whether the goal is to understand history better, or to understand medicine better, the study of history broadens and enriches our knowledge and understanding of human life (30).

The documentation of medicine in history has enabled physicians and scientists to place recent events and findings into context and to understand their significance. The most notable example of this today is in the formal reporting of research. Research questions and findings are routinely placed into historical context in order to provide a basis for evaluation of the research methods and findings as an extension of past work and as a contribution to knowledge in the field. Cassell notes that the study of medicine in history also helps us understand that medicine is not timeless or value-free, and that medicine has always been subjected to economic and social forces (4).

The contributions of history to medicine transcend the pragmatic, however, and add texture to the strands of humanism as delineated by Pellegrino. At the level of literary and educational ideal, history provides medicine with an important source and sense of continuity. Genevieve Miller ". . . maintains that the main value of medical history is in making the practitioner a truly 'educated person', that is broadening his range of experience beyond the provincial beliefs of his time" (30). By providing a framework for analyzing clinical concepts, history enables physicians to understand the practice of medicine and medical thought of different times. Our understanding of morbidity and mortality, for example, are directly related to events and/or developments that have taken place in the past. Intellectually, historical analyses of medicine have contributed to a broader understanding of the profession as a complex social system. As examples, "Neo-Marxist scholarship has directed attention to the part played by the medical profession in the maintenance of the class system, feminist scholarship has shown how medicine perpetuates gender roles" (31).

The study of history also enhances meaning in the clinical setting and directly facilitates the rehumanization of medicine. As Cassell has stated, ". . . patients *always* have histories" (4). Physicians take a patient's "history" in an effort to place the patient and his illness into context and, thus, perspective. This is where Pellegrino's second strand of humanism—the affective and behavioral—is addressed. Cultural historians show us how diseases and medical concepts are time-specific, directly related to the social, religious, or philosophical thought of the particular period (30). Thus, patients from cultural and social backgrounds different from their physician may come to the medical encounter with different sets of assumptions and expectations. The success of the encounter rests, in part, on the ability of the physician to understand those differences and to accommodate them in the transaction of medical care. Patients are not independent of the worlds in which they live, and through history physicians come to understand the impact of social context on patient care in general and on patients specifically. History thus is a

Now . . . consider this poem describing the same office visit:

Love is driving me crazy,
says the back of Scruggs' wife,
her hand turning the doorknob.
She stops and tugs the end of our talk
to a new place, as if it were a skirt
rounding her ironing board.
He's across the bed dead drunk,
she tells the x-ray boxes
and cocks her head around at me.
She steps from my room to her room,
a room without furniture -
He sold the couch last week
and took a bus to Ocean City -
where she stands by a stack of Scruggs' beer
in front of a window, ironing.
She puts up the iron. *Oh, God, I suffer*
from the power of inclination.
How my body changes
and the times change, but Scruggs . . .
That doesn't change. She wears a pair of pink
drawers and a white blouse, and sprinkles
and steams her traveling skirt.
This is the last straw, If the Vets
don't keep him this time, doctor,
I'm going to find a way to kill him
quickly, not piece by piece
like he killed me.

. . . in the poem we see the patient as a person whose story matters. She had her hand on the doorknob, ready to leave the office, when she began to tell me about her real concern, the fact that her alcoholic husband was drinking again. In her anger and frustration, she told me a tale about the ravages of love and hate. No wonder blood sugar was out of control (pp. 364-365).

Although the process of writing from the patient's point of view is enlightening in itself, this example highlights the value of the physician's listening to patients with the skills and sensitivities with which one reads stories, of seeing patients as more than numbers and "facts" on a page. Coulehan uses literature to move beyond chart notes and to see the patient as a person with an important story to tell. With interpretive skills honed on literature, physicians are better able to interpret the stories that are being told by patients.

The field of literature and medicine has thus evolved into one in which there is ". . . a fruitful interaction . . . an interaction that will enrich teaching and thinking about both works of literature and the work of caring for the ill" (38). Larry Churchhill (39) writes in the inaugural issue of *Literature and Medicine* that:

> . . . narrative has the power to *show* us, rather than *tell us about* the profound mystery of medical encounters. Literature makes this narrative available to us, displays it, rather than recasting, cloaking or analyzing it beyond recognition. Literature at its best lets be, for its own sake, and on its own terms, the human realities of medicine. Far from being artificial, the conjoining of literature and medicine is natural and even essential (p. 35).

This conjoining of literature and medicine is best facilitated and enhanced by interdisciplinary work—clinicians and humanities faculty working together, drawing on the strengths of their respective disciplines to provide insights that reveal the pattern that underlies the whole. We see the essential part of this relationship in Coles' (40) comments on the connections between stories and service.

> In the tradition of Emerson, Thoreau, Tolstoy, William Carlos Williams, and William James—each of whom tried to connect moral ideas to the lived life—my parents realized the link between stories and service. They knew that stories are a means of glimpsing and comprehending the world; they knew that service is a means of putting to use what has been learned, for in the daily events designated as service, all sorts of stories are encountered and experienced (p. xxiii).

Another important dimension of literature and medicine is the critique of literary works by feminists. By extending and emphasizing the connections made earlier by others between literature and social issues, these works provide insights into the clinical encounter and the profession of medicine. The examination of content, language, and images in terms of variables such as gender, race, and class has served to refocus the lens through which we view people in general and individuals in particular. One of the major contributions of literary criticism to medicine and medical education has been in the deconstruction of role stereotypes that have contributed to the dehumanization of medicine. Wear (41) describes how this happens in her literature classes for medical students:

> I believe that humanities inquiry—literature in particular—can confront critique, and unsettle learners. With that as a goal, my literature classes should be sites of uneasiness, of exploring preconceptions, of self-conscious examinations of values and beliefs. My classes should be sites of resistance from the taken-for-granted, a place where our thinking and actions are under scrutiny. . . . I propose that the medical humanities, literature in particular, be an outsider (outlaw?) discourse in medicine that challenges inequities, distortions, and abuses of power. Such inquiry would explicitly and directly challenge the insidious, cunning, but often covert sexism, racism, classism, religiosity and heterosexism of our culture, all reflected in the practice of medicine in the United States" (p. 3).

Viewed in this manner, literature and medicine specifically and the humanities in general are clearly on the margin, but on the margin of medicine as opposed to the margin of the humanities. Wear (42) describes the humanities as a ". . . community of resistance in the margins . . . " where ". . . we can use radical voices that speak directly and openly to those issues that compelled our existence in medicine in the first place" (p. 203). It is here, on the margin, that we find the intersection of disciplines—philosophers and physicians, basic scientists and humanists—that supports and reaffirms the presence and importance of human values in medicine and results in the textured tapestries that are the humanities in medicine. We will explore this important idea further in the last section of the chapter.

THE HUMANITIES IN UNDERGRADUATE, GRADUATE, AND CONTINUING MEDICAL EDUCATION

As noted earlier, a variety of social forces at work during the 1960's, including the call for relevance on college campuses, a widespread dissatisfaction with specialization in medicine and resulting maldistribution of medical care, and the renewed interest in family medicine with its acknowledged value on the individual as a whole and as part of a larger social unit, sparked conversation and interaction among those engaged in the various disciplines of the humanities and those engaged in various aspects of medicine. From this early and tentative interdisciplinary collaboration came the drive to integrate humanities into the fabric of the medical curriculum.

The effort to link the humanities and medicine gained momentum in 1965 with the formation of the National Endowment for the Humanities and Arts by act of Congress and, shortly thereafter, the founding of The Society for Health and Human Values (SHHV) in 1968. The SHHV was formed to provide faculty of all disciplines a formal forum for discussion of issues related to human values in health professions education. The 1970's saw the National Endowment for the Humanities (NEH) and private foundations providing significant funding of institutional programs and institutes dealing with the humanities and human values. The Institute on Human Values in Medicine (IHVM), for example, an arm of the SHHV, was established in 1970 with NEH funding. New York University in 1976, with funding from the Andrew W. Mellon Foundation, was able to create its university-wide Humanities Council.

Undergraduate Medical Education

In its first decade, the IHVM conducted national surveys, published descriptions of human values programs, and provided "resource site visits" to eighty medical schools. In 1972, the IHVM published detailed descriptions of teaching programs in twelve medical schools; in a 1982 survey conducted by the IHVM, 109 of the 122 U.S. medical schools responding reported human values courses and/or activities (43).

In 1984, the Association of American Medical Colleges (AAMC) published "Physicians for the Twenty-First Century", a report that was intended to review and provide guidance with respect to the general professional education of physicians (44). The Working Group on Personal Qualities, Values, and Attitudes declared that physicians:

> . . . should possess stamina, moral sensitivity and integrity, curiosity and creativity, the ability to cope with intellectual and emotional demands, and a commitment to help and work with others. They should value intellectual growth, science and the scientific method, social responsibility, and altruism. They should be respectful, modest, and compassionate toward their patients and toward other health professionals (44).

To these ends, the working panel recommended, among other things, ". . . that each medical school campus have at least one full-time humanist to lead research in these areas and to act as a catalyst and liaison with other course directors to ensure that humanities materials are integrated into the curriculum" (p. 185).

While it is unclear what impact the AAMC report may have had on the development and funding of the humanities in U.S. medical schools, more recent surveys show a continuing increase in the number and type of programs being offered under the "human values" rubric. Of the 114 U.S. medical schools responding to a survey from the Association of American Medical Colleges in 1985, 113 reported provided information on human values teaching programs at their institutions (45). This survey sought to:

> . . . obtain information on required courses designed to improve students ability to: 1) examine their values in relation to those of patients, 2) communicate effectively with patients, or 3) think critically about cultural, social and ethical issues arising in medical care (p. 1).

In the report of preliminary results of a survey conducted by Frank and Becker in 1992 (48), all 78 medical schools (60% of U.S. medical schools) responding to the first request for information reported offerings in ethics/human values. Seventy of these schools reported offering ethics/human values curricula; eight cited informal activities.

Over the decade spanning these surveys, institutions report an increase in the numbers of courses and activities that fall under the rubric of "human values" and of courses offered that contain human values components. The numbers reported by self-report surveys are of interest, but by no means provide a clear and detailed picture of content and the degree of intellectual integrity and coherence found within and across the boundaries of course titles. While these courses and activities, required and elective, span the four years of the medical curriculum, from the lists of courses provided by Bickel's survey, little seems clear about what is actually taught under the rubric of "human values", or how much time is actually devoted to human values topics and issues. Neither does Bickel's survey clarify whether these courses and activities are part of an institutionally developed and financially supported human values program that is integrated into the overall curriculum or whether they are isolated attempts on the part of various departments to introduce humanistic components into courses for which they have responsibility.

For example, a course entitled "Human Growth and Development" offered by a department of pediatrics is difficult to justify under the rubric of a "required human values course". Similarly, to include "ICM" as a human values course stretches the definitions of both human values and introduction to clinical medicine courses. This is not to negate the value of human components of courses, but rather to caution against placing too much weight on the inclusion of sporadic activities that do not fit into an overall humanities or human values conceptual framework defined in terms of the institutional curriculum.

Furthermore, it is unclear how many of these humanities programs would be termed successful. As noted by Pellegrino and McElhenny (43) in their review of "resource site visits" to 80 medical schools under the auspices of the IHVM between 1972 and 1982, the Institute proclaimed a human values program "successful" if it:

> . . . engaged its teachers and learners, was visible and respected outside its own confines, occupied a secure place organizationally, and if funding was assured. The degree of clinical involvement and 'spill-over' into other parts of the curriculum were additional indicators of success (p. 21).

In her report of the 1985 AAMC study, Bickel (45) noted that there existed significant barriers to integrating humanities programs into medical schools, primary among them: funding, already overloaded curricula, and departmental boundaries. These social and financial forces make developing and sustaining long-term integrated medical humanities programs as a prominent feature of undergraduate medical education extremely difficult.

Graduate Medical Education

The teaching of humanities in residency education has been less widespread and more focused in terms of concentration on medical ethics. In 1985, Bickel (45) noted that 42 medical schools reported having formally organized human values programs for residents—programs that took place on an on-going basis in at least one department. However, this number does not begin to account for the myriad of accredited residency education programs that exist today.

The most notable presence of the humanities in graduate medical education is found in the 1985 requirement of the American Board of Internal Medicine (ABIM) ". . . that all candidates for certification demonstrate a high standard of humanistic behavior in their professional lives" (47). To underscore the importance of this requirement, the ABIM has published a guide book in which they define what they mean by humanistic qualities (integrity, respect, and compassion), describe how graduate medical education programs can have an impact on their residents and fellows with respect to these qualities, suggest strategies for assessing humanistic qualities in trainees, and provide an annotated bibliography. Given the prominence of ABIM in the medical community and the number of internists trained each year, this guide certainly represents an important step. Other important issues for further work include the clarity of the requirements, accountability of training programs, and assessment of individual practitioners.

Continuing Medical Education

The humanities in continuing medical education is at best episodic. Despite the recognition that the humanities contribute to the development of health care professionals at all levels, little evidence of formal activity at this level exists.

The Kennedy Institute of Georgetown University and the Hastings Center both offer educational activities in the area of ethics that are appropriate for physicians. Isolated CME courses occasionally offer a session or two on ethical issues related to topics at hand, and a review of the education sections published bi-annually in the *Journal of the American Medical Association* showed few, if any, courses in medical humanities.

Limited educational opportunities for practicing physicians extend as well to medical school faculty. Compared to the variety and large numbers of other types of continuing medical education opportunities that are available, the opportunities for faculty development in the area of medical humanities are rare, and can accommodate few participants. Such faculty development programs are most often in the area of biomedical ethics and are frequently tied to grant funding of limited duration. Notable exceptions to this exist. The Center for Literature, Medicine, and the Health Care Professions, a collaborative project of Hiram College and Northeastern Ohio Universities College of Medicine, provides programs which explore how literature and the humanities relate with medicine. Critical to the healthy life of the paticipants (48) is the need to provide a full range of humanities programs medical school faculty and extend the interdisciplinary connections within medical schools.

MARGINALITY AND *MEDICINE AS HUMANITIES*

Medical humanities programs in undergraduate and graduate medical education occupy the margin. Such activities do not quite fit into the mainstream of what happens at the center of medicine, medical schools and/or hospitals. In this position of the discipline lies strength but also weakness and vulnerability.

Working along the margin provides opportunities for innovation in practice and theory that could not be realized otherwise. Recent scholarship on the process of specialization-fragmentation in disciplines has shown that when scholars from one discipline knowingly work on problems that are the focus of attention of scholars from another discipline, innovation in the humanities and social sciences occurs more often and with considerable impact. This process has been conceptualized as a two stage process—increased specialization leading to fragmentation into narrow subspecialties, and then as specialization approaches extreme limits, scholars work to integrate the fragments into hybrid fields (49). This process is a useful representation of the current state of subfields in literary theory, philosophy, sociology, and anthropology as they have connected with medicine and evolved into specific fields within medical humanities. Currently, some of the most conceptually innovative work resides along the boundary where medicine, philosophy, literary theory, political science, and micro-sociology intersect and engage in work on common issues and problems. Evidence for this view may be found, for example, in the work of Kathryn Hunter (39) on the ways of knowing in medicine; in the way Rita Charon has conceptualized and implemented ideas on the nature of transactions between physicians and patients as well as the way in which medical students can be educated in more humane ways (32, 33); in Howard Brody's theoretical and practical analysis of physician-patient relationships to empower all participants (28, 29);

in the works of Howard Waitzkin (50) and Susan Sherwin (26) on the influence of race, gender and social class in clinical encounters.

Working along the margin also increases the likelihood that the medical humanities will serve one of its most important functions—social critique. The distanced and reflective voices of the medical humanities punctuate the limitations of foundational knowledge in medicine and the tacit assumptions, customs and ritual performances of medicine.

At a practical level, however, there is reason to be concerned. Typically, there are fewer professionals doing interdisciplinary work at the margin. Perhaps because of the difficulty of this type of work, perhaps because of current forms of academic politics, perhaps because of decreasing financial resources available to most of our institutions of higher education, and most likely, because of some unknown mix of these and other factors, rarely does there emerge a critical mass of individuals committed to the advancement of medical humanities in our institutions of medical education. As a consequence, more often than not, these professionals have their time and energy dissipated in such a way that students, residents and physicians receive only a "snap shot" of medicine as humanities—an aperiodic, unsystematic view of the relationships between medicine and medical humanities. This social-organizational arrangement serves often to diminish the impact of the relationship—it becomes superficial and easily dismissed. There are, of course, important and notable exceptions to this representation, but they are *exceptions*.

Vulnerability is also associated with working along the margin. One source of risk is due to the political economies of institutions of medical education. In the time of budgetary restrictions, activities on the margin are most vulnerable to cutbacks in resources, personnel and funds. This is particularly true in situations where activities are on soft money lines and where organizational support resides exclusively in an administrator's *noblesse oblige* (while this might be a necessary condition it is certainly not sufficient for long term growth and development of a program). These situations serve to destabilize the relationship between medicine and the humanities.

Another vulnerability associated with working along the margin deals with one's professional identity. One often encounters difficulty in finding a personally satisfying balance point between being a part of the dominant field in order to reflect on and engage in its activities (e.g., being a medical sociologist doing good medical sociology) and at the same time remaining sufficiently distant from the center so as not to have one's role as critic be diminished. What complicates matters is that the medical humanist as social critic really has two responsibilities in this era of post-modernism. Given the current intellectual ferment in each of the humanities and social science disciplines, one must within these fields reflect critically on the intellectual positions as well as critique their connections with medicine.

Teaching, doing research and administering from the margin entail yet another vulnerability—one which some have recognized as a form of evangelism and hegemony (41). Individuals living as members of small communities of scholars define the particulars of work along the margin. This situation along with the current political economy of medicine and medical education have the potential for nurturing a situation in which medical humanities become another univocal "solution" to the ills of medical practice and education. At one and the same time medical humanities can be mystified and instrumentalized. If and when this happens we become what we criticize in medicine—another monolithic centrism, intolerant to other viewpoints and other less powerful voices.

An antidote for both the weaknesses and vulnerabilities we've discussed lies in reflective critical interdisciplinary practice along the boundary of medicine and humanities (some form of critical pragmatism, if you will). The challenge is in interdisciplinary teaching and collaborative research, where the collaborators are not only our colleagues from other disciplines but those people whom we are interested in understanding in greater detail. The difficult task is in making room for the practical and intellectual work of all those who have a vested interest in whatever we come to call problematic. To disentagle medicine and humanities either conceptually or practically is misguided. The work is at the level of relationships among the fields, not at the level of the separate disciplines. Because it places heavy responsibilities and resource demands on both individuals and organization, this idea may not be popular. Having visiting professorships in medical humanities is easier. Having one or two Grand Rounds devoted to medical ethics or a course in medical ethics for first-year medical students is easier. Asking a physician and a social scientist, usually overcommitted to begin with, to give a few lectures on the meaning of a biopsychosocial model of medicine to a freshman class is easier. Establishing an interdisciplinary program or department of medical humanities and social sciences with full-time faculty representing different professions, including medicine; a program or department with responsibilities for teaching and doing collaborative research across the continuum of medical education is more difficult. The first situations, all too common, represent *medicine and the humanities.* The last situation, all too rare is *medicine as humanities.*

AUTHOR'S ACKNOWLEDGMENT

We wish to gratefully acknowledge the helpful critique of this work by several colleagues. Comments and conversations with Delese Wear, Harry LeFever, Jack Coulehan, O.D. Kowlessar, Paul Durbin, and Lee Mullett have served to strengthen the work. Any remaining limitations are solely ours.

REFERENCES

1. Pellegrino, Edmund D. 1979. *Humanism and the Physician.* Knoxville: The University of Tennessee Press.
2. Thomasma, David C. 1982. "Capstone" Conference Workshops: Reflections on the State of the Art. In E.D. Pellegrino and T.K. McElhinney (Eds.), *Teaching Ethics, the Humanities, and Human Values in Medical Schools: A Ten-Year Overview.* Washington, D.C.: Institute on Human Values, Society for Health and Human Values.

3. Callahan, Daniel, Arthur Caplan and Bruce Jennings. 1984. *On the Uses of the Humanities: Vision and Application.* New York: The Hastings Center, Institute of Society, Ethics, and the Life Sciences.
4. Cassell, Eric J. 1984. *The Place of Humanities in Medicine.* New York: The Hastings Center, Institute of Society, Ethics, and the Life Sciences.
5. Mitchell, S. Weir. 1909 (1972 edition). *Doctor and Patient.* New York: Arno Press & The New York Times.
6. Osler W. 1904. Bed-Side Library For Medical Students. In *Aequanimitas, With other Addresses to Medical Students, Nurses and Practitioner.* London: H.K. Lewis, p. 389.
7. Rothstein, William G. 1987. *American Medical Schools and the Practice of Medicine: A History.* New York: Oxford University.
8. Lundmerer, Kenneth M. 1985. *Learning to Heal; The Development of American Medical Education.* New York: Basic Books.
9. Starr, Paul. 1982. *The Social Transformation of American Medicine: The Rise of a Sovereign Profession and the Making of A Vast Industry.* New York: Basic Books.
10. Flexner, Abraham. 1910. *Medical Education in the U.S. and Canada. A Report to the Carnegie Foundation for the Advancement of Teaching with an introduction by Henry S. Pritchett, Bulletin No. 4.* New York.
11. Duffy, John. 1993. *From Humors to Medical Science: A History of American Medicine.* Urbana, Illinois: University of Illinois Press.
12. Toulmin, Stephen. 1982. How Medicine Saved the Life of Philosophy. *Perspectives in Biology and Medicine, 24:*736-50.
13. Pellegrino, Edmund D. 1987. The Reconciliation of Technology and Humanism: A Flexnerian Task 75 Years Later. In Charles Vevier (Ed.), *Flexner: 75 Years Later: A Current Commentary on Medical Education.* New York: University Press of America.
14. Englehardt, H. Tristan and Edward Erde. 1984. Philosophy of Medicine. In Paul T. Durbin (Ed.), *A Guide to the Culture of Science, Technology and Medicine.* New York: The Free Press.
15. Pellegrino, Edmund D. 1993. *The Metamorphosis of Medical Ethics: A 30-Year Retrospective.* JAMA, 269(9), 1158-62.
16. Ross, William D. 1988. *The Right and the Good.* Indiana: Hackett Publishing Company.
17. Beauchamp, Thomas L. and James F. Childress. 1989. *Priciples of Biomedical Ethics.* New York: Oxford University Press.
18. Whitehead, Alfred N. 1925. *Science and the Modern World.* New York: Free Press.
19. Brody, Boruch. 1990. Philosophic Critique of Bioethics. *J. Medical Phil., 15,* 1-236.
20. Clauser, K.D. and B.A. Gert. 1990. A Critique of Principalism. *J. Medical Phil., 15,* 219-236.
21. MacIntyre, Alasdair. 1980. A crisis in Moral Philosophy: Why Is the Search for Foundations So Frustrating? In H.T. Englehardt and D. Callahan, (Eds.) *Knowing and Valuing.* Hastings-On-Hudson, NY: Hastings Center.

22. Jonsen, Albert R. and Stephen Toulmin. 1988. *The Abuse of Casuistry.* Berkeley: University of California Press.
23. McIntyre, Alasdair. 1988. *After Virtue.* Indiana: University of Notre Dame Press.
24. McIntyre, Alasdair. 1990. *Three Rival Views of Moral Enquiry.* Indiana: University of Notre Dame Press.
25. Jonsen, Albert R. 1991. Casuistry As Methodology in Clinical Ethics. *Theoretical Medicine, 12,* 295-307.
26. Sherwin, Susan. 1992. *No Longer Patient: Feminist Ethics and Health Care.* Philadelphia: Temple University Press.
27. Noddings, Nell. 1984. *Caring: A Femine Approach to Ethics and Moral Education.* Berkley University of California Press.
28. Brody, Howard. 1987. *Stories of Sickness.* New Haven, CT: Yale University Press.
29. Brody, Howard. 1992. *The Healer's Power.* New Haven, CT: Yale University Press.
30. Ziporyn, Terra. 1985. Historians Strive to Improve Perspective, Practice of Medicine. *J. Amer. Med. Assn.* 254(19):2713-2720.
31. Prioreschi, Plinio. 1991. Does History of Medicine Teach Useful Lessons? *Perspectives in Biology and Medicine* 35(1):97-104.
32. Charon, Rita. 1993. Medical Interpretation: Implications of Literary Theory of Narrative for Clinical Work. *J. of Narrative and Life History* 3(1):79-97.
33. Charon, Rita. 1986. To Render the Lives of Patients. *Literature and Medicine* 5:58-74.
34. Coles, Robert. 1988. Medicine and the Humanities. In *Times of Surrender, Selected Essays.* University of Iowa Press, Iowa City, IA, pp. 77-87.
35. Brieger, Gert H. 1982. *Arrowsmith* and the History of Medicine in America. *Mobius:* Special Issue: Medical Humanities. University of California Press, Berkeley, CA, pp. 32-38.
36. Coulehan, John L. 1990. Personal communication.
37. Coulehan, John L. 1992. Teaching the Patient's Story. *Qualitative Health Research* 2(3):358-366.
38. Hunter, Kathryn M. 1991. Toward the Cultural Interpretation of Medicine. *Literature and Medicine* 10:1-17.
39. Churchill, Larry R. 1982. Why Literature and Medicine? *Literature and Medicine* 1:34-35.
40. Coles, Robert. 1993. *The Call of Service: Witness to Idealism.* Boston: Houghton Mifflin Company.
41. Wear, Delese. 1993. Feminist Criticism in Literature and Medicine (in press).
42. Wear, Delese. 1992. The Colonization of the Medical Humanities: A Confessional Critique. *Journal of Medical Humanities* 13(4):199-209.

defect and we "lose" at the social lottery if our parents raise us next to a chemical plant which is spewing poison into the atmosphere (Daniels, 1985). In addition, we are at a disadvantage if we are harmed because of an accident. What health care often is able to do is to reverse or control unhealthy states over which persons would otherwise have no control. If health care is not distributed equitably, the consequence is that persons with poor health through no fault of their own will not be able to pursue their life plans with the same relative ease as do those persons who either have resources for health care available to them or those persons who have "won" in both the natural and social lottery.

Allocation decisions also reflect what a given society values as important in the delivery of medical care. For example, medical care in the United Kindgom is centered around the general practitioner. Primary practice and preventive medicine are the basis of the medical care system. It is quite different in the United States, where medicine is focused upon the rescue of persons who suffer from illness or accident. It is not only that this latter type of medicine is very expensive. If resources are scarce, it is also more difficult to decide that this or that particular person will not be rescued.

Current discussions of allocation of health care resources are important for another reason, related to the discussions going on nationally about health care in American society. If a given country's allocation of health resources is thought to be unjust, and there is no hope of reform, one author argues that persons will not voluntarily limit their use of health care resources, because they would believe that would be foolish. Through these discussions we articulate what kind of a society we want to be and articulate a consensus about what is more and less important. Thus discussions of allocation are important as part of any discussion of reform of the health care system (Callahan, 1991). But these discussions are not only important; they are also contested.

By now it should be clear that discussions of allocation presume two things, a shortage of resources and a claim that all actors are self-interested. Given that all the actors are self-interested, they will seek to obtain all the health care resources they need for themselves. It is obvious that this second presumption provides one of the difficulties in trying to fairly allocate health care resources. It colors one view of the physician patient relationship. Physicians are supposed to be loyal to the patient who is present to them and not worry about the health care system in general. Traditionally, physicians have been reluctant to take responsibility for allocation decisions because they argued that to do so would be to put them into conflict with their role to seek the best for their particular patient. Someone else should make the allocation decisions. Unfortunately, this often comes to mean obtaining as many resources for the patient as possible, because, this is what we should assume a self-interested patient would want.

Before discussing the details of the current allocation of health are in the United States, it is important to understand some of the different views that are popular in our society about how health care resources should be allocated. After that, there will be a discussion of some of the issues that are involved in determining what a fair allocation system might include.

DIFFERENT VIEWS OF ALLOCATION

There are a number of theories about how health care resources ought to be allocated. Not all of them will be discussed here, although the significant theories will receive some attention.

Some theorists begin with the claim that health care is not distributed equitably throughout our society and then argue that health care ought to be distributed based upon need. This is one of the most common positions for thinkers who stand in religious traditions. One version of it is as follows.

Given that one's health is not entirely within the control of a person, and that a person may have poor health for many factors outside of their control, persons should be given health care based upon their particular need. This will lead to a situation in which one person is given much more health care than another, but, no injustice is done if one person receives more health care than another if the one person in fact needs that health care in order to pursue their particular life projects. There may be limits upon the level of care society can afford to give, and these limits will have to be discussed but the starting point, it is argued, should be the needs of persons. Since health is such a special kind of good, both in terms of our possession of it and in terms of its instrumental nature for the pursuit of other goods, persons ought to think of needs as the basis of distribution of health care. Implicit in this perspective is a critique of any suggestion that health care should be distributed, as it is in the United States, based upon one's ability to pay. In short, the argument that health care should be distributed based upon need usually is a direct rejection of any application of market theory to the allocation of health care (Outka, 1974).

A second competing perspective on health care in our society is to claim that health care is a right. Rights language is often used in our society and this language is a powerful way of making claims. Thus it is attractive as a way of speaking about health care. Discussions of a right to health care may involve a number of factors. One author argues that these include equal access to appropriate services, equity in health states for all groups in society, mechanisms to evaluate and monitor health needs, and equitable social and political institutions which allow all groups participation in any discussion on the allocation of health care (Susser, 1993).

At the same time, rights language opens up a number of its own problems. First, there is a great deal of writing about different kinds of rights and those persons who wish to argue that health care is a right need to specify what kind of a right it is and against whom it can be claimed. Second, rights language is in principle unlimited (Glendon, 1991) and thus there has to be some discussion about the limitations one might put upon the rights claims to health care which persons could conceivably make.

One of the persistent worries of persons who wish to reform health care in the United States is what happened with the treatment of end stage renal disease. What began as an entitlement program with very limited goals and expectations for persons who were suffering from end stage renal disease has turned into a program which sustains persons originally thought not appropriate candidates for this therapy. A very small number of persons consume a relatively large proportion of health resources. Other nations limit the treatment of end stage renal disease and thus the financial commitments to therapies of this kind (Aaron, 1984). It is more difficult to do this in the United States.

The worry is that if a program which began as an entitlement for a small number of persons has become so expensive, health care for all understood as a right will become even more expensive. It is especially difficult when rights language is in principle unlimited. For this reason, it has been argued that any discussion of rights to health care has to include discussions about how rights to health care should be limited.

A third perspective on how health care should be distributed is associated with John Rawls. Rawls argues that justice requires that we should make our choices about justice in society behind a veil of ignorance. That is, Rawls is arguing that we should decide about the kind of society we want without knowing any of the particulars of our position in that future society. He argues that if we were to do this, we would choose a society in which all persons had liberty compatible with an equal liberty for all others, and that there should be only those inequalities that were to the advantage of the least advantaged in the society. What Rawls is trying to do is respect the autonomy of the individual and arrange a society which was efficient in the production of goods and services so that this worked to the benefit of all in the society. In the literature this is called a maximin system, in which one maximizes the benefits to the least advantaged in the society and will accept inequalities only if those inequalities benefit the least well off more than other groups in the society. Rawls thus eliminates discussions of formal equality at all points and persons could have differential access to health care in the society, as long as the least well off in the society are attended to and are better off than they would have been if everyone had been treated equally (Rawls, 1971). Applying this to health care, persons choosing a health care system would have no knowledge of their current health status. In addition, they would have to choose a system which would benefit the least well off and this would not necessarily mean a system with distributed health care equally to all.

A fourth perspective on health care argues that health care, like all other goods in the society, ought to be distributed based upon one's ability to pay. In brief, the market should work as the allocation mechanism within society. When this is a moral theory, instead of an economic one, it assumes that one has acquired one's wealth legitimately. Given the legitimacy of this acquistion, no wrong is done if some persons have enough wealth to afford health care and others do not. The focus of attention is justice in the acquisition of wealth and the inheritance of it and not upon one's health status (Nozick, 1974).

Note the implications of these four different perspectives. Three pay little attention to formal equality, one insists upon it. One system pays special attention to health care needs while the other three systems do not focus upon this feature. We are left with no clear consensus about how health care ought to be allocated. It could be argued that this would be expected. If one takes the view that we live in a very divided world, with many different conceptions of what counts as a good life, and what counts as a just health care system, with no conception of the good life or just health care system held in common, then no single theory of justice will satisfy (MacIntyre, 1981).

One potential implication of holding such a view is that *who* does the allocation becomes crucial. Theorists influenced by democratic theory argue that health care allocation decisions should follow the wishes of the electorate as closely as possible and not be left in the hands of experts. Of course, this too will be contested by those who insist upon rights to health care, as well as by those who argue for a distribution based upon needs. Persons who use ability to pay as the basis for the allocation of health care will also object to the possibility of a form of decision making which would relieve persons of their legitimately acquired wealth. At the end of the day, there is no single unifying theory in our society which has persuasive force.

This does not mean that some theories are not more or less adquate. As should be clear by now, this author thinks that the best case can be made for the distribution of health care on the basis of need. Other allocation schemes, which do not take both the arbitrariness and the incapacitating features of illness as seriously as this position, finally appear inadequate.

DISTRIBUTION OF HEALTH CARE IN THE UNITED STATES

It was noted above that there is no single unifying theory of a good life in this country and thus no theory which persuades all of us. One of the consequences of this is that discussions of the allocation of health care resources are made more difficult. At the macro level, if government officials decide that within health care, certain programs should no longer be funded, say, artificial heart transplants, there is no assurance that funds that would have been spent on the artificial heart will be wisely spent somewhere else. The same is true at the micro level. Resources not spent on this particular patient will not necessarily be wisely spent on the next patient. In both cases, this leaves little incentive to allocate resources at all.

It is obvious that the health care system in the United States is not based upon some conception of need nor is it based upon some kind of Rawlsian system. Nor does anyone argue that health care is allocated equitably in the United States. Some persons have available to them the best health care in the world, from excellent primary care all the way through multi-organ transplantation procedures. Other persons struggle to obtain the most uncomplicated preventive care and the simplest of therapeutic measures. One author comments that the United States limits primary and preventive care more than other industrialized democracies, limits tertiary care less, and use bureaucracy and price controls more than many other nations. The persons most affected by this form of allocation are the poor and those needing long term care. The persons most advantaged by such a system are specialist physicians who perform procedures and those persons who can afford their fees, either directly or through insurance (Higgins, 1991).

This is not to say that the allocation of health care is not a problem throughout the world. Indeed, the equitable distribution of health care is an issue no matter what the development of a particular society (Kilner, 1992). However, on a comparative basis, other industrialized countries more fairly distribute elementary or primary health care throughout their population. In making these claims, it should be understood that there is some evidence that Americans have exactly the health care system which they desire. Survey after survey reports that Americans think that no matter what the cost, high technology medicine should be used to try to save every life. The result in the United States is that the country supports high technology medicine with no agreed upon consensus about how that high technology medicine is going to be used.

There are three other features about the discussion of the allocation of health care resources in the United States which should be mentioned at this point. The current discussions about allocation take on a particular urgency because of the increasing expense of health care relative to other goods. In a short period of time, the United States has gone from spending 9% of the GNP to spending 14% of the GNP on health care. If that rate of increase continues, it will further constrain expenditures for other important social goods. Indeed, it has already constrained expenditures on other goods such as education and police protection.

Second, on a comparative basis, the 14% of the GNP spent on health care is quite high when compared to other countries. This compares to an average of 8-10% for most other industrialized countries (Reinhardt, 1993).

Third, the United States spends more on high technology health care than do other industrialized countries. Part of the reason for this may be practices which do not restrict access to high technology care. As mentioned above, in the United States treatment of end stage renal disease is funded through Social Security and is available to all who can benefit from it while kidney dialysis is restricted by age in Great Britain. This is just one example of how the United States tends to treat disease.

It could be argued that the percentage of GNP spent on health care and on high technology health care would be "worth it" if it led to better mortality and morbidity statistics for the United States. Most disturbing is the information which points to the conclusion that all of the extra resources which are spent on health care in the United States do not yield any significant advantage in terms of mortality and morbidity. Indeed, for certain subgroups within the population, mortality and morbidity in certain areas is quite high. For example, infant mortality in America ranks twenty-second among industrialized nations. However, white infant mortality ranks twelfth among industrialized nations. At the same time African Americans have an infant mortality rate twice that of whites in America (Mason, 1990).

There is one other characteristic of the United States health care system which has become a central issue. Relative to other industrialized countries, the United States is the only country, with the exception of South Africa, which does not have some form of universal health coverage. What this means in the United States is that many persons are without insurance for either basic health care or for the more expensive high technology health care. Typically, illnesses are left untreated when they can be treated easily and then turn to major hospital events when patients finally can put off seeking assistance no longer. Uwe Reinhart argues that this type of maldistribution is the primary ethical problem faced by the health care system in the United States. Reinhart points out that the issue is not simply that there are many persons without health insurance. The United States also permits insurers to refuse coverge to persons with chronic conditions. The system in the United States, according to Reinhardt, is a system which rations explicitly, based upon price and ability to pay. He compares this to implicit rationing, which, he argues, occurs in most other industrialized nations. (Reinhardt, 1993).

The next feature of the health care system, predictable in light of what has been said already, is that the United States has a unique distribution of physicians. Although there are more physicians per 1000 population than in other industrialized countries, there is a marked difference in the practice specialties of these physicians. In the United States, there are fewer primary physicians per 1000 population and many more technologically intense subspecialty physicians.

Following the above, not only is there an imbalance, relative to other countries, of physician specialties, but these specialties are located in urban areas. This means that a large part of the United States is underserved, relative to other countries.

It is this context which sets up the framework for the discussion of the ethics of the allocation of resources in health care. Most commentators, either religious or secular, have concluded that the allocation of health care resources in this country needs to be changed because, first, so many persons are without access to primary medical care, second, medical care is so heavily weighted towards expensive technological care, and third, the cost of health care has prevented this country from doing other things that need to be done. Those conclusions have set up the dynamic within which health care reform is discussed and is currently being decided. It is important that this conclusion not be seen simply as a pragmatic one. In the view of this author, given that health care ought to be based upon need, and given that health care in the United States is not distributed in this fashion, the inescapable conclusion is that the system is unjust. The poor and the unemployed, in particular, suffer the most under this system.

PROPOSALS FOR REFORM

Given that there are two central problems with the allocation of health care resources in the United States, cost and fair distribution, there are a variety of proposals for reform of the system. Different proposals focus on one or both difficulties of the current system.

First, no one disputes that many resources are not used wisely at the end of life. Patients are usually unwilling to have as much high technology medical care given to them as is routinely offered to them. Thus some commentators argue that one of the ways in which health care resources might be saved is for physicians to be more careful in the use of health care resources at the end of life. There are many difficulties with this proposal. The most important one is that physicians do not know in advance when the last illness will come. Thus they are inclined to continue trying to cure the patient. Second, it is also the case that what patients say they want

At the same time, if we take a broader view, it is arguable that the discussions taking place in the United States are part of a larger pattern of discussions taking place in the industrialized world. In those discussions, most countries have moved from health care which financed all the expenditures which health care professionals thought necessary to health care which is budgeted and where health professionals are asked to do what they can within budgetary constraints. The United States is the last industrialized country to make any moves in the direction of health care budgets.

It has to be recognized that there is one contrary movement within the United States. That is the move towards managed competition. The theory of managed competition is that health care systems will seek patients on the basis of quality and price. Presumably, health care consumers will be provided with enough information to be able to make intelligent decisions about the quality of the medical care being rendered.

This does make even the Clinton proposal odd in the context of a wider perspective. Canadians and Europeans control costs by limiting the capacity of the system, controlling prices, and aiming for global budgets. There is little management of the physician-patient relationship. The Clinton proposal would not aim to limit the capacity of the system but would aim at controlling the growth in costs, and would have some form of global budgeting. At the same time, physicians would still be subject to the kinds of direct supervision which is not found in other health care systems. All of the monitoring appartus which would inform consumers about the success rate of physicians would also act to constrain physicians in their activities (Reinhardt, 1993).

It should be clear by now that there is no consensus on how to proceed to allocate health care costs in the United States. This paper is written at the beginning of what promises to be an extended debate in this country, a debate which will entail not simply judgments about the facts of the matter, about the relative merits of the quality of the American health care system, but also judgments about the fairness with which health care is allocated within this country. It should be clear that on the latter point at least, this author thinks that we can do better.

REFERENCES

Aaron, Henry. 1984. *The Painful Prescription: Rationing Hospital Care.* Brookings Institution, Washington, D.C., pp. 191.

Anonymous. 1992. An Ethical Foundation for Health Care: an Emergency Medicine Perspective. Ethics Committee, Society for Academic Emergency Medicine. *Annals of Emergency Medicine* 21:1381-87.

Callahan, Daniel. 1987. *Setting Limits.* Simon and Schuster, New York, NY, pp. 256.

Callahan, Daniel. 1991. Symbols, Rationality, and Justice: Rationing Health Care. *American Journal of Law and Medicine:* 18:1-13.

Daniels, Norman. 1985. *Just Health Care.* Cambridge University Press, New York, NY, pp. 245.

Daniels, Norman. 1986. Why Saying No to Patients in the United States is So Hard: Cost Containment, Justice, and Provide Autonomy. *NEJM* 314:1380-83.

Glendon, Mary Ann. 1991. *Rights Talk*. Free Press, New York, NY, pp. 218.

Higgins, W. 1991. Rationing Medical Care. *Family Medicine* 23:292-6.

Jecker, N.S. 1992. Allocating Medical Resources in Rural America: alternative perceptions of justice. *Social Science and Medicine* 34:467-74.

Kilner, John. 1992. *Life on the Line*. Wm. B. Eerdmans Publishing Co., Grand Rapids, MI, pp. 349.

MacIntyre, Alasdair. 1981. *After Virtue: A Study in Moral Theory*. University of Notre Dame Press, Notre Dame, IN, pp. 252.

Mason, James O. 1990. Health Care in the U.S.: Facts and Choices. *Second Opinion* 13:22-29.

Nozick. 1974. *Anarchy, State and Utopia*. Basic Books, New York, NY, pp. 367.

O'Connell, Laurence J. 1993. The Park Ridge Center Goes to Washington. *The Center Line* 2:1.

Outka, Gene. 1974. Social Justice and Equal Access to Health Care. *Journal of Religious Ethics* 2:11-32.

Rawls, John. 1971. *A Theory of Justice*. Howard University Press, Cambridge, MA, pp. 607.

Reinhardt, Uwe. 1993. Reforming the Health Care System: The Universal Dilemma. *The American Journal of Law and Medicine* XIX:21-26.

Susser, Mevyn. 1993. Health Care as a Human Right: An Epidemiologist's Perspective on the Public Health. *American Journal of Public Health:* 83:418-426.

Medicine and Health Care Into the Twenty-First Century. Edited by S.K. Majumdar, L.M. Rosenfeld, D.B. Nash and A.M. Audet.

Chapter Thirty-Three

THE AGED AND HEALTH CARE: The Case of Pennsylvania

GEORGE A. SCHNELL[1] and **MARK MONMONIER**[2]

[1]Department of Geography
The College at New Paltz
State University of New York
New Paltz, NY 12561-2499
and
[2]Department of Geography
Syracuse University
Syracuse, NY 13244-1160

INTRODUCTION

Delivery of health care is now under revision at the nation's highest level, and expectations of far-reaching changes are widespread. At the intersection of the health-care debate and national concerns over Social Security and its many adjuncts is the aged population, with well-publicized concerns about longevity and quality of life. Although much of the debate addresses such economic and ethical issues as who pays or what treatments are provided, access to appropriate health care also involves geographic concerns with distance and local availability. This chapter examines the status of hospital and nursing-home facilities among the counties of Pennsylvania as they relate to the aged population—its distribution and trends from 1980 to 1990. Sources of data are the Pennsylvania State Data Center, the (Pennsylvania) State Health Data Center, and the U.S. Bureau of the Census.

THE AGED: DISTRIBUTION AND TRENDS

The population 65 and older in the United States in 1990 numbered some 31 million persons and constituted 12.5 percent of the total population. Compared to the national figures, Pennsylvania's are noteworthy—over 1.8 million were over 64, accounting for more than 15 percent of the Commonwealth's inhabitants. Indeed, in several sparsely populated counties, the elderly comprised as much as 18 percent of the population. Among states, the number of Pennsylvania's elderly residents ranked fourth behind California, Florida, and New York. In relative terms, Pennsylvania's 15.4 percent aged ranked second to Florida's 18.3 (1).

This section focuses on the distribution of the aged as well as their trends from 1980 to 1990. Since sheer numbers reflect the demand for medical services of those 65 and older, some maps show counts, and since ratios illustrate the relative importance of this cohort, other maps show percentages. The latter indicates the importance of the aged in each of the several counties—their political "clout" locally. To portray trends from 1980 to 1990, a similar series of maps portrays change as both an absolute increase or decrease and as a percentage rate.

Figure 1 (upper map) shows the number of inhabitants 65 and over in 1990 among Pennsylvania's counties. The greatest counts, 40,000 and more, were recorded in nine counties in the southeast, including Philadelphia and its four suburban counties, as well as Lehigh, Berks, Lancaster, and York. In addition, Allegheny and Westmoreland, the two most densely inhabited counties in the Pittsburgh region, and Luzerne and Lackawanna, the most populous of the anthracite counties in the northeast, round out the highest class. This group is thus comprised of Pennsylvania's 13 highest ranked counties in both total population and the aged (except for Luzerne and Chester, none of the group is more than two places off in its ranks on the two lists).

The lowest group shown on Figure 1 (upper map) is spread across the Appalachian Plateau from Forest in the west to Montour and Sullivan in the east. The others are Juniata and Fulton counties in south-central Pennsylvania. The same relationship as described above for the populous counties holds for the sparsely inhibited counties shown here. The relationship, however, is much more direct insofar as the seven are ranked the same for both measures, occupying the very bottom of the lists for size of total and aged populations (61st through 67th place).

Figure 1 (lower map) illustrates the percentage of county populations 65 and older in 1990. Not surprisingly, the patterns shown on the maps of Figure 1 are quite dissimilar—just two of the counties which appear in the highest category on the upper map are shown in that rank on the lower map, Lackawanna and Luzerne. These two anthracite-region counties are among the smallest in population size among the highest category shown on Figure 1, upper map. The remainder of the highest-percentage group on the lower map includes three of the other northeastern coal counties and three very sparsely inhabited counties—Cameron (5,913 total inhabitants), Forest (4,802), and Sullivan (6,104). Cambria and Lawrence, the remaining two, have over 163,000 and some 96,000 residents, respectively. Taken together, the two high-percentage classes are mostly in the west, as only Wayne and Montour counties join those in and near the anthracite area at 18 percent or more aged.

Change in the aged cohort over the 1980 decade is presented in two ways on Figure 2, the upper map showing the net number gained and the lower map showing the percentage increase. In the upper figure, the pattern is very much like the distribution of the number of aged shown on Figure 1 (upper map), on which the heavily populated counties occupy the first class. Note that the highest-ranking counties (growth of 8,000 or more) cluster largely in the southest, with additional concentrations of aged in Luzerne County, and in Allegheny and Westmoreland counties in the southwest; all counties with more substantial gains are metropolitan,

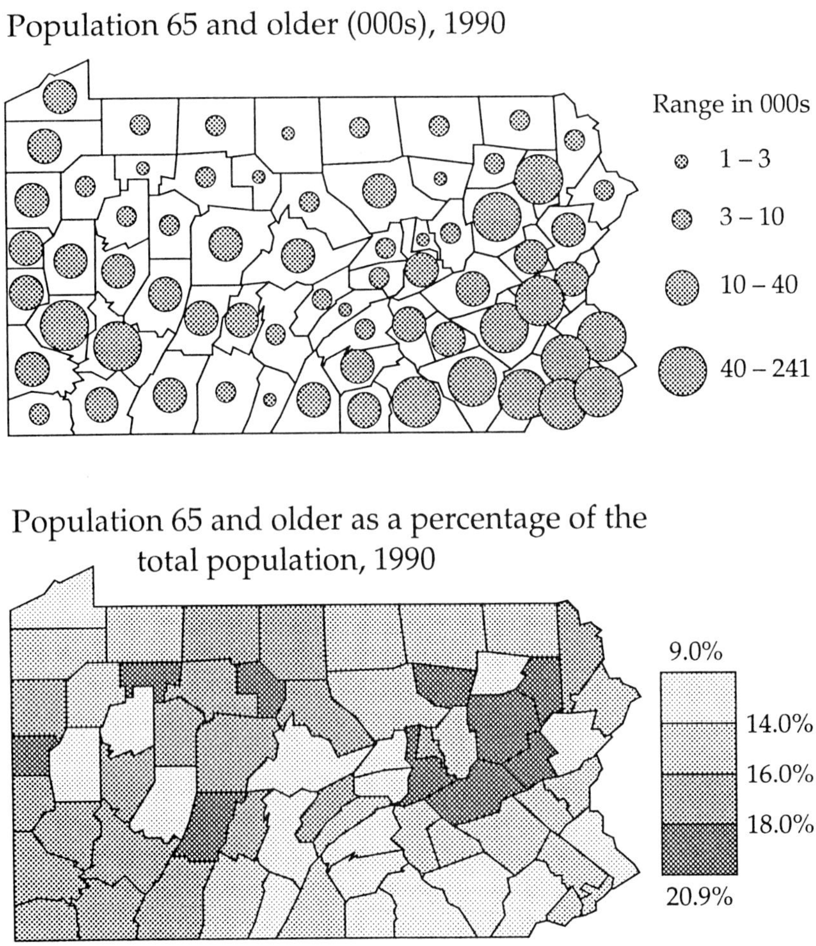

FIGURE 1.

with large numbers of residents of all ages. In contrast, the lowest category is concentrated in rural, sparsely inhabited counties in the northwest on the plateau, north of the anthracite belt, and in south-central Pennsylvania.

The lower map of Figure 2 illustrates change of those 65 and older for 1980-1990, by county, as a percentage of the 1980 aged population. The rapidly growing aged populations (gains of 30 percent or more) are found generally in counties with high-quality residential environments—Bucks and Chester counties suburban to Philadelphia; Lancaster, Adams, and Cumberland, extending westward from the Philadelphia region; Northampton, Monroe, and Pike in the Delaware Valley from the Lehigh Valley northward to the Poconos. In addition, Centre County has noteworthy residential amenities in State College and its environs due in large

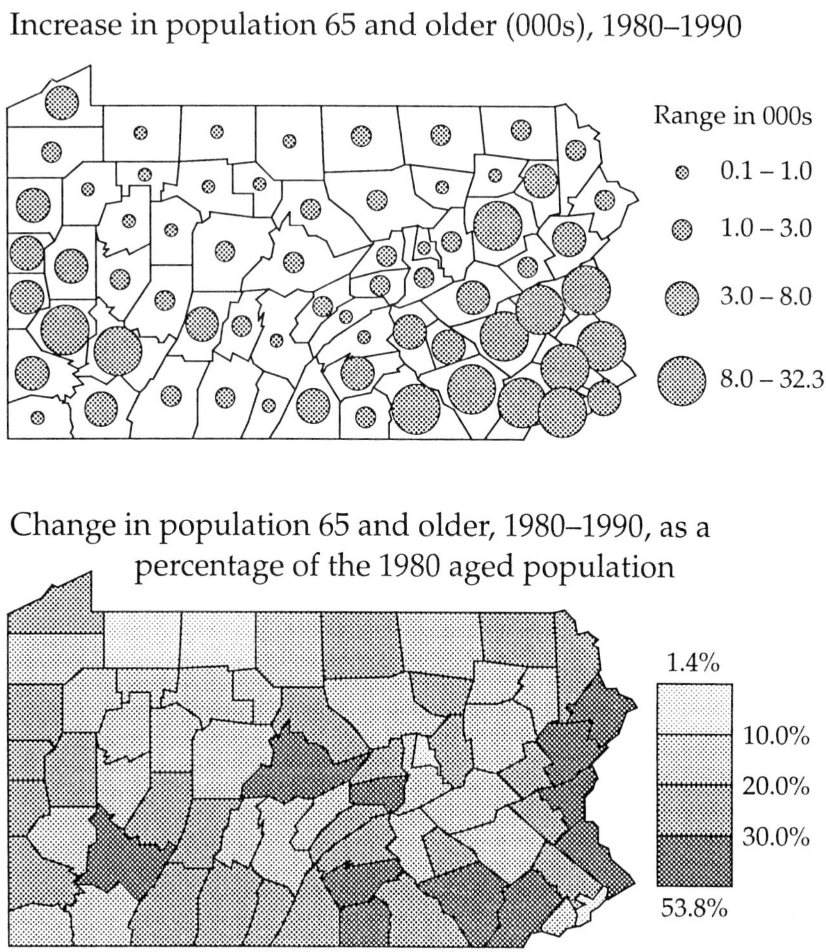

FIGURE 2.

measure to the presence of the Pennsylvania State University (2). Conversely, counties with the lowest percentage gains—Philadelphia and McKean (both recording 1.4 percent gains for their elderly residents)—have little in common. The two remaining in the lowest category, Warren and Montour (with 9.1 and 9.0 percent increases, respectively), occupy disparate locations in the Commonwealth but have relatively sparse populations.

To summarize, the distribution of aged reflects the distribution of the total population, with large numbers of elderly in Philadelphia and Pittsburgh regions and with generally significant numbers in the other metropolitan counties. Relatively, the greatest concentration of the aged is in the anthracite counties and those nearby, although the western half of the state has many more counties in the two higher classes than the east. Concerning growth, the aged recorded the greatest percentage gains in counties considered nice places to live—suburbs of Philadelphia and counties such as Lancaster and those in the Poconos along the Delaware River. Other prominent growth foci are Centre (3) and Union counties, where universities offer an array of educational, cultural, and recreational services open to residents, help foster attractive residential neighborhoods, and a wide range of retail services in the boroughs of State College and Lewisburg and beyond.

Counties with the greatest number of aged inhabitants obviously have the greater demands for services, including health care, but in smaller counties a smaller yet proportionally strong cohort of people 65 and older could well apply more political pressure. In counties where noteworthy aged growth was accompanied by growth of the total population (increases among the younger cohorts specifically), net in-migration of the elderly often bolstered aged gains brought about by residents 55-64 in 1980 who remained in the home county through the decade to add to the number of those 65 and older in 1990 (4). In counties where aged growth was relative, produced essentially by out-migration of younger residents, a *residual* aged population with a greater percentage of the total population in 1990 ensued. Counties representing the former case include Adams, Bucks, Centre, Chester, Cumberland, Lancaster, Monroe, Pike, and Snyder. Counties in which the aged cohort experienced only relative gains include Allegheny and Northampton.

Taken together, these leaders among counties in aged growth are diverse, encompassing municipalities that are among the wealthiest suburbs in the state as well as quite modest rural areas—reflecting aged diversity too (5). Although the eleven counties vary, the ability to keep their aged population after retirement is strong in most, and the attraction for aged in-migrants is evident in several of the group. For example, Bucks and Chester counties' aged residents are among the wealthiest in the state. In contrast, the counties of Monroe and Pike have lower-order socioeconomic status but, as popular recreation-vacation destinations close to the cities of New York and Philadelphia, retain many of those who attain retirement age and attract in-migrant retirees, many of whom know the Pocono area by having vacationed there over a period of years (6).

HOSPITALS, NURSING HOMES, AND THE AGED: GEOGRAPHIC ASSOCIATIONS

Directories published by the State Health Data Center of the Pennsylvania Department of Health provided a bed count, facility type, and type of control for each of the Commonwealth's 298 hospitals and 705 licensed nursing homes, as of 1991 (7). Aggregation by county yielded counts of hospital beds and licensed nursing-home beds comparable to census data on the aged population. In order to more closely reflect general health-care facilities serving local and regional aged populations, the hospital-bed totals include only "beds set up and staffed" and omit bed counts for 39 psychiatric hospitals, 17 rehabilitation hospitals, and 14 other specialized facilities dedicated to treating alcoholics, children, or diseases of specific sites, such as eyes and the feet—but include one "geriatric" hospital. Division by number of aged in 1990 yielded simple demographically adjusted measures reflecting each county's ability to respond to the acute needs and long-term care of its elderly residents.

Figure 3 describes variations among the Commonwealth's 67 counties in hospital-bed capacity, mapped as the number of staffed hospital beds per 1,000 elderly residents. The eleven counties in the map's two highest categories and lowest category are outliers requiring separate explanations. At the high end is Montour County, where an anomalously high ratio of 197.2 staffed beds for every 1,000 elderly residents reflects the presence in Danville of the Geisinger Medical Center. With 577 beds, Geisinger is the state's third largest hospital; its widely renowned staff and clinics serve patients throughout the northeastern United States. Three other counties with ratios above 40 are also regionally important medical centers: Bradford County (52.1 hospital beds per 1,000 aged) is home to the Robert Packer Hospital (with 326 beds in Sayre); Venango County (41.8 hospital beds per 1,000

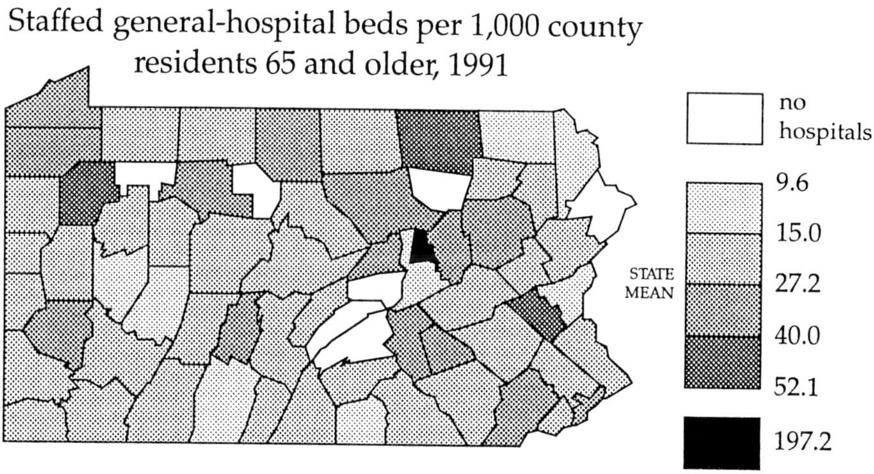

FIGURE 3.

elderly) is home to the Northwest Medical Center (with 238 beds in Franklin and 135 in Oil City); and Lehigh County (41.0 hospital beds per 1,000 elderly) has several large and medium-size hospitals, including Allentown Hospital (with 319 beds), the Lehigh Valley Hospital Center (with 514 beds, also in Allentown), and St. Luke's Hospital of Bethlehem (with 435 beds). At the low end are seven counties without general hospitals. Their aged populations range from 970 in Forest County, the state's least populous county, to 4,616 for Snyder County. These counties typically depend on neighboring counties for higher-order central-place services, found not far beyond the county lines in nearby centers such as Harrisburg (serving Perry County), Lewistown (serving Juniata County), and Sunbury (serving Snyder County). Distance and county size are also important. For instance, in Forest County, one of Pennsylvania's smaller rural counties, most of the population lives within 30 miles of hospitals in Titusville (Crawford County) and Oil City (Venango County). Similarly, in Cameron County, another small rural county without a hospital, most residents live within 30 miles of hospitals in St. Marys and Ridgeway (Elk County). Residents of remote parts of the Commonwealth's large counties commonly live more than 30 miles from the nearest hospital.

The three remaining classes in Figure 3 also reflect a dependence on hospitals in neighboring counties. Counties with hospital-bed ratios less than 40 but above 27.2, the statewide average, include the central counties of the Philadelphia (36.8), Pittsburgh (35.1 for Allegheny County), and Harrisburg (37.7 for Dauphin County) metropolitan areas, all of which are well endowed with large or numerous hospitals. Also in this group are several rural counties, such as Elk and Union, containing hospitals whose service areas extend well into neighboring counties. In the next lowest category, below the statewide mean but above 15.0 beds per 1,000 elderly residents, are several other metropolitan counties such as Berks (23.2), Lancaster (21.8), Westmoreland (20.6), and York (18.4), most likely overshadowed by larger medical centers within an hour's drive in Philadelphia, Pittsburgh, Harrisburg, Baltimore, Maryland, or Wilmington, Delaware.

The lowest category for hospitals (9.6 to 15.0 beds per 1,000) also reflects similar "shadow" effects enhanced by a unique combination of geographic situation and a prominent medical center. For instance, Northumberland County, which borders Montour on two sides, most likely has a comparatively low value (10.7 per 1,000) because of its proximity to Geisinger Medical Center, in Danville. Somewhat similar reasons probably account for below-average ratios in Northampton County (9.7), a small county just east of medically well-equipped Lehigh County, and Susquehanna County (13.6), situated north of Scranton, south of Binghamton, New York, and east of Bradford County (with the Robert Packer Hospital in Sayre). These shadow effects explain the frequent juxtaposition in Figure 3 of high- and low-ratio counties.

Figure 4 reveals a somewhat less fragmented pattern for long-term care, as measured by the ratio of licensed nursing-home-beds per 1,000 inhabitants 65 and older. With six categories delimited to identify comparatively low, high, and very high anomalies, the map indicates that ratios higher than the statewide average of 49.2 are common in the southeastern and northwestern parts of the Commonwealth and in the Susquehanna Valley north of Harrisburg, whereas lower-than-average rates are typical in northeastern and southwestern sections. The most notable exception is the below-average ratio of Philadelphia (36.2), which is offset by above-average ratios in the suburban counties of Bucks (63.6), Chester (54.0), Delaware (57.8), and Montgomery (58.3).

Some positive outliers are astonishingly high but none bear the imprint of a single massive medical center. Montour County, with the highest ratio (155.5 beds per 1,000 elderly), has four nursing homes with between 60 and 152 licensed beds—with no direct link to the Geisinger Medical Center readily apparent. A similarly anomalous above-average ratio for Sullivan County (149.0) reflects the presence of two nursing homes (one with 70 beds and the other with 120) in a county with a small elderly population. A single 100-bed nursing home in Forest County yields the Commonwealth's third highest rate, 103.1 beds per 1,000. The 14 counties comprising the three highest categories in Figure 4 generally have small elderly populations, less than 20,000 residents 65 and older, with substantially smaller aged cohorts in the two highest classes. The most notable exception is Lancaster County, with 55,469 elderly residents, a ratio of 74.4, and an astounding 32 nursing homes, many affiliated with Protestant groups such as the Brethren, Lutheran, and Methodist denominations. Only Allegheny, Bucks, Delaware, Montgomery, and Philadelphia counties have more licensed nursing homes. Church-affiliated nursing homes are prominent in other high-ratio counties, such as Adams (87.4), McKean (75.9), and Union (88.0). These fit the pattern of high-ratio counties in the southeast and northwest.

Equally apparent is a relative dearth of nursing-home beds in the southwest and northeast. All but one of the seven counties in the map's lowest category (21.7 to 35.0) are in Pennsylvania's southwestern quadrant, and the one exception (Pike County, with a ratio of 34.0) is in the northeast. Although Allegheny's

Licensed nursing-home beds per 1,000 county residents 65 and older, 1991

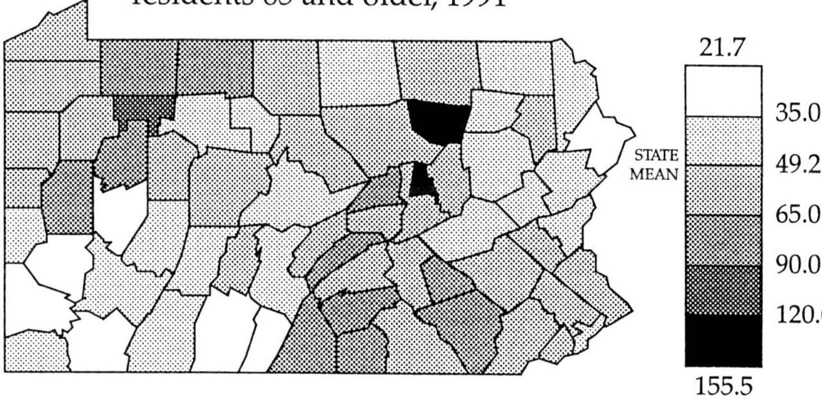

FIGURE 4.

Pennsylvania's elderly population, by the end of the decade of the 1990s the aged 75 and older will make up half of the total aged cohort. Although those 75 and older numbered less than 750,000 in 1990, their ranks are projected to swell by almost 200,000 in the decade ending by the year 2000. The facts are that those over 74 are most demanding in terms of the need for services but the relatively small cohort born in the period after the post-war baby boom yields a smaller labor force to pay taxes to fund the increasing demands for services by a growing aged population (8). Of special concern could well be the poorer populations resident in cities as well as the less fortunate inhabitants of remote and rural counties. Despite the projections, the activity directed toward the provision of a variety of elderly housing opportunities as well as growth of nursing homes could well encourage many of the Commonwealth's residents to remain after retirement and, if recent events are any indication, serve as an invitation to retiring out-of-staters.

REFERENCES AND NOTES

1. DeJong, G. 1992. The Graying of Pennsylvania's Elderly Population in the 1990s. Pennsylvania State Data Center. *News,* November 5, 3.
2. Many colleges are located in Pennsylvania's smaller municipalities and, through their educational and cultural offerings, contribute to the residential amenities of those places.
3. In local newspaper clippings obtained from the Centre County Planning Office, a series of construction plans and projects for aged housing and nursing homes were reported during the 1980s. The construction activity, along with State College's desirable residential characteristics, no doubt contributed to the county's 12th-place rank in Boyer, R. and D. Savageau. 1983. Places Rated Retirement Guide. Rand-McNally, Chicago. Lancaster County was ranked 74th in the same publication. Widespread construction activity during the 1980s was directed toward the burgeoning aged cohort—the growth of aged persons reported as residents of institutions (which equate essentially with nursing homes) rose in number statewide from 1980-1990 by almost 28,000, for a 37 percent increase.
4. Adams, Monroe, and Pike counties actually recorded gains in the population 55-64 in 1980 and 65-74 in 1990, gains that can be accounted for only by in-migration of that age group. Among the remaining eight counties in the top percentage growth category, all recorded declines in the 55-64 cohort as its members aged in place, died, or migrated in or out over the decade of the 1980s—but none approached the rate of decline experienced by the state. Pennsylvania's 55-64 age group declined by almost 55 percent but the counties in question had no percentage loss exceeding 25 (the percentage for Allegheny County) and most were well below that. On the importance of the 55-64 cohort in growth of the aged population, see Schnell, G.A. 1970. Factors Affecting Recent Trends of the Aged Population: A Case Study. *Aging and Human Development.* 1:219-320.

5. Data on income and poverty of the elderly reveal the range among the eleven counties with aged population gains of 30 percent or more. With the state median income at $15,852 in 1990, nine of the eleven counties exceeded the state's rate, as only Pike ($15,569 and ranked 19th) and Snyder ($13,228 and ranked 33rd) fell below that standard. The poverty threshold, based on estimates of the amount required to meet needs, was $5,947 for the single aged inhabitants and $7,501 for elderly married couples in 1989. Across the state, almost 190,000 aged residents were found to be impoverished by these standards, a figure amounting to 10.6 percent of those over 64 years of age. Although all but Allegheny among the eleven counties with the highest relative growth of the aged were under 10.0 percent on the aged poverty index, it varied from a low of 6.0 in Cumberland (ranked 2nd statewide) to Allegheny's 10.1 (38th). See Cornwell, G.T., G.F. DeJong, and J.M. Wilmoth, 1993. Sixty-Five Plus in Pennsylvania: County Demographic Profiles. Population Research Institute, the Pennsylvania State University, and the Pennsylvania State Data Center, Harrisburg, 17 and 18.
6. In a study of aged population in New York's Catskill Mountains, Lane and Pine discussed retirees as in-migrants. They reported that about one in four of their respondents who were fully retired were in-migrants, less affluent than retirees moving to western and southern United States retirement centers. They also found that the modal pattern involved spending vacations in a summer cottage which was improved over the years until it was habitable year round at retirement. Lane, W.C. and P.P. Pine. 1988. Catskill Counties Aging Study: A Study of Long-Term Residents and Relocated Retirees in Four Rural Counties in New York State. Final Report. Conducted under the auspices of a The Gerontological Society of America's Postdoctoral Program in Applied Gerontology.
7. State Health Data Center, Pennsylvania Department of Health. 1993. Directory of Pennsylvania Nursing Homes. Harrisburg; and ________. 1992. Directory of Pennsylvania Hospitals. Harrisburg. These data were supplied by the State Health Data Center, Pennsylvania Department of Health, Harrisburg, Pennsylvania. The Department specifically disclaims responsibility for any analyses, interpretations, or conclusions.
8. Cornwell, et al., *op. cit.,* 3 and 4.

Medicine and Health Care Into the Twenty-First Century. Edited by S.K. Majumdar, L.M. Rosenfeld, D.B. Nash and A.M. Audet. © 1995, The Pennsylvania Academy of Science.

Chapter Thirty-Four

RELIGION AND MEDICINE IN THE TWENTY-FIRST CENTURY
Convergence or Divergence Parallels and Crosses

EDWARD C. BRADLEY, S.J., M.D.
Clinical Associate Professor of Medicine
Special Counselor-in-Residence
Thomas Jefferson University
Philadelphia, PA 19107

INTRODUCTION

Both Religion and Medicine are relational and therefore have a relationship, one to the other. In the pages which follow, a brief historical review will indicate the common origin in subject, namely Man; the relational action of each to its particular object, namely, the Absolute for Religion and the Finite for Medicine; finally the influence of the Enlightenment on each. Man's desire to transcend can be complemented by his pursuit of science, yet it can also be compromised by his tendency toward Immanence, a concept of self-dependence, self-sufficiency, which recognizes nothing outside worldly reality, such that whatever goals man sets for himself, can be and / or will be attained within his history. No predictions will be found for the twenty-first century. The present is a mirror to the past and a possible lens for the future. Since the future is not merely a "happening" but rather a "decision," the reader is encouraged to wonder and decide for themselves. The twenty-first century will be what we decide it is to become.

Certainly the assigned topic for this chapter is one of the many indications of a heightened interest in the relationship between religious belief and the ideals of medical practice. In recent years, more and more medical schools have included in their curricula, at least as electives, courses in spirituality, the nature of the human person, religious-belief systems and their influences on patient-physician interaction. At this practical level of conduct, the profession of medicine seeks, as part of human society, clearer directives and guidelines to what can and should be done or avoided. Fundamental to these efforts is the essence of the human person, its rights, its freedoms, its responsibilities, its beginning, and its end. The great advances in technology and the ever-greater horizons in scientific understanding and interventional capabilities, have paradoxically raised the conciousness of the practitioner to a more profound appreciation of the art of medicine, the need for it. The role of physician and the role of patient are not enduringly mutually exclusive. The contrasting roles dissolve in time into the commonness of our personhood.

I have subtitled this presentation, convergence or divergence; parallels and crosses. The former, the question, is put forth mainly because of general introversion of philosophic thought and its effect on religion, understood in the terms I shall define below. It is a question to which no final answer will be given here for it is a question which must await answer in the mind and heart of each practitioner of the noble art. Contributing to the question of con- or di-vergence is the attitude frequently associated in an individual with a series of great successes or in a society which enjoys the wealth of scientific discovery. *That attitude is one of immanence;* a term defined in the introduction. Certainly, no one would contest the benefits of the great discoveries of this century and the next will probably surpass it. Nevertheless, succumbing to the temptation of self-sufficiency will sooner or later render us disappointed. My bias is clear.

In this chapter, I will begin with a review of the phenomenon of religion, its origins, its development, and its present condition. Much of this will relate to philosophic influences and will necessarily be brief. For purposes of this discussion, religion is viewed as man's relationship to the sacred, the holy, the wholly -other. There is no generally accepted definition. The difficulty in refining the concept is immediately evident when one realizes that two of the world's most populated sects, Buddhism and Taoism, do not have the notion of an Absolute, Personal, Transcendent Being still involved in the world. I shall use the term God for the sacred, the holy, the Absolute Transcendent Being which man seeks, searches for, denies, ignores, is terrified of, finds solace in. The existence of this Being is not self-evident and the demand for proofs of the existence of this Absolute Transcendent holds its own inherent contradiction, for proof must reach beyond the physical and purely rational into the realm without apprehension, the realm of the nonfinite, the incomprehensible, for finite definition. So in the final frustration of trying to prove this object of religion, God, through authority external to God, man must admit to the impossibility and the attempts must be seen as an invitation to faith.

There is something within man which seeks to transcend, to approach the transcendent. It is a prompting which is buried in the mystery of man. History gives evidence through language and symbol. *Mircea Eliade,* a historian of religion, explains of the primitive human, the human before technology, that the sensible objects of nature were not ends of adoration but were viewed as manifestations of the absolute mystery (1). The stars, the rock, the lightning-flash, the serpent, etc., are heirophanies, manifestations of the sacred. Nonliterate peoples worshipped the skygod or lord of the animals, or the earth goddess. Similarly, more sophisticated peoples—and I, in no way, wish to suggest an evolutionary basis to religion—expressed a need for the Divine. Whether that need was prompted to expression for the sake of cultural unity, political expediency, or dominance and survival, I must leave to historians. Suffice it to say, there is not a single culture which has been researched, which did not have "religion" at its base. Moreover, it could be concluded that their social structure, their art, their philosophic views and their morality, all depended so heavily on "religion." The movements of peoples, the conquests of tribe or nation over its neighbor brought some amalgamation of religious views. The polytheism of the Egyptians and Babylonians and Sumerians and the Greco-Roman Period reflected this, for example, in the changing of the names for their god of this-or-that and the fall from power of the gods of the vanquished. So numerous and varied did these designated gods become that a hierachy was formed and a supreme god was named. Even in their pantheons, which reflected the happenings on earth, there was a need to transcend to a higher plane. But we can reasonably question whether a concentration of gods can make God. Is not there something more beyond man's ability to understand, to confine to time and space? Is not man always seeking the More, the Absolute Transcendent? If we consider this as the basic premise of religion, then there can be no essential difference between the polytheism and monotheism of the religions of nature in which man seeks God through the hierophanies of the universe. The process is the same, differing only in the accidental. We then enter into an entirely new world of relationship with the Divine. It is absolutely new for the Absolute Other is actively involved in human history, as history and not myth. It is the ACT of God coming to meet man. Historically, that new world of religion was given birth in the life of Abraham. The transcendent Absolute made a covenant with man and henceforth man would be directed in what was good in relationships not only with God but also with his fellowman. A marked contrast appeared between the polytheistic and syncretic cults of the ancient world, those cults which were fusions of oriental religions with those of Greece and Rome in Hellenism, and the belief of Judaism. E.O. James expresses this difference in speaking of the Hebrew Prophets: "They insisted on a standard of conduct that would satisfy the demands of an ethically righteous God who had shown man which is good and what is required of him. The transcendent majesty inspired awe, loyalty, and obedience, which introduced a new standard of the "good life" (2). The Hebrew was to walk humbly *with* his God and although political and economic struggles would be experienced, the basic principles would be preserved because it was not merely the aspiration of man to possess the Good as life's value but it was the Absolute Transcendent condescending to communicate, to reveal, this value along the path of history. Covenanted monotheism came into existence and with Christianity this is expressed as reaching its fullness, with the Absolute Transcendent condescending to not only communicate through signs and prophets but be forever at communion *with* man in human nature.

Although religion, then, has always been part of man's life and although analytic comparisons were made even by the ancient Greeks, it was not until the period of the Enlightenment, beginning in the seventeenth century, that probings into causes for man's "irrational" belief systems began. Perhaps prompted by, in their judgment, an intolerant Absolutism of a presented Christianity, philosophers sought to grasp the very essence of phenomena as expressions of religion. Everything had to be reasonably explained and reasonably formulated. The relationship of man with God, if indeed the existence of such a being could ever be proved, was existent in only a passive way. Perhaps this God had created this world with all its marvelous natural phenomena, but it is now allowed to operate on its own and so too with man. There is no active engaging relationship. If there is a God, man has no dependence on that higher power because all that man needs to know is deposited in nature and awaits his discovery. In the final analysis, the God who is not active is dead and the immanent explanation of all reality is sufficient. "The absolute to man is his own nature," "God is the mirror of man" are two statements by one of the most influential of nineteenth century philosophers, Ludwig Feuerbach (3), which according to some, offered the complete criticism of religion. Human autonomy holds sway in that man is an end unto himself. So as not to labor further in the maze of philosophical influences on religion, let me end this section by asking: If man is an end unto himself and expectant of what can be discovered about himself will be discovered by his power of intellect, then to what or to whom does man direct his ageless need to transcend? Is man to return to mythological constructs? Is there a hierarchy of gods but no absolute? If man is sufficient unto himself, then ultimately man should be able to discover or mold the superman and the utopia. What will man do with this ultimate find and who will regulate the progress and declare the utopian state has been reached? Is there not inherent in this humanistic autonomy an erosion of human dignity and the reduction of, at the least, some to serve as purely means for the progressive few? Could moral conduct be expressed other than for its expedience? Human life itself would become a pawn to be sacrificed in the pursuit of the purely immanent. The sacred would be gone. Have we arrived?

When we review the history of Medicine, we trace the progress of yet another relationship, not as fundamental as religion but certainly profound and inspiring. It too begins with man; the innate desire to preserve his life, to shield his injury, to select his nourishment, to restore his health and vigor. As science seeks knowledge through causes, it can be said that primitive man was scientific, speculative, and practical; speculative in that every effect has a cause; practical in that the quest for knowledge is ordered to action. Like religion, medicine has a relationship to another. That relationship in the primitive was to another as the cause for the disease which sets the individual apart from the "normal." Here too is the assessment of a relationship. The cause was viewed as something mysterious, some higher power which removed something necessary for well-being or invaded to afflict the individual. What was the cause? It was some spirit responding to a violation of some tabu. Disease was thought of as a punishment from on-high because of some violation of tribal custom. That primitive assessment of illness is still expressed in the halls of twentieth century hospitals. What to do to afford healing of the afflicted? Summon the sorcerer, the witch-doctor, the divinizer, the priest! Let him work his special powers with incantations, noisy instruments or special brews! Manipulations, bloodletting, incisions are all described by Frederick Stenn, M.D., in his most interesting review of ancient, primitive, and Assyrian Medicine (4). In all the methods and means used by the ancients, the notion of the spiritual, the transcendent-other, was always of prime importance; superstitions admittedly and some we experience as enduring. Yet as bizarre as we might judge them today, they do indicate man's fascination with, need for, relation to the wholly-other. Priest, medicine-man, scientist, astrologer, source of wisdom, were all in one. The combination, priest-physician, continued into recorded history of Egyptian and Greek Medicine. Anthropomorphic polytheism included a god of healing, Aesculapius, under whose protection a guild of physicians was formed. Significant transition to a more objective, nonsuperstitious, brand of medicine entered with the Father of Medicine, Hippocrates. Disturbance in the humoral balance *within* the body was the immediate disorder and every disease was unique and initiated by external causes. Combining careful observation, speculative reasoning, and practical application, he brought medicine to birth as science and art. In the Roman period, and well into the Christian era, the greatest name is that of Galen who, aside from his neural and vascular discoveries, had a basic belief that all things in nature were created by an intelligent being and for a specific purpose and the body is but the tangible conveyer of the soul, and a corruptible one at that. Coupled with wars which destroyed centers of learning and a great pandemic, the attitude that spiritual matters were of sole importance did much to dim the flame of scientific inquiry. Medicine and religion were in conflict, a cross. While monasteries became the centers for healing in Europe and the repositories for whatever medical manuscripts survived, it was the Moslem and Judaic influences which did much to advance medicine. Although religious tabus and restrictions presented many crosses for the physician of the Middle Ages, it was the religious orders which established hospitals, lazarets, quarantines for those with contagious diseases, and leprosoria, to care for the sick and it was members of such religious groups who rekindled the flame in the darkness of ignorance. The period of the Enlightenment saw not only the multiplicity of philosophic views emerge but also an acceleration in medical science and its application, e.g., physiologic understanding, anatomical identification, the disciplined observations of patients' signs and symptoms, and the categorization of disease. As religion was impacted by the rationalists, medicine continued to advance with the discipline of empiric observation and reasoned explanations for disease and the rationales for treatment. That discipline has spawned innumerable discoveries and molded the practitioner of the noble art for our twentieth century. It is not the purpose of this chapter to enumerate them. Our relationship to the persons of the past, whose gifts we use, is sealed in the profession we share and is recorded in history. In our present age, the winds of scientific pursuit have propelled us at an even greater speed of medical advance.

We live in the most active century in medical history. Diagnostic techniques providing entry to the interior of human biology, antibiotics, surgical removal of diseased parts of the human anatomy and insertion of prosthetics, transplant surgery, the dawn of molecular synthesis and genetic engineering are but a few of the remarkable achievements. The human person can begin in a test tube and its life prolonged through technologic assists. Is there anything medical science cannot achieve?! Can we give life? Can we remove death? If we cannot effect these two extremes of the biologic existence in an absolute manner, surely the very nature of the human must transcend, ultimately and absolutely, the speculative and practical realms of his own genius. Certainly, the controversies regarding abortion and direct euthanasia evidence that, for many consciences, there is more to human life than the biologic "what." The heightened questions concerning personal rights, self-determination, duty, responsible obligation, moral conduct, and choice, clearly indicate a recognition of something more than medical science can provide answers for or reasonably ignore. The complexity of the biologic species will continue to unfold to the discoveries in the science of medicine but the complexity of the person will always remain both subject and object of its art.

What will Medicine be like in the Twenty-First Century? Ask the investigator, the geneticist, the molecular biologist, the physicist—those who dream the links in the chain of scientific progress and forge them! Ask the practitioner of the art and the answer will be that although insight into disease will be aided by discovery and computer technology, the physician-patient relationship will endure as the esssential mark of the profession.

What will Religion be in the Twenty-First Century? In the nineteen-sixties and seventies, there was a revolt among the youth dissatisfied with the course of technological civilization and religious traditions. Expressions of freespirit and individualized utopia were heard for a brief period, quickly replaced by a new religious movement evidenced by, and still growing, interest in meditation techniques, cults, and spirituality. This is an ambivalent phenomenon however. The recognized need to transcend the secularized, materialistic view of reality may be limited to merely another plane of humanistic objectives and, once again, by yet another claim to self-sufficiency, the immanence of man, in his pursuit of the better world and personal wholeness. Will religion endure? So long as man does and, in his quest for the good life, is mindful of his history, reflective on his failures and successes and is persistent in his efforts to gain insight and remains receptive to truth in his Enlightenment.

As religion is relational to the Other, so is medicine relational to an other; the former to the Absolute; the latter to the limited-like-self. Both the subject and object of each dynamic are shrouded in mystery, reasonable reality to be revealed in their fullness. Medicine and Religion are parallel in that each serves another person. They cross in the essence of reality and at the crux is the realization of who we are and are called to become.

REFERENCES

1. Eliade, M. 1959. "The Sacred and the Profane," ET by W.R. Trask. New York: Harvest Book, Harcourt, Brace & World Inc.
2. James, E.O. 1960. "The Ancient Gods." London: Weidenfeld & Nicolson.
3. Feuerbach, Ludwig. 1967. "Essence of Christianity." ET by G. Eliot. New York: Torchbook.
4. Stenn, Frederick. 1967. "The Growth of Medicine." Springfield, IL. Charles C. Thomas.

Medicine and Health Care Into the Twenty-First Century. Edited by S.K. Majumdar, L.M. Rosenfeld, D.B. Nash and A.M. Audet. © 1995, The Pennsylvania Academy of Science.

Chapter Thirty-Five

THE PHYSICIAN / PATIENT RELATIONSHIP

STEPHEN E. LAMMERS, Ph.D.
Professor of Religion
Lafayette College
Easton, PA 18042

INTRODUCTION

The physician / patient relationship has been the subject of renewed attention recently. All of the attention has not been sympathetic to the traditional idea of a relationship between physician and patient. For some writers, it is increasingly difficult to speak of a physician / patient relationship. One can speak in the language of the marketplace and use the terms provider / consumer relationship, but the older language is no longer appropriate. The traditional language has also been criticized for masking the inevitable conflicts between patients and physicians.

In such a situation, it has to be recognized that anything one says about the physician / patient relationship is going to be contested. Many voices and many perspectives are part of the conversation. What are some of them?

In the first place, physicians are concerned about the personal nature of this relationship, because they fear it is being lost in a kind of medicine which is increasingly impersonal. However, physicians often refer to the personal nature of the relationship as a way of justifying fee for service medical practice. Thus the form of the relationship is taken as justifying the physician's comfortable economic position (Rodwin, 1993).

Second, patients are concerned about the relationship because they fear that physicians do not understand just how differently physicians understand what is occurring to the patient from how the patient is experiencing her / his own illness.

Third, ethicists have written about the relationship in order to ground much of what they say about medical ethics.

Discussions of the physician / patient relationship often focus upon the changed context of medical care. During the past fifty years, the place where health care is given has moved from the doctor's office into the hospital. More recently, in an effort to save resources, hospitals have tried to do more and more procedures on an outpatient basis or in a clinic. One of the consequences has been that the level of patient acuity in the hospital has risen. Further, skilled nursing facilities are now often the places where patients recuperate from their surgeries or other hospital based interventions.

These different settings have an impact upon the physician / patient relationship. It always has been the case that the type of relationship was in part determined by the kind of medicine being practiced. Patients in hospitals generally are sicker and often are less able to participate in their own care. This is especially true if the physician sees patients in the intensive care unit. At the other end of the scale, rehabilitation physicians work with patients over a long period of time and come to know their patients well. The role of the physician here is quite different from the intensive care specialist and the rehabilitation physician often functions like a counsellor to a patient.

The same physician may actually have two different kinds of relationships within her practice. Pulmonary physicians who treat chronic obstructive lung disease will see their patients through a process of decline that may last many years. That same pulmonary physician may be asked to consult on a ventilator patient she has never seen before. The form of the relationship thus changes, depending upon the circumstances. Expecting the type of relationship in the one setting that is possible in another is simply not realistic. Close physician / patient relationships are more difficult when the setting is the technologically intensive hospital of the late 20th century.

As we shall see, there are some thinkers who take the hospital relationship as the norm and work from there. It should not be a surprise to anyone that given the different perspectives and the different reasons why the relationship is being examined, there are quite different views about what the relationship is and what might be done to enhance it. In what follows I will briefly summarize the dominant views on this subject and give some indication about the issues which have arisen as we move into the twenty-first century.

THE STRUCTURE OF THE RELATIONSHIP—THE DEBATE

The first issue which is in the background of much of the discussion is a judgment about the distribution of power between physicians and patients. Most commentators begin their discussion of the relationship between physician and patient by commenting on the disparity of power which is present.

In the perspective of those who argue that the relationship between the physician and the patient is inherently unequal, the patient presents herself to the physician doubly disadvantaged. First, she is ill and the illness raises questions about her own mortality and the limits of the body. Second, the physician (presumably) knows something about the body and the illness. Thus there is a disparity in knowledge as well as a disparity in perspective (Toombs, 1992).

Recently, writers have been more carefully specifying exactly what the disparity in outlook involves. Modern scientific medicine in the west involves looking for a disease which is the cause of the patient's current difficulties. Thus the physician approaches the patient as having a disease. The patient, however, comes to the relationship with the experience of something being amiss with the body and seeking healing or at least reassurance about this illness. The patient *lives* the illness whereas the physician *studies* the disease with the hope of curing it or alleviating its symptoms. Only a very sympathetic and imaginative physician can overcome this distance between the patient and herself (Cassell, 1993).

Given that there is a disparity of perspective between the physician and the patient in this view, how then should the relationship function? There are those who wish to think of the relationship between the physician and the patient as a contract. The emphasis here is not upon the disparity of power but upon the mutual responsibilities of both parties to the contract. Defenders of this view also wish to empower the patient and make it clear that the physician is to some extent the agent of the patient. A further advantage of the contract model is that it recognizes the limited nature of the relationship. In an era when some wish to put no limits on the professional, a contract model insists upon limits in the relationship from the very beginning. In short, defenders of a contractual understanding of the relationship wish to limit the responsibilities of both parties to the contract so that the inherent inequalities in the relationship will not dominate the entire relationship. In particular, the physician will not be allowed to dominate all decisions because of some supposed superiority in moral wisdom (Veatch, 1981).

The contractual view of the relationship is congruent with a more recent description of the relationship as that of provider and consumer. This view takes a market approach to medicine and the patient is seen as a consumer of medical services. In this view, the consumer supposedly gains some power to determine what medical care is going to be given. The use of market language is also a further attempt to encourage responsibility on the part of physicians and patients.

Another view which argues for a great disparity between patient and physician is that of Katz. He argues that inevitably there is conflict between patients and physician and that physicians go to great lengths to mask this conflict. One of the ways this is done is through not telling the patient all of the diagnostic treatment options and the potential risks and benefits associated with each. Katz argues that disclosure should be the norm of the relationship and that physician, as well as patients, should learn to live with conflict instead of avoiding it. Katz is working out of a contractual understanding with the end in view of making the terms of the contract more explicit to both patients and physicians (Katz, 1984).

There are others who think that a contract model in any form is not adequate to describe the relationship. Although it is true that patients and physicians should be encouraged to take responsibility for their actions, it is also important to recognize the continuing disparity between the two parties. Thus May introduces the idea that the relationship is a covenant, in which there is a candid recognition of a disparity of power and a demand that the person with the greater power, the physician, be asked to take greater responsibility in the relationship. Further, the physician should understand that the demand which is being placed upon her does not start as limited as a contract. Physicians do not know what they will be called upon to do at the beginning of the relationship and May wants them conscious of this fact. If they pretend that the relationship is like an ordinary contract, they will not be available for the patient precisely at the point when the patient needs them. May further wants the physician to extend her or himself to the patient and the difficulty with the contract model is that it encourages the physician to think of her/himself as a provider of services when, in May's view, so much more is at stake. The physician has to realize that part of what is being provided is not a service as such, but the presence of one person to another when one of the persons is ill (May, 1983).

In this perspective, a contractual understanding of the relationship is a good place to begin, but only to begin the discussion. Further, leaving the relationship open to contractual understandings also makes the relationship open to being co-opted by the language of the market. At that point, there is little relationship at all and there is a tension between market imperatives to seek one's own interest and professional requirements to act on the patient's behalf. To put this another way, if one takes market models seriously, there is no reason to trust the physician and the advice which she gives any more than one trusts any other provider of services in a capitalist economy. Further, markets are regularly closed off to persons because of their inability to pay. That is taken for granted when one has a market. Not all of us can afford Cadillac automobiles. The difficulty with the market model for health care is that what cannot be afforded may also be needed by the ill person for their basic health care.

SOME SPECIFIC DUTIES OF PHYSICIANS

There are arguments about what constitutes the most fundamental duties of physicians to patients and what constitutes the content of those duties. This section will review some of the most important questions that have arisen.

The classic maxim, is, "Do no harm!" The point of the maxim is that physicians are situated so as to bring great benefit to patients but, and this is necessarily the case, in the process of doing good, much harm can be the result.

Although this maxim appears simple, in practice it is not. Physicians regularly invade the body in order to bring benefit to patients. Given the way in which modern medicine is practiced, physicians must learn to balance real and potential harms to potential benefits to the patient. Most of the time, this balancing is not difficult. For example, the act of prescribing an antibiotic for an infection for a patient who reports no reactions to antibiotics, is usually not a problematic event. All the actions of a physician are not so simple however. It is quite possible that the activity of the physician may bring about precisely the result which the intervention is designed to avoid. This is true, for example, in the fields of cardiology and cardiac surgery, where interventions designed to prevent the occurrence of myocardial infarction may trigger that event.

A second duty of the physician is that of truthulness. Truthfulness is crucial because without it, the patient cannot be authentically involved in the decisions about future diagnostic options and about the benefits and risks of different therapeutic options. Only a theory of the physician / patient relationship in which the physician makes all the decisions for the patient could justify not emphasizing truthfulness. That theory is not under discussion here. Whether the theory of the relationship is based upon a contractual model or one which is more interpersonal, truthfulness is crucial. In the case of the contract theory, it is crucial for one of the parties to the contract to understand what she is being offered; in the other case, truthfulness is essential if the patient is to be enlisted in the process of healing. But truthfulness, in and of itself, is not the whole answer.

It is not always clear to whom the truth is owed. It is one thing to argue that the truth is owed to the patient but if the patient is suffering from a contagious condition, is the truth owed to others who are close to or intimate with the patient? Does it make a difference if those others are also patients of the same physician? The only point of agreement is that the physician should urge the patient to inform persons close to him or her but there is no uniformity as to what to do if the patient refuses to do this.

One of the ways in which the power of the physician can be limited is by assuring that the physician does not proceed with any process or procedure without the consent of the patient. This limitation on physician power, called informed consent, is not simply an important moral constraint but an important legal constraint as well. In the legal arena, it is justified on the assumption that the patient knows best what he or she wishes and that to assume otherwise is to violate the patient's right to control her/his body.

This statement of the duty only begins the discussion however. There are a number of difficulties. First, it is not clear what the standard of consent should be. There are a number of alternatives. One is that the physician is obligated to disclose all the information which is normally disclosed to patients in these circumstances. One looks to what other professionals disclose in these circumstances and makes an attempt to do likewise. This standard is professionally based. The second possibility is that the professional standard is insufficient and that the appropriate standard is patient centered. This standard is called the reasonable patient standard and requires the physician to disclose what a hypothetical "reasonable patient" wishes to know. Thus, even if professionals do not ordinarily disclose the risks of surgery to patients, it is reasonable for patients to want to know these things and thus these risks should be disclosed. The third possibility is that the patient centered norm is not enough. It is not just any patient who is with the physician at this moment; it is this particular patient. The physician must disclose what it is that *this patient*, at this time and place, wishes to know. That may be far more than the reasonable patient standard, or it may be less. The physician can only know if she seeks to find out from the patient what she wishes to know.

But the standard of information is informed consent is not the only problem. The second issue concerns the quality of the consent. It is not always simple to tell whether the patient is capable of assimilating the information which is being given by the physician. The patient may be slightly depressed, concerned, or too passive to ask the physician what she wishes to know. Any one of these matters can affect the capacity of the patient to consent to what the physician recommends should be done.

Some thinkers argue that patients must have a general capacity to decide matters; only then do they have the capacity to make decisions about medical care. This view is in the minority. The majority view is that patients need only have the capacity to decide the particular matter at hand. If the matter is of a life or death nature, then the standard for capacity must be higher than if the procedure is relatively trivial. Saying this, of course, does not solve all the problems of capacity. Often it takes a very insightful and patient physician to determine whether a patient has the capacity to decide on the particular matter under discussion.

Problems of capacity are among the most intractable in the discussion of informed consent. Patients present to physicians in myriad ways. If the question of capacity is doubtful and the matter is serious, courts may be asked to intervene to determine who should be making a decision in a particular case (Brock, 1987).

The obligation of confidentiality is another duty which grows out of the classical medical tradition. That obligation is under a great deal of pressure today. Consider the differences between the context of not revealing the secrets learned in the home by a solo practitioner on a house call and keeping confidential patient information in a modern hospital with an on-line patient data base. Literally hundreds of persons can have legitimate reasons to inquire about the status of a patient. In the recent past, they would have had to go to the unit and obtain the chart. In some hospitals, with well trained and conscientious unit clerks, this would have been no small achievement. Today, the person may be hundreds of miles away with access to the hospital mainframe.

If there is one obligation which needs discussion today, it is this one. I am not implying here that I think that the duty of confidentiality should be forsworn. What concerns me is that the features of modern hospital practice make it more and more difficult to understand just what the duty of confidentiality is. Many persons have access to patient information. This does not relieve the physician from keeping confidences, but again, in a context in which medicine is based upon team practice, it is crucial that all the members of the team are informed about crucial physiological, psychological, and social facts about the patient.

The obligation to keep confidence has also been limited by courts when patients threaten harm to others and the physician has reason to take the threats seriously. In a famous case in California, a family successfully sued a college which had a counselling service. The client of the counsellor threatened harm to the daughter. The daughter was not warned and she was killed by the man undergoing treatment. The court found in this case, the obligation to protect the public was a more important obligation than the obligation to keep confidences (Tarasoff v. Regents, 1976).

One of the most contentious aspects of current discussions of the physician/patient relationship concerns the discussion of managed care and the potential conflict which it introduces for patients and physicians. If one accepts one popular view of the patient and the physician, the patient could rely upon the physician to serve as her advocate and to make recommendations which were best for the patient. This assumed that the physician was not obligated to others. Indeed, one of the worries in the literature about sports team physicians and industrial physicians is that they have dual loyalties, in the one case to the team owners and in the other to the owners of the factory. In neither case, it was argued, could they be trusted to be concerned solely with the patient's well-being; the team and the firm would be strong competitors for the physicians' primary loyalty.

Marcia Angell argues that such a situation of double-agency of the physician is precisely what is being suggested by many as part of the solution to the health care crisis in the United States. Angell argues that the current fascination with managed care plans is a mistake, in that physicians in such plans will have great incentives to forgo necessary treatment in order to satisfy their employers. Angell is even more concerned about those plans which reward physicians for monies saved by not sending patients to specialists. Her argument is that physicians will have too great an incentive not to recommend specialists because the physician's income will be directly affected by such recommendations (Angell, 1993). Variants of this which concern physicians are insurance rating schemes, which evaluate the physician based upon how often she recommends that the patient see a specialist or how often the physician orders tests.

Of course, supporters of managed care do not agree. There seem to be two points here which are worth considering. The first is that there is some evidence that persons who have participated in managed care over a long period of time have as good a life expectancy as those who do not. The second point is that it is possible to insist upon a set of procedures so that patients are warned when therapies are not recommended. That is to say, it is one matter when the physician does not recommend a potential therapy because she thinks that it will not be efficacious; it is quite another if the therapy is not recommended because of its cost. The patient must be advised, certainly in the second case and probably in the first. In that way, patients would at least be warned about why the physician was failing to make a recommendation and they could seek advice on that physician recommendation. What would be problematic would be a system which encouraged physicians to limit care and in which patients were not aware of the limitations which were being applied and why they were being applied.

HIV infected patients and patients with AIDS have recently added a new/old dimension to the discussion of the physician/patient relationship. In the recent past, western medicine honored those physicians who continued to treat patients whose disease was a threat to physicians. Discussions of physicians fighting yellow fever in the 19th century would be only one example of this. With the advent of AIDS, many younger physicians, who were unfamiliar with either yellow fever or even more recently, tuberculosis, argued that they had no obligation to either accept HIV positive patients or to continue to treat them if they had been treating them previously. Unfortunately, often this rejection of the HIV patient was as much a rejection of a presumed lifestyle as it was a rejection of a patient with a specific disease.

As a result of intense discussions within the profession, it is generally agreed that physicians ought to continue to serve patients who present with HIV infection or with AIDS. Only physicians whose immune systems might be compromised or pregnant physicians are excused from this obligation. Physicians may refer patients to other physicians with more expertise when that proves to be necessary but they ought not to refuse to offer care within their competence. In particular, in emergency situations, and most medical residents today spend some time in emergency rooms, no patient should be turned away because of their medical condition (Arras, 1988).

HIV only brought to the fore the more fundamental issue of whether, and if so, under what conditions, physicians might terminate a relationship. The rest of that discussion has remained relatively stable, for example, the noncompliant patient. But the tension brought about by HIV positive patients remains in medical circles.

Another new issue, which depends upon advances in medical technology, concerns the question, "Who is the patient?" Previously, that question arose only if the physician was treating one patient who might be a threat to another patient or to someone else, say through the possibility of a sexually transmitted disease. In that case, both patients were independent entities. However, due to advances in obstetrics, the fetus can and does become a patient, in the sense that it can be the subject of efficacious treatment, and there is the possibility that there is a conflict between the physicians's duties to the woman and the physician's duties to the fetus. These conflicts can be minor, such as when the woman is not following diet restrictions; they can be more important, such as when harmful drugs are being used by the woman; and they can become intense, such as when the woman refuses to give permission for life-saving fetal surgery.

Now note that the conflicts only become possible in the latter case because of technological advances. These conflicts could not have been imagined before. Further, even the construction of the fetus as a patient is a contested event. Some commentators think that this is simply one more way in which medicine attempts to disempower woman. Both the technological event and the new construction of the fetus are necessary for the conflict to exist. What is clear is that there is little agreement about what to do. Physicians who emphasize fetal rights are going to argue that they should act as *parens patriae* in the interest of the fetus. Physicians who emphasize the right of anyone to determine what happens with their body will argue that unless the woman consents to what the physician recommends, there should be no intervention.

Experimentation upon human subjects further complicates the physician / patient relationship. In the first place, the norm of much experimentation, randomized double-blind experiments, means that the patient and physician lose some control over what treatment is being received. Second, there is the potential for the experimenter physician to be a double agent, first, for the experiment and second, for the patient. Third, there is the problem of fully informing the patient. The common difficulty is that the consent process for the experiment often is not as clear as it might be about the purpose of the experiment and the participation of the patient. Almost always, there is some phrase about hoped for patient benefit. What is not made clear to the patient is that the experiment can be a success even if the patient dies, as long as the sought after information is obtained. In that sense, the hoped for patient benefit is clearly secondary.

At the same time, experimentation is necessary to assess proposed interventions and to protect patients from unproven therapies. The hope is that more education about the purposes of experimentation, and more candor on the part of physicians will correct a continuing problem that afflicts the most vulnerable of patients, those patients for whom current therapies are useless (Office for Protection from Research Risks, 1993).

The very technology which is used in modern medicine has set up a situation of potential conflict between patients and physicians, in that patients fear that physicians will continue to use technology long past the time when there is some hope of meaningful recovery. This has been shown to be a difficult problem, because even when there is wide societal agreement about the usefulness of a given procedure, individual patients or their guardians might insist upon it. At the same time, the fear remains about unwanted treatment.

One way in which patients in the United States have of informing their physician of their wishes is an Advance Directive. Advance Directives usually take two forms, a living will or a durable power of attorney for healthcare. The living will documents the patient's wishes and the durable power of attorney identifies who should be consulted if the patient can no longer speak for herself. Neither becomes effective until the patient becomes incapacitated.

Since 1991, hospitals and other health care facilities have been required to ask patients if they have Advance Directives or if they wish more information about them. Some hoped that this process would cut health care expenditures at the end of life, in that the expectation was that patients would often refuse treatments they would otherwise be given. Until now, there is no research which shows this to be the case.

Although there is much discussion in the popular literature about the unavailability of physicians to patients and the ways in which physicians distance themselves from patients, physicians who are aloof and uncaring, the relationship is also threatened by physicians who are too familiar with their patients. Physicians who are sexually intimate with their patients, especially in psychiatry, are thought to exploit the vulnerability of their patients. A minority of physicians argue that sexual intimacy is permitted for therapeutic reasons in psychiatry but this rationale is not widely accepted in the profession.

CONCLUSION

This paper has outlined the various views of the physician / patient relationship and the implications of some of these views for some of the issues raised by the new advances in medical treatment. It should be clear from what has been said that there are some issues which persist and some which are new because of the new medical technologies.

It is also important to understand the contested nature of the relationship as a sign of vitality. Many of these issues would not have been present twenty years ago. That they have arisen again is a sign of life for medicine and not a sign of its demise. To put this another way. The fact that these issues have arisen is a sign that once again people are beginning to understand that medical care involves more than curing disease with new advances in technology. In addition, it involves thoughtful reflection about the limits and purposes of human life and medicine itself. In that sense, all of the discussion is a sign that medicine might become re-vitalized as physicians and patients think together about the various relationships between them.

REFERENCES

Angell, Marcia. 1993. The Doctor as Double Agent. *Kennedy Institute of Ethics Journal* 3:279-88.

Arras, John D. 1988. The Fragile Web of Responsibility: AIDS and the Duty to Treat. *Hastings Center Report* 18,2:10-20.

Brock, Dan W. 1987. Informed Consent, pp. 98-126. In: Donald VanDeVeer and Tom Regan, (Ed.) *Health Care Ethics: An Introduction.* Temple University Press, Philadelphia, PA, pp. 464.

Cassell, Eric J. 1991. *The Nature of Suffering and the Goals of Medicine.* Oxford University Press, New York, NY, pp. 254.

Katz, Jay. 1984. *The Silent World of Doctor and Patient.* Free Press, New York, NY, pp. 263.

May, William F. 1983. *The Physician's Covenant: Images of the Healer in Medical Ethics.* The Westminster Press, Philadelphia, PA, pp. 204.

Office for Protection from Research Risks. 1993. *Protecting Human Subjects: Institutional Review Board Guidebook.* Superintendent of Documents, U.S. Government Printing Office, Wasington, D.C., pp. 415.

Rodwin, Marc A. 1993. *Medicine, Money and Morals: Physicians' Conflicts of Interest.* Oxford University Press, New York, NY, pp. 411.

Tarasoff v. Regents. 1976. California Supreme Court.

Toombs, S. Kay. 1992. *The Meaning of Illness: A Phenomenological Account of the Different Perspectives of Physician and Patient.* Kluwer Academic Publishers, London, England, pp. 161.

Veatch, Robert M. 1981. *A Theory of Medical Ethics.* Basic Books, New York, NY, pp. 187.

Medicine and Health Care Into the Twenty-First Century. Edited by S.K. Majumdar, L.M. Rosenfeld, D.B. Nash and A.M. Audet. © 1995, The Pennsylvania Academy of Science.

Chapter Thirty-Six

COMPARING HEALTH CARE SYSTEMS: An Overview

MARILYN F. HARRIS, Ph.D.
Associate Professor of Pharmaceutical Administration and
Director of Professional Degree Programs
School of Pharmacy
Duquesne University
Pittsburgh, PA 15282

INTRODUCTION

The 1980's and early 1990's has been a time of dynamic change in the world. New boundaries have been drawn for many countries, there has been a decline in the world economies, the social fabric of many countries is facing new challenges, the rapid growth in technology has made available more information, and allowed the global community to grow, interact, and face many new problems. Health care has not been immune to these forces and it too is in a state of flux. This chapter will discuss the changing world development indicators that affect health. The indicators used to measure health status between countries will be used to compare countries. Some elements of the health care systems will also be used to indicate health status. Parallel developing trends are seen in most countries and will be discussed.

THE CHANGING WORLD SITUATION

Borders and Politics

The break-up of the Soviet Union, once a large homogeneous country politically with a national health care system identified as a socialist system by Roemer in his comparative typology, is now a microcosm of separate countries politically, economically and socially. As each country develops as a separate nation without the strong communist influence, there is a declining economy, a different ideology and the need for a new health care system that meets new directions and challenges. Yugoslavia, as it breaks into many nations, will not only face a new political basis but form new alliances and will need to build its infrastructure. These changes have affected much of the world and the formerly socialist economies (FSE) that have been classified as developed countries by various international agencies are experiencing the problems of many developing countries. China, often classified as a developing country, has moved rapidly, especially in health care, and now has a disease pattern similar to most developed countries. India has made great strides and although it still has many of the problems of the developing world, is moving to a stronger economy and improvement in health care. Decline in the economies and with it the inherent decline in health care is seen in many sub-Saharan and South American countries. More natural events, such as famine, earthquakes, tornados, etc. will affect the health of some and unnatural events, such as wars, will leave their devastation on some other countries.

Economic Decline

Since health care cost in comparative studies is frequently reported as the percent of GDP (Gross Domestic Product) or GNP (Gross National Product), it follows that this cost must be viewed relative to the economic growth and stability of the country. Economic growth for the world during the 1970's was 3.5 percent per year. During the 1980's, including 1991, it was 3.0% per year. This, however, does not show the difference between countries. Wide differences among countries are seen. The growth in GDP is quite dramatic between these two decades for a few countries. China and India both had exceptional growth. This growth is seen in these two countries in the four major production areas: agriculture, industry, manufacturing and services. The balance of the countries classified as low-income countries, show an average decline in growth from 4.8% to 3.7%. Individually, some countries in the low-income classification did, however, show modest growth including Bangladesh, Pakistan and Ghana. Most sub-Saharan countries showed a decline in percentage growth between the 70's and 80's.

Middle-income economies generally showed a slight decline in overall GDP growth over the two decades. Slight growth is, however, seen in the agriculture segment in some countries, which is one of the necessary components without which improvement in health status could not be expected. Lack of sufficient production in the agriculture sector, unless offset by growth of the industry and manufacturing segments, providing necessary funds to import food, would tend to affect negatively health status.

The group of countries classified as upper middle-income show a decrease in GDP growth between the decades. These countries primarily in South and Central America are in an area that previously had shown substantial growth. All segments of their production are similarly affected.

The high-income economies, in general, show decrease in overall production. However, some countries, i.e. the United Kingdom and Denmark, report slight increases. The declines in production with this group of countries tend to be less than with the countries in the other classifications. Generally high producers in all areas, the opportunity for further growth is much less. Decreases, however, indicate the overall decline in the world economies. This affects the spending in countries on health care and the need to be more cost effective. Affected also is development assistance, including assistance for health care, that this group of countries provides for many of the low and middle-income economies.

Education

Primary school is generally considered to include students ages 6-10 years while secondary school is 12 through 17 years and these classifications are used in Table 1.

The level of education of the mother affects the health of the family. Undereducated mothers tend to have low birth weight babies and high infant mortality, both indicators of overall poor health status of a country. Primary education, or lack thereof, has the greatest affect on the health of the family. Table 1 compares the level of education for selected countries and for their female population in 1970 and 1990. Universal education at the primary level is seen by 1990. This is an increase from 83% in 1970. Using income classification, the greatest increase in primary education is seen in the low-income group. However, in this group, although improvement is seen in all countries, there is a significant level of undereducation in countries such as Nigeria, Ethiopia and Sierra Leone. Although not reported in the table, Pakistan, which has an increase in GNP over the reported years, had a decrease in overall primary education level from 40% in 1970 to 37% in 1990. The female population, however, had an increase from 22% to 26%. Bangladesh, another country with modest economic growth, made significant increases in education level from 54% to 73% overall and from 35% to 68% among females when comparing 1970 and 1990. Attainment of secondary education is much less likely than primary education. Although level of primary education of the mother has the greatest affect on the health of the family, the higher the level of mothers' education also positively affects health outcomes of the family and the nation. Generally, only those countries in the high-income groups had high levels of secondary education in 1990. There is significant increase in educational level in all high-income countries from 1970 to 1990 at the secondary level. By 1990, secondary education is almost universal in this income group as is education of the female population. India and China again show significant increases between 1970 and 1990; however, almost 56% and 52% respectively of the population still does not receive secondary education.

Urbanization

Urban population is defined differently by countries, making comparisons difficult. However, broadly stated, about 50% of the world population resides in urban areas.

This has increased from about 35% in 1970. Urban populations are highest in the high-income economies. The lowest urban population is found in the low-income economies. In 1970, New York, Tokyo, Shanghai and London, in descending order, were the four largest cities in the world. It is estimated that Mexico City, San Paulo (Brazil), Tokyo and Calcutta (India), will be the four largest cities by the year 2000.

TABLE 1

Percent of Population Enrolled in Education
Selected Countries

	Primary				Secondary			
	Total		Female		Total		Female	
	1970	1990	1970	1990	1970	1990	1970	1990
Low-income economies								
China	89	135	—	129	24	48	—	41
India	73	97	56	83	26	44	15	33
Nigeria	37	72	27	63	4	20	3	17
Ethiopia	16	38	10	30	4	15	2	12
Sierra Leone	34	48	27	39	8	16	5	12
Lower-middle-income economies								
Philippines	108	111	—	110	46	73	—	75
Ecuador	97	—	95	—	22	—	23	—
Jamaica	119	105	119	105	46	60	45	63
Thailand	83	85	79	85	17	32	15	32
Turkey	110	110	94	105	27	54	15	42
Chile	107	98	107	97	39	74	42	77
Upper-middle-income economies								
South Africa	99	—	99	—	18	—	17	—
Venezuela	94	92	94	94	33	35	34	41
Brazil	82	108	82	—	26	39	26	—
Mexico	104	112	101	110	22	53	17	53
Puerto Rico	117	—	—	—	71	—	—	—
Korea	103	108	103	110	42	87	32	85
High-income economies								
Singapore	105	110	101	109	46	69	45	71
Italy	110	97	109	96	61	79	55	78
United States	—	105	—	104	—	92	—	91
Germany	—	105	—	105	—	97	—	103
Japan	99	101	99	101	86	96	86	97
Denmark	96	98	97	98	78	109	75	110
Canada	101	105	100	104	65	106	65	107
United Kingdom	104	107	104	107	73	84	73	85
World	**83**	**104**	**71**	**99**	**31**	**65**	**28**	**46**

Note: For some countries with universal primary education, the gross enrollment ratios may exceed 100 percent because some pupils are younger or older than the country's standard primary school age.

— data not available

Source: Adapted from World Development Report 1993. The International Bank for Reconstruction and Development, Oxford University Press.

The national population growth is not responsible alone for this growth. The major factor is movement of rural population to the cities. This has resulted in the dramatic increase in the size of cities in the demographically developing countries (DDC). With this population migration different health patterns emerge. In a rural setting, although it may be possible to grow a portion of one's food, lack of medical facilities and health care professionals, even at the primary health care level, put the rural population at a disadvantage. The poor who move to the city are frequently gathered in a ghetto or in the developing world in "septic fringes" surrounding the large megatropolis. More tuberculosis, cancer, especially lung cancer in men, mental illness and infectious disease are seen in the fringe cities. Some health care services are usually available and the support system built by displaced rural inhabitants often offsets the increase in exposure to disease, the lack of sanitation and water, and the increased psychiatric problems. Although conditions may be bad generally, the migrants stay because the situation is still better than in the rural setting.

Population

The total world population in 1991 was 5,350 million. The low-income economies, including China and India, accounted for 59% of this number. Middle-income population was 26% and high-income population was 15%. A review of average annual growth of population over the last decade shows an overall 1.7% average annual growth. The average annual increase for low-income countries is 2% and if continued at this rate would result in a doubling of the population by the year 2027, while the high-income segment had an average annual growth of 0.6% over the same time. It would take until 2111 for this segment to double. Population growth along with decrease in mortality especially among infants and children and increased life expectancy, may further increase population size in the short term. The low and middle-income countries, many of whom cannot currently meet their population needs, will be further strained to provide basic needs including health care. The concept of demographic transition introduced after World War II by Omran describes the shift in population demographics that follows decreased mortality and increased life expectancy. As the likelihood of a child reaching maturity increases, the family is less likely to have more children. Factors such as the family's ability to provide more than the basic necessities, the declining economic role of the children, and the mother's involvement in the work force also have been shown to contribute to the reduction in the number of children. Stationary population size is a goal for many health planners but a long-term one. Concern for improved living standards and quality of life for all people of the world is the overall goal. With the limited resources available, even if an equal distribution was possible, it becomes readily apparent that a slowing of population growth is necessary. History has shown that improved standards of living results in fertility declines.

MEASURING HEALTH

Basic Indicators

Two indicators frequently used to compare health status among countries are life expectancy and mortality. Life expectancy at birth calculations are based on the mortality rate at each age, not accounting for the total population at those age levels. Life expectancy at birth for selected countries is reported in Table 2. The sub-Saharan countries overall have the lowest life expectancy. China, also in the low-income group, has a life expectancy of 69, the highest. India, with a life expectancy

TABLE 2

Life Expectancy and Infant Mortality Related to Economic Resources Selected Countries

	GNP Per capita, (dollars)	Total health expenditure Per capita (dollars)	Life Expectancy (years)	Infant Mortality Per 1000 live births	
	1991	1991	1991	1970	1991
Low-income economies					
China	370	11	69	69	38
India	330	21	60	137	90
Nigeria	340	9	52	139	85
Ethiopia	120	4	48	158	130
Sierra Leone	210	5	42	197	145
Lower-middle-income economies					
Philippines	730	14	65	66	41
Ecuador	1,000	43	66	100	47
Jamaica	1,380	—	73	43	15
Thailand	1,570	73	69	73	27
Turkey	1,780	76	67	147	58
Chile	2,160	100	72	78	17
Upper-middle-income economies					
South Africa	2,560	158	63	79	54
Venezuela	2,730	89	70	53	34
Brazil	2,940	132	66	95	58
Mexico	3,030	89	70	72	36
Puerto Rico	6,320	—	76	29	14
Korea	6,330	377	70	51	16
High-income economies					
Singapore	14,210	219	74	20	6
Italy	18,520	1,426	77	30	8
United States	22,240	2,763	76	20	9
Germany	23,650	1,511	76	23	7
Japan	26,930	1,538	79	13	5
Denmark	23,700	1,588	75	14	8
Canada	20,440	1,945	77	19	7
United Kingdom	16,550	1,039	75	19	7
World	**4,010**	**323**	**66**	**85**	**53**

Source: Adapted from World Development Report 1993, The International Bank for Reconstruction and Development, Oxford University Press.

of 60, is similar to the overall average for Asian countries. The low-income group, excluding India and China but including the balance of Asia and Africa, has an average life expectancy of 55 years. The middle-income group of countries' life expectancy average is 68 years. The high-income economies have a life expectancy of 77 years. Overall, the world life expectancy is 66 years. There appears to be some correlation between GNP per capita and life expectancy. Japan, with the highest GNP per capita, also has the highest life expectancy. Switzerland also ranks high on both indicators. In the middle-income economies, both the low and upper groupings show less correlation between GNP per capita and life expectancy. The low-income economies also indicate some correlation between GNP per capita and life expectancy with China again being an exception. Another exception, Sri Lanka, with a low GNP per capita, has a life expectancy of 71 years—the only country besides China in the low GNP per capita category to have a life expectancy over 60 years. When health expenditure per capita is studied, less correlation is seen with life expectancy at all economic levels. The United States, with the highest per capita health care expenditure ($2,763), has a life expectancy of 76, while Japan, with a health care expenditure of $1,538, has a life expectancy of 79. Mexico, with a GNP per capita of $3,030, has the same life expectancy of 70 years as Korea, with a GNP per capita more than double ($6,330). The larger the amount of expenditure on health care by a country does not appear to indicate a longer life expectancy. It is possible that longevity is more related to the overall wealth of the country, but here again there appears to be other factors at play.

Another measure used to indicate the health of a nation is infant mortality. Infant mortality (0-1 years) globally was 53 per 1,000 live births for 1991. For the 22 high-income countries, mortality was 8 per 1,000. Among these countries, infant mortality ranged from a low of 5 per 1,000 in Japan to a high of 9 per 1,000 in the U.S. In the upper middle-income group, Portugal and Greece have the lowest infant mortality while South Africa and the Gabon the highest. The lower middle-income group ranged from a low of 11 per 1,000 in Czechoslovakia to a high of 115 per 1,000 in the Congo. The average of the other 38 countries in the middle-income group is 91 per 1,000. Child mortality, 0-5 years, has a similar trend. Median age at death is 5 years in sub-Saharan Africa, reflecting the high infant mortality rate in addition to the high risk to children. Median age at death for Asia is 42 years with China 64 years and India 37 years. In Asia, Sri Lanka has a median age at death of 73 years, signficantly higher than the rest of the developing countries in Asia. The median age at death globally is 55 years with a high in the high-income economies of 74 years. Table 3 ranks 10 countries in the high-income group for per capita expenditure on health care, % of GNP and mortality rates. The U.S., the highest spender per captia and as % of GNP, ranks 10, the lowest ranking, in infant mortality and in addition has low mortality rankings for child, men and women. Japan, with the lowest mortality rates at all ages, spends less as a % of GNP on health care than all countries except the United Kingdom. Clearly, the amount of funding for health care is not an indicator that better health care will result. Even in very poor countries, lower mortality rates do not seem to be related to size of health care budget. In comparing health care expenditures, especially among demographically developing countries, one must consider that most of the expenditure is not monetary but that a significant barter economy, operating in many countries, may play a significant part in improved health. This is believed to be one of the important factors in the significantly higher indicator numbers for China.

Feeding the World

In the low-income economic grouping, agriculture production increased from the decade of the seventies to the eighties. In the Middle Eastern crescent and most of Latin America, i.e. Mexico and Brazil, the agriculture production decreased. Asia's agriculture production increased over the same period. There was a decrease in those countries ravaged by war. Overall, agriculture production improved slightly but not enough to provide food to feed the total population of all countries. Most of the DDC do not provide enough food for their own use and since they do not have the resources to purchase food from other countries, a food deficit exists. Lack of food specifically results in many diseases. Not only are those malnourished more susceptible to developing diseases but they are also less likely to recover without disability. Childhood diseases, diarrheal and respiratory diseases, tuberculosis and malaria are the diseases most fatal to malnourished children.

The most prevalent symptoms of protein-energy malnutrition are stunting, low height for a given age, and wasting, low weight for a given height. These terms are used to measure health status in children. Thirty-nine percent of children age 2 to 5 years in sub-Saharan Africa have stunting, while 10% of the 1 to 2 year olds are wasted. India (65% stunting, 27% wasting) as well as other Asian countries (53% stunting, 11% wasting) show indication of greater protein-energy deficiencies than Africa. Forty-two percent of the population worldwide (2-5 years) are stunted and 12% in those age groups are wasted. The World Health Organization estimated

TABLE 3

Rank Order of Health Expenditure and Mortality Rates
Ten Countries

	Health Expenditure $ per capita	% of GNP	Mortality Rates Infant	Child	Men	Women
U.S.A.	2,763	1	10	9	8	7
Sweden	2,343	4	2	2	3	4
Finland	2,046	7	3	3	10	9
Canada	1,945	2	4	5	4	2
France	1,869	3	5	4	9	3
Japan	1,538	9	1	1	1	1
Italy	1,426	6	8	10	2	5
Australia	1,331	5	7	6	5	6
U.K.	1,039	10	6	7	7	10
Spain	831	8	9	8	6	8

Source: Adapted from World Development Report 1993, The International Bank for Reconstruction and Development, Oxford University Press.

that 780 million people worldwide are energy deficient. Iron deficiency is the most common mineral disorder. If the mother has anemia while pregnant, the child will start life undernourished. Iron deficiency reduces physical productivity and the child's ability to learn. Other nutrient deficiencies such as iodine cause mental retardation, development delay and stunting, while vitamin A deficiency accounts for vision loss and blindness. WHO estimates that approximately 14 million children have some degree of eye damage from Vitamin A dificiency.

Environment Effects

Lack of sufficient clean water and adequate sanitation are often cited as the major causes of the disease pattern in DDC. The high incidence of diseases transmitted via feces, diarrhea and intestinal worm infections, accounts for 10% of the diseases in these countries. WHO reports that 1.3 billion people in DDC lack clean water and 2 billion lack adequate sanitation. In India, over 80% of households do not have sanitation while in sub-Saharan Africa 62% do not. Worldwide, 40% of the population do not have adequate sanitation while 28% do not have sufficient clean water.

Indoor air pollution in some countries is a larger problem than the air problem in cities such as the large industrialized cities in China and India often cited in the press. Smoky huts in Nepal and Papua New Guinea have particulate levels much higher. Rural inhabitants who use coal in unvented or improperly vented fires indoors are as likely to develop respiratory disease and lung cancer as smokers.

Disease Patterns

Shift in health and disease patterns prior to the twentieth century, in the more developed countries, are closely associated with a rise in living standards and improved nutrition. The corresponding shift in developing countries, in the twentieth century, is initiated by medical progress, organized health care and disease control programs that are internationally assisted and financed, and largely independent of the socioeconomic level of the country. The disease patterns of the DDC and the FSE (formerly social economies) and EME (established market economies) are different. Table 4 ranks the major burden of disease in the DDC for 1990. The leading diseases reported for the DDC were respiratory infections for females and unintentional injuries for males. This latter disease grouping included both motor vehicle injury and falls. Cardiovascular disease was ranked second for females an third for males. The ranking for the combined FSE and EME (Table 5) ranked cardiovascular as the leading disease. Infectious diseases are not a leading cause of death in developed countries but are the major cause of disease in developing countries. Tuberculosis is the leading disease, followed by malaria. Measles is the third most prevalent infectious disease. In the developing world, communicable diseases are the major cause of death while in the developed countries, it is non-communicable disease. The communicable diseases are diseases that need public health programs and improved living conditions to alleviate, while the non-communicable diseases need public health programs directed at screening and lifestyle changes.

ELEMENTS OF THE HEALTH CARE SYSTEM

Financial Resources

In all countries, health care is financed from both government and private sources. In low-income countries, the public support of health is from general tax revenues and is usually for minimal health care including limited public health and frequently district hospitals that provide only very basic benefits to a small percentage of the population. Much of the population receives little health care. What is available is often traditional medicine and/or western drugs on the open market. These commodities are usually paid for by the individual at a very high price in relation to individual income. A small percentage of the wealthy, usually less than 5% of the total population, utilize the majority of health care. Many capital cities have a well-equipped hospital where the affluent can receive good health care. These services are not available to the general population. There is very little health insurance available for any economic grouping in the low-income countries. Traditional medicine is important to the overall health care and is being incorporated with

TABLE 4

Disease by Rank
Demographically Developing Countries (DDC) (1990)

Disease	F	M
Respiratory infections	1	2
Cardiovascular	2	3
Diarrheal diseases	3	4
Neuropsychiatric	5*	—
Unintentional injury	5*	1
Perinatal	4	5

*both 335,000 disability adjusted life years

Source: Adapted from World Development Report 1993, The International Bank for Reconstruction and Development, Oxford University Press.

TABLE 5

Disease by Rank
Formerly Socialist Economies (FSE) Plus
Established Market Economies (EME)

Disease	M	F
Cardiovascular	1	1
Malignant	2	2
Neuropsychiatric	3	3
Injuries unintentional	4	4
Injuries intentional	5	—
Musculoskeletal	—	5

Source: Adapted from World Development Report 1993, The International Bank for Reconstruction and Development, Oxford University Press.

western medicine in some of the more progressive country health care systems. As colonies, many of the developing countries received their health care through "mission" hospitals. Although most of the religious and other mission-type hospitals have been incorporated into the countries' health care system, some countries receive substantial development assistance for health care from both bilateral and multilateral government agencies and from private voluntary organizations (PVO). Many of the sub-Saharan countries receive a substantial percentage of their health care dollars from aid (Table 6). Sierra Leone received 33% of its total health care expenditure from development assistance in 1990. Mozambique and Tanzania receive 53% and 48% respectively of their health care expenditure in aid. Note, however, that the total health care expenditure for health care per capita for Mozambique and Tanzania is $5 and $4 respectively, indicating the total amount of aid even at approximately 50% is not large. China and India receive very little development assistance for health care.

As a country's economy improves, there is often a general increase in percent of

TABLE 6

Health Expenditure by Sector and Development Assistance Selected Countries 1990

	Percentage of GNP Total	Public Sector	Private Sector	Development assistance for health percentage of total health expenditure
Low-income economies				
China	3.5	2.1	1.4	0.6
India	6.0	1.3	4.7	1.6
Nigeria	2.7	1.2	1.6	6.4
Ethiopia	3.8	2.3	1.5	18.8
Sierra Leone	2.4	1.7	0.8	33.0
Mozambique	5.9	4.4	1.5	52.9
Tanzania	4.7	3.2	1.5	48.3
Lower-middle-income economies				
Philippines	2.0	1.0	1.0	7.8
Ecuador	4.1	2.6	1.6	7.0
Jamaica	—	—	—	—
Thailand	5.0	1.1	3.9	0.9
Turkey	4.0	1.5	2.5	0.5
Chile	4.7	3.4	1.4	0.7
Upper-middle-income economies				
South Africa	5.6	3.2	2.4	—
Venezuela	3.6	2.0	1.6	0.1
Brazil	4.2	2.8	1.4	0.4
Mexico	3.2	1.6	1.6	0.9
Puerto Rico	—	—	—	—
Korea	6.6	2.7	3.9	0.2

— data not available

Source: Adapted from World Development Report 1993, The International Bank for Reconstruction and Development, Oxford University Press.

health care dollars from the public sector. This is coupled with the political views of the country. The more socialized a country, the larger percent of health care expenditure that comes from the government. In the middle-income countries, generally this public support increases as development increases. Therefore, as expected, the lower middle-income countries receive less support for health care from the public sector than the upper middle-income countries.

The high-income countries receive the largest amount of their health care dollars from the public sector (Table 7). These government funds are supplemented by private funds. Health care is widely available in high-income countries for which they pay a significantly higher percentage of their GNP than countries in other economic groupings. Most of the countries in the high-income group have supplemental insurance which is a private option of the individual and in some countries provides a significant portion of the overall health care funding. The expenditure from the private sector ranges from a low in Norway of 5% to a high in the U.S. of 55%. The majority of the high-income countries provide 60% to 70% of the funding for health care from public funds. The established market economies, excluding

TABLE 7

Health Expenditure High-Income Countries 1990

	Total health expenditure U.S. dollars Per capita	GNP per capita, U.S. Dollars	Health expenditures as a percentage of GNP Total	Public Sector	Private Sector
High-income economies					
United States	2,763	22,240	12.4	5.5	6.9
Switzerland	2,520	33,610	7.5	5.1	2.4
Sweden	2,343	25,110	9.3	8.3	1.0
Finland	2,046	23,980	8.5	7.2	1.3
Canada	1,945	20,440	9.5	7.1	2.4
France	1,869	20,380	9.2	6.8	2.4
Norway	1,835	24,220	7.6	7.2	0.4
Austria	1,711	20,140	8.5	5.6	2.9
Denmark	1,588	23,700	6.7	5.6	1.1
Japan	1,538	26,930	5.7	4.2	1.5
Germany	1,511	23,650	6.4	4.6	1.8
Netherlands	1,500	18,780	8.0	5.8	2.2
Belgium	1,449	18,950	7.7	5.1	2.6
Italy	1,426	18,520	7.7	6.0	1.7
Australia	1,331	17,050	7.8	5.5	2.3
United Kingdom	1,039	16,550	6.3	5.4	0.9
New Zealand	925	12,350	7.5	6.2	1.3
Ireland	876	11,120	7.9	6.4	1.5
Spain	831	12,450	6.7	5.3	1.4
Hong Kong	699	13,430	5.2	1.0	4.2
Israel	494	11,950	4.1	2.1	2.1
Singapore	219	14,210	1.5	0.9	0.6

Source: Adapted from World Development Report 1993, The International Bank for Reconstruction and Development, Oxford University Press.

the U.S., provide universal or near-universal coverage through general revenue financing or compulsory social insurance. They tend to use global budgets and capped third party payments. The government is frequently the third party payer. France, Germany and Japan have premium based social insurance, while Norway, Sweden and the United Kingdom finance their health care through general tax revenue. The United States uses a combination of private voluntary insurance and general revenue taxes. The system is unregulated with fee-for-service compensation prevalent. High administrative costs are associated with it.

Human Resources

The health care professionals in a system range from primary care workers to the highly-trained medical specialists. In comparing health care systems, gross data on the number of physicians and the number of nurses is the most widely available and is therefore usually used (Table 8). There are 1.34 per 1,000 of physicians to

TABLE 8
Health Resources per 1,000 Population
Selected Countries

	Doctors 1988-92	Nurses 1988-92	Hospital beds 1985-90
Low-income economies			
China	1.37	0.69	2.6
India	0.41	0.45	0.7
Nigeria	0.15	0.90	1.4
Ethiopia	0.03	0.07	0.3
Sierra Leone	0.07	0.35	1.0
Lower-middle-income economies			
Philippines	0.12	0.37	1.3
Ecuador	1.04	0.31	1.7
Jamaica	—	—	—
Thailand	0.20	1.10	1.6
Turkey	0.74	1.11	2.1
Chile	0.46	0.37	3.3
Upper-middle-income economies			
South Africa	0.61	2.75	4.1
Venezuela	1.55	0.78	2.9
Brazil	1.46	0.15	3.5
Mexico	0.54	0.43	1.3
Puerto Rico	2.55	—	4.0
Korea	0.73	0.73	3.0
High-income economies			
Singapore	1.09	4.14	3.3
Italy	4.69	2.81	7.5
United States	2.38	6.66	5.3
Germany	2.73	4.64	8.7
Japan	1.64	2.95	15.9
Denmark	2.56	14.34	5.7
Canada	2.22	10.43	16.1
United Kingdom	1.40	2.80	6.3

Source: Adapted from World Development Report 1993, The International Bank for Reconstruction and Development, Oxford University Press.

population worldwide. This varies widely among country economic groupings. In the sub-Saharan countries there is an average of 0.12 per 1,000. A low of 0.02 per 1,000 is seen in several sub-Saharan African countries (Mozambique, Malawi, Rwanda and Guinea) with a high in Zimbabwe of 0.16 per 1,000. Asia (excluding China) has an overall average of 0.32 per 1,000. The EME have an overall ratio of 2.52 per 1,000 with a high in Italy of 4.69 per 1,000 to a low of 1.40 per 1,000 in the United Kingdom. The FSE have the highest ratio on average of 4.07 per 1,000 with a low of 1.79 per 1,000 in Romania and a high of 4.69 per 1,000 in the Russian Federation. Russia has the highest ratio of physicians to population of any country in the world. These statistics, however, do not show either the geographic distribution of the physicians within a country or the ratio of specialist to the general practitioner. It is generally recognized that even in countries with an oversupply of physician manpower, certain areas of the country may not have sufficient physicians to serve the population. Indeed, in the U.S., the government has designated certain rural and inner city areas as underserved. The percent of general practitioners to specialists also affects distribution as specialists tend to practice in major medical centers in urban areas. In addition, the cost of medical care will be higher the larger the number of specialists. In some of the upper middle-income countries, especially Latin America, the percent of specialists may be as high as 75% as in Chile. The percent of specialists in EME ranges from 25-50%. In Belgium, France, Germany and the Scandinavian countries, the regulatory bodies control the number of physicians trained including specialists. About one specialist to three general practitioners appears to be adequate and is higher than the ratio used in some managed care facilities in the United States. The overall increase in number of physicians in some DDC countries has not always lead to better health care of the population. The quality of the programs has sometimes been reduced as the number and specialization of physicians increased. The more developed the medical care, the more likely the physicians are to congregate around a major urban area with a technologically advanced hospital. In addition, the increased number of physicians trained has often lead to a higher migration to the EME, resulting in a more than adequate supply of physicians in some of the EME and a shortage in the DDC. Therefore, several EME countries have limited this migration in recent years.

The overall number of physicians must also be viewed in respect to the number of other health care workers. In many countries, more emphasis is being placed on training primary health care workers to practice at the entry level of the system. This concept, identified in China as the "barefoot doctor", the traditional health care worker in other countries and in the U.S., the physician assistant or nurse practitioners, to name a few, is an increasing segment of the health care providers. Statistics currently are not kept on these types of workers in enough countries to make comparisons. However, their numbers greatly affect the physician manpower needs of a country and must be considered when adequacy of health care manpower coverage is being discussed.

The statistics on gross number of nurses in a country are available. Worldwide there are 1.4 nurses for each physician. This tends to be higher in EME (2.1 nurses per physician) to 0.5 in Latin America and the Caribbean. The number of nurses in a country may be influenced by the number of other health auxiliary personnel used. There are, however, wide differences in the number of nurses which often has a cultural basis. In some countries, especially in Latin American countries, nursing is not considered a suitable profession for a daughter in many families. In sub-Saharan Africa, the number of nurses is high, an average of 5.1 nurses for each physician. Clearly, with the undersupply of physicians, as well as the greater geographic maldistribution of physicians, the nurse is very important. In fact, the nurse is the only health care worker available to much of the population.

In general, although the only data available on a consistent basis, the number of physicians and nurses do not give a good overall picture of the health care providers in a country. The number of other types of providers needs to be included to get a good picture of the adequacy of a health care system.

Physical Resources

The physical resources of a health system are often measured by comparing the number of beds available (Table 8). This, however, does not account for the trend worldwide, especially in EME, toward more home care and shorter hospital stays. However, the number of hospital beds does give an indication of the adequacy of physical facilities. In the EME, there are 8.3 beds per 1,000 of population with a high in Canada of 16.1 to 1,000 and a low of 3.9 per 1,000 in Ireland. The FSE have a ratio of 11.4 beds per 1,000 with the Russian Federation the highest at 13.8 beds per 1,000 and Poland the lowest with 6.6 beds per 1,000. The FSE countries, as with physicians, show a possible oversupply. The number of beds in sub-Saharan Africa overall is 1.4 per 1,000. In Asia, excluding India and China, the ratio is 1.8 per 1,000 and is 2.7 per 1,000 in Latin America and the Caribbean.

Types of Health Care

Most countries spend the major portion of their health care expenditure on curative medicine. Until this century, health care was not available to the majority of the population and a hospitalization was usually only at the end of one's life with the hospital considered as a place to die. As medical treatment advanced, this curative function of medicine became widely accepted as health care. Physicians and the health care professionals focused their effort on curing the patient. Hospitals became large edifices, well equipped with the latest technology. As more physicians specialized and technology became more advanced, physicans tended to congregate in medical centers often associated with Universities. These tertiary care treatment centers are costly and available to only a small portion of the population. Even in the lower-income economies, the major city usually has at least one tertiary care center around which the majority of the highly-trained physicians practice.

Secondary hospitals, often referred to as community or district hospitals, have somewhat less technology and fewer specialists. They are more numerous and more widely distributed. These hospitals, in all economies, service the majority of the population. In the low and middle-income economies, more attention to primary care, often through polyclinics, has developed. In each of the economies discussed, more attention is being given to primary care. However, primary care may mean different levels of care depending on the country. In the low-income countries, there may be efforts to train a large cadre of community health workers, especially for rural practice. In the EME, primary care may be provided by family physicians or general practitioners. In all countries, more attention is being given to preventive care. From an economic perspective, it is widely recognized that it is more cost effective to prevent a disease than to treat it after the disease has developed. Preventive programs in the DDC are frequently directed at communicable diseases, especially immunization, and health education focused on prenatal and infant care. Attention in these programs frequently is given to nutrition education as well. In the EME, preventive programs are usually focused on lifestyle change that will prevent non-communicable disease or improve quality of life in patients with chronic disease.

Organization

The EME have a wide range of systems of health care. These range from the highly government controlled system to a system based on a high degree of free enterprise. The less government control, the more pluralistic and decentralized is the system. The U.S. is an example of such a system. Overall, the priorities in the U.S. are based on individual wealth. This may change to some extent as the U.S. moves to a national health care system. On the other extreme, the system in Norway is highly regulated. A standardized package of benefits is available universally to all citizens. Health education is a significant part of the system. Hospitals are regionalized and numbers closely controlled. Preventive care is an important aspect of the system. Training of health professionals, including auxiliary personnel, is regulated by the government. Many EME countries have a mix of these two systems.

The FSE previously focused on children and industrial workers; however, most countries in this group had universal coverage. Preventive services were not a high priority. Overall the system has the highest number of health care workers including the highest ratio of physicians to population as well as the most hospital beds. With the breakdown of many of these economies, the control and regulations as well as universal coverage will change; however, the extent of change remains to be seen.

The middle-income countries, especially those in Latin America, are moving toward government control of the public sector with plans of universal coverage; however, the private sector operates with no government regulations. Country health plans in this region are influenced by many other cultures and some countries have attempted to include the traditional medicine of their indigenous Indian culture, the charitable hospital supported by the Roman Catholic Church, types of public health programs from North America, the modern European social security and the wealthy middle-class private medical care. The result has been major strides in some countries, especially during the late 1970's and early 1980's. This growth has slowed with the downturns in the economies in much of this area.

The low-income economies generally have a government plan focused on improved sanitation, control of infectious disease, and primary health care. However, the financial resources generally are spent on hospital services in the main cities, which primarily service the wealthy.

EMERGING TRENDS

The preamble of the Constitution of the World Health Organization, written in 1948, lists principles that are basic to the happiness, harmonious relations and security of all peoples.

> "Health is a state of complete physical, mental and social well-being and not merely the absence of disease or infirmity.
>
> The enjoyment of the highest attainable standard of health is one of the fundamental rights of every human without distinction of race, religion, political belief, economic or social condition, etc."

All member countries accept these principles as part of their contract with WHO. In 1978, at the Conference on Primary Health Care, held in Alma-Ata, Kazakhstan, the groundwork for the World Health Organization's main target, "the attainment by all citizens of the world by the year 2000 of a level of health that will permit them to lead a socially and economically productive life," decided in 1977 by the World Health Assembly, was set. This goal, now commonly known as "Health for all by the Year 2000," is a major focus of WHO and member countries are working toward this goal. Although the goal will not be met by all countries, it has helped to focus effort and most governments, including the United States, are pushing to broaden access to health care and to provide at least primary care to all citizens. This trend of equalization is widely seen among all countries.

As health care cost inflation has become prohibitive, even in countries in the EME group, governments are looking closely at cost containment. Along with equal access and cost containment, a greater control by government is emerging. Expenditures are being regulated to a greater extent, and countries are looking for more effective administration of the health care system in general. In addition, countries are starting to talk openly about rationing of health care with the result that a new meaning is emerging for ethics in health care.

Equalization of access, cost containment and greater control for the 1990s are emerging as the driving forces of health care in all countries of the world.

BIBLIOGRAPHY

Basch, Paul E. 1990. *Textbook of International Health,* Oxford University Press, Inc., New York.

Omran, A.R. 1982. *Epidemiologic Transition 1. Theory.* In J.A. Ross, (Ed). International Encyclopedia of The Population, Free Press, New York, pp. 172-175.

Raffel, Marshall W. (ed). 1984. *Comparative Health Systems: Descriptive Analyses of Fourteen National Health Systems.* Pennsylvania State University Press, University Park, PA.

Roemer, Milton I. 1977. *Comparative National Policies in Health Care,* Marcel Dekker, Inc., New York and Basel.

Roemer, Milton I. 1991. *National Health Systems of the World,* Oxford University Press, New York.

Saltman, Richard B. (ed). 1988. *The International Handbook of Health-Care Systems,* Greenwood Press, Westport, CT.

Scheiber, George J., Poullier, Jean-Pierre and Leslie M. Greenwood. 1991. "Health Care Systems in Twenty-four Countries," Health Affairs (Project HOPE), Milwood, Vol. 70, No. 3, pp. 22-38.

Spivey, R.N., Wertheimer, A.I. and T.D. Rucker (eds). 1992. *International Pharmaceutical Services, The Drug Industry and Pharmacy Practice in Twenty-Three Major Countries of the World,* Pharmaceutical Products Press, An Imprint of The Haworth Press, Inc., New York, London, Norwood (Australia).

World Development Report 1993. Investing in Health, World Development Indicators. 1993. The International Bank for Reconstruction and Development, Oxford University Press, New York.

Medicine and Health Care Into the Twenty-First Century. Edited by S.K. Majumdar, L.M. Rosenfeld, D.B. Nash and A.M. Audet. © 1995, The Pennsylvania Academy of Science.

Chapter Thirty-Seven

THE BRITISH NATIONAL HEALTH SERVICE

ROGER D. JENNINGS, MA C Chem FRSC
Cabinet Office
Office of Science and Technology
Albany House
84-86 Petty France
London SW1H 9ST England

INTRODUCTION

The British National Health Service (NHS) came into operation in 1948 following extensive discussions and negotiations which actually began before the end of the Second World War. It was at once heralded as a major advance in the provision of health services and one which would lead to a very rapid improvement of the health of the British public. To a large extent, the vision of the founders of the NHS has been fulfilled, although the system, as it exists today, is very different from that introduced in the late 1940s.

The underlying foundation, on which the entire NHS was built, was that health care should be free at the point of service; that appropriate preventive medicine should be available to the entire population of the United Kingdom, regardless of ability to pay; and that finance should be entirely through general taxation.

Whilst the latter two ideals remain true today, soon after the system started, it rapidly became clear that the first ideal could not be achieved in all circumstances. In order to limit excessive and inappropriate demand on dental and ophthalmic services, charges had to be introduced. Per item charges were subsequently made for individual pharmaceuticals. Although these charges have been steadily increased, even now, where need is greatest, such services are provided free of charge. Some

80% of drug prescriptions are dispensed free and the per item charge is only about \$7, irrespective of the actual cost of the pharmaceutical. It is, however, still true, as it was in the 1940s, that all services provided in the NHS by general practitioners, specialists and internists, and all hospital care, both in-patient and out-patient, are provided free of charge at the point of service to every person resident in the United Kingdom. The cost of this is still derived almost entirely from general taxation, with the Secretary of State for Health being politically accountable to Parliament for the provision of health care services.

STRUCTURE OF THE NATIONAL HEALTH SERVICE

The NHS serves a population of approximately 55 million people. The total spent on health care is about \$51 billion per year or 6.1% of the Gross Domestic Product (GDP). During the past 30 years, the percentage of GDP spent on health care in the United Kingdom has risen only slowly from 4% to 6.1%. This contrasts with most other developed nations where the percentage of GDP spent on health care is much higher. For instance, in 1991, the United States spent 13.5% of GDP on health care, a figure predicted to rise to 16% during the next few years. The United Kingdom is therefore spending \$1,035 per capita on health care, in contrast to the U.S. spending of \$2,869.

The Department of Health, itself, does not run the NHS. This function is carried out, directly and indirectly, by the Regional Health Authorities (RHAs). Currently, the United Kingdom is divided into 14 RHAs in England, with separate health departments covering Scotland, Wales, and Northern Ireland, where there are no individual regions. In October 1993, the Secretary of State for Health announced certain changes to the management structure for the NHS. These are shown in Figure 1. In essence, from April 1996 (subject to Parliament approving the legislation), the 14 RHAs will be reduced to only 8 Regional Offices of the NHS Management Executive (part of the Deparment of Health). The detailed functions of the Regional Offices have not yet been determined, but it seems likely that they will be responsible for compliance with the regulatory framework for the NHS; with managing performance of purchasers and providers; with dispute arbitration; with approving general practitioner fund holder applications and budgets; and with purchaser development.

The Departments of Health's role is normally to provide finance and specific general policy advice, without becoming involved directly in the day-to-day provision of health services. An example of this would be patient access to radiotherapy treatment. The Department of Health advises on the number of radiotherapy treatment machines per 100,000 population and the types and numbers of individual machines which should be available. It assesses the quality, safety, efficacy and cost effectiveness of individual machines. It is then up to the RHAs, in consultation with their individual hospitals, to decide which particular equipment to buy, where such facilities should be placed and how they will be staffed.

CHANGES TO THE NHS STRUCTURE

By April 1992, the structure of the Health Service had changed markedly. Prior to that date, each region was divided into a number of District Health Authorities, each providing health care for approximately 250,000 people. A typical District consisted of one or two acute hospitals, each with about 500 beds; a trauma unit and all other acute service facilities; short and long term psychiatric and mental health hospitals; maternity beds; and other minor specialties. Some of these hospitals were providing facilities for the entire Region.

In January 1989, the government published details of major changes to the structure of the Health Service (1). These changes are listed in Table 1.

One of the most important changes made under these revisions, is the second, which gives hospitals and other service providers the ability to apply for a new self governing status, known as NHS Trusts. By April 1994, approximately 450 of these trusts had come into being. Individual trusts have been set up, not only to operate hospitals but, for example, to manage psychiatric services and to operate

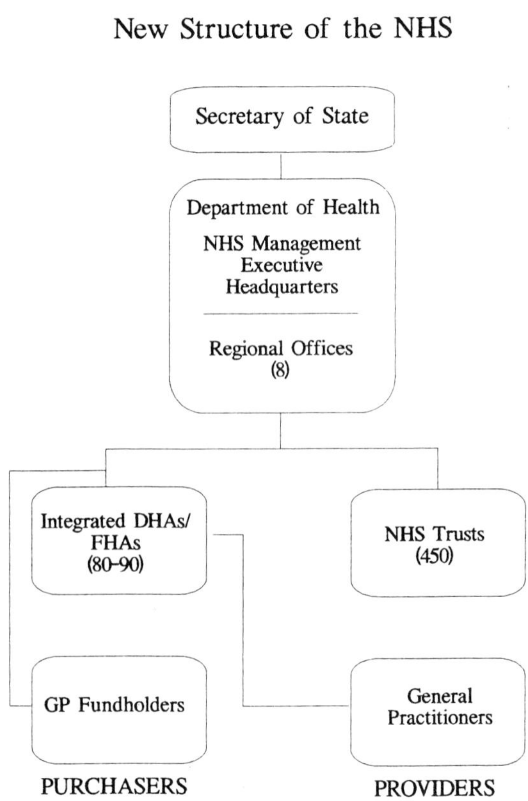

FIGURE 1.

laboratories. The key advantage which the trusts have, is a very much greater control over their own finances than was possible under the previous structure. Purchasers can now buy services from whomever they consider is able to provide these in the most cost effective manner. They even buy services from private hospitals, which now account for almost 10% of the total acute hospital beds available in England. Indeed, the private sector, which was growing, both in size and revenue until the NHS reforms were introduced, has now been hit by a combination of the worldwide recession and by the improvements to the NHS services to the extent that they are selling private hospitals to the NHS.

STAFFING OF THE NHS

With a staff of a little over 1 million, the NHS is one of the largest employers in the world. There are some 1,560 hospitals, of which 860 have acute beds. Of just over 68,000 doctors, 20,000 are specialists and 35,000 general practitioners. In addition there are 485,000 nurses. There are far fewer administrators among the 450,000 other staff than in many health care systems financed through third-party payer systems since there is no billing process.

For the most part, hospital doctors are salaried employees of the NHS, although many specialists do some private practice in addition. General practitioners operate under a contract. Those who are not part of a fund holding practice receive a per capita fee for each patient registered with them, with greater amounts for children, pregnant women and the elderly. There are incentives for general practitioners to meet the high immunization targets and to provide screening services for women, such as PAP smears, on a regular basis.

The health care system, in Britain, depends very strongly on the general practitioner as a primary provider of health care services. Each member of the public

TABLE 1

The Government's Proposals

1. To make the Health Service more responsive to the needs of patients, as much power and responsibility as possible will be delegated to local level.
2. To stimulate a better service to patients, hospitals will be able to apply for a new self-governing status as NHS Hospital Trusts.
3. To enable hospitals which best meet the needs and wishes of patients to get the money to do so, the money required to treat patients will be able to cross administrative boundaries.
4. To reduce waiting times and improve quality of service, to help give individual patients appointment times they can rely on, and to help cut the long hours worked by some junior doctors, 100 new consultant posts will be created over the next three years.
5. To help the family doctor improve his services, large GP practices will be able to apply for their own budgets to obtain a defined range of services direct from hospitals.
6. To improve the effectiveness of NHS management, regional, district and family practitioner management bodies will be reduced in size and reformed on business lines, with executive and non-executive directors.
7. To ensure that all concerned with delivering services to the patient make the best use of resources available to them, quality of service and value for money will be more rigorously audited.

is registered with a local general practitioner. Except in emergencies, all patients must go first to their general practioner who either provides appropriate treatment, there and then, or refers them to a hospital based physician. Self referral is not allowed. Under the fifth of the government's major proposals (see Table 1), general practitioners in large group practices are able to become fund holders themselves to manage their own budgets and buy defined services directly from hospitals for their patients. This gives them very much greater freedom to send their patients to hospitals with minimal waiting lists, even if these hospitals are a few miles further from the patient's home than the local hospital with a longer waiting list. The result of this and other measures has been a massive drop in waiting lists as can be seen from Figure 2. From a total of 50,000 patients waiting more than two years for certain elective procedures in September 1991, by April 1993 there were only 291 such patients. By April 1994, there were some 6,000 GP fund holders.

QUALITY OF SERVICE

Although the NHS is markedly less expensive to operate than health care systems in most other developed nations, the provision of service and the health of the public is often superior. For instance, life expectancy for males at 72.6 years is one year greater than that for the U.S. Infant mortality at 7.4 per thousand live births is below the average of 10.0 in the United States and well below the United States inner city level of 15.0. Pre-school immunization rates are very high, averaging over 95%. The

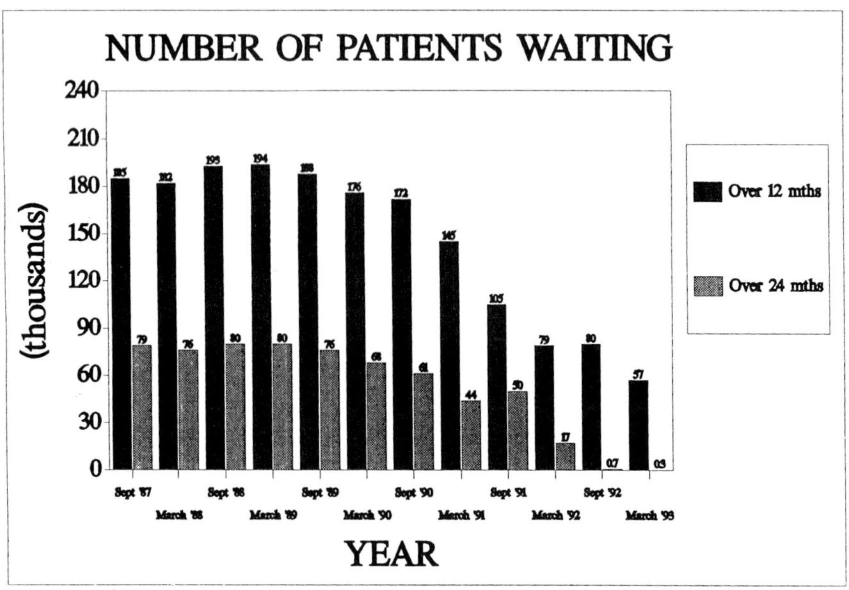

FIGURE 2.

screening program for neo-natal hypothyroidism (which leads to cretinism) and for phenyl ketonuria achieves coverage of virtually 100%, thus reducing very markedly the financial burden which would otherwise be placed on society, if such infants were not treated quickly enough.

All this is made possible by the efficient use of resources. Hospital facilities are, for the most part, adequate without being lavish. There is less tendency to over test patients and the provision of expensive equipment such as magnetic resonance imaging has been kept considerably below that of, for instance, the United States. In part, this is because of a different opinion about the most cost effective use of such imaging techniques, but in part because hospitals are not in direct competition with one another to obtain finance from patients and their third-party payers. Hospitals are not required to keep buying the latest technology, which frequently may stand idle for most of the day, just to attract patients. The percentage of costs attributable to administration are considerably less for an NHS hospital, than for those in other countries where the cost of billing the patient contributes markedly to high overheads.

The United Kingdom is not a litigious nation and the rules governing litigation are different in some respects from those in other countries. In the United Kingdom, the losing party is generally required to pay the costs of the winning party and lawyers involved in such litigation do not often take on cases on the basis of a share of the award. Malpractice premiums have risen considerably in the United Kingdom in specialties such as obstetrics and gynecology, but they are nowhere near the levels found in the United States. Consequently, doctors' earnings do not have to include a large element to pay for such high premiums.

Just because services are provided free, it does not mean that they are necessarily available immediately on demand. As stated earlier, the period of waiting for minor procedures has fallen markedly in the last two years. Although in some circumstances, the *number* of people waiting may have grown, the *length* of wait has been reduced.

In some circumstances, hospitals that were built at the end of the last century are still in use, although slowly and steadily, these are being replaced by modern facilities. The total number of beds in the NHS has fallen considerably since 1948. However, this is primarily as a consequence of improvement to treatment. No longer are patients required to spend days, or even weeks, in hospital in most circumstances. There has also been a considerable move toward treatment of patients on a day-surgery basis.

FUTURE FOR THE NHS

The Conservative government has stated, categorically, it is not their intention to privatize the NHS. Despite the introduction of Trust status for the majority of hospitals and health providers, the government still retains ultimate control. There will certainly not be moves towards a system dominated by private insurance companies and private hospitals. The government will continue to be, by far, the major provider of health care finance. What is likely to occur over the next few years is the completion of the move of virtually all health care services to Trust status and a further improvement of the services offered to patients. Waiting lists will never disappear, but they will be reduced beyond their current, already generally acceptable levels. Dental and ophthalmic services will continue to develop outside the NHS and it is likely that the majority of dentists will offer private treatment. There will, however, be provision for those who are unable to pay for basic dental treatment to get such services free of charge.

The future of the NHS looks good and a system not dissimilar to the current one is likely to be flourishing well into the 21st century.

REFERENCE

1. Working for Patients; Her Majesty's Stationery Office, London. 1989.

Medicine and Health Care Into the Twenty-First Century. Edited by S.K. Majumdar, L.M. Rosenfeld, D.B. Nash and A.M. Audet.

Chapter Thirty-Eight

HEALTH CARE IN FINLAND

MARKKU PEKURINEN, DPhil, Docent
Director of the Health Services Research Ltd.
Tarkk'ampujantu 10B
Fin 00150
Helsinki, Finland

INTRODUCTION

Geographically, Finland is the fifth largest country in Europe, but its population is less than 5 million. Around 60 percent of the labor force work in services, 30 percent in industry and construction and the remainder in agriculture.

Throughout the 1980s, economic growth was better than in other OECD countries. But at the beginning of the 1990s, the environment changed dramatically. Deregulation of the money markets created an unprecedented credit boom, with companies and individuals going into debt. Lack of competitiveness in European markets and the collapse of trade with the former USSR lead to a steep fall in exports.

Today Finland is undergoing the most severe recession in this century. Gross domestic product (GDP) has been falling around four and a half percent annually for three years in a row. The unemployment rate has reached 20 percent. The economic situation is not yet threatening the health care system, although expenditure growth has levelled off and providers are adjusting their behavior to diminishing resources.

EVOLUTION

Finnish health care policy has been characterized by step-by-step improvements. After the Second World War, the provision of maternal and child health services became a top priority. In the 1950s and 1960s, the emphasis shifted to building a national hospital network, which absorbed most of the growth in resources. Primary care received less attention and continued to be limited mainly to maternal and child health.

In 1964 the National Sickness Insurance reform was launched, with the aim of increasing the use of outpatient services (mainly provided by the private sector) by lowering the economic barriers to eligibility. It was supposed to reimburse up to 60 percent of fees and the aim was to guarantee equal access for all citizens regardless of their ability to pay. It was assumed that changing monetary incentives on the demand side would lead to increased use and thereby to increased and equitable supply.

At the beginning of the 1970s, cross-national comparisons and national follow-up studies showed that the health of the population was relatively poor and improving only slowly (Purola et al 1971, Kohn and White 1976). The 1964 reform had improved service use and individual choice, particularly for people living in wealthy towns who were willing and able to pay. But it failed to meet all the need for services because of the patchy and inadequate supply of primary care.

In the early 1970s, policy-makers faced a number of problems. For example, 90 percent of public health care resources were absorbed by specialized care. It was argued that a broader range of services was needed. The 1972 primary health care reform was the key to shifting the emphasis towards primary health and towards greater regional and social equity in the supply and use of health services.

While the 1964 reform relied on the markets and focused on the demand side, the 1972 reform relied on planning and focused on the supply side by reforming financing, administration and planning systems (Pekurinen et al. 1987, Saltman 1988). A uniform state subsidy system was created to increase resources for primary care. All primary care services were brought under local control through a network of health centers. A uniform strategic planning system was created to cover all public health care services.

In the 1980s, decision-making gradually shifted from the central government to the provincial authorities. At the beginning of the 1990s, Finland is following the Zeitgeist and is carrying out major health care reforms which will radically change the system.

ORGANIZATION

The provision of health services in Finland has traditionally been a public responsibility. Today, 75 percent of production and 79 percent of financing is public (Figure 1). Municipalities run by elected councils, which levy an income tax (ranging from 14.5 to 19.5 percent of income, depending on the municipality), are responsible for organizing services for their residents.

Health care is divided into primary and specialized care, both of which are further divided into outpatient and inpatient care. Both types of service are operated by municipalities, or federations of municipalities. Each municipality nominates representatives to the politically accountable board of a federation.

In principle, the structure is hierarchic. To obtain treatment patients go first to their local health center or to a private practitioner. If they cannot be treated there, they are referred to the outpatient department of the district, central or university hospital. District hospitals (N = 34) provide services in the most common specialties (mainly surgery, internal medicine and gynecology) near patient's residence. Central hospitals (N = 21) handle all common specialties. Five of them are university teaching hospitals that give treatment in rarer and more demanding specialties. In practice, the supply of hospital services is fragmented and most hospitals treat a broadly similar spectrum of patients. Patients have fairly direct access to the hospital system and about 15 percent are admitted to hospitals without referral (Piirainen et al. 1992).

FINANCING AND MANAGEMENT UNTIL 1992

Health services are jointly financed by local authority and state taxes with modest co-payments by patients. Primary health care services are mostly free of charge. Some municipalities, however, levy a differential charge which is around US$9 per health center visit. For hospital inpatient care a patient pays a fixed per diem, around US$20. Hospitals and health centers operate under a fixed prospective budget and charge municipalities according to the number of bed-days and outpatient visits provided using average cost figures. Doctors and other staff receive fixed monthly

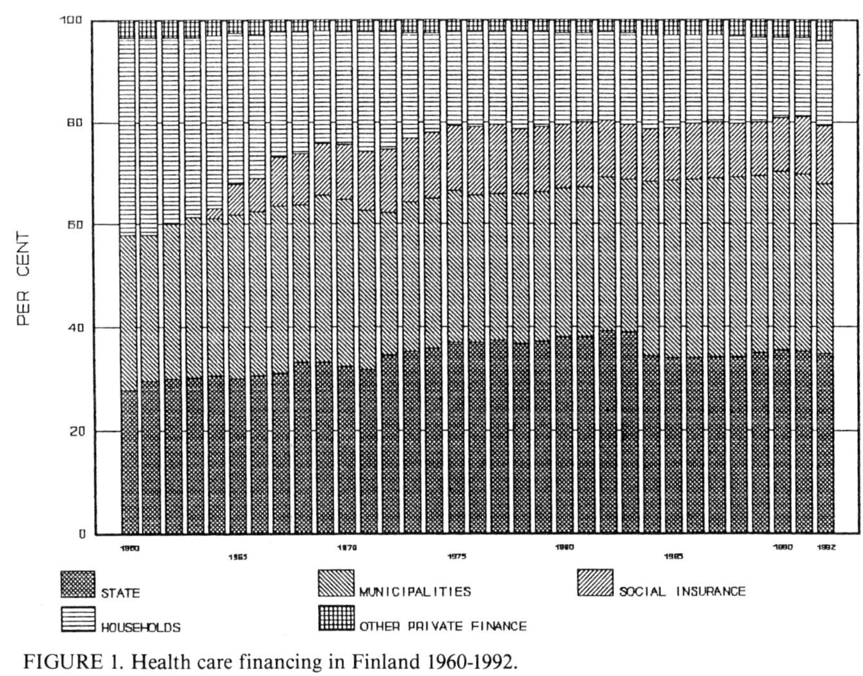

FIGURE 1. Health care financing in Finland 1960-1992.

salaries. In 1992, average monthly salary range for doctors was US$3,000 - 4,500 (junior doctor - senior doctor) and for nurses US$1,800 - 2,300 (registered nurse - head nurse [CSOF 1993]).

Until 1992, the state subsidy system reimbursed 29-66 percent of the costs of a patient's care incurred by the municipality. Subsidies were paid directly to hospitals and health centers, but the amount depended on the financial status of the municipality in which the patient lives: the richer the municipality, the smaller the state's financial contribution. Hospitals and health centers billed the net costs (gross costs minus state subsidy) to the municipalities. The subsidy was the same for running costs and capital costs in both primary and specialized care, as well as for social services. The municipality thus had no financial incentive to prefer health care to social services, or primary to specialized care.

Until 1992, decision-making and service provision were strongly decentralized, while allocation of staffing and capital resources were centralized. National priorities were implemented by a steering mechanism based on state subsidies and on a strategic planning system which also allocated new resources to hospitals and health centers.

Each year, the cabinet approved a national plan which determined the general guidelines for health care and new posts and investments entitled to subsidy. The Ministry of Social Affairs and Health allocates the new resources to provincial authorities which distributed them to health centers and hospitals. Municipalities could create posts at their own expense, but they rarely started and maintained activities which were not state subsidized.

The planning and state subsidy system in fact bound the increases in health care resources to the annual state budget, which determined the total amount of subsidies provided by the central government. Since the subsidy was substantial, it provided a major incentive for municipalities to use tax money to develop health care, yet it enabled central government to influence resource allocation and to decide the total amount of resources (Pekurinen et al. 1987).

TRENDS IN HEALTH SPENDING

The proportion of gross domestic product devoted to health care has been increasing more slowly in Finland than in most of the OECD countries (from 3.8 percent in 1960 to 9.4 percent in 1992), while staffing and capital resources have been expanding in step with others (Figure 2).

Spending is determined primarily by the numbers of posts and beds. Labor is undoubtedly the most significant factor, accounting for 75 percent of spending. A substantial fall in health service wages relative to other sectors, from the end of the 1960s until the mid-1980s, and the rapid economic growth of the 1980s, made it possible to expand the health care sector rapidly without increasing the proportion of health spending in the GDP and without running into great financial difficulties (Häkkinen 1988).

At the beginning of the 1990s, the situation has changed radically and this year, mainly due to the severe economic slump, Finland will spend well above the OECD average on health.

WHERE ARE WE NOW

The infrastructure of the Finnish health care system is now almost complete. In 1993, the country will spend around 10 percent of its GDP on health. But it is clear that in the foreseeable future, the only affordable way to respond to increasing demand will be to improve productivity (services/expenditure) and efficiency (effectiveness/expenditure).

The health care financing and management system Finland adopted 20 years ago had several important strengths. It was a factor in bringing about a below-average growth for the OECD in the GDP spent on health. It also resulted in a shift of resource allocation in favor of outpatient care (Figure 3). But the hospital sector still dominates. Around 44 percent of cash is allocated to inpatient care. Finland has an exceptionally high bed-stock, aroung 135 beds per 10,000 inhabitants which is 38 percent above the OECD average (OECD 1990).

WHERE ARE WE HEADING?

Current concerns are primarily managerial, such as how should the provision of services be organized; how should hospitals and health centers be funded, and how to create genuine competition between them, in particular between hospitals?

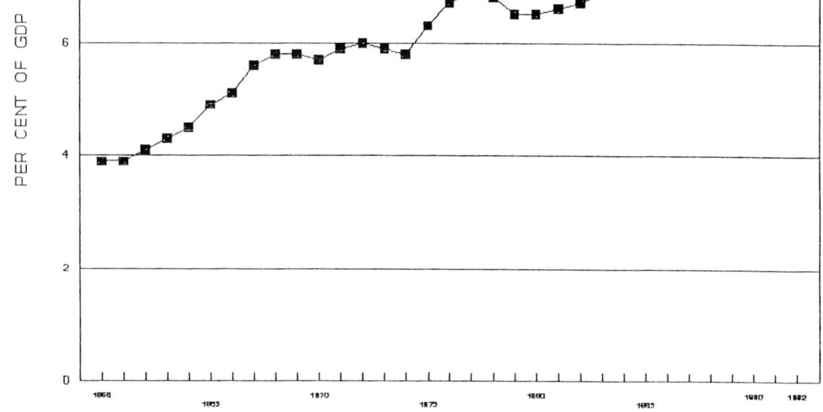

FIGURE 2. Health care expenditure as a proportion (%) of the Gross Domestic Product (DGP) in Finland 1960-1992.

Three separate management reforms which are currently under way will change the present system profoundly. They are state subsidy reform, hospital reform and primary care reform.

STATE SUBSIDY REFORM

In 1993, the retrospective cost-based state subsidy system was replaced by a system based on anticipated spending for all welfare services. The reform will affect health care dramatically. The subsidy is to be paid directly to the municipality, and the amount is a proportion of the municipality's anticipated health care spending, based on the six criteria of size, age structure, morbidity (as appoximated by standardized mortality) and population density, as well as on the area and financial status of the municipality. Although the subsidy is ring-fenced for health care use, the municipality is free to use the money as it wishes. It may keep any efficiency-gains.

National strategic planning is confined to setting national policy priorities and to allocation of major investment resources. Municipalities will thus gain more economic power, freedom and responsibility for service provision. So in theory, they are able to force hospitals to compete and so achieve cost-savings.

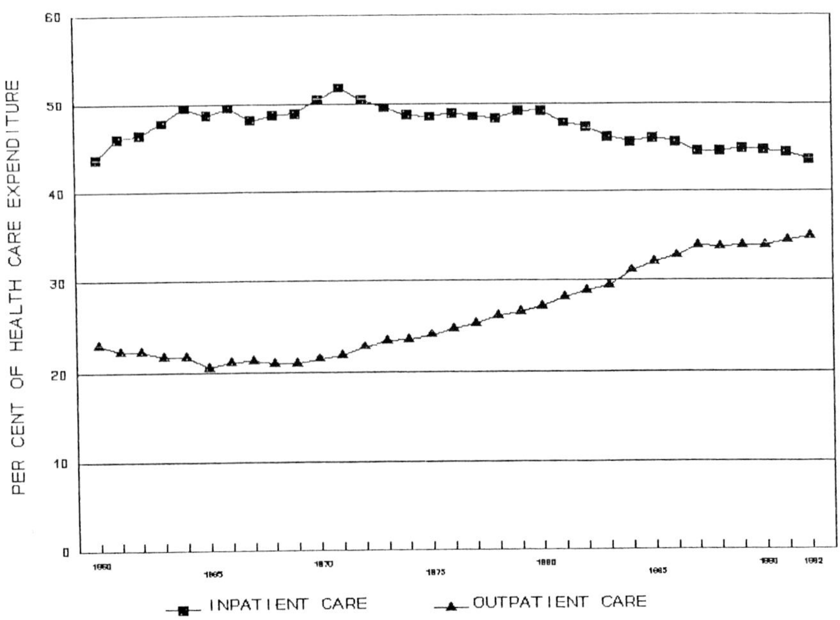

FIGURE 3. Structure of health care expenditure in Finland 1960-1992.

HOSPITAL REFORM

The hospital reform that came into force in 1991 brought all the hospitals within a health care region under single management, creating 21 economically powerful regional monopolies. Each is responsible for organizing hospital services for that region. From 1993, hospital budgets will gradually become open-ended, and hospitals will be paid by the municipalities according to the number of bed-days and outpatient visits. They will charge municipalities the full costs of treatment according to specialty-specific cost figures. Exceptionally high costs of care and costs of special duties by hospitals will be shared within the hospital region by the member municipalities.

It is believed that deregulated charges, together with the opportunity to supply services freely to all municipalities around the country, will stimulate competition between hospitals and it is claimed that cost and quality of care will become decisive factors in competition. Yet it remains unclear how costs are to be assessed, how quality is to be defined and how genuine competition can be generated.

PRIMARY CARE REFORM

Primary care reform aims to develop a personal doctor system, a concept introduced several years ago as a means of solving some of the major problems in primary care. The basic idea is simple. Each GP will be responsible for providing primary medical services for a population. Personal doctors will be paid according to a three-tier salary-scheme comprising a basic allowance (based on experience and training), a capitation fee (based on the size and case-mix of the list) and a fee for service (based on the services provided). Experimental research evidence has shown that this approach improves continuity of care and increases patient satisfaction (Vohlonen 1989) and that the related pay scheme encourage efficiency (Pekurinen et al. 1991). Extensive development research is attempting to discover if a similar approach is applicable to other primary care activities as well as health related social work (Aro et al. 1993).

FROM COST-CONTAINMENT TO COST-EXPANSION?

While the hospital and state subsidy reforms are likely to cure some of the defects in the present system, there is a danger that they could destroy the strengths of Finnish health care.

Both reforms claim to improve efficiency by stimulating public competition, although it is not obvious how competition would emerge. While the hospital reform created 21 economically strong hospital regions, the state subsidy reform will increase the power of the 455 municipalities. As most of the municipalities are economically weaker than the hospital regions, it is unlikely they will have sufficient power to force hospital monopolies to compete with each other.

Moving from closed prospective budgets to open-ended reimbursement for hospitals may lead to a faster growth rate in expenditures during the first few years following the reforms, although deepening financial problems in the municipalities may partly offset this.

The diminished role of national strategic planning will free health care markets from centralized steering, and this will give municipalities more freedom and power over what services to provide. While voters may gain more influence, the reform may increase the power of professional organizations at the local level and there are fears that the hospital-intensive service model may increasingly dominate primary care.

REFERENCES

Aro, S. and M. Liukko (Eds.). 1993. Population in Primary Health Care - Evaluation of a demonstration project in 1989-1992. In Finnish with English summary. Stakes, Reports 105. Helsinki.

CSOF. 1993. Wages and Salaries 1993:17. Central Statistical Office of Finland, Helsinki.

Häkkinen, U. 1988. Costs, financing and prices of health care in Finland 1960-1985. Social Insurance Institution, Series M:65, Helsinki.

Kohn, R. and K.L. White. 1976. Health Care. An International Study. Oxford University Press. London.

OECD. 1990. Health Care Systems in Transition. The Search for Efficiency. Paris.

Pekurinen, M., Vohlonen, I. and U. Häkkinen. 1987. Reallocation of resources in favor of primary health care: the case of Finland. World Health Statistics, 49, 313-325.

Pekurinen, M., Vohlonen, I. and H. Sintonen. 1991. Redefining incentives in primary medical care: Results of a Finnish demonstration project. In Lopez-Casasnovas G. (ed.). Incentives in Health Systems. Springer-Verlag, Heidelberg, pp. 224-238.

Piirainen, H., Pekurinen, M., Vohlonen, I. and P. Paunio. 1992. Potilasvirtatutkimuksella tietoja toiminnan kehittämiseen. Sairaala, 2, 25-26.

Purola, T., Nyman, K., Kalimo, E. and K. Sievers. 1971. Sairausvakuutus, sairastavuus ja lääkintäapalvelusten käyttö. Kansaneläkelaitoksen julkaisuja A:7. Helsinki.

Saltman, R. 1988. National planning for locally controlled health systems: the Finnish experience. Journal of Health Politics, Policy and Law, 13, 27-51.

Vohlonen, I. (ed.). 1989. Personal Doctor Program. Data, results and conclusions of the Finnish study. In Finnish with English summary. Health Services Research by the National Board of Health in Finland, No. 50. Helsinki.

Medicine and Health Care Into the Twenty-First Century. Edited by S.K. Majumdar, L.M. Rosenfeld, D.B. Nash and A.M. Audet.

Chapter Thirty-Nine

THE FUTURE OF THE HEALTH SERVICES: The Hungarian Model

GYULA KINCSES

President of the Committee for Structural Changes
in Health Care of the Ministry of Health
Member of Parliament, Ministry of Welfare
Budapest
Arany J.u. 6-8 H-1051
Hungary

INTRODUCTION

The Economic Aspects of Health Care

The provision and financing of health care is a general and serious challenge in the last years of the 20th century and it is not solely the problem of the change of regime in the post-Stalinist States. In all countries where there is a system based on central distribution, there is dissatisfaction with low efficiency and continuously rising costs, while at the same time in the fee-for-service systems the growth of costs is even more dramatic and uncontrollable. The cause of the problem is probably that in the second half of the 20th century, the democratic States treated the question of equity in health care (equal opportunities for access) as a question of top priority, in keeping with the recommendation of WHO (World Health Organization). By the nineties, medical science and medical technology have developed to such a level that with their present economic performance, countries are unable to balance the operating and investment costs with the equal access attained and the age pattern changed. The conflict of "technically possible and economically feasible" has not been a new idea in the literature of the late eighties. Some authors (5) believe that the problem lies in the general crisis of the welfare States and in the protracted recession of recent years. The author's view is more pessimistic: the conflict arises not from the passing economic crisis which will be resolved sooner or later, but we are faced with a fundamental conflict which is insoluble without a new social consensus.

This conflict can be expected to deepen by the 21st century since the development curve of science is exponential while that of the economy, in the best of cases, is only linear. The principle of "everything for everyone at any time" can almost certainly not be realized. This gap is even wider in the post-Stalinist countries since the promise here was very great: comprehensive, high standard free-of-charge health care as the automatic entitlement of citizens. While we led the field in promises, we lagged far behind in economic performance with the result that the contradiction between demands and reality has reached alarming proportions.

This state of affairs forces us to draw three conclusions:

1) The question of health care systems must be treated not as a narrow professional issue but as a fundamental question of society. The entire society—and not the medical profession, social insurance or the minister for health—must decide that the population:
   - insists on the existing access and level of health care, in which case it also accepts the financial consequences involving a fundamental shift in priorities.
   - or it decides that the present burdens and expenditures cannot be increased any further without threatening the stability of the economy as a whole, in which case it accepts restriction based on a rational compromise.
2) The basic attitude of the health profession is service on the basis of the Hippocratic Oath, providing the highest possible level of care in the interest of the patient (the patient's interest is the supreme command, but I will decide what the patient's interest is . . .). It follows from this, that any attempt at restriction aimed at controlling costs and preserving the capacity to function, comes up against the resistance not of the population, but above all, of the health services. This was also found in Germany, where introduction of the GSG (Gesundheits Struktur Gesetz), which contained certain restrictions, was most strongly opposed by the sector of industry and trade serving the health services, followed in the second place, by physicians and with the least objections raised by the population. It is important to create an awareness that the health services can no longer maintain their aristocratic isolation but must recognize that questions of health care cannot be treated outside the macro context of the economy.
3) It is not solely through the health services that an improvement can be achieved in health status. According to the standpoint of WHO, the health services are responsible for only 11% of health status, while the curative services consume a substantial part of health-related costs. It must be decided whether the State prefers health care or health itself (Figure 1). A subsequent cost explosion can

only be curbed if the cause of health does not remain the private affair of the relevant ministry, but becomes an intersectoral attitude shaping governmental policy as a whole

It can be seen that the inadequacy of health resources is not a temporary or regional problem, but a serious challenge for the next century that can only be resolved through the detailed renegotiation of the problem. To find an optimal solution, we need to know the nature of health care costs and, since the countries of the former socialist system represent a condensation and projection of the worldwide problems, a knowledge of the Hungarian answer to the questions could be instructive.

The Nature of Health Care Costs

Seen from the viewpoint of the policy-maker, health care costs have only one predictable characteristic: they are steadily rising and intervention for any purpose whatsoever, only increases the growth in costs (7). It is, therefore, generally well-intentioned dilettantism to expect a reduction of costs from any solution containing market elements. In the best of cases, the introduction of market elements (performance-based distribution, prospective payment systems, etc.) can only slow down the rate of cost increase, or reduce the specific cost and increase efficiency. This is not an insignificant result, but greater efficiency and the reduction of specific costs generally leads, not to a reduction in total costs, but to an increase in the quantity and quality of services provided. It can be concluded, in general, that the

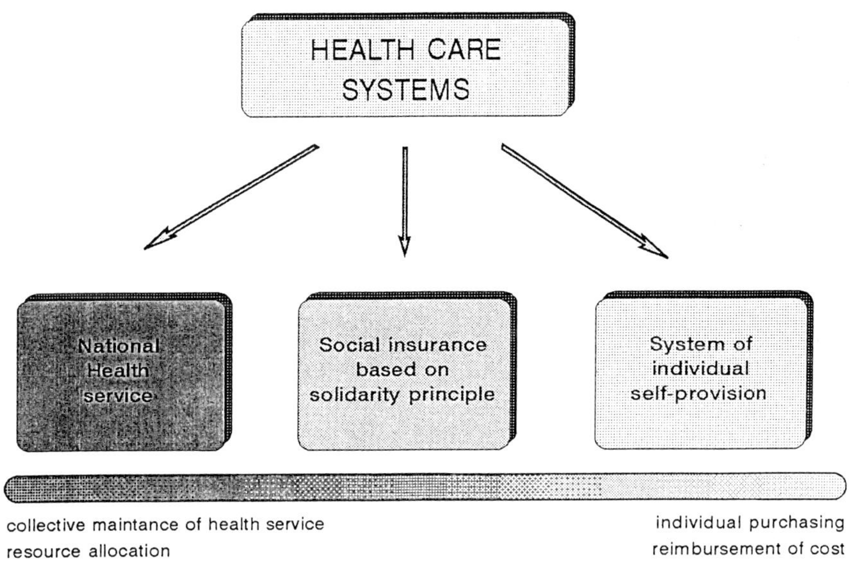

FIGURE 1.

aggregate of health care costs, fundamentally, does not depend on the structure or system of distribution, but is a question of a social compact, that is, it depends on how much the country concerned is prepared to spend for this purpose. Accordingly, the controllability of health care costs depends on the extent to which the financing of health care expenditures is centralized in the given country. In the case of a National Health Service (NHS) and a single-insurer social insurance model (contributions set centrally), the volume of health care costs is determined by the budget and the incorporation of market elements only changes the technique of distribution. The financing is based on resource distribution. If the source in health care costs is diffuse and multisectoral, the financing is based on recognition of costs and is difficult to control. If total expenditure (the source) in the given country can be kept under control or reduced by the law because costs are determined centrally (NHS, single-insurer social insurance model), the market elements will compensate for the restriction of the source, and unchanged services can be obtained at a lower cost.

The explanation of this is to be sought in the unique nature of the health care market. Where market relations prevail, it can be generally found that demand determines supply. Health care is an exception to this. Here, the situation is the reverse: the supply determines the demand. With the expansion of the economic possibilities, the density of services increases, differences in regional access disappear, causing an increase in utilization of the service, a growth in demand. The answer is to be sought in an analysis of the concept of demand. Demand can be defined as the sum of two factors, the size of which depends on the need and the resource available for its satisfaction. In my opinion, the need is the more decisive of the two since, if the need is strong enough, it creates the resources required for its satisfaction through a reordering of priorities at a macro level.

Health care need has two specific characteristics.

a) *The extent of the need.*

Needs can be basically divided into two groups. Some needs are inelastic, that is, they are objective and their size can be defined. The others are elastic, that is, their quantity cannot be determined in a precise way. In the case of inelastic needs, it is easy to determine the limit above which consumption cannot be raised, and, if the supply exceeds this level, a buyers' market arises which in theory, is capable of ensuring the best level of supply at the lowest attainable price. But the demand for health care does not behave in this way because the needs are inelastic and cannot be measured objectively. There is more than a grain of truth in the common saying that there is no such thing as a healthy person, only a patient who has not been assessed properly. In this way the quantity of health services is determined not by the need, the health status of the population, but by the capacity and accessibility of health care services. (The author is familiar with the objection raised by economic theorists that human needs cannot be increased in an unrestricted way through supply because the competition of the gratification that can be obtained from other goods sets a limit to the demand. However, this limit acts above such a high level of consumption that it falls far outside the limits of affordability. Therefore, within the domain of the realistic, it is justified to suppose a linear relationship.) Accordingly, the concept of buyers' market must be interpreted quite differently in the case of needs which are elastic: the effect of the buyers' market will not be a fall in prices and a spontaneous, self-regulating retriction in the number of service sites, but an increase in utilization and the growth of health care expenditures in keeping with the growth in supply.

b) *The definability of the need.*
The other special characteristic of health care need is that the need is determined not by the consumer but by the provider of the service. In the majority of cases, the patient is unable to control his own need and, in this respect is forced to rely on the provider of the service, the health service. On the part of the doctor, the determination of need is, inevitably, tinged by subjective elements. If the doctor, as the provider of a service, also has a financial interest in the quantity of the care, he is able to increase demand at will. In the opposite case (in a baseline financing system), in the absence of a financial incentive the service could respond by holding back care. This is why the volume of services is growing in the tariff systems and it also explains the long waiting lists in the British and Irish health systems.

On the basis of all this, it seems fair to say that market competition, the creation of a buyers' market—as a principal instrument—is unsuitable for regulating the quantity and quality of health care services, and for reducing prices.

The development of public health, health education, central screening and prevention programs are all very important systems determining the life of a country, but they, naturally, all have cost implications. Health education increases the public's demands, screening in itself causes additional utilization, and the treatment of the cases detected also raises the costs. It is a false illusion to think that the principle of "prevention is easier than cure" has the effect of reducing health care costs. Prevention and screening can improve a nation's life expectancy, but they cannot reduce the costs of health care—on the contrary, they increase them, although they can be expected to produce better outcomes. This train of thought is not intended to prove the inexpediency and economic inefficiency of prevention; I simply consider it my duty to draw attention to the oversimplified approach that proclaims the cost-saving effect of prevention in health care. As a result of prevention, concrete savings can be anticipated at macro level, as a result of the active years of life gained and the reduction in sick pay and disability pensions, but these savings do not appear in the place where the investment was made. As an economic result, even over the long term, the most that can be expected is a slower growth of costs. Prevention is the fundamental duty of a State, but it has serious economic conditions that must be ensured in the interest of the increased longevity that can be lived in acceptable quality.

Factors Influencing Health Care Costs in a Decisive Way

Kühn (10) has given a very pithy summary of the great variety of health care systems in the developed countries, pointing out that no conclusion can be drawn from a comparison of the cost level in the different countries, since differing systems can be equally costly, and even with identical systems the growth in costs can differ greatly. Similar conclusions can be drawn from other comparative studies (7, 8). Despite this, objective economic relationships must exist in health care, too. The difficulty in finding the answer arises from the fact that the health care systems cannot be described by one single parameter. Some of the factors influencing costs are to be found within the health care system while others are outside it, and the cost influencing effect of the latter is stronger. In the following, an attempt is made to sum up the most important factors in determining the volume of health care expenditures.

a) *The macro environment of the society.*
The general wage and price level, the legal environment, the state of the economy and the influence of social equality are of decisive importance and these factors are the most important in determining the trend in health care costs. The volume of the costs is decisively the result of a social bargain, which fundamentally depends on the breadth of the generally ensured access, but the costs of health care cannot be separated from the general level of prices and wages in the country concerned. A cost analysis of the effect of the macro environment on health would require a separate study, since health care is responsible to the smallest extent, for health status, but environmental hazards, the lack of health protection and health promotion, the change in the age pattern, all cause additional costs for health care.

b) The macro system of health care.
The second most important characteristic is probably the nature of the health care system as a whole. The basis of the classification here is, principally, the resource side and the provision of general access. The countless solutions can be divided into three main groups:
• the National Health Services (NHS),
• social insurance based on the Solidarity principle,
• the system of individual self-provision.
The above classification is, of course, an arbitrary simplification, since the number of variations is enormous, in fact, it could be said that no two countries have the same health system. It can be seen from Figure 1 that the transition from national health services to a systems based on individual self-provision, is actually a continuum. On the one hand is a central organization, distributing resources and administering as a collective buyer and owner, while at the other extreme is the purely market system based on individual responsibility, individual buying and cost-based prices.

In general, it can be said that central systems are always the cheapest (Great Britain, Hungary, etc.), while the pluralist systems of individual self-provision are the most expensive (USA).

c) *The extent and role of privatization in health care.*
With the disintegration of the former Socialist Block and the worldwide economic recession, the strengthening of privatization is a gradual process. This, together with the demand for the incorporation of market elements, raises the

expansion of privatization in health care too. At the same time, because of its expected effects, the question of privatization in the field of health care must be handled with caution.

- Privatization involves investment and capital, by its' nature, likes to see a return. The costs of this return further add to the operating costs that are already difficult to cover.

- The other, deeper reason, is that privatized health care is always more expensive than care based on the social insurance principle. The explanation is very simple: price formation in the private sphere is based on recognition of the actual and concrete costs and inputs, while in the social insurance systems it is based on the central distribution of resources. Accordingly, price formation in the private sphere "builds from the bottom up", taking individual inputs and individual expectations as its point of departure, while social insurance price formation does not deal with individual inputs and needs.

  It follows logically from this that the cost level of a country's health system is largely determined by the proportion of the participation of the private sphere. If central services (and price formation) dominate, then the private sphere is obliged to adapt to it, that is, its prices will not be too high because it can charge more for the higher standard of private care only up to a certain limit compared to the social insurance coverage which is otherwise free, or available, cheaply. The reverse is also true: if private care dominates in a country, the prices of central care will be adapted to it. This is the explanation for the seeming contradiction: if the DRG system is so cost-efficient, then why is Medicare so expensive in the US?

- The other illusion in connection with privatization that must be dispelled for reasons of economic efficiency, is that sector neutrality can be introduced freely and at will. The utilization of health care services is proportionate, not to the number of diseases, but to the quantity and accessibility of service sites. The unlimited authorization of private businesses leads to a rapid increase in the volume of utilization and thus to a rapid growth in costs. This does not mean that privatization should be banished from the health services. The conclusion which can be drawn is that, in the field of mass care, private contractor arrangements can be recommended only for the operation of the existing services (which means transfer not of the ownership but the right of operation), while the task of real privatization could be the differentiated satisfaction of differentiated demands, providing a higher standard of service for a very narrow stratum.

d) *The system of financing (distribution, reimbursement).*

The cost level in health care is also determined by the system of distribution applied.

Two basic principles can be found:

- if the financing is based on resource distribution it is cheaper than the systems based on cost reimbursement,
- the cost level of systems encouraging increased performance is always higher.

It is now the generally accepted view that the baseline based on budget planning are the cheapest but the least efficient, while the fee-for-services type systems based on a tariff system, are the most expensive and in addition their efficiency is also questionable. Most reform processes hope to achieve a solution from introduction of distribution based on the normative principle which on one hand, can be used to control costs and on the other, can increase efficiency. The view that extension of co-payment rationalizes use and thus reduces total costs can also be regarded as accepted.

e) *The structure of health care service.*

Compared to the above factors, the structure of health service probably has the least—although still quite considerable—economic effect. The health services are generally characterized by a two-tier system of services. The conventional classification distinguishes primary health care and specialized care. It is only up to this point that there is full agreement. One approach equates primary health care fundamentally with the system of family physicians and specialized care with outpatient and inpatient specialized care. The other approach, is based on the spatial location of the patient and treats outpatient and inpatient care as the two levels. International experiences show that the most economical structure is one based on the family physician system, where the family physician has an important function as gatekeeper.

The question of economic efficiency has come to the focus of attention in the developed countries. It is known from the excellent overview by Y.W. van Kemenade (8) that all of the developed European countries want to change their health care systems. The debates are largely over the conflict of centralization versus marketization. In my opinion, the two things should not be brought into confrontation. The most efficient and the least costly health care system can be achieved if the resource side, planning and investment, that is, resource and capacity are under strong central control, but performance-oriented market elements dominate in the system of distribution (reimbursement).

THE TRANSFORMATION OF THE HUNGARIAN HEALTH SERVICES

The Background

The development of Hungarian health services must be seen in their historical context. Modern social insurance based on the solidarity principle looks back on a past of more than 100 years. A developed public health system was created in the interwar years. After 1948, in keeping with the Socialist system, market and pluralist elements were eliminated in the health care delivery system and a Soviet type State Health Service was created, financed from the budget without any systematic principle, treating health care, pensions and social policy as a single whole and directed from above, with the promise of comprehensive, high standard, free-of-charge health care as the automatic entitlement of citizens.

We inherited a health care delivery system with a large capacity that was over-used and under-funded, in which the black market represented the sole incentive system.

The Aim and Instruments of Reform

To solve these problems, we elaborated a system based on the solidarity principle and also containing market elements, as the complete restructuring of the health services.

The main features of this are:

- separation of the functions of social insurance, the tasks of the State, local governments and social welfare,
- capacities are to be brought into line with needs,
- real access is to be ensured,
- citizen-oriented, personalized care,
- strengthening of the preventive approach in primary health care,
- spread of modern technologies to replace inpatient care.

The aim above listed have been attained with the following three basic steps:

1) Creation of health care operating on an insurance basis.
2) Introduction of a bipolar health care structure based on free choice of doctor.
3) Introduction of a performance-based incentive system and rational system of economic management.

The aim of the insurance principle is to spread burdens on the basis of the solidarity principle, to clarify sources and functions and to create the possibility of control.

The introduction of a bipolar health care structure based on free choice of doctor is intended to eliminate duplications, strengthen primary health care, encourage definitive care and personalize treatment.

The aim of performance-based distribution is to achieve equitable resource allocation which in turn, rationalizes economic management. Performance-based distribution can also be the indirect and sensitive instrument for the regulation of capacity in keeping with actual demands.

The elaboration of the reform was the result of a number of years of consistent workshop work, preliminary studies and series of experiments (1, 2, 3, 4, 5, 6) and it is being introduced in stages to achieve its final form at the end of a three-year period. Accordingly, the State and decentralized tasks have been separated in a number of steps, the public health service system has been created, social insurance shaped on the basis of the solidarity principle, and sector-neutral, performance-based financing introduced.

THE NEW FINANCING SYSTEM IN HUNGARIAN HEALTH SERVICES

In elaborating the new system of distribution in Hungarian health services, in harmony with the system of health policy goals, normative financing was adopted as the basic principle. The normative, performance-based distribution makes the resource allocation more equitable and at the same time is outcome-oriented and assists in the rationalization of economic management and the identification of internal reserves.

The Financing of Primary Health Care

This is based on age-adjusted capitation, supplemented with various allowances. Technically, the new financing system for primary health care is linked to the free choice of doctor to whom the patient gives the control stub of the insurance card. Reimbursement is based on the age-adjusted capitation which gives the physician differentiated point values corresponding to the intensity of activity required in 5 age groups. The physician also has a correction index based on qualification and period of service.

In order to balance incomes and prevent the formation of excessively large districts, the receipts from the practice diminish degressively, on the average, above 1800 patients.

The allowance: the practice receives a fixed sum in support, to maintain the doctor's office. The amount of this support depends on the nature of the settlement (town, village, farm) and practice (adult, children and mixed), the location of the practice and the number of residents to be served. Only doctors with an obligation to serve a given area are entitled to the allowances. 70% of the receipts are performance-based. Since 1st July 1993, receipts of practices have been based solely on the above principles.

Social insurance pays a fee for operation of the doctor's office on a sector-neutral basis. The operator may be the local government, an institution, foundation or company, or the doctor may have a practice in his own medical office or in one rented from the local government. The advantages of the new system of primary health care which has been introduced are:

- It is aimed at replacing the previous disease-centered, specialist-oriented treatment with citizen-centered (not only patient!), personalized care,

Health care Financing in Hungary

Primary health care (GP)
- age-adjusted capitation
- allowances
  - location of practice
  - qualification of physician
  - supplementary service

Specialist care
- itemized-service payment (fee for service) based on:
  - WHO/ICPM classification
  - adapted values of the German point system

Inpatient care
- active beds
  - diagnosis related groups
- long-term care
  - severity adjusted bed-day

The financing can be controlled and planned since it is based on simple and calculable data and ad hoc uses do not have a substantive influence on the costs.
- The financing is linked to basic screening of the population which is of inestimable significance for both prevention and public health.

Outpatient Specialist Care

The reimbursement system for the financing of outpatient specialist care is activity financing (fee for service) based on a point system. The classification and coding of the activities have been based on WHO's International Classification of Procedures in Medicine (ICPM).

Financing by services rendered could cause costs to become uncontrollable and this could easily endanger the liquidity of social insurance. For this reason, at the time of introduciton, only the so-called floating point technique can be used.

At the time of introduction of the new system the institutions receive 70% of their previous budget as a baseline allocation and the performance-based payment rates represent only a smaller proportion of their revenues. The baseline will be gradually eliminated in annual stages and when this is achieved, sector-neutral, itemized financing will become the actual practice.

The New Financing System in Inpatient Care

The Financing of Active Beds

The financing of active beds is based on the DRG system and the principle applied is inpatient case financing. Classification is made on the basis of the parameters of the inpatient episode. The system is the adaptation to Hungarian conditions of the system of Diagnosis Related Groups (DRG) in use in the United States. The essence of the adaptation is the following: the American reimbursement principle, the algorithm is introduced, but it is based on parameters measured in Hungary. It is an important feature that, at the time of introduction, we have applied, not the expected or optimal parameters, but have set out, in the regulation, the time duration and weighting numbers actually corresponding to the Hungarian average. This creates the possiblity for identifying internal reserves.

The Financing of Chronic Beds

Care provided over a long period that cannot be determined in advance, provided largely because of the need for nursing care and in a separate organizational form, belongs in the category of chronic (long term) care. The basis of financing is the length of stay and the classification is based on the parameters of the department. The payment rate for this is not uniform but depends on the nature of the department, and is indexed by the average nursing, treatment and materials cost intensity.

It is generally valid for specialist care, that the revenues of the institution are determined as a whole, on the basis of the performance of the individual departments and social insurance does not reimburse the department but the institution. The system of internal distribution is not regulated in the legislation but simultaneously, with the introduction of the performance-based financing, the institutions have been exempted from previously rigid budget rules.

Under the influence of the above measures, a two-tier system of health care, giving priority to primary health care (GP) is taking shape in the Hungarian health service, based on resource distribution containing market elements and social insurance on the solidarity principle (insurance obligation for the whole population, compulsory insurance, the payment is in proportion with incomes and health services are not independent from it).

The Republic of Hungary has succeeded in transforming its health care system, in the space of three years, an achievement unparalleled in the region. The new regulation that has been elaborated is largely of a framework nature and will gain its final form over the course of many years, through self-developing and self-correcting mechanisms.

SUMMING UP

The fundamental problem of health care systems in the 21st century will be creating the source for health care on a standard and with access that correspond to the level of development of the society. It can be anticipated that the viable systems will be those where:

- an intersectoral attitude is decisive in policymaking for health care,
- the capacity of health care service is regulated centrally, balancing out regional inequalities,
- coverage is provided by full or quasi full social insurance based on the solidarity principle, which will not necessarily be organized in a single institution, but will definitely be based on the central and uniform setting and collection of contributions,
- the financing of health care institutions is based on normative resource distribution containing market elements.

Table 1 shows the recommended distribution of tasks in welfare systems.

TABLE 1

System of Social Security and the Distribution of Tasks

	Pensions		Social policy	Public Health		Health Care Services	
	Basic	Supplementary		Prevention	Function as Authority	Investment	Operating Cost
State	Guarantee		XXXXX	XXXXX	XXXXX	XXX	XX
Local Government			XXXXX	XXX	XX	XXXX	XX
Social Insurance	XXXXX	XX		X			XXXXX
Commercial Insurance		XXXX		X		X	X
Employer		XX	X	XX		X	
NGO		XXXX	XXX	XXX		X	XX
Citizen		XX	XX	XXX			X

REFERENCES

1. Elgondolások az egészségügy reformjáról. 1988. (Ideas on the reform of health care. In Hungarian) Task-Force on Health Care Reform, Ministry of Health and Social Affairs.
2. Program of Action for the Renewal of Hungarian Health Care. 1991. Ed: István Mikola. Orvosi Hetilap, Aug. suppl.
3. Kincses, Gyula. 1991. A magyar egészségügy finanszírozási és strukturális rendszere. 1991. (The financing and structural system of Hungarian health care. In Hungarian) Lege Artis Medicinae (LAM), Aug. suppl.
4. Kincses, Gyula: Az egészségügy átalakításának feladatai 1992-1994. 1992. (Tasks for the transformation of health care, 1992-1994. In Hungarian) Lege Artis Medicinae, (LAM), Sept. suppl.
5. Orosz Éva. 1992. Egészségügyi rendszerek és reformtörekvések. (Health systems and reform aspirations. In Hungarian) Budapest. Foundation of the Institute for Political Studies.
6. Boján, Ferenc and Éva Belicza. 1992. A homogén betegségcsoportok betegosztályozási rendszerének alkalmazása a kóházi ellátá elemzésében. (Use of the DRG system in the analysis of hospital care. In Hungarian) Lege Artis Medicinae, (LAM), 2, 12, 1164-1171.
7. Bondár, Éva. 1993. Egészségügyi kiadásaink és a nemzetköi tendenciák. (Our health expenditures and the international trends. In Hungarian) Lege Artis Medicnae, (LAM), 3, 4, 364-371, 1993.
8. Kemenade, Y.W. van. 1993. Health care in Europe: The finance and reimbursement systems of 18 European countries. Zoetermeer: National Council for Public Health, 96 p.
9. Hoffmann, H. 1993. Internationale vergleichende Analysen von Gesundheitssystemen. (International comparative analysis about health care. In German) Artz und Krankenhaus, 66, 6, 227-232, 1993.
10. Kuhn, H. Das Krankenhaus zwischen Markt und Dirigismus. (Hospital between market and commanding. In German) Manuscript, in press.

admission committee then weighs each applicant's credentials, among them the examinee's total score in the NUEE, which is most heavily weighted. No interview is given and recommendation letters for the students are not required. High school grade point average is given some consideration in the admission process. In the 1991/92 academic year, 59,075 students matriculated into medical school (Table 1. Note: The number does not include military medical school matriculants). In 1990, where the data are available, the ratio of matriculants to applicants was 1:4. Among them 53.8 percent were females. The mean age of the entering class of 1990 was 19.4 (2).

TABLE 1

Number of Matriculants, Medical Students, and Graduates and Program Classification in the Academic Year of 1991-1992 by Major Areas

Specialty +	Matriculant	Student	Graduate
Clinical Medicine	33,781	125,584	16,745
Chinese Medicine	5,287	20,967	4,259
Preventive Medicine	2,708	11,227	2,687
Pharmacy	2,175	7,204	1,925
Dentistry	1,270	6,139	1,332
Pharmacy in Chinese Medicine	1,710	5,706	1,295
Acupuncture	1,374	5,525	1,181
Health Testing	1,582	5,324	1,149
Pediatrics	839	4,046	734
Nursing Care	861	2,639	629
Administration in Medicine	448	1,423	413
Radiology	634	2,420	580
Legal Medicine	192	1,254	344
Otolaryngology	437	1,963	263
Pharmacology, Chemistry	147	597	257
Chem. & Bio. Medicine	315	1,064	206
Bio. Medicine Engineering	175	704	188
Basic Science	264	691	100
Pharmacology	90	406	44
Data & Inf. in Medicine	49	115	35
Radiology Therapy	29	80	21
Anesthesiology	104	241	12
Statistics in Health	0	0	10
English in Medicine	21	81	0
Other	4,583	9,507	1,565
Total	59,075	214,907	45,974
Program:			
5- or 7-Year*	32,603	154,552	30,883
3-Year**	26,472	60,355	14,991

Note:

+ The specialties are arranged in a descending order of number of graduates;

* Bachelor of medicine (5-year) or master of medicine (7-year) were issued upon graduation;

** Certificate of medicine was issued upon graduation.

Source: Chinese Health Statistics Digest, 1991. Ministry of Public Health, Beijing, China.

There were a total of 214,907 medical students in school during the 1991/92 academic year and 45,974 graduated in that year. (Table 1). The total number of students in 112 WM schools was 182,709 and 32,198 in the 30 CM schools.

Curriculum. The curriculum emphasis varies among medical schools, however, the major departments in WM schools are clinical medicine which includes most specialties in medical fields, preventive medicine, dentistry, pharmacology, medical laboratory and nursing care. For CM school, the major departments are clinical Chinese medicine, pharmacology in Chinese medicine and acupuncture. It should be noted here that there are only two colleges of pharmacy in the nation and therefore most pharmacists and all dentists are graduated from respective departments within western-medicine oriented medical schools. There are a few relatively new majors in the school curriculum such as English in medicine and statistics in health care.

There are three types of programs currently available in the higher institutions of medicine: 3-, 5-, and 7-year. The most popular and widely accepted program is the five-year program in which high school graduates spend 5 years of study in medical school and obtain the bachelor of medicine degree upon graduation. This five-year curriculum usually comprises the basic sciences (first two and one half years) and the clinical sciences (the remaining two and one half years). More than half of the medical students in China are currently in such a program. A continuation or expansion of this 5-year program is the 7-year program where students spend an additional two years in medical school in order to obtain the degree of master of medicine upon graduation. Research oriented curriculum is strongly emphasized in this program. Satisfactory completion of a thesis (including defense of thesis) is also required in the 7-year program.

The 3-year program requires that high school graduates spend three years in medical school and obtain a certificate of medicine upon graduation. Those programs are especially popular among local-government-sponsored medical schools, which are oriented to provide basic or primary health care for a larger population in rural areas and in some sectors of urban areas. Most schools can only have 3- or 5-year programs. All key medical schools have a 7-year program.

It should be mentioned here that in addition to the three types of regular medical education programs, there are quite a large number of middle-level medical schools which have been developed in the past decades to meet the special needs of rural health care and for taking care of the basic needs of factory workers and miners. This includes 517 schools which produce nurses, clinical physicians assistants, public health doctor assistants, medical technical assistants, among others. In 1990, where the data were available, approximate 90,000 students enrolled in the middle-level schools. The length of training in these schools ranges between three to four years and a diploma is issed upon graduation.

Residency Training. The post-graduate residency program is usually fixed for five years. The first two years of residency is clinical rotations in all major specialites of internal medicine, surgery, pediatrics, obstetrics and gynecology. The remaining three years of residency is specially oriented for the development of clinical skills and knowledge. Physicians are not required to obtain a license to practice. However, a medical school diploma is required before hospitals or clinics can hire medical practitioners.

Health Personnel, Hospital and Health Care System

Physicians. Physician refers to those who have graduated from WM or CM medical schools and obtain at least a certificate of medicine or above. There were 1,746,825 active clinical physicians in China in 1991 (See Table 2 for the number of physicians in both categories of high-level and middle-level personnel) in a total of 49 specialites or subspecialties. For a nation with a population close to 1.2 billion (exact figure of 1.158 billion in 1991 [1]), the physician to population ratio is about 145

TABLE 2

Number and Percent of Health Personnel in China in 1991[1]

High Level Personnel*	Number	Percent
Physicians in WM	1,065,223	21.2
Physicians in CM	240,818	4.8
Combination of CM & WM	4,892	0.1
Nursing with BS	439,106	8.7
Pharmacologist	163,541	3.3
Lab Research Associate	82,543	1.6
Other	69,464	1.4
Subtotal	2,065,587	41.1
Middle Level Personnel**		
Physicians in WM	346,795	6.9
Physicians in CM	89,097	1.8
Nursing with Certification	572,837	11.4
Gynecology Assistant	59,731	1.2
Pharmacist	165,514	3.3
Lab Technicians	72,764	1.4
Other	94,277	1.9
Subtotal	1,401,015	27.9
Lower Level Personnel	518,372	10.3
Other		
Technology Assistant	91,265	1.8
Administrators	408,819	8.1
Other staff	540,076	10.7
Subtotal	1,040,160	20.6
Total	5,025,134	100.0

Note:

[1] WM refers to those graduated from western medicine oriented school and CM refers to those graduated from Chinese medicine oriented school.

* High level personnel refers to those who obtain at least bachelor degree or above;

** Middle level personnel refers to those who obtain certificates upon graduation from medical school. Most of them were the graduates from 3-year school program.

Source: Chinese Health Statistics Digest, 1991. Ministry of Public Health, Beijing, China.

physicians per 100,000 population. The total number of physicians graduated from WM medical schools increased about 20 times in the last four decades, whereas a corresponding figure of population increase was 2.1 times. In 1990, where the data was available, 36.6% of the WM graduates were internists (including those in general internal medicine and some of its subspecialties), followed by surgery (14.6%); obstetrics/gynecology (8.7%), public health (6.0%) and pediatrics (5.4%). There is no department of family practice or general practice in medical school in China. Primary care in China usually refers to those in internal medicine, pediatrics, public health, obstetrics and gynecology. In recent years, the concept of general/family practice has been introduced into China. However, its development as a specialty is still in an experimental stage.

Nurses. Nurse refers to those who graduate from nursing school and obtain a certificate of nursing or above. It specifically refers to the nurses of both high level and middle level personnel (Table 2). There are 1,011,943 nurses in the country and currently there are 490 nursing schools or vocational training schools. Nursing school usually enroll students who have graduated from junior high school and for 3- or 4-years of training, they obtain the nursing certificate or school diploma. The ratio of nurse to physicians is 1:1.73.

Lower-level Health Personnel. This group refers to those who do not receive certificates of medicine or a school diploma but who work in the medial fields. Most of them are medical assistants, lab assistants, or village health workers working in township hospitals or village clinics in rural areas (Table 2). (The total number is 518,372). It should be noted that most village health workers have to have some medical clinical study and training up to one year in the county-level medical training schools. They do not receive a certificate after completing the training. However, the county health care department may issue permits for them to practice medicine.

Hospitals. Table 3 shows the classification of hospitals, beds, and personnel in the nation. The hospitals in China are classified largely into three types: those in or above county level, the township hospital, and village clinics/clinical health maintenance and disease prevention units. The occupancy rates of hospitals is 89.1%. (Hospital occupancy rate = ([days per capita x population] / 365 x hospital beds.) It should be noted that health clinics play a crucial health support role for a majority of patients in the nation. Their medical and health services are very much similar to the services provided by family physicians or generalists in most western countries. In 1990 where the data were available, the total number of patient visits was about 2.4 billion, and about 2% of those were hospitalized. Note here also that in recent years, there has been a trend of increased numbers of private clinics and practitioners.

Health Care System. A planned and regulated system of health care delivery is provided to all people of the nation. Specifically, universal health care coverage is used for all employees whereas a fee-for-service system is used mainly for those who are unemployed, most of them live in rural areas.

All employees receive medical and health care free. This includes primary care, care in specialty/subspecialty areas, prescription drugs used in disease treatment, operations, eye/dental care, childhood immunization, and abortion. Patients also obtain their salary in full for up to a period of 3 months per year, while required to stay in the hospital. Pregnant women have up to 6 months of salary paid in order to stay-at-home during or after the delivery. Those who retire (60 for men and 55 for women) can also obtain 60% to 100% of full coverage of medical care. Usually, employees of factories, mines, and industrious enterprises can also obtain 50% of health care coverage for direct members of the family. For the employees of other government agencies and non-profit institutions, the coverage for members of a family is not available.

China's economic reform brings more private-owned factories and business into the scene in the recent decade and the health care coverage for the employees working in those units is an issue yet to be resolved. The current policy does not require the employers in those units to pay for their employees' health care insurance.

About 80% of the nation's population are not regular employees of institutions or working units. They are peasants and farmers working in rural areas. The health care coverage for those people is through what is called "three-level protection and health care networks" referring to county hospital, township hospital, and village clinic. All primary medical and health care is provided on the first level of village clinics or sometimes under the guidance of health care personnel on the second level of township hospitals. Those working in village clinics or health care units in the township hospital are usually graduates from the middle- or lower-level medical schools or the county vocational training school. The patients are charged much less in those units, or hospitals below the county level, than in most of the high-level technology-oriented hospitals. However, the peasants or farmers have to pay for prescription drugs for themselves and their families. This raises a great concern among health care policy makers of the nation, to which we turn in the next section.

TABLE 3

Percent of Hospitals, Beds, and Personnels by Type of Hospitals in 1991

Type of Hospital	Hospital (%)	Bed (%)	Personnel (%)
County or above	6.5	63.5	51.8
Township	23.0	24.4	18.2
Other Hospital	0.6	2.0	1.4
Vocational Institute	0.3	4.2	1.1
Emergency Clinic	61.6	3.1	12.0
Specialty Prevention Center	0.9	1.1	1.1
Immunization Center	1.7	0	3.7
Women and Children Clinic	1.4	0.5	1.4
Drug Testing Center	0.9	—	0.4
Health Care Institution	2.6	1.0	1.9
Research Institution	0.2	0.2	0.7
College of Pharmacology	—	0	2.1
School of Pharmacology	—	0.1	1.2
Private Medical Clinic	—	0	3.0
Total Percent*	100.0	100.0	100.0
Total Number	209,036	2,991,859	5,025,134

Note:
* The percentages may not add up to 100 because of rounding error.

Source: Chinese Health Statistics Digest, 1991. Ministry of Public Health, Beijing, China.

PROBLEMS IN HEALTH CARE AND MEDICAL EDUCATION

Health Care Coverage in Rural Areas. The issue of lack of health care coverage for peasants in rural areas has been noted as early as the 1950s when the People's Republic was founded. The Chinese government has been exerting great efforts to resolve this situation.

In the past several decades, roughly 2.3 percent of the government's financial expenditures have been on health care. The amount of the government's subsidies to health care has proved inadequate in addressing the issue of accessibility of large numbers of its population living in rural areas. In the recent decade, there has been rapid economic development in these rural areas, however, a corresponding figure of expenditure on health care is not seen.

Inaccessibility of health and medical care in China's rural areas is directly related to physicians' maldistribution. The pattern of physicians' distribution is roughly divided into four time periods since 1949 (3). The first period of 1949-1954 was the time when a series of mass programs to eliminate epidemic and infectious diseases were carried out in the rural areas. There were about 50,000 health personnel in total in China in the early 1950s and few were living in the rural areas. Therefore most health care services in the rural areas were provided by the health personnel with a minimum medical training (usually a few months or so). This type of health care mass programs proved to be the most effective way, at least in the early 1950s, of reducing diseases and promoting health. The second period of 1955-1965 witnessed a healthy development in every aspect of the health care system in rural areas. The government made a great investment of manpower, materials, finances in a process of establishing what is called "three-level protection and health care networks". The services of medical and health care to peasants were provided through the third level of village clinic where a cooperative reimbursement system was implemented. The obvious lack is high quality of health care including qualified physicians and equipment. The Networks were not fully established until the third time period of 1966-1978. This was a time of turmoil with an onset of the "Cultural Revolution" where a great deal of destruction of the health care system took place, particularly in the areas of medical education, teaching and research. A large number of high-level physicians and health care personnel were forced to go to the countryside to receive re-education from the peasants. A side-effect of this executive order was a great improvement of middle-level and lower-level health personnel's clinical skills under the guidance of those high-level physicians. The "barefoot doctors" became a popular name in every household of rural areas. The fourth period started in 1978 when China's economical reforms were initiated. Economic reform brings change in health care sectors such as establishing private health care practitioners in support of most public health care hospitals or clinics already in existence. However, one major problem which arises from such reform is that a large number of health care personnel have left rural areas or changed their profession. The Three-Level Network is in an unsteady position. Peasants have difficulty getting access to health care as needed. The differences of health care accessibility between rural and urban areas, although narrowed to some extent over the years, remain to be addressed. For instance, physician to population ratios in the city was 3.22 per thousand in 1980, and 2.92 per thousand in 1991, whereas corresponding figures were 0.76 and 0.97 for 1980 and 1991, respectively, in rural areas which include county and below county levels (1). Several models have been proposed and implemented to change this pattern of physician maldistribution. This includes programs of encouraging or requiring medical school graduates to serve in rural areas for a certain period of time, physician rotation programs which set a time frame during which rounds are carried out by higher level health personnel to serve patients in those areas, and change of recruitment policy by admitting more students from those areas with the obligation of returning to those areas after graduation.

It seems that both factors of accessibility of peasants to health care and the psychological needs and satisfaction of physicians working in these areas need to be carefully weighted in order to achieve positive outcomes. As such, in recent years, a large number of vocational health schools, lower-level medical training schools, and short health-training medical programs in regular medical schools were developed in order to meet the need of peasants' accessibility to primary care.

A great increase in the number of health personnel, particularly those in middle- and lower-levels, will lessen the degree of inaccessibility of medical care in rural areas. As hospitals are subsidized tremendously by government, including personnel training (free of charge), equipment, and technical support, peasants are charged far lower fees, for their medical and health care services, than they would be in the hospitals above the county level. This is also partly due to the large number of health care jobs completed by a large number of health care assistants (roughly about 1.2 million) who are trained in a short period of time in county health schools and then become active health care providers in the rural areas of China.

Imbalance in Ratio of High-Level Physicians to Middle- or Lower-Level Physicians and in Ratio of Physicians to Nurses. As seen in Table 2, the number of high-level medical and health care personnel in both WM and CM categories is more than that of middle-level personnel, which in turn is more than of lower-level personnel. This maldistribution of educational level of health care personnel poses a problem of inaccessibility of medical care in rural areas, as most high-level personnel tend to stay in well-established technology-equipped larger hospitals in urban areas. This also increases workload on high-level personnel as most work that might be accomplished by middle- or lower-level health personnel are actually performed by high-level personnel. This partly results in unnecessary increase in cost of health care.

Table 2 also shows an imbalance in ratio of physicians to nurses, particularly in high-level personnel. One reason that has been widely cited for a lack of nurses is low pay and heavy workload. In China, where a larger proportion of the population is living in the countryside, a large number of health care personnel serving in those areas are certainly required. Nurses are desperately needed in order to accomplish this objective.

Control of Communicable and Leading Death-Cause Diseases. In recent years, there has been reported an increase in frequency of communicable diseases including tuberculosis, hepatits A, digestive diseases and schistosomiasis. More Acquired

Immunodeficiency Syndrome (AIDS) cases are detected every year since 1985 when the first case was reported in China, although the number is extremely small in comparison with other western countries. Up to 1993 in 22 provinces in China, of 1,159 confirmed carriers of the human immunodeficiency virus (HIV), which causes AIDS, 947 are Chinese and 212 are foreigners or overseas Chinese (4). It is projected that by the year 2000 the number of HIV carriers in China will reach 100,000 and number of patients with AIDS will be around 20,000 (4). The National Association of Sexually Transmitted Diseases and AIDS Control and Prevention was formed to help the government organize prevention activities. Other chronic diseases, such as cancer, heart disease, and respiratory disease remain the major threat to the people's health. Most of those diseases are preventable and curable if detected early and treated effectively. Therefore, the long-advocated policy of "prevention first and treatment second" should continue and be implemented effectively.

Medical Education and Evaluation. Lack of unified national medical education system remains a problem. Students' evaluation process is carried out mostly by individual medical schools and comparisons of quality of students between medical schools has been used experimentally and with some success (5) but problems remain to be solved.

Accreditation of medical schools and hospitals poses another concern. This becomes especially urgent as more medical schools, most of them secondary or vocational schools, are becoming operational each year, and more graduates from these schools obtain residency training in hospitals or clinical units which have never been officially recognized through a formal accreditation process. Even for those schools and hospitals which have been known for quite some time, a regular inspection and renewal of their status as teaching and educational institutions is certainly needed.

Physicians and health personnel need constant improvements in their knowledge base, clinical skill, and adjustment of professional attitudes. In a world of constant change and development, physicians have to keep up with those changes. Lack of units such as continuing education within medical schools and hospitals is apparent. The problem of lack of continuing education becomes especially apparent for middle- and lower-level health personnel, as they represent the major force of providing care to the underserved in rural areas.

Other Problems Arising in Economic Reform. There is a growing awareness that much illness is societally-induced, due to lifestyle and environmental factors. Cigarette smoking, for instance, becomes increasingly popular, particularly among the teenage population in the nation. It has been estimated that half of the world's new smokers, by the next century, will be in China (6). Heart and respiratory diseases have long been known to be related to smoking behavior. Preventing or reducing such behavior is difficult because it involes fundamental changes in individual and societal values.

There is also significant evidence that social functioning, health and well-being can be seriously affected by job insecurity and unemployment. As China moves from a planned centralized economical system to a market economy, unemployment rates are increasing, and certainly it will demand more psychological and mental adjustment among individuals and in the public at large. Universal medical and health care coverage will be tested in such a changing environment.

MEDICINE IN CHINA IN THE 21ST CENTURY

China's government is committed to economic reform, so we are committing ourselves to health care reform. This reform is overwhelming, in terms of both its scope and magnitude. As such, we set up goals and specify the actions yet to be accomplished by the 21st century.

Goal. A general development of the Chinese economy in the past decades and further improvement in the 1990s has and will continue to improve general health of the nation. Life expectancy, for instance, has double in the past four decades and reached 69 years in 1992. Infant mortality rates have been reduced by twofold in the same time period and reached a historical low of 14.0 per thousand in urban areas and 37.5 per thousand in rural areas in 1991, where the data were available. Health care reform will bring significant changes in a number of areas including universal health care, health administration, medical education and evaluation, among others.

Goals are specified in the following:

- Universal medical and health care coverage for all people by the year 2000;
- Life expectancy expected to reach 71 years;
- Infant mortality rates expected to reduce to 30 per thousand in the nation;
- Ratio of health care personnel to population will be 380/per 100,000 population among them 120/per 100,000 for high-level medical and health care personnel;
- 60% of health care assistants or lower-level health personnel will obtain at least associate degree of medicine through re-training programs.

Health Care System. The top priority will concentrate on the health coverage for peasants and health care in rural areas. This requires further consolidation and development of "Three-Level Protection & Health Care Network" in rural areas. Health personnel training schools and programs will be expanded. Specifically targeted programs will be encouraged and funded, if possible. Successful programs will be rewarded and popularized. The government will increase its budget for rural medical and health care in the next few years in order to help establish and strengthen the Network in these areas. Medical schools should encourage their graduates to provide services and care in rural areas and provides some re-training programs for lower-level health personnel. The financial reward of health care personnel working in the countryside should be equal to or higher than village officials in the areas.

Chinese medicine, in combination with western medicine, has proved to be an effective way for health maintenance and protection, disease prevention and treatment. The programs of combining both schools of medicine should be encouraged and developed. Emphasis will be given to status and function of Chinese medicine in combination with western medicine. It is important to discourage unhealthy behaviors and increase the state of general health of the nation.

Aging Population. China's population is increasingly becoming aged. The government's report (2) indicated that in 1990 about ninety-seven million out of a total 1.13 billion population is 60 years of age or older, consisting of 8.6% of the total population. This proportion of aged population is estimated to be increasing steadily in the future. China is a developing country and a rapid increase of aged people will put greater pressure on the national health care system and will eventually lead to the development of more comprehensive health insurance for the aged. Geriatrics is still a new area in medicine in China and will certainly require more attention in the foreseeable future.

Medical School and Educational Research. Regular 5-year medical school programs are a basic component of medical education in producing high-level health personnel for the nation and should be further strengthened. At the same time, 3-year programs, which produce most of middle- and lower-level health personnel, will be further expanded. The past decade has witnessed a tremendous increase in the number and variety of health training schools, including the establishment of adult medical education institutions (7). The products of these schools—health care assistants and other lower-level health personnel—play a significant role in providing primary care in rural areas. It is expected that the trend will continue. However, quality assessment of these schools and of its product should be given careful attention.

We need the best and brightest high school graduates to enter medicine. The admission process has to weight different aspects of the applicants, not just the NUEE score. NUEE score is and should be one of the most important aspects, but other qualities, such as personal characteristics and overall performance in high school, should be seriously considered.

The quality of health personnel is directly connected to overall quality of health care of the nation. Medical school students of today are the future providers of health care to the nation. Evaluation of the students not only serves as a tool of medical school quality maintenance, but as a necessary means of maintaining a high quality of the health care system into the next century. However, lack of a systematic way of evaluating students, both in cognitive and non-cognitive aspects, is apparent, particularly in the clinical phase of medical education. It will become a major new issue facing medical educators. A scientifically-sound objective way of examining students' clinical skills requires further study.

The content of curriculum has to reflect the newest development of medicine in the world. Faculty of medical schools should keep pace with such development and bring it into the classroom. Healthy competition among students or among schools is necessary and should be encouraged.

Accreditation of medical schools will be carried out. National accreditation committees will be formed to supervise such a process. Experts and medical educators have to be recruited from the nation to actually carry out the procedures and actions.

In summary, quality assessment of medical schools, of teachers and faculty, will all be on tomorrow's agenda of medical school administrators. It is expected by the next century, China will implement national examination of medical school students, certification examination of physician and health personnels, and regular assessment and certification of medical schools.

Hospital Reform. Hospitals have acquired a great deal of government's financial subsidies and funding over the past decades. As a result, lack of efficiency in administration and overstaffing of personnel become major problems. Rising costs of hospital expenditures, particularly in the use of high technology equipment, is

Medicine and Health Care Into the Twenty-First Century. Edited by S.K. Majumdar, L.M. Rosenfeld, D.B. Nash and A.M. Audet. © 1995, The Pennsylvania Academy of Science.

Chapter Forty-One

MEDICINE AND HEALTH CARE IN NIGERIA INTO THE 21ST CENTURY

KAYODE O. ADENIYI, Ph.D., FIAES, FELIX I. ANJORIN, MBBS, FMCP (Nig), FWACP, JOHN T. MOMOH, MBBS, FRCS (C) and JOSEPH A.M. OTUBU, MBBS, Ph.D., FRCOG

Faculty of Medical Sciences
University of Jos
P.M.B. 2084
Jos, Nigeria

INTRODUCTION

Medical care in Nigeria has gone through undulating patterns from the traditional African medical care with its variable levels from the utilization of crude herbs to the chanting of incantations for apparent medicinal purposes followed by the advent of the early Christian missionaries who brought with them refined, western type medical care, an era of hopefulness to replace despondency. However, the area of this positive influence was often limited by poor communication, and the increasing population resulted in demand outstripping available supply.

Government health care facilities which came later to complement missionary efforts were seen by the people to be obviously less efficient than the Christian missionary facilities due to less dedication to work in the government facilities and a more regular "syndrome" of "out-of-stock" for drugs and reagents in the government facilities.

The rudimentary health care program in Nigeria has, however, gradually metamorphosed into district primary health care services (dispensaries and comprehensive health facilities), offering basic first aid and preventive services, secondary medical facilities, (made up of district general hospitals) and tertiary health institutions (made up of specialists and teaching hospitals). The graduation in available facilities enables referrals to be made from primary to secondary and subsequently to tertiary health care facilities. The strengthening of the primary health care facilities in the last 8 years has improved services to the rural areas, emphasizing more of preventive measures at the grassroots, where about 80% of the population resides.

Private and missionary health care facilities such as those provided by Catholic, Church Missionary Society (CMS), Sudan Interior Mission (now Evangelical Churches of West Africa EWCA), and Baptist Churches are now largely offering services at primary and secondary health care levels to complement existing government facilities. The recent emergence of private tertiary health care facilities like the Eko Hospital in Lagos and Igbinedion Hospital in Okada near Benin City is a welcome development in trying to reduce the need for overseas trips for specialized medical care.

In this chapter, therefore, we shall be discussing the historical background of health facilities, primary, secondary and tertiary health care and then discuss what the future holds as a result of projections from the past and present status of health care in Nigeria, with its teaming population of 88 million, making her the most populous African nation.

HISTORICAL BACKGROUND

Nigeria today has a system of health care delivery based on the model of Western Europe and America. Prior to the establishment of this system of health care, Nigeria had its own system of traditional medicine.

The traditional medical practice of the various ethnic groups in Nigeria developed through attempts of the various groups to deal with the exigencies of illness. Traditional medicine in Nigeria was holistic, involving preventive and curative roles. It involved the acquisition of knowledge of preventive and curative agents such as herbs, trees, magic, etc. It also involved learning of techniques and skills of communication not only with the patients but also with causative agents in ill-health such as spirits, ancestors, etc. Individuals trained in herbal therapy acquired the knowledge of the various trees and herbs needed for cure. Those involved in the field of bone-setting acquired the knowledge about the human body, knew the various joints and learned the techniques of manipulating them. Traditional healers that cured through the act of spirit-possession "knew the entire spirit world". Training in traditional medicine was based on apprenticeship in which trainees came directly under the tutelage of an appropriate specialist.

Disease etiology was simple at that time. These etiological factors included curses, witchcraft, bad medicine, sorcery, ancestral punishment, spirit attack, magic and strains in social relations.

Traditional medicine still enjoys some support today due to its nature of "holistic healing". In contrast to modern medicine, which focuses largely on disease as biological process and provides therapeutic regimens to deal with biologic organisms, traditional medicine "deals" concurrently with both the psychological and physical needs of patients. It addresses itself to both the body and mind of patients.

In general, traditional healers held a monopoly for practice before the arrival of allopathic medicine. This dominance has been attributed to three distinct factors; traditional healers external relations with the supernatural, their socio-economic position within society and their healing skills. The interplay of these three factors made the healers a respected and feared class, even by chiefs, in certain communities.

Modern allopathic medicine came to Nigeria prior to actual colonial conquest from early to mid-nineteenth century. It arrived as a package, with therapeutic techniques developed, tried and somewhat perfected, in Europe and America. While the missionaries were the first to organize modern health care, full establishment occurred in the colonial days of Nigeria's transition. The first real attempt to train personnel for the health services in Nigeria was taken with the establishment of an experimental medical school by the CMS missionaries at Abeokuta in 1862. The school collapsed in 1864. It would reappear that missionary organizers of the school set standards too high. The colonial state established a Dispensary Attendant School in 1920 at Calabar. The Yaba College, Lagos was established in 1930 for the training of medical assistants and shortly after this, the Ibadan Medical College was created in 1948. The college was affiliated with the University of London. It continued to be the only medical training institution until 1954 when another medical school was established in Kano. The Kano medical school was similar to the Yaba medical school and offered diploma training for practice only in Northern Nigeria. It admitted no students after 1958 and was finally closed down to give way to the more universally acceptable and comprehensive training program at Ibadan.

October 1st, 1960 marked an end of an era in Nigeria's transition. It was the day in which colonial rule terminated. The state which emerged at the end of colonial rule was very different from its colonial forebearer. Concerned with development, the state realized the centrality of health. Health was and still is seen as a vital factor in raising productivity and an important stimulant for development.

In general, the state's intervention in health care has been characterized by the following:

(a) High level of activity and dominance.
(b) Maintenance of orthodoxy in the pursuit of health which led to the sustenance of colonially inherited methods and strategies for health development.
(c) Use of selection mechanisms which involve the support of private enterprise in health and avoidance of measures such as strong legislations to curtail the excesses of private medicine; lack of legislation on occupational health and failure to take adequate measures against environmental degradation arising out of the operation of capital.

Post-colonial Nigeria saw the growth of more medical colleges to address the problems of shortage of doctors in the country. The Third National Development Plan (1975-1980) provided for the accelerated expansion of medical colleges and facilities for the training of full fledged doctors. As of today, Nigeria has twenty medical schools, the highest in Africa. The philosophical foundations of current health care in Nigeria are rooted in orthodoxy, in which health personnel are trained for curative roles. This slant gives little help in solving the problems at hand. In reality, the health needs of the country are for basic social amenities to enhance the quality of life: mass immunization, environmental sanitation and health education to deal with easily preventable diseases. This pattern would have required an integrative approach between the various professionals that are involved in health care delivery.

THE CURRENT HEALTH CARE PATTERN IN NIGERIA

Nigeria's health policy has essentially been formulated to ensure health through the provision of health services. The approach remains, in the main, curative, involving the creation of structures and establishments for health services provision. The fundamental goals of health policy have required the training of more personnel to achieve a better practitioner: patient ratio of 1:2000 (presently 1:4379), the building of more hospitals and clinics and expansion of existing ones and the procurement and better distribution of drugs and other supplies for curative services. In effect, Nigerian health care policy is based largely on curative medical service provisions.

According to Lamberstan (1972), health care is the sum total of care provided by all health disciplines. It comprises more than diagnosis, treatment and cure, during acute and chronic illness; it also includes health education, health maintenance, prevention, early case finding and rehabilitation. A distinction should therefore be made between medical care which focuses on illness and disability and health care which is concerned with the total spectrum of health and illness services.

Overemphasis on curative medical services in Nigeria remains one of the fundamental explanations for the failure of the state's attempt at improving the health situation in Nigeria. Table 1 demonstrates that Government financial allocation has favored curative as against a preventive approach to health care.

The situation became worse in the 1980s, when the expenditure for preventive services reached a low mark of less than 1% of the Government health expenditure.

TABLE 1

Allocation of Capital Expenditure on Health Program 1970-1974

Type of Service	Federal Government N (Million)	State Government N (Million)	Total N (Million)	Percentage
Curative Services	28.370	58.334	86.700	72.0
Preventive Services	1.880	17.625	19.500	16.0
Training Program	1.830	8.625	10.460	9.0
Others	0.200	3.592	3.790	3.0
Total	32.280	88.180	120.450	100

Source: Goverment of Nigeria. Second National Development Plan 1990/94 Lagos: Government Press.

Recently, because of the global call for improved health for all by the year 2000, the state has re-evaluated its health policy with added emphasis on prevention. The emphasis is on primary health care (PHC). Expanded programs for immunization (EPI) and early detection and treatment of ailments clearly demonstrate an acknowledgment of the signficance of prevention in the Government health policy.

There has been steady progress in the re-orientation of the national health system towards Health for All. As a first step, a National Health Policy was developed. The policy which is founded on the national philosophy of social justice and equity has committed the Government and peoples of Nigeria to the attainment of Health for All Nigerians by the year 2000, emphasizing the primary health care approach. It has as it's goal, the establishment of a comprehensive health care system which shall operate at three levels—primary, secondary and tertiary—with the three levels maintaining a continous relationship with one another. Such a relationship is to facilitate the process of technical consultation or supportive supervision emanating from the tertiary to the secondary and to the primary levels and then the referral of patients from primary care to the secondary and then tertiary levels. The fostering of such relationships is one of the main roles of Teaching and Specialist Hospitals in the process towards making Health for All a reality in Nigeria.

The present National Health Policy and strategy to achieve Health for All Nigerians was a product of the 4th National Development Plan in 1981. Essentially, Primary Health Care is a function of local government. Secondary Health Care and the Supervision of the implementation of PHC is a function of state governments, while the federal government provides Tertiary Health Care and supervises the implementation of the National Health Policy in the entire federation.

The Policy provides for the establishment of a National Managerial Process for determining goals, flexible planning, Programmed Budgeting, implementation and evaluation. The National Health Policy also provides for the local government to evaluate and train traditional medical practitioners to fit into appropriate slots in the PHC Scheme.

PRIMARY HEALTH CARE

According to the World Health Organization (1968), "Primary Health Care (PHC) is essential health care made universally accessible to the public through their full participation and at a cost that the community and country can afford". It is therefore community-based and closest to the people. It has long been argued that community medicine is what needs to be emphasized in the developing countries, for it is within the community that diseases arise and develop.

In the search for health for all, PHC was launched in Nigeria in 1987 and it represents the front line in the battle for good health. It is the basis of the National Health Policy and the emerging National Health System in Nigeria. In its 1987 document, the Nigerian Government identified the role and functions of PHC as the provision of general health services of a preventive, curative, promotive and rehabilitative nature to the population as the entry point of the health care system.

The provision of care at this level is largely the responsibility of local governments with the support of State Ministries of Health. Private Medical Practitioners also provide health care at this level. This level of health care is quite clear and it encompasses grass-root level institutions such as health clinics, primary health centers, maternity centers and homes, Child centers, dispensaries and family planning clinics.

The data presented in Table 2 below show that primary health care facilities constitute the majority of health care institutions available nationwide. They accounted for about 92 percent of all institutions, 63% government owned and 29% privately owned. Most common among these institutions are the dispensaries, perhaps the most prevalent form of rural health facilities which account for about 21 percent of all health facilities. Next in importance to these are the health clinics and Primary Health Centers each of which encompasses about 13 percent of all institutions while

TABLE 2

Inventory of Health Facilities by State

States	TCH	SPH	IDH	GH/DH (u)	CHC	HC	PHC	MC	D	FPC	PF	O	Total	%
Abuja (FCT)	—	—	—	1	4	15	—	—	—	1	6	—	107	0.93
Akwa Ibom	—	2	6	13	5	102	7	18	11	—	45	15	224	1.94
Anambra	1	3	5	30	24	98	98	57	53	58	796	—	1223	10.60
Bauchi	—	—	—	4	1	2	2	3	16	—	—	—	32	0.28
Bendel	1	—	—	44	—	143	55	202	248	—	247	24	964	8.36
Benue	—	—	3	21	—	24	56	50	179	—	255	13	631	5.47
Borno	1	—	—	13	13	82	4	—	215	8	20	—	356	3.09
Cross-Rivers	1	4	1	11	3	11	82	4	9	—	25	—	151	1.30
Gongola	—	2	—	14	—	63	—	13	144	—	34	—	270	2.34
Imo	—	1	1	12	—	88	—	—	86	56	389	—	143	5.58
Kaduna	1	1	1	10	1	58	12	8	—	59	187	—	338	2.93
Kano	1	5	—	14	17	4	67	5	358	1	86	2	530	4.60
Katsina	—	—	—	8	1	31	11	19	13	11	22	—	116	1.01
Kwara	1	1	—	26	1	—	36	—	—	—	74	—	139	1.21
Lagos	1	4	—	7	1	59	12	64	85	62	627	1	922	8.00
Niger	—	—	1	9	6	—	33	21	—	26	47	4	147	1.28
Ogun	1	—	—	5	4	5	16	162	51	—	23	—	327	2.84
Ondo	—	5	49	12	29	43	—	191	229	88	149	—	795	6.90
Oyo	2	—	—	21	5	27	22	232	338	44	322	9	1022	8.86
Plateau	1	—	—	9	5	1	28	24	24	—	113	—	205	1.78
Rivers	1	2	3	30	10	207	50	—	—	94	166	—	563	4.88
Sokoto	1	—	—	9	1	394	1001	5	319	62	32	—	1824	15.82
Total =	14	30	70	323	131	1457	1592	1108	2468	580	3687	68	11529	100.00

Key to Table 2:

TCH = Teaching Hospitals; SPH = Specialist Hospitals (Psychiatric, Orthopaedic, etc.); IDH = Infectious Disease Hospital; GH = General Hospitals; DH (u) = District Hospital/District Health Unit; CHC = Comprehensive Health Center; HC = Health Clinics; PHC = Primary Health Center; MC = Maternity/Child Center/Home; D = Dispensary; FPC = Family-Planning Clinic; PF = Private facilities and NGIS; O = Others (Rehabilitation Center).

Source from Survey of secondary Health Care Facilities, in Nigeria. A report for the Federal Ministry of Health by Health Aid Limited, August 1989.

trailing closely behind them are the maternity centers (about 10 percent of all institutions).

The Federal Government developed national objectives for the implementation of PHC and indicators to measure progress in the attainment of these objectives. As part of this effort, the Monitoring and Evaluation (M&E) Division of the PHC Department of the Federal Ministry of Health established a PHC monitoring system which collects routine statistics from five levels: the home, the community, the health facility, the district, and the local government areas. Table 3 below shows the national objectives as well as the sources of data used to decide whether the objective has been met.

TABLE 3

Indicators for Measuring Progress for PHC Program (From Nig. Bull. Epid. 2[1]:1992)

PHC Topic	Primary Health Care National Ojective by the year 1992	Source of Data
EPI Coverage	80% of Children will be fully immunized with I BCG, 4 Polio 3 DPT/OPV and I Measles at one year of age	Special-coverage Surveys/M&E Forms/Children 0-12 months = 4% population
Ante-Natal Care	50% of pregnant women will be fully immunized with 3 doses of Tetanus Toxoid	Special Surveys, Including Home-based adult records/M&E forms Pregnant women = 5% Population WRA = 20%
Nutrition Pregnant Women	90% or more of newborns will have birth weight of 2500gr. or more	M&E forms on pregnancy outcome survey of Home based Health Cards
Nutrition Children 0-3 years	90% of Children 0-3 years old will have a weight for age above the 3rd percentile	M&E growth monitoring forms. Survey of growth monitoring (0-3 year old) = 15# population
Health Care Coverage Pregnant Women	70% of deliveries will be attended by a health worker or trained Traditional Birth Attendants (TBA)	M&E forms on Pregnancy outcome survey
Family planning	10% of women in reproductive age group will use modern family planning	M&E forms on Family planning Survey/Village Health Ward VHW records
Access to Health Services	80% of the population will live within 5kms or 1/2 hour of a health facility of VHW	Survey/Maps
Portable Water	40% of the population will live within 300 meters of a source of potable water	Survey
Latrines	60% of the population will live within 50 meters of VHW of a pit latrine or toilet	Survey
Essential drugs	80% of VHW/Health facilities will have 80% essential drugs available continuously	Essential Drug programs monitoring forms/surveys

Key to Table 3:

PCH = Primary Health Care; EPI = Expanded Program on Immunization; DPT = Diphtheria, Pertussis, Tetanus; OPV = Oral Polio Vaccine, M&E = Monitoring & Evaluation; TBA = Traditional Birth Attendant; VHW = Village Health Ward; WRA = Women in reproductive age.

Each local Government area is to set its own level of attainment for the objectives based on its health problems and resources.

The Nigerian Government has achieved much under the Primary Health Care System. Each year since 1988, the M&E Division has produced a situation analysis based on reports submitted by the 1986 model Local Government Areas (LGAS). These reports were circulated among the states and LGAS which were using the M&E PHC reporting systems. This chapter presents some information from the 1991 report.

THE EXPANDED PROGRAM ON IMMUNIZATION (EPI)

In the 1970s, epidemiologists calculated that nearly five million of the world's children died each year, and about the same number became crippled, blinded or disabled after suffering from vaccine preventable (VP) diseases; measles, tetanus, poliomyelitis, tuberculosis, whooping cough (Pertussis) or diptheria. As a response, the World Health Organization (WHO) Inititated EPI.

Immunization in Nigeria dates back to the control of yellow fever and smallpox. The Federal Ministry of Health in collaboration with World Health Organization (WHO) and UNICEF, launched pilot EPI projects in two states in 1975. The program began nationwide in 1979 and it is aimed to immunize 75-85% of children between 0-24 months old.

In the years between 1979-1984, only 5-10% of the children were vaccinated and there was little impact on the VP diseases. As recently as 1984, about 200,000 Nigerian children were still dying every year of these preventable diseases. Things improved dramatically with support from UNICEF, Rotary International/Polioplus, WHO and the United States (USAID). The 1991 survey revealed that 95.5% of Children 12-23 months old had been vaccinated with BCG, 81.1% had received DPT3/OPV3 and nearly 85% received measles vaccine. Nigeria, thus, achieved the 1990 goal of 80% immunization.

Since January 1991, the target population for EPI has been children in the first year of life.

ANTE-NATAL CARE

As part of this effort, Nigeria planned to immunize 80% of pregnant women by 1993, and to immunize 80% of all women aged 15-45 years by 1995 with tetanus toxoid (TT). This, combined with hygienic child-birth practices, will work together to eliminate tetanus in neonates. The results of the 1991 National Immunization Coverage Survey were encouraging. Nearly 60% of mothers of children 0-11 months old had correctly received two doses of tetanus toxoid (TT).

Nigeria's policy has since shifted from giving 2 doses of TT to pregnant women to a 5 dose schedule.

ENVIRONMENTAL HEALTH ACTIVITIES

PHC workers reported in 1991 that for every 1000 population, there was:

- 1 new well dug
- 1 new stand pipe
- 4 new latrines
- 40 houses inspected
- 5 food premises inspected

Although a lot has been achieved in the promotion of health in Nigeria using PHC, much needs to be done to make health for all Nigerians realizable. The first National Workshop on the National Health Policy, held in Kaduna in 1990, suggested the following recommendations for implementation in order to make PHC more functional:

1. Proper monitoring of the quality and effectiveness of PHC.
2. Improvement of the Maternal and Child Health components of PHC.
3. Secondary and tertiary health care units should give more support to PHC.
4. Managerial capability at the local government level should be strengthened.
5. Improvement in funding of PHC at local government level.
6. The medical schools should be compelled to reorientate their curricula so that the ideas of PHC are taken into congnizance in the training of medical students.

SECONDARY HEALTH CARE

This is the apex of the Health Care Delivery System at the State level and operates through the services of General Hospitals which are situated at each local government area Headquarters in each state. Referral cases, especially most surgical operations, are made from the district or village Health Services to the General Hospitals. According to the Federal Ministry of Health, the level of Secondary Health Care exists to provide specialized services to patients referred from the Primary Health Care level through out-patient and in-patient services at hospital centers for general, medical, surgical and pediatric patients. It is also expected to provide administrative training and technical support to and supervision for the subordinate level. For this, it is expected to have access to services and facilities covering laboratory, diagnostic bloodbank and physiotherapeutic features. In terms of location, these facilities are conceived of essentially as urban and semi-urban institutions and they are expected to be at the intermediate level either in the district, divisional, zonal or state locations.

The predominant type of establishment at the secondary health care level is the General and District Hospital. Table 4 clearly shows this. Of the total of 454 institutions recorded as comprising the public secondary health care sector in 1989, 323 of them, about 71.15 percent, were General or District Hospitals.

The distribution of secondary health sector (Table 4) reveals that it is not only an underdeveloped sector numerically, but it is also slanted in favor of certain metropolitan centers. If it is to serve its function as an intermediate level in the National Health Care Delivery System, then a more even distribution of the establishments, particularly at each local government, is required. However, it needs to be pointed out that the private sector seems to have fitted into the gap created by the under development of the Secondary Health Care Subsystem. Considering the variety both of ownership and interests of this sector, there is the need to systematically devise, not only enabling strategies for a more effective private sector presence but, also, positive measures for the protection of the rights of the individual users.

The acceptance of and provision of primary health care at the community level appears not to be presently matched by well spread efficient and optimally functional secondary health care facilities. Yet, each local government area is expected to have at least one secondary health care facility to serve as the apex of the health care delivery system in that area.

TABLE 4

Public Secondary Health Care Facilities by States in 1989

	GH/DH (U)		CHC		Total	
State	N	%	N	%	N	%
1. Abuja (FCT)	1	20.0	4	80.0	5	1.10
2. Akwa Ibom	13	72.22	5	27.78	18	3.96
3. Anambra	30	55.55	24	44.45	54	11.89
4. Bauchi	4	80.0	1	20.0	5	1.10
5. Bendel	44	100.0	—	0.0	44	9.69
6. Benue	21	100.0	—	0.0	21	4.63
7. Borno	13	50.0	13	50.0	26	5.73
8. Cross River	11	78.57	3	21.43	14	3.08
9. Gongola	14	100.0	—	0.0	14	3.08
10. Imo	12	100.0	—	0.0	12	2.65
11. Kaduna	10	90.90	1	0.10	11	2.42
12. Kano	14	45.16	17	54.84	31	6.83
13. Katsina	8	88.88	1	0.12	9	1.98
14. Lagos	7	87.50	1	12.50	8	1.76
15. Kwara	26	96.29	1	3.71	27	5.95
16. Niger	9	60.0	6	40.0	15	3.31
17. Ogun	5	55.55	4	44.45	9	1.99
18. Ondo	12	29.26	29	70.73	41	9.03
19. Oyo	21	80.77	5	19.23	26	5.73
20. Plateau	9	64.28	5	35.71	14	3.08
21. Rivers	30	75.0	10	25.0	40	8.81
22. Sokoto	9	90.0	1	10.0	10	2.20
Total	323	71.14	131	28.85	454	100.0

Key to Table 4:

GH = General Hospital; DH (U) = District Hospital/District Health Unit; CHC = Comprehensive Health Center.

Source from Survey of Secondary Health Care Facilities in Nigeria; a report for the Federal Ministry of Health by Health Aid Ltd., Aug. 1989.

TERTIARY HEALTH CARE

Tertiary health care, which is at the apex of the National Health System, consists of highly specialized services which provide care for specific diseases and conditions of specific groups. It consists of teaching hospitals, specialist hospitals, orthopedic, eye, psychiatric, maternity and pediatric hospitals. These often are centers of high level research, training and the source of provision of specialized services in the clinical, scientific, diagnostic and technological spheres. This level exhibits greater capital and technological intensity than the other levels.

Table 2 above shows that tertiary health care exhibits the smallest proportion of facilities. It accounts for 0.1 percent of all recorded health institutions in Nigeria. Teaching Hospitals, which operate at the highest level of specialization, sophistication and expertise come last with only 14 being recorded nation-wide. Next in the league of least-represented facilities is the specialist, which consist of 30 establishments nationwide accounting for 0.26 percent of all the health establishments in Nigeria. The Infectious Diseases Hospitals number 70, accounting for 0.60 percent of health establishments.

THE FUTURE

As we look forward to the change from the twentieth into the twenty-first century, the gains of the last decade, mostly under the leadership of Professor Olikoye Ransome-Kuti, former Federal Minister of Health who emphasized preventive and first aid measures at the rural community level, need consolidating. The Expanded Program on Immunization which should incorporate vaccination against hepatitis B virus infection, if strengthened, will witness further decline not only in the childhood killer diseases—diptheria, pertussis, tetanus, measles, poliomyelitis and tuberculosis—but a decline in post-hepatitic liver cirrhosis and primary liver cell carcinoma.

Although the search for a malaria vaccine still continues, it is hoped that success may come later to help in combating this disease, which constitutes a major cause of morbidity and mortality.

The present emphasis on exclusive breast-feeding in the first 4-6 months of life, the drive combating childhood diarrheal diseases and malnutrition and population control measures are likely to manifest their positive effects later with the production of a better and healthier citizenry.

However, these gains are not likely to be realized to the fullest without improved agricultural input to produce adequate food for the population, which is still growing. Communication must also be improved to many rural areas which are partially cut off, especially during the rainy season.

The problem of a deteriorating economy appears to have come to stay with us as we turn into the twenty-first century, with the attendant hardship, especially on the low-income sector of the society. Indeed, the transformation from a largely free health care system in the 1950's and 1960's to a system which is becoming increasingly more expensive, is threatening in the 1990's to make modern health care outside the reach of the common Nigerian. Political instability, when it occurs, as it not infrequently does, worsens the economy and further increases the already heavy economic burden of the average Nigerian. Political engineers must, therefore, ensure a more favorable political climate.

The pandemic infection with the human immunodeficiency virus (HIV) has not spared Nigeria and indeed the Auto-immune Deficiency Syndrome (AIDS) has become a reality as we approach the end of the twentieth century. The future must witness a more aggressive and coordinated health education drive to stem the tide of the astronomical increase in this deadly disease as the search for a suitable vaccine continues.

The effect of increasing change in life-style from a physically active to a sedentary existence in offices, homes and cars by the urban Nigerian, coupled with increasing stress and low fibre, high-fat diet are already beginning to become manifest in the 1990's, resulting in the emergence of atherosclerotic arterial disease in the middle-aged Nigerian. Especially in the hypertensive smoker, ischaemic heart disease is therefore likely to pose a greater threat to the health of the Nigerian urban dweller in the twenty-first century. While we moiunt an aggressive health education program, our tertiary health institutions, in particular, must prepare to tackle problems arising from our changing diet and life-style.

REFERENCES

1. Alubo, S.O. 1985. Underdevelopment and Health Care Crisis in Nigeria. Medical Anthropology No. 9:319-335.
2. Gusau, G.A. 1992. A Political Economy of Medical Education in Nigeria. PhD. Thesis. University of Jos.
3. Ityavyar, D.A. 1989. African Traditional Medicine with reference to "wholistic" view of sickness and health care. In: Ikenga Mituh and O. Ojoade (Ed.) Nigerian Cultural Heritage. Onitsha: IMICOP Publishers 223-226.
4. Lamberstan, E. 1972. Perspective on Physician Assistants. Nursing Outlook 20(11):32-36.
5. Federal Republic of Nigeria.
   1970. Second National Development Plan 1970-74, FMO, Information, Lagos.
   1975. Third National Development Plan 1975-1980. Federal Ministry of National Planning, Lagos.
   1981. Fourth National Development Plan 1981-1985. Federal Ministry of National Planning, Lagos.
   1987. National Policy and Strategy to achieve health for all by the year 2000. Federal Ministry of Health, Lagos.
   1989. Survey of Secondary Health Care Facilities in Nigeria. Compiled by Health AID Limited. Federal Ministry of Health, Lagos.

1991. Nigerian Bulletin of Epidemiology, Vol. 2, No. 3. Federal Ministry of Health, Lagos.
1992. Nigerian Bulletin of Epidemiology, Vol. 2, No. 3. Federal Ministry of Health, Lagos.
1992. Nigerian Bulletin of Epidemiology, Vol. 2, No. 1. Federal Ministry of Health, Lagos.
6. World Health Organization
1968. Training of Medical Assistants and similar personnel, Technical report services. No. 385, Geneva.

Medicine and Health Care Into the Twenty-First Century. Edited by S.K. Majumdar, L.M. Rosenfeld, D.B. Nash and A.M. Audet. © 1995, The Pennsylvania Academy of Science.

Chapter Forty-Two

HEALTH CARE SYSTEM IN ISRAEL: An Historical Perspective

SHIFRA SHVARTS, Ph.D.
Faculty for Health Sciences
Ben Gurion University, Beer Sheva
84105, Israel

INTRODUCTION

As in many western countries, the issue of the health care system in Israel has never left the public agenda. In recent years, the system was characterized by the decline in government funding of health care, which was followed by substantial labor unrest, consumer dissatisfaction and substantial growth in private health care and small sick funds (health organizations, providing comprehensive health insurance and medical care). Political change in Israel has brought up the question of who should be the provider of health services for the people and what should be the future character of the Israel health care system.

For almost 80 years, long before the establishment of the state of Israel in 1948 (1), the Israeli health care insurance system, which today covers the vast majority of the 5 million people of the country, is dominated by a single major health insurance and medical care organization, the Kupat Holim Klalit (the General Workers' Sick Fund) (2). Kupat Holim is part of Israel's Labor Federation—the Histadrut Union. Kupat Holim's special role in Israel's health care system is a result of both its size, its strong mutual aid orientation and its extensive political affiliation with the Labor Federation and Labor Party, the dominant powers in Israeli

"The Convention confirms the vital need of a joint sick-fund for the workers of Erets [land s.s.] *Israel and abroad, to deal with matters concerning all of them. The fund should be financed by the members' savings on the basis of mutual guarantee and help" (7).*

This decision can be regarded as the milestone in the foundation of the workers' sick fund in Israel, later known as Kupat Holim, by which today, 83 years after that convention, more than 75% of Israel's five million people are insured (8).

In the years 1912-1918, three similar district workers' sick funds were established by regional workers' organizations: the "Judea Workers' Sick Fund", the "Samaria Workers' Sick Fund", and the "Galilee Workers' Sick Fund". These were named after the three regions in the country in which most of the workers were concentrated. Sick rooms run by nurses were soon opened in almost every village. Hospitalization services were provided by the "Shaar Zion Community Hospital" in Jaffa (9), according to an agreement of the workers' sick funds with the Hebrew Medical Association, founded in 1912. In 1920, after the British occupation of Israel and the end of World War I, the three regional workers' organizations were merged into the General Labor Federation (the Histadrut Union). The regional workers' sick-funds were integrated and functioned within the framework of the Labor Federation as one body, named the General Sick-Fund - Kupat Holim (3, 6).

The Early Days of Kupat Holim

Unlike all workers' sick-funds in other countries, which were established in the aftermath of the Industrial Revolution with urban worker concentrations, the Workers' Sick-Fund in Israel was founded in the village. The village has continued to be the model for medical work of Kupat Holim. That model is based on small clinics in agricultural settlements and workers' districts, enabling every patient to obtain medical care close to his residence and to establish personal ties with its physician.

In parallel with the establishment of workers' sick funds, the Hadassah Medical Organization, a branch of Hadassah Womens' Zionist Organization of America, in 1918, stepped in to assist the Jewish community in Israel (10). Hadassah's idea was to set up a new system of health care services, based on American standards. Administered from abroad, Hadassah engaged in sanitary and anti-malaria work, opened six hospitals in the main cities as well as outpatient clinics. Hadassah focused its work primarily on children, from birth through adolescence, and school health programs. These programs led later to the establishment of a country wide network of maternal and child health care centers, a public service free to all, which functioned successfully until today (11). In 1921, according to an agreement between the Hadassah Medical Organization and Kupat Holim, Hadassah financed the costs of medicines and buildings for Kupat Holim, while the latter was responsible for the practical provision of services.

During the years 1922-1930, years of extensive agricultural settlement in Israel and the erection of many workers' settlements around the larger towns, the clinic network of the Kupat Holim has expanded. Membership increased to 20% of the Jewish population of 165,000 people, and 85% of the worker settlement population (12). In spite of this great expansion, the financial situation of Kupat Holim did not improve, and even worsened, as a result of the economic crisis of the Jewish community in Israel during the twenties. From its inception, Kupat Holim suffered severe financial deficits. The membership fees covered no more than 60% of the expenditure. An employers' health levy did not exist and only few employers agreed to partake in the costs of health services for their employees. In 1925-1927, the crisis of the fourth wave of immigration to Israel aggravated the situation of Kupat Holim, bringing it close to bankruptcy. In 1926, the World Zionist Organization came to the aid of Kupat Holim by appointing an inquiry commission "to examine the condition of Kupat Holim" (13). The commission mandate was to check the functioning and the organization of Kupat Holim and the entire community health care system, in order to improve its financial situation and efficiency. The findings of the commission showed a great measure of wasteful administration, and a large portion of centralization in Kupat Holim, that prevented the introduction of local efficiency and adjustment to local needs.

That inquiry commission was the first in a long series of commissions, established during the next 68 years, to examine the functioning and organization of the health care system in Israel. The questions put before the commission, its fundings and recommendations continue to follow the health care system throughout those years. In the wake of the 1926 commission, two parallel inquiry commissions were appointed in 1927, the aim of which was to recommend a reorganization program for the entire health care system of the Jewish populations in Israel. The recommendation of both commissions was to establish a National Health Authority for health services, funding and policy determination and supervision. It was recommended that this authority should be granted to Hadassah or to the Jewish Community Health Committee. Kupat Holim, according to the recommendation, should be financed and supervised by that authority. In 1929, the combination of civil disorder among the Arabs population of Israel and the world economic crisis which affected the Hadassah Medical Organizations, resulted in termination of the reorganization program, leaving both Kupat Holim and Hadassah to function as two independent entities.

The Hadassah - Kupat Holim agreement, which functioned well in the early twenties, met many difficulties towards the end of the decade. Repeated changes in Hadassah directors, financial crises, interference of the Hadassah management with the work of Kupat Holim, and medical-ideological disagreement regarding the administration of medical needs in the workers' settlements caused a break between the two organizations. Eventually, Kupat Holim decided not to depend anymore on the hospitalization services of Hadassah, and established its own hospitalization system.

The first Kupat Holim hospital, "The Emek Hospital" [The Valley Hospital] (14), was opened in 1930 and functioned very successfully, providing hospitalization services to Kupat Holim members. The success of the hospital and Kupat Holim's ability to tackle the tasks of building and operating of the institution, created a turning-point in Kupat Holim policy. Until that time it had focused on primary medicine, but now it had expanded its activities to include hospitalization services, central urban clinics and an independent supply of medicines. Kupat Holim choose to step forward towards the creation of an independent medical system.

Development of the Sick Funds and the Membership Issue

During the 30s, the Jewish population in Israel grew to 500,000 and contained many workers living in the cities. With the arrival of hundreds of immigrant physicians from Germany, Kupat Holim activities expanded significantly (15). The "Beilinson" Hospital with a nursing school was built near Tel Aviv; an "Investment Fund" of Kupat Holim was founded for financing the planning and building of new institutions, and scores of neighborhood-clinics were built in the large towns.

The membership question was one of the most difficult issues Kupat Holim had to overcome. At the beginning, the Histadrut-Union did not force its members to join Kupat Holim. This created a situation, in which a significant number of Union members were not members of Kupat Holim. To change this situation, Kupat Holim reapeatedly appealed to the Labor Federation Council (which functioned also as the board of directors of the Union) to force mutual membership. By that, Kupat Holim hoped to increase the numbers of its members mainly from the ranks of the Histadrut-Union in order to improve its financial situation. In 1927, the Labor Federation convention decided to accept the Kupat Holim appeal and to force mutual membership in the Union with membership in Kupat Holim. The practical meaning of this decision was that membership in Kupat Holim depended on Union membership and vice versa. Compulsory membership in the Union with Kupat Holim, increased Kupat Holim membership to over 30% of the Jewish community in Israel. From that moment, Kupat Holim became the central insurance fund in the health services of Israel (3). The political and social developments which occurred in Israel in those years also influenced Kupat Holim. Hadassah Medical Organization founded the "Amamit Sick Fund" [Popular sick fund] as an alternative for workers who did not want to become members of the Kupat Holim. The social ostracism of the Revisionist movement (a right of center, activist-oriented, founded by Zeev Jabotinsky in 1925) in Israel in 1933 (16), caused many physicians and members of the Revisionist party to leave Kupat Holim. It brought about the founding of the "National Workers' Sick Fund".

The great number of immigrant German-Jewish physicians brough about the development of several primary medical institutions and the founding of additional independent sick-funds such as "Maccabi Sick Fund", the "Assaf Sick Fund", the "Physicians' Treasury Sick Fund", etc. These organizations constituted a competition for the Kupat Holim, drawing a significant number of upper middle class members and diminishing the alternative income sources of Kupat Holim. On the other hand, the large number of immigrant Jewish physicians from Germany, who remained in Kupat Holim, improved its health care services. The integration of the

German Jewish physicians, coming from mid-European medical schools, into a centralized-socialist institution such as the Kupat Holim, posed severe ideological dilemmas regarding the character of the medical service Kupat Holim, wished to grant its members and the position of the physicians in its ranks. These dilemmas emerged at the end of World War II and during the beginning of the struggle towards the birth of the state of Israel in 1948 (15, 17).

HEALTH CARE SERVICES IN THE EARLY YEARS OF THE STATE (1948-1953)

In May 1948, the state of Israel was established. Government ministries were organized and a Health Ministry took over the Mandatory Government Department of Health. Soon after, regional health bureaus and an epidemiological service were formed. The state extended its responsibility for the health services through a partial national health service invested particularly in hospital construction and operation, in preventive services to mothers and children (18) and in operating hospitals which belonged to the Mandatory Government. At the same time, a Military Medical Service was formed to operate military hospitals, serving the Israeli Defense Forces during the War of Independence.

At the time of establishment of the state, David Ben Gurion, Israel's "founder" and first prime minister, asked Moshe Soroka, head administrator of Kupat Holim for many years and the leading authority in health administration in pre-state years, to take upon himself the management of the Israeli Military Medical Service (19). Ben Gurion's assumption was that when the war was over, Soroka and Kupat Holim would lead and be head of the National Health Service. The appeal to Kupat Holim was only natural, since Ben Gurion, from his first days as secretary of the Labor Federation, attributed great value to the political and organizational potential of the Kupat Holim. Undoubtedly he wished to secure that source of influence within the Labor Movement. On the other hand, Ben Gurion wanted to impose the principle of nationalization throughout the health services as was later to be done in the field of education. However, that was possible only with the consent of Kupat Holim and through the appointment of a leading Kupat Holim personality to head the national health care services. Soroka and Kupat Holim turned down Ben Gurion's proposition. This act put off Ben Gurion's idea to nationalize medial services, placing Kupat Holim apart from the political administration, which was just being formed, and raised a bitter dispute over the future nature of the medical services in Israel (17).

The Military Medical Service developed rapidly and established sixteen military hospitals, mainly in previous British medical facilities, in existing buildings, barracks, military camps, etc., serving both soldiers and civilians. All professional positions were occupied by enlisted Kupat Holim doctors and volunteers from abroad. The combination of serving wounded soldiers and civilian patients would become a unique source of administrational and political power, turning the hospitals into first rate institutions. The military hospitals attracted many Kupat Holim physicians, thus making it obvious that this medical service was a serious rival, about to deprive Kupat Holim of its monopoly.

In October 1948, the government decided to share in the cost of hospital beds for both at Kupat Holim as well as military hospitals by 200 Israeli pounds per bed (about $50). This effectively increased the Kupat Holim budget by 20% and encouraged a significant increase in the numbers of beds (17). Kupat Holim perceived this as an opportunity to win the struggle with the Military Medical Service. Kupat Holim believed that the growing number of beds would prevent physicians from leaving and at the same time make the Kupat Holim so large and complex an organization that it would be impossible to nationalize. In 1949, Kupat Holim enlarged its hospitals by adding more beds and new buildings and expanded its network of clinics.

At the end of 1948, only 53% of the 650,000 Jewish community population were insured, most of these (about 80%) were insured through Kupat Holim and the rest through other sick funds. During the next two years of statehood, the population of the state doubled to 1.2 million people, mainly by a flow of immigrants from Europe and from Arab countries, and within ten years, the population reached 2.1 million people. The percentage of insured people increased dramatically during those years and reached the level of about 90% (16, 18).

The role of Kupat Holim in insuring the new immigrants was dominant. Provision of health care services to the new immigrants became yet another issue in the continuous struggle between the Kupat Holim and the State health services. Both sides knew the benefits which could be establishing in handling the new immigrants, large budgets as well as options for expansion. Kupat Holim and the Jewish Agency, which was responsible for the immigrants' reception and initial settlements, reached an agreement which stated that the new immigrants would be granted automatic health insurance through Kupat Holim immediately upon arrival and at reduced rates. The agreement encouraged most of the new immigrants to join the Labor Federation in order to get Kupat Holim services, the growth of which surpassed, by far, the growth of the population in general. Both the Ministry of Health and Kupat Holim expanded their medical facilities in order to cope with the increasing demand for health services. The number of hospitals in the state had been increased from ten to twenty and many primary care clinics were opened in the new areas.

In 1950, Dr. H. Sheba, leading authority in the Military Medical Service who was both a physician and a socialist, was appointed as the Director General of Israel's Ministry of Health (16, 17). Dr. Sheba, with full support of Ben Gurion, was in favor of nationalizing of the health services whereas Kupat Holim, headed by Soroka, raised strong opposition, knowing that it meant weakening the organization. Ben Gurion's support of Dr. Sheba was important, but he had to back down because his opponents were his labor party colleagues. These colleagues, heads of the Labor Federation, fought to preserve the Kupat Holim hegemony in order to secure and establish the position of the Labor Federation in the formative stage of the state of Israel. Against this background, nationalization of health services was put off again. The Ministry of Health had been deprived of its strength, which thus made it an easy target for coalition manipulations (16, 17).

For reasons of financial and management efficiency, it was decided in 1953 to transfer all military hospital facilities to the Ministry of Health which has become the major provider of hospitalization services. This transfer was actually the final stage in shaping the general health system in Israel. From then on, both the Ministry of Health and Kupat Holim concentrated mainly on preserving their status while continuing the ideological struggle over the future image of the health system.

The rivalry between Kupat Holim and the Ministry of Health has continued since then. Considering its origins, even prior to the State, Kupat Holim acted to continue its former dominant role in the health services. With financial support from abroad Kupat Holim acted in order to expand its services rapidly, by building more hospitals and community clinics, using its traditional priority status over the Ministry of Health. The Kupat Holim's fast growth created a large gap between its facilities and those of the government. Other sick funds were trying to follow and compete with Kupat Holim by opening more clinics. In order to finance their growth, the sick funds demanded an increase in government financial support. The conflict between sick funds that expected no government involvement in decision making on one hand and the demand for increasing government financial support on the other hand, created a system that lacked incentives for increasing efficiency and not taking into account costs of services. It led to one of the basic problems that the Israel health care system is facing today.

THE ISRAELI HEALTH CARE SYSTEM - ACHIEVEMENTS, PROBLEMS AND PROSPECTIVE

Characteristics of the Present Israeli Health Care System

At present, Israel has a population of about 5,000,000 people, 83% Jews and 17% non-Jews, most of them Arabs. The major part of the population lives in urban areas and the country is considered one of the middle-income countries. About 8% of Israel's GNP is allocated to health, similar to that allocated by western European countries. In 1988, the average life expectancy was relatively high: 77.0 for females and 73.6 for males (19).

Israel's health care system is characterized by its high rate of health insurance among the population (Jews and Arabs). Even though health insurance is not mandatory in Israel, 96% of the population is insured, meaning that in general, the Israeli population is well protected by health care coverage (19). The high rate of health insurance of the total population was kept high mainly because payments to sick funds depended on income and family status, and services were distributed on the basis of need and not on the ability to pay. In addition, in 1973, the Israeli government passed a health insurance bill. According to the bill, every employer is mandated to pay a health tax in order to cover part of his employees health insurance premiums, this covered about 30% of the national expenditure for health (19). The employers health tax is another means to maintain the high rate of health insurance among workers of all kinds. From the sociological point of view, the employers' health tax together with the sick funds' payment regulation gives most of the people in Israel a sense of quality, equity and social security. In general, these principals were based on the old Jewish tradition of mutual aid and a sense of community and the social nature of the society.

The sick funds are the major providers of health care and medical services in Israel. Today, four major sick funds are in operation (18): 1. Kupat Holim—the General Workers' Sick Fund - 3.7 million members, 75% of the population (Jews and Arabs); 2. Maccabee Sick Fund—700,000 members, 14% of the population; 3. National Sick Fund—200,000 members, 4% of the population; 4. United Sick Fund—150,000 members, 3% of the population.

The Ministry of Health, the principle public health agency in the state, is functioning as the supreme body for licensing the medical and paramedical profession, as well as for implementing all health related legislation passed by the Israeli parliament. Since the 50's, preventive medicine and primary care has improved and expanded markedly, both among the Jewish and the Arab communities.

Over twenty general hospitals are presently operated in Israel containing about 13,000 beds. The Ministry of Health operates nine general hospitals which contain 40% of the public beds in Israel, while Kupat Holim operates eight general hospitals, with 20% of the public beds, and the Hadassah Medical Organization operates two general hospitals with 3% of the public beds. The system also includes 16,000 geriatric and psychiatric hospital beds. Most of the geriatric and psychiatric hospitals are operated by the Ministry of Health and are private entities. The State's ratio of total hospital beds to population is about 6.5 beds per 1000 people, one of the lowest among western countries (20).

There are about 15,000 physicians in Israel (20), most of which are salaried public workers. The ratio of physicians' to the population is more than 1 to 350, one of the highest in the world. This relatively high number of physicians together with the strong primary care services is one of the reasons for the low hospitalization rate in the country.

The Ministry of Health operates a successful community health service: 850 maternity and child health care centers, a nation wide public network, free to all, with high accessibility and availability to most of the community. It provides health education programs and current services to mothers and children, including an immunization program for babies from their first days until the age of five. About 460 centers are operated directly by the Ministry of Health, the others are operated by Kupat Holim, the National Sick Fund and the municipalities. The rate of immunization among babies and children is about 85% of the total population, higher than in western Europe. The nation's immunization program maintains the low rate of infant mortality at about 7.5 per 1,000 live births for Jews and an average of 10.7 for the total population. Side by side with the maternity and child health care centers, the system operates over 2000 community oriented primary care clinics all over the country, most of them (about 1300 clinics) operated by Kupat Holim (21). The nation wide distribution of primary care clinics and maternity and child health care centers came into being mainly to over come the variations in health conditions among new immigrants and established citizens, to fill in economical gaps and to give the people equal access to health care services.

As for medical education in Israel, there are four medical schools which are affiliated with the major universities in the country. The Hebrew University Medical School associated with Hadassah; the Tel Aviv University Medical School; the Technion Medical School in Haifa and the Ben Gurion University Medical School associated with Kupat Holim. The Ben Gurion Medical School runs a special program of community oriented medical education with an emphasis on family physician specialization (22).

The Major Problems of Israel's Health Care System – The Netanyahu Commission Findings

As described above, Israel has built a substantial and comprehensive health care system during its 45 years. This system provides voluntary health insurance for almost all of the population, based on mutual aid and social justice, with no connection between a patients' needs and ability to pay. The system is responsible for its expenses and is keeping a reasonable position among the western countries in the percentage of the GNP which is allocated to health. The system is built in a community oriented fashion and provides to consumers good accessibility (23). However, this system suffers today from a series of severe problems that heavily influence and weaken its ability to function as a national health care system, resulting in a substantial crisis in the last decade.

Growing consumer expectations during a period of rising standard of living as well as an increased consumer awareness of modern western health care services has increased public dissatisfaction with the present health care services. Examples include lack of sensitivity to the privacy of the patient and freedom of choice in selecting physicians, issues which were not adequately addressed by the public health care system. A major complaint of the population has focused on the heavy bureaucratization of health care.

The last decade has been characterized by prolonged labor unrest in the Israeli health care system, with a low level of employee satisfaction and motivation among the medical profession, who felt that they are underpaid by the public system. Financial and moral decline on the part of the physicians was accompanied by growth of under-the-table medicine. This all caused a lack of incentives for increasing efficiency (23).

In addition, there is some indication of decline in the quality of health care services as compared to western societies, with increasing consumer dissatisfaction. Among the indicators are: a slower improvment in life expectancy of women compared to Europe; a lag in improvement in combating infant mortality; a relatively high rate of mortality from ischemic heart diseases; and the fact that incidence of certain infective diseases is still high even though the percentage of children receiving immunization is relatively high. There is also a feeling of a decline in the technological advances of the Israeli health care system, mainly related to budget constriction (23).

These problems, of service and costs, have accompanied the health care system in Israel since the establishment of Kupat Holim, long before the state was even established. During all of those years, more than eleven inquiry commissions have been established in order to evaluate these problems and to recommend solutions (13). The last and most influential commission was the Natanyahu Inquiry Commission, established by the Israeli government in June 1988 with the mandate to "Inquire into the Functioning and Efficiency of the Health Care System" (18, 21). The Commision mandate was to analyze the Israeli health care system and to recommend changes needed to be taken in order to improve it. The Commission was headed by the Honorable Justice Shoshana Natanyahu and included leading professional authorities in the Israeli health care system including Prof. M. Shani, then the Director General of Sheba Medical Center near Tel Aviv, and presently the Director General of Israel Ministry of Health and Prof. S. Pinchas, Director General of Hadassah Medical Center, in Jerusalem.

The commission identified that the major cause of problems for the health care system was the fragmentation and the unclear division of decision making power between the Ministry of Health, the Ministry of Finance and Kupat Holim. The Ministry of Finance, which determines the health care budget, tried over the years to reduce costs and to control wage policy without professional analysis of the actual needs of the system. Kupat Holim, which is the nation's larger provider of services, wanted to ensure its hegemony in the health care system (16, 23). This fragmentation has hindered the Ministry of Health's ability to define and implement a clear and consistent national health policy. In addition, the fact that the Ministry of Health is engaged in the operation of a large portion of the public hospitals, serving as both the provider and regulator, creates a source of conflict of interest. The political weakness of the Ministry of Health, usually controlled by small political partners fo the Labor Party on the one hand and the dominant role of Kupat Holim and the Labor Federation in policy decisions and budget sharing on the other hand, ensures that key policy decisions can be influenced by political and other nonprofessional considerations. Due to the lack of overall coherent policy, important topics, such as preventive medicine and health education, manpower planning, technology improvement, etc. have not been given the proper priority (23).

As for the financing and budgeting procedures of the health care system, the commission pointed out that the budget of the Ministry of Health is determined by the Ministry of Finance without considering the actual and real growth needs of the system in light of population growth, population aging and technological advances. The budget is developed, more as a consequence of bargaining between the Ministry of Finance and the Ministry of Health than from relevant reasoning. Against the request of the Ministry of Finance to restrict expenditures and to keep national expenses for health services on a constant level, there are increasingly expensive costs, resulting from both new technologies and expectations of the population to improve health care services (24).

The commission pointed out that since the division of responsibility in the provision of services between the government and the insurers (the sick funds) has not been spelled out in legislation, the health care system in Israel is characterized by ad hoc financial help and subsidies given without definite criteria, many times after the deficit has already been accumulated. The fact that cost of services is not considered as a high priority element in the providers' considerations and was not rewarded, led to lack of incentives for increasing efficiency in the system and to the creation of substantial queues which exist while expensive equipment lies idle (23, 24).

The Natanyahu Commission Recommendations - The Debate and the Future of the Health Care System

In 1990, the Natanyahu Commission presented its recommendations to the public. The report was highly regarded and was adopted both by the previous Minister of Health, E. Olmart, from the Likud Party (right), and the present Minister of Health, H. Ramon, from the Labor Party, as the future health care system of Israel. Since then, these recommendations have been the focus of the public debate, the result of which will determine the future nature of the Israeli health care system.

The commission's recommendations were guided by three principle criteria, widely accepted by the Israeli public, reflecting a social consensus across the country:

a. The basic value of social justice and mutual aid in the Jewish tradition ("All Israel are guarantors of one another", Mishna, Shavuot, 39:1) and in the state of Israel;
b. Modern values of a western society such as benefits versus costs (to the individual and society), effectiveness, quality and freedom of choice;
c. Pragmatic considerations of the impact that those changes will have on the individual and society from the point of view of economical ability, social acceptance and the participation of professionals in the process of implementing the recommendations (18).

The central and most revolutionary recommendation of the Commission was the essential need to pass a National Health Insurance Law. The proposed law would supply universal health insurance coverage by the sick funds, ensure freedom of choice among sick funds, define a minimum benefits package, define how the health system would be financed and provide a legal basis for government regulation of the insurers.

In addition to the currently guaranteed packages by the sick funds, the proposed benefit package would include institutional long term care, psychiatric care, additional preventive services, treatments abroad which could not have been carried out in Israel and dental services.

As for the Ministry of Health, the Commission defined a need for its organization. The role of the Ministry as a provider of hospitalization services should be ceased and health care services would only be supplied by not-for-profit sick funds. The Ministry would focus on planning and policy making, quality assurance and health system financing. A separate National Health Authority would be set up in order to control the regulation of the health services provision system.

The public health care system would be financed primarily by payroll taxes on employers and employees, to be collected by the National Insurance Institute, with supplementary funding from government general revenues and other sources. The sick funds would cease to set premium rates and would no longer collect premiums directly from their members.

The Commission recommended, that in order to improve efficiency and competition between providers, services provision should be decentralized, on a regional basis (including both sick funds and hospitals), under the supervision of a regional branch office of the National Health Authority. All hospitals should be run as self financed, non-profit entities. Consumers would have complete freedom of choice among sick funds. Sick funds would be not-for-profit entities and hospitals would compete to sign hospitalization contracts with sick funds within their region.

While many observers have expressed support for the Commission's general finding and recommendations, and while some concrete steps have already been taken toward their implementation, some key recommendations were bitterly criticized. A major criticism related to the social values upon which the Commissions recommendations are based. The forced separation of Kupat Holim and the Labor Federation was noted as an interference with the people's rights to organize as they wish and with the right of voluntary organizations to organize internally as they chose. Furthermore, future expansion of private services in public hospitals will enlarge social gaps and increase inequity in health services, especially in peripheral regions.

Critisizm regarding the organizational and the financial part of the recommendations noted that taking away the insurance function from the sick funds would make them mere governmental executors. It would eliminate healthy economical competition on price as well as on quality among sick funds. A future increase of government involvment in health care finance and organization, through the National Health Authority, would lead to a substantial increase in administrative costs and decreased efficiency in the long run. The regionalization recommendation was criticized as inappropriate for a small country like Israel as it will create duplication of services and eliminates economies of scale as well as its future effect on the quality of services in peripheral regions.

Almost all reviewers noted and emphasized that the problems of financial contribution and obligation of the government and the Ministry of Health were not solved. The Commission did not address a financial procedure that will guarantee minimal government investments in health care services. As in many other areas, if all financing will be administered by the government, it could give the Treasury the possibility to manage and manipulate the health budget not for health necessities, increasing once more the politicization of the system.

However, the core of the public debate over the proposed health insurance law is its future impact in the Israeli political arena. The central political question that arises is "who will dominate the health care system". Acceptance of the National Health Insurance Law would significantly increase government involvement and control over the system. At the same time, it would reduce the dominance of Kupat Holim in health services and through it, the hegemony of the Labor Federation in the Israeli political, economical and social arenas. Furthermore, the acceptance of the law would reduce the affiliation of Kupat Holim and the Labor Federation, which has been maintained for many years by the mandatory joint membership between the two organizations and by the direct collection of membership fee by the Union. This separation of Kuapt Holim from the Labor Federation would strip it of a large portion of its political power and financial base. It would weaken the social and political ideology of mutual aid and provision of services on the basis of needs and not on the basis of ability to pay, an ideology that has shaped Israeli society and its health care services from its beginning.

EPILOGUE

The Natanyahu Commission report was presented to the public in August 1990, raising sharp public criticism and political dispute. In February 1993, after three years of delay, the Israeli government confirmed the initiative of the Minister of Health, Chaim Ramon, for the enactment of a National Health Insurance Law. This initiative is currently being considered by the Israeli Parliament and is a source of bitter political dispute within the Parliament and the Labor Movement which is in control of the government (25). In February 1994, the Israeli government, effected by the political dispute over the proposed law, decided to delay again and for unlimited time, the enactment of health insurance law (26).

Will the political powers in the Israeli Parliament bridge the political and ideological gap and pass a Health Insurance Law in the future? Can the Israeli health care system be changed by legislation? What will be the future of the Israeli health care system? In a political system such as the Israeli multi party regime, with many balances of power, a drastic change of the system through a legal process is hard to achieve.

System's changes can be brought about only by focusing on a small number of changes over long period of time. For a over-centralized and over politicized system, such as the Israeli health care system, which has functioned in this manner for so many years, the chances to achieve a dramatic change are small. It is more likely that the current fee and competitive economy, supplemented by internal changes within the framework of the Labor Federation, has a better chance by legislation to achieve changes in the Israeli health care system. From a historical point of view, reviewing prior inquiry commissions and failed reforms in Israeli society in general and in the health care system in particular, it is most likely that the issue of the health care system and the debate over political aspects of the health insurance law, will continue to remain on the Israeli public agenda in years to come.

ACKNOWLEDGEMENT

The author acknowledges Prof. S. Kottek (the Hebrew University); Prof. Z. Tzahor, Dr. Zwanger, Prof. S. Glick, Prof. S. Moses, Prof. H. Doron and Prof. D. Chernichovsky (Ben Gurion University in the Negev), for their encouragement and guidance during her research on the History of the Israeli Health Care Services. Special thanks to Mrs. E. Aridor, the health policy correspondent of "Haaretz", who kept me informed of the political developments surrounding the National Health Insurance Law in the last few months, while I was abroad. Prof. T. Brown, Dr. D. Mukamel and Dr. J. Zwanziger (the Department of Community and Preventive Medicine), and Dr. S. Skupsky, University of Rochester, New York, were kindly enough to read and comment on the manuscript.

During the course of writing this review, I made use of many of the publications of the Health Policy Research Unit of the JDC-Brookdale Institute, headed by Dr. Bruce Rosen. Of special importance to me, during the course of writing the present review, was their English Language Overview of the Natanyahu Commission Report issued as an internal report. This report as well as many valuable discusstions with Dr. Bruce Rosen and his colleagues during the last five years were mostly regarded.

NOTES AND BIBLIOGRAPHY

1. The geographical region of the present State of Israel (including the occupied territories of Gaza and the West Bank) has been called in the past 100 years with several names: *Jerusalem Region* during the Ottoman period until 1918; *Palestine* during the British Mandate years 1917-1948. For simplicity, the common name *Israel* is used throughout the review; both for the pre-state and the state periods.
2. The name Kupat Holim means in Hebrew Sick Fund. The origin of this name is the German "*Fabrikkrankenkassen*", the 19-century workers' sick funds, established in Germany (1884) by Chancellor Otto von Bismark as part of the German Social Insurance. H. Shryock, *The Development of Modern Medicine,* the University of Wisconsin Press, 1979.
3. Shvarts, S. 1989. "The Development of Health and Medical Services in Israel 1838-1948", *The Netanyahu Commission Report, National Inquiry into the Financing and Efficiency of the Health Care System,* Jerusalem, May (internal report).
4. Since the percentage of Arabs in Israel is less than 20% of the population, I have mainly concentrated on the evolution of the health services among the Jewish community. The description of the present situation of the health care system in Israel, which will be discussed in the last section of this review is also relevant to the Arab population as part of the Israeli community. In general the Arab population of Israel is served by the same health care system and is subjected to its achievements and problems as any citizen of the state. N. Reiss, *The Health Care of the Arabs in Israel,* Westview Special Studies on the Middle East, Westview Press, Boulder, San Francisco, Oxford, 1991. As a less developed community within Israel, there are some specific problems of that community which will not be discussed in the present review. Also not described and discussed in the present review is the health care system of the Arab population in the occupied territories.
5. Shvarts, S. 1988. "Religion, Community and Politics in the Establishment of the First Jewish Hospitals in Jerusalem During the 19th Century", *Koroth,* (9)7-8.

6. Tzahor, Z. 1987. *Israel's Political Roots,* Hakibbutz Hameuchad, Tel Aviv.
7. Labor Archives-Lavon Institute, section VI-122-18, minute of assembly; Z. Tazahor, *On the Road to Yishuv Leadership, The Fomrative Years of Histadrut,* Yad Ishak Ben Zvi Publication, Jerusalem 1981.
8. *The Health of the People is the Wealth of Society.* 1992. Kupat Holim, Health Insurance Institution of Israel, Archdut Press, Tel Aviv.
9. Shvarts, S. 1989. "Shaar Zion Hospital - The First Community Hospital in Palestine", *Koroth,* (9)9-10.
10. Levin. 1973. *Balm in Gilead,* Schocken Books, New York. American Association for Labor Legislation Archive, Cornell University, Dr. Issac M. Rubinow's Files.
11. Palti, H. et al. 1990. "Process and Outcome Evaluation of Preventive Care for Infants in Two Types of Practices", Department of Social Medicine, Hadassah School of Public Health, Hebrew University, Jerusalem, in - *The Netanyahu Commission Report, National Inquiry into the Functioning and Efficiency of the Health Care System,* Jerusalem. I.
12. Giladi, D. 1973. *Jewish Palestine During the Fourth Aliya Period (1924-1929),* Am Oved, Tel Aviv.
13. Shvarts, S. 1994. "By Needs or by Capability, 67 Years to the First Commission of Inquiry on the Subject of Kupath Holim", *Harefua* (Medicine), March.
14. Nadav, D. 1992. *The Emek [Valley] Hospital Durith The 20s.* Yad Tabenkin, Israel.
15. Niderland, D. 1984. "The Influence of Doctors From German Origin on the Development of Medicine in Israel in the Years 1933-1948", *Cathedra,* 30: 11-161.
16. Halevi, H.S. 1979. "The Pluralistic Organization of the Israeli Health Care System", *Betachon Sociali,* 17(3):5-49,; A. Doron "Medical Services in Israel - a Different Perspective", *Bitachon Sociali* (Social Security), 17(3):51.
17. Zertal, E. *Days and Deeds,* Machbarot L'esifrut Publication House, Tel Aviv 1975; R. Bondi, *Sheba-Every Man's Physician,* Zmora, Bitan, Modan-Publishers, Tel Aviv, 1981; Y. Zalmonovitch, *Histadruth, Kupath Holim, Government,* Haifa University, 1981.
18. 62; 1990. *The Netanyahu Commission Report, National Inquiry into the Functioning and Efficiency of the Health Care System,* Jerusalem, I, II.
19. Metz, H.C. (ed.). *Israel, a Country Study,* Federal Research Division Library of Congress, Area Handbook for Israel, Washington, 1990; I. Beiran, L. Ore, L. Epstein, "Mortality Trends Among Jewish and Non-Jewish men in Israel. Israel Journal on Medical Sciences", 1991, 27(1):38-42.
20. Statistical Bulletin of Israel, 39 (1988) in The Netanyahu Commission Report, ibid 18.
21. *Kupat Holim, Health Insurance of Israel.* 1993. Achdut Press, Tel Aviv; The Netanyahu Commission Report, ibid 20, I, pp. 38;187;196;397;427.
22. Glick, S., L. Naggan, M. Prywes. 1987. "The Beer Sheva Experiment", *Israel Journal of Medicine,* Jerusalem.

23. Rosen, B. (ed.). *The Netanyahu Commission Report: Background, Contents and Initial Reactions.* An English language overview prepared by the Health Policy Research Unit of the JDC-Brookdale Institute, Jerusalem 1992; G. Ginsberg, A. Israeli, S. Penchas, "Israel's Expenditure on Health Services", *Israel Journal on Medical Sciences,* 1990, 26(11):625-9; Z. Rotstein, M. Shani, "Do We Really Spend Enough on Health Services in Israel?" *Israel Journal on Medical Sciences,* 1990, 26(11):630-2.
24. Cohen, M.A. and T. Barnea. 1992. "Private Outlets for Public Limitations: The Rise of Commercial Health Insurance in Israel", *Journal of Health Politics, Policy & Law.* 17(4):783-811.
25. *Letter to the Members.* H. Haberfeld, General Secretary of the Labor Federation, 13 Dec. 1993; *Haaretz, daily newspaper (Israel), 17 Dec. 1993, p. 4; Memorandum to the Public,* The State of Israel, Office of the Minister of Health, Jan. 4, 1994; *Haaretz,* 7 Jan. 1994, p. 12; *Yedeot Hacharonot,* daily newspaper (Israel), 6 Jan. 1994, p. 8.
26. *Yedeot Hacharonot,* 5 February 1994, p. 3; *Haaretz,* 5 February 1994, p. 4 (editorial).

Medicine and Health Care Into the Twenty-First Century. Edited by S.K. Majumdar, L.M. Rosenfeld, D.B. Nash and A.M. Audet. © 1995, The Pennsylvania Academy of Science.

Chapter Forty-Three

SOUTH AFRICAN HEALTH CARE - A SYSTEM IN TRANSITION

BRUCE L.W. SPARKS, M.D.
Chairman
Department of Family Medicine
Medical School
University of the Witwatersrand
York Road, Parktown 2193
Johannesburg, South Africa

SUMMARY

The South African health care system has been characterized by inequities and discrimination shaped by, among other factors, the policy of apartheid and its social and economic implications. In this chapter, the author attempts to briefly summarize the development of the South African health care system over the last 50 years and to indicate how, in 1994, the debate has almost completed a full circle, with similar pleas for social justice, equity, and universal free health care for all, which were called for in 1944.

INTRODUCTION

South Africa, a country comprising nearly 40 million people, is a society in transition, a transition from a political system which has excluded the majority of its people from participating in its government and which in its social and economic consequences, has entrenched inequality and discrimination at every level of daily life. The health care system of South Africa, despite notable achievements and excellent academic standards, has reflected the general inequalities of the society

---

This chapter was submitted for publication early in 1994. In April 1994, South Africa's first fully democratic elections were held, and the country now has an interim Government of National Unity, led predominantly by the African National Congress. The 'Homelands' have been reincorporated into a united South Africa. A new health policy is being drafted.

which produced it. Many health professionals, hope that 1994, the year in which a new and representative government will come into power, will also mark the transition to a more equitable, accessible and appropriate health care system for all. South Africa's present health care system is typical of many countries that have a powerful tertiary health care structure, supported by very competent academically-linked specialist services, and where very little of the health care budget is spent on primary and preventative services. This is compounded by the presence of a well-developed private health care system catering mainly to the needs of the more affluent white population.

Until recently, all South Africans were classified in terms of the Population Registration Act as either African, coloured (mixed race), Asian or white. While this classification is totally abhorrent, it should be realized that in South Africa, *'this classification has certain objective consequences. Where people may live, the kind of education they are likely to receive, the jobs that are open to them, the public health facilities they will use and the kind of political representation they are permitted, are all substantially affected by the racial category to which they are assigned. These in turn all have important consequences on health* (1). Therefore, despite their offensive connotations, these terms will be used in this chapter for the puposes of discussion. The term 'black' is a generic term which includes African, Indians, and Coloureds, as opposed to those who are 'white'.

BACKGROUND TO THE PRESENT SITUATION

The origins of racial discrimination and inequality in South Africa may be traced back hundreds of years, through its Dutch and British colonial history. However, the policy of separate development, or apartheid as it was termed, was formalized by the Nationalist Party when it came into power in 1948. They have been in power ever since. Four years earlier, the report of the National Health Services Commission (the Gluckman Report) (2) had been published. The commission was one of several commissions established by the United Party Government in response to the social tensions and problems of the 1930's and 1940's, and was to *'investigate and recommend the best measures to be adopted for ensuring adequate health services for all sectors of the population'* (2). Among the many inadequacies in the health system of the time, it identified that:

- health services were *'disjointed and haphazard, provincial and parochial'*;
- health services were not *'available to all sections of the people'* of the country;
- services were *'mainly directed, not to the promotion and safeguarding of health, but to the cure of ill-health'*;
- medical education was unbalanced and concentrated on complicated clinical and surgical entities and not enough on problems of women and children, and industry-related diseases.

Among other recommendations, the report called for the establishment of a National Health Service with free care provided by a National Health tax; a network of community health centers; a referral chain of hospitals from general practice to tertiary teaching hospitals, with access determined only by the need of each case; and the phasing out of private practice. DeBeer summarizes the gist of the recommendations as a health service that would *'be rationally planned to make the best use of available resources, be decentralized but well coordinated, provide health care of equal quality to all'* (3). Due to the change in government, the recommendations of the Gluckman Report were never implemented. DeBeer continues *'There is no simple way that a society built on division, oppression and exploitation could accommodate a health service premised on unity, equality, and the elevation of the needs of all above the needs of the privileged elite.*

Since the time of Gluckman, there have been repeated calls for a more equitable health care system. Thus, for example, in 1955, the well known Freedom Charter of the African National Congress (ANC) was announced. In relation to health care, it stressed the importance of preventative services and special care for mothers, young children, the aged, orphans, and the mentally ill (4). The principles and objectives of the Charter too, were never implemented and soon thereafter, the ANC was banned and many of its leaders were imprisoned or went into exile.

The 1970's and 1980's saw a never ending spate of critics of the health care system, under the control of the Nationalist government (5, 6, 7, 8, 9). In 1979, Savage, a notable South African sociologist, typified the brunt of these critics, *'(T)he leading characteristic to be mentioned, typifying the social organization of South African medicine, is that it is dominated and controlled by whites and is deeply permeated by the structure of apartheid. Its own professionals are trained in different institutions according to their skin colour and paid differentially. . . Similarly, gross segregation runs throughout the bulk of medical facilities available to the population and thus inevitably many, if not most, of these facilities are not equal either in terms of their physical capacities, physical quality or in terms of the quality of care that they are able to offer. There can be no other country in which the duplication of expensive facilities on an unequal basis on the grounds of colour can be the norm. . . . That a few blacks in some homelands can help decide about the framework of medicine in limited geographic areas merely gives emphasis to the far more important feature of the the general exclusion of blacks in the control and design of the national system of health care'* (10).

Savage's last sentence refers to the duplication of health departments, ministries and services in the 10 ethnically divided territorial administrations for Africans, known as homelands, that were eventually created in South Africa. Four of these have become fully independent states since 1977, while the remaining six have obtained self-governing status. The remaining territory became known as 'white South Africa'.

A further chapter in apartheid's history was the constitutional reform of 1983 that resulted in a tricameral parliament and its own three 'own affairs' departments of health. *'The gist of this reform was that it granted greater political self-determination to the coloured* (mixed race) *and the Indian* (Asian) *population groups, but then, once more, on a racially differentiated basis, in the form of a tricameral government with separate representative councils for whites, coloureds and Indians. Blacks were specifically excluded from this dispensation because their 'political development' had to be realized through the homelands, though provision was now made for the establishment of black local authorities in black communities'* within white areas (11). This meant that South Africa and its 'homelands' were favored with 14 ministers of health! The coordination and rationalization of health services were in shambles! The delivery of health care was made even more complicated by the provisions of the Health Act of 1977, that divided the functions and responsibilities of the health sector down to the point of service delivery, between the Department of Health (State), the Provincial Health Authorities, and the health departments of local authorities. Thus, for example, if parents require immunization for their children, they must consult the local authority clinic, the Provincial clinic would dispense antibiotics for a tonsillitis, and family planning would be attended to by the state clinic. In some instances, all three services are housed within the same building but with totally separate staff and salary structures, facilities and answerability, while in some geographical areas, one or more of these services could be absent (12).

PRESENT HEALTH SYSTEM

Health Indicators

As can be gathered from this brief contextual background, there is marked racial inequity in the health delivery system of South Africa and its 'homeland' states. The impact of SA's racial policy may conveniently be summarized by reviewing selected health indicators. These indices reveal both the current inadequacies of the healthy system and by implication, suggest the challenges facing the new government. While it must be stated that race is an important determinant of health status in SA, it *'is not to deny that there are other important determinants of health status, most notably social class. Indeed, race is probably only a significant factor to the extent that apartheid has ensured that there is a close correlation between race and class* (1).

Health statistics in South Africa are far from adequate, particularly for those of black communities (13, 14). Recent population census figures are considered to be relatively inaccurate and populations of the 'independent' homelands are excluded from the recent census counts. In addition under-reporting affects most morbidity and mortality data (15).

Table 1 shows estimates of the total South African population by population group, for the years 1990 to 2005 (1). These figures were adjusted for under-counting and include populations of all the homelands.

Some 44% of the total population live in the 10 homeland areas (which constitute 14% of the country's total surface area) (16). It is evident from the figures that the 37% expected increase in the population in the next 15 years is mainly accounted for by a 33% increase in the African population. The population pyramid of South Africa is characteristically broad-based, typical of developing countries, who have a high proportion of the people under the age of 15 years. Accurate and reliable employment figures are difficult to obtain, but it is estimated that 18.3% of economically active persons (i.e. working, unemployed and looking for work) are unemployed (16) This has resulted in a marked increase in informal employment activities. Estimates of the number of people living in informal settlements and backyard shacks in 1992 ranged from 3.5 million to 10 million (10-26%) (16).

The impact of the Acquired Immune Deficiency Syndrome (AIDS) epidemic on the population is difficult to predict, but it is expected that the most profound effect of the epidemic will be seen in the 15-49 year age group, as well as in those under 4 years (17). It is also estimated that by the year 2000, there will be about 4.1 million people in South Africa infected with HIV and cumulative deaths would amount to 602,000. By 2005 the epidemic should plateau. It is felt that the population is unlikely to be reduced, but that the growth rate will probably decrease (18).

It should also be noted that there is a recent major demographic shift of the population to urban and peri-urban areas, but with there still being a significant increase in the rural population (19, 20). Resources will have to be reallocated to meet the increasing and specific needs of urban and rural areas.

Morbidity and Mortality

The infant mortality rate (IMR) is an indicator not only of the health status of infants but also of the whole population, their socioeconomic conditions and the utilization, availability, and effectiveness of health care (21). The rates for SA as stated by the Minister of Health in 1992 are indicated in Table 2.

Rural Africans and Coloureds have IMRs at least 2.6 times higher than those in urban areas (1). Postnatal deaths are an important contributor to IMRs in Africans and Coloureds, most deaths being due to gastro-enteritis and respiratory infections (23, 24). By comparison, the IMR for the continent of Africa is 109 and that for Western Europe 8 per 1000 live births.

TABLE 1

South African Population Size by Population Group, 1990-2005 in millions (1)

	1990	1995	2000	2005
African	28.259	32.515	37.260	42.509
Coloured	3.244	3.527	3.782	4.006
Indian	0.978	1.053	1.122	1.178
White	5.052	5.249	5.427	5.590
Total	37.533	42.344	47.591	59.70

TABLE 2

Infant Mortality Rates for South Africa and 'Homelands'/ 1000 live births in 1992 (22).

	Africans	Coloureds	Indians	Whites
SA (Excl. Indep. Homelands)	52.8	28	13.5	7.3
Non-Homeland areas	50			
Non-Independent Homelands	54.4			
Independent Homelands	59.8			

Conditions of concern in South Africa, as in most African countries, include tuberculosis, measles, HIV and AIDS, malnutrition, mental illness and physical trauma. Of particular concern, at present, is what has become known as 'political' violence within certain 'black townships' and rural areas in the country. Although political issues are important in many instances, the causes are much more complex, but will not be discussed in this short chapter. In addition, the statistics may be distorted by cases of criminal violence which have received political status. The 1993, consolidated figures for 'political' violence in South Africa are shown in Table 3.

There was a 24.7% increase in politically linked deaths in 1993, compared to 1992, while the recorded injuries are 24% less than the 1992 total (25). There is relatively little information regarding the grades of morbidity associated with the injuries nor the resulting dysfunction.

Certain cases of infectious or contagious conditions are subject to compulsory reporting or 'notification'. Tuberculosis is the most frequently notified disease in South Africa, accounting for 61% of all notifications in 1987 (26). Possible causes for this include, poor socioeconomic circumstances related to increased urbanization, poverty, unemployment, over-crowding, HIV infection, a high total infected pool of 6-10 million people, and increasing drug resistance (16, 27, 23). It affects mainly the African and Coloured populations. Relative to whites, Africans were 14 times and Coloureds 32 times more likely to be notified with TB (1). It is thought that almost half the cases of tuberculosis are unreported and these are more likely to be African patients. In the 5 years leading up to 1990, the total case load had increased by 41% from 88,268 in 1985 to 124,635 cases in 1990 (28).

Measles is the second most important notifiable disease in SA (16). It is potentially preventable through effective immunization, and is a potentially lethal childhood disease, particularly in children with lowered immunity, such as occurs in malnutrition. While the number of measles notifications continues to be high, ranging from 43.1 per 100,000 for Africans to 3.8 for whites in 1989, recent immunization programs have almost halved these figures. It is, however, still vitally important that high levels of vaccination coverage be sustained.

Health Personnel

South Africa is more fortunate than many of the other African countries to the North, since it has an infrastructure of well trained professional health workers. The country as a whole, has 8 medical schools, 34 nursing colleges and

TABLE 3

'Politically' Related Deaths and Injuries in South Africa During 1993 (25)

	PWV Area	Natal	Other Areas	Total
Deaths	2,001	1,975	388	4,364
Injuries with survival				4,339

(PWV = Pretoria, Witwatersrand & Vereeniging)

16 University-based nurse training programs. The number of professional personnel and estimated traditional healers in South Africa are indicated in Table 4 (1, 11, 16).

Although it would appear from the figures in Table 4 that there are sufficient doctors, it must be realized that most doctors are concentrated in metropolitan areas. Ratios, therefore, vary from 1:564 in some urban areas to 1:150,000 in localized rural areas (1).

There are many other recent significant changes and initiatives within the South African health care system which I am unable to detail here. These have included calls for more emphasis on primary health care; initiatives within medical schools to more community-based health worker education; and moves towards various systems of managed health care within the private sector. Only some 24% of the population have access to any health insurance (16). Financing of health care is an increasing problem and as the priorities change so too will the demands. Expenditure on AIDS/HIV alone increased from R5,4m (US$1,6m) in 1991/92 to R20,9m (US$6,3) in 1992/93 but even this is acknowledged as being insufficient in view of the seriousness of the epidemic (16).

Thus, the challenges facing any new government will be to address the legacies of apartheid and separate development in all spheres, including the health sector. They will also have to meet the expectations and needs of a disempowered and disadvantaged majority without alienating and scaring off the private practitioners who have enjoyed the freedom of uncontrolled and affluent practice.

The Future South African Health Care System?

Given the significant recent political and social changes in South African society, it is obviously difficult to accurately predict what the structure and nature of the future government will be, let alone its health system. However, the African National Congress (ANC), whom it is generally believed will be a significant player within the new government, recently published a draft of their long awaited health strategy for the future, 'A National Health Plan for South Africa' (29). This plan calls for the establishment of a national health system by July 1994. It is remarkable that many of the main features of the plan are almost identical to those in the Gluckman Report of 1944, mentioned earlier in this chapter. Have we come full circle?

The report and its accompanying press release states *'that high quality care for all in South Africa is affordable, within the current level of total health care*

TABLE 4
Health Personnel in South Africa (1, 11, 16).

	Specialists	Non-specialists	Total	Ratio to Population
Doctors (Jan. 1994)	6632	18,743	25,375	1:1,537
Nurses (1991)			140,460	1:270
Dentists (1991)			3,944	1:9,634
Pharmacists (1991)			9,058	1:4,195
Traditional Healers (1992)			±250,000	1:155

expenditure. SA spends R550 (about US$166) *per person, per year on health care (6.5% of GDP). This is ten times what the World Bank estimates is needed to provide basic health care for all. It is the lack of coordinated planning, the mismanagement of resources and the inefficiencies in both the public and private sectors that result in South Africans getting, at the moment, so little for their money.'*

The main features of the plan include a vision of health for all; a strong emphasis on primary health care with special programs for women, children, the elderly and other vulnerable groups; a single National Health System (NHS); quality control of health services; greater authority will be given to district health authorities, including the control of private ('independent') practitioners; curricular reform in health worker training; and community accountability and participation in planning policy. Of concern to those in the private sector are the suggested curbs on development of this sector, remuneration capping, and restriction of licenses to practice in certain areas. It is envisaged that the private sector will be complementary to the public sector, which in turn will be strengthened and made more attractive to health care personnel. Underpinning the whole plan is a 'Code of Patients' Rights' and a 'Code of Ethics for the NHS'.

Will this plan have the same fate as that of the 1944 Gluckman Report? It will not be an easy transition, faced with the many agendas and 'turf' structures within the health sector including the vested interests of a powerful private sector. There is also concern whether the new government will have the infrastructure and ability to implement the strategy. But fortunately there is a general commitment and willingness to change. In the words of DeBeer, *'It means that we must commit ourselves, not only to the provision of good health care, but to the creation of a society in which a National Health Service as envisaged by Dr. Gluckman becomes not desirable—but possible'* (3).

REFERENCES

1. Rispel, L. and G. Behr. 1992. *Health Care Indicators: Policy Implications.* Johannesburg: Centre for Health Policy.
2. Gluckman Commision. 1944. *Report of the National Health Services Commission UG30/1944;* Pretoria: Government Printer.
3. DeBeer, C. 1985. Explaining the present: Why health services do not meet the needs of the population. In *NAMDA Conference 1985: Towards Health Care For All.* Zwi AB & Saunders LD (Eds.). Johannesburg: NAMDA; 58-59.
4. Marcus, G. 1985. *The Freedom Charter: A Blueprint for a democratic South Africa.* Johannesburg: Centre for Applied Legal Studies (Wits).
5. Botha, J.L., Bradshaw, D., Gonin, R. and D. Yach. 1988. The distribution of health needs and services in South Africa. *Soc Sci Med;* 26:845-851.
6. DeBeer, C. 1984. *The South African Disease: Apartheid Health and Health Services. Johannesburg:* South African Research Services.
7. Loening, W. 1981. *Primary health care in Natal and KwaZulu. Durban:* SA Instit of Race Relations (Natal Coastal Region).
8. Andersson, N. and S. Marks. 1988. Apartheid and health in the 1980's. *Soc Sci Med*; 27(7):667-81.

9. Price, M. 1986. Health care as an instrument of Apartheid policy in South Africa. *Health Policy & Planning;* 1(2):158-70.
10. Savage, M. 1979. The political economy of health in South Africa. In *Economics of Health in South Africa.* Westcott G. & Wilson FAH (Eds.). Johannesburg.
11. vanRensburg, HCJ, Fourie, A. and E. Pretorius. 1992. *Health care in South Africa: Structure and dynamics.* Pretoria: Academica.
12. *Government Gazette 26.05.1977 Health Act, act no 63 of 1977.* 1977. Pretoria: Government Printer.
13. Botha, J.L. and D. Bradshaw. 1985. African vital statistics-a black hole? *S Afr Med J;* 67:977-981.
14. Jinabhai, C.C., Couvadia, H.M. and S.S. Abdool-Karim. 1986. Socio-medical indicators of health in South Africa. *Int J Health Serv;* 16:163-176.
15. Department of National Health and Population Development. 1987. The 1985-census. *Epidemiological Comments;* 14(1).
16. South African Institute of Race Relations. 1993. *Race Relations Survey 1992/93.* Johannesburg; South African Institute of Race Relations.
17. Doyle, P.R. 1991. The impact of AIDS on the South African population. In: *AIDS in South Africa: The Demographic and Economic implications.* Johannesburg: Centre for Health Policy, University of the Witwatersrand; 9-25.
18. Centre for Health Policy. 1991. *AIDS in South Africa: The Demographic and Economic implications.* Johannesburg: Centre for Health Policy, University of Witwatersrand.
19. Urban Foundation. 1990. *Population Trends: Demographic Projection Model.* Johannesburg: Urban Foundation.
20. Urban Foundation. 1990. *Population trends: Policies for a new urban future series: Part I.* Johannesburg: Urban Foundation.
21. World Health Organization. 1981. *Development of indicators for monitoring progress towards health for all by the year 2000.* Geneva: World Health Organization.
22. Venter, R. In: The *Star* 9, April 1992. Johannesburg: The Star.
23. Bradshaw, D., Botha, H., Joubert, G. Pretorius, J.P., Van Wyk, R. and D. Yach. 1987. *Review of South African Mortality (1984).* Parow: South African Medical Research Council (Institute of Biostatistics).
24. Yach, D and J.L. Botha. 1986. The use of age - and cause specific proportional mortality ratios to compare causes of death in South African children in 1980. *S. Afr J Epi and Infection;* 1.
25. Human Rights Commission. 1994. *Summary report on repression & year end review.* Johannesburg: Jan.
26. Strebel, P.M. and J.R. Seager. 1991. Epidemiology of tuberculosis in South Africa. In: Coovadia H.M., Benatar, S. (eds.). *A century of tuberculosis: Perspectives from South Africa.* Cape Town: Oxford University Press.
27. Böhm, L. 1992. A new face of TB. *SAMJ;* 82(2):75.
28. *SANTA TB News.* Nov 1991. Johannesburg: South African National Tuberculosis Association. 1991.
29. African National Congress. 1994. *A National Health Plan for South Africa.* Johannesburg: ANC. Jan.

Medicine and Health Care Into the Twenty-First Century. Edited by S.K. Majumdar, L.M. Rosenfeld, D.B. Nash and A.M. Audet.

Chapter Forty-Four

HEALTH CARE SYSTEM IN ARGENTINA

ROBERTO O. ARATA, M.D.
Associate Dean
Faculty of Medicine
Maimonides University
Buenos Aires, Argentina

INTRODUCTION

Socioeconomical Situation

During the four year period, 1990-1993, Argentina established economic adjustment policies in order to control the hyperinflationary process of the eighties. The success of these policies allowed for a decrease in the consumer price index (CPI). Actually, the inflation index in April 1993 was 1.0%. This index decrease was accompanied by slight improvements in production but strong macroeconomical distortions.

Private and Public sectors carried out important programs of personnel reduction in 1990-1992.

The impact of these modifications on income and employment and upon the quality of life in Argentina during 1988-1992, has been correlated by the work of the Executive Committee for the Study of Poverty in Argentina.

The methodology used for the quantification of poverty and indigency in Greater Buenos Aires, showed 34% and 6.6% of the population were found below these lines in 1988 and 20.2% and 2.4% in 1994. This decrease suggests a higher impact of the adjustment on middle income sectors, with 2.2 million people still persisting in a situation of critical poverty.

Education

Education varies with the province. The rates of pupils who completed elementary school is 62.9% for the country.

Population

The National Census of Housing and Population (1991) estimated the Argentine population at 32,608,687 inhabitants.

Argentina reduced its proportion of the total continental population from 10.8% in 1950 to 7.3% in 1991.

Some characteristics revealed ten years before were stressed once again: concentration in urban sites and large geographics areas remaining impopulated.

The decrease in child mortality and death rate in the early eighties raised life expectancy from 65.4 years for men and 72.1 years for women in 1975-80 to 67.3 and 74 years respectively in 1985-90.

ANALYSIS OF MAIN HEALTH PROBLEMS

In 1990, the country had a general mortality rate of 8.0 per thousand and a childhood mortality rate of 25.6%. Analyzing death rates, we observe a progressive rise of heart disease, malignancies and cerebrovascular diseases. The epidemiological bulletins of the National System of Vigilance of Diseases (Secretary of Health, Ministry of Health and Social Welfare) provide a tool for the analysis of morbidity due to infectious diseases, in 1989-1992, with historically comparable incidence rates.

Chagas Disease is the most parasitic endemic disease. In January 1992, the first case of cholera was reported. The most important epidemic areas were those experiencing poor hygiene and labor conditions in a context of structural poverty and margination.

AIDS experienced a doubling of the number reported cases each year. The prevalent nutritional problem in Argentina is chronical malnutrition caused by extreme poverty. This affects 10% of schoolage children and is associated with deficits of iodine and iron.

HEALTH SYSTEMS IN ARGENTINA

Characteristics

The health sector in Argentina is complex, as it has never been integrated or coordinated.

Health care is provided by and is under the control of the National Governments, Municipalities, Social Security Hospitals, Private Hospitals and Independent Physicians.

Three subsectors can be identified: Public, Social Security Organizations, and Private.

This produces a heterogeneous system which differs according to the place of residence, occupation and income level of the residents.

The public subsector offers services by means of three areas: National, Provincial and Municipal. The users are in general low-income groups, theoretically under the social security subsector but with limited access to benefits due to economic reasons, geographical areas with scarce facilities, or if these exist, they do not provide the required technical services.

The infrastructure of the public sector is extensive but it has lost excellence in the last 20 years, with respect to medical attention, teaching and research.

This has resulted because of limitations in attention, low quality services, lack of medical and surgical materials, scarce personnel in the provincial hospitals and poor conditions of maintenance and repair services.

The Social Security subsector is made up of 337 agencies, 82.6% of which are coordinated by a central organization. The remaining 45 (13.3%) correspond to provincial, municipal, Congressional and army Social Security organizations. This subsector has poor infrastructure and acts mainly as a financial source, dealing with the private sector in all services that it offers. The quality of health care differs according to the income of the users; the fact that workers associated with the same corporation, with equal income, receive different quality medical attention, is caused by geographic factors.

The private subsector consists of two main groups: health professionals providing independent services to private patients or to affiliates of social security organizations or paid systems, and hospitals controlled by social security organizations.

There are also non-profit institutions supported by homogeneous groups, such as ethnic community hospitals. The private sector had 31.4% of the beds in the country in 1985 and has expanded its number of beds in recent years (1991).

The sector has 50-60% of sophisticated equipment spread among its 2,000 organizations of diverse complexity, located in the major cities of Buenos Aires, Cordoba, Rosario and Mendoza.

Installed Capacity and Production of Services

The primary network of health care consists of 6,456 health establishments, without hospitalization services, which carry out health promotion activities, preservation and outpatient medical care. 30% are located in the city of Buenos Aires and in the Province of Buenos Aires.

The country has 3,180 hospitals containing 147,000 beds, five beds per 1,000 population (second only to Cuba in Latin America). 68% are in the public sector, Social Security or the army, and 32% belong to the private sector.

Health Care Economic Situation

In 1985-1992, health care expenses were 8.4% of the gross national product, about US$ 190 per capita.

In 1985, expenses for health care consisted of 22.7% in the public sector, 39% for social security and 38.1% for the private sector.

The percent of the participation of Social Security Organizations increased steadily: 22.8% in 1970, 35.8% in 1980 and 39.2% in 1985.

In 1993, the percent of this participation decreased to 35%.

The public sector grew between 1970 and 1980 but after that time experienced a severe contraction. There was a decrease in the participation of the national public sector in total health care costs.

There was recovery in private expenditures in health care which was similar to that of the corporations, to a point that was between these and the Private System, they cover 80% of the total costs in health care.

This steady growth of the private sector is supported by an adequacy in available resources: about 2,000 physicians, 47,000 beds and high utilization of medications which amounts to nearly US$ 50 per capita.

This has had the following consequences:

1. The weakening of the public sector assisting low income populations.
2. A big increase in private expenditures that could be caused by migration of the population in search of more efficient services.

Human Resources

Estimations in recent years indicated that the health care work force consisted of around 400,000 people (more than 4% of the economically active population). This force presents the characteristics of an inverted pyramid in which professionals outnumber technicians and assistants (90,000 physicians; 22,000 dentists, 29,000 pharmacists, 9,500 biochemists; 4,000 obstetricians, 13,000 physiotherapists; 25,000 psychologists; 16,000 nurses; 25,000 nursing assistants; 90,000 technicians and 95,000 administrators). Source: Census of Human Resources, Secretary of Health. According to estimates of the World Bank, 1989. Argentina has an especially great supply of physicians, with a ratio of 270 per 100,000 population, the highest of any country in Latin America. All but two of the ten medical schools are operated by national or provincial governments, and they observe a policy of open admissions.

Argentina is the country with the highest number of medical students per inhabitant: 50-60 students of the first year of medicine per 100,000 population.

Although many students who are admitted fail, there are still more than 8,000 medical graduates each year.

PERSPECTIVES AND TRENDS OF HEALTH SYSTEMS IN THE NEXT DECADE

As we have stressed, the 1989 hyperinflation has modified all rules. Sanitary structures have not been modified. A new model is supposed to be configured but its exact characteristics are difficult to predict. At present, the National Secretary of Health has reduced National Institutions and finished the transfer of hospitals to the provinces. The provinces and the Municipality of Buenos Aires are affected by serious financial problems and will have to deal with intense reductions in their functional organization.

At the present time, the central entity of Social Security has no power to make decisions because of legislation which deregulates the system of Social Security, undermining the National System of Health Security, made law in 1988 and never was enforced. The most important decisions concerning the health care sector are made by the Economic Ministry, as is the case of the transfer of hospitals or the reform of the System of Social Security.

Private investors are excited about the possibility of intervention in the financing of medical services or private retirements.

In the last three years, we have been observing significant trends for the future sanitary system.

1. Institutionalization of medical care with assistance and technological support through professional groups of different specialties.
2. Promotion of generalist physicians, family doctors, counteracting the premature specialization of professionals but related to institutions which act in a political frame orientated toward primary health care.
3. Coordination of integrated network of services.
4. Categorization of sanitary facilities.
5. Normatization of medical care through algorithms in diagnosis and treatment, binary questionnaires (YES-NO) in order to provide differential diagnosis and selection of the adequate treatment.
6. Rationalize the market of pharmaceutic products, discouraging unnecessary consumption.
7. Development of evaluation programs for high quality medical care.

As we can see, the future organization of the health care system shows characteristics which allow us to expect a different configuration in the immediate future. We can expect: Institutionalized medical care, rationalization of the services and therapeutic resources of assistance, a marked development of evaluation mechanisms, a rationalization of the public structures of health administration and administrative decentralization of public hospitals.

BIBLIOGRAPHY

Roemer, Milton I. 1991. "National Health Systems of the World" Vol. 1. The countries. Oxford University Press.

Saltman, Richard B. 1988. "The International Handbook of Health Care Systems". Greenwood Press, Inc.

"Las condiciones de salud en las Americas" ("Health Conditions in the Americas"). 1990. Organizacion Panamericana de la Salud. Vol. II. Publicación Científica N° 524.

Paganinin, J. "Los Desafíos de los Servicios de Salud en la Década del '90" (Challenges in Health Services in the 1990") OPS-OMS, Buenos Aires, 1992.

Gonzalez García et al. 1989. "El Gasto en Salud y en Medicamentos" ("Health Care and Medicine Expenditure"), Argentina 1985. Estudio CEDES, Ed. Humanistas, Buenos Aires.

Donabedian, "La calidad de la Atenció Médica" ("The Quality of Medical Care"), 1984. La Prensa Médica Mexicana, México.

Sonis, A. 1984. "Roles del Hospital Moderno, Perspectiva Argentina" ("Modern Hospital Roles, Argentina Prospects") Medicina y Sociedad Vol. 7, N° 1 y 2, Bs. As.

INDEC. 1989. "Módulo de utilización y gastos en Servicios de Salud" (Utilization and Expenditure Module in Health Services"), Mayo.

INDEC. 1981. "La Pobreza Argentina" ("Argentine Poverty"), Serie Estudios N° 1, 2da. Ed., Buenos Aires.

Minujin, Scharf A. 1989. "Estructura del hogar y lineas de pobreza" ("Home Structure Poverty"), INDEC, documento de trabajo N° 8 Buenos Aires.

Arc, Hugo. 1993. "El territorio de las decisiones sanitarias" ("The Field of Sanitary Decisions") Ed. Hector Macchi.

Medicine and Health Care Into the Twenty-First Century. Edited by S.K. Majumdar, L.M. Rosenfeld, D.B. Nash and A.M. Audet.

Chapter Forty-Five

CANADA'S HEALTH CARE SYSTEM: A Qualified Success

RAISA B. DEBER, Ph.D. and
SHARMILA L. MHATRE, Ph.D.
Department of Health Administration
Faculty of Medicine
McMurrich Building
University of Toronto
12 Queens Park Crescent West
Toronto, Ontario M5S1A8
Canada

Canada's health care system combines single-payer financing for hospital and medical care with private delivery. Health status measures are good to excellent, in international terms, and Canadians appear highly satisfied (1-3). Indeed, Canada has been pointed to by some U.S. health policy analysts as a possible model for the U.S. to emulate (4-7). However, there are ominous signs. Canada has been hard hit by the world economy. Organization for Economic Cooperation and Development (OECD) data reveals that its health care spending, as a proportion of GDP, is now second only to that of the United States, and deficit-plagued governments are seeking to reduce public spending. It is unclear whether the health care system will survive temptations to erode it (8-10).

It is important to recognize that there is no national "Canadian health care system". Constitutionally, health care is not "Canadian" because Canada's constitution placed health under provincial jurisdiction; Canada instead has a series of 10 provincial and 2 territorial government-run health insurance programs. Any U.S. equivalent of the Canadian plan would not consist of a Washington-run plan (e.g., U.S. Medicare), but would consist of a series of state-level plans which would meet specified national goals and objectives. Operationally, Canada does not have a "national health system" like those of the U.K. or Scandinavia because, with a few exceptions (e.g., provincial psychiatric hospitals in some provinces), health care providers are not public employees. A U.S. equivalent of "the Canadian way" would involve substituting a single payer for the myriad of insurance plans which currently exist to reimburse private providers, but would not involve somehow nationalizing health care delivery. Finally, Canada does not have a "health care system" because service delivery in general remains decentralized and largely uncoordinated, although recent initiatives in some provinces are attempting to remedy this.

Nonetheless, there are strong similarities among the provincial programs. There are, however, considerable fiscal disparities across provinces. Therefore, to accommodate the belief that all Canadians are entitled to roughly equivalent levels of services, the national government plays a role in "equalizing" fiscal capacity. Accordingly, Ottawa incrementally entered into a series of cost-sharing programs which have intertwined health policy and "fiscal federalism" (11, 12). Initially, it provided grants to the provinces for specific purposes (e.g., hospital construction, training of public health workers, etc.). In the mid 1950s, the federal government agreed to pay approximately half the costs of qualifying provincial insurance plans for hospital and inpatient diagnostic services, as long as a set of national terms and conditions were adhered to. The *Medical Care Act* (1966) established a similar arrangement for insuring physician services. By 1971, all Canadian provinces had set up complying plans for hospital and medical insurance, and this marks the completion of Canadian Medicare. The development of the system has been well described elsewhere (13, 14).

The national terms and conditions were reaffirmed by the 1984 *Canada Health Act,* and remain in effect as of this writing. To receive federal funds, provincial plans must adhere to the following principles:

- universality (with very few exceptions, everyone must be covered);
- comprehensiveness (all "medically required" services provided in hospital or by doctors must be covered, although it is important to recognize that the definition does not force coverage of services which were not included in the earlier cost-shared programs. Accordingly, coverage of out-patient pharamaceuticals, home care, assistive devices, etc. is at the discretion of the individual province, but not included in the *Canada Health Act* provisions);
- accessibility (there must be "reasonable access", with no co-insurance or deductibles permitted for insured services);
- portability (inter-provincial agreements must be signed to provide coverage for individuals when they are in other provinces; there are also limited provisions for paying for elective care and emergency out-of-country care); and
- public administration (i.e., there is no longer a role for private insurance for insured services).

In consequence, hospital and medical care for "medically necessary" conditions is fully insured, without co-payments or deductibles. Provinces may chose to extend coverage for other types of services not required under the *Canada Health Act,* such as public health, community mental health, health promotion, dental, drugs, ambulances, assistive devices, or long term care. Some of these programs are targeted to special groups (e.g., those on welfare, the elderly); many involve means testing and co-payments. Health and Welfare Canada estimates that about 72% of health

Another set of considerations arise from ideology and politics. What level of discrepancy across provinces is tolerable? The answer clearly depends upon whether people are seen as citizens of Canada (and thereby entitled to roughly equal levels of services), or whether a more "provincial rights" viewpoint is taken (20). What role will markets play, and what is the role of government? Social democratic parties see health care as a "merit good" with little role for the private sector; conservatives see it as yet another market commodity. What role should ability and willingness to pay play in the allocation of services (21)? What are the implications of the recognition that health is influenced by environment, housing, wealth, education, and other factors well beyond the scope of the health care system? It has been suggested that we are now practicing "flat of the curve" medicine, and that additional resources devoted to medical care will not lead to increases in health status (22, 23). Can that justify a shift of resources away from medical care? Will the public accept this?

One key difference between Canada and the U.S. is that few Canadian health economists and policy analysts believe in the primacy of markets *per se* for regulating necessary medical services (22). They point to international evidence to suggest that mixed public-private systems tend to be more expensive and less cost-effective (24). A perennial issue is that of user fees. Evans refers to this as a "zombie"—an issue which should be dead, but keeps lurching about and doing damage (25). In general, Canadians have been opposed to "two tier" medicine as a matter of philosophy, while Canadian health economists argue that direct charges to patients for medically necessary services are ineffective and counterproductive. Their arguments include the following: any fees high enough to outweigh their collection costs are likely to deter the poor, without cutting total costs (since physicians can still induce demand among those more able to pay); without the monopsony bargaining power over fees characteristic of single payers, total costs are likely to increase with negative consequences for national economic competitiveness; equity is impeded if access to needed care is based on financial resources; the only country relying heavily upon consumer co-payments—the U.S.—is hardly a model of cost control (26). To date, these arguments have been accepted; indeed, many health ministers begin by advocating for user fees, but change their views after being briefed on the subject. However, as efforts to contain costs appear to threaten access to desired services, public support for the user fee option has grown, and the "zombie" may return to vitality.

Another element is the issue of societal expectations as to what a health care system can and can not do. In most industrialized countries, the standards of what it is to be healthy have significantly increased. People no longer expect to put up with disability. Consumers have higher expectations concerning the quality of food in hospitals, or accommodations, or the amount of time they should have to wait before receiving services. Needs-based planning which does not take sufficient account of demands is unlikely to be politically tenable (27).

Another challenge comes from the changing definition of health. Recognition that health is far more than the absence of disease means that more and more things can be classified as "health care". Should coverage be expanded to include long term care, or dental care, or outpatient drugs? To what extent should a health care system address issues of wellness? As the boundaries become more elastic, the scope for service provision grows. Should the public system help pay for such services as prevention of family violence, fitness programs, nutrition, social support, or friendly visiting? Where should the line be drawn? If income is related to health, do we have to support income redistribution? And if we can't afford everything, how do we ration? In general, most Canadians would agree that rationing should be based on need and appropriateness. Other approaches, however, are possible. An "Oregon-style" approach would allow the public to decide what they would pay for the poor, and allow the more affluent to "top up" coverage for themselves. Waiting lists ration according to urgency, allowing those wishing elective procedures to wait (28). Debates abound about, for example, whether people should be able to jump the queue if they can pay extra (recognizing that the public has highly subsidized the training and infrastructure in the first place), or whether allocation should be solely on need/ability to benefit. Often lost in the debate is whether unnecessary care is worth getting at any price, and why, if care was not necessary, people would want to buy it at all.

These philosophical questions become more pressing because of economics, and questions about the carrying capacity of the economy. If the recession continues, will Canada have to move towards lifeboat ethics, and debate who to toss overboard? At present, there is general agreement that there is enough money in the system, but that the political implications of reallocating resources may be severe. Health care spending is, in many cases, health care incomes. Just as those generating the "administrative waste" in the U.S. system will fight fiercely to preserve their share of the health dollar, so will communities fight to preserve jobs and incomes arising from providing health care services, whether or not these are necessary for the health of their population. Will providers make less money than they're used to doing? Will the skill mix be altered? Will the role of denominational hospitals change? Will institutions have to change their roles? Will individuals have to travel for (preferably better) care? Such questions are clearly political dynamite, and governments vary considerably in the extent to which they are ready to play with fire.

The potential trouble spots can be related to the terms of medicare. Will coverge remain universal, or will it be "targeted" to those in need, even at the risk of increasing total costs and decreasing national competitiveness?

How comprehensive will coverage be? At present, provinces are engaged in "keeping down with the Jones" and limiting coverage for those services not required by the *Canada Health Act* (especially drug benefits). Consideration is also being given to definitions of medical necessity, including deinsurance of selected items (29). In Ontario, for example, newborn circumcision, benign skin lesions, port wine stains, and *in vitro* fertilization are among the items being scrutinized. Other provinces are engaging in similar exercises. To the extent that such services will still be provided, this effort results in shifting costs rather than containing them, and diverts governments from addressing the structural problems of the system. Deinsuring may also serve to perpetuate the fee-for-service system and provide an opening for market forces; uninsured services are likely to continue being provided, but at higher costs.

Will portability agreements break down, particularly if one province has more generous coverage than its neighbors?

Finally, will there be a role for private insurance to pick up the services vacated by the public plans?

Governments unwilling to challenge the basic terms of medicare are thus looking more carefully at means by which they might improve the effectiveness of the system.

An easy approach is to reduce "fraud" and "abuse" in the system. For example, the newspapers have voiced suspicions that many Americans, particularly those in border cities, have been taking advantage of Canadian health insurance. Coverage for illegal immigrants, foreign visitors, and other non-residents is also being scrutinized. Although these factors may be important in particular communities, however, they are neither the major problem, nor the major target.

An important set of trends is the effort to shift emphasis from doctors and hospitals towards community-based care and alternative providers. Ontario, for example, integrated midwives into its system in 1994. Provinces are increasing emphasis on community health centers, home care, wellness education, and similar efforts. In consequence, the proportion of health spending devoted to institutional care has been decreasing, fuelled by technological advances which permit less invasive forms of therapy.

The reduction in length of stay and the trend towards day surgery has meant considerable oversupply of hospital capacity. This is being downsized dramatically, while patient volumes have increased. The effort to achieve genuine savings through rationalization of institutions (including closures) is moving more slowly. Inertia, local pride, and institutional loyalty are strong. In consequence, a number of provinces are seeking to delegate the difficult decisions to regional levels of government, including setting up regional structures. Hospital boards have been abolished in a number of provinces, replaced by regional boards some of which are also given the power to allocate regional budgets. Regionalization has evoked some local concerns, as it represents a transfer of control from local providers to a more centralized bureaucracy. It is also unclear how cross boundary issues will be dealt with; catchment areas do not always match bureaucratic boundaries, and people may live and work in different areas. The determination of the size and boundaries of regional units can also be fraught with conflict; in provinces such as Saskatchewan, regions can be as small as 12,000 people, which implies that they would be appropriate only for primary care (and that mechanisms would have to be developed to allow "risk pooling" in such a small population). The ultimate fate of these regionalization efforts remains unclear. Their strong potential advantages—which may or may not be realized—are the ability to incorporate more needs-based planning, the potential for breaking the inertia preventing necessary restructuring from taking place, the ability to reallocate resources to where they would make the greatest contribution to population health, and the premise that local communities have a better sense of their own needs than do provincial bureaucrats.

Considerable interest has also been expressed in having clinical practice better guided by technology assessment and outcomes research. Centers for technology assessment/clinical epidemiology have set up nationally, and in a number of provinces. The potential for "appropriateness" research to improve the cost-effectiveness of current practice appears promising. This move towards more effective and appropriate care is underway in a number of Canadian hospitals under the rubric of Continuous Quality Improvement. Strategies for ensuring that guidelines will be studied, adapted in practice, updated, and evaluated are critical for success. In the long run, many argue that such efforts will have to be coupled with reforms to provider payment mechanisms, such that there is no connection between reimbursement and clinical judgment (30).

Government has also embarked upon a public education campaign to affect demand by informing people about when care is, and is not, needed. The instructions that patients with the flu should consider chicken soup rather than antibiotics has received particular attention.

It is unclear whether these measures will be given time to work. The keen hope of most Canadians appears to be that the economy will improve, and remove the necessity of making tough choices about a highly popular, and quite successful, social program.

REFERENCES

1. Blendon, R.J. and H. Taylor. 1989. Views on health care: public opinion in three nations. *Health Affairs;* 8(2):149-57.
2. Blendon, R.J., Leitman, R., Morrison, I. and K. Donelan. 1990. Satisfaction with health systems in ten nations. *Health Affairs;* 9(2):185-92.
3. Mhatre, S.L. and R.B. Deber. 1992. From equal access to health care to equitable access to health: a review of Canadian provincial health commissions and reports. *International Journal of Health Services;* 22(4):645-68.
4. Marmor, T.R. 1993. Commentary on Canadian health insurance: lessons for the United States. *International Journal of Health Services;* 23(1):45-62.
5. Woolhandler, S. and D.U. Himmelstein. 1991. The deteriorating administrative efficiency of the U.S. health care system. *N Engl J Med;* 324(18):1253-8.
6. United States General Accounting Office. 1991. *Canadian Health Insurance: Lessons for the United States.* Report to the Chairman, Committee on Government Operations, House of Representatives, Washington, D.C.: GAO.
7. Deber, R.B. 1993. Canadian medicare: can it work in the United States? Will it work in Canada? *Am J Law Med;* 19(1 & 2):75-93.
8. Evans, R.G. 1993. Health care reform: "The issue from hell". *Policy Options;* 14(6):35-41.
9. Deber, R.B., Baker, G.R. and S.L. Mhatre. 1992. Review of provincial systems. In: Davis, S.M. ed. *Health Care. Innovation, Impact and Challenge.* Queen's University, Kingston: School of Policy Studies/School of Public Administration; 9-23.
10. Adams, O., Curry, L. and R.B. Deber. 1992. *Public and Private Health Care Financing: Literature Review and Description.* Ottawa: Curry Adams & Associates.
11. Olling, R.D. and M.W. Westmacott. 1988. *Perspectives on Canadian Federalism.* Scarborough, Ontario: Prentice-Hall Canada Inc.
12. Milne, D. 1986. *Tug of War.* Toronto: James Lorimer & Company Publishers.
13. Taylor, M.G. 1987. *Health Insurance and Canadian Public Policy: The Seven Decisions That Created the Canadian Health Insurance System and Their Outcomes.* Kingston: McGill-Queen's University Press.

14. Evans, R.G. and G.L. Stoddart, eds. 1986. *Medicare at Maturity: Achievements, Lessons & Challenges.* Calgary: University of Calgary Press.
15. Lomas, J., Charles, C. and J. Greb. 1992. *The Price of Peace: The Structure and Process of Physician Fee Negotiations.* Centre for Health Economics and Policy Analysis Working Paper Series 92-17, Hamilton: McMaster University.
16. Lomas, J., Fooks, C., Rice, T.H. and R.J. Labelle. 1989. Paying Physicians in Canada: Minding our Ps and Qs. *Health Affairs;* 8(1):80-102.
17. Barer, M.L. and G.L. Stoddart. 1991. *Toward Integrated Medical Resource Policies for Canada.* Vancouver: University of British Columbia Centre for Health Services and Policy Research.
18. Thompson, A. 1991. *Federal Support for Health Care.* Ottawa: HEAL, The Health Action Lobby.
19. Thompson, A. 1991. *Financing Health Care.* Ottawa: HEAL, The Health Action Lobby.
20. Deber, R.B. 1991. *Regulatory and Administrative Options for Canada's Health Care System.* Background paper prepared for HEAL, (The Health Action Lobby) Ocober 8.
21. Deber, R.B. 1991. Philosophical underpinnings of Canada's health care system. *Can-US Outlook*; 2(4):20-45.
22. Evans, R.G. 1984. *Strained Mercy: The Economics of Canadian Health Care.* Toronto: Butterworths & Co.
23. Evans, R.G. and G.L. Stoddart. 1990. Producing health, consuming care. *Soc Sci Med;* 31(12):1347-63.
24. Organization for Economic Cooperation and Development. 1990. *Health Care Systems; in Transition: The Search for Efficiency.* OECD Social Policy Studies No. 7, Paris.
25. Evans, R.G. 1992. U.S. influences on Canada: can we prevent the spread of Kuru? In: Deber, R.B., Thompson, G.G., eds. *Restructuring Canada's Health Services System: How Do We Get There From Here?* Toronto: University of Toronto Press; 143-8.
26. Stoddart, G.L., Barer, M.L., Evans, R.G. and V. Bhatia. 1993. *Why Not User Charges? The Real Issues.* Discussion paper: The Premier's Council on Health, Well-being and Social Justice, September.
27. Saltman, R.B. and C. von Otter. 1992. *Planned Markets and Public Competition: Strategic Reform in Northern European Health Systems.* Philadelphia, PA: Open University Press.
28. Naylor, C.D. 1991. A different view of queues in Ontario. *Health Affairs;* 10(3):110-28.
29. Deber, R.B., Ross, E. and M. Catz. 1993. Comprehensiveness in Health Care. Ottawa: HEAL, The Health Action Lobby.
30. Wright, C.J. 1991. The fee-for-service system should be replaced. *CMAJ;* 144(7):900-1, 903.

Medicine and Health Care Into the Twenty-First Century. Edited by S.K. Majumdar, L.M. Rosenfeld, D.B. Nash and A.M. Audet. © 1995, The Pennsylvania Academy of Science.

Chapter Forty-Six

HEALTH CARE IN BERMUDA

HON. QUINTON LANCELOT EDNESS, CBE, JP, MP
Minister of Health, Social Services and Housing
P.O. Box HM 1195
Hamilton HM EX
Bermuda

INTRODUCTION

Bermuda is a small group of islands located 586 miles east, southeast of Cape Hatteras, North Carolina. The islands cover an area approximately 20.5 square miles and have a maximum elevation of about 260 feet. The climate is subtropical, mild, frost-free and humid. The maximum temperature is 88 degrees Fahrenheit, while the minimum temperature is 65 degrees Fahrenheit; the annual rainfall is 55 inches. Hurricanes during the season May to November are the only potential cause of natural disasters.

Permanent settlement began on the islands in 1609 and Bermuda is the oldest self-governing British Dependent Territory. It has a parliamentary system of government. A Cabinet of 11 members is appointed by the Premier. The Legislature consists of a Senate, whose 11 members are appointed by the Governor and a House of Assembly with 40 elected members.

There are virtually no natural resources on the island and it must import almost all of its consumable goods. The economy is based almost entirely on tourism and international company business. About one third of the work force is engaged in wholesale/retail trade, one third in restaurants, and hotels; another third is engaged in community, social and personal services.

The country generally shows a small balance of payments surplus; the Bermuda dollar (BD$) is pegged to the U.S. dollar on an equal basis and inflation is estimated at under 6% per annum. Per capita annual income is over US$ 22,000. The recent recession, however, has had an adverse effect on the island's balance of payments resulting in a decrease in Government revenues.

Education is free in public schools and compulsory up to the age of sixteen. In 1993, a total of 10,403 students were enrolled in both government and private primary and secondary schools, and the Bermuda College. The literacy rate has been estimated as being as high as 97%.

Living standards are high, with good housing and well developed transportation and communication systems. Roads are of a good standard and there is a well-developed public transporation system (bus, taxis and ferries). Private care ownership is high, although restrictions limit this to one vehicle per household. One hundred percent of the population has safe drinking water available in their homes, as well as a hygienic waste disposal.

DEMOGRAPHIC CHARACTERISTICS

The island's population was estimated at 58,990 in 1993. According to the 1991 Census, the population was 58,480. Fifty-two percent of the population were female and 48% were male. The annual growth rate fell slightly to 0.7%. The island has an 'aged' population. In 1991, 9% of the population was 65 years or older. The median age of the population increased from 29 years in 1980 to 31 years in 1991. The population distribution by age group is shown in Table 1.

The racial composition of population has not changed significantly over the past decade. In 1991, 58% of the island's residents were black and 42% white and other races. Data from the census indicate that 75% of the Bermuda-born population was black while the foreign-born population was primarily comprised of whites and other races (79%). There was a significant increase in the foreign-born population since the last census.

Over half of the population belong to three religious groups, Anglican (27%), Catholic (15%) and African Methodist-Episcopalian (12%).

In 1991, 13% of the population aged 16 years and older held university degrees, compared with 8% in 1980. Eighty-four percent of this population had completed secondary level education.

The island's labor force increased during the period of 1980 to 1991 by 12%. The number of females in the work force increased by 17%, males by 8%. Women now

TABLE 1

Selected Age Distributions, 1991

Age	Number	Percentage of Total Population
0-4	4,051	7
5-14	7,354	13
15-44	29,684	51
65 and over	5,396	9

Source: The 1991 Census of Population, Census Office Bermuda.

constitute 48% of the work force. Economic expansion during this period occurred primarily in the financial sector of the economy. However, as the economy entered the recession, unemployment levels reached unprecedented levels. The unemployment level reached 6% in 1991, triple the 2% recorded in 1980. The median annual household income recorded in 1991 was US$ 48,588, a change of 16.4% since 1988 when household income was last measured.

There were 22,430 households on the island in 1991. There has been a shift from multiple family member households to smaller households with the average number of persons per household dropping from 2.93 in 1980 to 2.61 in 1991.

Selected demographic indicators are shown in Table 2.

HEALTH STATUS OF THE POPULATION

General Mortality / Morbidity

In general, Bermudians enjoy good health as measured by standard indicators. Life expectancy for females is 78 years compared with 70 years for males. Although life expectancy at birth has continued to improve, the difference between the sexes has continued to widen. Mortality and morbidity patterns have remained the same over recent years. Mortality rates for the population as a whole have not changed significantly. The crude death rate was 8.6 per 1,000 population in 1993. While the birth rate has declined, the infant mortality rate has improved. Selected vital statistics are shown in Table 3.

TABLE 2

Demographic Indicators

Bermuda - 1991	
Estimated population	58,460
Population density (inhabitants per sq. mile)	3,160
Annual growth rate (%)	0.7%
Population: 15 years of age (%)	19.5%
Population: 65 years of age (%)	9.0%
Birth rate (live births per 1,000 inhabitants)	16.4
Mortality rate (deaths per 1,000 inhabitants)	8.09

Source: Department of Health, Bermuda, 1992.

TABLE 3

Selected Vital Statistics

	1960	1970	1980	1990
Birth rate	28.2	20.4	14.6	15.2
Death rate	8.5	7.4	7.3	7.5
Infant mortality	31.5	15.1	13.9	7.8

Source: Department of Health, Bermuda.

Fertility has declined since the 1970's. The general fertility rate in 1993 was 66.0 per 1,000.

In 1993, the leading causes of death on the island were: malignant neoplasms, diseases of the heart, cerebrovascular diseases, AIDS, accidents and violence, pneumonia, diabetes, renal disease and chronic liver disease.

Incidence rates for sentinel health events (i.e., uncontrolled diabetes, uncontrolled hypertension in adults) are not readily available. The major, current health problems for Bermudians include cancer, ischaemic heart disease, fatal cerebrovascular disease (stroke), HIV infection and AIDS, and accidents (motor vehicle).

Heart Disease

Death rates for heart disease remain unacceptably high. In 1993, one of every five deaths was due to ischaemic heart disease. Up through 1992, heart disease was the leading cause of death.

Cancer

One of every four deaths, was attributed to cancer and cancer has increased in frequency as a cause of death. Rates have increased gradually, primarily as a result of increases in deaths from cancer of the breast and the lung. The major types of cancer include: breast, lung, colon and stomach.

HIV/AIDS

Incidence rates for sexually transmitted diseases have not altered significantly over the past five years. Reported cases of gonococcal infections have declined, while the rates of reported cases of syphilis, chlamydia and non-specific urethreitis have increased slightly. The rate for herpes has remained about the same.

Human immunodeficiency virus (HIV) infection and the acquired immunodeficiency syndrome (AIDS) are a major public health problem on the island. AIDS was first reported in 1982; at the end of 1993, a total of 247 cases were recorded. Two hundred and thirteen persons with AIDS have died. Females accounted for 20.2% of all reported cases. The majority of cases (90.4%) have occurred in the 20-49 year age group while one pediatric case has been recorded. Of the cases reported, 47.4% were reported in intravenous durg abusers and 28.7% in homosexual or bisexual men. The percentage of cases occurring in intravenous drug users has gradually declined while there has been an increase in cases in homosexual and bisexual men and among the heterosexual partners of persons infected with HIV.

Accidents

Accidents are a major public health problem with significant morbidity and mortality. Although alcohol analyzers have been introduced, and road safety campaigns are on-going, fatalities from motor vehicle accidents remain high. Accidents represent the major cause of death in the 15-34 year old age group. Males are affected disproportionately.

Health of Children and Youth

Maternal and child health indicators are good. In 1993, over 95% of pregnant women received prenatal care; 99% were fully immunized against tetanus and all births took place in hospital. A total of 4.1% of newborns had a birth weight of 2,500 grams or less compared with 1992 when there were 7% low birth weight infants.

In 1993, there were 9 deaths of infants under 1 year of age and the infant mortality rate was 9.6 per 1,000 live births. The main causes of death were congenital anomalies and conditions originating in the prenatal period. Over the past decade, the infant mortality rate has ranged from a high of 13.5 in 1986, to 3.2 in 1988.

For infants up to 1 year old, respiratory diseases were the leading cause of hospitalization. For children 1-14 years old, the leading causes were respiratory diseases and accidents.

In youths 15-19 years old, accidents were the leading cause of death and one of the major causes of hospital admissions along with pregnancy and respiratory diseases.

The incidence of vaccine preventable diseases is low. Immunization against all five of the common preventable childhood diseases (measles, rubella, DPT, polio and mumps) have been maintained at consistently high levels. Reported cases of mumps and measles declined considerably after the introduction of the triple vaccine MMR in the 1980's. Immunization against H. influenzae was introduced in 1990.

Obesity is a public health concern. Approximately 90% of children in the 5-15 years old age group have weight for age. There is some obesity in this age group.

Decreases in the incidence of dental decay have been dramatic over the past decade and oral health in children is generally excellent. This is largely attributed to a preventive dental care program for infants and children, that provides free fluoride treatment. The voluntary school-based program has maintained high participation levels.

Health of Adults

According to the 1991 Census, 33,581 persons, over 57% of the total population were between the ages of 25 and 64 years. The most important causes of mortality and morbidity in this segment of the population were chronic diseases and accidents and violence. Substantial increases in mortality occurred in the population 25-44 years old, between 1985 and the present. These increases were due primarily to deaths from AIDS, particularly in males. The leading causes of deaths in 1993 for persons 25-34 years old were accidents. AIDS was the main cause of mortality in those 35-44 years old.

The major causes of hospital admissions for adults aged 25-44 years include childbirth and accidents. For those aged 50-64 years, diseases of the circulatory and digestive systems and cancers are the leading causes.

Pharmacists

There are 38 pharmacists who provide a range of services from retail pharmacy to clinical pharmacology. Most pharmacists are employed on a salaried basis.

Regulation of Health Care Providers and Training

Licensing is required for most health professions. Regulation of physicians is provided through the Bermuda Medical Council under the Medical Practitioners Act, 1972. Nurses are registered with the Bermuda Nursing Council on an annual basis, while pharmacists are regulated through the Bermuda Pharmacy Council. Dentists are licensed by the Bermuda Dental Board as shown in Table 6.

Allied health workers are registered with the Council on Professions Supplementary to Medicine, under the Professions Supplementary to Medicine Act. There are currently no provisions under legislation for the registration of nurse practitioners or physicians assistants.

Legislation governing psychologists has been drafted. There are no regulations on counselors.

No medical schools or graduate medical education programs exist, continuing

TABLE 5

Allied Health Personnel

Category	Number
Physiotherapists	15
Speech-Language Pathologists	7
Nutritionists / Dietitians	9
Medical Lab Technologists	40
Radiographers, etc.	23
Occupational Therapists	15

Source: Council on Professions Supplementary to Medicine, Bermuda, 1994.

TABLE 6

Health Care Professions

Category	Regulatory Body	Professional Association
Physicians	Medical Council	Bermuda Medical Society
Dentists	Dental Board	Bermuda Dental Association
Nurses	Nursing Council	Bermuda Nurses Association
Pharmacists	Pharmacy Council	Bermuda Pharmaceutical Association
Nutritionists / Dietitians	Council on Professions Supplementary to Medicine	Bermuda Dietetic Association
Physiotherapists	Council on Professions Supplementary to Medicine	Bermuda Physiotherapy Association
Psychologists		Bermuda Psychological Association
Opticians / Optometrists	Opticians Board	

Source: Chief Medical Officer, Bermuda.

medical education is required for hospital based physicians. Refresher courses and a degree program for trained nurses have been developed at the Bermuda College in conjunction with overseas institutions. A training program for emergency medical technicians (EMT's) has recently been established.

HEALTH CARE DELIVERY

Primary health care servives are delivered from private physicians offices, government health centers and hospital outpatient clinics. Additional ambulatory care services are provided through specialty clinics and the emergency room at the hospital. A significant proportion of primary health care is delivered through the private sector. The majority of physicians and dentists are independent, private practitioners. Most other health care providers are employed on a salaried basis by the hospitals, the public health service or by private physicians.

There are no health maintenance organizations (HMO); independent practice associations (IPA); or preferred provider organizations (PPO's). There are no provisions for pre-paid medical care.

Medical Practice

There are a small number of multi-specialty group practices and a limited number of partnerships involving specialists. The majority of physicians are self-employed and in solo practice. Salaried physicians are found in the public health service and in the hospitals.

Primary care physicians (including internists and pediatricians) constitute 50% of all physicians in active practice. General practitioners (family physicians) and other primary care physicians serve as gatekeepers and co-ordinate care and control access to other specialists. Access to primary care is generally available on demand. Office visits are a major portion of physician patient contact. Almost all physicians have admitting privileges at the hospitals.

Public Health Services

Responsibility for providing public health service rests with the Department of Health. The department is mandated to provide disease prevention and control, and health promotion services for the island. It serves as a regulatory agency, and monitors food safety, water and air quality. It also provides for a variety of public health services including personal health and dental health as well as environmental health services.

The public health service is substantially involved in providing personal health services and administers a number of traditional public health programs including: maternal and child health, school health, immunization, communicable disease control, as well as home health care (including, health visiting and district nursing and select specialized care, i.e., AIDS), rehabilitation, health education and health promotion programs. Services are generally categorical in nature and are provided across socioeconomic lines.

The delivery of public health services is facilitated by the division of the island into three health regions. The department operates a health center in each of these regions. These centers offer antenal care, family planning services, immunizations, child health and other primary care services as well as dental clinics for children.

Private voluntary agencies assisted by Government provide some specialized services, (i.e. community based oncology nursing, personal services for HIV infected persons, etc.).

Hospitals

There are two acute care hospitals on the island; the King Edward VII Memorial Hospital, a general (community) hospital with 234 beds; and St. Bredan's Hospital, a psychiatric hospital with 166 beds. The King Edward VII Memorial Hospital also has 90 geriatric and rehabilitation beds. Both hospitals are operated by the Bermuda Hospitals Board which is appointed by the Government. The Board is a corporate body which can be sued. It delegates day to day responsibility for the running of the hospitals to an Executive Director; he is assisted by a number of senior managers, including a Chief of Staff, and a Director of Nursing and Patient Services at each hospital. Medical Staff Committees representing the physician staff are involved in the running of the hospitals as well. There are no private hospitals on the island.

The general hospital provides diagnostic and treatment services for patients with a variety of medical conditions (surgical and non-surgical). Services include: Medicine, Surgery, Pediatrics, Obstetrics and Gynecology, Rehabilitation and Geriatrics. In addition the hospital provides some specialized and intensive services, including oncology, medical and surgical intensive care, and renal dialysis. A neonatal care unit is being developed. Both hospitals undergo periodic accreditation reviews by the Canadian Council on Hospital Accreditation.

The average length of stay at the general hospital was 8.7 days per admission in 1993; this has remained stable for several years. Average occupancy was 75% and there were 63,905 patient days.

There are no urgent care or freestanding outpatient surgery centers. Outpatient surgery is provided through the hospital. There were over 29,238 patient visits to the Emergency Room in 1993.

In addition to its specialty, ambulatory care clinics, the general hospital operates a primary care clinic for indigent patients.

There are no secondary, or tertiary referral hospitals on the island. However, there are traditional links for the provision of tertiary care with the U.S.A., U.K., and Canada.

Funding for the hospital is provided through a variety of mechanisms, including: insurance and Government subsidies. The Government provides an operating grant to the psychiatric hospital.

Mental Health Services

Mental health services are provided through psychiatrists, psychologists, a psychiatric social worker and mental welfare officers attached to St. Bredan's, the only psychiatric hospital on the island. St. Bredan's provides care and treatment for both mentally ill and mentally handicapped individuals. The hospital operates a day hospital, an outpatient clinic and provides community based services. It maintains a half-way house and is developing additional supported facilities in the community.

With the exception of one psychiatrist in private practice, all of the consultant psychiatrists on the island are employed by the Hospitals Board on a salaried basis.

Long-Term Care Facilities

Long-term care facilities are operated by the Hospitals Board and the Government. Skilled nursing care facilities include Lefroy House, with 57 beds and the Extended Care Unit at the general hospital, with 90 beds. A hospice facility for the terminally ill, Agape House was opened in 1991; it provides care for individuals with AIDS and other terminal illnesses. It is operated by the Hospitals Board and partially subsidized by public funds. There are eleven residential care facilities for the elderly including nursing homes that provide limited nursing care and personal services and domiciliary care homes that provide room and board and limited assistance with personal services. Most of these facilities are partially funded through public monies.

HEALTH CARE FINANCING

The health care system is financed through a variety of mechanisms. Health services are either paid through an insurer, by a government agency or by consumers. There is no universal, publicly funded health insurance. Hospitalization insurance is mandatory for all employed and self-employed persons. Both employers and employees contribute to hospitalization insurance; employers must contributed 50% of the premium costs. Insurance coverage is nearly universal; there is some over insurance. Administration of Hospital Insurance is provided through the Hospital Insurance Commission. Insurance sold by private companies and public agencies is regulated through the Commission, and must provide mandated, minimum benefits (the Standard Hospital Benefit).

Health insurance schemes are provided through private companies, public agencies and employers. Government employees are insured through the Government Employees Health Insurance Scheme, while several major employers operate 'approved schemes' to cover their employees. The Hospital Insurance Commission operates a health insurance plan as well, the Hospital Insurance Plan. This plan has an annual open enrollment period designed to ensure access to health (hospitalization) insurance for all residents of the island.

There are no restrictions on direct payment to providers by consumers, and physicians may bill patients for charges in excess of standard insurance reimbursement or agreed fee schedules.

A Mutual Reinsurance Fund covers dialysis, kidney transplants, diabetes education and counseling, anti-rejection drugs, hospice care and long-stay (in-hospital) patients. It is funded through a compulsory levy on all health insurance premiums collected, and was introduced to spread the cost of high risk claims among all insurers. The fund is administered by the Commission as well. Hospitalization is provided free-of-charge to children and the aged; this is covered through a Government subsidy to the Bermuda Hospitals Board. The subsidies to the hospitals are also administered by the Commission.

Public health services are generally free, or provided at modest cost, they are funded through general revenues.

The prevailing method of payment for doctors and dentists is fee-for-service. there are no government controls on physicians' fees; however a fee schedule for hospital based physician services is established on an annual basis by agreement between the Bermuda Medical Society and the Health Insurance Association of Bermuda.

Government determines overall increases in hospital fees, and regulates the acquisition of major equipment and services.

HEALTH POLICY

Government health policy places emphasis on several areas including: maternal and child health, health of the school-age child, community nursing for the elderly, dental health, control of communicable diseases, mental health, and alcohol and drug abuse. Population groups designated for special attention include mothers and infants, school-age children, and the elderly. Public policy on health is based on the following:

1. Government should be the provider of last resort, and should serve as the guarantor of public health.
2. All residents of the island should have the opportunity to participate in determining the priorities of the health care system.
3. Individuals, the community and the government share responsibility to maintain the public health and assure conditions in which the individual can maintain and improve his or her health status.

FUTURE DIRECTIONS

In response to community concerns about escalating health care costs and the quality of health care on the island, Government initiated a comprehensive review of the health care system in 1993, involving providers, consumers, the government and the insurance industry. The review is focused on four major areas: health care costs, financing, quality and needs assessment.

The general practitioner or family physician will probably continue to play the role of 'gatekeeper' and control access to secondary care. It is likely that the island will develop more formal arrangements with preferred providers in the U.S.A. and Canada for tertiary care and some secondary care in an attempt to meet the challenge of increased costs. Insurers are facing increased pressure to expand coverage and increase benefits, particularly for the treatment of addictions and preventive services.

Both the Public Health Service and the Bermuda Hospitals Board have focused on the development of additional ambulatory and community-based services, and greater integration of existing community services, particularly for the elderly. There are already expectations that these services should be funded through insurance.

REFERENCES

Bermuda Hospitals Board. 1993. *The Bermuda Hospitals Board Annual Report.*

Bermuda Hospitals Board. 1994. *Report of the Statistical Analyst.*

Bermuda, Department of Health. 1993. *Report of the Chief Medical Officer.*

Bermuda, Department of the Registry General, Ministry of Labour and Home Affairs. 1989. *Report of the Registrar General.*

Bermuda, Department of the Registry General, Ministry of Labour and Home Affairs. 1990. *Report of the Registrar General.*

Bermuda, Statistical Department, Ministry of Finance. 1992. *Digest of Statistics,* No. 16.

Bermuda, Statistical Department, Ministry of Finance. 1993. *Bermuda Facts and Figures.*

Bermuda, Census Office. 1993. *The 1991 Census of the Population.*

Subject Index

A

B

C

D

E

F

G

H

I

J

K

L

M

N

O

S

T

U

V

W

Y

Z